Economic Analysis

Theory and Application

Economic Analysis

Theory and Application

S. Charles Maurice
Professor of Economics
Texas A&M University

Owen R. Phillips
Associate Professor of Economics
University of Wyoming

Sixth Edition

IRWIN

Homewood, IL 60430
Boston, MA 02116

© RICHARD D. IRWIN, INC., 1970, 1974, 1978, 1982, 1986, and 1992

Cover photograph: Fundamental Photographs, New York

Sponsoring editor: Gary Nelson
Project editor: Ethel Shiell
Production manager: Ann Cassady
Interior designer: John Rokusek
Cover designer: David Jones
Compositor: J. M. Post Graphics, Corp.
Typeface: 10/12 Times Roman
Printer: R. R. Donnelley & Sons Company

Library of Congress Cataloging-in-Publication Data

Maurice, S. Charles.
    Economic analysis: theory and application / S. Charles Maurice,
Owen R. Phillips. — 6th ed.
        p.   cm.
    Includes bibliographical references and index.
    ISBN 0-256-08209-X
    1. Microeconomics.   I. Phillips, Owen R.   II. Title.
HB172.M38   1992
338.5'21—dc20   91–33904

Printed in the United States of America
  2 3 4 5 6 7 8 9 0 DOC 9 8 7 6 5 4 3 2

PREFACE

This text is designed for undergraduate courses in basic microeconomics—the theory of market value and distribution. Throughout all of its editions, this text has held to two major objectives. The primary goal is to present the basic fundamentals of price theory in a clear and understandable way. A secondary, but important, purpose is to illustrate both how these fundamentals of price theory can be applied to the solution of actual decision-making problems and how they can be used to gain an understanding of the functioning of markets.

To meet these goals, we continue to combine numerous applications with the theoretical tools developed in each chapter. In this edition of *Economic Analysis,* we have increased our emphasis on applications of economic theory by discussing the application as the theory is developed. Many of the concepts are developed in a real-world context using numerical examples. In this way, we hope to impress upon students that the application of price theory is an integral part of economics and not just an "aside" to the fundamentals of the theory.

We also have attempted in this edition to show that economic theory is an important tool that can be used to understand and interpret the economic events that are discussed every day in the news. To this end, in each chapter we have included boxed-off analyses of actual news stories, magazine articles, opinion columns, and TV stories. We have entitled these analyses "Economics in the News." In these applications, we typically summarize an article or news story. In the vast majority of cases, this is a recent article or story. Next, we use the theoretical tools developed in the text to show how the news can be interpreted by the theory. In this way we stress the economic approach to thinking about current issues and we reinforce the fact that economics is an extremely useful tool for understanding the world. We believe that this change to the use of "Economics in the News" will make the application of economic analysis more up-to-date and "newsy" than the applications used in previous editions and in other texts. We have tried to drive home the point that economic concepts are a critical part of arriving at many real-world decisions and conclusions.

For the same purpose, we also have incorporated questions titled "Applying the Theory" into almost every chapter. These segments sometimes summarize a news story or column and then ask students to provide the analysis. In other cases, questions are asked that make students think more carefully about the concepts. Solutions to "Applying the Theory" are provided at the end of the chapter. In this way, students will be able to practice with the tools of economics as they work through the text.

Some things have not been changed in this sixth edition. We continue to present the basics of microeconomic theory. We continue to emphasize that a substantial portion of microeconomics is based on the theory of optimizing behavior, which, in turn, uses simple marginal analysis. After reviewing the concepts of demand, supply, market equilibrium, and elasticity in Chapters 2 and 3, Chapter 4 is devoted to the principles of unconstrained and constrained optimization. We emphasize that economic decision making is based on the principles of maximizing or minimizing an objective function. Decisions are made to maximize net benefits, to minimize the cost of achieving a given level of benefits, or to maximize the benefits attainable at a given level of cost. We know of no other text that introduces the theory this way. Economics is a decision science that has broad application to daily living. When developing the theory of consumer behavior, in Part III of the text, and the theory of the firm in Parts IV through VI, we consistently refer back to the principles set forth in Chapter 4 to show that microeconomic theory is a specific case of the general theory of optimization.

As in all previous editions, there is no calculus in the text. Although the theoretical exposition is complete and rigorous, only graphical and algebraic exposition is used. The major topics of the text remain as before: market basics, consumer behavior, production and cost, market structures, input demand, and welfare analysis with discussions of the causes of market failure. Last, and certainly not least, we have continued to include many technical and analytical problems at the end of each chapter, beginning with Chapter 2. Many previous adopters of *Economic Analysis* have told us that these problems are one of the most appealing features of the text. About half of these problems are new to this edition, and in some chapters more than half are new.

Several parts of the text have been changed. We consider this edition to be a major revision of the fifth. Two entirely new chapters have been added: Chapter 11 is an introduction to market structures, and it contains a general overview of the theories of firms and industries. In this chapter, different market structures are introduced and defined before a more detailed exposition in the chapters that follow. Chapter 21 presents several recent theories on the role of information in markets. Information and market failure are discussed along with other concepts in microeconomic theory that are relatively new in the body of literature.

Several chapters have been thoroughly reorganized. At the request of adopters, elasticity is now presented more completely in a separate chapter. The chapter on production has been divided into two chapters, short-run and long-run production. The theory of perfect competition is now divided into two chapters, one dealing with the theory of the perfectly competitive firm and the other with the theory of the perfectly competitive industry. In Chapter 16, the material on the use of game theory in oligopoly analysis has been greatly expanded. This material is relatively rigorous but nonmathematical.

Most pages contain changes from previous editions; this was done frequently to make the exposition more clear. Embarrassingly, several adopters of the fifth edition have pointed out material that is confusing. We have tried to eliminate or clarify these sections, for example, the concept of the elasticity of substitution in production theory. Although this edition has been expanded to 21 chapters, the book is not much longer than the previous edition. We have tried to make most of the chapters shorter and more focused.

All in all, *Economic Analysis* remains a traditional text in the basics of microeconomic theory. We are committed to writing a complete and rigorous undergraduate text without the use of calculus. We believe the changes we have made in this edition continue to move us in that direction. We have tried to keep the theoretical material, the applications of the theory, and the problems fresh and up-to-date, and we hope we have succeeded. We have tried to show students that although economic theory is at times rather abstract, it is a relevant and useful approach to understanding how the economy functions.

We would very much appreciate hearing comments, suggestions, and criticisms from instructors and students. We can be reached either through our publisher or directly at the department of economics at Texas A&M University or the University of Wyoming.

We are grateful for the many suggestions we have received from students and instructors who have used *Economic Analysis* in the past. We wish to thank our colleagues at Texas A&M and the University of Wyoming for their help. We greatly appreciate the help from Niccie McKay of Trinity University for many useful suggestions and comments during the early stages of the revision. We also appreciate the excellent reviews and suggestions of Carl Kogut of the University of South Florida, Patrick M. Boarman of National University San Diego, Wayne A. Jesswein of The University of Minnesota-Duluth, and Thomas M. Lucid of Ithaca College. We only wish that we had time to incorporate more of their suggestions into the final version. Finally, we thank Tricia Ofczarzak, Mary Strouch, LeDawnna Clancy, Mary Mesa, and Christine Stimson for their excellent typing services and support.

S. Charles Maurice
Owen R. Phillips

CONTENTS

PART IV   Production and Cost, 257

PART V   Industrial Organization, 373

PART VI   Input Demand, 577

PART VII   Welfare and Market Imperfections, 645

Economic Analysis

Theory and Application

PART I

Introduction

1
Scope of Economics

CHAPTER 1

Scope of Microeconomics

1.1 Introduction

You are beginning a course in microeconomics. In this course you will learn a great deal about how markets work, how firms and consumers make decisions, how these decisions affect the functioning of markets, and how government activities affect these decisions.

You will learn the answer to many interesting and intriguing questions such as: (1) Why do people purchase what they do? The answer isn't as obvious as you might think. To put the question differently, why don't you buy things that you want *and* can afford? (2) Why do firms charge the prices they do; why is bread $1.09 a loaf, coffee $3.35 for a 26-ounce can, and a Toyota, $12,500? (3) Why are some firms huge and others quite small? Why are automobiles and beer produced by a few giant firms, whereas shirts and dresses are produced by a large number of small firms? (4) Why do athletes such as Michael Jordan and Steffi Graf or rock stars such as Sting and Madonna make astronomical incomes, whereas school teachers and telephone linemen, who are arguably more useful, make far less. For that matter, why do coal miners make more than teachers? (5) Why do your out-of-pocket expenses, such as books, tuition, and room and board greatly underestimate the cost of your college education?

All of these questions, and many others similar to these, deal with microeconomics. In this course you will not only learn the answers to these and similar questions, but you will also learn how to approach and answer such questions for yourself. You will learn how to analyze the way people, as consumers of goods and services and at the same time sellers of their labor time and possibly other factors of production, and business firms, as producers of goods and services and also employers of resources, interact to decide which goods and services are produced, how much is produced, and what prices are charged. You will learn to predict the effects of consumer and producer decisions on the functioning of markets and on your own life.

An understanding of microeconomics is important for two reasons: First, because microeconomics concerns individual decision making, this course will help you make better decisions at whatever you do. Second, and far more important, informed, educated people understand how markets function. An understanding of markets is as important a characteristic of an educated person as a knowledge of history, literature, or political science. A voter who understands markets is able to predict the effects of changes in wage and tax laws, for example. Many promises are made during political campaigns; some are potentially feasible, others are not. A good understanding of how markets work can help weigh the feasibility of proposed public programs.

A large part of what you read in newspapers or news magazines or hear on TV news deals with microeconomic issues. Many TV channels and newspapers have economic or financial specialists reporting. A few recent examples are news stories and editorials about economic conditions in the Soviet Union, the effects of oil spills off the Alaska shore line, increases in the minimum wage and the establishment of a "training wage," strikes in baseball, new energy alternatives such as cold fusion, and the passage of tougher environmental regulations. Informed citizens should understand the implications of these events; similar ones appear in the news every day. They should be able to interpret and analyze the discussion of these events and in some cases predict the effect on their own lives and on the economy.

In this course, you will learn the fundamentals of microeconomic theory and see how economists use the theory to analyze economic questions. Economics is essentially a way of thinking about problems. This economic way of thinking does not change just because economists have acquired somewhat more sophisticated theories or tools of analysis than those set forth in the text.

This chapter will give you a brief preview of what is to come. It discusses the role of microeconomics in understanding the functioning and performance of markets. It then describes how theory is used in economics and introduces some fundamental themes that appear again and again throughout the text. The chapter closes with a discussion of the structure and the style of the text.

1.2   Microeconomics: The Study of Markets

As we noted, microeconomics is concerned with the study of consumers and producers as decision makers. Consumers make up the demand for a good or service. Producers provide the supply. Microeconomics deals with the interaction of consumers and producers for a good or service. Collectively, buyers and sellers compose a market. A market can be loosely defined as follows:

Figure 1–1   The Circular Flow

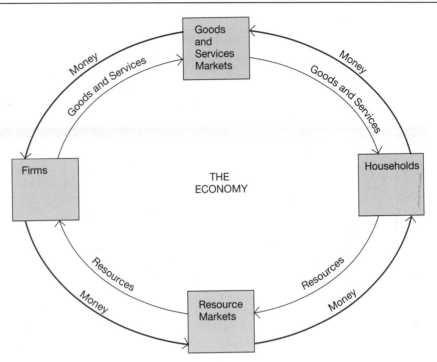

Definition

A market is the collection of buyers and sellers who willingly exchange a good or service.

A market as we know it can take many forms. Examples of formal markets located in a specific place are the New York Stock Exchange or the Chicago Commodities Exchange. Buyers and sellers in these markets actually meet face to face and trade stocks and certificates of ownership for selected commodities like wheat or pork bellies. But markets exist for *everything* that is bought and sold. There are markets for automobiles, personal computers, engineers or accountants, and apples or grapes. Markets need not be located at a specific place like the New York Stock Exchange. The only thing essential to the definition of a market is that voluntary exchange takes place. Markets can be international, national, regional, or local. A market may exist for one and only one product or service produced by a firm, or a market may cover a rather broad spectrum of products if consumers view the products as good substitutes.

Figure 1–1 shows a simplified picture of how exchange creates and fuels an economy. It shows the function of markets in an economy. This picture is called a circular flow. In this simple hypothetical economy, households are buyers, and they live in the box labeled "Households." Firms are producers, and they are located in the box labeled "Firms."

Each period—daily, weekly, monthly, or whatever—households bring their resources (their labor, land, or capital) to the many *resource markets*. The firms purchase or hire these resources each period with money. The firms use the resources they purchase or hire to produce goods and services, which they sell in a market. In one form or another these are finished products. The households use the money they earn from selling their resources to purchase the produced goods and services. These are consumed in the household box. As you can see in the figure, the money flows through the outer circle, while goods, services, and resources flow through the inner circle. The process is repeated the next period and each period thereafter. This is how an economy works. Buyers are sellers, and sellers are buyers. The income received in one market lets individuals spend in another. If one part of the chain is broken, the economy breaks down. The result is a recession or a depression. For example, if households stopped selling labor, what would firms do? Certainly they would close, and the economy would literally shut down.

Even though the circular flow diagram in Figure 1–1 is extremely simple, it gives a good picture of the role of markets in a real economy. It would be easy to add some additional features to make the picture a bit more realistic and a bit more complicated. For example, we could add a box for banks. Some households and firms would save some of the money they earn and accumulate interest. Other firms and households would borrow the money, paying interest, to finance the purchase of more goods and services.

Some of the households' income could also be spent to purchase goods and services from foreign firms, which may, in turn, use the money to buy goods and services from firms in this economy. Also, firms could purchase some resources, for example capital, from other firms. People in the households could produce for themselves some of the goods and services they consume (e.g., home repairs, child care, housecleaning, and lawn maintenance). Finally, we could add a box for government. Government would take money from households and firms in the form of taxes, then buy goods and services from firms and distribute them to citizens or citizen groups.

Notwithstanding these possible complications, Figure 1–1 illustrates how real markets function. In this course you will study how markets work, why they work, and the way they work. You will learn how the decisions of households and firms and the activities of government affect the functioning of markets. You will also learn how to analyze a large number of important questions that are concerned with the functioning of markets.

1.3   The Role of Theory

Most of this text will involve theory. We, therefore, want to explain what a theory is and how theory is used in economic analysis. Perhaps you have heard statements such as, "That's OK in theory, but what about the real world?" Theory, however, is not merely idle speculation about events or individual decisions. Theory is designed to apply to the real world. It enables economists to understand how the economy functions in a way that otherwise would be impossible.

Theory can be defined in several ways:

Definitions

A theory is (1) a coherent group of general propositions used as principles of explanation for a class of events; (2) a plausible explanation of how facts are related that isolates the determinants of the events being explained; (3) an abstraction from the real world that approximates reality and makes real-world events easier to understand; (4) a logical explanation of an event or occurrence that focuses upon the most important causes of the event and ignores all possible causes that are unimportant or insignificant.

In short, theory is a way of abstracting or simplifying events in the real world in order to make the real world easier to understand. The purpose of theory is to make sense out of confusion. Theory helps economists to explain and make predictions about events in the real world, even though the theory abstracts away from many actual characteristics of the real world.

Economists use theory to examine and analyze buyers and sellers and markets, because markets can be incredibly complex. Consumers can choose among thousands and thousands of goods and services. With all of these choices, why do consumers purchase the goods and services they do? Even making a selection from the menu at the restaurant can be complicated. Many things may enter into the decision: Recommendations from the waiter or waitress. The reputation of the restaurant. The prices. What your friends are going to order. How much money you have. How hungry you are. If you are on a diet.

The manager of the restaurant also makes complicated decisions every day. How many entrees to cook? What prices to charge? How many cooks and waiters or waitresses to hire? How should the restaurant be decorated? Should order out be provided, or are only sit-down customers served? How long should the restaurant stay open? You can see how difficult it would be to determine and predict how much of a good every consumer would purchase if everything that influenced a decision is taken into account. Consider how difficult it would be to determine and predict each producer's decision when every possible factor is considered.

Economists are interested in explaining why and how consumers and producers *in general* make buying and selling decisions in a market. For this reason economists are interested in market behavior. They study the behavior of the group of consumers in the market and firms that are collectively in a market. They can ignore the tremendous number of unimportant or irrelevant influences on some specific individual's consumption decisions or some specific firm's production, pricing, or hiring decisions. They use theory in order to concentrate on and isolate the most important determinants of buyer demand and producer supply and to analyze the effects of changes in these important determinants.

The theory of consumer behavior is an example of such a simplifying theory. When analyzing why a person chooses to purchase a given amount of some good, economists ignore relatively extraneous influences, such as the decor of the store, the disposition of the salesperson, weather conditions, traffic conditions, and so on. These and many other things may have some effect on the purchases of some people at some times, but they are not important in general for the questions economists want to answer, and there are too many such things for anyone to take them all fully into account. In analyzing consumer behavior, economists usually concentrate specifically on the price of the good in question, consumer income, and the prices of goods that are close substitutes. Economists believe these three variables capture the most important influences on the purchasing decisions of consumers. As you will see in this text, economists construct theories that concentrate on these determinants of buyer and seller behavior, and they ignore the many other variables.

The use of theory is by no means confined solely to economics. Meteorologists use theory to abstract away from unimportant determinants of the weather in order to concentrate on only the most important forces when making predictions. Engineers, chemists, physicists, and other scientists all use theory to make discoveries. The discovery of nuclear energy was based on a theory. When scientists working at the University of Utah and other universities announced that they had done experiments creating energy from cold fusion in the spring of 1989, physicists throughout the world did not know if they had discovered anything because there was no theory to explain it. In order to proceed further, scientists developed new theories and attempted to replicate findings based on these theories. When, on election nights, the TV networks miraculously announce the correct results, based upon a tiny proportion of votes counted, within minutes after the polls close, the predictions are made using sampling theories developed by statisticians.

The ability to use theory and abstract away from or ignore everything that is insignificant to an economic problem enables economists to come to grips with the issue at hand without becoming bogged down in unimportant details. Economists reach conclusions using relatively simple assumptions about behavior, while ignoring factors that *could* affect the conclusion but in all likelihood will not. Economic theory, therefore, provides a formalized structure or method of analysis for answering economic questions.

The simplicity or complexity of a theory depends to some extent upon the problem to be analyzed. For some problems, the assumptions of the theory are quite simple and the effects of only a few or even only one influence are considered. For other problems, the assumptions are less simple, and more influences must be taken into account. In this sense a theory is similar to a road map: the type of map that is used depends on what it is used for. For example, if you want to drive from Los Angeles to Houston, you would probably use the state maps of California, Arizona, New Mexico, and Texas, showing only the major highways. A more detailed map with all of the minor roads would be confusing and you might well get lost. If, when you got to Houston, you wanted to drive to the downtown business section, you would then use a city map, showing the major streets. If you wanted to go to a specific address downtown, you would use even a more detailed map, showing every downtown street.

This text follows a similar approach. We will use the simplest assumptions possible to explain a particular question, and we will not complicate things with a large number of realistic but unnecessary assumptions. For example, when we analyze consumer behavior, we will generally assume that a consumer purchases only two types of goods with a given level of income. Obviously, people buy more than two goods, but we can explain why people buy a given amount of any specific good and the effect of a change in the price of a good using the two-good assumption just as well as we could using the assumption of a multitude of goods without the added complexity of the latter case. Similarly, when explaining a firm's output and pricing decisions, we will assume that the firm produces only a single type of good, knowing full well that most firms produce a variety of goods and services. The single-good assumption allows us to explain firm behavior almost as accurately as would be the case if we used a more complex, multiple-good assumption. And the analysis is much less complicated.

Because we will use simplifying assumptions that may not be completely realistic, we want to warn you at the beginning of the course that a theory is not totally realistic. It is not designed to be. The theories in the text are designed to explain and predict conditions in the real world, even though the assumptions are not completely descriptive. As you will see, economic theory is an extremely valuable tool for analyzing, explaining, and predicting economic events and human behavior.

Keep in mind the following principle:

Principle

Real world economic events and human behavior are determined by many influences that are, when considered as a whole, confusing and difficult to interpret. Theories permit economists to cut through this mass of data and explain many aspects of human behavior and make sense out of the otherwise incomprehensible array of facts. Abstracting from many of the extraneous details in the real world, they can simplify economic analysis. A good theory simplifies in order to concentrate upon only the most important determinants of behavior, while retaining the fundamentals of the economic problems to be addressed.

1.4 Some Fundamental Themes

Before you get very far in this text, you are going to notice several fundamental topics that appear again and again. Because these topics appear so often and are so important, you should be aware of them from the beginning. They are the topics of (1) scarcity, (2) forgone opportunities, (3) marginal decisions, (4) equilibrium, and (5) optimization. This section gives a brief discussion of each.

1.4.1 Scarcity

Scarcity means that no society or economy has enough productive resources to produce enough for people to have everything they want. People in wealthy societies can have more of what they want than people in relatively poor societies, but people in the wealthiest society cannot have all the goods and services they want. There simply aren't enough resources and, most important, one of these resources is time. Choices must be made because of scarcity. Because choosing between alternatives is so pervasive throughout economics, some people have even called economics "The Science of Choice."

If people cannot have everything they want, they must choose within the limits set by their income and the time available. Consumers choose which goods and services to purchase. Firm managers choose which goods and services to produce and how to produce them. Workers choose which jobs to take, within the limits set by their ability and training. People choose how to spend their leisure among many possible alternatives. The fact that you are taking this course means that you have chosen to obtain a college education rather than to work full time and earn income. You and everyone else must make choices because you and everyone else cannot have everything that is desired.

Economics will teach you how people make choices. Even more important, economics will show you the implications of peoples' choices and how these choices affect the economy.

1.4.2   Forgone Opportunities

For every choice made there are forgone alternatives. The opportunity cost of a particular choice is the value of the best alternative that must be given up when that choice is made. If you choose to study tonight rather than go to a movie, your next best alternative, the opportunity cost of studying, is the implicit value you place on the enjoyment from the forgone movie. If you choose to go to the beach over spring break, the opportunity cost may be the new CD player you would have otherwise purchased with the money you spend on vacation plus the implicit value to you of the alternative use of your time. Anytime you buy something, the opportunity cost is the value of the other goods and services you would have otherwise purchased. When you are in college, the opportunity cost is the income you could have earned working at the job you would have taken if you had not gone to college.

People who own firms and use their money to buy capital equipment for their firm bear the opportunity cost of the interest they could have earned had they bought bonds with the money. People who choose to manage the firms they own bear the opportunity cost of the income they could have earned had they worked for another firm.

Choices by governments involve opportunity costs also. For example, the opportunity cost of increased spending on national defense may be the value of sacrificed spending on, say, education or public housing. Economists are sometimes fond of reminding people of the cost of government programs. Those who argue in favor of such programs practically never talk about their cost—what must be given up. The local newspaper may print an editorial that pleads persuasively that this city " . . . desperately needs a science and math magnet school." The editorial generally makes no mention of the cost of the school. Will other local programs be cut? Will taxes be raised? If so, the opportunity cost is the reduced consumption of the citizens. Another editorial may argue for more police protection, not just on the major streets but in all neighborhoods, right down to the most obscure cul-de-sac. Certainly a worthy goal, but what will be given up?

Economists try not to ignore cost. When evaluating the desirability of any activity, private or governmental, they consider both the benefits and the cost. In this text, you will frequently encounter benefit/cost analysis—weighing the benefits against the cost. In this text, we will continue to emphasize that all choices are accompanied by an opportunity cost.

1.4.3   Marginal Decisions

An important tool used to study how consumers, firms, and even governments should make decisions compares benefits and costs at the margin. Decisions at the margin necessarily involve small changes in a choice variable. When economists study decision making at the margin, they assume that when people make choices they consider the consequences of small changes in some activity or variable over which they have control; these are choice variables. For example, when we examine consumer behavior, we consider the effect on a consumer's happiness of a small increase or decrease—one unit—in the consumption of some specific good or service. In the theory of the firm, we will focus upon how a firm's profit is affected by small changes in the firm's level of output or usage of a particular input. By looking at the margin, we can determine the conditions under which a consumer can obtain the greatest happiness from a given level of income, or the output or input level for which a firm can attain the highest possible level of profit. By continuing to look at the effect of small changes, we can determine when no further changes can make the consumer any better off or earn the firm any more profits. We can discover when the consumer achieves the greatest happiness from a given income, or the firm, the largest possible profits. Maximizing a goal such as happiness or profit is an example of equilibrium.

1.4.4   Equilibrium

Equilibrium is defined as follows:

Definition

> Equilibrium occurs when no one has any motivation to change his or her choices. An equilibrium can change when some variable previously held fixed or beyond the control of the decision maker changes.

The preceding subsection mentioned two such equilibrium situations. When no change in the allocation of a given income among goods and services can make a consumer any better off, that consumer is in equilibrium. The consumer is achieving the highest possible satisfaction from that income and has no reason to change. If something external to the consumer changes, such as income or the price of a good, the consumer will usually change the allocation of goods and services and reach a new equilibrium.

If no increase or decrease in a firm's output or price can increase its profits, that firm is earning the highest possible profit and is in equilibrium. If something external to the firm changes, such as the wage that must be paid, the firm will change its output or price and reach a new equilibrium, which maximizes its profit under the new situation. Finally, for the market as a whole, where no single buyer or seller has any control over price, if all buyers can purchase all they want and all sellers sell all they want at the prevailing market price, that market is in equilibrium. No participant in the market has any incentive to change, but if something external to the market changes, the equilibrium price and quantity will probably change.

The concept of equilibrium is important because it enables economists to predict and explain the effect of changes in important economic variables. For example, assuming consumers seek an equilibrium, economists can explain and predict the effect of a change in the price of a good or a tax on that good on consumers' purchases of the good. Similarly, if producers maximize their profit, economists can explain and predict the effect of a technological improvement or a tax on the output or price of a good. As you will see, much of the predictive power of economics depends on comparing movements from one equilibrium to another after there is a change in a variable external to the equilibrium. Analysis of changes between equilibria is called *comparative statics*. Comparisons of two equilibria typically involve examining the effect of small changes in variables and are therefore examples of marginal analysis.

1.4.5   Optimization

As you will see, most description of economic behavior is based upon the assumption that people optimize. This means that people, who are forced to make choices, try to choose among different alternatives so as to attain the maximum possible net benefit.

Some everyday situations where you or someone else has wanted to optimize will help show the importance of this topic:

1. You have three tests coming up and a fixed amount of study time. How should you allocate the study time among the three courses so as to maximize the grade point average for the courses?
2. You are planning to buy a new car. How much time should you spend shopping for a low price so as to minimize the total cost in terms of the price of the car and the cost of the time spent shopping?
3. You are running for a class office and have an extremely limited advertising budget and limited time. How should you allocate your budget and time so as to maximize the number of expected votes for yourself?
4. You have a given weekly food budget. What food should you buy to give yourself the maximum pleasure and the necessary level of nutrition?
5. How should you allocate your fixed amount of charitable contributions to do the most "good."

All of these and many more such everyday decisions can be answered using simple economic theory. You will also see throughout this text that a great deal of economic analysis uses the assumption that decision makers try to solve questions such as these.

When we set forth the theory of consumer behavior—how consumers make purchasing decisions—we will use the assumption that consumers try to choose the particular combination of goods and services that yields the highest possible level of satisfaction from a given level of income. When we develop the theory of the firm, we will assume that managers try to set the level of output, the price, the level of advertising, or any other decision variable that will yield the largest profit to the firm. Or the manager chooses the particular combination of resources to produce any given level of output that enables that output to be produced at the lowest possible cost. Furthermore, as you will see, there are several other theories of economic behavior that are also based on an assumption that market participants optimize.

Using the assumption of optimizing behavior and a bit of simple logic, we will determine the equilibrium condition at which the optimum result is attained—the maximum or sometimes the minimum value of an objective. Then we will discuss what this equilibrium condition means in terms of the consumer's or the firm's allocation decision and in terms of the performance of the market.

From time to time we will discuss the implication of certain changes in government policy such as changes in taxation, ceiling prices, and regulations, assuming market participants optimize. We will begin with an equilibrium in which consumers, firms, or both are optimizing. Then the change in policy will change an externally imposed variable. Assuming the decision makers adjust in an optimal way, we will compare the new equilibrium to the original one in order to analyze the effect of the change in policy.

1.4.6   How Realistic Is Economic Theory?

As we have stressed, you will see the five topics we have just discussed emerge frequently in the theoretical analysis of economic behavior. We must caution you, however, that sometimes, when you are reading, you may wonder whether buyers and sellers really do behave and markets really do function in the way set forth by the theory. In other words, how realistic is economic theory?

First, it is obvious that everyone must make choices. Even if someone had enough income to purchase everything desired, there would not be enough time to consume it all. And, the vast majority of people do not have enough income to purchase everything desired. Second, since people must make choices, each choice must have, by definition, an opportunity cost. Thus, the concepts of choice and opportunity cost are certainly accurate descriptions of actual, real-world situations.

Third, with regard to individuals making decision at the margin, this is the way consumers and producers do make choices. Most people consider the effect of relatively small changes in their consumption patterns at any given time. Most firms consider the effect of relatively small changes in price, production, or resource usage when making decisions. Therefore, marginal analysis is a rather realistic way of examining behavior and is certainly useful.

The assumption that market participants optimize is less realistic, but no less useful in economic analysis. Do people actually try to allocate their income so as to squeeze the maximum possible happiness out of that income? Do firms try to gain the maximum profit possible or produce any given output at the minimum possible cost? Do people and firms, when making decisions, always try to achieve the greatest gain? The answer is: not exactly and probably not all of the time. For example, people do not continually calculate so as to maximize their satisfaction at every moment. This would be too time-consuming. Firms do not continually adjust their levels of output or resource use so as to maximize profit at all times. This would require too many adjustments and would be too expensive. Finally, in a world of uncertainty, consumers and firms would not have all of the information required to attain precisely the maximum level of utility or precisely the largest possible profits or the lowest possible cost of production. Gathering all of the necessary information would be too expensive.

Nonetheless, the assumption of optimization is pervasive in economic theory for two reasons. In the first place, consumers and firms do make adjustments. People do adjust their consumption patterns in response to changes in externally determined variables such as prices or income. They would try to adjust in a way to make themselves better off after the change. It's hard to imagine a family changing its purchasing patterns deliberately to make the family members worse off. Likewise, it seems improbable that workers change jobs in order to become unhappier, or firms change their prices in order to reduce profits or switch the inputs they use in order to increase their costs. Thus, we can clearly assume that people make decisions in order to move closer to an optimum, even though they may not exactly achieve it.

Recall the previous discussion of the use of theory in economics. Theory is not designed to be an accurate description of any specific individual or firm. Theory is a way of explaining and predicting behavior in general. Theories based upon the assumption of optimization do give, as you will see, good explanations and predictions, even though they are not precise descriptions. The predictions of the theories that you will learn to use in this course have been tested many times with statistical data, and in the vast majority of the tests, the real-world data are consistent with the predictions of the theories. Although these tests do not prove the truth of the theories, the consistency of the results leads economists to believe that the theories are useful. Therefore, the assumption of optimization is used in economic theories because it is a general description of human behavior and is useful in explaining and predicting that behavior.

Finally, consider the realism of the assumption of equilibrium. As we implied and as you will see, a consumer is in equilibrium when no adjustment in the bundle of goods and services purchased can make the consumer better off. A firm is in equilibrium when no change in output or price can increase the firm's profit, or no change in input usage can lower the cost of producing a given level of output. A market is in equilibrium when all buyers can buy all that they wish to buy and sellers can sell all that they wish to sell at the going market price. In all of these equilibria no market participant, firm or consumer, has any incentive to change price, output, the amount purchased, or anything else under a buyer's or seller's control.

Is equilibrium a realistic description of real-world markets? In a narrow sense, the answer is "no." As noted above, consumers and firms do not continually adjust their consumption, prices, output, and resource use so as to achieve an optimal outcome at every moment. Prices and output do not continually adjust in most markets so that the markets are always cleared.

Nevertheless, assuming buyers and sellers move toward an equilibrium is an extremely useful way of describing market behavior. Because there is a *tendency* for consumers, firms, and markets to adjust and move toward equilibrium, the equilibrium conditions give a good basis on which to predict how consumers and producers will react to changes in market conditions. Perhaps most important, equilibrium, based upon optimizing behavior, yields predictions about economic behavior that are consistent with real-world observations.

Therefore, when you encounter in this text theories of individual behavior and markets, do not worry whether the theory presents a totally realistic description of the real world. As we have emphasized, theory is designed to give a good general explanation of how markets work and to yield predictions consistent with what is observed. Finally, these economic theories based on assumptions of optimization and equilibrium, although not perfect, are the best that economists have been able to come up with: best in the sense of the best explanations and the most accurate predictions.

1.5   Structure of the Text

Let us briefly discuss the material covered in this text. Microeconomics, the subject matter of the book, is concerned with analyzing and explaining both individual consumer and producer behavior and how consumers and producers interact in a market. Microeconomics does not focus on the behavior of aggregates in an economy, such as the behavior of *all* households or *all* businesses in an economy. In microeconomics, you will study the forces that affect relative prices—why the price of one good or resource rises or falls relative to the prices of other goods or resources—but not the forces that affect the general price level or cost of living.

Microeconomics is the study of markets, markets for goods and services and markets for resources, as pictured in the circular flow. We will, therefore, first present a general description of how markets function. In this general description, we will not attempt to explain the behavior of each firm and each household that participates in the markets. The behavior of the market participants in general is the subject of the majority of the text.

The major body of this text is divided into three sectors, as is typically the case in microeconomics. The first broad area is the behavior of an individual consumer and groups of consumers in a market. Consumer behavior determines the demand for goods and services in the markets. The second major area is the behavior of firms and industries as sellers of goods and services. This behavior determines the supplies of goods and services. The third area concerns the behavior of households, as sellers of resources, and firms and industries, as buyers of resources. This section looks at theories of resource distribution. Here we will discuss the forces that affect the payment to the owners of resources—labor, capital, land, management. These payments are in the form of wages, salaries, interest, and rents.

Keep in mind throughout this course that the major factor limiting the amount of goods and services that a society produces and consumes is the amount of resources in the society available to produce goods and services. Clearly, as either the technology improves or the resources owned by people in the society increase, the society can have more of some goods without giving up some other goods. During any one period of time, the total supply of resources limits the total amount of goods possible, and if the society wishes more of certain things, it must give up some other things that are also desired. The society experiences scarcity, and scarcity is the subject of study for economists.

1.6   Style of the Text

We have tried to make this text as easy to understand as possible. This is not to say that everything you read will be simple. On the contrary, you will encounter some difficult concepts, but they will be presented in an understandable fashion.

To help you grasp the important ideas presented in each chapter, we have identified and classified them as a *definition, relation,* or *principle*. These headings are highlighted in bold type in the body of the text immediately following or even preceding the theoretical discussion. They highlight important concepts and will be an important part of your study of microeconomics.

Throughout the text we will apply the basic theory to specific questions. These applications typically extend the fundamental assumptions of the theory in order to address some real-world issue. For example, the basic theory of consumer behavior explains how people choose what goods and services to purchase. An application would extend the theory to analyze the effect of inflation upon purchasing decisions. Another application would extend the general theory of the firm to consider the effect of taxation on a firm's price and output decisions. These applications will show you how economists use economic theories to answer questions about what is happening in the economy and will illustrate the relevance of the theories you will learn.

Throughout the text you will encounter two types of material that is blocked off from the main body of the text. One type is labeled "Economics in the News" and the other type "Applying the Theory."

"Economics in the News" will first present a brief synopsis of a recent news story or editorial that deals with some issue in microeconomics. We will then discuss the article or editorial. Sometimes we will simply show how a theory explains the behavior or events described in an article. At other times we will analyze statements or opinions in order to show, using a theory, why these statements are either correct or incorrect. Or, we will discuss the implications of the events that are discussed in order to predict, based upon a theory, the consequences of these events. The articles and stories are taken from newspapers, magazines, journals, and TV news programs. "Economics in the News" is designed to help you understand and analyze the economic news you read and hear.

"Applying the Theory" is designed to give you practice using microeconomic theory. You will be asked a question that can be answered using only the theory you have learned. These will not be technical questions that merely ask you to reproduce the graphs or tables from the text using different numbers. Neither will the answers to the questions require you to make extensions or additions to theory you have already learned. The questions will be taken from the news, or sometimes they will be realistic but hypothetical questions. Our answers will be at the end of each chapter. You should, however, try to answer the questions yourself and use our answer only as a check. We might warn you that some of the questions do not have a single, clearly correct answer. This will be noted in our discussion.

The following examples will give you a good idea of what to expect in the material that is blocked off.

Economics in the News

The High Cost of Going to College

Business Week, May 1, 1989, reported that the tuition costs of going to college rose dramatically, but the value of going to college rose substantially also if you measure it relative to the value of not going to college. According to Frank S. Levy, an economist at the University of Maryland, real wages (net of inflation) of college graduates had risen over the past decade while the real wages of high school graduates had fallen. Consequently, the gap between the value of a college and a high school degree widened. In 1979, the average male college graduate age 25 to 34 earned 18 percent more than a high school graduate of the same age. From 1986 to 1989, the advantage had increased to 43 percent more. The advantage for women college graduates had increased also, but not as dramatically. This trend reversed what happened in the 1970s when college graduates lost ground relative to high school graduates.

During the 1970s there was an oversupply of college graduates. Levy noted that beginning in the 1980s blue-collar workers were getting squeezed out of manufacturing jobs by foreign competition and technological change. More high school graduates competing for fewer manufacturing jobs led to lower wages not only in manufacturing but also in the service sector, where many blue-collar workers were seeking employment. Finally, high school graduates were having trouble getting manufacturing jobs because of more sophisticated job requirements.

According to *Business Week,* what happened to the opportunity cost of choosing not to go to college? The opportunity cost of taking a job immediately after high school had risen, because the earnings of a college graduate relative to a high school graduate of the same age increased substantially—from 18 to 43 percent more. Thus, the cost of not attending college had increased. Furthermore, because high school graduates were having trouble getting good manufacturing jobs, implying lower average wages, the benefits of taking a job after high school decreased.

What is the opportunity cost of someone attending college? As the *Business Week* article pointed out, the tuition cost of college had risen dramatically, which increased the opportunity cost of college. However, *Business Week* ignored what had happened to another, perhaps more important, opportunity cost of attending college. This opportunity cost is the sacrificed income that could have been earned had a student chosen to take a job rather than attend college. (If you don't think this cost is important, stretch the point to the extreme and think of what you might do if Steven Spielberg offered you $1 million a year to come to Hollywood and star in his movies. Would you quit college?) Since high school graduates were having a hard time getting jobs and the jobs were paying

(continued)

less, this part of the opportunity cost had fallen and offset, at least partially, the higher tuition cost. The point here is that costs do not have to involve out-of-pocket monetary expense; they also can be something that is implicitly sacrificed.

What predictions can be made from the analysis of the article? The opportunity cost of college had fallen (ignoring tuition) while the opportunity cost of taking a job after high school had risen. (Or, as the article expressed it, the value of a college education rose—ignoring the fall in opportunity cost—while the value of taking a job after high school fell.) One would expect that this change in relative costs would induce some, perhaps many, high school graduates, who would otherwise have taken jobs, to postpone income and go to college in response to the lower cost. (Note that we said "some" or "many" not "all"; some people could not get into college, even if they wanted to, and some would not attend, even if they could.)

The increase in the number of college graduates and relative decrease in the number of people with only a high school degree should decrease the salaries of college graduates relative to high school graduates in the future. That is, one would expect the salaries of college graduates to remain higher than that of high school graduates, but not quite as much higher.

This should give you some idea of what to expect when you come upon "Economics in the News." We went into a bit more detail in our analysis here than we will later in the book, because by then you will have more experience analyzing such articles on your own. If we had used the information in the article as an "Applying the Theory" section, it would have appeared as follows.

1.1   *Applying the Theory*

On May 1, 1989, *Business Week* reported that the average salary of male college graduates 25 to 34 years old increased from 18 percent more than that of high school graduates of the same age in the 1970s to 43 percent more by the late 1980s. High school graduates at the time were having a difficult time getting higher paid manufacturing jobs because of more sophisticated requirements. What does this information imply about salaries of college graduates relative to high school graduates in the future? Use the concept of opportunity cost.

Finally, each chapter, except Chapter 1, ends with two sets of problems. The first set falls under the heading of "Technical Problems." Here, the solutions are frequently expressed in quantities or money units. They are designed to reinforce your understanding of market mechanics. The second set is given the name "Analytical Problems." These problems are similar to those in "Applying the Theory" and are more thought-provoking. They are intended to help you apply the theory presented in the chapter in a wide variety of market contexts. These analytical problems are more difficult, and you might not be able to answer all of them. They are learning tools to keep you thinking and to promote discussion with your fellow students and instructor.

Of course, each chapter, including this one, will conclude with a summary to help tie things together.

1.7 Summary

Microeconomics is concerned with the study of markets. Markets are composed of buyers and sellers who exchange a certain good or service. The study of microeconomics enables one to understand how market participants make decisions and to predict the consequences of such decisions. The circular flow diagram in Figure 1–1 shows graphically how households and firms interact in markets. Households sell their resources in resource markets to firms, which use the resources to produce goods and services. Households use the money they earn from selling their resources to purchase the goods and services in markets. Thus, the circular flow gives a highly abstract picture of how important markets are to an economy.

Theoretical material makes up a majority of this text. Theory necessarily abstracts away from all but the most important aspects of the topic or problem to be examined. The world is too complex for us to consider every aspect of an issue. Theory is designed to explain and predict the implications of economic behavior in general, not the behavior of any specific individual or firm. Thus, a theory may not be totally realistic and may not precisely fit a particular situation. It is not supposed to be.

The text is divided into three broad general sections: (1) The theory of consumer behavior explains the decisions of consumers of goods and services. (2) The theory of the firm explains the decisions of firms as producers and sellers of goods and services. (3) The theory of distribution explains the decisions of individuals as sellers of resources and firms as buyers of resources and how resource markets function.

In this course you will encounter five fundamental topics.

1. Scarcity. Everyone cannot have everything desired. Resources are scarce. Thus, everyone must take decisions that involve choosing between alternatives.
2. Forgone Opportunities. Every choice has an opportunity cost—the next best alternative that must be given up if a particular choice is made.
3. Marginal Decisions. Decisions at the margin consider the effect of small changes in choices on other economic variables or outcomes. Economic theory frequently deals with making the best decisions at the margin.
4. Equilibrium. Equilibrium results when no individual in the group under consideration has any incentive to change unless some variable external to the group changes.
5. Optimization. The assumption that people optimize—try to achieve the maximum benefits or minimum costs in a given situation—is frequently used in economic theory.

This chapter is designed to give you a brief preview of the scope and structure of the text. Now we will begin developing the theories and showing you how to apply these theories to problems. We urge you to work through the sections that will enable you to apply the theories for yourselves and to try to solve the problems at the end of the chapters. In economics, as in mathematics, riding a bike, playing tennis, and speaking a foreign language, one learns by doing. These problems will give you plenty of practice doing economics. We want you not only to learn economics but also to learn how to do and use economics and think like economists.

PART II

Market Basics

CHAPTER 2

Demand and Supply

2.1   Introduction

Economics is concerned with the problem of scarcity. Goods are scarce because the resources used to produce them have alternate uses. When there is market exchange, prices will allocate scarce goods and services. A fundamental task of economics is to analyze the factors that determine prices and the quantities sold in markets. These factors are usually separated into two categories: those affecting the demand for a good and those affecting supply. The purpose of this chapter is to explain what demand and supply are and show how they determine price and the quantity sold.

Demand and supply schedules give a visual picture of what happens in a market. Sometimes the picture is a table; sometimes it is a graph. Either way demand and supply are without a doubt the two most important tools in economic theory. By looking at how demand and supply interact, a story can be told about how the two sides of the market work toward deciding what price and quantity will prevail. If we know what demand and supply are, we can predict how prices and quantities will change when one of the schedules change. The ability to predict changes or to expect no change in the market illustrates that demand and supply are powerful tools when we have to make decisions and plans. The decision to buy now or later, for instance, is in part decided by whether we think prices will rise or fall in the future. Knowing the factors that determine price movements helps people make more informed decisions.

Thomas Carlyle, the man who named economics "the dismal science," stated: "It is easy to train an economist: teach a parrot to say Demand and Supply." This is an epigram that has survived because it is humorous and contains a certain amount of truth. Demand and supply are such important tools of analysis that we will devote several chapters to investigating the underlying forces behind them. In this chapter, however, we will discuss what demand and supply are and, more specifically, how they determine prices and quantities sold in markets.

2.2   Individual and Market Demand Schedules

An individual's, or a household's, demand schedule for a specific commodity is the quantity of that commodity the person (or household) is willing and able to purchase at each possible price during a particular time period. For example, if someone is willing and can afford to buy at the grocery store during the week, 2 pounds of chicken at $3 a pound, 4 pounds at $1 a pound, or 5 pounds at $.50 a pound, these prices and quantities would be part of that person's demand schedule for the commodity. To get the full schedule we would have to extend the list of prices, but the schedule would show that consumers are willing and able to buy more at lower prices than they are at higher prices. Such behavior is so pervasive it is referred to as the *law of demand*. If you doubt the law of demand, try to think of a specific item you would buy in larger amounts if only its price were higher.

Perhaps you can think of cases when you bought more as price increased. But this was probably because the price change caused you to think differently about the product or made you expect future price increases. Many factors can affect expectations, and these can *change* the demand schedule, which is different than arguing that as price goes up people buy more on the same demand schedule. Considerable portions of this and later chapters are devoted to analyzing the law of demand. We now assume the following is correct: people are willing and able to buy more at lower prices than at higher prices.

Principle

An individual's demand schedule is a list of prices and corresponding quantities that an individual is willing and able to buy at each price during some time period. Quantity demanded increases as price decreases.

2.2.1   Markets and Demand Schedules

Suppose a large group of people go to the grocery store weekly to buy chicken. When they arrive the grocer requests that each person turn in a list indicating the number of pounds he or she is willing and able to purchase that day at each price: $.50, $1.00, $1.50, $2.00, $2.50, $3.00 and so forth. The grocer then adds up the amounts that each person is willing and able to buy at each of the prices and gets the figures shown in Table 2–1. The table shows a list of prices and corresponding quantities that consumers demand per period of time at each price on the list. This list of prices and quantities is called a *market demand schedule*. It is the sum of the demand schedules of all individuals in the market. Because people are willing and able to buy more at lower prices than at higher prices, quantity demanded and price vary inversely in the market.

Table 2–1   Market Demand Schedule

Pounds Demanded		Price per Pound
500	....	$3.00
2,000	....	2.50
3,500	....	2.00
5,000	....	1.50
6,500	....	1.00
8,000	....	.50

Principle

The market demand schedule is the sum of the quantities that all individual consumers in the market demand at each price. In the market, quantity demanded increases as price decreases.

At this point it looks as though economists overemphasize the importance of price to buyers and ignore other factors that also affect quantity demanded, such as advertising and service at the grocery store. This criticism can be concisely stated by using the letter f for the symbol "function of" or "depends upon." If we let Q_d represent the quantity of a certain good and P its price, the accusation that economists think Q_d is only a function of P can be expressed as

$$Q_d = f(P),$$

or Q_d depends on P.

Frequently, this is the way economists model demand; nevertheless, they recognize that many forces other than price determine the quantity demanded. The common practice is to hold other influences constant and focus on either price or just a few important variables. Economists do not say price is the sole influence on purchases—but they say that price generally has a *very important effect* on quantity purchased. To analyze the effect of price, economists hold constant other variables and concentrate on the relation between quantity demanded and price— the relation shown by a demand schedule.

When using demand schedules, you should bear in mind what some of the other things are that can influence quantity demanded. First, a consumer's income affects the amount demanded at any price. For some commodities, an increase in income will cause consumers to demand more of a particular commodity at each price. For other commodities, an increase in income will cause consumers to demand less at given prices. Thus, the effect of income on quantity purchased can be the same as the effect of price or just the opposite.

Economists classify goods as *normal* or *inferior* according to the effect of changes of income on demand. A good is a normal good if a change in income causes a consumer to demand more of the good at a given price when his/her income increases and less of the good when his/her income decreases. A good is an inferior good when a change in income causes a consumer to demand less of that good at a given price when his/her income increases and more of the good when his/her income decreases.

Second, the prices of other goods are held constant. For any price of a particular good other prices affect the quantity of that good purchased. For example, suppose both chicken and pork have been selling for $2 a pound, and the price of pork falls to $1 per pound. Consumers would probably buy less chicken when pork is relatively cheaper than they would when chicken and pork are the same price. When consumers switch to another good because the price of the good they now buy increases, the two goods are substitutes in the market. Pork and chicken are an example, Nike and Reebok shoes are another, and two different brands of gasoline are likely to be substitutes. Consumers also might buy less of a second good when the price of what they now buy increases. These goods are complements. For example, if the price of rice goes up, shoppers may buy less chicken as a result. A rise in gasoline prices could lead to fewer purchases of tires because consumers will drive less. Thus, depending on whether the price of a substitute or complement rises, the demand for a particular good can increase or decrease.

Third, changes in consumer's tastes can affect how much of a good is demanded at a given price. If some influential movie or television stars report in an interview that they eat no meat, some consumers who wish to imitate them would probably buy less meat, including chicken, at the prevailing price. Tastes are influenced by advertising. This is why ads exist. Many different strategies are employed by advertisers to increase demand for a product. Basketball shoes are endorsed by the well-known stars, for instance, a Wendy's burger is compared favorably to the competition, or buying an Oldsmobile is claimed to keep you young and sexy. Many factors can influence tastes, and these factors and their importance are constantly studied by marketing experts.

Finally, people's expectations affect demand. When people think the price of a good is going to rise, they have an incentive to increase their rates of purchase before the price rises. On the other hand, expecting prices to fall causes some purchases to be postponed. All kinds of things can affect someone's expectations about future prices: the threat of war, a technological breakthrough, new government legislation that might deregulate a market are some examples. When people don't have better information, a product's relative price may be used to judge the quality of a good. Expectations can be based on the current price itself rather than on predicted changes. People might use a rule of thumb that when price is high they expect high quality. They believe price is connected with how well the product is made.

Economists do not believe that quantity demanded is simply a function of price. To summarize the discussion, if we let M represent the consumer's income, $\bar{P}$, the prices of other goods, T, tastes, and V, expectations, economists assume that

$$Q_d = f(P,M,\bar{P},T,V),$$

and there may be other influences, some peculiar to the good studied. The point is, however, that when economists set forth demand schedules such as the one shown in Table 2–1, they do so *ceteris paribus,* or under the assumption that all other things that may affect quantity demanded remain the same.

Figure 2–1   Market Demand Curve For Chicken

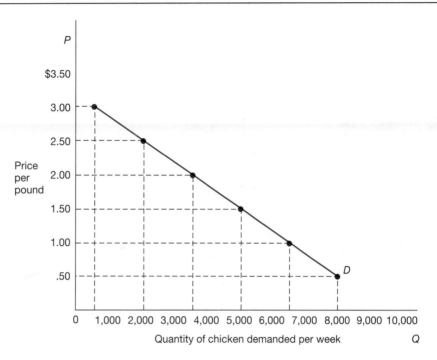

2.2.2   Demand Curves

Quite often, it is more convenient to work with a graph of demand, rather than a table. Figure 2–1 is the graph of the demand schedule shown in Table 2–1. Each price-quantity combination ($3.00, 500), ($2.50, 2,000), and so on, is plotted, and then the six points are connected by the curve labeled *D*. Whenever we draw a demand curve, price will always be on the vertical axis, and quantity will be on the horizontal axis.[1] This demand curve indicates the quantity of the good consumers are willing and able to buy per period of time at every price from $3.00 to $.50. Since consumers demand more at lower prices, the curve slopes downward. When deriving a demand curve from a set of price-quantity data, we assume that price and quantity are infinitely divisible. Price can be any number between $3.00 and $.50; quantity demanded also can be any number between 500 and 8,000. This assumption sacrifices some realism because consumers usually cannot buy fractions of units, but this sacrifice is more than counterbalanced by the gain in analytical convenience from having smooth curves in the graphs.

[1]By convention, when graphs are drawn, the variable on the vertical scale is dependent on the variable measured by the horizontal scale. So, we have reversed the role of *P* and *Q* from our discussion above and drawn the graph in such a way that *P* is a function of *Q*, rather than *Q* being a function of *P*. Technically, the curve in Figure 2–1 is an inverse demand curve. We will continue, however, to refer to it as the demand curve.

Figure 2–2   Shifts in Demand for Chicken

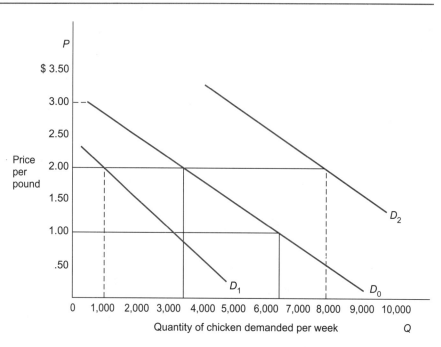

2.2.3   Shifts in Demand

When price falls and consumers purchase more of a good, other things remaining the same, we say that *quantity demanded* increases. When price rises and less of a good is purchased, we say *quantity demanded* decreases. We do not simply say that demand increases or decreases; this refers to a shift in the schedule or curve. Demand is a list or schedule of prices and quantities demanded at each price. In a graph, this curve shifts only if one or more of the factors held constant when deriving demand changes. For example, if the incomes of consumers change, causing them to demand more of a good at each price than they did previously, we say the demand for that good increases. If the change in income causes consumers to demand less of a good at each price than they did before, then demand decreases.

When one or more of the variables held constant when deriving demand changes, demand changes. Figure 2–2 illustrates such a change. In the figure, D_0 is the demand for chicken, reproduced from Figure 2–1. At a price of $2 per unit, consumers want to purchase 3,500 pounds of chicken per period. If price falls to $1, quantity demanded increases, along D_0, to 6,500 pounds.

Now, begin with demand D_0 and a price of $2. Suppose that consumers' taste for chicken is reduced, perhaps because of a scientific discovery that chicken is high in cholesterol. This change in taste causes demand to decrease (shift to the left) to D_1. Now consumers demand only 1,000 units per period of time at the price of $2. In fact, at every price, consumers are willing and able to buy less of the good after the shift than before. This shows a *decrease in demand*.

Now return to the original demand, D_0. At \$2, consumers once again wish to purchase 3,500 pounds of chicken. Suppose now that the price of pork, a close substitute for chicken, increases significantly, causing the demand for chicken to increase (shift to the right) to D_2. At \$2, consumers purchase 8,000 units per period, and at every other relevant price they will buy more than before. This shows an *increase in demand*. It is worthwhile to repeat, if demand is D_0 and price falls from \$2 to \$1, other things remaining the same, we say that *quantity demanded* changes from 3,500 to 6,500, but demand does not change. An increase or decrease in demand means the entire schedule has shifted to the right or left. The distinction between a change in quantity demanded and a change in demand may be summarized as follows.

Relation

When price falls, other things remaining the same, quantity demanded rises. When price rises, quantity demanded falls. When something held constant in deriving the demand curve changes, demand increases or decreases. An increase in demand indicates that consumers are willing and able to buy more at each price on the schedule. A decrease in demand indicates they are willing and able to buy less at each price. Changes in demand are represented by shifts in the demand curve; changes in quantity demanded are shown by movements along the original demand curve.

Finally, it should be remembered that demand curves can shift for demographic reasons. A market can grow, shifting the demand curve to the right simply because population increases in a region. Demand can fall because population decreases. The age, education, race, gender, and religion of buyers can have a big impact on demand. These demographic characteristics play a big part in determining the tastes of consumers. As populations grow older, for instance, they will shop less for those items frequently purchased by young households—baby cribs, tricycles, and swing sets—and more for those items purchased by more mature households, for example, increased medical care and luxury automobiles.

Economics in the News

Trends Show Chicken Is a More Popular Meat[2]

Since 1955, consumption of chicken in the United States has risen dramatically. Thirty years ago, per capita consumption of chicken was about 14 pounds per year. Presently, it is more than 60 pounds per year. This represents a more than four-fold increase in consumption. You can probably think of several reasons for the increased popularity of poultry. Health concerns about eating red meat and other meats with high cholesterol have surely changed the tastes of many consumers. However, the health concern may

(continued)

---

[2]This report is based on the article by Robert Bishop and Lee Christensen, "America's Poultry Industry," *National Food Review*, January-March 1989, pp. 9–12.

have been a bit selective; from 1975 to 1987 the average American consumption of sugar and sweeteners increased 29 percent. Also, chicken has been sold and packaged more conveniently in recent years. Fryers have gone from the uncut bird to being packaged and cut as breast fillets and chicken nuggets. Fast-food chains have had a tremendous influence toward popularizing chicken nuggets among young consumers, and chicken processors have attained much of their recent growth through selling ready-to-eat chicken parts to fast-food outlets. Overall, the proportion of whole chicken sales to total processed sales has dropped from 74 percent in 1968 to 28 percent in 1985, while cut-up parts and processed chicken increased from 26 percent to 72 percent.

Despite changing tastes and increased convenience, which have acted to *increase demand,* growth in the industry also must be attributed to price decreases. Declining prices have acted to increase the *quantity demanded.* In 1955, the per-pound price of chicken was more than the per-pound price of hamburger. A pound of hamburger cost about as much as 11 ounces of a whole fryer. In 1987, the price of a pound of hamburger was equivalent to the price of 27 ounces of chicken. Taking account of inflation and converting prices to what they would buy in 1967, the price of chicken in 1955 would have been 68.8 cents a pound, whereas it was just 22.7 cents a pound in 1987. This represents a 67 percent decline in the real price. Over the last 30 years, tastes, product quality (e.g., convenience of consumption), and income have changed. These and other factors are influencing consumption. But the law of demand is at work in the market for poultry. As price goes down, consumption increases.

To summarize our introduction of demand schedules, Figure 2–3 presents a general picture of three schedules. All are downward sloping, reflecting the law of demand. Beginning with schedule D_0, if price falls from P_1 to P_2 quantity demanded increases from Q_1 to Q_2. This is a movement along the same schedule. An increase in demand means the schedule shifts to the right, say from D_0 to D_1. Consumers now demand more at every price. In the figure, Q_3 is demanded at P_1. Also, demand can decrease. This is pictured as a movement to D_2. Now, less is demanded at each price. At price P_1 only Q_0 is purchased. Remember that demand depends on many other factors besides price. When any one of these changes, there is a shift in the schedule. Movements along a demand curve illustrate how price alone influences the quantity purchased.

2.3   Market Supply Schedules

To gain an understanding of supply, suppose a number of grocers sell prepared chicken in the same market. All the grocers can order as much as they want from meat processors at any time. One particular grocer is willing to sell 100 pounds per week if the price per pound is $.50 per pound. If the price of chicken were $1.00 a pound, the grocer would be willing to sell more—say 200 pounds. The higher price induces the grocer to devote more time and store space toward selling

Figure 2–3   Demand Shifts Summarized

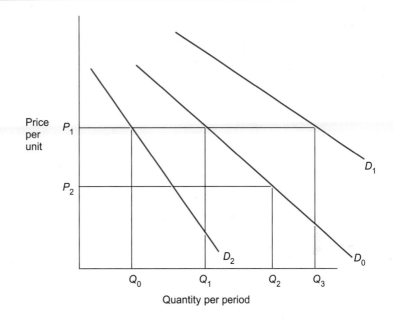

chicken because selling chicken is more profitable at the higher price. A still higher price of $1.50 a pound would be required to induce sales of 300 pounds a week, and so on. The grocer allocates time and store space to make as much money as possible. It naturally follows that higher prices are required to induce the grocer to reallocate more time and space to chicken.

A portion of the grocer's supply schedule might, therefore, be as follows:

Quantity Supplied (pounds)	Price per Pound
100	$ .50
200	1.00
300	1.50
400	2.00
500	2.50
600	3.00

This table shows the minimum price that induces the grocer to supply each amount on the list. Note that, in contrast to demand analysis, where price and the quantity demanded vary inversely, price and quantity supplied move in the same direction. Each price on the supply schedule shows the minimum price necessary to induce sellers to voluntarily offer each possible quantity for sale. Generally, for supply schedules, an increase in price is required to induce an increase in quantity supplied.

Table 2–2   Market Supply Schedule

Quantity Supplied (pounds)	Price (per pound)
11,000	$3.00
9,000	2.50
7,000	2.00
5,000	1.50
3,000	1.00
1,000	.50

Just as the market demand schedule is the sum of the quantities demanded by all consumers, the market supply schedule shows the sum of the quantities that sellers (firms) supply at each price.

Definition

Supply is a list of prices and the quantities that a seller or group of sellers (firms) are willing and able to offer for sale at each price in the list per period of time.

2.3.1   Supply Schedules and Supply Curves

Consider the market supply schedule in Table 2–2. This table shows the minimum price necessary to induce grocers to supply, per week, each of the six quantities listed. In order to induce greater quantities, price must rise. For example, if price increases from $2.00 to $2.50, stores will increase the quantity supplied from 7,000 to 9,000 pounds. Figure 2–4 shows a graph of the schedule in Table 2–2. It is called a *supply curve*. Table 2–2 and Figure 2–4 are examples of the two most common forms of describing a supply schedule.

You might ask why the supply curve in Figure 2–4 has the shape that it does. Why, for example, does a price of $2.50 rather than a price of $2.00 induce a quantity supplied of 9,000? Why isn't a lower quantity supplied at each price in the list? The reason given so far is that more of a good is supplied at higher prices because suppliers, at the higher prices, can earn greater profits. If a supplier observes a rise in price and does not have any increase in cost, profit will go up on all the units sold, and more profit can be earned by selling more.

Over time, however, these profits are usually competed away by new sellers entering the market. In the long run, prices will tend to just cover the cost of providing the good. Hence, in the long run, supply curves show the costs of producing and selling. An upward-sloping schedule shows that sellers generally experience increasing costs as more is produced and sold. As more is produced, resources are taken from progressively more valuable activities. Therefore, higher prices must be paid to obtain the use of these resources, and this increases the cost of doing business.

Figure 2–4 Market Supply Curve

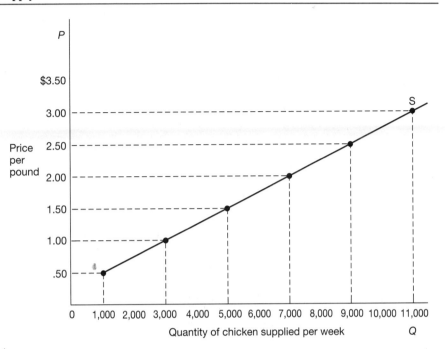

While it is *usually* the case that supply curves slope upward, there is no law of supply that says they *always* slope upward. Over some ranges of quantity, the supply curve may be flat. This indicates that sellers are willing and able to provide these quantities at one price. Flat supply curves mean that it is easy for producers to increase production. So, the slightest increase in price brings forth larger quantities from producers who are already in the market or from new entrants. It would indicate, too, that the cost of attracting additional resources to produce and sell the good is not rising.

As in the case of demand, we have illustrated a supply curve in which the quantities offered depend only on the price of the good. This is a simplification. Supply curves depend on other factors. When these factors change, the supply curve will move to the right (downward) or left (upward). A move to the left or an upward shift means that less is offered at each price. A move to the right or a downward shift means more is offered at each price. We will briefly highlight four factors that are generally held constant when drawing a supply curve and will shift the supply curve when they change.

First, technology is assumed to be unchanged along a supply curve. If technology improves and a more efficient method of production is discovered, firms generally increase the amounts they are willing to supply at each price, shifting the supply curve to the right. Such a shift is called an increase in supply. It is hard to imagine a deterioration in technology, which causes firms to adopt a less efficient method of production and to decrease supply. However, certain types of governmental regulations, such as pollution controls or worker safety restrictions, can have a similar effect. In such cases, firms are forced by the regulations to use a production process that they would not otherwise use. This could have the effect of a less efficient production process, and it could shift supply to the left.

Second, the prices of all inputs used to produce the good are held constant. A decrease in the price of labor or the price of raw materials (e.g., crude oil) will increase firms' costs of production and shift the supply curve to the left (decrease supply), reflecting the fact that suppliers require a higher price for each quantity to cover their higher costs. A fall in the prices of some factors of production will shift supply to the right (increase supply).

Third, the prices of related goods (in production) are held constant. Goods related in production are other goods that the firms can produce using essentially the same resources. For example, generally wheat and corn can be grown on the same land, so the price of corn is held constant when deriving the supply of wheat. If the price of corn rises, corn becomes relatively more profitable and, at a given price of wheat, some farmers will switch from wheat to corn. This switch causes the supply of wheat to shift to the left (supply decreases). If the price of corn decreases, the supply of wheat increases as some farmers switch from corn to wheat.

Finally, expectations of producers about the future, especially expectations about the future price of the good, are held constant along supply. If producers expect the price to be lower in the future than they previously expected, some firms would sell a portion of their inventory now before the price falls. This would have the effect of shifting supply in the present period to the right (increase supply). Expectations of a higher price in the future would have the opposite effect of decreasing present supply as some firms build up inventories, hoping for a higher price.

2.3.2 Shifts in Supply

When firms offer a greater quantity of a good for sale because the price of the good rises, thereby staying on the same supply curve, we say that *quantity supplied changes,* and in this case *increases*. This is not the same as a shift of the supply curve. When one or more of the factors held constant for a supply curve changes, the entire schedule changes, indicating that firms are induced to supply more or less at each price on the schedule. In this case, *supply changes*.

Consider Figure 2–5, in which S_0 is the initial supply curve for chicken shown in Figure 2–4. If price falls from $2.00 to $1.50, the quantity supplied decreases from 7,000 to 5,000, other things remaining the same. This change simply reflects a movement down the existing schedule. On the other hand, if technology changes and supply increases to S_2, firms now wish to offer 11,000 pounds at a price of $2, and they wish to offer more units for sale at each price in the entire range of prices. Such a shift is called an *increase in supply*.

A leftward shift in supply from S_0 to S_1 indicates a *decrease in supply*. Firms now are willing to sell only 2,500 pounds of chicken at $2 a pound, and at every other price over the range, grocers are willing to sell less than before.

Figure 2–5   Shifts in Supply

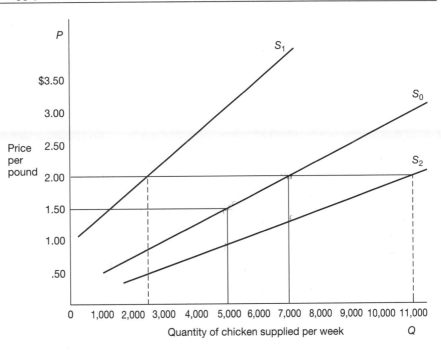

When price rises (falls), other things remaining the same, quantity supplied rises (falls). When something that was held constant in deriving supply changes, for example, the prices of inputs or technology, supply increases or decreases. If firms are induced to offer more (less) at each price, supply has increased (decreased).

2.4   Market Determination of Price and Quantity

The separate study of supply and demand provides the background for the analysis of their interaction, which determines market price and quantity. A primary reason for separating supply and demand is to isolate the factors that determine each, so that we can analyze the market effects of changing these factors. In this section, we combine the supply and demand curves and examine their interaction in the market.

2.4.1   Market Equilibrium

Suppose that in the market for chicken at the grocery store, buyers and sellers have the particular demand and supply schedules set forth in Tables 2–1 and 2–2, respectively. These schedules are combined in Table 2–3. Notice that at high prices

Table 2–3 Market Demand and Supply

Price	Pounds Supplied	Pounds Demanded	Excess Supply (+) or Demand (−)
$3.00	11,000	500	+ 10,500
2.50	9,000	2,000	+ 7,000
2.00	7,000	3,500	+ 3,500
1.50	5,000	5,000	0
1.00	3,000	6,500	− 3,500
.50	1,000	8,000	− 7,000

of $2.00, $2.50 and $3.00 per pound, the quantity supplied exceeds the quantity demanded. For the week, grocers have more chicken at the counter than they can sell. At the low prices of $.50 and $1.00 a pound, the quantity demanded exceeds the quantity supplied. Now customers who come late in the week find the grocer sold out.

Whenever quantity demanded exceeds quantity supplied, we call this situation *excess demand* (sometimes called a shortage). An increase in price will cause quantity demanded to decrease and quantity supplied to increase; that is, excess demand will decrease when price rises, as shown in the table. Consumers are willing and able to buy less as price rises, and firms are willing and able to sell more. When the quantity supplied exceeds the quantity demanded, there is *excess supply* (sometimes called a surplus). A reduction in price causes a reduction in quantity supplied and an increase in quantity demanded; thus, a price reduction reduces excess supply.

Suppose the prevailing price in the market is $2 a pound and 3,500 pounds are demanded. Because 7,000 pounds are offered for sale, there is an excess supply of 3,500 pounds at that price. To reduce their unwanted inventories, the grocery may decide to reduce their average price to $1.00 and cut back the quantity supplied to 3,000 pounds. Because customers now demand 6,500 pounds at $1.00, excess demand is now 3,500 pounds. At any price above $1.50 per pound grocers will experience excess supplies or *surpluses* of chicken. Prices below $1.50 per pound will cause excess demand or *shortages*. Consumers, unable to purchase all they want at this low price, will act to bid up the price in the attempt to buy more. The grocers, seeing that they are running out of chicken and noticing consumers asking for more chicken, will raise the price. At the price of $1.50, quantity supplied equals the quantity demanded. There is neither excess demand nor excess supply, and the equilibrium price is said to be $1.50. The equilibrium quantity sold is 5,000 pounds.

There are pressures brought on buyers and sellers to move toward the point where supply and demand are equal in a market. A price above the equilibrium causes inventories for a seller to build. Storage costs rise or there may be spoilage, which there would be for fresh meat. To avoid problems connected with excess supply, sellers tend to reduce price. Buyers, shopping for the lowest prices, will

Figure 2–6   A Market Equilibrium for Chicken at the Grocery Store

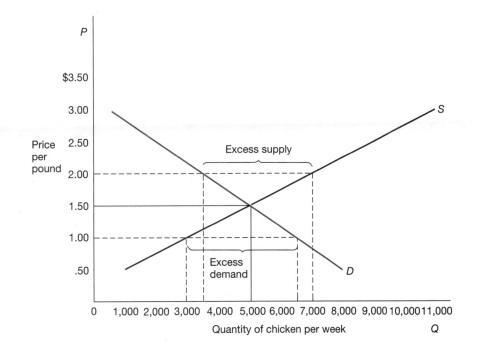

go to the grocers who reduce their prices the most, putting pressures on all grocers to reduce their prices. In summary, building unwanted inventories causes sellers to reduce prices.

Excess demand or a shortage, in contrast, means grocers can sell the amount they supply at higher prices. Shortages make customers unhappy because they cannot buy as much as they want at the prevailing price. To keep stock on hand grocers have the incentive to raise prices. The higher prices reduce the shortage and, to the grocer's joy, increase profits. A shortage will continue in the market described above until the per-pound price of chicken is raised to $1.50. Similarly the building up of inventories at prices above $1.50 will be eliminated only when the per pound price is brought down to $1.50.

Figure 2–6 has combined the demand curve shown in Figure 2–1 and the supply curve shown in Figure 2–4. Three possible scenarios are illustrated at prices of $2.00, $1.50, and $1.00. The graph shows that at $2.00 there is a surplus measured by the horizontal distance between the two schedules. From Table 2–3 you already know this surplus is 3,500 pounds. As prices fall, the distance between the schedules is reduced until supply equals demand at $1.50 a pound. At $1.00 a pound, the figure shows that more is demanded than is supplied. This excess demand is once again measured by the horizontal distance between the two schedules. As prices increase from $1.00 up to $1.50, the distance decreases until shortages are eliminated at the price of $1.50 per pound.

Figure 2–7   Market Equilibrium

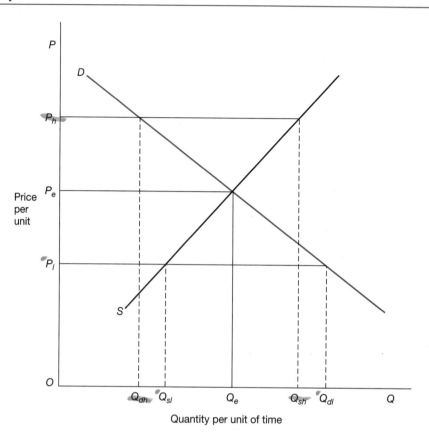

Quantity per unit of time

2.4.2   The Market Equilibrium Picture

We can express an equilibrium solution in general with a graph. In Figure 2–7, D and S are the market demand and supply curves. It is clear that P_e and Q_e are the only price and quantity at which the quantity demanded equals quantity supplied.

If price happens to be P_h, a price higher than P_e, producers supply Q_{sh}, but only Q_{dh} is demanded. An excess supply of $Q_{sh} - Q_{dh}$ develops. This surplus accumulates for the producers, and producers are induced to lower the price to keep from accumulating unwanted inventories. At any price above P_e, there is an excess supply, and producers will lower price. On the other hand, if price is P_l, demanders are willing and able to purchase Q_{dl}, while suppliers are only willing to offer Q_{sl} units for sale. Some consumers are not satisfied, and there is an excess demand of $Q_{dl} - Q_{sl}$ in the market. Since their demands are not satisfied, consumers bid the price up and sellers raise the price. As price rises, quantity demanded decreases and quantity supplied increases until price reaches P_e and quantity is Q_e. Any price below P_e causes shortages, and the shortages cause the price to rise. Given no outside influences that prevent price from rising or falling, an equilibrium price and quantity are attainable. This equilibrium price is the price that clears the market, and both excess demand and excess supply are zero in equilibrium.

Principle

When price is above the equilibrium price, quantity supplied exceeds quantity demanded. The resulting excess supply induces sellers to reduce price in order to sell the surplus. When price is below the equilibrium price, quantity demanded exceeds quantity supplied. The resulting excess demand causes the unsatisfied consumers to bid up price and sellers to raise price. Since prices below equilibrium are bid up by consumers and raised by sellers, and prices above equilibrium are lowered by producers, the market will converge to the intersection of supply and demand.

Economics in the News   **Why Are New Car Sales So Low?**

The Wall Street Journal (January 5, 1990) reported that auto executives at the North American International Auto show professed to be puzzled. They quoted the head of Ford's North American automotive operations, "I wish I could explain why [U.S. auto] sales fell off to the extent they did. I've heard all sorts of explanations and none of them make any sense."

The Journal's response: "Except, it seems, the most elementary explanation of all: New cars, particularly those from the Big Three U.S. automakers, cost too much."

In 1989, U.S. auto sales fell 6 percent from 1988. It was the industry's worst year since 1984. *The Journal* noted that during the 1980s, car prices had risen faster than family income. In 1980, it took 18.7 weeks for the average American family to earn the price of the average car. That figure had remained constant for more than a decade. By 1989, however, it took 24.9 weeks to earn the $15,281 price of the average new car.

A few, though not many, auto executives acknowledged that price is a key issue. The head of Mitsubishi's U.S. division stated, "A few years ago, everybody said that $10,000 was a lot to pay for a new car. Now it's hard to find something for under $10,000."

Prices essentially were above equilibrium. The auto companies were supplying more cars than consumers were demanding at those prices. Car inventories were piling up as the theory predicts. What did the manufacturers do about this? More later.

2.4.3   Demand Shifts

A new equilibrium is established when either the demand curve or supply curve shifts. We can often predict the up or down movements in price and quantity when something held constant along supply or demand changes. Comparing the old equilibrium to the new equilibrium is called a *comparative statics* exercise. We begin such an exercise by considering changes in demand.

Suppose demand increases, meaning the demand curve shifts to the right. If supply is held constant, this shift usually leads to greater quantities purchased and higher prices, as illustrated in Figure 2–8 for the market for chicken. In the figure,

Figure 2–8   An Increase in Demand for Chicken at Grocery Stores

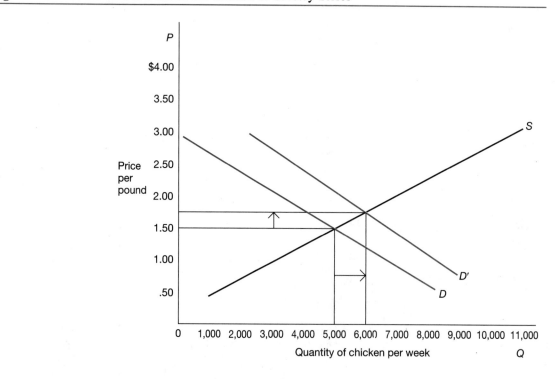

Figure 2–9   A Decrease in Demand for Chicken at Grocery Stores

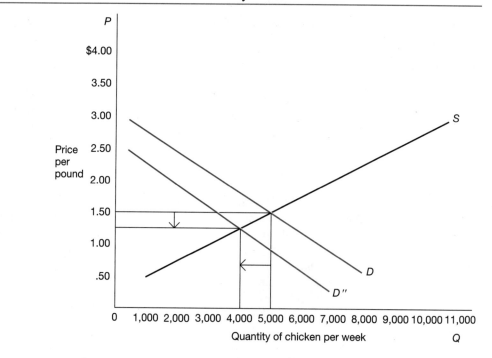

D and S are the demand and supply curves from Figure 2–6. Equilibrium price and quantity are, as before, $1.50 and 5,000. Now, let the price of pork, a substitute for chicken, increase. The demand for chicken increases to D'. The new demand curve intersects the supply curve at a price of $1.75 per pound and a quantity of 6,000 pounds. The increase in demand has caused an increase in price and quantity sold. As long as supply slopes upward and is not perfectly vertical or horizontal, both price and quantity sold will always increase when demand increases. The flatter is the supply curve the less price will increase when demand increases. For a horizontal supply schedule, an increase in demand will lead to larger quantities sold but no change in price. A vertical supply schedule, on the other hand, will lead to higher prices but no change in quantity sold when demand increases.

Figure 2–9 illustrates the effect of a decrease in demand. Begin once again with the original demand for and supply of chicken at D and S. Price and quantity sold are again $1.50 and 5,000. Now let consumers' income decrease. If chicken is a normal good, the demand for chicken would decrease to D''. This shift to the left in demand causes the new equilibrium price to fall to $1.25 a pound and the quantity sold to decrease to 4,000 pounds. Price falls and the quantity sold declines when demand decreases, as long as supply is upward sloping. Only quantity, however, will change if the supply curve is horizontal; only price will change if the supply curve is vertical.

To summarize, when supply is upward sloping, an increase in demand causes both price and quantity sold to increase, and a decrease in demand causes both price and quantity sold to fall.

Economics in the News

Valdez Cleans Up after Oil Spill

In 1989 the tanker Exxon Valdez hit a reef, causing the largest oil spill in North American history near Valdez, Alaska. Two weeks after the huge spill *The Wall Street Journal* (April 10, 1989) reported that an influx of oil men, reporters, environmentalists, scientists, and generic opportunists had poured into the town of Valdez, doubling its size. Many more people were expected. Most of the newcomers brought cash.

The Journal spoke of the tremendous rise in prices. An ordinary steak was selling for $19.95 in restaurants. A five-minute cab fare from the airport increased from $3 to $11. Boat charters increased 50 percent to $1,800, and helicopter fares shot up from $400 an hour to $550. The prices of hotel rooms rose accordingly.

A spokesman for Alaska's fish and game department lamented, "There's something absurd about this. People will try to make a buck off of anything." What was absurd? The rush of people to the little town caused a large increase in the demand for products typically purchased by visitors. The supply of these products was basically fixed given the short period of time since the spill, causing a great shortage of these products. Given your knowledge of the working of supply and demand in markets, what else could have happened? Prices had to be bid up, sometimes by a very large amount. Otherwise, how would the limited supplies of these products have been allocated? Supply and demand in real markets work just the way the theory says they do. When demand increases, prices rise.

Figure 2–10   An Increase in the Supply of Chicken at Grocery Stores

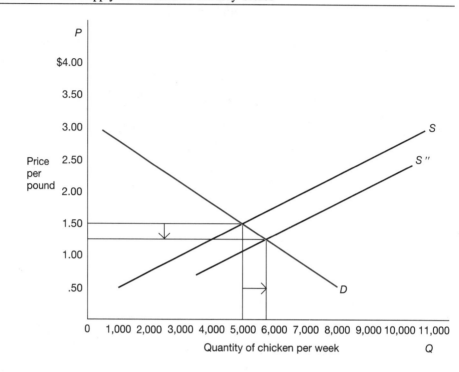

Quantity of chicken per week

2.1   *Applying the Theory*

An article in *Newsweek* (May 21, 1990) discussed the sharp downturn in the prices restaurants throughout the country, particularly the finer restaurants, were charging for meals. The owner of one elegant restaurant, whose average check had fallen from $65 to $50, stated, "The golden rule of this business has always been to build up your check. Frankly, the thought of actively lowering the check to improve business had never occurred to me."

Newsweek pointed out several reasons for lowering the check: an economic downturn, new tax laws that limit the deduction for expense account dining, the change of many baby boomers to baby's parents with less time for dining out, and maybe even a growing distaste for the excesses of the 1980s. Why would these events cause restaurants to lower their prices?

2.2   *Applying the Theory*

In the "Economics in the News" that discussed slumping new car sales early in 1990, we pointed out that new car sales were low because prices were too high. The automobile companies realized the problem but actually did not lower their prices. Instead, in an effort to spur sales, they offered large rebates, up to $2,000

Figure 2–11   A Decrease in the Supply of Chicken at Grocery Stores

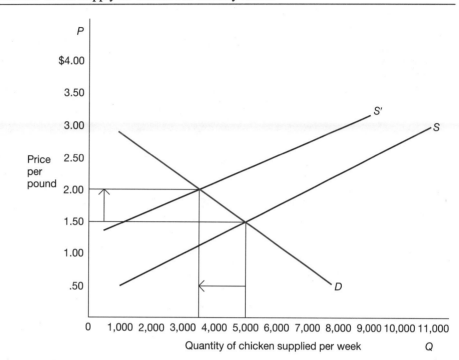

on some models, and extremely low interest rates for financing new cars. Why would these firms react this way and not simply drop their prices?

2.4.4   Supply Shifts

Figures 2–10 and 2–11 show how the equilibrium price and quantity sold change when supply increases and decreases, respectively, while demand is unchanged. In both figures, *D* and *S* are the original demand and supply curves from Figure 2–6. The equilibrium price and quantity sold are $1.50 and 5,000. An increase in supply, shown in Figure 2–10, as the shift to S'' causes greater equilibrium quantities to be sold at a lower price. The rightward shift of supply generates a new equilibrium price of $1.25 a pound and sales of 5,570 pounds a week.

Figure 2–11 shows the leftward shift in the schedule, or, in this case, a decrease in supply. Begin again with the original demand and supply, *D* and *S,* giving the original price and quantity sold of $1.50 and 5,000. Now supply decreases to *S'*. When supply decreases and demand remains constant, the equilibrium price rises and the quantity sold declines. In Figure 2–11 price increases to $2.00, an increase of $.50, and quantity sold falls to 3,500, a reduction in sales of 1,500 pounds. To summarize, when demand remains constant, an increase in supply causes price to fall and quantity sold to rise; a decrease in supply causes price to rise and quantity sold to fall.

Economics in the News

Who Pays for "Saved" Jobs?

Politicians, many unions, and a large number of U.S. corporations frequently push for restrictions on imported goods such as tariffs and quotas. Those favoring such restrictions say that these restrictions save jobs in U.S. firms that would otherwise be lost to foreign competition. However, as a *Newsweek* article, "Tremors of a Trade War" (September 9, 1985), pointed out, most economists are opposed to such restrictions and favor free trade.

One economist who was quoted in the article estimated that the cost to consumers of quotas on imported footwear, rejected by the Reagan administration, would have been $50,000 to $60,000 for every job saved. Another economist estimated that 1983 auto quotas raised the price of Japanese cars in the U.S. market $920 to $960 each and the price of domestic cars by $370. Economists who work for the Federal Trade Commission estimated that the 1984 extension of steel quotas cost consumers $113,622 per job saved in the steel industry.

The reason jobs saved by quotas mean higher costs to consumers is a simple exercise in supply and demand analysis. Quotas decrease the supply of imported goods and therefore the supply in the U.S. market of the good on which the quota is placed. A quota simply restricts the amount of a good that can be imported and sold in the United States. The reduction in supply drives up the price of the good, both domestic and foreign produced. This protects U.S. producers, to some extent, from foreign competition and, ostensibly, keeps open some U.S. manufacturing plants that would otherwise close in the face of foreign competition. In this way, some U.S. jobs that would be lost are supposedly saved. The cost of protecting these jobs is, however, borne by consumers who pay higher prices for the goods. Furthermore, many economists doubt that even through the use of quotas these jobs and less efficient plants are actually saved in the long run.

2.3   Applying the Theory

Newsweek introduced an article on measures being considered by Congress to clean up the air, "Keep Holding Your Breath," June 4, 1990, in the following way: "For nine years, every time the Clean Air Act of 1970 came up for renewal, Congress managed to duck. It just couldn't resolve wrangles between lawmakers looking out for the interest of the automobile and other industries and those more concerned with cleaning up the muck that passes for urban air."

The major measures being considered were regulations on the amount of pollution automobiles could emit and the type of fuels cars could burn. Besides the automobile and other industries and those concerned with clearing up the muck, who else may have some interest in the effect of such measures?

2.4.5   More Comparative Statics

When just one of the curves, either supply or demand, shifts, we have shown in the above cases how price and quantity change. Before we finish our discussion of equilibrium in the market, we want to show how a market equilibrium is disturbed when *both* the demand and supply schedule change.

Figure 2–12   Effects of Supply and Demand Shifts

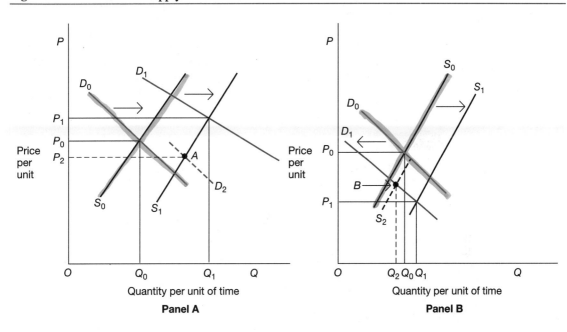

Panel A

Panel B

When supply and demand change simultaneously, the direction of change in price and quantity is not immediately apparent. In Panel A, Figure 2–12, D_0 and S_0 are the initial demand and supply curves. Their intersection determines the equilibrium price and quantity, P_0 and Q_0. Now, suppose supply increases to S_1 and demand increases to D_1. The result is that price rises to P_1, and the quantity sold rises to Q_1. While quantity always increases when both demand and supply increase, price may increase, decrease, or even remain the same, depending on the relative magnitudes of the shifts. Suppose supply shifts to S_1, but demand shifts only to the position indicated by the dashed demand curve D_2 crossing S_1 at A. With this shift, quantity still rises (although by a lesser amount), but price now falls to P_2. Furthermore, by constructing the change in supply or demand still differently, we can cause price to remain at P_0 while quantity increases.

To see the effect of a decrease in both supply and demand, consider D_1 and S_1 in Panel A as the original curves. Next, let them both decrease to D_0 and S_0. Quantity and price decrease from Q_1 and P_1 to Q_0 and P_0. While quantity always decreases when both curves decrease, price need not fall, and indeed may rise or remain constant.

Panel B, Figure 2–12, shows the effect of an increase in one curve accompanied by a decrease in the other. Let supply *increase* from S_0 to S_1 and demand *decrease* from D_0 to D_1. Price falls from P_0 to P_1 and quantity rises from Q_0 to Q_1. While price *must* fall when supply increases and demand decreases, quantity need not increase. Suppose that, while demand shifts to D_1, supply increases only to the position indicated by the dashed supply schedule S_2 crossing D_1 at B. The new equilibrium entails a price reduction (although not so large as before), but now quantity decreases to Q_2 rather than rising to Q_1. The effect on quantity depends on the relative strength of the shifts. To see the effect of a decrease in supply accompanied by an increase in demand, simply assume that demand shifts from D_1 to D_0 and supply from S_1 to S_0. Price must rise. In this illustration, quantity decreases, but depending on the size of the shifts in the curves, quantity may change in either direction. We can summarize the effects of shifts in demand, shifts in supply, and shifts in both (assuming the general case of upward sloping supply curves) in the following:

Principle

(1) When demand increases (decreases), and supply remains constant, both price and quantity increase (decrease). (2) When supply increases (decreases), and demand remains constant, price falls (rises) and quantity rises (falls). (3) When both demand and supply increase (decrease) quantity increases (decreases), but price can either increase or decrease, depending on the relative magnitude of the shifts. (4) When supply and demand shift in opposite directions, the change in quantity is indeterminate, but price always changes in the same direction as the shift in demand.

2.5   Derived Demand in Input Markets

Thus far our discussion of demand and supply has focused upon markets for consumption goods. For a full understanding of markets, it is helpful to distinguish two types of buyers: one who buys the product for consumption and another who buys the good in order to use it to produce something else. The latter type of buyer has a *derived demand*. Most shoppers in grocery stores and other retail outlets are buying for their household's consumption. The determinants of the quantity they demand have already been discussed: the product's price, income, the prices of some other goods, tastes, and expectations.

Derived demand, on the other hand, depends on the demand of customers for the product the buyer sells. For example, a buyer who owns a restaurant is probably buying chicken to serve in the restaurant. This person's demand is determined by the patrons who come to the restaurant. If restaurant goers did not want much chicken on the menu, the restaurant owner would not be buying much chicken, but more of another type of meat, or perhaps no meat at all. Derived demand curves are therefore determined by the preferences of those to whom the buyer sells. There are several important types of derived demand. We will touch on them here, but these markets will be discussed in more detail in later chapters.

2.5.1   The Demand for Materials

The restaurant owner who buys chicken wholesale to prepare dishes for the menu views chicken as a material in the production process. The unprepared chicken is combined by chefs with other ingredients in recipes and presented to diners. The chicken and other meats are viewed as raw materials that are transformed by a chef.

The demand for chicken by restaurants depends on how much diners demand. If the chef is good, business will be good and the restaurant will demand more of the raw material, here chicken. If the chef is bad, progressively less chicken will be demanded by the restaurant as people go elsewhere. Business, and as a consequence the demand for materials, may depend upon the tastes of diners in general. As people dine out more often, the demand for poultry dishes increases, and the restaurant owners will demand more chicken.

Every production process generally requires raw materials. The makers of apparel require cloth, automobile makers use steel, and steel makers require iron ore, the production of electronic equipment takes micro chips, and so on. The demand for these materials is derived and depends on the choices made by consumers who are downstream in the production process. Frequently, in the case of materials *intermediate markets* are distinguished from *final demand* markets. In the latter case, buyers make a purchase for consumption, in the former, purchases are made to produce something that is, in turn, sold.

Notwithstanding the difference between derived demand and the demand for consumption goods, the demand for materials and the demand for all other inputs in the production process are always downward sloping. Both types of demand obey the law of demand. In the case of materials used to produce other goods, when the price of the input falls, buyers of the input will find it more profitable to purchase more of the input at lower prices. They will, if they can, substitute the lower priced input for inputs with unchanged prices. For example, in the case of chicken, restaurant owners will buy more chicken after its price decreases, and perhaps they will feature more chicken dishes on the menu or even lower the price of chicken dishes, hoping to sell more.

Furthermore, as was the case for consumer goods, the supply of materials—and almost all other inputs—is generally upward sloping. Finally, and perhaps most importantly, the price and quantity sold of material and other inputs are determined in the market where demand and supply are equal.

Economics in the News

Health Concerns Have Increased the Derived Demand for Poultry and Fish[3]

During the years 1980 to 1987 consumption of poultry, chicken, and turkey increased 30 percent. Consumption of fish and shellfish rose 20 percent, and consumption of beef fell 4 percent. The per capita consumption trends are shown in the table that follows. Although the relative price of poultry decreased, a big reason for this change in consumption is that the tastes of consumers were changing during these years. Health concerns about cholesterol led consumers to seek meats with lower fat content. This has made poultry and fish better substitutes for beef. As health concerns over red meat have mounted,

(continued)

[3]Pounds of boneless equivalent meat. Source: Michael Harris, "Spending on Meat, Poultry, Fish, and Shellfish," *National Food Review,* October-December 1988, p. 34.

the demand curves for chicken and fish have shifted out, showing an increase in the quantities consumed.

Most of the increase in consumption has come through households eating out more. This has led restaurants, especially the fast-food types, to increase the number of chicken and fish items on their menus. Five years ago, fast-food outlets were just test marketing fish and chicken sandwiches. Chicken nuggets had just been introduced. Today, every chain has several ways to prepare white meat. Restaurant demand is totally derived. It is the increase in demand by patrons, sparked by health concerns, that has led to restaurants offering more chicken and fish entrees.

Poultry and Fish Consumption Have Steadily Increased in the 1980s (annual per capita consumption)

Year	Poultry		Total	Beef	Fish and Shellfish
	Chicken	*Turkey*			
1980	34.5	8.3	42.4	72.1	12.8
1981	35.5	8.5	44.0	72.7	12.9
1982	36.5	8.5	45.0	72.4	12.3
1983	37.0	8.9	45.9	73.8	13.1
1984	38.2	9.0	47.2	73.6	13.7
1985	39.8	9.5	49.4	47.3	14.4
1986	40.6	10.5	51.1	74.1	14.7
1987	43.4	11.9	55.3	69.2	15.4

2.5.2 Capital Markets

Capital, broadly defined, includes all the equipment and machinery that is used in production. Capital markets bring together the buyers and sellers who participate in the exchange of productive machines and equipment. Sometimes capital is sold outright to a buyer; at other times, it may be leased to the user.

The demand for machines and equipment is totally derived, because the function of capital is to produce goods and services. A pizza oven is capital, for example. Its purpose is to bake the pizza demanded by the customers of the pizza parlor. If the parlor is selling a lot of pizzas, it may purchase a personal computer to help manage its finances. This is also capital. The demand for the computer comes from the business the restaurant has generated. Capital comes in all forms and shapes, and some is very specialized or tailored for a specific purpose. Other kinds of capital are used widely across different industries and are easily adapted to different purposes.

The derived demand for capital is sensitive, as you would expect, to the price of the product or service produced by the capital. If the demand for pizza increases, it is likely that pizza prices would rise. The profits of the pizza parlor would go up, and the owner would be able and willing to pay more for an oven. Demand for ovens would increase, and it is likely that their prices would rise too.

Another important determinant of the demand for capital is interest rates. Often the buyers of capital are unwilling or unable to pay the price of machines and equipment without borrowing money. The buyer agrees to pay the lender installments on the loan as the capital is used in production. If the interest rate on the loan is low, the buyer's payments are lower, and this makes the purchase of capital more attractive. Higher interest rates make the payments higher. The buyer of the machinery or equipment must then earn more profits to meet these higher payments. The buyer may decide that the higher profits are not possible or very unlikely and, therefore, will not purchase the capital; the risk of losing money is too great. Declining interest rates generally spark capital investment in markets. Rising interest rates cause investment to decline.

The supply of capital is generally upward sloping. Capital is a manufactured good, so the reason for the upward slope is the same as that used to explain the positive relation between price and quantity supplied in any market. The equilibrium price and quantity are determined, as would be expected, by supply and demand.

2.5.3   Labor Markets

The demand for labor time is also a derived demand. Producers hire workers only if they can sell the goods and services they offer in the marketplace. A seller experiencing an increase in demand will produce more of a product and likely raise the price. This, in turn, will increase the demand for labor time; more workers will be hired or overtime for existing workers will increase. It is likely that a sustained increase in demand will cause wages to rise. A decrease in the producer's demand will act to reduce the demand for labor time. Less labor is used if the producer does not sell as much.

An increase in demand for chicken at the grocery store sets into motion an increase in demand for labor at several different levels in the production chain. First, an increase in business at the grocery store may cause the grocer to add more people to the staff, especially in the meat section. But the grocer may also hire more checkers and carry-out people. When the grocer buys more prepared meat from the meat packer, the packer may increase its demand for labor to process poultry. When packers buy more poultry from farmers, farmers may increase their use of labor in order to raise more chickens.

The demand for labor in general depends on the demand for the good or service produced. Increased quantities, linked with increased prices, will increase the value of labor time and, therefore, will increase demand. Conversely, decreased quantities along with lower prices will decrease the value of labor time and will decrease demand.

2.4   *Applying the Theory*

On November 27, 1987, *The Wall Street Journal* reported, "Undergraduate enrollment in computer courses is down nationwide, and fewer students are majoring in the field or indicating they want careers working with computers. Meanwhile many companies are struggling to fill computer jobs. The shortage of computer professionals . . . now appears likely to worsen over the next few years, educators and industry officials say." A research study found that the percentage of college freshmen who aspired to careers as computer programmers or computer analysts declined by more than half—from 8.8 percent in 1982 to 3.3 percent in 1986. The percentage planning to major in computer science fell from 4.5 percent in 1983 to 1.9 percent in 1986.

Aside from possible reasons for the decline in computer science majors, which *The Journal* discussed, what predictions would you make about the occupation of computer scientists in the short term and the long term?

2.5.4   The Demand for Land

Why does coastal acreage sell for many thousands of dollars in California, whereas prairie land in Nevada and Utah can be bought for practically nothing? Location has much to do with the price of land. An old saying among real estate agents is that the three most important determinants of land prices are location, location, and location. Land has a derived value to buyers because of its location. For residential owners the value depends on where it is located relative to a person's work place, schools, parks, roads, and shopping malls. Commercial owners want land that is easily accessible to potential customers. Land with an ocean view is desired because of the view. If it is located near work places and schools, it becomes even more desirable and therefore more costly.

Land is also valuable because it is productive. There is much valuable land in rural Kansas, Iowa, Indiana, Nebraska, and other states that have large agricultural industries. If the land is well suited for growing corn and corn sells at a high price, the land will have a high derived demand, and it is likely that such land will sell at high prices. The land is expensive because the corn is expensive, not the other way around. Many times we forget about derived demands and make the mistake of thinking that corn is expensive because the land is expensive. A resource is valuable because of what it can be used for. Whether it is materials, capital, labor time, or land, these inputs in a production process have value because of the demand for what is produced.

Economics in the News   **Why Do Home Prices Differ So Much?**

A news story in the *Houston Post* (May 8, 1990) about housing prices in various cities throughout the United States and Canada presented some information that, at first glance, seemed rather astonishing. The Coldwell Banker Home Price Comparison Index compared prices for a single-family, 2,200-square-foot dwelling, with four bedrooms, 2 1/2 baths, a family room, and a two-car garage. The average price varied from $916,666 in Beverly Hills, California, the highest priced city, to $81,666 in Corpus Christi, Texas, the lowest. Three other California cities had average prices between $869,00 and $636,700. The average price for the same home was $121,413 in Houston, Texas, and $84,833 in

(continued)

Oklahoma City. Averages in the 197 other cities surveyed fell all along the range, from the above-$500,000 range to the below-$90,000 range.

Why would there be such a huge disparity in home prices? People in Beverly Hills don't pay 10 times more for a can of coffee, a pound of steak, a BMW, or a VCR than people in Corpus Christi. A TV, an automobile of a given type, or a six-pack of beer may differ some in price in the various cities, but not much. Remember, the price survey was for essentially the same house in each market, so differences in the quality couldn't account for the difference. Certainly differences in building regulations could make the cost of building a house a bit more in some cities than in others, but that would not account for such huge differences. Differences in wage rates for construction workers in various cities may account for slight differences in the cost of construction.

However, the major factor that probably accounts for most of the differences is a unique property of one resource, land: Land cannot be moved, other resources can. When a family buys a home, it also buys the land on which the home is built. As the population of a city grows, the demand for homes in that city increases, just as the demand for most other goods increases. The quantity supplied of these other goods can increase after demand increases. The quantity of land supplied cannot increase; the supply is vertical, or very close to it. All of the materials, tools, and workers needed to build a house can be brought in from other areas. Land on which to build the house cannot be brought in.

Thus, the increase in the demand for houses increases the demand for, and therefore the price of, land. Because of the nearly vertical supply of land, the higher price of land does not cause more to be supplied. Cities whose population is large and growing, relative to the amount of land in the city, will have much higher home prices compared to cities with a lot of land, relative to the size of the population.

We might note some cities have placed tight restrictions on the areas that can be developed for new housing. These restrictions benefit those who already own homes by driving prices up, and they harm newcomers in the cities who want to buy homes.

2.5.5   Summary

Even though the demand for resources, or inputs in the productive process, is a derived demand, the markets for resources work in the same way as markets for goods and services. The derived demand for a given type of material, capital, labor, and land is downward sloping. Firms demand more of a resource, the lower the price of that resource. In general, the supply of a particular type of resource is upward sloping, with the exception of land. Resource owners generally will supply more the higher the price of the resource.

Supply and demand in the market for a given resource determine its price and the quantity that is exchanged. If price is above equilibrium, and there are no governmentally enforced restrictions such as a minimum wage, the resource price will fall until supply is equal to demand. If price is below equilibrium and there are no restrictions, the resource price will rise until supply equals demand. Thus in resource markets, as in markets for goods and services, the equilibrium price and quantity exchanged are determined by the equality of supply and demand. The price and quantity will change if either supply or demand shift, in exactly the same way as described for goods markets.

A large part of the remainder of this text will be devoted to the theoretical underpinnings of supply and demand and to the important role of prices in a market economy. In fact, prices are so important for the functioning of markets that some courses in microeconomics are simply called "Price Theory." Therefore, in the remainder of this chapter we want to give you a brief preview of the basic function of prices in a market economy.

2.6 The Role of Prices in Markets

Almost everything that people consume has a price, but sometimes prices are not determined by a market. In some countries, the explicit existence of markets is forbidden. In the Eastern Bloc countries, for instance, the private selling of consumer goods has historically been against the law. Only recently have markets been allowed to develop. Previously, the government has overseen the production and distribution of nearly all goods and services. Prices were set by a government committee that had little regard for supply and demand. Prices were usually set too low, and consumers formed long lines to get their "allocation" of the good. Instead of prices eliminating excess demand, limits were set on the amount each consumer could purchase, and lines determined who made a purchase. In many communist countries the rule of allocation has been "first come, first served."

2.6.1 Prices as Rationing Devices

When markets are allowed to freely operate, there is no need for rationing rules. Rationing always limits the amount that can be purchased by a buyer. In a market, consumers ration themselves by the choices they make. Given income, prices, and the menu of goods and services available, consumers choose the mix of commodities that they believe will give them the greatest benefit. When the price of a good rises, usually substitution takes place. Buyers will purchase less of the relatively more expensive item and more of substitute items that are now relatively less expensive. The capability to substitute when prices change in a market is the way rationing is accomplished in a freely operating market.

Those consumers who continue to buy the product after a price increase are the buyers who most desire the good and are able to pay the higher price. Hence, those who are willing to pay the higher price are those who get the good. Those who are not willing, or perhaps not able, to buy the good make a substitution.

Therefore, if supply and demand determine the price in a market, this ensures that goods and services go to those who value them the most. Clearly, anyone who purchases a good at the market price values that good by at least as much as the price. The price paid for a good is the value of the other goods and services that are forgone. This represents the opportunity cost of the purchased good. Alternatively, anyone who chooses not to purchase the good at the market price is not willing to pay the opportunity cost and, consequently, does not place as high a value on the good as those who choose to purchase it.

*Economics in
the News*

Perestroika Is a Painful Process in the Soviet Union[4]

Many changes have occurred in the Soviet Union. *Glasnost* now allows citizens to discuss their troubles and to openly criticize government policy. Previously, dissent was forbidden by law. Gorbachev's regime has also undertaken *perestroika* in the Soviet economy. The Soviet government is releasing its strict control of the economy. Until recently, freely operating markets did not exist within the law. All exchange was tightly controlled by the 18 million bureaucrats, who directed all terms of trade by setting prices and the quantities traded between two parties. Usually, prices were set too low and quantities were restricted. As *perestroika* gets off the ground, *glasnost* makes it plain that the Soviet people are tired of shortages.

The typical Soviet citizen continues to stand in long lines to buy bread, soap, matches, and meat. Meat is particularly scarce. These lines take up much of an individual's nonworking time. The produce of some farmers with private farm plots and some of the produce from collective lands are now being sold in open-air markets. This is a bright spot for *perestroika*. Fruits and vegetables are becoming more plentiful. But productivity, especially in agriculture, remains low. The average worker has no incentive to do well, since pay is not based on performance. Profits are not kept by the enterprise earning them. There is no incentive to work hard, because wages do not increase and other workers are critical of someone setting a faster pace.

Until productivity increases in the Soviet Union, *perestroika* will be painful. Markets will exist, but the standard of living is not likely to rise much. Certainly, the long lines will to some extent be reduced, but at freely determined market prices it may be that many workers are neither willing nor able to buy at posted prices.

2.6.2   Prices as a Signaling Device

As you have seen, prices ration goods and services to their highest valued use. Prices have another important function in a market economy: They signal producers to produce more when consumers want more of a particular good or service, and they signal producers to produce less when consumers want less of a particular good or service.

As we have emphasized, whenever consumers wish to purchase more of a good, the demand for that good increases. The increase in demand causes the price of the good to increase. Because the price is higher, that good becomes more profitable for firms to produce and sell, and they increase the amount they offer for sale. Therefore, the higher price caused by the increase in demand acts as a signal for producers to produce more. Producers do not increase production out of the goodness of their hearts or because of any innate desire to benefit society. They produce more when consumers demand more because it is more profitable to do so.

[4]This account, written prior to the breakup of the Soviet Union, is based on John Ehrlichman, "How A Russian Really Lives," *Parade*, April 15, 1990, p. 4–7.

When consumers want less of some good, demand decreases. The decrease in demand drives down the price of the good, causing firms to offer less for sale because the good is less profitable. Therefore, a reduction in price acts as a signal to firms to produce less.

In a society without a freely functioning price system, there is no way for government decision makers to respond to changes in consumers' desire for the product even if they wanted to. Government sets the price, typically too low, and the level of output, typically too low also. Then the goods are rationed to the consumers who are first in the line.

Some people object to the price system based on consideration of equity: some people, because of income differences, get more than others. Nonetheless, based upon principles of efficiency, the price system is a more efficient system for rationing scarce goods and services and signaling the desires of consumers to producers than any other system that has been discovered.

2.6.3 Market Equilibrium

An equilibrium exists at points where the supply and demand schedules intersect. There is neither excess supply nor excess demand. However, the existence of a market equilibrium in theory does not mean markets *are* always in equilibrium. Indeed, there are so many factors that can affect the movement of supply and demand curves that there is probably at any given time some shifting taking place for one or both schedules. This movement may create shortages or surpluses in the market. Prices will begin adjusting toward equating the quantity supplied with the quantity demanded. And while this is happening, some other factor underlying the schedules may change to cause another shift. Readjustment toward an equilibrium starts all over.

Markets are dynamic—that is, they are generally in a state of change. Hence, equilibrium is rarely achieved, but the tendency toward equilibrium is ever present. Constantly changing demand and supply do not mean a supply and demand equilibrium is a useless concept. Even though an equilibrium may not be achieved, its existence helps us predict how prices will change when there is excess demand or supply. The definition and description of market equilibrium has been the theme of this chapter. Prices above the intersection of supply and demand create excess inventories that bring downward pressure on prices. Prices below the intersection create shortages that cause prices to rise. As a market moves toward equilibrium, pressures in one direction or the other abate and finally cease once the price exactly matches the intersection of the two market schedules.

2.5 *Applying the Theory*

The Wall Street Journal (January 11, 1990) reported that oil prices had surged because gasoline inventories had decreased, 10 to 15 million barrels below normal. Explain fully, using demand and supply, how the process worked. This is a fairly difficult application, requiring the analysis of two markets, one with a derived demand.

2.7   **Summary**

Demand is a list of prices and of the corresponding quantities that consumers are willing and able to buy per period at each price. Quantity demanded varies inversely with price. The entire demand schedule changes when something held constant in deriving demand changes. Among these are income, tastes, the prices of other goods, and expectations.

Supply is a list of prices and the corresponding quantities that will be supplied per period at each price in the list. Typically, price and quantity supplied are directly related. Changes in technology, the price of inputs, and the prices of related (in production) goods will shift the entire schedule.

When price in a market is such that quantity demanded equals quantity supplied, the market is in equilibrium. Prices below equilibrium cause excess demand (or a shortage). If prices are not fixed, they will be bid up. Prices above equilibrium cause excess supply (or a surplus). If prices are not fixed, they will be bid down. When supply and demand change, equilibrium price and quantity will change.

Every day, economists use simple demand and supply analysis to solve complex problems and to answer questions dealing with these curves. However, one must be careful about deciding how these underlying factors affect market price and output. In the next chapter, we apply the model of supply and demand in selected market problems. We do this to give you more familiarity with the model and to extend the theory in certain directions.

In all cases, there are two fundamental concepts to remember. First, on the demand side of the market, when the price of something falls, more is demanded; when the price of something rises, less is demanded. Second, for supply, as prices rise, in general, more will be offered for sale; when prices fall, less will be offered.

Answers to   *Applying the Theory*

2.1   All of these factors would be expected to decrease the demand for meals in fine restaurants. Dining out is probably a normal good. An economic downturn would decrease some people's income and would therefore decrease the demand for restaurant meals. New tax laws that decreased the proportion of a meal that is tax deductible would decrease the number of "business meals" demanded at each price. People having less time for dining out because of children and distaste for excesses (hard as that is to believe) represent a change in tastes that would lower demand. The reduction in demand caused the prices of restaurant meals to decline.

2.2   It's not certain why car manufacturers did not simply lower prices. The rebates did act as a price reduction. The much lower interest rates (loans are a complement good to new cars) made it cheaper to finance a new car, which most people do, and had the effect of increasing demand. Automobile firms probably resorted to these tactics rather than lowering price, because they could drop the rebates and low finance charges after the slump was over and inventories were depleted, without having to raise car prices. Holding sticker prices steady would spare automakers from consumers' irritation over price increases.

2.3   Consumers of cars and gasoline would certainly have an interest. The measures being considered would increase the cost of manufacturing automobiles. This would cause the supply of automobiles to decrease and consequently drive up the price of new cars. Also, the primary alternative clean fuel, methanol, has only half the energy content of gasoline and would require bigger tanks or more refueling, which would also raise the cost to consumers.

2.4   In the short run, because of the probable steep slope of the supply of computer scientists and analysts and the increase in the demand for people in this occupation, salaries would be expected to rise sharply. The *Journal* noted that average starting salaries for computer science graduates had already increased 15 percent. Industry experts were predicting even greater increases in salaries. In the long run, the higher salaries would induce more and more students to take computer courses and major in computer science. The supply, therefore, should become less steep in the long run when enough time has elapsed for these students to be graduated. Salaries should fall some, relative to what they were in the short run, but remain above what they were at the time of the article.

2.5   There are two markets: the market for gasoline and the market for oil, the demand for which is in large part derived from the demand for gasoline, which is, as you know, refined from oil. The demand for gasoline probably increased, causing a shortage of gasoline. However, refiners keep inventories of gasoline, which were drawn down to fill the shortage. The refineries wanted to buy more oil in order to refine more gasoline and to replenish their inventories. This increased the demand for oil, driving up the price of oil. Later, when the price of gasoline rose, the explanation given consumers was that costs went up because oil prices rose and dealers' costs rose. The real reason was the increase in demand.

Technical Problems

1. In Figure E.2–1, the demand curve has the equation $P = 80 - (1/3)Q_d$ and the supply schedule is $P = 20 + (1/5)Q_s$.

   a. Find the equilibrium price and quantity from the equations. Note: In a market equilibrium $Q_d = Q_s$, there is one quantity (Q) and one price (P) at the intersection of supply and demand. To find the P and Q, set the demand and supply equations equal to each other. Since $P = P$, $80 - (1/3)Q = 20 + (1/5)Q$. Find Q using algebra. Then to get P substitute your solution for Q into either the equation for supply or the equation for demand. Is your answer consistent with the figure?

   b. From the graph at a price of 50, what is excess supply? From the graph at a price of $40, what is excess demand?

   c. At a price of $50, what is total consumer expenditure on the commodity? Total expenditure is the price multiplied by the quality sold. At a price of $40, what is expenditure?

   d. Starting at the equilibrium price, does total consumer expenditure rise or fall as price goes to $50?

2. For the demand equation $P = 80 - (1/3)Q_d$ and the supply equation $P = 20 + (1/5)Q_s$:

   a. Graph the equations and find the equilibrium from your figure. Now find the equilibrium P and Q using algebra. Are your answers consistent?

   b. Calculate the new equilibrium price and quantity when demand is kept the same but supply changes to $P = 100 + (1/5)Q_s$. Does this new equation represent a decrease or increase in supply? Show the new supply curve in the graph you drew in part *a*.

   c. Calculate the new equilibrium price and quantity when supply is kept at $P = 20 + (1/5)Q_s$ but demand changes to $P = 100 - (1/3)Q_d$. Does this new

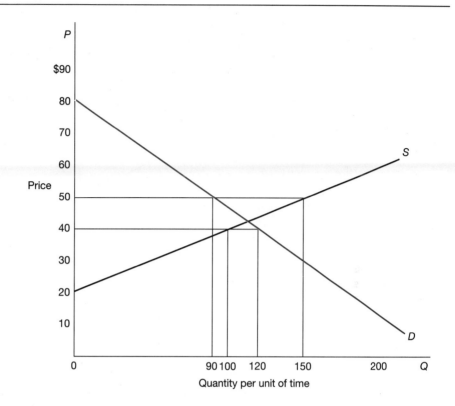

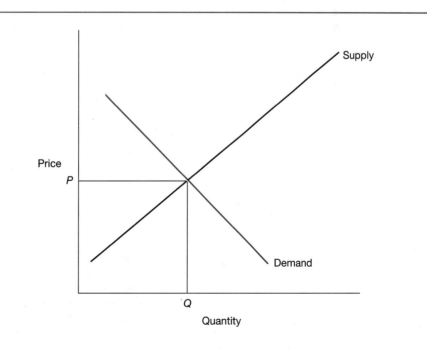

Figure E.2–3

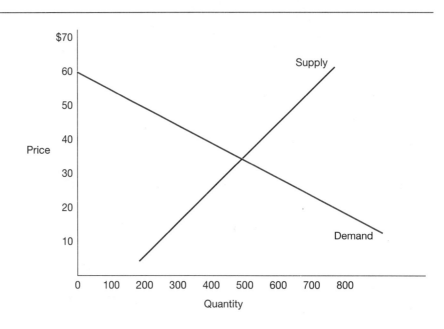

equation represent an increase or decrease in demand? Show the new demand
curve in the graph you drew for part *a*.

  d. Calculate the equilibrium when demand changes to $P = 100 - (1/3)Q_d$ and
supply changes to $P = 30 + (1/5)Q_s$. Is price higher or lower than before
there were any changes? Draw a new graph of this equilibrium.

3. Use Figure E.2–2 to answer this question. The figure shows demand and supply
curves in a market. With these demand and supply curves, equilibrium price and
quantity are, respectively, P and Q. For each of the following events: What
happens to demand and/or supply? What is the immediate effect at the original
equilibrium price? What happens to the equilibrium price and quantity? Return to
the *original* demand, supply, and equilibrium price and quantity to answer each
part of the question.

  a. The price of a substitute good (for consumers) decreases.

  b. The price of a complement good (for consumers) decreases.

  c. The good is normal and consumer income decreases.

  d. The wages of workers used to produce this good increase.

  e. Technological improvements occur in the industry.

  f. The price of another good that firms selling in the market can produce
decreases.

  g. Consumers expect the future price of this good to be higher than they
previously expected, and the rent on the land on which this good is produced
decreases.

  h. Sellers expect the price of the good to be higher than they previously
expected, and the price of a substitute good (for consumers) increases.

4. Use Figure E.2–3, showing demand and supply in a market, to answer this

question. Return to the original demand, supply, and equilibrium price and quantity to answer each part of the question.

   a. With the demand and supply curves in the figure, what will be equilibrium price and quantity?

   b. A wage increase in the industry causes firms to be willing and able to supply 150 fewer units at each price in the list. At the original equilibrium price there is now a_____of_____units. The new equilibrium price and quantity will be $_____and_____units.

   c. Return to the original demand and supply. A reduction in income causes consumers to demand 300 fewer units at each price in the list. At the original equilibrium price there is now a_____of_____units. The new equilibrium price and quantity are $_____and_____units.

   d. Return to the original demand and supply. Now, a technological improvement causes firms to be willing to supply 150 more units of output at each price in the list. At the original equilibrium price, there is now a_____of_____units. The new equilibrium price and output will be $_____and_____units.

   e. Return to the original demand and supply. Now, an increase in the price of a substitute good causes consumers to demand 150 more at each price in the list. At the original equilibrium price there will be a_____ of _____. The new equilibrium price and output will be $_____ and _____units.

5. How would the following events affect the demand and/or supply of hamburgers in a city and the equilibrium price and quantity?

   a. A large decrease in the price of pizzas.

   b. Fast-food stores offer a half-price sale on french fries.

   c. The price of beef increases substantially.

   d. A scientific study announces that beef causes premature wrinkling and baldness.

   e. A new automatic burger machine reduces production costs by 50 percent.

   f. All high school and college students receive a weekly stipend of $150 from the government.

6. How would the following events affect the demand and/or supply of houses in a particular area and the equilibrium price and quantity of houses.

   a. Interest rates increase substantially.

   b. The wages of carpenters, bricklayers, painters, and electricians rise.

   c. The prices of bricks and lumber fall.

   d. A new manufacturing plant opens, and many new workers move into the area.

   e. A recession causes a great deal of unemployment and many businesses close down.

   f. The rent on apartments increases.

7. Explain why, in the case of land in an area, price is a good rationing device, but it does not perform well as a signaling device.

8. Note each of the following shifts in demand and supply and determine the effect on equilibrium price and quantity. In each case the effect on one of the variables is determinant, and the other variable can either increase or decrease.

   a. Supply and demand both increase.

   b. Supply and demand both decrease.

   c. Supply increases and demand decreases.

   d. Supply decreases and demand increases.

Analytical Problems

1. If you owned a retail store, how would you know if the price is either "too high" or "too low"?

2. Economists typically draw demand curves as continuous curves, indicating that the quantity is continuously divisible. However, everyone knows that people buy goods such as automobiles in increments of one, two, and so on. In light of this knowledge, how can we justify the use of continuous demand curves? Hint: From 1973 to 1986 the average age of cars in the United States rose one third to 7.6 years, whereas the price of cars rose 530 percent faster than family incomes over this period.

3. *The Wall Street Journal* (January 3, 1990) reported that total airline industry capacity is expected to rise 6 percent, whereas passenger demand, as measured by revenue passenger miles, is likely to rise only 2 percent to 3 percent, according to an industry analyst. To fill all those extra seats, the airlines are going to have to stimulate demand by lowering fares for the most price-sensitive consumers, particularly vacation travelers, analysts said. What is wrong with these statements? How would you describe the situation?

4. *The Wall Street Journal* (January 4, 1990) reported that the sales of new homes had increased strongly. An economist at the National Association of Home Builders said that the rise "reflects the decline in interest rates over the past few months." Given that this economist was correct, describe what happened in terms of supply and demand.

5. Analyze critically the following statement that reflects what people often believe: A decrease in supply causes an increase in price. However, the increase in price causes a decrease in demand, which, in turn, causes an offsetting decrease in price.

6. After an oil spill from the tanker Mega Borg in the summer of 1990 off the coast of Texas, many environmental groups called for a ban on offshore drilling, although spills from offshore rigs are practically nonexistent. Why might a ban on offshore drilling cause more oil spills from tankers?

7. An article in *Newsweek,* "Big Oil's Gusher of Woe," December 19, 1983, showed a graph with years from 1970 through 1983 plotted along the horizontal axis and barrels of oil per day, measured in millions of barrels, along the vertical axis. The line in the figure rose rather steadily from 1970 to 1980, and then it fell sharply thereafter. This figure was labeled, "World Oil Demand." What did the figure probably show? Also in the article was a prediction by Gulf Oil that "crude-oil demand will remain essentially flat through the mid-1980s." What did this prediction probably mean?

8. This question anticipates later material. Suppose you have paid $50 for a pair of 50-yard-line tickets to a major bowl game. You find that you and your guest cannot attend the game. Many people want to buy your tickets and offer much more than $50, but the antiscalping law in your state makes it illegal to sell the tickets for more than the $50 you paid. How would you decide whom to sell the tickets to? Are there other ways to solve the problem?

CHAPTER 3

Elasticity and Market Analysis

3.1   Introduction

Now that we have introduced demand and supply curves, we can analyze the way the shape of these curves describes the sensitivity of quantity demanded or quantity supplied to changes in price. In the market for some goods, consumers will reduce their purchases a great deal when price rises, or they will greatly increase the amount purchased when price falls. Consumers in such markets are said to be *sensitive* to price changes. In other markets, consumers change the amount purchased very little when price changes. In these markets, consumers are relatively *insensitive* to price changes. We should emphasize, however, that even in markets in which consumers are relatively insensitive, quantity demanded falls when price rises and rises when price falls, but not very much. The law of demand holds in all markets.

The sensitivity of quantity demanded to changes in price is measured by *demand elasticity;* it shows the relative responsiveness of quantity demanded to changes in price. The sensitivity of quantity supplied to changes in price can be described by *supply elasticity*. The elasticity of supply measures the responsiveness of the quantity supplied to a change in price. In some markets, the quantity supplied may change very little when price changes, whereas in others, there may be a large change in quantity supplied.

For both demand and supply, sensitivity to a price change can be crudely gauged by how steep or flat the demand or supply curve is. A steep curve indicates little change in quantity when price changes. A flat curve represents large quantity changes for a given change in price. You will see, however, that slope is a rough but not a reliable measure of sensitivity, which is why elasticity is used to determine sensitivity.

Approximately half of this chapter is concerned with the concept and calculation of demand and supply elasticity. We will begin by giving you a precise definition of elasticity, and then we will explain why elasticity is a much better measure of the sensitivity of consumers and firms to changes in price than the slope of the demand and supply curves. We will then discuss how demand elasticity affects total expenditure, or the total amount consumers spend on a good, after the price of the good changes. Economists who do applied work are frequently interested in how total expenditure changes when there is a movement along a demand curve. People in business are greatly interested in the effect of a change in price on their sales revenue; this is equivalent to the total expenditure made by consumers. We will also discuss why in some markets consumers are quite sensitive to price changes, whereas in other markets they are relatively insensitive. Finally, we will discuss the concept of supply elasticity, and we will mention rather briefly some other elasticities used by economists.

The second half of this chapter describes how equilibrium price and quantity are affected when a market is forced away from its equilibrium. What happens depends on the elasticity of demand and supply, and we will show how elasticity affects the results of such movements away from equilibrium. One example of markets forced away from equilibrium occurs when prices are pegged above or below the price that would exist at the intersection of supply and demand. We call this intersection the natural equilibrium. Prices above the natural equilibrium are called *price floors;* prices below the equilibrium are called *price ceilings*. We also explore the impact of a tax, for example, a sales tax, on items sold in a market. These taxes have the effect of shifting the supply, and sometimes the demand, schedule to create a new equilibrium. The impact of price floors, price ceilings, and taxes on prices and quantities in a market depends crucially on the elasticity of demand and supply. This is why we develop these topics in conjunction with elasticity.

3.2   The Concept of Elasticity of Demand

We begin with the idea that the slope of a demand curve gives some indication of how sensitive consumers are to a price change in a particular market. If demand is steeply sloped, consumers do not change the quantity demanded of a good much when its price changes. If demand has a gentle slope, consumers change their quantity demanded a great deal when price changes. However, for reasons we will discuss below, the slope of demand is not a reliable indicator of consumer sensitivity in a market. Therefore, economists use a measure of sensitivity called the elasticity of demand, defined as the *ratio of the percent change in quantity demanded to the percent change in the price*. Algebraically, demand elasticity (E_D) is

$$E_D = - \frac{\% \text{ change in quantity demanded}}{\% \text{ change in price}} = - \frac{\%\Delta Q_D}{\%\Delta P} = - \frac{\Delta Q_D/Q_D}{\Delta P/P}$$

$$= - \frac{\Delta Q_D}{\Delta P} \cdot \frac{P}{Q_D}.$$

where Δ means "the change in" and Q_D and P denote, respectively, quantity demanded and price. Since price and quantity demanded vary inversely, the minus sign is used to make the coefficient positive.

From the formula, you can see that the relative responsiveness of quantity demanded to changes in price measures the ratio of the proportional change in quantity demanded to the proportional change in price. The larger the elasticity of demand, the greater the percent change in quantity demanded after a given percentage change in price. Therefore, a high E_D indicates that consumers are quite sensitive to changes in price. A low E_D means that consumers are not particularly sensitive to price changes.

Suppose E_D equals 3. This means that the percent change in quantity demanded is three times as large as the percent change in price; for example, if price increases 10 percent, quantity demanded will decrease 30 percent. Or, if E_D equals 1/2, the percent change in quantity demanded is half as large as the percent change in price; if price increases 10 percent, quantity demanded will decrease only 5 percent.

3.2.1 Classification of Demand Elasticity

Economists classify demand elasticity into three categories. Demand is *elastic* if $E_D > 1$; that is, $|\%\Delta Q_D| > |\%\Delta P|$ over a given range of demand. The larger E_D is, the more elastic is demand—that is, the more responsive quantity demanded is to a change in price. Demand is *inelastic* if $E_D < 1$; that is, $|\%\Delta Q_D| < |\%\Delta P|$ over a given range of demand. The smaller E_D is, the more inelastic is demand—that is, the less responsive quantity demanded is to a change in price. Finally, demand is *unitary* if $E_D = 1$; that is, $|\%\Delta Q_D| = |\%\Delta P|$.

As we demonstrate below, it is usually not accurate to say that a given demand curve is wholly elastic or inelastic. In many cases, demand curves have both an inelastic and an elastic range, along with a point or range of unitary elasticity. With this measure we can also determine, over a certain range of prices, which of two demand curves is more elastic. This comparison proves very helpful in analyzing many public issues.

3.2.2 Percentage Changes Are Used to Measure Sensitivity

As we noted above, the slope of a demand or supply curve gives a rough approximation of how sensitive the quantity demanded or supplied is to changes in price. Specifically, slope shows how units of the measured quantity change when price, however measured, changes. Elasticity, which is defined in terms of *percentage* changes in quantity and price, not the numerical changes, is a more reliable measure of sensitivity. We will demonstrate why this is so in terms of demand elasticity, but the demonstration applies equally well to supply elasticity.

The problem with using numerical changes in quantity demanded and price is that this measure is affected by the units of quantity or the units of price that measure demand. To show this, the demand schedule for chicken at the supermarket, discussed in Chapter 2, is reproduced in columns 1 and 2 of Table 3–1 below. Two more columns have been added. In the third column, pounds are converted to

Table 3–1   Market Demand Schedule in Pounds and Ounces

(1) Pounds Demanded	(2) Price per Pound	(3) Ounces Demanded	(4) Price per Ounce
500	$3.00	8,000	$.19
2,000	2.50	32,000	.16
3,500	2.00	56,000	.13
5,000	1.50	80,000	.09
6,500	1.00	104,000	.06
8,000	.50	128,000	.03

ounces. The fourth column shows the price of chicken per ounce. Let the effect of a change in price on quantity demanded be given by the ratio, $\Delta Q_D/\Delta P$ where Δ means again a "change in." Using pounds and increasing the quantity demanded from 500 to 2,000 pounds, the change in quantity demanded is $\Delta Q_D = 2,000 - 500 = 1,500$. From the table, the decrease in price that caused the increase in quantity demanded is $\Delta P = \$2.50 - \$3.00 = -\$.50$. Thus the responsiveness of quantity demanded to price between these two combinations in the schedule is

$$\frac{\Delta Q_D}{\Delta P} = \frac{1,500}{-\$0.50} = -3,000.$$

You can calculate and see that between any two price-quantity combinations, measured in pounds, in Table 3–1 $\Delta Q_D/\Delta P$ equals $-3,000$. This is because the demand curve associated with this schedule (Figure 2–1 in Chapter 2 and reproduced as Figure 3–1 below) is a straight line. Price is plotted along the vertical axis and quantity along the horizontal axis, and the slope of the demand curve is $\Delta P/\Delta Q_D$, which is the inverse of the ratio used above, $\Delta Q_D/\Delta P$. Along the straight line demand $\Delta P/\Delta Q_D$ ($= -1/3,000$) is constant for any change in Q_D and P. Thus, the ratio $\Delta Q_D/\Delta P$ is also constant and equal to $-3,000$ for any change in P and Q_D.

We could have measured the quantity units in ounces as Table 3–1 shows. All of the pound quantities in column 1 are converted to ounces by multiplying each entry by 16 (e.g., $8,000 = 500 \times 16$) since there are 16 ounces to a pound. The price per ounce in column 4 is derived by dividing each entry in column 2 by 16. Thus, the first entry in column 4 is $\$3.00 \div 16 = \$.1875 \approx \$.19$ (the symbol $\approx$ means "approximately equal to"). Therefore columns 3 and 4 can also be used to measure the ratio $\Delta Q_D/\Delta P$. When price falls from $.19 to $.16, the quantity demanded increases from 8,000 to 32,000 ounces; in this case

$$\frac{\Delta Q_D}{\Delta P} = \frac{32,000 - 8,000}{\$0.16 - \$0.19} = \frac{24,000}{-\$0.03} = -800,000.$$

And, between any other two price-quantity combinations measured in ounces, $\Delta Q_D/\Delta P$ equals $-800,000$. This a dramatic change from the ratio measured in pounds. This change happens solely because of a change in the units of measure. Consumers have not changed. Demand has not changed. Because slope can be

Figure 3–1   Market Demand Curve for Chicken

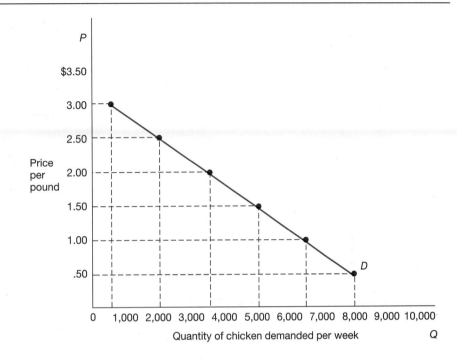

changed by changing how price and quantity are measured, it behooves us to measure the sensitivity of quantity demanded to a change in price in a way that does not depend on the units used to measure demand. As we noted previously, this measure is the ratio of the percentage change in quantity demanded to the percentage change in price (E_D).

3.2.3   Algebraic Calculation of Point Elasticity

The equation

$$E_D = - \frac{\Delta Q_D}{\Delta P} \cdot \frac{P}{Q_D}$$

(the last term in the above definition of E_D) is sometimes referred to as the point formula for the elasticity of demand, because elasticity at any point on a demand curve can be calculated by using this formula. A particular point on a demand curve gives the price and quantity demanded, so we know what P/Q_D in the formula is. All that is left to find is $\Delta Q_D/\Delta P$, but this term is, as shown above, simply the inverse of the slope of the demand curve. We calculated this term, for instance, from Table 3–1 when the demand for chicken at the supermarket was measured in ounces as well as pounds.

Recall that $\Delta Q_D/\Delta P$ for the demand schedule in Table 3–1 when quantity is measured in pounds is $-3,000$. At a price of $2.50 a pound, sales are 2,000 pounds. Hence, the elasticity of demand at this price and quantity is:

$$E_D = -\frac{\Delta Q_D}{\Delta P} \cdot \frac{P}{Q_D} = -\frac{(2,000 - 500)}{(\$2.50 - \$3.00)} \cdot \frac{\$2.50}{2,000}$$

$$= -(-3,000) \cdot \frac{\$2.50}{2,000} = 3.75.$$

It does not matter how the units are measured, with elasticity you always get the same answer. Suppose that demand has been measured in ounces. Any quantity in column 1 would be that quantity times 16; any price in column 2 would be that price divided by 16. Thus, the point elasticity formula in ounces would be

$$E_D = -\frac{\Delta Q_D}{\Delta P} \cdot \frac{P}{Q_D} = -\frac{(16 \times 2,000 - 16 \times 500)}{\$2.50/16 - \$3.00/16)} \cdot \frac{\$2.50/16}{16 \times 2,000}$$

$$= -\frac{(2,000 - 500}{\$2.50 - \$3.00} \cdot \frac{\$2.50}{2,000} = 3.75,$$

which is the same as before. The formula causes the multiplying and dividing by 16 to cancel, resulting in the same measure of elasticity no matter how the units are measured.

Recall that we said demand curves generally have different elasticities at different price-quantity combinations and are generally elastic over some ranges of combinations and inelastic over others. Since at $P = \$2.50$ per pound and $Q_D = 2,000$ pounds, $E_D = 3.75$ and demand is elastic at this combination. Now, consider a price of $1.50 and quantity of 5,000. Since $\Delta Q_D/\Delta P = -3,000$ for any change in price, elasticity at this new combination is

$$E_D = -\frac{\Delta Q_D}{\Delta P} \cdot \frac{P}{Q_D} = -(-3,000) \cdot \frac{\$1.50}{5,000} = .9$$

Thus, at this lower price and higher quantity, $E_D < 1$, so demand is inelastic. You can calculate E_D at every other price and quantity in Table 3–1 and see that E_D decreases and demand becomes less elastic, as price falls and quantity increases. Demand is elastic at higher prices and inelastic at lower prices. This relation holds for any straight-line demand, because $\Delta Q_D/\Delta P$ is constant; as P falls and Q_D rises P/Q_D becomes smaller, so $(\Delta Q_D/\Delta P)(P/Q)$ decreases along the demand curve.

3.2.4 Elasticity and Total Expenditure

The elasticity of demand determines how total expenditure on a good changes when there is a movement along the curve. Total expenditure (TE), is simply price times quantity demanded, or

$$TE = P \cdot Q_{D'}.$$

From Figure 3–1, which is reproduced from the demand curve for chicken at the supermarket in Figure 2–1, Chapter 2, and from the demand schedule in Table 3–1, we can calculate the total expenditure at any point on demand curve D. At a price of $2, market sales are 3,500 units. Total expenditure is, therefore, $TE =$ $2 \cdot 3,500 = \$7,000$. If sales rise to 5,000 units after the price falls to $1.50, expenditure becomes $1.50 \cdot 5,000 = \$7,500$, which represents an increase in total expenditure. At a price of $1.00, sales rise to 6,500 and total expenditure falls to $1.00 \cdot 6,500 = \$6,500$. Thus, over one range of demand, when price falls and sales rise, total expenditure increases. Over another range, when price falls and sales rise, total expenditure decreases.

The reason total expenditure can either increase or decrease as price changes is because along any downward sloping demand curve P and Q_D move in opposite directions and, consequently, have offsetting effects on expenditure. Specifically, a decrease in price alone would tend to decrease expenditure, whereas the resulting increase in quantity would tend to increase expenditure. The effect on total expenditure depends on which force dominates—the decrease in price or the increase in quantity demanded.

Therefore, the effect of a change in price and quantity on total expenditure must depend on the elasticity of demand over the range of the price change. If demand is elastic over the range, the percentage change in quantity is greater than the percentage change in price. Because the change in quantity dominates, a decrease in price and the resulting increase in quantity cause total expenditure to increase; conversely an increase in price and a decrease in quantity cause total expenditure to fall.

The reverse happens if demand is inelastic and the percentage change in price is greater than the percentage change in quantity. Now, the price effect dominates the quantity effect. An increase in price and decrease in quantity cause total expenditure to rise. Alternatively, it can be stated that if demand is inelastic a decrease in price and increase in quantity will cause total expenditure to fall. If demand is unitary elastic, the percentage changes in price and quantity are equal. The two effects exactly offset each other, and total expenditure does not change when price and quantity change.

In the previous example from Figure 3–1, total expenditure rose when price fell from $2.00 to $1.50. Demand is elastic over this range. Total expenditure fell when price fell from $1.50 to $1.00. Demand is inelastic over this range.

Another graph can help you visualize how price and quantity interact to determine the effect on total expenditure of a movement along the demand curve. In Figure 3–2, a seller sets a price of $p,$ and operates at point b on the demand curve. Price is then raised by the amount ΔP until the seller is at point a on the curve and sells ΔQ_D fewer units. We refer to total sales at this point as Q_D. Before the price increase, total expenditure or total revenue on the seller's product was the sum of the two areas $B + C$. After the price rise, revenue becomes the areas $A + C$. The difference in revenue is easily seen to be the difference between shaded areas A and B. For a price increase, total revenue rises if area A is greater than area $B;$ it falls if area A is less than area $B;$ and it stays the same if area A equals area B.

If expenditure increases when price increases ($A > B$) demand is inelastic. With inelastic demand, price and total expenditure move in the same direction. When price rises, expenditure rises; when price falls, expenditure falls. If expenditure decreases when price increases ($A < B$), demand is elastic. With elastic demand price and total expenditure move in opposite directions. When price rises, expen-

Figure 3–2   Change in Total Expenditure from a Price Increase

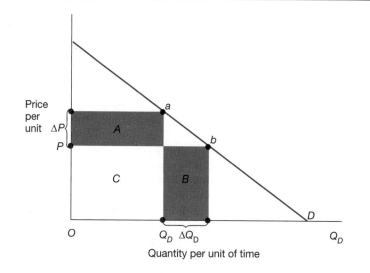

diture falls; when price falls, expenditure goes up. If demand is unitary elastic (*A* = *B*), expenditure does not change when price moves up or down. These relations between price movements, changes in expenditure, and elasticity are summarized in Table 3–2.

We can use the demand curve in Figure 3–2 and the definition of elasticity, $E_D = (\Delta Q_D/\Delta P) \cdot (P/Q)$, to prove that when price increases and total expenditure goes up, demand must be inelastic over this range. If expenditure rises as price rises in Figure 3–2, area *A* > area *B*, or from the figure the relation is

$$Q_D \cdot (\Delta P) > P \cdot (\Delta Q_D).$$

Dividing the right side by the left side gives

$$1 > \frac{\Delta Q_D}{\Delta P} \cdot \frac{P}{Q_D} = E_D.$$

This proves that when total expenditure rises after a price increase, demand elasticity is less than one.

If total revenue goes down when price rises, we reverse the inequality; in the figure, area *A* < area *B*, so

$$Q_D \cdot (\Delta P) < P \cdot (\Delta Q_D).$$

Again, dividing the right side by the left side

$$1 < \frac{\Delta Q_D}{\Delta P} \cdot \frac{P}{Q_D} = E_D$$

showing that demand elasticity is indeed greater than one when total revenue falls for a price increase. It is left as an exercise for the student to show $E_D = 1$ when area *A* = area *B*.

Table 3–2   Relations between Demand Elasticity and Total Expenditure (TE)

	Elastic Demand	Unitary Elasticity	Inelastic Demand
Price rises	TE falls	No change in TE	TE rises
Price falls	TE rises	No change in TE	TE falls

3.2.5   The Arc Elasticity Formula

We have shown how elasticity is calculated using the point elasticity formula when one is interested in the elasticity at a given point on demand. However, the point formula is not a good measure of elasticity when considering the elasticity between two points on the demand curve. If the point formula is used over a range between two price-quantity relations, certain biases come up in selecting the price (P) and quantity (Q_D) used in the calculation. As an example, consider the demand schedule given in Table 3–3. Suppose price falls from \$1.00 to \$.50, and quantity demanded rises from 100,000 to 300,000. Total expenditure then rises from \$100,000 to \$150,000. From the summary in Table 3–2, demand is elastic over this range since total expenditure increases when price decreases.

Let us now compute E_D beginning at $Q_D = 100,000$ and $P = \$1$ using the point formula

$$E_D = -\frac{\Delta Q_D/Q_D}{\Delta P/P} = -\frac{(100,000 - 300,000) \div 100,000}{(\$1.00 - \$.50) \div \$1.00} = -\frac{-2}{1/2} = 4$$

As expected from the change in total expenditure, the coefficient is greater than one. But some caution must be exercised. The changes in Q_D and P are definitely known from Table 3–3, but we really do not know whether to use the values $Q_D = 100,000$ and $P = \$1.00$ or the values $Q_D = 300,000$ and $P = \$.50$. Try the computation with $P = \$.50$ and $Q_D = 300,000$:

$$E_D = -\frac{(300,000 - 100,000) \div 300,000}{(\$.50 - \$1.00) \div \$.50} = -\frac{2/3}{-1} = \frac{2}{3}.$$

It actually looks as though demand is inelastic, despite the fact that we know it is elastic because total expenditure increases.

The difficulty lies in the fact that elasticity has been computed over a segment of the demand curve and not at a specific point. We can get a much better approximation by using the *average* values of P and Q_D over the range in which they change. That is, for two points on a demand curve, (Q_0, P_0) and (Q_1, P_1), we should compute elasticity using what is known as the "arc formula." Arc elasticity, $\overline{E}_D$, is

$$\overline{E}_D = -\frac{Q_1 - Q_0}{(Q_1 + Q_0)/2} \div \frac{P_1 - P_0}{(P_1 + P_0)/2} = -\frac{Q_1 - Q_0}{Q_1 + Q_0} \div \frac{P_1 - P_0}{P_1 + P_0},$$

Table 3–3   Demand and Elasticity

Price	Quantity Demanded	Total Expenditure	Elasticity
$1.00	100,000	$100,000	
			Elastic
.50	300,000	150,000	
			Unitary
.25	600,000	150,000	
			Inelastic
.10	1,000,000	100,000	

where subscripts 0 and 1 refer, respectively, to the initial and the new prices and quantities demanded. Using this formula for the previous computation, we obtain:

$$\bar{E}_D = -\frac{(300,000 - 100,000)}{(300,000 + 100,000)} \div \frac{(\$.50 - \$1.00)}{(\$.50 + \$1.00)} = \frac{3}{2}.$$

Demand is indeed elastic when allowance is made for the discrete, or finite, changes in price and quantity demanded. As a rule, when calculating elasticity along a segment of the demand schedule you should use the arc formula, or $\bar{E}_D$. If you calculate elasticity at or very near to a point on the demand curve, you should use the point formula. You can calculate arc elasticity between $.50 and $.25 and see that $\bar{E}_D = 1$ and between $.25 and $.10 and see that $\bar{E}_D < 1$, as expected.

Principle

Demand is said to be elastic, of unitary elasticity, or inelastic according to the value of E_D. If $E_D > 1$, demand is elastic; a given percentage change in price results in a greater percentage change in quantity demanded. Small price changes result in bigger changes in quantity demanded. When demand is elastic, total expenditure increases (decreases) when price decreases (increases). When $E_D = 1$, demand has unitary elasticity, meaning that the percentage changes in price and quantity demanded are precisely the same. Total expenditure does not change when price changes. Finally, if $E_D < 1$, demand is inelastic. A given percentage change in price results in a smaller percentage change in quantity demanded. When demand is inelastic, total expenditure decreases (increases) when price decreases (increases).

3.2.6   Graphical Computation of Elasticity

The point formula for demand elasticity can be rewritten and expressed in geometric terms, in order to allow us to compute demand elasticity from a graph of the demand curve. We can then immediately compare the relative price sensitivity of two demand curves and have a way of estimating elasticity at a point on a curve of any shape.

Figure 3–3   Estimation of Point Elasticity

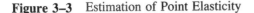

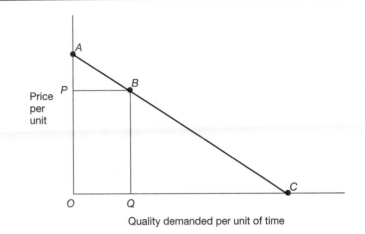

Quality demanded per unit of time

Let us consider the case of a linear demand curve such as that shown in Figure 3–3. The point elasticity at any price and quantity, such as P and Q at point B, can be computed as the ratio of QC/OQ, or OP/AP. These ratios are estimates of the elasticity at a point for very small changes in price and quantity, and each proves useful in different contexts. To prove that these ratios measure elasticity, recall that $E_D = -(\Delta Q/\Delta P) \cdot (P/Q)$. The ratio P/Q is geometrically OP/OQ, but, since $OQ = PB$, P/Q is also equal to the ratio OP/PB. The negative slope of the curve is $\Delta P/\Delta Q_D$, the inverse of $\Delta Q_D/\Delta P$. Referring to Figure 3–3, $\Delta P/\Delta Q_D = AP/PB$, so for the inverse we have $\Delta Q_D/\Delta P = PB/AP$. Therefore,

$$E_D = -\frac{\Delta Q_D}{\Delta P} \cdot \frac{P}{Q_D} = \frac{PB}{AP} \cdot \frac{OP}{PB} = \frac{OP}{AP}.$$

Similarly, since we may also set $OP = BQ$, the ratio OP/OQ is equal to BQ/OQ, and from the figure we see that slope $\Delta P/\Delta Q_D$ may also be written as BQ/QC, giving

$$E_D = -\frac{\Delta Q_D}{\Delta P} \cdot \frac{P}{Q} = \frac{QC}{BQ} \cdot \frac{BQ}{OQ} = \frac{QC}{OQ}.$$

Using the two geometric expressions for elasticity of demand, we can readily show how elasticity along a linear demand curve changes. At the midpoint of a linear schedule, elasticity is unitary. We can locate a point on DD', the linear demand curve in Figure 3–4, where $OQ = QD'$. This is the midpoint of a linear curve. It is also the point where demand has unitary price elasticity, since $E_D = QD'/OQ = 1$. Next, consider any quantity to the left of Q such as Q_1. At Q_1, $E_D = Q_1D'/OQ_1 > 1$. The coefficient of price elasticity is greater than unity at any quantity to the left of Q. Finally, at any point to the right of Q, say Q_2, the coefficient of

Figure 3–4   Ranges of Demanded Elasticity for Linear Demand Curve

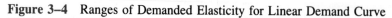

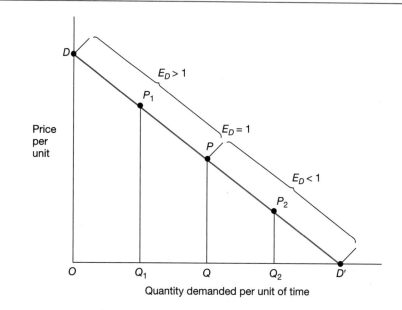

Figure 3–5   Computation of Point Elasticity for Nonlinear Demand Curve

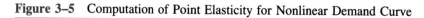

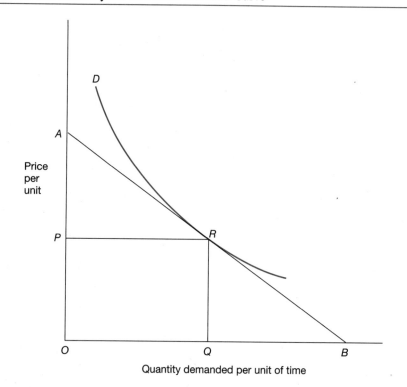

Figure 3–6   Relative Elasticities of Two Intersecting Demand Curves

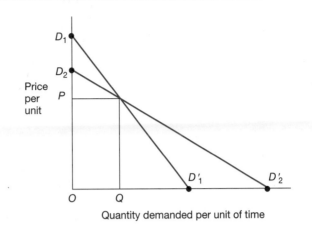

price elasticity is $E_D = Q_2D'/OQ_2 < 1$. Over this range, demand is inelastic. These observations deserve to be emphasized:

Relation

For a linear demand curve: (1) demand is elastic at higher prices, (2) has unitary elasticity at the midpoint, and (3) is inelastic at lower prices. Therefore, in the case of linear demand, elasticity declines as one moves downward along the curve.

When demand is not linear, as in the case of D in Figure 3–5, one can easily approximate point elasticity in the following manner. Suppose we want to compute the elasticity of D at point R. First, draw the straight line AB tangent to D at R. For very small movements away from R along D, the slope of AB is a relatively good estimate of the slope of D. We may estimate the elasticity at R by using either of the above elasticity ratios

$$E_D = \frac{QB}{OQ} = \frac{OP}{AP} \gtreqless 1.$$

These formulas also help us compare the relative elasticities of two or more demand curves. Figure 3–6 illustrates two intersecting demand curves. To intersect, they must have different slopes. Although elasticity is not the same as slope, it is possible to show, in this example, that the demand curve with the steeper slope is less elastic. It is a straightforward application of the geometric ratios for elasticity. By applying either formula, you can see that D_1D_1' is less elastic for any price and quantity than D_2D_2'. For instance, let E_{D1} be the elasticity of the steeper schedule and E_{D2} the elasticity of the less steep demand schedule. Then at the intersection of the schedule,

$$E_{D1} = \frac{QD_1'}{OQ} < \frac{QD_2'}{OQ} = E_{D2} \text{ or } E_{D1} = \frac{OP}{PD_1} < \frac{OP}{PD_2} = E_{D2}.$$

Figure 3-7 Relative Elasticities of Two Nonintersecting Demand Curves

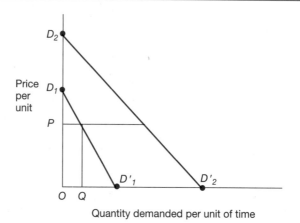

You can pick any other point on the price or quantity axis when demand curves intersect and apply either formula to get the same result, the steeper curve is always less elastic.

The curves in Figure 3–7 do not intersect nor are they necessarily parallel. By now, observation should tell you which curve is more elastic. At price P, for demand curve D_1D_1', $E_{D1} = OP/PD_1$, but for the curve D_2D_2', $E_{D2} = OP/PD_2$. The numerators are equal for both ratios, but the denominator is smaller for D_1D_1'. Hence, at any given price DD_1' is the more elastic schedule. As long as linear schedules do not share the same endpoints, the curve with the smaller quantity demanded at every price has the greater elasticity of demand at a given price. These results may be summarized by the following principle:

Principle

Slope is not elasticity; at any price, demand curves with different slopes may have the same elasticity, whereas curves with the same slope may have different elasticities.

3.1 *Applying the Theory*

Suppose that you own a small manufacturing business and find out that the price you are charging is on the inelastic portion of the demand for your product. What would you do?

3.3 Factors Affecting Demand Elasticity

Whether demand is elastic or inelastic is frequently an important consideration in making government policy and business decisions. For example, if the demand for wheat is elastic, an increase in the price of wheat would result in a proportionately greater reduction in quantity demanded. Farmers would obtain smaller total revenue from the sale of wheat. If the government established a minimum wheat price above the market equilibrium price, wheat sales would be reduced (as would farmers' incomes, unless the price support were accompanied by a minimum sales guarantee). On the other hand, if the demand for wheat is inelastic, as it probably is over the relevant range, a minimum price above the equilibrium price would increase farmers' total revenue.

Price elasticities can take on a wide range of values. For any given demand curve, two basic factors determine price elasticity: the availability of good substitutes and the time period of adjustment. These factors are related: a long adjustment period gives consumers more time to shop for suitable substitutes in the event of a price increase. If the adjustment period is sufficiently long, substitutes can be developed when none was present earlier.

3.3.1   Substitutes

The more and better the substitutes for a specific good, the greater its price elasticity will be at a given set of prices. Goods with few and poor substitutes—wheat and salt, for example—will always tend to have low price elasticities. Goods with many substitutes (wool, for example, which can be replaced by cotton and synthetic fibers) will have higher elasticities.

Substitutability implies that there is a great deal of difference between the market elasticity of demand for a good and the elasticity of demand faced by one seller in the market. For example, if all of the gasoline stations in a city raised the price of gasoline five cents a gallon, total sales would undoubtedly fall off, but in the absence of close substitutes, probably not very much. If all the Exxon stations—but no others—raised the price a nickel, the sales of Exxon gasoline would probably fall substantially. There are many good substitutes for one brand of gasoline at a lower price. If only one service station raised the price of gasoline, its sales in the long run would probably fall almost to zero. Some people might continue buying there (perhaps the owner's close relatives), but the availability of so many easily accessible substitutes would encourage most customers to trade elsewhere, since the cost of finding a substitute service station is so small.

3.3.2   The Period of Adjustment

Time also affects the elasticity of demand for a commodity. Consider the following example. Congress has passed legislation to deregulate the price of natural gas piped across state lines. Suppose the immediate effect of deregulation is an increase in the average price of a cubic foot of natural gas. What predictions would you make, using your knowledge of demand theory and information about the real world, on the effect higher prices will have on the quantity of natural gas demanded immediately after deregulation, and then after a rather long period of time, say two to five years?

We examine first the very near future, say within a year after deregulation. The theory of demand says that when the price of something increases, people demand less. In most cases, however, businesses and households already have their gas-using appliances and equipment installed. During a very short period of adjustment, households and businesses will respond by decreasing their use of natural gas, but it is difficult to quickly switch to an alternative fuel. We would expect the use of natural gas to fall some, but gas would not be particularly responsive to an increase in price.

Given a longer period of adjustment, users of natural gas can decrease consumption much more. Even though manufacturing plants that use gas are already built, some can convert to alternative fuel use. In the last 10 years, many industrial and utility boilers have, in fact, been designed to switch between two fuels. Households, if they have a relatively long time to adjust, can replace gas furnaces and air conditioners with electricity. Builders of new homes can insulate better. People can increase the insulation in older homes and install storm windows. In summary, if people think the price increase is permanent, the longer the time period that consumers have to adapt to a price change, the more elastic is the demand for the product. This adaptation can be in response to a price increase or decrease.

Economics in the News

Recent Estimates of Meat Elasticities Show Chicken Demand Less Elastic than Beef

It is difficult to estimate the elasticity of demand for specific products because factors that affect demand are frequently changing. Over time the demand curve can be shifting. This makes it difficult to be certain that the quantities sold at two different prices are on one demand curve rather than on two curves. Nevertheless, estimates are made. Recently, agricultural economists James Eales and Laurian Unnevehr estimated the demand elasticity for chicken and beef.[1] They did it in two ways, First, they treated chicken and beef as meat aggregates along with pork and a category for other food. In a second study, they broke chicken and beef into two categories each, "whole birds" and "parts" for chicken and "hamburger" and "table cuts" for beef.

When meats were aggregated, they found the following elasticities:

Meat Group	Elasticity of Demand
Chicken	0.267
Beef	0.570

When chicken and beef were broken into product groups, they found the following elasticities:

Product Group		Elasticity of Demand
Chicken:	Whole birds	0.677
	Parts and processed birds	0.610
Beef:	Hamburger	2.593
	Table cuts	0.684

(continued)

[1]James Eales and Laurian Unnevehr, "Demand for Beef and Chicken Products: Separability and Structural Change," *American Journal of Agricultural Economics*, August 1988, pp. 521–32.

By comparing the meat group and the product group estimates, you can see that the product groups have larger elasticities than the meat groups for beef and chicken. Elasticity measures the sensitivity of purchases to a price change. All other things held constant, the more abundant the substitutes are for a product, the more elastic will be the demand. The presence of substitutes makes it easier for consumers to switch from one product to another when prices change, and this increases the sensitivity of quantity demanded to price. The fact that product group elasticities for chicken and beef are higher means that different cuts of chicken are substitutes for each other and different cuts of beef are substitutes for each other. The presence of these substitutes is hidden by looking at the elasticity of demand for chicken as an aggregated product. Similar reasoning holds true for beef.

3.4   Other Elasticities

The formulas for the point elasticity of demand and the arc elasticity are not unique to economics. Elasticity measures are used in physics and engineering to determine how sensitive one related variable is to another. Even in economics, there are other kinds of elasticities. For example, in the next section the elasticity of supply is discussed. It is the percent change in the quantity supplied of a good, relative to the percentage change in price.

3.4.1   Income Elasticity

There is also the concept of income elasticity that will be discussed in a later chapter. It is a measure of the sensitivity of purchases to changes in income. Income elasticity is the percent change in the quantity of a good purchased, relative to the percent change in income. It is a ratio like demand elasticity, except income rather than price changes.

3.4.2   Cross-Price Elasticity

Another important elasticity that is discussed later is cross-price elasticity. This ratio measures the sensitivity of the purchases of one good when the price of another good changes. It is the ratio of the percent change in good X purchased when the price of good Y changes by some percent. The formula for cross-price elasticity is very similar to demand elasticity, except that the price of good Y is changing rather than the price of good X. Sometimes it is necessary to distinguish between the elasticity of demand and cross-price elasticity. The elasticity of demand expression E_D is then referred to as a good's *own price* elasticity.

3.2   *Applying the Theory*

During the mid-1980s, the price of gasoline began to fall, which obviously had an effect on automobile sales. A GM executive was quoted by *The Wall Street Journal* (February 4, 1986) as saying that a sustained 10 percent decline in gasoline prices would generate about a 4 percent increase in U.S. car sales, roughly the equivalent of a 4 percent decline in the prices of autos themselves.

Based on this information, what is the own-price elasticity of demand for U.S. cars? What is the cross-price elasticity of demand for U.S. cars with respect to the price of gasoline? Are cars and gasoline substitutes or complements? What would you predict would happen to gasoline sales if the price of automobiles fell?

3.5   Supply Elasticity

Similar to the case of demand, the coefficient of supply elasticity measures the relative responsiveness of quantity supplied to changes in price *along a given supply schedule*. The computation technique is the same as that used for demand elasticity

3.5.1   Definition and Computation of Supply Elasticity

The coefficient of supply elasticity is defined as

$$E_S = \frac{\text{\% change in quantity supplied}}{\text{\% change in price}} = \frac{\Delta Q_S/Q_S}{\Delta P/P} = \frac{\Delta Q_S}{\Delta P} \cdot \frac{P}{Q_S},$$

where ΔQ_S is the change in quantity supplied, and ΔP is the change in price. Since price and quantity supplied, P and Q_S, are assumed to change in the same direction, when P falls (rises), quantity supplied falls (rises). Therefore, the term E_S is always positive. Similar to demand, supply curves can be elastic, unitary, or inelastic. If the percentage change in quantity supplied exceeds the percentage change in price, supply is elastic and $E_S > 1$. If the two percentages are equal, supply has unitary elasticity and $E_S = 1$. If the percentage change in quantity supplied is less than the percentage change in price, supply is inelastic and $E_S < 1$.

The more elastic is supply, the more responsive is quantity supplied to price changes over a given range of supply. This tells us something about the shape of a supply schedule. If E_S is large, the supply curve will be close to horizontal, and, as the curve becomes horizontal, the coefficient will approach infinity. A small E_S indicates the supply curve is steep, and as the curve becomes vertical, the coefficient gets closer to zero. Table 3–4 shows the elasticity of supply for the schedule illustrated in Figure 2–3. This supply curve is a straight line. The inverse of its slope can be calculated using any two price and quantity combinations; we use the first two quantities and prices shown in Table 3–4:

$$\frac{\Delta Q_S}{\Delta P} = \frac{11,000 - 9,000}{\$3.00 - \$2.50} = \frac{2,000}{\$.50} = 4,000$$

The elasticity at each point on the supply curve (point elasticity) can be found by multiplying 4,000 by any price-quantity ratio (P/Q_S) determined by a point on the supply curve. For $Q_S = 11,000$ and $P = \$3.00$ the elasticity of supply is

$$E_S = \frac{\Delta Q_S}{\Delta P} \cdot \frac{P}{Q_S} = 4,000 \cdot \frac{\$3.00}{11,000} = 1.09.$$

Table 3–4 Supply and Point Elasticity

Quantity Supplied	Price	Elasticity
11,000	$3.00	1.09
9,000	2.50	1.11
7,000	2.00	1.14
5,000	1.50	1.20
3,000	1.00	1.33
1,000	0.50	2.00

As we move down the supply schedule toward lower prices and quantities, E_S becomes larger so the supply schedule becomes more elastic, as shown in the last column of the table. Conversely, with a straight-line supply, supply becomes less elastic as price and quantity supplied increase.

Just as in the case of demand elasticity, supply elasticity can be calculated at a point, as we just did, or between two points on a supply schedule. When supply elasticity is calculated between two points, the arc elasticity formula is used in order to get around the problem of deciding on a base point. The arc elasticity formula for supply is the same as the arc formula for demand, except for the use of quantity supplied, rather than quantity demanded:

$$\overline{E}_S = \frac{Q_1 - Q_0}{(Q_1 + Q_0)/2} \div \frac{P_1 - P_0}{(P_1 + P_0)/2} = \frac{Q_1 - Q_0}{Q_1 + Q_0} \div \frac{P_1 - P_0}{P_1 + P_0},$$

where Q_1 and Q_0 are the quantities that firms want to supply at P_1 and P_0, respectively. Consider the following segment of a supply schedule.

Price	Quantity Supplied
$20	4,000
15	2,000
10	1,000

The arc elasticity of supply for a price change between $20 and $15 and a quantity change between 4,000 and 2,000 units is, using the above formula,

$$\overline{E}_S = \frac{Q_1 - Q_0}{Q_1 + Q_2} \div \frac{P_1 - P_0}{P_1 + P_0} = \frac{4,000 - 2,000}{4,000 + 2,000} \div \frac{20 - 15}{20 + 15}$$

$$= \frac{1}{3} \div \frac{1}{7} = 2.33.$$

Since $\overline{E}_S$ is greater than 1, supply is elastic over this range. It is left to the reader to show that $\overline{E}_S = 1.67$ between prices of $15 and $10.

It is important to mention that, unlike demand, we do not relate elasticity of supply to changes in revenue. Price and quantity vary directly. An increase in price increases quantity supplied and, hence, increases revenue whether supply is elastic or inelastic.

Figure 3–8   Calculating Supply Elasticity

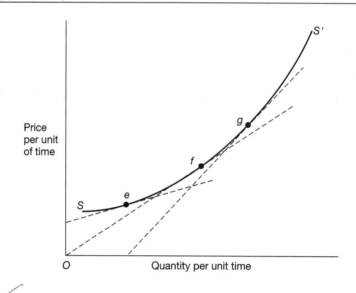

3.5.2   A Graphical View of Supply Elasticity

Geometrically, it is possible to tell at a glance whether a supply curve at a certain point is elastic, inelastic, or unitary. Consider the curve in Figure 3–8, with points *e*, *f*, and *g* and the corresponding tangent lines at each point. For any point on a supply curve, if the tangent line intersects the vertical axis above the origin, supply is elastic at that point; if it passes through the origin, it has unitary elasticity; and if it cuts the horizontal axis, supply is inelastic.[2] You can see from Figure 3–8, without any computation, that at a point *e* supply is elastic, at point *f* supply is

---

[2]Proof: Each of the tangent lines in Figures 3–8 is of the form $P = b + aQ_s$. For such linear forms, the slope $\Delta P/\Delta Q$, is "*a*" and the intercept is "*b*." If we divide both sides of the linear equation by Q, after rearranging the order of terms we obtain:

$$\frac{P}{Q_s} = a + \frac{b}{Q_s}.$$

Because the elasticity of the supply curve at each point approximately equals the elasticity of the tangent at that point, this information helps us determine the elasticity of the supply curve. Observe for a positive supply slope ($a > 0$):

$$E_S = \frac{\Delta Q_s}{\Delta P} \cdot \frac{P}{Q_s} = \frac{1}{\Delta P/\Delta Q_s} \cdot \frac{P}{Q_s} = \frac{1}{a} \cdot (a + \frac{b}{Q_s}) = 1 + \frac{b}{aQ_s}.$$

At point *e* in Figure 3–8, the intercept, *b*, is positive; thus, $E_S = 1 + (b/a)Q_s > 1$ and the supply curve is elastic. More generally, if the tangent at a point intersects the vertical axis, supply is elastic at that point. If we know "*a*" and "*b*," we could even estimate the elasticity. At point *f*, $b = 0$, so $E_S = 1$. If the tangent line goes through the origin, we know the elasticity of supply is unitary. Finally, at point *g*, the intercept is negative for the tangent line and $E_S < 1$; and a tangent cutting the horizontal axis means the supply curve is inelastic.

unitary elastic, and g describes a point on the supply schedule that is inelastic. It follows that any straight-line supply that intersects the vertical (horizontal) axis is elastic (inelastic) over its entire range.

3.5.3 Determinants of Supply Elasticity

The responsiveness of quantity supplied to changes in price depends, in a very large measure, on the ease with which resources either can be drawn into the production of the good in question, in the case of a price increase, or can be withdrawn from production of that good and attracted into production of other goods, in the case of a price decrease. If additional quantities can be produced only at much higher costs, a large increase in price is needed to induce much more quantity supplied. In these cases, supply is rather inelastic. On the other hand, if more will be produced at a relatively small increase in cost, quantity supplied is quite responsive to price changes, and supply is rather elastic.

Suppose the price of a particular good increases. If the resources used to produce that good are readily accessible, in the sense that more of the resources can be purchased without substantially increasing their prices, and if production can be increased easily, supply would be more elastic than would be the case if the additional resources are obtainable only at sharply increasing prices. For a price decrease, elasticity depends on how rapidly resources can be released from production of the good in question and moved into the production of other goods.

One can also think of the elasticity of the supply of people to an occupation. For some occupations, a small increase in the average wage or salary induces rapid entry into that occupation. Thus, supply is elastic if entry is easy. For other occupations, the supply is more inelastic because entry is induced only at a much higher wage. The elasticity of persons into an occupation depends on how easily people can enter the occupation after a wage increase and how willing they are to enter that occupation. In the case of wage decreases, elasticity depends on how rapidly people leave the occupation.

The length of the adjustment period is a crucial determinant of supply elasticity, in the case of either goods and services or entrants into an occupation. Clearly, if suppliers have more time to adapt to a change in price, the quantity supplied is more responsive, and supply is more elastic. Over a very short period of time, supply is generally quite inelastic.

Economists frequently distinguish between momentary, short-run, and long-run supply elasticity. For example, consider the supply of lawyers. Three supply curves for lawyers are shown in Figure 3–9. Begin with L_M, the momentary supply of lawyers. At any instant, there are L_M lawyers, and this number cannot be changed. Suppose the average income of lawyers rises from P_0 to P_1. Because the number of lawyers cannot be increased in response to the increase in income, the vertical supply curve L_M is infinitely inelastic.

Within a reasonably short period of time, however, the increase in the average income of lawyers will induce an increase in the number of lawyers, perhaps from L_M to L_{SR}. The increase in income will induce some retired lawyers to begin practice

Figure 3–9   Effect of Time of Adjustment on Supply Elasticity

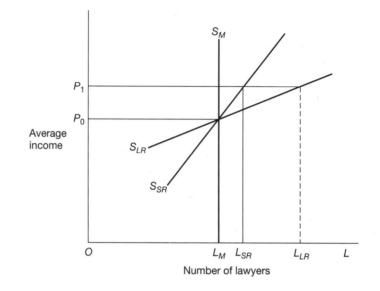

again, and some business people with law degrees will be induced to leave their companies and enter law practices. The resulting short-run supply curve is S_{SR}, the supply curve when a reasonably short period of adjustment is permitted. This curve is more elastic than is L_M because, when some adjustment time is permitted, quantity supplied is more responsive to price changes.

The long-run supply curve is S_{LR}, which allows sufficient time for *all* adjustments to be made. (We shall define short run and long run more precisely in Chapter 8.) In this example, higher average incomes will induce more college graduates to enter law school, and the period of adjustment is long enough to permit them to begin practicing law. Alternatively, if average income declines compared to those of other professions requiring similar periods of training, the number of lawyers will decline appreciably. The long-run supply curve S_{LR} is more elastic than S_{SR} because quantity is more responsive to price when sufficient adjustment time is permitted.

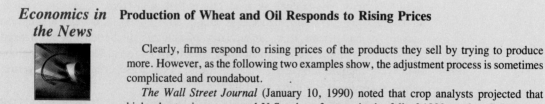

Economics in the News   **Production of Wheat and Oil Responds to Rising Prices**

Clearly, firms respond to rising prices of the products they sell by trying to produce more. However, as the following two examples show, the adjustment process is sometimes complicated and roundabout.

The Wall Street Journal (January 10, 1990) noted that crop analysts projected that high wheat prices prompted U.S. wheat farmers in the fall of 1989 to plant 7.5 percent more acres of wheat than they did a year earlier. This was the second consecutive year

(continued)

of an increase in wheat acreage. The price of wheat had risen $1 over two years, one third of the increase coming in the last year. The response however was not instantaneous. Farmers waited to see if the price rise was permanent. Furthermore, a 7.5 percent increase in acreage planted does not necessarily translate into a 7.5 percent increase in wheat. *The Journal* pointed out that subzero temperatures in December probably damaged some of the young crop in Southern Plains states. Furthermore, stockpiles of wheat had been decimated by a previous drought. Thus, at the time it was difficult to predict how elastic the supply of wheat actually would be in response to the rise in price.

The Wall Street Journal (January 4, 1990) also predicted a large increase in U.S. oil production in 1990 in response to higher and more stable oil prices. The number of oil rigs in service was expected to increase 11 percent in 1990. Furthermore, a survey found that oil companies were expected to increase spending for exploration by about 10 percent in 1990. Much of the increase in drilling was in response to a 13 percent forecasted increase in the price of natural gas, a by-product of oil.

In the case of both oil and wheat, producers responded to the increase in price, but in the momentary situation output could be increased very little (supply was almost perfectly inelastic). However, after several months, when the long run would be attained, the increase in output was expected to be much larger after the price increase. It takes a certain amount of time to increase output. The length of the time period of adjustment depends on the product in question, which determines how quickly producers can switch resources to its production.

3.6   Floor and Ceiling Prices

There are two things that governments know how to do: create a shortage and create a surplus. Shortages and surpluses can be created simply by legislating a price below or above the equilibrium price. Governments have decided, in the past, and probably will decide in the future, that the price of a particular commodity is or will be either "too high" or "too low" and proceed to set a "fair" price. Without evaluating the desirability of such interference, we can use demand and supply curves, along with the concept of elasticity, to analyze the economic effects of two types of interference in a market: the setting of minimum and maximum prices.

3.6.1   Price Ceilings

If the government imposes a maximum, or ceiling, price below the market equilibrium, the effect is to cause a shortage of that good. In Figure 3–10, a ceiling price, P_c, is set on a good. No one can legally sell the good for more than P_c, per unit, which is below the equilibrium price, P_e. At a price of P_e the quantity would be Q_e. However, at the ceiling price, only Q_s is offered for sale; but at this price Q_d is demanded. The excess demand or shortage in the market is therefore the amount $Q_d - Q_s$. Since quantity supplied is less than quantity demanded at the ceiling price, there must be some method of allocating the limited quantity, Q_s, among all those who are willing and able to buy the larger amount, Q_d. The sellers

Figure 3–10   Effect of Ceiling Price

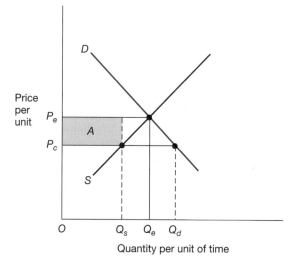

Quantity per unit of time

may devise a method—perhaps consumers have to stand in line. Those first in line get the good; those last in line don't get any. Suppliers may garner special customers on the basis of under-the-counter offers. Or underground markets may develop by which goods become available to customers on a cash only basis at a black-market price above the officially set price. Sometimes the government rations the available amount through ration coupons. In any case, when price ceilings are set, the allocation either is based on nonmarket considerations or the market mechanism functions less effectively outside the law.

Notice, however, that some consumers may benefit from price ceilings. Those who are fortunate enough to get the Q_s at the ceiling price pay less than if the equilibrium price had prevailed. Figure 3–10 shows the income transfer away from the producers to the consumers. Before the price ceiling, buyers paid P_e for all Q_e units they purchased. When the lower price is installed, they pay P_c. Area $A =$ $(P_e - P_c) \cdot Q_s$ represents the gain to those buyers who are fortunate enough to be able to purchase Q_s units of the good at P_c. Area A represents the saving in terms of the reduced amount of income they spend on the good. This represents the transfer of income from producers to consumers.

Some consumers, however, are harmed by the price ceiling. There is a shortage of $Q_d - Q_s$ units that buyers would be willing to purchase at a price above the minimum price at which the good is supplied. This is called the distortion of the ceiling price. As we will show later in this section, the amount of the distortion or shortage depends upon the elasticity of supply and demand over the relevant range of prices. Also, we must not forget the costs involved from standing in line, or avoiding the law if illegal markets should arise, to allocate the good.

Economics in the News

Sometimes Price Ceilings Are Hard to Enforce

In November 1988, California voters approved Proposition 103, which was designed to roll back automobile insurance rates 20 percent, then freeze them for at least a year. *Business Week,* "California Insurers Won't Roll Over," February 27, 1989, commented, "It sounded so simple—too simple it turns out."

Business Week noted that several insurers appealed to the California Supreme Court and some raised their rates before the bill went into effect. Others revoked many policies. Two large companies tried to quit the state; one of these companies was forced to reinstate the 1,900 policies it had refused to renew after the bill was passed. The president of a company that was refusing to write any new California policies until the Court had ruled on the legality of the bill predicted, "There won't be any private insurance business in California within two years." This is probably an overstatement; nonetheless, as in the case of all ceiling prices, one can predict a shortage of insurance in California in the future, unless some changes, such as deregulation, are made.

3.3 Applying the Theory

Several cities in the United States, including New York City, have rent control laws that set the maximum rent that can be charged for many apartments and houses. Several economists have blamed rent control for a large part of the homeless problem in these cities. They have also asserted that rent controls primarily help those who are better off and hurt the poor. What would be their reasoning behind these assertions?

3.6.2 Price Floors

In contrast to price ceilings, the government may feel that the suppliers of the good are not earning as much income as they "deserve" and, therefore, sets a minimum, or floor price. We show the results of such an action in Figure 3–11. Dissatisfied with the equilibrium price and quantity, P_e and Q_e, the government sets a minimum price of P_f. Since the law of demand cannot concurrently be repealed, consumers demand less (Q_d) at the higher price. Producers want to supply Q_s, at the higher price, so an excess supply or surplus of $Q_s - Q_d$ develops. In order to maintain the price P_f, the government must find some way to limit supply, or it must agree to purchase the excess.

One way to make producers keep output at Q_d is for the government to simply restrict production at Q_d by law. The vertical dashed line above supply at this output then becomes the new supply curve, and a price of P_f would clear the market. For those producers lucky enough to sell the Q_d units of output, area B represents an income transfer from consumers to producers; $(P_f - P_e)$ more revenue is earned on every unit sold, so the increase in revenue is $(P_f - P_e) \cdot Q_s$. However, buyers are not helped by price floors. No matter how many units are purchased, they pay more per unit. Furthermore, some producers wish to sell more than Q_d at P_f, but

Figure 3–11   Effect of Floor Price

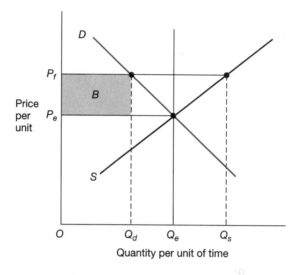

they are not allowed to. The excess supply of $Q_s - Q_d$ represents the distortion in the market.

Alternatively, the government may agree to purchase the excess supply, $Q_s - Q_d$, at the floor price. Consumers still pay P_f for Q_d units, so revenue represented by area B is still transferred from consumers to producers. Producers, however, are even better off in this instance than they would have been had supply been restricted to Q_d. Taxpayers, through government, transfer $P_f \cdot (Q_s - Q_d)$ to producers. As you can see from the figure, the sum of this transfer from taxpayers plus the amount consumers pay to producers is much larger than the revenue producers would have earned, $P_e \cdot Q_e$, had the market been permitted to attain equilibrium.

The government farm price support program is by far the most prominent example of price floors in the United States and in many other countries. The U.S. government uses a combination of two methods of supporting the price floors in agriculture: it restricts supply somewhat, and it purchases the surplus. As we will show later in this section, the amount of excess supply and the amount of the transfer to producers after a price floor is imposed depends on the elasticity of demand and supply in the market.

3.4   *Applying the Theory*

This problem is from the article, "American Consumers Get Milked. . . Again," in *The Margin* (January-February 1989). This article describes the effect of government support prices in the milk market.

The U.S. government sets prices for milk above equilibrium. The surpluses are used to make manufactured products such as butter, cheese, and cottage cheese. The government then buys whatever surplus there is of these products, which is approximately 10 percent of total dairy products.

Economists use elasticity measures to estimate the effect of such programs. The above article used the estimate .63 as the elasticity of demand for milk. It estimated that the price of milk would be 23 percent lower in the absence of price supports. At the time per capita milk consumption was 27.1 gallons per year. Based on these estimates how much would per capita milk consumption increase if the support prices were eliminated? Elasticity estimates for cheese and butter are .52 and .73 respectively. Assuming the price of all dairy products would fall 23 percent in the absence of support prices, how much more cheese and butter would be consumed?

3.6.3   Stable Prices and Temporary Shortages or Surpluses

We should emphasize that certain temporary shortages or surpluses may not be governmentally caused. For example, cities have experienced serious natural gas shortages during extreme cold spells. Many people have blamed these shortages on the fact that gas shipped interstate was subject to a regulated ceiling price below the market equilibrium. It is true that more households and firms will want and use gas than would be the case with a market-determined price, but some shortages probably would, and even should, occur with no ceiling price.

Why? Consider that when a gas shortage occurs, it is almost always during an extreme cold spell, for example, during a 50-year low in temperatures. Clearly, a publicly or privately owned gas company would not construct pipelines and storage capacity to accommodate all users during such a cold spell. This would not be cost efficient. Also think of the political implications if the city, or even a private utility, drastically raised prices to consumers during a freezing blizzard, when the demand for gas would increase dramatically. Citizens would march on city hall and vote differently in the next election. Therefore, cities or utilities rely on a gas capacity sufficient to handle the vast majority of winters, but not the extremes. When one of the rare, extremely cold periods occurs, cities generally ration by eliminating or reducing some industrial users and asking for voluntary reductions from customers.

The situation is analogous to the problem of snow removal in the Sunbelt. Every few years, the South gets a snow storm—light by most northern standards, paralyzing by local standards. Practically everything comes to a standstill until the snow melts. Would snow removal equipment be economical? Of course not. Such an expense to alleviate some inconvenience every few years would be extremely costly.

Similarly, during the summer of 1980, Dallas, Texas, experienced the hottest two months in its recorded history. Heavy air-conditioning usage caused periodic shortages of electricity. Should the electric company have increased prices to consumers? Over 100 people died from the heat. What do you think the reaction would have been to a large price increase?

Similar conditions apply to businesses. Movie theaters sometimes turn away customers from a popular movie. They also have a surplus, sometimes a very large surplus, of seats for other movies. Prices could be used more effectively to ration seats, but theaters would be constantly changing their prices, depending on the movie and the time it was shown. Such behavior would cause poor public relations. Movie goers, uncertain of the price they would pay, might prefer entertainment with stabler prices, and the long-run profits of theaters could fall. Similarly, retailers face the problem of the proper size of inventory to hold. Too much stock can get very costly to store, too little turns customers away. Over the long run, an inventory is held to maximize profits, but because there is a cost of storage, shortages can sometimes occur at the going price.

3.6.4   Elasticity and Distortion from Price Ceilings and Floors

The amount of excess demand created by a price ceiling and the amount of excess supply caused by a price floor depend on the elasticity of demand and supply. If we call the excess demand or excess supply created by the set prices the amount of distortion from government interference, then the distortion is smaller the less elastic is the demand or supply schedule. This is a reasonable observation, because these elasticities measure the sensitivity of quantities to price changes. If the quantities do not change much, that is, the schedules are inelastic, then the distortion will be small when a different price is set. If the schedules are quite elastic, the quantities will change a great deal and the distortion will be large.

A variety of examples can be constructed, but a frequently used graph shows the impact of a less elastic demand schedule on the excess supply created by a price floor. As noted previously, price floors are common in United States agricultural markets. They exist for virtually all grain and dairy products. In many of these price support programs, the federal government agrees to buy the excess supply created by the high price. The amount the government must purchase depends on how sensitive supply and demand are to the higher price.

In Figure 3–12, suppose the equilibrium price of a particular type of grain is $3 a bushel. The government, however, has set a price floor at $4 a bushel. With demand curve D and supply curve S, the excess supply is $1,600,000 - 800,000 = 800,000$ bushels of grain. If the government buys this many bushels of grain, the cost to the taxpayer is $4 \cdot 800,000 = \$3,200,000$. Now, imagine a less elastic demand schedule at the equilibrium. Figure 3–12 shows one labeled as D'. Since D' is clearly steeper than D, it is less elastic in equilibrium. At the $4 price floor, there is less distortion. Excess supply is the difference $1,600,000 - 1,000,000 = 600,000$ bushels and the taxpayers pay $2,400,000 to producers. The amount of distortion has gone down by 200,000 bushels of grain and the cost to the taxpayers by $800,000. The distortion would be less if the demand were even less elastic than shown. Also, it would decrease if the supply schedule were less elastic than shown.

Figure 3–12   Distortion from a Price Floor

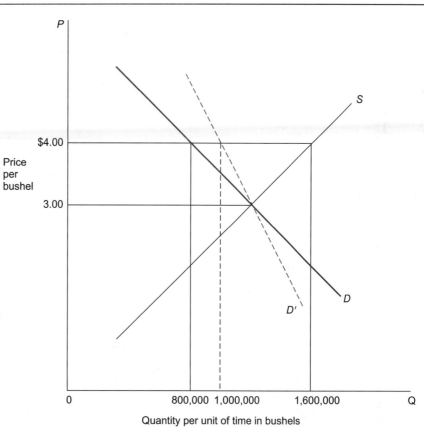

Quantity per unit of time in bushels

As an exercise, assume that a price ceiling of $3.50 is set in this market. Determine the resulting excess demand or shortage for each demand curve and compare.

We can summarize the preceding discussion with the following two principles:

Principle

A ceiling price is a price set by government below equilibrium. It is illegal for sellers to charge a higher price. A ceiling price causes consumers to demand more at that price than sellers are willing to supply. The difference between quantity demanded and quantity supplied is called excess demand or a shortage, and it represents the distortion in the market. The greater the elasticity of demand and/or supply, the larger the shortage. When a ceiling price is imposed, sellers or government must find a way to ration the available supply to consumers.

A floor price is a price set by government above equilibrium. A floor price causes sellers to want to sell more at that price than consumers are willing to buy. The difference between quantity supplied and quantity demanded is called excess supply, or a surplus. The greater the elasticity of demand and/or supply, the larger the surplus. When a floor price is imposed, government frequently limits the quantity supplied to the amount demanded or purchases the surplus.

3.7   The Effect of Taxes in Markets

An excise tax is a tax directly related to either the number of units sold or the price of a particular commodity. Excise taxes are always collected from the seller. If the tax is based on the number of units sold, it is often called a unit tax. The classic example of a unit tax is the excise tax collected on gasoline sold to motorists. It is not based on the price of gasoline, but on the number of gallons pumped. Alternatively, the tax may be a fixed percent of the sales price, in which case the excise tax is also known as an ad valorem tax. Sales taxes on consumer goods in most cities and states are examples of ad valorem taxes.

We will use supply and demand to study the market effects of excise taxes, looking first at the unit tax and then turning to ad valorem taxes.

3.7.1   Market Effect of a Unit Tax

Suppose your state legislature is debating the establishment of or an increase in a state unit tax on gasoline. Typical claims made by legislators are that such a tax will cause motorists to conserve on gasoline, and the added tax revenue is necessary for road improvement and construction. In contrast, some lawmakers may oppose the tax on the grounds that sellers will pass the full tax or its increase on to the consumer, who is taxed heavily enough already. Economic tools we have already developed will shed some light on these arguments and the controversies surrounding excise taxes.

Let us turn to a theoretical analysis of a unit tax with the tools of supply and demand. Suppose D in Figure 3–13 is the demand for gasoline in the state, and S is the present supply of gasoline prior to the tax imposition. Therefore, 1,000,000 gallons and a $1.25 price per gallon are, respectively, quantity and price.

A unit tax simply means that for every gallon of gasoline sold, the seller must pay a stipulated amount to the state. This payment shifts the supply curve upward (decreases supply). Demand does not shift. The consumer who pays $1.25 for a gallon of gasoline presumably does not care what portion of the price goes to the seller and what portion goes to the government. Consumers demand so much at $1.25 and at every other price, no matter what part goes to the government. Sellers, on the other hand, do care what portion of the price goes to the government and what portion they can keep. At a price of $1.25 a gallon, stations are induced to supply a million gallons per week in the market. This means that they themselves must receive $1.25 a gallon to supply this amount.

Figure 3–13   The Effect of a Unit Tax on Gasoline Sales

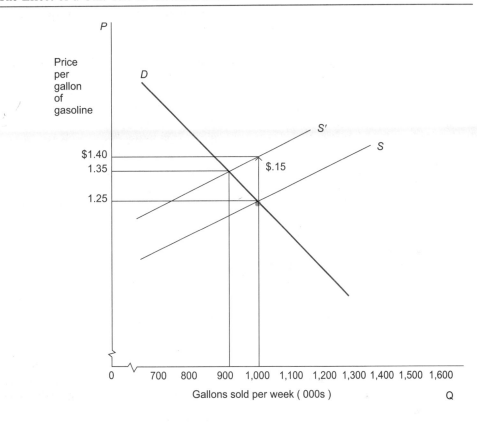

Suppose a tax of 15 cents a gallon is imposed. In order to induce suppliers to supply 1 million gallons a week, the price must be $1.40 a gallon, because only in this way can suppliers keep $1.25 for themselves. In Figure 3–13 an arrow is drawn upward from the $1.25 price to show that with the $.15 tax suppliers must receive $1.40 in order to continue offering 1 million gallons a week. At every quantity, suppliers must receive 15 cents a gallon more to induce them to supply the same amount.

The original supply schedule S therefore is shifted upward by $.15 everywhere. This creates a new schedule in the figure labeled S'. A new supply curve changes the market equilibrium. You can see that the intersection of the new supply S' and D is at a price below $1.40. The new price of gasoline is $1.35 and the quantity sold is 900,000 gallons a week. The price of gasoline, as a result of the tax has risen by 10 cents. The 15 cent tax levied by the government must still be paid. So 5 cents of the tax is absorbed by the sellers when the new equilibrium is established and 10 cents is paid by consumers in the form of higher prices. The government collects $135,000 in taxes: 15 cents per gallon times the 900,000 gallons sold.

The full tax is not passed on to the consumer as is often asserted. Figure 3–13 shows that if producers tried to raise the price to $1.40 a gallon there would be excess supply in the market. Inventories would build up and producers would be forced to lower prices in order to sell their stocks. The only time consumers would pay the entire tax would be when demand is perfectly inelastic, or vertical. In general, the more inelastic is demand, the more price rises after a tax is imposed, and the greater the share of the tax paid by consumers in the form of higher prices. This should not be a surprising conclusion. Goods with inelastic demands are relatively insensitive to price—when prices rise, consumers are not willing to reduce their consumption as much as would be case for a more elastic demand. Therefore, the more inelastic the demand, the less quantity is reduced after a given tax, the more tax receipts collected by government, and the greater the proportion of the tax that is shifted to consumers in the form of a higher price. Conversely, the more elastic is demand, the more quantity is reduced, the less the tax receipts collected by government, and the lower the proportion of the tax shifted to consumers in the form of a higher price.

You can see the effect of demand elasticity on equilibrium price and quantity in Figure 3–13 by drawing in a new, more inelastic (steeper) demand than D, passing through the original pre-tax equilibrium point. Compare the new after-tax equilibrium price and quantity with those shown in the figure. Do the same thing with a more elastic (less steep) demand passing through the original pre-tax equilibrium.

Supply elasticity also affects the shares of a unit tax paid by the buyer and seller; we can show that the more inelastic is the supply curve, the smaller is the proportion of a unit tax passed on to consumers, and the smaller the reduction in quantity after a tax. Figures 3–13 and 3–14 have identical demand curves for gasoline. The difference between the graphs is that Figure 3–14 has a less elastic supply schedule upon which the tax is levied. The upward shift in supply is still $.15 everywhere, so the government is collecting 15 cents on every gallon of gasoline sold. The less elastic supply curve results in a price increase to consumers of 7 cents; the rise is from $1.25 to $1.32 a gallon. Previously in Figure 3–13, the increase was 10 cents. By comparing the figures you can see that the consumer pays a smaller portion of the tax when supply is less elastic, the reduction in sales is smaller and the government collects more tax revenue.

Although this point is easy to see in the graphs, the reasoning behind this conclusion can be put into words. The key to understanding why price does not change so much is to think about what a less elastic supply means. It tells us that sellers are not as sensitive to price. In the extreme case of perfect inelasticity, they want to sell a given quantity of the good no matter what the price may be. Therefore, when the tax is levied, sellers are willing to pay the entire amount of the tax in order to maintain sales. Comparing Figures 3–13 and 3–14 once again you can see that the tax reduced sales to 900,000 gallons of gasoline in the first case, but the reduction was just to 920,000 gallons in the second case. In summary, when supply is elastic, sellers are more willing to adjust the quantity supplied rather than pay the tax themselves. In contrast, when supply is inelastic, the quantity sold adjusts very little, so sellers tend to absorb more of the tax.

Figure 3–14   The Unit Tax Share When Supply Is Less Elastic

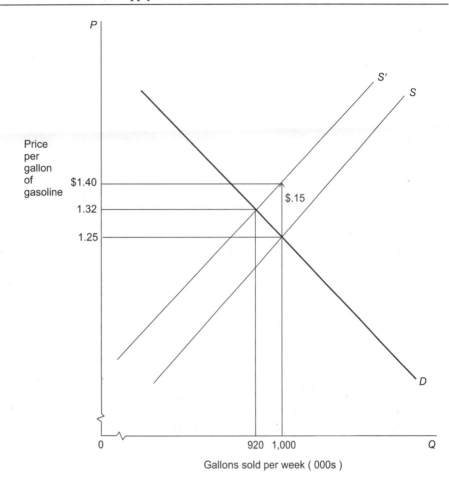

Gallons sold per week (000s)

3.7.2   Ad Valorem Taxes

When the excise tax is an ad valorem tax the impact on prices and quantities is conceptually the same as a unit tax. The tax shifts the supply curve upward, and who pays what portion of the tax depends on the elasticities of demand and supply. However, with a percentage tax, the amount of tax depends on the price of the commodity. Let us focus our attention on the supply curve, which tells us how much sellers offer at each possible price. If a 10 *percent* ad valorem tax is placed on sellers, they would require their old price plus 10 percent more to supply the same amount.

Because supply curves have a positive slope, a higher price is necessary to induce sellers to offer larger quantities in a market. As prices rise to induce larger quantities, the absolute amount of the tax, *t,* must therefore rise. Remember, *t* is a constant percentage of the sales price; as the sales price rises, so does the amount of tax

Figure 3–15   The Market Effect of an Ad Valorem Tax

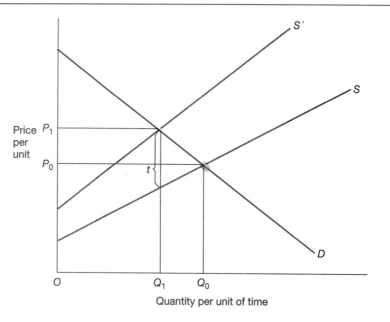

paid. If the sales tax on a bicycle is 10 percent, then a $100 price tag means the tax is $10, but if the price jumps to $150, the tax becomes $15.

Figure 3–15 shows generalized supply and demand curves. The vertical difference between the supply curves S and S' is the amount of the tax. At sales of Q_1 this distance is labeled t, but you can see that it gets larger as sales increase, because the market price is higher. The before-tax equilibrium is at price P_0 and quantity Q_0; the tax shifts the new equilibrium to P_1 and Q_1. Compared to the old equilibrium, prices are higher and the quantity sold is less.

At the new equilibrium quantity, the tax paid to the government on each unit sold is the distance t. This is more than the change in price from P_0 to P_1. Hence, part of the tax is paid by the consumer—this is the difference between the old and new price—and the rest is paid by the seller.

3.7.3   Government Revenue

The amount of tax revenue collected by the government is always equal to the tax, t, times the numbers of units sold. Letting T be tax revenue, then

$$T = t \cdot Q.$$

In Figure 3–13, when the $.15 tax was imposed and sales fell to 900,000, the tax revenue collected by the government would be

$$T = \$.15 \cdot 900,000 \text{ gallons} = \$135,000.$$

For any *t*, tax revenue is less, ~~the greater the fall in quantity sold after the tax is imposed~~. Tax authorities prefer to tax goods that are not sensitive to price changes on either the demand or supply side of the market (e.g., gasoline, cigarettes, and liquor). These kinds of goods represent reliable sources of income to governments, because they have demand schedules that are relatively inelastic.

Economics in the News

What Would Be the Effect of a Tax on Gasoline?

The following statements are excerpts from "Economic Trends," *Business Week,* January 30, 1989. This article discussed the effect of a proposed increase of 25 cents a gallon in the federal excise tax on gasoline. The purpose of the increase would be to raise a large amount of tax revenue, which would be used to decrease the budget deficit.

1. Gasoline taxes are a big potential revenue source, with each penny-per-gallon hike producing roughly $1 billion per year in gross tax receipts, or $25 billion from a 25 cent increase.
2. To be sure, some analysts claim that the net gain in revenue would be far less, once the reduced demand and lower economic output induced by the tax hike are factored in.
3. [An economist with a large brokerage firm] notes that the impact on demand would be very modest over the short term.
4. [Another economist] believes that a tax hike may well fall more heavily on gasoline refiners than consumers . . . profit margins have been so large recently that refiners may be forced to absorb much of the tax increase in order to continue to maximize gasoline output.

There are several problems with these statements. In 2 and 3, demand will not be reduced after a tax increase; quantity demanded will fall. These mistakes are frequently made in the popular press. Statement 1, as statement 2 indicates, implicitly assumes a perfectly inelastic demand. At the time, approximately 100 billion gallons of gasoline a year were sold. A 25 cent tax would raise $25 billion in taxes only if consumers did not decrease consumption. The extent to which sales would decline depends on elasticity.

Statement 4 is more subtle. If the tax hike falls more heavily on refiners, and if refiners may be forced to absorb much of the tax increase, it must be the case that demand is very elastic—not much is shifted to consumers in the form of higher prices because consumers are quite sensitive to price increases. The more elastic is demand, the more consumers reduce purchases. This would mean that an excise tax on gasoline is a poor source of government revenue. Most estimates indicate that the demand for gasoline is relatively inelastic. Such a tax would be a good source of government revenue, but most of the tax would be passed along to consumers in the form of higher prices. The fact that refiners are making large profits has nothing to do with the effect of a tax on prices. Furthermore, refiners don't try to maximize output. They could have increased their output anyway, merely by lowering their prices if that was what they wanted to do. Firms want to maximize profits, not output.

3.8   Summary

Elasticity is one of the most important tools economists use in the study of markets and consumer behavior. This chapter defined and applied the concepts of elasticity of demand and elasticity of supply. Additional elasticity definitions will be brought up in later chapters. In all cases, elasticity is measured in the same way: it is the ratio of a percentage change in one variable to a percentage change in another. For the elasticity of demand

$$E_D = -\frac{\text{Percent change in quantity}}{\text{Percent change price}}.$$

It measures the sensitivity of the quantity of a good demanded to a change in the good's price. There is a point formula and an arc formula for elasticity of demand. The point formula measures elasticity at one point on the demand curve and, therefore, measures elasticity at one price and quantity. The arc formula gives the average elasticity between two points, and it should always be used when calculating the percent changes between two points.

Elasticity of supply measures the sensitivity of the quantity offered for sale when the market price changes. The same formulae discussed for demand elasticity apply to the elasticity of supply E_S. However, for a supply schedule when prices rise, the quantity offered generally rises, and when prices fall, the quantity offered generally falls. The relation is direct, so E_S is always positive. For demand the relation is indirect; rising prices lead to lower quantities purchased and falling prices lead to more purchased. E_D is therefore a negative number but economists frequently ignore the sign when reporting demand elasticities.

The elasticity of demand determines how the expenditure of a consumer or consumers in a market changes when price goes up or down. Expenditure is equivalent to the revenue collected by a seller or sellers in a market. $E_D > 1$ means demand is elastic, and expenditure falls (rises) when price rises (falls); $E_D < 1$ means demand is inelastic, and expenditure rises (falls) if price rises (falls). Finally $E_D = 1$ is unitary elasticity; expenditure remains constant when price goes up or down.

The elasticity of demand and supply indicate how much distortion is caused in the market when prices are adjusted through price ceilings or floors and excise taxes. Distortion is the excess demand or supply at the adjusted price. Distortion is less, the less elastic is demand or supply. When taxes are levied, the revenue collected by government is greater the less elastic is demand.

Answers to   *Applying the Theory*

3.1   If you want to increase your profits, and presumably you do, you would increase your price and reduce the quantity you sell. Since demand is inelastic on the portion of the demand curve your price is on, the increase in price would increase consumer expenditure on your product. Also, the reduction in the quantity you sell would reduce your costs of production. Both effects would tend to increase profits. No individual firm would knowingly sell on the inelastic portion of its demand curve. However, supply and demand *in the market* may easily result in a *market* price on the inelastic part of demand.

3.2 From the information given, the own price elasticity of demand is unitary, since 4 percent/4 percent = 1. The cross price elasticity is 4 percent/ − 10 percent = − .4. The goods are complements since a fall in the price of gasoline leads to a rise in car sales. A fall in the price of cars would probably lead to a rise in gasoline sales, but the cross-price elasticity of gasoline regarding car prices would not necessarily be − .4.

3.3 A rent control on apartments or houses is really just a price ceiling. More people want to rent than there are apartments available. Thus, there is a shortage of housing. Because they cannot raise rents, housing owners let some of their apartments deteriorate and even become uninhabitable. Many believe that this decline in the amount of housing has forced some people onto the streets. Because more people want housing than there is housing available at the ceiling prices, some observers believe that owners will rent to those who have the highest income. These people are more desirable tenants because they, presumably, will take better care of the property. The prediction is those who are better off get housing at lower prices, and some of the poor get no housing or possibly substandard housing.

3.4 If the elasticity of demand for milk is .63, then $- \%\Delta Q_D / \%\Delta P = .63$, so $-\%\Delta Q_D = .63 \cdot \%\Delta P$. Since price would fall 23 percent in the absence of a support price

$$-\%\Delta Q_D = .63 \cdot (-.23) \text{ or } \%\Delta Q_d = .145.$$

Quantity would rise 14.5 percent; therefore, per capita consumption would be

$$1.145 \cdot 27.1 = 31,$$

or approximately four gallons more. For cheese, using the same formula,

$$-\%\Delta Q_D = .52 \cdot (-.23) = -.12, \text{ or } 12 \text{ percent.}$$

And for butter

$$-\%\Delta Q_D = .73 \cdot (-.23) = -.168, \text{ or about } -17 \text{ percent.}$$

Technical Problems

1. The following are the demand and supply functions for a hypothetical product

$$Q_D = -.6P + 18$$

$$Q_S = .4P - 2.0$$

   a. Plot these functions on a graph.
   b. Calculate the elasticity of demand and supply at the equilibrium.
   c. Suppose a \$1 tax is placed on all units sold. What is the new supply curve? Calculate the new equilibrium. What is the change in price?

2. The following table shows four points on a straight line demand schedule.

Price	Quantity Demanded
\$80	200
60	400
40	600
20	800

Figure E.3–1

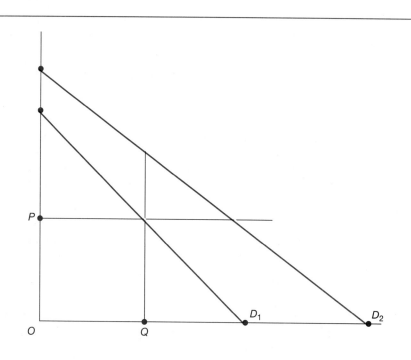

First calculate $\Delta Q_D/\Delta P$.
- *a.* Calculate the point elasticity of demand at each price-quantity combination.
- *b.* Calculate the arc elasticity of demand between pairs of price-quantity combinations when price goes from 80 to 60, 40 to 20, and 80 to 20.
3. "I earn $20 a week and spend it all on chocolate donuts, no matter what the price." What is the person's elasticity of demand?
4. *a.* In Figure E.3–1, use the graphical method (along with a ruler) to calculate the elasticity of each D_1 and D_2 at price P, then at quantity Q. Compare.
   b. In Figure E.3–2 use the graphical method (along with a ruler) to calculate the elasticity of D_1 and D_2 at price P and quantity Q. Compare.
5. An athletic director at a college recently raised ticket prices from $12 to $15 per game. Sales went down 8 percent. The director said, "With the 25 percent increase in ticket prices, dollar volume has increased about 16 percent." Is this claim consistent with what you know about demand elasticity? Find the elasticity of demand in this case, assuming the demand schedule is stable.
6. *a.* If the elasticity of demand for gasoline is .8, what would be the effect on the quantity of gasoline demanded if its price increases 10 percent.
   b. If the elasticity of demand for wheat is .5, what would be the effect on the price of wheat if the quantity of wheat increases 10 percent.
   c. If a 10 percent increase in the price of mopeds causes a 15 percent decrease in the quantity of mopeds demanded, what is the elasticity of demand for mopeds.

Figure E.3–2

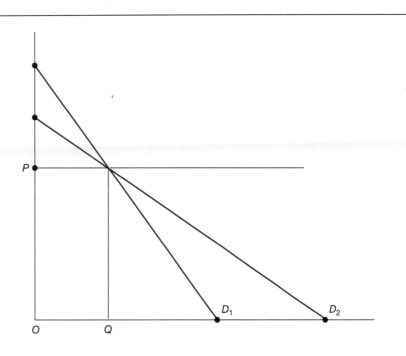

Figure E.3–3

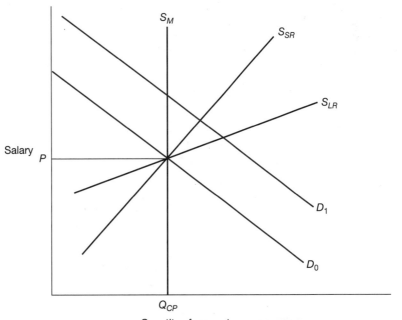

Figure E.3–4

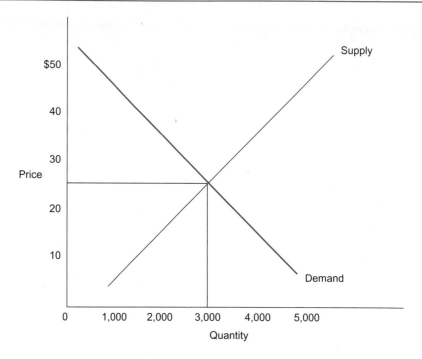

Figure E.3–5

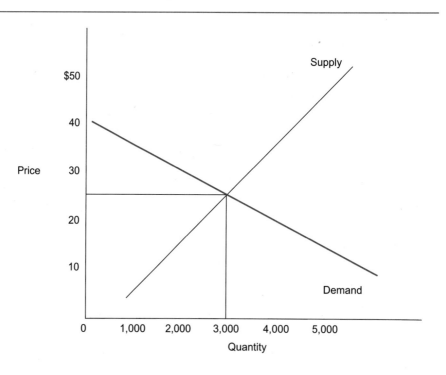

7. Assume the demand for CD players is elastic over the relevant range. Are the following statement true or false? Explain why.
   a. When the price of CD players decreases, the quantity demanded of CD players increases.
   b. When the price of CD players decreases, the quantity demanded of CD players increases, but by relatively less than the increase in price.
   c. When the price of CD players decreases, the total expenditure on CD players increases.
   d. If the price of compact disks decreases, the demand for CD players will probably increase.

8. In the Figure E.3–3 S_M, S_{SR}, and S_{LR} are, respectively, the momentary, short-run, and long-run supply curves for computer programmers. D_0 is the original demand for programmers, so P and Q_{cp} are the salary and quantity of programmers employed. The demand for programmers increases to D_1.
   a. Compare the effect of the shift in demand on the salary and number of programmers employed in the momentary situation, the short run, and the long run.
   b. Discuss the role of price (salary) as both a rationing device and a signaling device in the momentary situation, the short run, and the long run.

9. What would be the probable effect on the long-run elasticity of supply in the following situations?
   a. The supply of surgeons, if the American Medical Association requires an additional year of residency to become a surgeon.
   b. The supply of widgets, if a decline in the gadget industry causes a drop in the wages and an increase in the unemployment rate of gadget makers, who can be easily trained to make widgets.
   c. The supply of airline pilots, if the mandatory retirement age of pilots is changed from 60 to 55.
   d. The supply of Picasso paintings after Picasso died.

10. Figure E.3–4 shows demand and supply in a market. Clearly, equilibrium price and quantity are $25 and 3,000 units. There is presently no tax on the product.
    a. What would be the effect of a floor price of $35?
    b. What would be the effect of a ceiling price of $20?
    c. What would be the effect of a unit tax of $10 on equilibrium price and quantity? What is the amount of the tax borne by producers, and government tax revenue?

11. Figure E.3–5 shows demand and supply in the same market. Supply is the same as in problem 10 and equilibrium price and quantity are the same, $25 and 3,000. However, demand is more elastic than before in the neighborhood of $25. There is now no tax on the product.
    a. What would be the effect of a floor price of $35?
    b. What would be the effect of a ceiling price of $20?
    c. What would be the effect of a unit tax of $10 on equilibrium price and quantity? What is the amount of the tax borne by producers, and government tax revenue?
    d. Compare your answers under the more elastic demand to those obtained in problem 10, and discuss the effect of demand elasticity in the case of a floor price, ceiling price, and unit tax.

Analytical Problems

1. Excise tax authorities find themselves torn between the need to tax items that promise a high and steady flow of revenue and the desire not to tax "necessities." Explain this conflict. On items that provide a good tax base, who bears the burden? Explain.

2. Some people say that without government price support programs farmers could not afford to grow some crops like cotton; therefore, no cotton would be grown in the United States without the support program. Analyze.

3. Some legislators want to put higher taxes on liquor and cigarettes because they assert that people, particularly poor people, spend too much of their income on liquor and cigarettes and not enough on other goods, such as food. If extra taxes are levied on liquor and cigarettes, people would spend less money on the "bad" things and more money on other "good" things. Evaluate this statement, using the concept of elasticity.

4. Analyze the effect of time on the elasticity of demand for the following products:
   a. Bread.
   b. Motorcycles.
   c. Gasoline.
   d. Electricity.
   e. Movie tickets.
   f. Cigarettes.

5. *The Wall Street Journal,* January 11, 1990, reported that the price of oil had surged because inventories of gasoline had decreased, from 10 to 15 million barrels below normal. Explain, by using demand and supply, what happened.

6. We classify, in the text, the supply of workers to jobs or occupations into momentary, short-run, and long-run supply. For the following jobs or occupations, about how long would you predict it would take for equilibrium to be attained along the long-run supply curve after an increase in demand? Explain your answer.
   a. Medical doctors in the United States.
   b. Medical doctors in Iowa.
   c. Retail clerks in California.
   d. Automobile workers in the United States.
   e. High school teachers in the United States.
   f. High school teachers in Texas.
   g. Math teachers in the United States.

7. What would be the effect of a large increase in tuition at a specific university? At all universities? Consider the effect of time.

8. Suppose a consumer with a fixed income spends all of that income on two goods, burgers and fries. The demand for burgers is inelastic. If the price of burgers rises, will this person buy more or less fries? Explain. What if the demand for burgers had been elastic?

9. A minimum wage is a floor price set above the equilibrium. As with any floor, more is supplied than is demanded. In this case, more people want to work than firms are willing to hire; that is, some people are unemployed. What type of workers do you think would be unemployed?

10. A federal excise tax (unit tax) is placed on several products. Among the most important products are gasoline, cigarettes, and alcoholic beverages. Explain why these products were chosen.

11. Many economists believe that the taxes on the three products in problem 10 are regressive because poorer people bear more of the tax than wealthier people in proportion to their income. Why would this be so?

12. Many universities with successful athletic programs set the price of tickets to football and basketball games far below the equilibrium price—more people want seats than there are seats available. Why would they do this? How are the seats allocated, particularly the better seats?

13. Why would many buildings and homes in cities such as San Francisco be extremely warm on infrequent hot days, whereas buildings and homes in cities such as Houston would be cooler on days with the same temperature. Can't people in San Francisco afford air-conditioning? For that matter, Houston becomes practically paralyzed on the infrequent days when it snows. Can't Houston afford snow removal equipment?

14. Why don't theaters increase their price when the manager can see that there are more people in line to see the movie than there are seats? By the way, how would you feel if you went into a restaurant, ordered a steak, and the waiter told you that there was one steak left but two people ordered it and then offered to auction off the steak to the higher bidder. Airlines actually do something to this effect when a flight is overbooked. People are offered bonus flights to take a later flight, and the bonus is raised until the market is cleared. Not many people seem to object.

CHAPTER 4

The Theory of Optimizing Behavior

4.1 Introduction

Life is filled with decisions or choices. You and everyone else make many choices every day. Some choices are relatively unimportant, such as what groceries you will buy this week or how long you will study tonight. Others are major decisions: What career you will prepare for, what university you will attend, what kind of a car you will buy.

When making such decisions, you, like most other people, probably try to make the choice that you believe will give you the greatest satisfaction or benefit (or in some cases the least dissatisfaction or lowest cost) of all possible alternatives. Such decisions require a method of *optimization* or involve *optimizing behavior,* the subject of this chapter. Everyone practices optimization. Few people, when making a choice, would knowingly choose an alternative that they think would make them worse off than some other possible alternative.

A vast number of economic problems and large parts of this text are concerned with optimization. For example, consumers try to obtain the maximum satisfaction from a given income, producers want to produce a given output at the lowest possible cost, firms attempt to maximize profits, and investors want to obtain the maximum returns from potential investments.

Since optimization plays an important role in this text, and in the whole body of economic analysis, we want to set forth some fundamental principles of optimizing behavior before going further. A thorough understanding of these principles will significantly decrease the difficulty of understanding the theoretical material developed in later chapters. All of the theories of decision making described later in this text will follow the principles set forth in this chapter.

Optimizing behavior falls into one of two general categories: *constrained optimization* and *unconstrained optimization*. We will briefly discuss both types of optimization before developing the decision-making rules in detail.

4.1.1   Constrained Optimization

Suppose a decision maker must choose among two or more levels of activities. Each activity requires that a variable such as time or money expenditure be decided upon. These are called choice variables. Increases in the level of an activity give benefits to the decision maker but also impose costs. The decision maker wants to choose the choice variable so as to attain the greatest benefits possible from a given level of cost. Alternatively, the problem may be to achieve a specified level of benefits at the lowest possible cost. Such problems involve constrained optimization.

Definition

Constrained optimization takes one of two forms: *constrained minimization* or *constrained maximization*. Constrained minimization involves making choices that yield a specified level of benefits at the minimum possible cost, in terms of money or time. Constrained maximization involves choices that yield the maximum possible level of benefits attainable within a specified level of cost. In the first case, the constraint is the total benefits sought. In the second case, the constraint is the specified cost.

In constrained minimization, a decision maker is faced with several ways of achieving a specific goal. (If there is only one way, the choice is predetermined and there is no problem.) Each possible method of achieving the goal involves a cost. The problem is to choose the method with the lowest cost.

For example, suppose a student has tests tomorrow in mathematics and economics, and wants to make an average grade of 90 on the two tests (not necessarily a 90 on each test). The grade on each test will depend on the amount of time the student spends studying a subject—so study time is the choice variable. The student's objective is to minimize the total time spent studying while making a 90 average. There are many ways to attain the goal of a 90 average: study math enough to make a 95 and economics enough to make an 85, or economics enough to make a 98 and math enough to make an 82, or any other combination such that

$$\text{(math grade + economics grade)}/2 = 90.$$

An average score of 90 is the constraint; that is, this score is the requirement that must be achieved. The problem is to find the one way that involves the least total studying time for the two courses. (We will show how to solve this problem later in the chapter.)

Another example of a constrained minimization problem that you will encounter later in the text is a business firm that can employ several combinations of resources to produce a desired level of output and wants to choose the combination that costs the least. A third example would be a governmental agency that wants to accomplish a specific goal, such as a desired level of purity in a river or lake, at the lowest possible cost.

Rather than minimizing, sometimes the problem is maximizing. In constrained maximization problems, a decision maker chooses among several combinations of activities, each of which yields a different level of benefits but involves the same level of cost. The decision maker chooses the combination that yields the largest amount of benefits possible within the set cost. In this type of problem the constraint is the specified cost, and the objective is the highest possible benefits attainable within that cost.

For an example of constrained maximization, return to the student who has tests tomorrow in math and economics. Suppose this student, rather than striving for a 90 average, now decides to allocate six hours of study time so as to attain the highest average possible. Study time is fixed, and a maximum grade is desired. In the minimization problem, the grade average was fixed, and the minimum study time was desired. For both optimization problems, the grade in each test will depend on the amount of time the student spent studying that subject. There is a special relation between this maximization problem and the minimization problem. The constraint in the minimizing problem, average grade, becomes the choice variable in the maximizing problem. And the choice variable in the minimizing problem, total study time, is the constraint in the maximization problem. When minimization is replaced by maximization the choice variable and constraint are switched. Constrained maximization is called the *dual* of constrained minimization and vice versa.

An important constrained maximization problem that appears later in the text concerns a firm that chooses the allocation of resources from all allocations possible at a specified level of cost, so as to produce the largest output possible. Note that this is the dual of the previously mentioned cost minimization problem. Another constrained maximization problem you will encounter later in the text is a consumer who wants to choose the combination of goods and services, from all possible combinations that can be purchased from the consumer's income, so as to yield the highest level of satisfaction.

These two kinds of constrained optimization are so closely related that you do not have to learn one rule for constrained minimization and another for constrained maximization. The optimizing rules, as you will see, are identical for both problems.

4.1.2   Unconstrained Optimization

Now assume that a decision maker must choose the level of some activity or choice variable, which, as always, yields benefits and imposes costs. The objective is to attain the highest possible *net benefits* (benefits minus costs). Such problems are referred to as unconstrained optimization.

Definition

Unconstrained optimization takes one of two forms: *unconstrained maximization* or *unconstrained minimization,* Unconstrained maximization involves choosing the level of an activity, which produces benefits but has a cost. The objective is to attain the greatest possible net benefit—total benefits minus total cost. Unconstrained minimization involves choosing the level of some costly activity, for which the benefit is the reduction in a cost. The objective is to achieve the lowest possible total net cost.

An example of *unconstrained maximization* is a jogger who receives satisfaction from burning calories and better fitness while running but also bears a cost from the pain of exercise. The longer the run, the greater the fitness and the more calories burned, but there is also increased pain. The jogger chooses the amount of exercise time to maximize net benefit, the difference between the gains and pain. A second example may be the government increasing tax receipts by hiring more IRS agents. The government hires the number of agents for which the additional net receipts—increases in tax payments, less the cost of agents—is greatest. Finally, the unconstrained maximization problem you will encounter most often in this course is a business firm choosing its sales, advertising, or the quantity of inputs to maximize its net profit. The firm seeks the greatest difference between the revenue from the activity and the cost of the activity.

An example of *unconstrained minimization* is a store that is hiring security guards to reduce its loss from shoplifting. The store would hire the number of guards, who cost money, to achieve the lowest total cost of security and shoplifting. Hence, the firm wants to minimize the sum of the two costs, where an increase in expenditure on security reduces the cost of theft. A similar problem would be a factory hiring inspectors in order to minimize the cost of sending faulty merchandise to customers. Inspectors and faulty parts both cost the factory money, but they have an inverse relation. The goal is to minimize the total net cost. In both of these problems the costs counteract each other and the reduction in one cost could be considered a benefit in an unconstrained problem. Unconstrained minimization problems are less frequently encountered in economics than maximization problems and can always be cast in the form of maximization.[1] The solution to any unconstrained optimization problem is the same for any situation. It involves a study of decisions at the margin.

4.2 Marginal Analysis

All optimization problems involve both benefits and costs. An optimal outcome is achieved by comparing the marginal benefits from an activity with the marginal cost of that activity. The marginal benefit (MB) of an activity is the addi-

---

[1]For example, consider the shoplifting problem. Additional guards reduce theft and, therefore, increase the store's profit. Additional guards cost the store money. The store hires the number of guards that maximize its profit from that activity.

Table 4–1   Output and Number of Workers

(1) Number of Workers (W)	(2) Output (Q)		(3) Marginal Benefit
0	0		
		>	20 = (20 − 0)
1	20		
		>	15 = (35 − 20)
2	35		
		>	10 = (45 − 35)
3	45		
		>	5 = (50 − 45)
4	50		
		>	2 = (52 − 50)
5	52		

tional benefits that are derived per unit increase in an activity. The marginal cost (MC) of an activity is the additional cost generated per unit increase in the activity.

4.2.1   Marginal Benefit

Some examples of marginal benefits from an additional unit of an activity are:

1. An improved course grade from an additional hour spent studying.
2. The increase in a firm's revenue or income from producing and selling an additional unit of output.
3. The increase in a person's satisfaction from consuming an additional bowl of ice cream.
4. The increase in output forthcoming when a firm hires an additional worker.

In economic theory there are special names for marginal benefit in many of these examples. As the theory is developed here, the new vocabulary will be presented in definitions. But, the definitions are simply new names for marginal benefit. From these examples it is readily seen that marginal benefit may be difficult to actually measure. Improved grades may be measured by a better grade point average (G.P.A.). The revenue of a business is measured in dollars. These are easy cases. Satisfaction in the previous example 3 is much more difficult, and it may be impossible to measure for a person. How can people tell you how happy they are about eating ice cream? The same problem is present in example 4. Output can be at times very difficult to measure. Schwinn makes bicycles. Wendy's makes hamburgers. But what is the output of a university? Students graduated? Does a bachelor's degree count the same as a master's degree? What about research? How is that measured?

As we develop the theory, we will assume that benefits can be measured, but in practice this can be difficult.

You will see marginal benefits illustrated in two ways: as a table, when the activity and resulting benefits vary discretely, and as a graph, when the activity and resulting benefits vary continuously. Table 4–1 is an example of discrete variation. Columns 1 and 2 show the output a firm can produce using zero through five workers, when the level of usage of all other resources (for example, capital) is held constant.

The third column of the table shows the marginal benefit to the firm from hiring each additional worker. The marginal benefit is measured by the additional units of output produced by the firm. Column 3 also reflects the frequently made assumption that the marginal benefits from additional units of an activity decrease as the level of the activity increases. In Table 4–1, because the number of workers increases by one unit at a time, the marginal benefit is simply the increase in output, as shown in column 3.

In some tables, the activity changes in increments other than one. For example, suppose a firm's output, the number of workers a firm hires, and the resulting increase in the level of output are as follows:

(1) Number of Workers (W)	(2) Output (Q)	(3) Incremental Output	(4) Average Incremental Output ($\Delta Q/\Delta W$)
20	1,000		
		800	800/10 = 80
30	1,800		

In this case, output increases by 800 (from 1,000 to 1,800) when the number of workers increases by 10 (from 20 to 30). This increase, in column 3, is called *incremental* output (or, in general, incremental benefits). Each of the 10 additional workers adds, on average, 80 additional units of output (shown in column 4). This is similar to marginal output (or, in general, marginal benefits) and is called average incremental output. It is the average marginal output of the 10 additional workers. Frequently, increases at the margin are made in increments other than one unit. Sometimes this is the only way increases in an activity like production can be made. For this reason, the average marginal output will simply be called the marginal output, and more generally, average marginal benefit for some incremental increase in an activity will be called the marginal benefit.

Returning to Table 4–1, suppose now that the number of workers and the resulting output, shown in Table 4–1, can vary continuously rather than increasing only in discrete amounts. The number of workers can take on any value because the firm can hire part-time workers. For example, the firm can hire 1.25 workers, 5.376 workers, or any other amount of workers. In this case, the relation between workers and output is shown graphically in Figure 4–1 to reflect the assumption of continuity.

Figure 4–1   Marginal Output of Workers

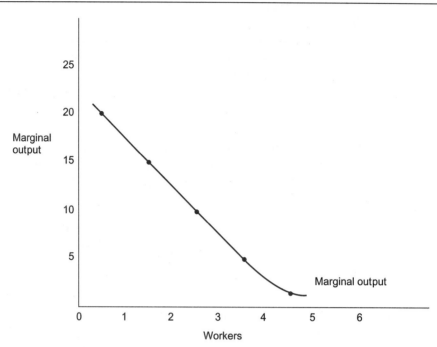

Each of the five observations for marginal benefits or marginal output in Table 4–1 is shown as a point on the curve. The points are then connected to reflect the assumption of continuity. The additional output that every increase in labor usage between zero and five can produce can be read from the graph. Each marginal output in column 3 of the table is plotted between the two values of the number of workers to reflect the fact that the marginal value is for a change in the number of workers, not for a specific worker. This is important when the data vary continuously.

Frequently, marginal values that vary continuously will appear in a graph without first appearing in a table. The interpretation of such graphs is straightforward. For example, suppose a person's satisfaction from eating ice cream can somehow be measured. The line labeled *MB* in Figure 4–2 shows the marginal benefit from additional pints of ice cream per month. Marginal benefit is measured along the vertical axis and pints of ice cream along the horizontal. Because any amount of ice cream can be eaten, not just in increments of one pint, the amount of ice cream and, therefore, the marginal benefit vary continuously.

The simplest way to interpret the graph is to read from the vertical axis the marginal benefit enjoyed from each additional pint of ice cream. A third pint of ice cream would add 35 units of satisfaction, the ninth pint of ice cream would add 20 units of satisfaction, and so on for every addition in the amount of ice cream

Figure 4–2   Marginal Benefit of Ice Cream ($\Delta TB/\Delta IC$)

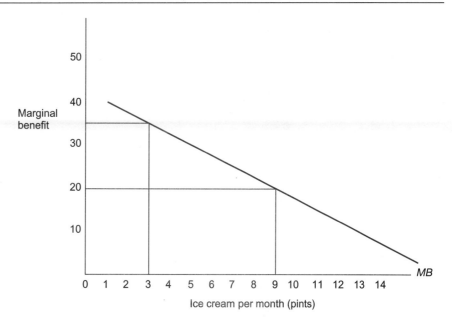

consumed per month.[2] This interpretation of graphs showing marginal benefit is used frequently in microeconomic theory.

4.2.2.   Marginal Cost

Some examples of the marginal cost of an increase in an activity are:

1. The perceived cost to a student of an additional hour spent studying.
2. The increase in a firm's cost from producing an additional unit of output.
3. The additional money a consumer must spend to buy one more unit of a good or service.
4. The increase in a firm's cost from hiring an additional worker.

As is the case with marginal benefits, we will show marginal cost in a table (for discrete variations) or in a graph (for continuous variation). In each case marginal cost (MC) is the additional expense of more unit of the activity.

The interpretation of marginal cost from a table or graph is similar to the inter-

---

[2]This interpretation of the graph is useful but somewhat loose, because the graph shows marginal benefits for infinitesimally small increases in ice cream (IC). For example, we stated that the 9th pint has a marginal benefit of 20. Consider a smaller increase of 1/2 pint (from 8.5 to 9 pints) that adds 1/2 as much total benefit (TB) as one pint, 10 units. Thus, $MB = \Delta TB/\Delta IC = 10/(1/2) = 20 =$ the marginal benefit per pint for the smaller increase. Or an even smaller increase in ice cream from 8.9 to 9 pints adds 1/10 as much benefit as a pint, or 2 units of benefits. In this case the marginal benefit per pint is $2/(1/10) = 20$. Thus, the simple interpretation is a good approximation for the purpose of this text.

Figure 4–3 Marginal Cost Curves

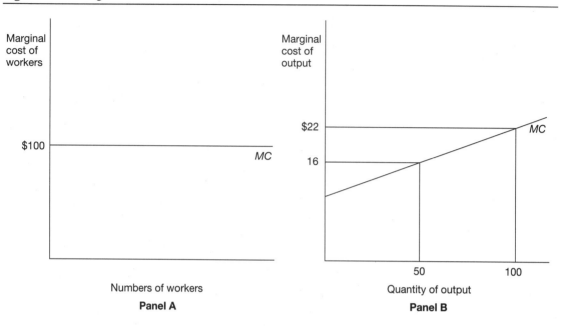

Panel A

Panel B

pretation previously discussed for marginal benefits. Figure 4–3 shows two types of frequently assumed marginal cost curves. Panel A shows the marginal cost (along the vertical axis) to a firm of hiring additional workers (along the horizontal axis). The wage rate is assumed to be $100 a day per worker. Therefore, the marginal cost of each additional worker is constant, and the marginal cost curve is horizontal at $100. Each additional worker hired adds $100 a day to the firm's cost.

The marginal cost curve in panel B shows the marginal cost to the firm (along the vertical axis) of producing additional units of output (along the horizontal axis). In this case, the marginal cost curve is upward sloping, reflecting the assumption that each unit of output increases the firm's cost by more than the preceding unit of output. From the figure, the 50th unit of output produced adds $16 to the firm's cost, the 100th unit of output adds $22 to cost, and so on. (As you will see in later chapters, the marginal cost of additional units of output typically decreases over a lower range of output, then increases thereafter.)

If the level of an activity changes in units other than one, the additional cost is the incremental cost, and the additional per-unit change in the activity is the average incremental cost. For example, if a 20-unit increase in output causes total cost (TC) to increase $100, the average incremental cost is ($\Delta TC/\Delta Q$ = $100/20 = $5). Because quantities may only increase in increments other than one, average incremental cost may be the best measure of marginal cost. The cost per unit from such an increase will often be referred to as the marginal cost.

We can now develop the simple rules for solving constrained and unconstrained optimization problems. You will see that these rules involve comparing marginal benefits and marginal costs.

4.3 Unconstrained Optimization

Because the theory of unconstrained optimization is simpler than the theory of constrained optimization we will begin with unconstrained optimization. The fundamental concept involves comparing the marginal benefits and marginal cost of an activity. Once this principle is understood, everything follows directly. To demonstrate the principle, we turn first to the maximization decision.

4.3.1 Unconstrained Maximization

Suppose that some activity yields benefits—measured in dollars of income. The greater the level of the activity, the greater the benefits; however, it is also true that the higher the level of the activity, the higher is the cost in dollars. Thus for each additional unit of the activity chosen, the individual receives added benefits, but has to pay additional costs. As before, the additional benefit from an additional unit of the activity is the marginal benefit; the additional cost from increasing the activity by one more unit is the marginal cost of that unit.

The task of the decision maker is to choose the level of activity that maximizes the total benefit received less the total cost of the activity. This maximizes the net value of the benefits received.

To illustrate the decision-making process, let's consider an extremely simplified problem. During the 1988 presidential campaign, there was a great deal of talk about increasing tax revenues, without raising tax rates, by collecting a larger amount of delinquent taxes. Opponents of the plan argued that the cost of implementation would exceed the increase in revenues. The problem is one of unconstrained optimization.

Suppose a hypothetical branch office of the IRS believes it can increase the amount of taxes it collects by hiring additional IRS agents to check returns and to collect taxes. The more agents, the more taxes collected: these increased taxes are the benefits to the government from the activity of hiring agents. More agents can be hired, but they must be paid: this is the cost of the activity.

Assume that the IRS office estimates the additional tax revenue per year, *over and above* what would be collected using the present staff, for each relevant number of additional agents hired. Columns 1 and 2 of Table 4–2 show the *additional* receipts from hiring zero through nine additional agents. Column 3 shows the additional or marginal receipts from hiring each of the additional nine agents. For example, increasing the number of agents from two to three increases the additional receipts from $260,000 to $340,000; thus, the marginal receipts from hiring the third agent is $80,000. Column 3, therefore, gives the marginal benefits from additional agents. (This table reflects a typically used assumption that marginal benefits decrease as the activity increases.)

Suppose the going salary of prospective agents is $48,000 a year, and the IRS office can hire all the agents it wants at this salary. In this case, the marginal cost of each additional agent is $48,000. Comparing the marginal benefits with the marginal cost determines the number of agents that would maximize the net additional tax revenue. From the table, each additional agent hired, from the first

Table 4–2   Additional Tax Revenue from Additional Agents

(1) Additional Agents	(2) Additional Tax Revenue		(3) Marginal Tax Revenue
0	0		
		>	$150,000
1	150,000		
		>	110,000
2	260,000		
		>	80,000
3	340,000		
		>	60,000
4	400,000		
		>	50,000
5	450,000		
		>	40,000
6	490,000		
		>	22,000
7	512,000		
		>	8,000
8	520,000		
		>	1,000
9	521,000		

through the fifth, adds more to tax receipts than the cost of hiring the additional agent. For example, the third agent would add $80,000 to tax receipts at a cost of $48,000, yielding a net return of $32,000. Similarly, the fourth would add a net return of $12,000, and the fifth, $2,000. The sixth would reduce net revenue by $8,000 because revenue would increase $40,000, but the total salary payment would increase $48,000. Thus, the IRS office would hire five new agents at a total cost of $240,000. Because hiring five more agents would increase tax revenue $450,000, the net increase is ($450,000 − $240,000) = $210,000. You can verify that five more agents would maximize the net additional tax revenue.

This example is an illustration of the following principle:

Principle

To attain the maximum possible benefits net of cost, a decision maker should increase the level of an activity if the marginal benefits from another unit of the activity are greater than the marginal cost of that unit. The activity should be reduced if the marginal benefits from the last unit are less than the marginal cost.

The preceding discussion was used as an example of activity with benefits and costs that varied discretely. It is easy to generalize the principle of unconstrained maximization to the continuous case. Assume that an activity, A, generates both benefits and costs, in this example measured in dollars. Figure 4–4 shows the marginal benefits and marginal cost from additional units of the activity. Marginal

Figure 4–4   Unconstrained Maximization

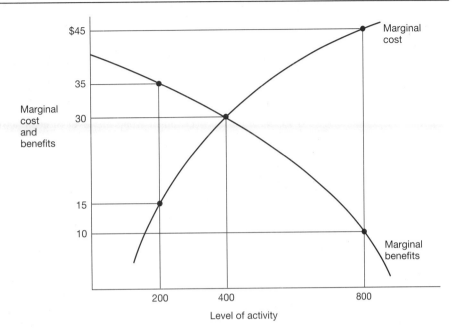

Level of activity

benefits decrease and marginal cost increases as the activity increases. Each increase in the level of the activity from zero to 400 produces more additional benefits than cost, because marginal benefits exceed marginal cost over this range. For example, suppose the decision maker mistakenly chooses 200 units of the activity. If the activity is increased by one unit, benefits would increase approximately $35 but cost would increase only $15, for a *net* increase of $20. Each additional increase in the activity up to 400 would increase benefits more than cost, resulting in an increase in net benefits.

The activity would not be increased beyond 400, where marginal benefits and marginal cost both equal $30. Increases beyond 400 units would increase cost more than benefits, resulting in a decrease in net benefits. For example, suppose 800 units of the activity are mistakenly chosen. The last unit added $45 to cost (*MC* = $45) and only $10 to benefits (*MB* = $10). Therefore, the activity could be reduced by one unit, reducing cost $45 and benefits $10. The one-unit reduction in the activity would, therefore, increase net benefits by $35 (= $45 − $10). Because marginal cost is greater than marginal benefits for every unit of the activity beyond 400, each reduction from 800 back to 400 would reduce cost more than benefits, resulting in an increase in net benefits. Thus, net benefits are maximized at 400 units of the activity where marginal benefits equal marginal cost at $30.

Principle

When an activity provides benefits and imposes a cost, net benefits are the total benefits from the activity minus the total cost of the activity. For a continuously variable activity, net benefits are maximized when the level of the activity is chosen so that the marginal benefits from the last unit of the activity equal the marginal cost of that unit.

$$MB = MC$$

This principle is the same when a decision maker chooses the level of two or more activities, each of which provides benefits and imposes a cost. Any activity should be increased if its marginal benefit exceeds its marginal cost. Any activity should be decreased if its marginal cost exceeds its marginal benefit. Thus, total net benefits from all activities are maximized when the level of each activity is chosen so that its marginal benefit equals its marginal cost.

Principle

If a decision maker chooses the levels of activities 1, 2, . . . , N, the total net benefits from all activities are maximized when

$$MB_1 = MC_1$$
$$MB_2 = MC_2$$
$$\cdot \qquad \cdot$$
$$\cdot \qquad \cdot$$
$$\cdot \qquad \cdot$$
$$MB_N = MC_N$$

You will encounter the principle of unconstrained maximization in two important theories: the theory of the firm and the theory of input choice. In the theory of the firm, a firm chooses the level of output, and in some cases the level of output and price, so as to maximize its profit, which is revenue from selling the output minus the cost of producing the output. In the theory of input choice, a profit-maximizing firm chooses the level of usage of one or more inputs, which produce output and, therefore, generate revenue and also impose costs. In both cases, the principle that marginal benefits equal marginal cost applies.

4.1 Applying the Theory

On July 25, 1988, *Business Week* published a story about change in the marketing strategies of two giant competitors, Procter & Gamble (P&G) and Colgate. This story reported that P&G was beginning to make managers more accountable for profits, whereas previously the company believed that if managers concentrated on gaining volume and market share, the profits would follow. P&G had been making poor returns on its investments throughout the 1980s. The story also mentioned that Colgate was selling more brands of detergents than it needed, and it reduced the number of brands from seven to four. How do these two management decisions fit within the context of the theory of unconstrained maximization?

4.3.2 Unconstrained Minimization

Unconstrained minimization problems typically involve activities that reduce a cost a decision maker must pay. This reduction in cost is the marginal benefit from the increase in the activity. However, increases in the cost-reducing activity can be obtained only at some other expense. This expense is the marginal cost of the activity.

One example of a cost-minimizing decision would involve shopping. Suppose you want to buy a particular type of automobile, but want to search among the different dealers for a low price. Here, your goal is to minimize net price. How long should you search? Shopping has potential benefits—the possible reduction in price from an additional day spent shopping. Shopping also has a cost, in time or in the salary you would lose taking a day off from work. You would want to shop an additional day if you think that the reduction in price you would have to pay exceeds the lost salary from taking the day off. If the expected price reduction is less than the lost salary, you should not shop. This example clearly involves comparing marginal benefits, the expected price reduction, with marginal cost, the lost day's salary, in order to minimize total cost.

As another example, suppose a firm is experiencing a considerable amount of product damage in its shipping department. The engineers recommend an extensive program of inspection and damage control. The goal is to minimize the net cost of product damage. How much damage control should the firm undertake?

Assuming that we can divide the damage control activity into units—number of inspectors, units of handling equipment, and so on—each additional unit of damage control reduces the amount of breakage and, therefore, reduces the cost of breakage to the firm. But each unit of control costs the firm money—the inspectors must be paid a salary. Should the firm add more units of damage control? Yes, if an additional unit of control reduces the damage cost by more than the cost of that unit of control. Clearly, the firm would not employ another unit of damage control if it costs more than the resulting reduction in damage cost. The firm would increase damage control until the marginal benefit (reduction in breakage cost) equals the marginal cost (additional cost of the damage control).

The same principle applies to many other cost-reducing activities, such as spilling ore during unloading, reducing shoplifting in a store, or even the cost of polluting the environment. In all such activities the following principle applies:

Principle

To minimize cost, a cost reduction activity should be continued if its marginal benefit exceeds its marginal cost. The activity should be reduced if the marginal benefit is less than the marginal cost. If the activity is continuously variable, the optimal amount of a cost-reducing activity is the level at which the marginal benefit of the last unit equals its marginal cost.

This principle is closely related to the one discussed for unconstrained maximization. And indeed the two principles should look alike since expenditures taken to control a cost have the marginal benefit of reducing expenses. The principle of unconstrained cost minimization is shown graphically in Figure 4–5. It is much like Figure 4–4. At each level of the activity up to A, the marginal benefits—the additional reduction in cost—from another unit of the activity is greater than the marginal cost of an additional unit of the activity. Beyond A the marginal cost exceeds the marginal reduction in cost. Thus, the decision maker should choose A

Figure 4–5   Unconstrained Minimization

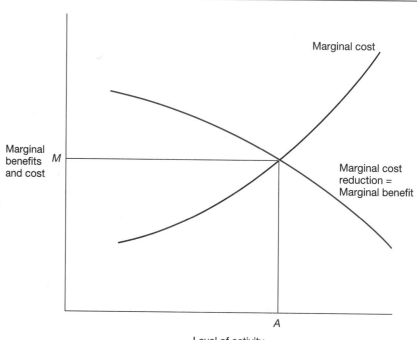

units of the activity, at which the marginal benefits and marginal cost both equal M.

Therefore, the rule is the same for unconstrained maximization and minimization: choose the level of an activity at which the marginal benefits equal the marginal cost. When more than one activity can be chosen, choose the level of each activity so that its marginal benefits equal its marginal cost.

Unconstrained minimization is encountered in economic theory much less frequently than unconstrained maximization. The primary reason is that all of a firm's minimization decisions can be analyzed within the framework of maximization, as shown by the previous examples.

Economics in the News   **Was Exxon Merely Minimizing Cost?**

In the spring of 1989, the Exxon Valdez, an oil tanker owned by the Exxon Corporation, ran aground off the coast of Alaska, spilling tons of oil into the water and onto the shore. It was the largest oil spill ever in North America. As you may recall, the wrath of the media, politicians, and the general public against Exxon was fierce. People were asking, "Couldn't this accident have been prevented? Why did Exxon let it happen?"

(continued)

According to an editorial by Michael Edesess in the Houston *Post,* June 28, 1989, the answers may well be "yes, it probably could have been prevented, and, although Exxon certainly did not want the spill to occur, the probability that such a spill would occur was a direct result of Exxon's policy." The editorial reported that a participant in a Denver symposium on economics and the environment asserted that Exxon's decision not to spend more on oil spill prevention and preparedness was probably its best economic decision. According to this participant, *The cost of reducing the likelihood of a spill like the recent one in Alaska would have been greater than the cost of damage control and compensation."*

This analysis sounds as though Exxon chose the level of a cost-reducing activity— measures to reduce the probability of a large oil spill—such that the expected marginal benefits equaled the marginal cost. Exxon obviously knew that it was liable for some damages and would have to pay some of the clean-up costs in case of a spill. Any investment that lowered the probability of a spill would lower these expected costs, which would be a benefit. But additional investment could be made only at a cost. Exxon was simply minimizing net cost in the way predicted by the theory.

Edesess went on to suggest a way of significantly reducing the probability of such spills in the future. He noted that the cost to the public will be much greater than the investment Exxon could have made to prevent the spill. These costs that Exxon did not pay were costs to the taxpayers of cleaning up the spill, costs in lost animals and fish, costs to people living near the Alaska coast, and so forth. Since Exxon pays only a small part of these costs, the extra investment was not warranted, because the benefits of cost reduction were less than if Exxon had to pay the full cost. The editorial implied that Exxon took this into consideration. Edesess argued that if there had been a law in effect that would have forced Exxon to reimburse the public and affected private parties for damage caused by the Valdez oil spill, the company would likely have opted for prevention (or more measures to reduce the probability of a spill) as the best economic decision. However, many observers believe that Exxon will be forced to pay through lawsuits.

In terms of the theory of unconstrained minimization, this argument says that if Exxon, or any other company, knows that it will have to pay all of the cost of an oil spill, the benefits of additional investment undertaken to lower the probability—and hence the expected cost—of a spill will be much greater than they would if the public pays a large part of the cost. Since the marginal cost of the additional investment would not be affected, the optimal level of prevention investment, at which expected marginal cost reduction (benefits) equals marginal cost, would be much higher.

We might note that costs imposed upon the public but not paid by the person or firm causing the costs are called externalities, a topic covered later in the text.

4.3.3   All-or–Nothing Optimizing Decisions

All of the optimization rules we have discussed thus far involve choosing a particular level of an endeavor that maximizes net benefit. This type of problem is by far the most frequently encountered in economic theory. However, some extremely important optimization decisions made by individuals and firms do not follow this pattern exactly, but the same general principles as those we have set forth do apply. Such decisions involve choices that cannot be marginally or even incrementally adjusted.

Such choices require a sizable commitment of resources. This commitment does not allow someone to make marginal adjustments to maximize net benefits or minimize net costs. And making the choice may mean other alternatives are closed to the person. One example of such a decision problem is the choice of a career or an occupation. Someone who chooses to study to become a lawyer does not practice law part time, medicine part time, and teach economics part time. Someone who chooses to be a plumber cannot also be an electrician or carpenter. An athlete who chooses to be a professional baseball player usually does not also play professional football. (Bo Jackson, who was an allstar outfielder with the Kansas City Royals and a running back with the L.A. Raiders, was, of course, an exception. Most people are not quite so talented and must specialize in a single occupation.) Because of the time and education cost to become proficient in one career, other careers become prohibitively expensive. For many decision makers the alternative is not a reasonable option.

A firm that builds a factory of a particular size does not build half a factory in California and half in New York. The commitment is made in one location, with no choice to marginally produce in both. For another example, firms typically choose to specialize in one line of products, because the resources invested to produce these products are specialized. The choice of a major at a university is similar. A major commits a student to specialize in a course program. Switching is a costly proposition, frequently so costly that the alternative is not available.

Such decisions are all-or-nothing decisions. You either choose to be a doctor or you don't. A firm chooses to build in California, or it chooses to build in New York. A student generally chooses one major at a university. Certainly once the decision is made, the decision maker can choose among different levels of the activity. A doctor can choose how many hours to work, a firm can choose how much to produce in the factory, and the student can choose how much to study. But the primary decision—the decision that must be made before the other decisions—is a choice among mutually exclusive alternatives. Nonetheless, people making all-or-nothing decisions do compare the costs and benefits of the available alternatives and choose the alternative that they expect will yield the highest total benefits net of total costs.

A person choosing between law and medicine would compare, among other things, the expected satisfaction of the professions (a benefit), the expected incomes of the two professions (a benefit), the expected amounts of time required in school (a cost), the expected amount of working time (a cost), and the prestige involved (a benefit). This person would then choose to enter the profession with the highest expected benefits minus expected costs. If we consider all of the benefits as marginal benefits and all of the costs as marginal costs, the person obviously chooses the profession for which marginal benefits net of the marginal costs are the greatest.

4.2 *Applying the Theory*

1. After finishing medical school, graduates must choose the specialty in which they will serve their period of hospital residency. The lengths of these residencies differ from specialty to specialty. The choice of the area of

residency determines the doctor's area of specialization for his or her working life. A recent study of residency choice found that the three variables that affected the probability of a particular specialty being chosen were expected income, expected hours of work, and the length of the period of residency. Which is a benefit and which is a cost? Why? Which variable do you think would have the greatest effect? In which direction? The least effect? Why?

2. From a column by Dale Robertson on the sports page of the Houston *Post,* May 31, 1989: Bill Wood, the general manager of the Houston Astros baseball team was thumbing through his son's book on Michael Jordan, his son's favorite athlete and arguably the best basketball player in the National Basketball Association. Mr. Wood noticed several pictures of a young Michael Jordan "proudly wearing his little league uniform" and immediately wondered, "How did we (baseball) lose this guy? . . . An athlete like Jordan would have been a major star at anything he chose." Given that the latter statement is probably correct, what about the former? Why did Mr. Jordan choose to star in basketball rather than baseball?

4.4 Constrained Optimization

In the introduction to this chapter, we stressed that in all constrained optimization problems a decision maker tries to allocate two or more activities in order to attain a specified goal at the minimum possible cost (minimization) or to maximize the benefits attainable at a specified cost (maximization). Every activity provides benefits to the decision maker and also imposes costs. We will show that the rule is the same for both constrained minimization and constrained maximization. The constrained optimization rule is somewhat more difficult than the unconstrained optimization rule, and is not obvious at first glance, or even second. After a little explanation and a few examples, however, the rule should become clear.

4.4.1 Constrained Minimization: A Special Case

Let us begin the development of the constrained minimization rule with a simple hypothetical problem. Recall the earlier example of a student who wanted to make an average grade of 90 in two exams, economics and math, by studying the least amount of time. This student knows that generally the more time spent studying a subject, the higher the grade in the subject. In fact, the student makes a list of the expected grade on each exam for hours of time studying each course from zero to six hours. The list for economics is in columns (1) and (2) in Table 4–3, and the list for math is in columns (4) and (5). The marginal benefit of studying economics each additional hour is the expected increase in the economics grade and is shown in column (3). The marginal benefit of studying mathematics each additional hour is the expected increase in the math grade and is shown in column (6). The marginal cost of studying an additional hour for each course is the value of the student's time at an activity other than studying. For simplicity, we measure the marginal cost as one hour, realizing that the value of an hour varies from student to student.

Table 4–3　Study Time and Test Grades

Economics			Mathematics		
(1) *Study* *Time* *(hours)*	*(2)* *Expected* *Grade* *(percent)*	*(3)* *Marginal* *Benefit*	*(4)* *Study* *Time* *(hours)*	*(5)* *Expected* *Grade* *(percent)*	*(6)* *Marginal* *Benefit*
0	20%		0	43%	
		> 　30			> 　20
1	50		1	63	
		> 　20			> 　15
2	70		2	78	
		> 　12			> 　10
3	82		3	88	
		> 　10			> 　6
4	92		4	94	
		> 　4			> 　4
5	96		5	98	
		> 　2			> 　2
6	98		6	100	

The task is to allocate hours so that the average grade, and therefore the total grade, increases as quickly as possible. If no time is spent studying, the economics grade is 20 and the math grade is 43, which obviously gives an average grade less than 90. The student must allocate hours where he or she is most productive in terms of the additional grade until the average of 90 (total of 180 percentage points) is achieved.

The first hour goes to economics, where it adds 30 points, rather than to math, which adds only 20. The second hour in economics and the first in math will add 20 points in either subject. Thus, the student is indifferent, and we will say the second hour goes to economics and the third to math. This is not yet enough time studying because the average grade is only $(70 + 63)/2 = 66.5$. Therefore, the fourth hour should be added to math, because the second hour spent studying math would add 15 points, whereas the third hour spent studying economics would add only 12. The fifth hour is allocated to economics, where the additional grade, 12 percentage points, is higher than the additional grade of the third hour in math. You can confirm that 3 hours spent in economics and 2 hours in math do not lead to the desired goal of 90. Therefore, the sixth hour is added to economics for a total of 4 hours in economics and the seventh hour is added to math for a total of three hours in math. The marginal benefit of each of these two hours is equal, 10 points in each course. This allocation of study time gives the desired average grade, $(92 + 88)/2 = 90$. You can confirm that this allocation is the least costly method, in terms of hours spent studying, of achieving an average of 90. For example, studying economics three hours for a grade of 82 and math five hours for a grade of 98 gives the desired average of 90, but it costs the student eight hours of time rather than seven.

We can express this optimal allocation of study time in terms of an optimization rule: In order to obtain the desired grade average of 90 with the least amount of study time, the time should be allocated so that the goal is attained and the marginal benefit, the higher grade, from the last hour spent studying each course is the same. That is,

$$\frac{MB_E}{P_E} = \frac{10}{1} = \frac{MB_M}{P_M} = \frac{10}{1},$$

where MB_E and MB_M are, respectively, the marginal benefits of the last hour spent studying economics and math and P_E and P_M are the price, or cost to the student, of an hour spent studying each course, in this case one hour.

To see that the above equality must hold if the cost in terms of time is to be minimized and the goal attained, suppose that the student had simply looked at the list in Table 4–3, noted that five hours studying math for a grade of 98 and three hours studying economics for a grade of 82 give the desired average of 90, and chose this allocation. Therefore, with this allocation the above equality does not hold:

$$\frac{MB_E}{P_E} = \frac{12}{1} > \frac{MB_M}{P_M} = \frac{4}{1}.$$

Time should be taken away from math, where the marginal benefit per hour is lower, and added to economics, where the marginal benefit per hour is higher. In this way the goal can be achieved at a lower cost in terms of time. The student can spend one more hour on economics, raising that grade from 82 to 92 for a marginal grade increase of 10 points. The time spent studying math can be reduced enough to reduce the math grade by 10 points, thereby keeping the average at 90. The student can spend two hours less studying math because the fifth hour would have added four points and the fourth six points to the total. The expected math grade falls to 88, so the average remains 90. The total study time falls from eight to seven hours. The equality $MB_E/P_E = MB_M/P_M$ now holds.

4.4.2   Constrained Minimization Generalized

In the above example, the marginal benefits of the last hour spent studying each course were the same when the cost of attaining the desired goal was minimized because the cost of an hour spent studying each course was the same. We can easily generalize the above rule for cases of cost minimization when the cost or price the decision maker must pay for each activity is not the same. Suppose a decision maker wants to allocate two activities, A and B, so as to achieve a given goal at the lowest possible cost, this time expressed in dollars. The cost or price to the decision maker of activities A and B are, respectively, P_A and P_B. The marginal benefits of the last unit of A and B are, respectively, MB_A and MB_B. The goal can be attained with several different allocations of A and B. The cost minimizing allocation is the one for which the goal is met and

$$\frac{MB_A}{P_A} = \frac{MB_B}{P_B},$$

or the marginal benefits per dollar spent on the last unit of each activity are the same. For example, suppose the marginal benefit of the last unit of A is 20 and the price of A is \$5. This means that each dollar spent on the last unit of A added 4 units of benefits. If the marginal benefits from the last unit of B are 40 and the price of B is \$10, each dollar spent on the last unit of B added 4 units of benefits also. Thus the cost of attaining the goal is minimized.

If $MB_A/P_A > MB_B/P_B$ and the goal is met, dollars should be taken away from B, where the marginal benefit per dollar is lower, and added to A, where the marginal benefit per dollar is higher. In this way, the goal can be met at a lower cost. The use of B should be reduced and the use of A increased so as to hold total benefits at the desired goal until the marginal benefits *per dollar* for the last unit of each activity are equal. Alternatively, if $MB_A/P_A < MB_B/P_B$, the use of A should be reduced and the use of B increased, again holding total benefits at the desired goal, until the equality holds.

Let's look at a hypothetical example that shows how this rule applies. Suppose a store has a sales goal of 20,000 units during a week, which it wants to attain with the lowest possible advertising expenditure. It can allocate its advertizing to newspaper ads and TV ads to attain the goal. The price of a newspaper ad, P_N, is \$100 for each ad, and the price of a TV ad, P_{TV}, is \$400 each. At these prices, the firm is going to choose 5 newspaper ads and 10 TV ads, which can attain the desired goal. Total advertising cost would therefore be

$$\$100 \cdot 5 + \$400 \cdot 10 = \$4,500.$$

The firm believes that the marginal benefit (additional units of sales) from the last newspaper ad, MB_N, would be 400 units and the marginal benefit from the last TV ad, MB_{TV}, would be 1,200 units of sales. With this allocation

$$\frac{MB_N}{P_N} = \frac{400}{100} = 4 > \frac{MB_{TV}}{P_{TV}} = \frac{1,200}{400} = 3.$$

The marginal benefit per dollar spent on the fifth newspaper ad, 4, is greater than the marginal benefit per dollar spent on the last TV ad, 3.

Suppose the store decides to cancel the tenth TV ad. Since the marginal benefit of that ad is 1,200 units, its sales from TV advertising would fall by 1,200. To keep total sales at 20,000, it must pick up 1,200 more units of sales from newspaper advertising. Ignoring for now the diminishing marginal benefits as an activity increases, the store could add three more newspaper ads, each of which adds 400 units of sales (the marginal benefit from a newspaper ad is 400), for an increase of 1,200 units from newspaper ads. Sales remain at 20,000 because the reduction in sales from TV ads was exactly offset by the increase in sales from newspaper sales. However, the cost of TV advertising decreased \$400, while the cost of newspaper advertising increased only \$300 with three more ads at \$100 each. Sales remain the same, but advertising cost falls from \$4,500 to \$4,400.

Note that in this example, and in all other cases, the marginal benefit alone is not the important thing to look at in cost minimization. TV ads had a marginal benefit greater than newspaper ads. The important thing is the *marginal benefit per dollar* spent on the last unit of each activity. The marginal benefit per dollar for newspapers was greater than for TV.

Anytime the marginal benefits of the last unit of an activity per dollar cost are greater for one activity than for another, cost can be reduced and the same level of benefits can be maintained by increasing the activity for which the marginal benefits per dollar are higher and reducing the other activity just enough to keep total benefits constant. Therefore, for any two activities, A and B, if

$$MB_A/P_A > MB_B/P_B \text{ or } MB_A/P_A < MB_B/P_B,$$

the cost of attaining the desired level of benefits can be reduced by increasing the activity for which the marginal benefits per dollar are higher and reducing the other activity. It must follow then that when the inequality holds, cost is not being minimized. Thus, constrained minimization requires

$$\frac{MB_A}{P_A} = \frac{MB_B}{P_B}.$$

Generally, in all cases of constrained optimization in this text, when an activity increases, the marginal benefits, and hence the marginal benefits per dollar, will fall, and when an activity is reduced the marginal benefits, and hence the marginal benefits per dollar, will rise. Therefore, when, for example, $MB_A/P_A > MB_B/P_B$, if A increases and B decreases, total cost will decrease, MB_A/P_A will decrease, and MB_B/P_B will increase until $MB_A/P_A = MB_B/P_B$. Only at this allocation will the cost of attaining the desired level of benefits be at the minimum.

We can summarize the above analysis in the following principle:

Principle

When several different combinations of two activities, A and B, can be used to achieve a specified goal or objective, the lowest cost combination of activities occurs when the objective is met and $MB_A/P_A = MB_B/P_B$, for the last unit of each activity; that is, when the marginal benefits per dollar spent on the last unit of each activity are the same. If $MB_A/P_A > MB_B/P_B$ ($MB_A/P_A < MB_B/P_B$) the use of A should be increased (decreased) and the use of B should be decreased (increased) while the objective continues to be achieved. This decision rule minimizes the cost of achieving a goal. It is almost always the case that as A increases (decreases), MB_A falls (rises); as B decreases (increases), MB_B rises (falls). As A is substituted for B or B is substituted for A while the objective is held constant, cost will continue to decline until the above equality holds, which is said to be the constrained minimization equilibrium condition.

If the rule $MB_i/P_i = MB_j/P_j$ gives the cost minimizing allocation of any two activities, i and j, it also must hold for all activities when two or more can be chosen. This establishes the following principle:

Principle

If benefits can be produced by n activities, $A_1, A_2, \ldots A_n$ and the total cost of producing any given level of benefits depends on the level of usage of each activity, to produce a fixed level of benefits at the minimum cost, the marginal benefit of the last unit of each activity divided by the cost of that unit must equal the marginal benefit of the last unit of every other activity used divided by its cost, or

$$\frac{MB_1}{P_1} = \frac{MB_2}{P_2} = \cdots = \frac{MB_n}{P_n}.$$

This relation must hold for any constrained minimization problem.

In this text you will frequently come across the method we just used for establishing the general rule for constrained minimization. We first will state an equilibrium rule for optimizing behavior. Then we will assume a decision maker is not allocating according to the equilibrium rule and show that a reallocation always can make the decision maker better off. Thus, if any allocation other than that given by the rule is not optimal, the allocation given by the rule must be optimal. In the above analysis, any time the marginal benefits per unit of cost of the last unit of each activity are not equal, the activities can be reallocated and cost can be reduced. If all inequalities are ruled out by demonstration, the equality between marginal benefits per dollar must give the cost-minimizing allocation of attaining a desired level of benefits.

Economics in the News

Employee Bonuses May Decrease Costs

A Knight-Ridder News Service feature reported that a survey of 330 company executives found that employee "time theft" in the form of employees arriving for work late, leaving early, claiming unwarranted sick days, socializing on the job, taking extra long lunches and coffee breaks, talking on the phone, and other nonproductive activities cost $170 billion in company time in 1986. This lost time was, on average, 4 1/2 hours per worker a week. *Business Week*, November 7, 1988, reported that many corporations, from giants to small firms, had begun paying profit-sharing bonuses not only to top management but also to middle managers and white-collar workers. A major purpose of the bonuses was to induce employees to be more productive—to shirk less—in order to increase the firm's profit.

Why should firms voluntarily pay some of their profits to induce workers to work harder? This can be answered within the framework developed above. Management may have believed that it could reduce the total cost of attaining a desired level of total work effort by paying incentive bonuses to reduce shirking, thus reducing the total number of workers and/or supervisory personnel. Since the bonuses would give workers a stake in the profits, they would have more incentive to work harder. If this is correct, the marginal increase in work effort per dollar spent on bonuses would be greater than the marginal increase in effort per dollar spent on additional workers (at the same rate of shirking) and/or additional supervisors. The increase in the cost of bonuses would, therefore, be more than offset by the reduction in the cost from hiring fewer workers and/or fewer supervisors. When the marginal increase in work effort per dollar spent is equal for bonuses, workers, and supervisors, the firm is minimizing the cost of attaining any desired level of work effort, when these are the only choice variables.

Table 4–4   Study Time and Marginal Benefit in Three Classes

Study Time (hours)	Statistics Grade	Marginal Benefit	Economics Grade	Marginal Benefit	Mathematics Grade	Marginal Benefit
0	50%		53%		65%	
		> 13		> 12		> 10
1	63		65		75	
		> 10		> 8		> 5
2	73		73		80	
		> 7		> 5		> 4
3	80		78		84	
		> 5		> 3		> 3
4	85		81		87	
		> 4		> 2		> 2
5	89		83		89	
		> 3		> 1		> 1
6	92		84		90	

4.4.3   Constrained Maximization: A Special Case

We stated at the beginning of this section that the same constrained optimization rule applies for both minimization and maximization. Recall that in a constrained maximization problem, the decision maker wants to allocate activities so as to achieve the maximum level of benefits possible from a given level of cost. Just as we did for minimization, we will now discuss why the same rule applies to constrained maximization.

Similar to the beginning of the minimization discussion, we begin here with another student preparing to study for exams the next day. This less fortunate student has three exams—statistics, economics, and mathematics—to study for. This student's objective is to allocate nine hours of study time, in order to maximize the total of the scores on the three exams (and therefore maximize the average score). The student's assessment of the grade in each exam for each amount of study time is shown in Table 4–4. The marginal benefits (or additional percentage grade points) from each additional hour of study time in each subject are given next to each grade column.

From the table you can see that if the student spent no time studying, the grades would be 50 in statistics, 53 in economics, and 65 in mathematics. If one hour of study is spent on a subject, that hour would add 13 points to the statistics grade, 12 points to the economics grade, or 10 points to the mathematics grade. So, the first hour of study would be allocated to statistics, where the return is highest. The second hour would be allocated to economics, since it would add 12 points to the grade in this subject but only 10 in each of the others. The third and fourth hours are spent studying statistics and math, since the grade increases are 10 points in each of these subjects, but only 8 in economics. Following this allocation rule, the fifth hour would go to economics and the sixth to statistics. The student's nine-hour study time constraint leaves three more hours of study time. You can see that the added test points from an additional hour of study time in each subject are now the same—five. Thus, the student would allocate one more hour to each course.

Therefore, optimal allocation of the nine hours would have the student spend four hours studying statistics, three hours studying economics, and two studying math. The total expected points would be 243, with an average grade of 81. This is the highest average possible with the nine-hour study constraint. (You can verify this by trying to reallocate the nine hours in different ways.)

This allocation decision is simply a specific application of the principle set forth above. The cost (in hours) of allocating an additional hour to a particular course is what is given up during that hour, or for simplicity one hour. The marginal benefit of allocating an additional hour to a particular course is the grade increase that would result. The optimization rule is to allocate so that

$$\frac{MB_S}{P_S} = \frac{MB_E}{P_E} = \frac{MB_M}{P_M},$$

where P_S, P_E, and P_M are simply the cost in time (one hour) of studying statistics, economics, or mathematics, and MB_S, MB_E, and MB_M are the marginal benefits or increased grade from the last hour spent studying statistics, economics, and math.

Using the above table with the allocation proposed, the ratios of marginal benefits to costs for the last hour spent in each course are

$$\frac{5}{1} = \frac{5}{1} = \frac{5}{1},$$

where 5 is the number of points that can be added to the test scores in any of the three subjects, and 1 is the hour of time given up to study that subject. The marginal benefit for the last unit of expenditure in time is the same for all three subjects, and the nine-hour constraint is met. The student maximizes the total and the average grade possible, given the constraint.

4.4.4   Constrained Maximization Generalized

To generalize somewhat, assume that a decision maker wants to choose the levels of two activities, A and B, so as to maximize the total benefits possible from a given level of cost. Increases in each activity produce both additional benefits, MB_A and MB_B, and involve additional costs (in dollars), P_A and P_B. Suppose the activities are chosen so that the cost constraint is met; $MB_A = 200$ and $MB_B = 300$, for the last unit of each activity, and $P_A = \$50$, and $P_B = \$150$.

$$\frac{MB_A}{P_A} = \frac{200}{50} = 4 > \frac{MB_B}{P_B} = \frac{300}{150} = 2.$$

The marginal benefit per dollar spent on the last unit of A is twice that of B. The use of B can be reduced by one unit; cost would fall $150, but the marginal benefits from the last unit, 300, would be lost. To keep the total cost constant, the $150 saved from the reduction in B would be used to buy three more units of A at $50 each. If each of the three additional units add approximately the same benefits as the last unit (200), total benefits increase 600 from the three-unit increase in A. The net result is an increase of 300 units of benefits—the reduction in B caused a reduction of 300 units and the increase in A led to an increase of 600 units.

The decision maker should continue to increase A and decrease B, keeping cost constant, as long as the inequality holds. Since, as is generally the case, MB_A falls as A is increased and MB_B rises as B is decreased, the maximum benefits will be attained when

$$\frac{MB_A}{P_A} = \frac{MB_B}{P_B}.$$

No adjustment of the levels of A and B at the specified cost can increase benefits. Thus, benefits are maximized under the cost constraint when the marginal benefits per unit of cost for the last unit of each activity are the same.

This problem can be generalized even further by assuming no specific numerical marginal benefits or costs. Simply assume that

$$\frac{MB_A}{P_A} < \frac{MB_B}{P_B}.$$

This allocation of A and B cannot be optimal. It is possible to take away $1 of A, for which the marginal benefits are lower, spend the dollar on B, for which the marginal benefits per dollar are higher, and increase total benefits. Since $1 was taken from A but added to B, the same level of cost is maintained. The dollar reduction in A reduced benefits by MP_A/P_A; the dollar increase in B increased benefits by MB_B/P_B. Since the marginal benefits per dollar spent on B are higher, total benefits will rise. The decision maker will reallocate dollars from A to B, until the marginal benefits per dollar for the last unit of each activity are equal, assuming diminishing marginal benefits from each activity.

Thus, we have ruled out inequalities as the combination of A and B that yields the maximum benefits obtainable under the cost constraint. Only if the equality holds ($MB_A/P_A = MB_B/P_B$), will the decision maker maximize the benefits forthcoming under the given constraint.

We have established the following principle:

Principle

When several different combinations of two activities, A and B, can be used to produce benefits and each activity involves a cost, the highest level of benefits that can be produced at any specified level of cost occurs when the cost constraint is met and

$$\frac{MB_A}{P_A} = \frac{MB_B}{P_B}$$

for the last unit of each activity; that is, when the marginal benefits per dollar spent on the last unit of each activity are the same. If $MB_A/P_A > MB_B/P_B$

$(MB_A/P_A < MB_B/P_B)$, dollars should be taken away from $B(A)$ and added to $A(B)$, maintaining the same level of cost. This reallocation increases total benefits. As A increases (decreases), MB_A falls (rises); as B decreases (increases) MB_B rises (falls). As A is substituted for B or B is substituted for A while cost is held constant, benefits will continue to increase until the above equality holds, which is said to be the constrained maximization equilibrium condition. It is identical to the previously developed constrained minimization equilibrium condition.

The same rule holds when there are more than two activities that can only be obtained at a cost; a budget constraint must be met, and each activity has positive but declining marginal benefits per dollar. Any time the inequality $MB_i/P_i \gtrless MB_j/P_j$ holds for any pair of activities, i and j, dollars should be taken away from the activity yielding less marginal benefit per dollar and added to the activity yielding more. In this way, total benefits increase while the budget constraint is met until $MB_i/P_i = MB_j/P_j$.

The following principle has been established:

Principle

With a given budget constraint and costs of activities $A_1, A_2, \ldots A_n$ of P_1, $P_2, \ldots P_n$, maximization of the total benefits obtainable within the given budget requires that:

$$\frac{MB_1}{P_1} = \frac{MB_2}{P_2} = \ldots = \frac{MB_n}{P_n}.$$

The marginal benefit from each dollar spent on the last unit of each activity employed must be equal for all activities.

4.4.5   Zero Usage of an Activity

To conclude the analysis of constrained optimization we will briefly discuss the case in which it is optimal to use none of a given activity, even though the first unit of the activity would, if used, have positive marginal benefits. Consumers who want to maximize the satisfaction possible from a given income do not choose to purchase every good available. Many goods that are not purchased are desirable to a consumer, and they are affordable. Likewise, a firm that is trying to minimize the cost of producing a given level of output may not use every type of input, even though some of these inputs have positive marginal benefits.

The reason for not using any of an activity follows directly from the theory. Suppose a decision maker can choose a combination of three activities, A, B, and C, in order to maximize the benefits with a specified cost or minimize the cost of attaining a given level of benefits. The decision maker would use A and B but not C, if the constraint is met (cost or benefits) and

$$\frac{MB_A}{P_A} = \frac{MB_B}{P_B} > \frac{MB_C}{P_C}$$

for the last units of *A* and *B* and the first unit of *C*. The marginal benefits possible from the first unit of *C* are positive, but the marginal benefit per dollar is less than that of the last unit of *A* or *B*. If any *C* is used, some amount of *A* and *B*, where the marginal benefit per dollar is higher, would have to be given up. Dollars cannot be taken away from *C* and added to *A* and *B*, because nothing is spent on *C*. Thus, the entire budget is spent on *A* and *B*.

Such cases are called *corner solutions* to the constrained optimization problem. Although corner solutions can be important, we will generally concentrate on situations in which positive amounts of all relevant activities are used, and we will ignore unused activities.

4.5   Summary

If you understand the principles of optimization developed in this chapter, you should have little difficulty understanding most of the theoretical analysis in this text. Most of the theories you will learn involve some type of constrained or unconstrained optimization problem. In each case, the rules of maximization and minimization are the same. Most types of optimization problems use marginal analysis—the effect of small changes in one economic variable on another economic variable.

In an unconstrained maximization or minimization problem, a decision maker wishes to obtain the highest possible net benefits (benefits less costs) from an activity that provides benefits but also produces costs. Optimization occurs when the marginal benefits of the last unit of the activity equal the marginal cost of that unit. All unconstrained minimization problems, in which the decision maker chooses the level of an activity so as to obtain the lowest net cost, can be expressed as an unconstrained maximization problem.

In constrained maximization problems, a decision maker chooses the combination of activities, $A_1, A_2, \ldots A_N$, that provides the largest benefits possible at a given level of cost. In constrained minimization problems, a decision maker chooses the combination of activities, $A_1, A_2, \ldots A_N$, that can produce a given level of benefits at the lowest possible cost. In the first case, the goal is maximum benefits, and the constraint is the level of cost. In the second case, the goal is minimum cost, and the constraint is the desired level of benefits.

In both types of optimization problems, the optimization rule is that the cost or benefit constraint is met, and, for all activities that are used,

$$\frac{MB_1}{P_1} = \frac{MB_2}{P_2} = \ldots = \frac{MB_N}{P_N}$$

where MB_i is the marginal benefit of the last unit of the *i*th activity and P_i is the price or cost of the last unit of the *i*th activity. Alternatively stated, the marginal benefit per dollar spent on the last unit of each activity must be the same for every activity used. For any activities not used, the marginal benefit per dollar of the first unit of that activity would be less than the marginal benefit per dollar of the last unit of all the other activities that are used.

The most frequently encountered unconstrained optimization problems in microeconomics, and hence in this text, is a firm that chooses its level of output so as to maximize its profit. Increases in output can increase a firm's revenue, what it receives from selling its product, but they can also increase a firm's cost, what it must pay to produce the product. In other maximization problems, a firm also chooses the price at which it sells the product, as well as its output, and in some cases it chooses its level of advertising. In all cases, the firm maximizes profit by choosing the level of the activity at which marginal benefits equal marginal cost.

Three major theories that use the principles of constrained optimization will be developed in this text. The theory of production assumes that firms choose the levels of the inputs they employ in order to produce a given level of output at the lowest possible cost or to produce the largest output possible at a given level of cost. The theory of consumer behavior assumes that consumers choose the goods and services they purchase so as to attain the highest level of satisfaction possible from a given level of income. The theory of labor supply assumes that workers choose the amount of time they work and the amount of leisure they enjoy so as to attain the most satisfaction possible during a specified period of time. Several extensions of the theory will be made, but the fundamental assumptions of constrained optimization will be used and the optimizing rule will be the same.

Answers to *Applying the Theory*

4.1 It appears that the management of P&G had been concerned primarily with the benefits—that is, the revenue or volume—from its choices, such as price, output, number of brands, and so on—and only secondarily with the cost of these activities. Therefore, the levels of the activities were chosen to maximize revenues rather than profits, and profits consequently suffered. To induce category managers to maximize profits, P&G began basing the financial rewards to these managers on profits earned.

In the Colgate case, the activity or choice variable was the number of detergent brands. Colgate must have believed that the marginal benefits (revenues) of the fifth through seventh brands were less than the marginal costs of producing and selling these brands. The company thought that by eliminating these brands the reduction in revenue would be more than offset by the reduction in cost, and, therefore, profit would increase. Colgate was using marginal analysis.

4.2 1. The data in the study indicated that a higher income increased the probability a particular specialty would be chosen. Income is a benefit. The longer the expected hours worked and the longer the period of residency, the lower the probability that a specialty would be chosen. These are costs. Even though longer periods of residency reduce a physician's lifetime earnings, this was the least important variable. Expected hours of work was the most important. There was no way to quantify other possibly important variables such as prestige and job satisfaction.

4.2 2. Perhaps only Mr. Jordan knows why he chose basketball rather than baseball, or any other sport. We can only speculate. We do have a bit of evidence, however, that may give some insight into how such talented individuals decide which career to pursue. One of us taught a student several years ago, a straight-A economics major, who was all-American in both football and baseball his senior year. He was drafted by the National Football League and a major league baseball team. He said that he considered all of the costs and benefits of each sport—income, expected career length, and so on—and it came down to one point. In baseball a player generally spends several years in the minor leagues before he knows if he will make it in the majors. In football a player either makes it or not in his first year. The student chose football so he would know immediately; if he didn't make it, he planned to go on to law school and begin a new career. He starred in the NFL, went to school during the off season, and is now a successful businessman. Big choices are frequently made on the basis of small marginal differences.

Technical Problems

1. A manufacturing firm believes that it can increase sales to environmentally concerned consumers and, therefore, net revenue by decreasing air pollution in the plant. It estimates that the marginal cost function for reducing pollution by installing new capital is

$$MC = 50P,$$

where P represents a reduction of one unit of pollution. It also feels that for every unit of pollution reduction the marginal increase in net income (MB) is

$$MB = \$800 - 30P.$$

How much pollution reduction should the firm undertake?

2. A firm making auto parts is having quality problems along its assembly line. The marketing division estimates that each defective part that leaves the plant costs the firm $20, on average, for replacement or repair. The engineering department recommends hiring quality inspectors to sample for defective parts in order to reduce the number of defective parts shipped. After extensive research, a management team comes up with the following schedule showing the number of defective parts that would be shipped for several numbers of inspectors.

Number of Inspectors	Average Number of Defective Parts per Day
0	120
1	85
2	55
3	35
4	22
5	12
6	6
7	3
8	1

The daily wage of people qualified to be inspectors is $150.

a. What is the marginal benefit (in dollars) of each additional inspector?

b. How many inspectors should the firm hire?

c. What would your answer be if the wage rate were $100?

d. What would your answer be if the average cost of defective parts is $10 and the wage rate remains $100?

3. A firm has the option of advertising on TV, radio, and in newspapers. It has a weekly advertising budget of $2,300 and wishes to maximize the number of

units sold. Its estimates of the increase in weekly sales from ads in each of the three media are in the table that follows.

| | Increase in Units Sold | | |
Number of Ads	TV	Radio	Newspaper
1	40	15	20
2	30	13	15
3	22	10	12
4	18	9	10
5	14	6	8
6	10	4	6
7	7	3	5
8	4	2	3
9	2	1	2
10	1	0	1

The prices of each type of ad are

TV	$300 each
Radio	$100 each
Newspaper	$200 each

a. How should the firm allocate its advertising budget among the three media?

b. Show that the allocation you suggest satisfies the condition for constrained optimization.

c. If the advertising budget is reduced to $1,100, how many ads should be purchased in each of the media?

4. A large shipping firm has established a minimum standard of necessary truck maintenance and repair. It can use a combination of skilled mechanics and unskilled labor to perform the maintenance. The maintenance supervisor believes that any of the following combinations of unskilled and skilled labor would achieve this minimum maintenance requirement.

Skilled Mechanics	Unskilled Labor
2	30
5	22
8	15
12	8

The table shows that if less unskilled labor is used, more skilled mechanics must be added, and vice versa. Clearly the two are substitutable.

Assume the going wage for skilled mechanics is $180 a day and the wage for unskilled labor is $40 a day.

a. Which combination results in the least cost for the required maintenance?

b. If the combination you suggest is optimal and the marginal benefit of a skilled mechanic is 90, what is the marginal benefit of unskilled labor?

c. If the price of unskilled labor rises to $80 a day, what combination would the firm choose?

5. Jones, who likes to play golf, budgets $140 a month for green fees. There are two golf courses in town; one (X) has a green fee of $10, and the other ($Y$) charges $25 to play. The more expensive course is nicer. Jones has the following schedule of benefits from playing at each course.

Time Played	Benefit from X	Benefit from Y
1	90	200
2	150	400
3	200	550
4	240	650
5	270	725
6	290	800

   a. What is the marginal benefit of playing on course X a second time? On course Y a second time?

   b. What is the optimal number of times to play golf on each course?

6. Assume that in this high-tech world you can measure the additional or marginal satisfaction of individuals for each unit of any good purchased and consumed. Suppose you test some person who consumes 12 pizzas and 14 burgers a week, and you find that the last unit of pizza consumed has a marginal satisfaction rating of 18, whereas the last burger adds 12 to the happiness index. When you ask the cost of each, you learn that a pizza costs $6 and a burger costs $3. What would you advise this person to do? Why? What advice would you give if the price of a burger was $4?

7. A city government does not know how much it should spend upon crime prevention (police, prisons, etc.). It knows the more it spends on prevention, the greater the percentage of thieves who are arrested and convicted. The greater the rate of arrest and conviction, the less crime will be committed. (People will commit fewer crimes the higher the probability that they will go to jail; criminals are optimizers also.) The fewer crimes that are committed, the smaller the loss from crimes. Figure E.4–1 shows the marginal cost (in $000) of increases in the rate of conviction and the marginal reduction in crime cost to society of increases in the rate of conviction.

   a. Suppose the city is presently spending enough on prevention so that the rate of conviction is 40 percent. From the figure, estimate the *net benefits* of spending enough on prevention to achieve a small increase in the rate of conviction.

   b. Suppose the city spends enough on crime prevention to attain a 70 percent conviction rate. What would be the net benefit of a small reduction in spending that causes the conviction rate to decrease?

   c. What rate of conviction should the city try to achieve?

8. A business firm is losing money. Its sales revenue is $100,000 and its cost is $120,000. Of this cost, $40,000 must be paid no matter what its output is, even at zero output. The other $80,000 is a variable cost that increases with the rate of output, and would not have to be paid if the firm produces zero output. Should the firm continue producing, losing $20,000, or should it shut down and produce nothing? Why? What if the fixed part of cost is $10,000, not $40,000?

9. Two activities, A and B, produce benefits. The marginal benefits of A and B are shown, respectively, in the left and right sides of Figure E.4–2.

   The marginal costs of A and B are constant at $MC_A = $5 and $MC_B = $4.$ The decision maker wants to choose the combination of A and B that can

Figure E.4–1

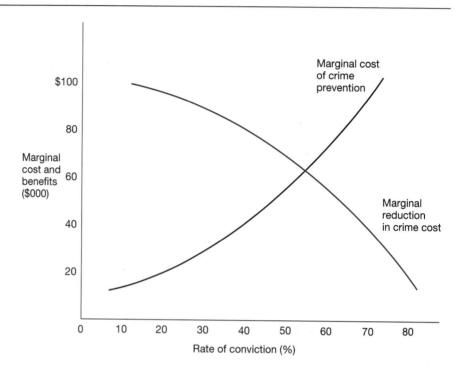

Figure E.4–2

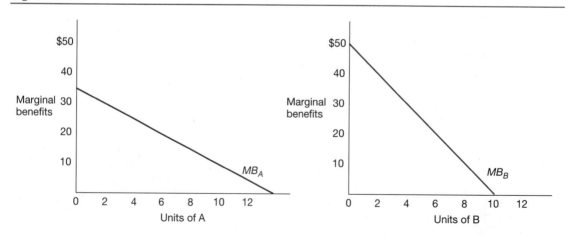

produce a specified level of benefits at the lowest possible cost. Among the many possible combinations of A and B that can produce this desired level of benefits are the following combinations: $2A$ and $9B$, $4A$ and $6B$, $6A$ and $4B$, and $8A$ and $3B$.

    a. What combination should the firm choose? Why?

    b. Suppose the person wants to produce the highest level of benefits at a cost of $44? What combination should the firm choose? Why?

    c. Suppose in part *a* of the question $MC_A = \$6$ and $MC_B = \$1$. What combination should the firm use?

    d. Now assume that the marginal benefits graphed along the vertical axis are expressed in dollars. The constant marginal costs of the two activities are again $MC_A = \$5$ and $MC_B = \$4$. The objective now is to produce the highest total net benefits from using the two activities. What amounts of A and B should be used?

    e. In terms of this question, explain the difference between constrained and unconstrained optimization?

10. Two activities, A and B, produce benefits and costs. A decision maker is using 20 units of A and 15 units of B to produce a specified level of benefits at a given cost. At this combination of inputs $MB_A = 20$ and $MB_B = 60$; marginal cost is constant at $MC_A = \$10$ and $MC_B = \$20$.

    a. Show arithmetically how the activities can be reallocated to produce the given level of benefits at a lower cost.

    b. Show arithmetically how the activities can be reallocated to produce a higher level of benefits at the same level of cost.

Analytical Problems

1. In each of the cases below identify the goal and the constraint.

    a. A hospital wants to maintain 300 beds at the lowest possible cost.

    b. A university has a budget and seeks to maximize the number of students.

    c. An auto maker tells a product subdivision to manufacturer as many cars as possible on a $200 million budget.

    In each case, do the goals create the "right" incentives for the decision maker? How might incentives be "wrong"? In general, discuss the difficulty of defining the correct goal for a decision maker.

2. A newsletter from the director of the computer center of a large state university stated that, as the authorized usage of the central computer facilities had grown, so has the unauthorized use. Malicious usage had "increased dramatically during the past year. While constituting a small percent of the usage (much less than 1%), any is too much."

    a. Is any unauthorized usage "too much"?

    b. When would any unauthorized usage be "too much"?

3. Baseball teams frequently have promotions at which they give away gifts, such as balls, bats, briefcases, travel bags, radios, and so forth. (*The Wall Street Journal*, May 7, 1986).

    a. Why and under what circumstances would teams do this?

    b. An owner of a promotional firm stated, in the case of one giveaway, "While the calculators [the items given away] cost only $2 to $3, the perceived value of a calculator is as high as the perceived value of the ticket." What would be the effect if this is true?

4. In 1987, corporations spent $6.5 billion on consumer premiums, up 5.6 percent from the year before (*Newsweek,* May 16, 1988). What would be the marginal benefits and marginal cost of premiums? How many premiums would a firm give away with its products?

5. People keep some of their money in pure checking accounts, some in money market accounts, which pay interest, and some in certificates of deposits, which pay a higher rate of interest. How would a depositor decide how much of the total deposit to put in each type of account? Discuss in terms of marginal cost and benefits.

6. Consumers shop for lower prices for some products they want to buy.
   a. How much time should be spent in price search?
   b. In general, for what kind of goods would consumers undertake the most price search? The least?

7. The speed limit on many of the nation's interstate highways was raised from 55 MPH to 65 MPH.
   a. What would be the costs and benefits of this increase?
   b. How could you determine whether an even further increase to 75 MPH would be optimal?

PART III

Theory of Consumer Behavior

CHAPTER 5

Theory of Consumer Behavior: Utility Maximization

5.1 Introduction

When we introduced demand and supply in Chapter 2, we assumed downward sloping demand curves without formally deriving them. Since demand is based on the way consumers act in the market, you must understand consumer behavior to fully understand the determinants of demand. This chapter and the next two describe the theory of consumer behavior and the relation between this theory and the theory of demand. First, the tools of analysis are developed; then these tools are used in Chapter 6 to establish how consumer behavior determines demand, with particular emphasis on explaining why market demand curves are negatively sloped. Chapter 7 applies the theory of consumer behavior in several different contexts.

In this chapter we will explain why a consumer chooses a particular bundle of goods and services and not some other bundle. Why does one person consume none of some good, such as Bruce Springsteen tapes, whereas someone else with nearly the same income may own all of his recordings? Why does someone buy seven Big Macs a week, while someone else buys only two, or none?

The theory of consumer choice is straightforward. You, as a consumer, have a given income and desire goods and services. Your income probably prohibits you from purchasing everything you desire. Therefore, you must make decisions about what goods to purchase during a given week, month, or any other period of time. Essentially, you have an allocation problem: how to best spend your income.

If you would like a new bike, why would you choose not to purchase one? Don't say you can't afford it. You could if you gave up enough other things. The reason you don't purchase a bicycle is that the added satisfaction received from owning one is not sufficient to compensate you for what you would be forced to give up. Why don't you eat out more? Or rent a larger apartment? The answer is that you have decided not to, given the other things on which you choose to spend your limited income. Because of limited income, people are forced to give up other goods when they choose to have more of some particular good or service.

The fundamental analytical tool in the economic theory of choice is the concept of *marginal utility*. Marginal utility is the change in consumer satisfaction from a one-unit change in the amount of a good consumed. For someone to choose more of one good and less of others, the marginal gain from the good chosen must outweigh the marginal loss from giving up the other goods. Consumers start with a particular mix of goods, then make marginal changes in order to reach more preferred bundles.

This is the basic theory. A consumer is constrained or restricted by both a limited income and the prices that must be paid for the goods. Consumers attempt to reach the most preferred level of consumption possible, given these constraints. Once they attain this level, they cannot become better off by giving up some goods in order to get others.

This sounds like a familiar story. The theory of consumer behavior is an application of the principle of constrained maximization set forth in Chapter 4. An individual maximizes benefits, given a constraint, when the additional or marginal benefits from the last unit of each choice activity per dollar spent on that activity is the same for all activities. In the theory to be developed here, the consumer wishes to maximize utility under the constraint of a limited income. Maximization occurs when the marginal utility from each good or service purchased per dollar cost is equal for all goods and services chosen.

5.2   Basic Assumptions

The theory of consumer behavior makes some simplifying assumptions in order to go directly to the fundamental determinants of consumer behavior. These assumptions allow us to abstract away from less important aspects of the decision process in order to concentrate upon the most important aspects. Before proceeding, we present a working definition of utility:

Definition

Utility is a consumer's perception of his or her own happiness or satisfaction.

Several assumptions are important in utility analysis. We discuss these assumptions in the following subsections.

5.2.1   More Is Preferred to Less

The first assumption is that consumers prefer to have more of something rather than less. For any consumer, holding all other things equal except the amount of one good, increasing the quantity of this good will increase the consumer's level of utility. This assumption is not intended to describe consumers as greedy hoarders of everything in sight. Although you might be acquainted with people who are like this, a consumer may prefer more in order to be better able to provide for others. For instance, a doctor may prefer more medical equipment to less, in order to provide better care for patients. Parents may want more food on the table for their children. People may want to be richer so they can give more to charity, making the donors happier. A person's utility or satisfaction can be increased by helping others, so consumption in economics has a rather broad meaning. Consumption of something means having control over its disposal. Hence, consumers may prefer more to less for a variety of reasons. Whatever the reason, it is assumed that a person is better off with having more than less.

5.2.2 Information

Second, we assume that each consumer knows the full range of goods available in the market, the price of each good, and that these prices will not be changed by his or her actions in the market. Also, consumers know what their income will be during the planning period. Given this information, each consumer is fully aware of how much of any combination of goods and services can be purchased. Prices and income determine the budget constraint for a utility maximizer. Economists say a consumer maximizes utility subject to a budget constraint.

Admittedly, to assume consumers know everything about prices and the availability of goods and services and that they can perfectly predict their income is an abstraction from reality. Consumers have only a fairly accurate notion of what their income will be for a reasonable planning period, not complete knowledge, and they can only estimate some prices, not quote them exactly. And some products exist that a consumer is not even aware of. No consumer actually succeeds in the task of spending a limited income to maximize satisfaction. Usually this failure is attributable to the lack of accurate information. Yet a more or less conscious effort to attain maximum satisfaction, given imperfect information, determines an individual's demand for goods and services; so, the assumption of complete information does not distort a buyer's tendency to maximize and allows us to concentrate on how consumption choices are made.

5.2.3 Utility at the Margin

A helpful tool in presenting the theory of consumer behavior is a definition of utility at the margin. This is the marginal benefit from consuming the last unit of a good. As mentioned already, it is called marginal utility.

Definition

Marginal utility is the addition to total utility that is attributable to the addition of one unit of a good to the current rate of its consumption. The marginal utility of some good X depends on its rate of consumption as well as the rates of consumption of other goods.

Marginal utility will have the abbreviation *MU,* and for a specific good a subscript will be attached. So, the marginal utility of good X will be represented as MU_x. Thus marginal utility, MU_x is the benefit of one more unit of good X.

Marginal utility is defined for a one-unit change, but sometimes changes consist of more than one unit. For example, a good can be bundled together in packages of several units, say a six-pack or case, and then the increment increases utility at the margin. Marginal utility then is written in general as

$$MU_x = \frac{\Delta U_x}{\Delta Q_x}.$$

For more than one-unit changes, this is the average benefit of the incremental increase.

When economists think about utility in this way, and this was the view of utility theory at the turn of the century, they believe that as an individual increases consumption of a good, marginal utility will decline. This is referred to as the *principle of diminishing marginal utility.* Each additional unit of a good consumed per unit of time adds to total utility, but it adds less to a consumer's satisfaction than the previous unit. For example, one scoop of ice cream might yield five units of utility, two scoops, nine units, and three scoops, 11 units of utility. The marginal utility of the second scoop is four, whereas the marginal utility of the third scoop is two units of utility. Marginal utility declines as consumption increases.

Economists in the early part of the 20th century used the concept of diminishing marginal utility to explain the law of demand. According to the theory, if marginal utility declined as more of a good was consumed, consumers would be less willing to pay as much for the next unit. This explanation led directly to a downward-sloping demand schedule. Though the concept of marginal utility is a helpful tool for learning about consumer behavior, it carries with it the assumption that utility can be measured. Recall the above example that the first scoop of ice cream yielded 5 units of utility, two scoops yielded 9 units, and so on. How can utility be measured? And what are the units? Measurability is a strong assumption.

5.2.4   The Nonmeasurement of Utility

The current theory of consumer behavior went through a long period of development. The earliest approaches to the theory of demand were based on the notion of a subjective and precisely measurable level of satisfaction. In terms of its measurability, utility was thought to be *cardinal.*

Cardinal measurability implies that the difference between two numbers is itself numerically significant. For example, how many apples someone possesses is cardinally measurable; four apples represent twice as much as two apples. In contrast, measurement is ordinal if items can only be ranked. For example, if one item is ranked second and another fourth, it does not mean the item with a rank of four is twice as desirable as the item with a rank of two. Both ordinal and cardinal measures rank items. The difference is that, in an ordinal system, one can say only that x is greater than y, whereas in a cardinal system, it is possible to say by how much x exceeds y.

The cardinal measurement of utility is no longer an essential ingredient to the theory of consumer behavior. All of the propositions that were once derived under the assumption that utility was measurable can be derived with the weaker set of assumptions that consumers can rank goods in terms of their preferences.

5.2.5 Ranking

The most critical assumption to the theory of consumer behavior is that each consumer can rank, according to his or her preferences, all conceivable bundles of commodities. That is, when confronted with two or more collections of goods, a consumer is able to determine an order of preference among them. For example, assume a person is confronted with two choice sets: (a) a grilled chicken sandwich, fries, and a Coke or (b) a quarter-pound hamburger, fries, and a Diet Pepsi. The person can say one of three things: I prefer the first bundle to the second, I prefer the second to the first, or I would be equally satisfied with either.

When evaluating two bundles of goods, an individual either prefers one bundle of goods to the other or is indifferent between the two. Since we will use the concepts of preference and indifference frequently, it is essential to understand them thoroughly now. If a consumer prefers one group of goods to another, he or she obviously believes a higher level of satisfaction will be gained from the preferred group. The less-preferred bundle would, in the opinion of the consumer, give less utility than the other. If a person is indifferent between two bundles, he or she would be perfectly willing to let someone else (or perhaps the flip of a coin) determine the choice. In the consumer's mind, either bundle would yield the same level of utility.

Much of what follows is based on the consumer's ability to rank groups of commodities. This is a relatively weak requirement. We can show why by listing some of the things we are not saying about consumer preferences and indifference. First, we do not say that the consumer estimates *how much* utility or *what level* of satisfaction will be attained from consuming a given bundle of goods. Only the ability to *rank* is required. Second and related to the first point, we do not imply that an individual can say *how much* one bundle of goods is preferred to another. Admittedly, a consumer might say that one group of goods is desired a great deal more than another group, and perhaps just a little more than still another group. But *great deal* and *just a little* are imprecise terms—their meanings differ from one person to another. Third, we do not say that consumers *should* choose one bundle over the other, or that they will be better off if they do. It is only necessary that the individuals who do the consuming rank bundles in their own order of preference.

When a consumer can rank bundles of goods, we assume that the consumer's preference pattern possesses the following characteristics. Given three bundles of goods (A, B, and C), if an individual prefers A to B and B to C, then A is preferred to C. Similarly, if someone is indifferent between A and B and between B and C, the individual must be indifferent between A and C. Finally, a consumer who is indifferent between A and B, but who prefers B to C, must prefer A to C. This assumption obviously can be carried over to four or more different bundles. If individuals can rank *any pair* of bundles chosen at random from all conceivable bundles, they can rank *all conceivable bundles.*

A real-world consumer who *purchases* one good rather than another does not necessarily prefer the chosen good. If you drive a Ford Escort rather than a Mercedes, we cannot infer that you prefer a Ford to a Mercedes. If the Mercedes costs less than the Ford at the time of purchase, and you were aware of this, we could make this inference. If, as was probably the case, the Mercedes cost much more, we can say nothing. If the two goods are presented at equal price, and you choose one over the other, we can say that you prefer that good. Or, if two goods are priced differently and you choose the higher-priced good, we can again deduce that you prefer that good. But if you choose the lower-priced good, we can say nothing.

In summary, utility theory depends on consumers having well-established preferences. With their preferences consumers can:

1. Establish a rank ordering among all bundles of goods.
2. Compare pairs of bundles and know that A is preferred to B, B is preferred to A, or B is equivalent to A.
3. In more than two-way comparisons, if A is preferred (indifferent) to B and B is preferred (indifferent) to C, A must be preferred (indifferent) to C.

5.3   Indifference Curves and Maps

Using the assumptions set forth above, we can now introduce a tool that is fundamental to the theory of consumer behavior: indifference curves. Indifference curves describe the tastes consumers have for one good relative to another.

Definition

An indifference curve pictures in a graph all of the combinations of two goods that yield the same level of total utility. Thus, a consumer is indifferent among any combinations of the two goods on the curve.

For analytical purposes, let us consider a consumer who can choose between two different goods, X and Y, each continuously divisible in quantity.[1] These goods could be anything: two different kinds of meat such as beef and chicken, a choice between buying more clothing or shelter in a family household, or it could be a choice between more beds or more nurses in a hospital. Later in the text we will name X as some good in particular and let Y represent a composite bundle of goods and services on which all other income is spent.

5.3.1   An Indifference Curve for Two Goods

Figure 5–1 shows an indifference curve for two goods, hamburger and chicken. Quantities of hamburger are plotted on the vertical axis and quantities of chicken are plotted along the horizontal axis. This indifference curve shows all the com-

[1]Admittedly, the possibility of continuous variation in quantity is perhaps less frequently encountered than "lumpiness," but this assumption permits a great gain in analytical precision at the sacrifice of very little realism. The assumption that bundles consist of no more than two separate goods enables us to analyze the problem of consumer behavior with two-dimensional graphs. This assumption is made, therefore, purely for simplicity of exposition. With the use of differential calculus, bundles of any number of different goods can be handled. But the analytical results based on two goods are exactly the same as those based on more than two. The gain in simplicity outweighs the loss of realism.

Figure 5–1   An Indifference Curve for Hamburger and Chicken

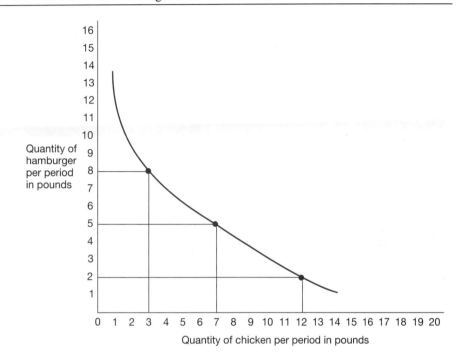

Quantity of hamburger per period in pounds

Quantity of chicken per period in pounds

binations of hamburger and chicken that are viewed by the household as equivalent. For example, 8 pounds of hamburger bundled with 3 pounds of chicken is equally as good as 5 pounds of hamburger and 7 pounds of chicken. And this package is equally as good as 2 pounds of hamburger combined with 12 pounds of chicken. Each bundle of meats on the curve gives the same level of utility to the consumer. This curve shows that the two goods pictured can be substituted for one another to maintain some constant level of utility. More of one good must be given to the consumer when some of the other is taken away.

5.3.2   Indifference Maps

An indifference map is a graph that shows a set of indifference curves. Figure 5–2 shows a portion of this consumer's indifference map consisting of just four indifference curves labeled I–IV. Many more such curves exist; indeed, there are an infinite number in the family, each one describing the combinations of X and Y that yield a particular level of utility. Returning to curve I, a consumer considers all combinations of X and Y on indifference curve I to be equivalent (for example, $20X$ and $42Y$, and $60X$ and $10Y$); these combinations yield the same utility, and the consumer is indifferent among them. All combinations of goods on indifference curve II (say $50X$ and $30Y$) are superior to any combination of goods on I. Likewise, all combinations on curve III are superior to any combination on curve II. Each

Figure 5-2   An Indifference Map

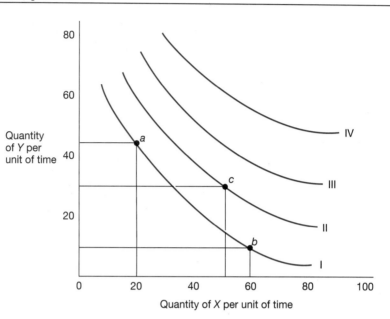

indifference curve that lies above another indifference curve represents combinations of X and Y that are considered superior to, or capable of yielding more utility than, every combination on the lower curve. At every utility level designated by a particular indifference curve, the consumer is willing to substitute X for Y or Y for X at some rate to remain on the same curve.

Since X and Y are assumed to be continuously divisible, each indifference curve in Figure 5-2 specifies an infinite number of combinations that yield the same amount of satisfaction. It is important to note that the specific utility numbers attached to curves I, II, III, and IV are immaterial. The numbers might progressively be 5, 7, 12, and 32, or 96, 327, 450 and 624, or any other set of numbers that *increase*. For the theory of consumer behavior, only the position and shape of the indifference curves matter. Since a precise measurement of utility is unnecessary, the theory of consumer behavior does not have to be based on the stronger concept of cardinal utility. The indifference curves and the capability to order preferences are all that are required in choice theory. All bundles of goods situated on the same indifference curve are equivalent; all combinations lying on a higher curve are preferred.

Relation

A consumer regards all bundles yielding the same level of utility as equivalent. The locus of such bundles is called an indifference curve because the consumer is indifferent among the particular bundles consumed. The higher, or further to the right, an indifference curve, the greater the underlying level of utility. Therefore, the higher the indifference curve, the more preferred is each bundle situated on the curve.

5.4   Characteristics of Indifference Curves

Indifference curves have four characteristics that are important for the discussion of consumer behavior. All but the fourth property are based on the consumer's ability to rank consumption bundles and on the assumption that the consumer always prefers more to less. For the sake of simplicity, assume once again that there are only two continuously divisible goods, X and Y. The indifference map is drawn with an X and Y axis. These axes define a *commodity space*.

5.4.1   Each Point in the Commodity Space Is on the Map

The first property is that each point in the commodity space lies on one, and only one, indifference curve. This is because each point in the commodity space represents some specific combination of the two goods and, therefore, some specific level of utility. Beginning at any point, it is possible to take away Y and add X or take away X and add Y in an infinite number of ways and leave the consumer with the same level of satisfaction. So, each point in the plane must lie on an indifference curve, and since all bundles can be unambiguously ranked, each lies on only one indifference curve. For obvious reasons, when graphing an indifference map, only a relatively few curves are used to represent the entire map. But remember, an infinite number of indifference curves lie between any two indifference curves that are drawn.

5.4.2   Indifference Curves Do Not Intersect

A second characteristic, and one that follows immediately from the first, is that indifference curves cannot intersect. In Figure 5–3, I and II are indifference curves, and the points W, S, and R represent three different bundles (or combinations of X and Y). Bundle R must clearly be preferred to bundle S because it contains more of both goods. Bundles R and W are equivalent because they are situated on the same indifference curve. In like manner, the consumer is indifferent between bundles W and S. Recall that if a consumer is indifferent between A and B and between B and C, he or she must be indifferent between A and C. In this case, R and W are equivalent, as are W and S, so R must be equivalent to S. But, as previously mentioned, R is preferred to S because it contains more of both goods. Intersecting indifference curves, such as those shown in Figure 5–3, imply that consumers are not consistent about ranking bundles of products.   *so Ind. curves cannot intersect*

5.4.3   Indifference Curves Have Negative Slopes

A third property of indifference curves is that they are negatively sloped. This property is based on the assumption that a consumer prefers a bundle with more goods to one with fewer. An upward-sloping indifference curve would indi-

Figure 5–3   Indifference Curves Cannot Intersect

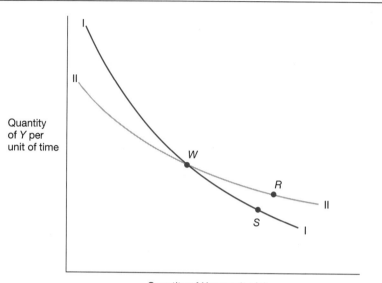

cate that a consumer is indifferent between two combinations of goods, one of which contains more of both goods. The fact that a positive amount of one good must be added to the bundle to offset the loss of some amount of another good (if the consumer is to remain at the same level of satisfaction) implies negatively sloped indifference curves. More X requires less Y to keep the consumer at the same level of utility.

5.4.4   Indifference Curves Are Convex

The fourth and final property is that indifference curves are convex. Each curve must lie above its tangent at every point, as illustrated in Figure 5–4. The convexity of indifference curves does not follow from the capability of consumers to consistently rank consumption bundles, but it comes from empirical observations showing that consumers generally value diversity and consume a number of different commodities. As we will show later, if the indifference curve were not drawn as pictured in Figure 5–4, utility maximization would lead to specialization rather than diversification in consumption. The predictions of our model would then contradict observation.

We could argue that if marginal utility always declines as more of a good is consumed—the principle of diminishing marginal utility—then indifference curves must be convex. As discussed already, diminishing marginal utility means that the more of a commodity a consumer has, the less valuable an additional or marginal unit is; conversely the less of a good a consumer has, the more valuable an additional or marginal unit is. Along an indifference curve, a consumer, such as the one shown

Figure 5–4   Indifference Curves Are Convex

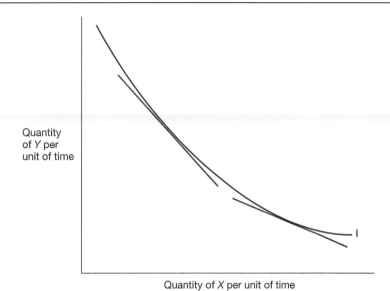

Quantity of Y per unit of time

Quantity of X per unit of time

in Figure 5–4, would be willing to give up less and less Y for an additional unit of X as Y decreases, because Y is becoming more valuable as less Y is consumed. As X increases, it becomes less valuable. If the consumer must get more X in return for giving up each additional unit of Y, the indifference curve must be convex. For example, a person at a football game who has four hot dogs (graphed as good Y) and one soft drink (graphed as good X) might be willing to trade two hot dogs for another soft drink. Alternatively, if the same person had only two hot dogs and two soft drinks, he or she would be willing to give up less than two hot dogs for an additional soft drink. In all likelihood, several soft drinks would be required to coax even one hot dog away.

The results of this section may be summarized in the following way:

Relation

Indifference curves have the following properties: (a) some indifference curve passes through each point in commodity space, (b) indifference curves cannot intersect, (c) indifference curves slope downward to the right, and (d) indifference curves are convex.

5.5   Marginal Rate of Substitution

The essential feature of utility theory is that different combinations of commodities give rise to the same level of utility. This condition enables us to draw indifference curves and maps. An indifference curve shows how one commodity can be

Figure 5–5 The Marginal Rate of Substitution

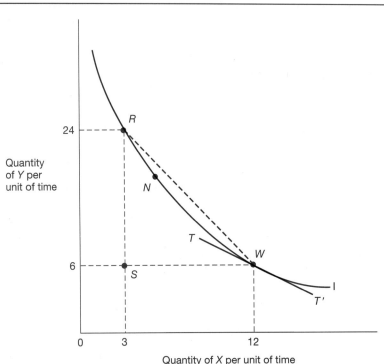

Quantity of X per unit of time

substituted for another so that the consumer remains just as well off as before, or remains on the same indifference curve. Indifference curves enable us to observe the *rate* at which a consumer is willing to substitute one commodity for another in consumption. As we will show, a consumer attains maximum utility from a limited money income when choosing a combination of goods such that the rate at which he or she is *willing* to substitute goods along an indifference curve is the same as the *rate* at which market prices *permit* substitution. Therefore, to understand utility maximization, one must understand the rate of substitution on an indifference curve.

5.5.1 Substitution and Consumption along an Indifference Curve

Consider Figure 5–5. On this indifference curve the consumer is indifferent between bundle *R*, containing 3 units of *X* and 24 of *Y*, and bundle *W*, containing 12 units of *X* and 6 of *Y*. Starting at point *W* and then going to point *R* the consumer is willing to give up 9 units of *X* for 18 more units of *Y*. We could also start at point *R* and go to *W*; then the consumer is willing to give up 18 units of *Y* for 9 more units of *X*. The *rate* at which the consumer is willing, on average, to substitute *X* for *Y* along an indifference curve is the change in *Y* divided by the change in *X*. We write this as:

$$\left|\frac{\Delta Y}{\Delta X}\right| = \frac{RS}{SW} = \frac{24 - 6}{3 - 12} = -\frac{18}{9} = -2.$$

This ratio measures the average number of units of Y the consumer is willing to forego in order to obtain one additional unit of X over the range of consumption pairs under consideration holding utility constant.[2] The consumer is willing to give up two units of Y in order to gain one more unit of X. Stated alternatively, the ratio measures the amount of Y that must be sacrificed (two units) per unit of X gained to remain at precisely the same level of utility.

In our subsequent use, we would find it cumbersome to have the minus sign on the right-hand side of the above equation. We therefore define this rate of substitution as

$$-\frac{\Delta Y}{\Delta X} = \frac{2}{1}.$$

The rate of substitution given by the ratio above is obviously the negative of the slope of the broken straight line joining points R and W. The ratio could be quite different between two alternative points, say N and W. But, as point R moves along the indifference curve toward W, the ratio RS/SW becomes closer and closer to the slope of the tangent TT' at W. In the limit, for extremely small movements in the neighborhood of point W, the negative of the slope of the indifference curve, which is the negative of the slope of its tangent at W, is called the *marginal rate of substitution of X for Y*.

Definition

> The marginal rate of substitution of X for Y measures the number of units of Y that must be sacrificed per unit of X gained so as to maintain a constant level of utility. The marginal rate of substitution is given by the negative of the slope of an indifference curve at a point. It is defined only for movements along an indifference curve, never for movements among curves.

We will use the letters MRS to denote the marginal rate of substitution of X for Y in consumption or, more generally, the marginal rate of substitution of the good plotted on the horizontal axis for the good plotted on the vertical axis. Also, since we want the MRS to be positive, and since $\Delta Y/\Delta X$ is necessarily negative, the minus sign must be attached. We write

$$MRS_{x \text{ for } y} = -\frac{\Delta Y}{\Delta X},$$

where the subscript "x for y" indicates that the consumer is taking more X for less Y along an indifference curve. In the graph we are moving down the indifference curve.

5.5.2   Diminishing MRS

The assumption that indifference curves are convex, which means that the slope of the curve decreases, implies that the MRS of X for Y diminishes as X is substituted for Y along an indifference curve. This is illustrated in Figure 5–6.

---

[2]The ratio is, of course, negative, since the change in Y associated with an increase in X is negative. This type of relation results directly from the assumption of negatively sloped indifference curves.

Figure 5–6   Diminishing Marginal Rate of Substitution

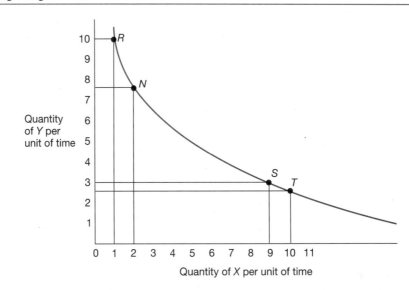

On this indifference curve, R, N, S, and T represent four bundles of X and Y located on the curve. Consider a movement from R to N. In order to maintain the same level of utility, the consumer is willing to sacrifice slightly more than two units of Y to gain one more unit of X. Now consider the consumer situated at S who then moves to T. To gain one more unit of X, the consumer now is willing to give up approximately 1/2 a unit of Y. Thus near the top of the indifference curve, around point R, the *MRS* is about 2.25. Near point T it is about .5. A convex indifference curve will always have a relatively high *MRS* near the top where the quantity of X is small and that of Y is large. The *MRS* will become smaller as the consumer moves down the indifference curve as the quantity of Y becomes smaller and the quantity of X larger. Convexity of an indifference curve means that when a consumer has a lot of Y (at the top of the curve), it is easy to give up Y for more of good X. But as the consumer gives up more and more Y, it becomes more valuable and, as a consequence, more difficult to give up Y for more X. Hence the *MRS* gets smaller.

Diminishing *MRS* is further illustrated in Figure 5–7, this time without actual numbers. For the indifference curve shown, N, R, and S are three bundles that yield the same level of utility. The horizontal axis is measured so that $OX_1 = X_1X_2 = X_2X_3$. We look first at the movement from N to R and see that the *MRS* between N and R is

$$\frac{OY_1 - OY_2}{OX_2 - OX_1} = \frac{Y_1Y_2}{X_1X_2}.$$

Similarly, for a movement from R to S, the *MRS* is

$$\frac{OY_2 - OY_3}{OX_3 - OX_2} = \frac{Y_2Y_3}{X_2X_3}.$$

Figure 5–7   Diminishing *MRS*

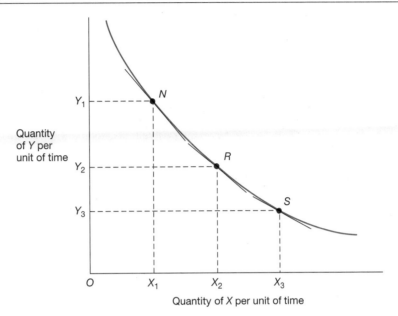

By construction, $X_1X_2 = X_2X_3$, but, from the figure you can see that $Y_1Y_2 > Y_2Y_3$. The *MRS* is less moving from *R* to *S* than from *N* to *R*. Diminished *MRS* is also shown by the decreasing (in absolute value) slopes of the tangents at *N*, *R*, and *S*.

5.5.3   Marginal Utility Approach

As already mentioned, the early economists who developed the theory of consumer utility assumed that utility was actually measurable and had a numerical value. They went on to reason that the more of one good consumed, the greater the total utility, but each *additional* unit of the good consumed added less to total utility than the previous unit. They thought it possible to also measure diminishing marginal utility.

We can tie the marginal utility a consumer receives from one more unit of goods *X* and *Y* to the marginal rate of substitution. For this exercise marginal utility can be: (a) the increase in utility from a small increase in the consumption of a commodity, holding the level of consumption of all other commodities constant or (b) the decrease in utility from a small decrease in the consumption of a good. Small changes may be increments less than one unit, but they can be possibly more than one unit for illustration.

Assume now that utility (U) and marginal utility (MU) are measurable and depend on the consumption rate of two goods, X and Y. Next, let the consumption of both X and Y change by a small amount. We can represent the total change in utility resulting from the changes in X and Y as

$$\Delta U = [(MU_X) \cdot \Delta X] + [(MU_Y) \cdot \Delta Y].$$

The terms in parentheses, MU_X and MU_Y, refer to the marginal utility of X and the marginal utility of Y. This expression means, for example, that if X increases by two units, and the marginal utility of each is five while Y increases by three units and the marginal utility of each is four, utility increases by 22 units: $(5 \cdot 2) + (4 \cdot 3)$. If marginal utility is the same and X increases by four units and Y decreases by five units, total utility remains constant; that is $(5 \cdot 4) + (4 \cdot (-5)) = 0$.

Since an indifference curve represents the locus of all combinations of X and Y among which the consumer is indifferent, utility must remain constant along any indifference curve. Thus, ΔU equals zero for any movement along an indifference curve. From the equation above, for very small changes in X and Y, and always remembering that $\Delta U = 0$ along an indifference curve, we can write the above equation for ΔU as

$$\Delta U = 0 = [MU_X \cdot \Delta X] + [MU_Y \cdot \Delta Y].$$

Rearranging terms by subtracting $[MU_X \cdot \Delta X]$ from both sides, we obtain

$$- [MU_X \cdot \Delta X] = [MU_Y \cdot \Delta Y].$$

Then dividing both sides of this equation by $-[\Delta X \cdot MU_Y]$, results in

$$\frac{MU_X}{MU_Y} = -\frac{\Delta Y}{\Delta X},$$

where $-(\Delta Y/\Delta X)$, as you already know, represents the slope of the indifference curve, which we have called $MRS_{x \text{ for } y}$. The ratio of marginal utilities is equivalent to the marginal rate of substitution; therefore, we can write

$$MRS_{X \text{ for } Y} = \frac{MU_X}{MU_Y},$$

after substituting for $-(\Delta Y/\Delta X)$.

Thinking of X and Y as specific goods may help you interpret this expression. Consider hamburgers (Y) and soft drinks (X), then picture a graph (or construct one for yourself) where the number of burgers is plotted on the vertical axis and the number of soft drinks is plotted on the horizontal. When a consumer has numerous burgers, the marginal value of one more is relatively low. Similarly, when the number of soft drinks is low, their marginal value is high. Thus, the MRS, the ratio of the marginal utility of soft drinks to that of hamburgers, is relatively high. Now suppose the individual substitutes drinks for burgers (X for Y in the previous notation). Increasing the rate of consumption of soft drinks decreases their marginal utility, while reducing the rate of consumption of hamburgers increases their marginal utility. The substitution of soft drinks for hamburgers must lead to a decrease in the $MRS_{x \text{ for } y}$.

5.5.4   The Importance of Substitution

Although the concept of indifference curves is useful in developing the theory of demand, measuring and plotting actual indifference curves for real people is extremely difficult. Economists have attempted such measurement—using both people and animals—with varying levels of success. But the *actual measurement and graphing* of indifference curves are not really important to those who use utility theory.

It is the *concept* of these curves that is most useful. A decision maker in a business must recognize that employees, for example, have subjective rates of trade-off between income and working conditions. The *MRS* indeed expresses what we can think of as a rate of exchange. To be more specific, some of our recent Ph.D. graduates have gone to work in economics departments where research is important, while others have joined faculties where research is not required. The teaching load—number of classes to be taught by a recent Ph.D—has been on average higher when research is not required. There is a trade-off between the faculty working conditions; less research means higher teaching loads. Universities also recognize that faculty members are willing to trade some amenities, such as preferred seating at football games and preferred parking facilities, for income. These trade-offs result from different tastes reflected in the shape of each individual's set of indifference curves. Any business that seeks to maximize employee benefits with limited resources for compensation must make its decisions based on a comparison of its employees' marginal values and willingness to substitute.

Government decision makers must also recognize the importance of substitution. Consumers of government products (constituents) do not want zero schools and perfect streets or perfect schools and no streets. Government officials must realize that there is a trade-off between the two that would be preferred. Even within a school system, there is a trade-off between teaching and classroom facilities.

Perhaps most important, any student of economics must realize that all goods have some substitutes. There are very few goods—probably no goods—that you are now consuming that you would not give up some amount of in order to obtain some amount of other goods. Don't say I would not give up food because I would die. You wouldn't have to give up *all consumption* of a large group of goods. We only said that there is some amount of other goods for which you would be willing to give up some amount of the food, or some type of food, you are now consuming. Virtually all consumers make trade-offs among goods. In very few cases is it essential that someone consume exactly the same amount of a particular good. We can think of some examples, of course, mostly medical, such as a given amount of medicine without which the patient would die, or a weekly treatment on a kidney machine. But these absolutes are rare.

Therefore, don't make the mistake, unless you are trying to convert someone to your point of view, of making statements like, "It is essential that the school increase classroom space by 20 percent" or "The city must double its recreational area in five years." Each of these "essentials" has some potential substitutes in the minds of consumers. The concept of the indifference curve allows us to better understand the concept of substitution.

Economics in the News

There Is a Trade-off between Convenience and Environmentalism[3]

Increased convenience for consumers is frequently at odds with ecology. Many convenient products are not biodegradable, for instance. Specifically, foam cups and plates do not degrade and are toxic when burnt. Paper plates and cups are better suited for waste because paper does degrade and is not toxic when burned. But fast-food restaurant owners are quick to point out that consumers prefer plastic and maintain that they lose business whenever they attempt a switch to paper. Paper plates are not as sturdy as the plastic variety and paper cups are more apt to leak, especially with hot liquids. In some markets, plastic containers are important because they allow consumers the convenience of squeezing out a liquid or paste. Ketchup in plastic squeeze bottles now accounts for about a third of all sales. Squeezability is important for many other consumer goods, including glues, makeup, toothpastes, and first-aid items.

Another conflict between convenience and sound ecological practice arises over the disposable diaper. Cloth diapers can be cleaned and reused many times, but cleaning isn't convenient. Diaper manufacturers have not yet devised a disposable diaper that is totally degradable. Yet disposable diapers have steadily gained popularity in the diaper industry, as parents seek more convenient changes. There is also the increased use of plastic in the manufacturing of automobiles and trucks. Plastic is used mainly to reduce the cost of production, and automobile weight is reduced as it replaces metal. Plastic parts are also less expensive to replace. But the plastic cannot be recycled the way scrap metal has been for decades. For the consumer, automobile prices are kept down, but the car is less degradable.

Although it may appear that consumers are behaving inconsistently, campaigning against toxic waste but at the same time keeping their babies in disposable diapers, a more correct interpretation of such behavior is that a better environment and convenience are substitute desires for consumers. On an indifference map, a cleaner environment and product convenience are labels on the vertical and horizontal axes of a commodity space.

5.1   Applying the Theory

During the 1980s, corporate bonds known as *junk bonds* came into prominence. These bonds typically were issued either by companies that were a bit shaky financially or by new companies getting started on a new product. These bonds carry a much greater risk of default, particularly if the economy is hit by a recession. Furthermore, investors are subject to a substantial loss of their principal if the issuing firms aren't doing well. In fact, market analyst Jane Bryant Quinn reported in *Newsweek,* March 27, 1989, that such investors had lost an average of 14 percent of their principal over the past 10 years.

---

[3]This report is based on "Ecology and Buyer Wants Don't Jibe," *The Wall Street Journal,* August 23, 1989, p. B1

Why would investors ever want to purchase junk bonds when so many highly rated corporate bonds and safe U.S. treasury bonds are available?

5.6   Budget Lines

In this chapter thus far we have set forth a method of analyzing what a consumer is willing to do or wishes to do. The theory of indifference curves describes the tastes of consumers. Tastes reflect desires or what the consumer wants to do. Recall from Chapter 2, however, that demand indicates both what consumers are willing or wish to do and what they are able to do. We will now discuss a way to analyze what a consumer is *able* to do, given a limited budget.

5.6.1   Income Constraints

If all consumers had an unlimited income—in other words, if there were an unlimited pool of resources—there would be no problem of "economizing," nor would there be "economics." Since this utopian state does not exist, even for the richest members of society, people are compelled to determine their behavior in light of limited financial resources. For the theory of consumer behavior, this means that each consumer has a maximum amount that can be spent per period of time. The consumer's problem is to spend this amount in the way that yields maximum satisfaction.

Suppose a grocery shopper has $25 to spend at the meat counter this week. The household shopper has already decided to divide purchases between chicken and hamburger. The average price of chicken is $1.25/pound and the average price of hamburger is $1.50/pound. Table 5–1 shows a partial list of combinations of chicken and hamburger that can be purchased for $25 at these prices. All six entries in the table add up to spending $25 at the meat counter as the table shows in the last column.

These combinations of hamburger and chicken are only a few of the many possible combinations. Assuming hamburger and chicken are continuously divisible, all combinations can be plotted in a graph. Figure 5–8 shows the six combinations listed in Table 5–1 and all other possible combinations of hamburger and chicken that the consumer may buy for $25. In the figure, if a consumer chooses any mix of hamburger and chicken that lies exactly on the line, this represents an expenditure of $25. Any combination inside the line means less is spent; any combination outside the line means more than $25 is spent. If $25 is a strict limit, points above or to the right of the line are unattainable. The line graphed in Figure 5–8 is the consumer's budget line or *budget constraint*.

Notice that the endpoints of the budget line indicate how much the consumer can purchase if just one item is bought, either all hamburger and no chicken, or all chicken and no hamburger. The table and the graph show that if all of the $25 is spent, 16 2/3 pounds of hamburger is the maximum quantity that can be bought, and 20 pounds of chicken is the maximum amount of chicken. These endpoints can always be found by dividing the budget or income available, in this case $25, by the price of the good. Thus, 16 2/3 = 25/$1.50 and 20 = 25/$1.25.

Table 5–1   Selected Combinations of Beef and Chicken that Can Be Purchased for $25

Quantities of Hamburger (pounds)	Quantities of Chicken (pounds)	Total Expenditure
16 2/3	0	16 2/3 · $1.50 + 0 · $1.25 = $25
15	2	15 · $1.50 + 2 · $1.25 = $25
10	8	10 · $1.50 + 8 · $1.25 = $25
5	14	5 · $1.50 + 14 · $1.25 = $25
2 1/2	17	2 1/2 · $1.50 + 17 · $1.25 = $25
0	20	0 · $1.50 + 20 · $1.25 = $25

Figure 5–8   The Budget Constraint for Beef and Chicken

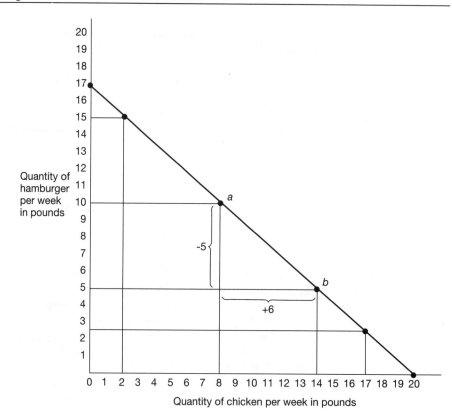

It can be shown that the slope of a budget line is the ratio of the two prices, with a minus sign because the slope of the budget line is negative. Suppose in Figure 5–8 we move from point *a* to point *b*. We start with the bundle consisting of 8 pounds of chicken and 10 pounds of hamburger and move to 14 pounds of chicken and 5 pounds of hamburger. The slope will be

$$\frac{\text{Change in quantity of hamburger}}{\text{Change in quantity of chicken}} = \frac{5 - 10}{14 - 8} = \frac{-5}{6}$$

as shown in the figure. Recall now that chicken (P_c) was priced at $1.25/pound and hamburger (P_h) at $1.50/pound. If we take the ratio with a negative sign we get

$$-\frac{P_c}{P_h} = -\frac{\$1.25}{\$1.50} = \frac{5}{6}.$$

Hence, the ratio of the price of the good on the horizontal axis to the price of the good on the vertical axis with a negative sign is the slope of the budget line.

5.6.2   The Budget Line in General

We continue to assume that there are only two goods, *X* and *Y,* bought in quantities Q_x and Q_y in order to develop the general concept of a budget line. Each consumer is confronted with market-determined prices, P_x and P_y, of *X* and *Y* respectively. The consumer has a known and fixed money income (*M*) for the period under consideration. *M* is the maximum amount the consumer can spend, and we assume that it is all spent on *X* and *Y*.[4] The amount spent on *X* is ($Q_x \cdot P_x$). The amount spent on *Y* is ($Q_x \cdot P_y$). These expenditures must be equal to the consumer's money income. Algebraically,

$$M = Q_x \cdot P_x + Q_y \cdot P_y , \qquad (5\text{–}1)$$

which is the formula used to get total expenditure in Table 5–1. This equation can be expressed as the equation for a straight line. Solving for the quantity Q_y—since *Y* is generally plotted on the vertical axis—we obtain

$$Q_y = \frac{M}{P_y} - \frac{P_x}{P_y} Q_x . \qquad (5\text{–}2)$$

Equation 5–2 is plotted in Figure 5–9. The first term on the right-hand side of Equation 5–2, M/P_y, shows the amount of *Y* that can be purchased if no *X* is purchased. This amount is represented by the distance *OA* in Figure 5–9; thus, M/P_y (or point *A*) is the vertical intercept of the equation.

[4]In more advanced models, saving may be considered as one of the many goods and services available to the consumer. Graphical treatment limits us to two dimensions; thus, we ignore saving. This does not mean that the theory of consumer behavior precludes saving—depending on preference ordering, a consumer may save much, little, or nothing. Similarly, spending may, in fact, exceed income in any given period as a result of borrowing or from using assets acquired in the past. The *M* in question for any period is the total amount of money to be spent during the period.

Figure 5–9   Budget Line

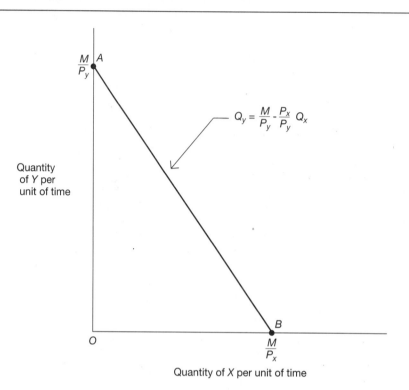

Quantity of X per unit of time

In Equation 5–2, $-P_x/P_y$, the negative of the price ratio, is the slope of the line. To see this, consider the quantity of X that can be purchased if Y is not bought. This amount is M/P_x, shown by the distance OB in Figure 5–9. Since the line obviously has a negative slope, its slope is given by

$$-\frac{OA}{OB} = -\frac{\dfrac{M}{P_y}}{\dfrac{M}{P_x}} = -\frac{P_x}{P_y}.$$

The line in Figure 5–9 is a general form of the budget line. The slope is the negative of the ratio of the price of X to the price of Y.

Definition

The budget line represents all combinations of goods that can be purchased if the entire money income is spent. Its slope is the negative of the price ratio. Its vertical intercept is income divided by the price of the good plotted along the vertical axis. Because a consumer is assumed to spend all income on X and Y, any bundle purchased by an individual must lie on the budget line.

Figure 5–10   Changing Money Income

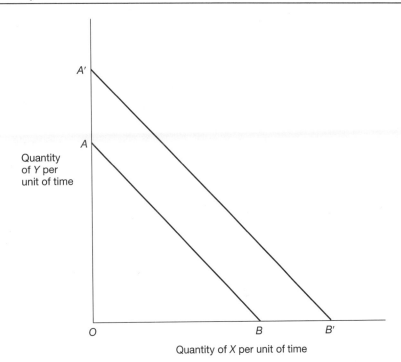

5.6.3   Shifting the Budget Line: Income Changes

In much of the analysis that follows, we are interested in changes in quantities purchased resulting from changes in price and money income, both represented graphically by changes in the budget line. Consider first the effect of a change in money income, the prices of goods remaining constant.

Any given budget line represents the set of all possible consumption bundles for a consumer at a given set of relative prices and money income. If the customer's money income increases at the original set of commodity prices, the set of consumption possibilities must increase. Since the increase in money income allows the consumer to buy more goods, the budget line is pushed outward, and since prices are not changed, the slope of the budget line does not change. Therefore, an increase in money income causes an outward parallel shift in the budget line. Similarly a decrease in money income, prices remaining constant, causes a parallel inward shift in the budget line. In Figure 5–10, budget line AB is associated with a lower income than is budget line $A'B'$. The slope of AB and $A'B'$ are equal, because the price ratio remains constant as the change in money income shifts the budget constraint upward or downward as income increases or decreases. Recall that the intercepts of the budget line are income divided by the prices of X and Y. So the distance OA' is greater than OA because $M'/P_y > M/P_y$, where M' is the

Figure 5–11   Changing the Price of X

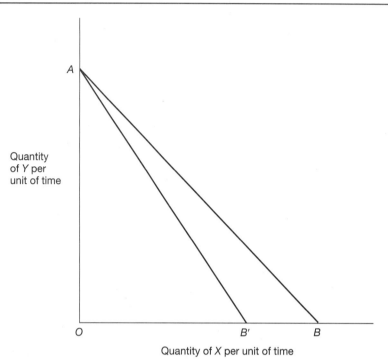

larger income. Likewise, the distance OB' is greater than OB because $M'/P_x > M/P_x$.

5.6.4   Shifting the Budget Line: Price Changes

Figure 5–11 shows what happens to the budget line when the price ratio changes with money income held constant. Assume that money income and the prices of X and Y are such that the relevant budget line is AB. The slope of the line is $- (P_x/P_y)$. Holding money income and the price of Y constant, let the price of X increase. Since P_x increases, P_x/P_y increases also. The budget line becomes steeper and, in this case, is the budget line AB'. The intercept on the Y axis remains the same because M/P_y remains constant. In other words, if income and the price of Y remain constant, the consumer can purchase the same amount of Y by spending the entire income on Y, regardless of the price of X. You can see from the graph that an increase in the price of X rotates the budget line inward, the Y-intercept remaining fixed. Of course, a decrease in the price of X pivots the budget line outward.

Alternatively, and perhaps more directly, the price change can be explained as follows. At the original price, P_x, the maximum purchase of X is M/P_x, or the distance OB. When the price rises to P'_x, the maximum purchase of X is M/P'_x, or the distance OB'. An increase in the price of X is shown by pivoting the budget line to the left around the vertical intercept. A decrease in the price of X is represented by a rotation to the right.

Relation

> An increase in money income, prices unchanged, is shown by a parallel shift of the budget line—outward and to the right for an increase in money income and in the direction of the origin for a decrease. A change in the price of X, the price of Y and money income constant, is shown by rotating the budget line around the vertical intercept—to the left for a price increase, to the right for a decrease.

5.7   Utility Maximization

All bundles of goods (combinations of X and Y) on the budget line are available to consumers in the sense that their income allows them to purchase these quantities if they wish. This line is established by the fixed money income and the given prices of the commodities. A consumer's indifference map shows the rank ordering of all conceivable bundles of X and Y. The principal assumption on which the theory of consumer behavior is built is that *a consumer attempts to allocate a limited money income among available goods and services so as to maximize utility*. Given this constrained goal, you will recall from Chapter 4 that marginal benefit per dollar should be set equal across the commodities in the bundle.

5.7.1   Maximizing Subject to a Limited Money Income

Graphically, we can visualize the consumer as being constrained by a limited money income that permits consuming only bundles of goods along the budget line. The consumer chooses the particular bundle along the line that is on the highest attainable indifference curve. In this way, the highest possible preference level is achieved.

The utility maximizing solution is depicted in Figure 5–12. The portion of the indifference map represented by the four indifference curves drawn in that figure indicates preferences among different combination of goods. Similarly, the budget line specifies the different combinations the consumer can purchase with the limited income, assuming all income is spent on X and Y, and the prices have not changed for X and Y.

The consumer cannot purchase any bundle lying above and to the right of the budget line and, therefore, cannot consume any combination lying on indifference curve IV. Some points on curves I, II, and III are, however, attainable. Moreover, as already discussed, an infinite number of indifference curves lie between curves I and III. Therefore, all points on the budget line between W and S are touched by some indifference curve, and if we extend the map to include curves below I, all points above W and below S are touched by some curve. Each point on the budget line yields some specific level of utility. Four of the infinite number of attainable combinations are represented by points W, E, R, and S.

Suppose the consumption bundle a consumer chooses is located at W. Without experimenting, the consumer cannot know for certain whether W represents a maximum position. However, let the individual move to combinations above and below W, along the budget constraint. Moving upward lowers the level of utility to some

Figure 5–12   Consumer Optimization

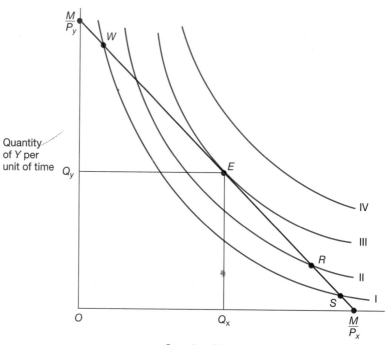

Quantity of X per unit of time

indifference curve below I, but moving downward puts the person on a higher indifference curve. Continued experimentation will lead the consumer to move at least as far as E, because each successive movement down the budget line moves him or her to a higher indifference curve. Continuing to experiment, however, by moving away from E, the consumer would locate on a lower indifference curve with its lower level of satisfaction and would, accordingly, return to the point E.

Similarly, if a consumer were situated at R, small movements would cause the substitution of Y for X, thereby moving this person in the direction of E. No point except E is optimal, because each successive substitution of Y for X brings the consumer to a higher indifference curve until point E is reached. The position of maximum utility—*or the point of consumer optimization*—is attained at E, where an indifference curve is just tangent to the budget line. At point E, the consumer would purchase Q_x units of X and Q_y units of Y.

5.7.2   Further Description of the Tangency

As you will recall, the slope of the budget line is the negative of the price ratio, the ratio of the price of X to the price of Y. Also recall that the slope of an indifference curve at any point is called the *MRS* of X for Y. The point of utility maximization is defined by the condition that the *MRS* must equal the price ratio (P_x/P_y).

The interpretation of this proposition is straightforward. The *MRS* shows the rate at which the consumer is willing to substitute X for Y. The price ratio shows the rate at which prices permit substitution of X for Y. Unless these rates are equal, it is possible to change the combination of X and Y purchased to attain a higher level of satisfaction. For example, suppose the *MRS* is two—meaning the consumer is willing to give up two units of Y in order to obtain one unit of X. Let the price ratio be unity, meaning that one unit of Y can be exchanged for one unit of X in the market. In this case, the indifference curve is steeper than the budget line. The consumer is at a point like W in Figure 5–12 since $MRS > P_x/P_y$. Clearly, the consumer will benefit by trading Y for X, since he or she is willing to give up two Y for one more X, but only has to give up one Y for one more X in the market. Generalizing, unless the *MRS* and the price ratio are equal, some exchange can be made to move the consumer to a higher level of satisfaction.

Principle

The point of consumer equilibrium—or the maximization of satisfaction subject to a limited money income—is defined by the condition that the *MRS* of X for Y must equal the ratio of the price of X to the price of Y.

5.7.3   Marginal Utility Interpretation of Optimization

At the beginning of this chapter, we gave a rather simplified intuitive explanation of utility maximization subject to a budget constraint. We argued that, if a consumer could give up some amount of a good and gain more satisfaction from purchasing some amount of another good for the same total expenditure, such substitution would occur. We can set forth this explanation a bit more formally now, using the marginal utility interpretation of indifference curves.

Recall from Section 5–5 that, along an indifference curve

$$MRS_{x \text{ for } y} = \frac{MU_x}{MU_y}.$$

At the equilibrium, the condition for utility maximization occurs when the $MRS_{x \text{ for } y}$ is equal to the slope of the budget line. Both are negative slopes, so the sign is omitted.

$$MRS_{x \text{ for } y} = \frac{P_x}{P_y}.$$

Therefore, in equilibrium it is also true that

$$\frac{MU_x}{MU_y} = \frac{P_x}{P_y}, \text{ or}$$

$$\frac{MU_x}{P_x} = \frac{MU_y}{P_y}.$$

(Note that this is the condition for constrained maximization developed in Chapter 4.) This is the equilibrium condition for any two goods X and Y, but it applies to the entire menu of goods and services a buyer purchases. For all goods i, j, k, and so on, the utility maximizing condition is

$$\frac{MU_i}{P_i} = \frac{MU_j}{P_j} = \frac{MU_k}{P_k} = \cdots$$

This relation provides an alternative view of the condition for consumer equilibrium. Dividing the marginal utility of a commodity by its price gives the marginal utility per dollar's worth of the commodity bought. In this light, we can restate the condition for utility maximization as the following:

Principle

To attain maximum satisfaction, a consumer must allocate money income so that the marginal utility per dollar spent on the last unit of each commodity is the same for all commodities purchased.

To help you see the sense of this principle, let's work through a numerical example. Suppose a consumer's income, M, is \$100 and $P_x = \$2$, $P_y = \$4$. Current purchases of X and Y are 30 and 10 units, respectively, so the consumer is spending the entire \$100 on X and Y. At these quantities $MU_x = 30$ and $MU_y = 40$; that is, at these quantities the marginal benefit of the last unit of X is 30, however benefit is measured, and the marginal benefit of the last unit of Y is 40. Can the consumer raise total utility when income is limited to \$100? Note first that

$$\frac{MU_x}{P_x} = \frac{30}{2} = 15 > \frac{MU_y}{P_y} = \frac{40}{4} = 10.$$

In this example, the consumer gets more utility per dollar at the margin from X than from Y. We conclude that in order to maximize utility, more X should be bought, and less Y should be purchased. If the buyer purchases one less unit of Y, releasing \$4 in income, two more units of X can be bought since P_x is \$2. Utility from the two additional X will then increase by about $2 \cdot 30 = 60$, while the decrease in utility from the sacrificed unit of Y is 40. Utility has increased by 20 $(= 60 - 40)$, while the expenditure on X and Y is unchanged. Whether the consumer should keep switching to X from Y depends on what the MU_x and MU_y are after this first change. Continuing to follow the principle set forth above always results in maximum utility.

Suppose, at the current allocation of income, the marginal dollar spent on X yields a greater marginal utility than the marginal dollar spent on Y. That is, suppose

$$\frac{MU_x}{P_x} > \frac{MU_y}{P_y}.$$

Reallocating one dollar of expenditure from Y to X will, therefore, increase total utility, and it must do so until the marginal utility per dollar's worth is the same for both commodities. This equalization will occur as X is substituted for Y because, as X increases MU_x declines, while MU_y increases as the amount of Y falls.

Alternatively, if

$$\frac{MU_x}{P_x} < \frac{MU_y}{P_y},$$

a dollar taken away from X will reduce utility less than the increase in utility obtained from spending the dollar on additional consumption of Y. The consumer will continue to substitute away from X toward Y until the marginal utility per dollar expenditure is equal, because MU_x increases and MU_y falls while prices remain constant.

Economics in the News

"We're Number 5" May Not Be Bad

In 1990, Buick extensively advertised that a survey of over 26,000 new car buyers revealed that Buick was the only American car line ranked in the top 10 in initial quality—according to owner-reported problems during the first 90 days. Buick featured in its ads a list of the top 10 automobiles in the survey, in which it was ranked fifth: behind Lexus, Mercedes-Benz, Toyota, and Infiniti and ahead of Honda, Nissan, Acura, BMW, and Mazda. All of these other nine car lines are Japanese or German.

In his nationally syndicated column, "High Five Is Goodbye Wave, not the Symbol of Quality," August 23, 1990, columnist George Will somewhat berated Buick for bragging about *only* being fifth. He stated that the boasts of winning college football players and their fans that "We're Number One" may be "mistaken, and the passion may be disproportionate to the achievement, but at least it is better than chanting 'We're Number Five'."

Mr. Will noted that "various American economic interests are resorting to anti-Japanese commercials to sell their products" and that such ads imply, "Don't expect us to measure up to the big boys—the ones overseas." He wanted Americans to become "impatient and censorious about lax standards (We're Number 5) that are producing pandemic shoddiness in everything from cars to art to second graders' homework." Mr. Will ended his column: "Americans would feel better, and might be more inclined to buy Buick, if they saw an ad reprinting the list above, but with a text that says: 'Fifth place is not nearly good enough for Americans to brag about. And until we do better, we apologize!'"

We don't want to criticize Mr. Will's argument that U.S. firms should not be running anti-Japanese ads or that many U.S. firms are not producing products up to the quality standards of many foreign firms. We do want to point out, however, that his criticism of Buick's boast of being number five as indicative of shoddy American quality may not be valid. In fact, it may be great to be "Number Five."

The annual auto issue of *Consumer Reports*, April 1990, gave the following list prices of the top 10 automobile lines for their medium-size models, the category of most Buick models:

1. Lexus $35,000
2. Mercedes-Benz $48,000 (avg.)
3. Toyota $21,500
4. Infiniti $38,000
5. Buick $15,000 (avg.)

6. Honda $14,500 (compact)
7. Nissan $18,000
8. Acura $26,000
9. BMW $37,000 (avg.)
10. Mazda $25,000

(continued)

Buick is priced lower than all the other cars but the Honda Accord, a compact car listed because Honda did not produce a medium-size car. Honda, which was ranked below Buick and is a compact, was only $500 below Buick. All of the other models were priced higher, some more than double. Of the cars ranked above Buick, Toyota's price was 40 percent higher, and the prices of the others were two to three times that of Buick.

Following the approach used in the theory of consumer behavior, consider the quality per dollar cost of a car:

$$\frac{\text{Quality of the Brand}}{\text{Price of the Brand}}$$

For the top-ranked automobile, Lexus, to have more quality per dollar—

$$\frac{\text{Quality of Lexus}}{\text{Price of Lexus}} > \frac{\text{Quality of Buick}}{\text{Price of Buick}}$$

—Lexus would have to have 2 1/3 more or better quality than Buick, because its price is 2 1/3 higher. Mercedes-Benz would have to have 3.2 times the quality of Buick, Infiniti, 2 1/2 more, and Toyota 40 percent more. Because the cars ranked 7 through 10 were higher priced and ranked lower in quality, they could not have more quality per dollar. Since Buick's price was only 3 percent higher than Honda's, Buick would have to have only a bit more than 3 percent more quality to be ranked higher in quality per dollar.

Based upon a measure of quality per dollar of cost, Buick could easily be ranked higher than fifth. Quite possibly, "They really are number one," and should not be disparaged quite as much as Mr. Will did. Perhaps Buick should not have apologized in its ads as suggested, but, instead, should have said, "We're Number One (or maybe Number Two) in quality per dollar."

Of course, initial quality isn't the only feature of a new car that gives utility: there are mileage, comfort, acceleration, looks, and so on. And, after all, it is the marginal utility of a car per dollar of cost that is relevant for consumer decision making. This example does, however, show the importance of price when making comparisons of product characteristics.

We might note that a survey by *Money* magazine (reported in the *Houston Post,* September 10, 1990) did consider quality relative to price. This survey was based upon analysis by education experts who investigated how well 1,000 public and private U.S. colleges deliver "quality relative to price." The list of the top 10 in this category excluded some extremely distinguished universities and included some that may surprise you. For your information the top 10 were, in order,

1. Cooper Union for the Advancement of Science and Art
2. Cal Tech
3. Rice University
4. New College of the University of South Florida
5. SUNY at Geneseo
6. SUNY at Binghamton
7. Trenton State College
8. SUNY at Albany
9. University of Virginia
10. University of Florida

Figure 5–13   Corner Solution

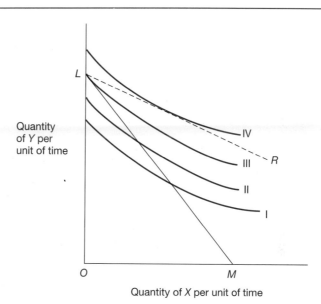

5.7.4   Zero Consumption of a Good

To this point, the discussion has focused on a consumer who chooses some positive amount of both X and Y, regardless of relative prices. The theory of consumer behavior, however, allows consumers to spend their entire income and purchase none of some specific good. They maximize utility by buying just one of the two goods.

One set of theoretical circumstances under which a consumer would choose to spend the entire income on (say) good Y and none on X is depicted in Figure 5–13. Given the budget line, LM, and the indifference map represented by curves I, II, III, and IV, the highest level of satisfaction attainable from the given money income is at point L on indifference curve III. The consumer chooses to purchase L units of Y (or M/P_y units) and no units of X. This point need not be a point of tangency where the MRS equals the price ratio, although it could be such a point. Economists call such a situation a corner solution. In this case, the price of X is so high relative to the rate at which a consumer is willing to substitute X for Y that the consumer chooses to purchase no units of X. It is literally the case where the consumer finds X too expensive. In terms of the constrained optimization rule for two goods, at zero consumption of X it is the case that

$$\frac{MU_y}{P_y} > \frac{MU_x}{P_x},$$

and all income is spent. That is, the marginal utility of the first dollar spent on X would be less than the marginal utility per dollar spent on the last unit of Y. Note, however, that for a sufficiently large decrease in the price of X relative to the price of Y (say to a price ratio depicted by budget line LR), the budget line could become tangent to some indifference curve above III (curve IV) at a point where both X and Y are purchased. The consumer will purchase some positive amount of X if its relative price decreases sufficiently.

For a wide choice of goods, and not simply a two-good picture, a corner solution, where the consumer purchases none of good X, results when

$$\frac{MU_x}{P_x} < \frac{MU_i}{P_i} = \cdots = \frac{MU_j}{P_j},$$

for all goods i, j, and so on, where the ith and jth goods are purchased in positive amounts. The consumer spends the entire income, yet the marginal utility per dollar for the first unit of X is less than the marginal utility per dollar spent on the last units of all other goods that are purchased. Perhaps you do not own a BMW—you say you cannot afford one. Conceivably you could buy one, perhaps by borrowing the money. So, if you do not own one, it must be that the alternative expenditure on goods that you consume gives more utility *per dollar* than the BMW would, even though a BMW would give more total utility than your present automobile. Stated differently, one does not consume some good X when the $MRS_{x \text{ for } y}$ (where Y is any other good that is consumed) is less than the price ratio, P_x/P_y, and total income is exhausted.

5.7.5   Other Corner Solutions

It was mentioned earlier that empirically, consumers prefer variety in their consumption bundle. Theoretically this does not always have to be true; in fact, we have just used indifference curves and budget constraints to show that corner solutions can exist. We illustrated in Figure 5–13 a situation where only good Y was consumed, but it remained possible, given a change in relative prices, that the consumer maximized utility by consuming both X and Y. If we did not have convex indifference curves, but other shapes as shown in Figure 5–14, utility maximization would always occur at the corner, if there was a unique maximization point at all.

In Panel A of Figure 5–14, the indifference curves are strictly *concave*—they lie below their tangent lines at each point. The budget line is represented by LL'. The consumer optimizes by seeking the highest indifference curve touching the budget line. Usually, this is where the indifference curve and income line are tangent, but at point E, the tangency of indifference curve I and LL', the consumer actually minimizes the utility attainable with the given income. The highest attainable indifference curve is reached by moving upward along LL' until the consumer eventually hits point F on indifference curve II. At this point, the consumer purchases no X and spends the entire income on Y. It will always be the case when indifference curves are strictly concave that corner solutions are the point of consumer equilibrium. Consumers will never choose a variety of products when they maximize satisfaction.

Figure 5–14   Indifference Maps that Are Not Convex

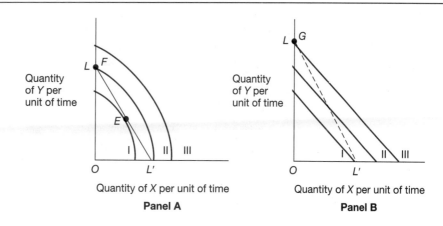

Panel A — Quantity of Y per unit of time (vertical), Quantity of X per unit of time (horizontal)

Panel B — Quantity of Y per unit of time (vertical), Quantity of X per unit of time (horizontal)

What kind of tastes would give a consumer concave indifference curves? The very shape of such a curve argues against variety. Starting at either endpoint, where only X or only Y is consumed, and moving along the indifference curve we see that the consumer is willing to give up more and more units of X or Y for each additional unit of the other good in order to remain at the same level of utility. In other words, variety is undesirable from the consumer's point of view. Indeed, when any budget line is added to the indifference curves in Panel A, it simply determines which corner of the graph maximizes utility.

Panel B shows some linear indifference curves. The budget line LL' is dashed to avoid confusing it with an indifference curve. Here, the marginal rate of substitution is constant; that is, the consumer is always willing to trade X and Y at the same rate, no matter how much the consumer has of each good. Since both the constraint and indifference curves are linear, there can be no optimizing tangency. If the lines have different slopes, the consumer maximizes utility at a corner, point G. The problem becomes unmanageable if the budget line and indifference curves have the same slope. Imagine the situation: one indifference curve perfectly superimposed over the budget line. No other indifference curves would even touch the constraint. The consumer would certainly know what level of utility was optimal, but would not know what mix of goods to consume on that indifference curve, because there would be an infinite number of optimal consumption bundles. Our theory would, therefore, predict indeterminant behavior. This does not accurately describe the real world—most consumers have definite ideas about what they want to purchase.

Panels A and B of Figure 5–14 are the two basic forms that indifference curves might take, other than the smooth convex shapes we have been using in our discussion. The result of the analysis is that the indifference maps in Figure 5–14 allow consumers in equilibrium little (or no) variety and/or substitution in their consumption of goods and services. Because this is generally not true of most consumers, we will continue working with the convex curves introduced at the beginning of this chapter.

Economics in the News

Psychologists and Economists Observe Inconsistent Preferences

Studies have shown that people are not always consistent about the choices they make. Two psychologists, Amos Tversky and Daniel Kahneman, have shown that people can change their preferences when the choice between two alternatives is reworded.[5] The way choices are presented to people is called *framing*. Kahneman and Tversky in their experiments have presented subjects with the following choice problem:

1. You've decided to see a Broadway play and have bought a $40 ticket. As you enter the theater, you realize you've lost your ticket. You can't remember the seat number, so you can't prove to the management that you bought a ticket. Would you spent $40 for a new ticket?

Most people answer no; they decide not to buy another ticket. We might think the lost ticket is the same as losing $40 in cash, and we might say to ourselves if we bought another $40 ticket the show would effectively cost us $80, which would indeed be the cost after buying two tickets.

But consider a slightly different circumstance:

2. You've reserved a seat for a Broadway play for which the ticket is $40. As you enter the theater to buy your ticket, you discover you've lost $40 from your pocket. Would you still buy the ticket? (Assume you have enough cash left to do so.)

Now the most likely answer is yes. Yet there really is no difference in the two cases. In both we might think the effective price of a ticket is $80. The only difference between the cases is that we lose the actual ticket in case A and the money to buy the ticket in case B. The way the problem is presented, however, makes most people answer differently in the two cases.

David Grether and Charles Plott, two economists, report similar results.[6] College students were given a choice between picking a ball from bingo cage A or bingo cage B. Each bingo cage had 36 balls numbered 1 to 36. In cage A, if ball 1 was picked, the subject lost $1 from a $7 balance. Any other selected ball paid $4. Hence, the probability of losing was 1/36; the probability of winning $4 was 35/36. If the game were repeated many times, a person could expect to win, on average, $3.86 [1/36 · (−1.00) + 35/36 · 4.00]. The rules for the other cage, cage B, were that balls 1–25 meant a loss of $1.50. Balls numbered 25–36 gave the subject a $16 payoff. If this game were played a lot, winnings would on average be $3.85 [25/36 · (−1.50) + 11/36 · 16.00]. Subjects were free to choose which bingo cage they wanted to play. A total of 273 subjects participated in the experiment. Of this number 99 chose to pick from bingo cage A. At the same time students were asked which cage was worth more to them to play; that is, what was the value of playing cage A or cage B? Of the 99 who chose to play A, 69 (70%) thought it was worth more to play B. Preferences definitely seem to be inconsistent for these people. If it was worth more to play B, why not choose to play B? For the 174 subjects who chose to play B, 22 (13%) thought it was more valuable to play from cage A. These people also show inconsistency in their behavior. It would seem that subjects would choose to play the game that they thought yielded the greatest value.

[5]See A. Tversky and D. Kahneman, "Judgment Under Uncertainty: Heuristic and Biases," *Science,* September 1974, pp. 1124–31.

[6]See D. Grether and C. Plott, "Economic Theory of Choice and the Preference Reversal Phenomenon," *American Economic Review,* September 1979, pp. 623–38.

5.8 Summary

In this chapter, we have developed the basic tools necessary to analyze consumer demand theory. Foremost are the concepts of indifference curves and budget lines. An indifference curve shows combinations of goods among which a consumer is indifferent. A consumer's preferences are reflected by all of the indifference curves that make up his or her indifference map. The slope of an indifference curve shows the rate at which a consumer is willing to substitute one good for another in order to remain at a constant level of utility. The slope is called the marginal rate of substitution.

The marginal rate of substitution can be related to marginal utility, which is the change in total utility caused by a one-unit change in a good's consumption. The marginal rate of substitution between two goods is the ratio of the two marginal utilities.

The budget line indicates combinations that the consumer is able to purchase with a given money income. The price ratio given by the market is the slope of the budget line. A change in money income moves the budget line inward or outward, parallel to the old line. A change in commodity prices pivots the budget line.

Generally, a consumer maximizes utility where the budget line is tangent to the indifference curve. This occurs for two goods X and Y when

$$MRS = \frac{MU_x}{MU_y} = \frac{P_x}{P_y} \text{ or } \frac{MU_x}{P_x} = \frac{MU_y}{P_y}.$$

For more than two goods, this same equality holds when utility is maximized. This is an important relation. Total benefit from consumption is maximized when the consumer equates marginal benefit per dollar across all goods consumed. It is a specific case of the constrained optimization problem discussed in Chapter 4.

Whenever

$$\frac{MU_x}{P_x} > \frac{MU_y}{P_y}$$

the per dollar utility from X at the margin is greater than the per dollar utility from Y. The consumer can increase utility by consuming more X and less Y, provided income is not already all spent on X, and the consumer maximizes utility at a corner on the indifference map. If the sign on the inequality is reversed, the consumer should spend more on good Y. In general, whenever there is not equality or

$$\frac{MU_x}{P_x} \lessgtr \frac{MU_y}{P_y}$$

the consumer should increase consumption of the good that has the greater marginal value per dollar and should continue doing this until equality is reached or all income is spent on just one good.

Answers to *Applying the Theory*

5.1 Trade-offs. These junk bonds typically have a much higher yield than the safer bonds. Corporations issuing these bonds are less stable financially than other companies and are forced to pay high interest rates to induce investors to take the risk of purchasing the bonds. The investors are willing to trade some amount of security for the higher yield. Quinn noted that junk-bond funds had come out winners because of their super-high rates of interest, which brought them comfortably into the black. These investors, therefore, have a marginal rate of substitution between security of return and high yields.

Technical Problems

1. Assume that an individual consumes three goods, X, Y, and Z. The marginal utility (assumed measurable) of each good is independent of the rate of consumption of other goods. The prices of X, Y, and Z are respectively $1, $3, and $5. The total income of the consumer is $65, and the marginal utility schedule is as follows:

Units of Good	Marginal Utility of X (units)	Marginal Utility of Y (units)	Marginal Utility of Z (units)
1	12	60	70
2	11	55	60
3	10	48	50
4	9	40	40
5	8	32	30
6	7	24	25
7	6	21	18
8	5	18	10
9	4	15	3
10	3	12	1

   a. Given a $65 income, how much of each good should the consumer purchase to maximize utility?
   b. Suppose income falls to $43 with the same set of prices; what combination will the consumer choose?
   c. Let income fall to $38; let the price of X rise to $5 while the prices of Y and Z remain at $3 and $5. How does the consumer allocate income? What would you say if the consumer maintained that X is not purchased because he or she cannot afford it?

2. The indifference curve I in Figure E.5–1 shows combinations of X and Y among which a consumer is indifferent.
   a. What is the consumer's MRS between combinations given by points A and B? B and C? C and D? D and E? Are your calculations consistent with the typical assumption about the slope of indifference curves? If so, in what ways?
   b. By drawing a tangent to I and calculating the slope of the tangent, what is the consumer's MRS at point B? at C? at D?
   c. What can you say about a combination that consists of 50Y and 40X? Of 30Y and 20X?

3. In Figure E. 5–2, suppose a consumer has the indicated indifference map and the budget line designated LZ. You know the price of Y is $5 per unit.
   a. What is the consumer's income?
   b. What is the price of X?

Figure E. 5–1

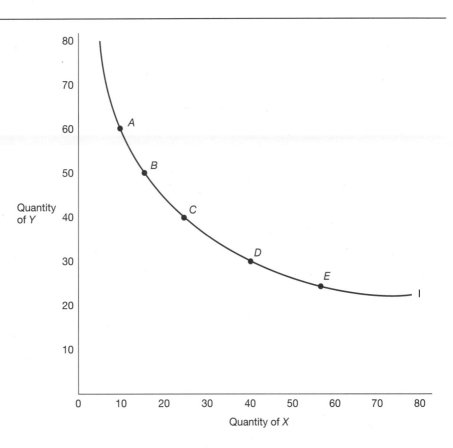

c. Write the equation for the budget line *LZ*.
d. What is the slope of *LZ*?
e. What combination of *X* and *Y* will the consumer choose? Why?
f. Explain precisely in terms of *MRS* why the consumer would not choose combinations designated by *B* or *C*.
  Suppose the budget line shifts to *L'Z'*.
g. At the same prices, what has happened to money income?
h. What combination is now chosen?
i. Draw the relevant budget line if money income remains at the original level (designated by *LZ*), the price of *Y* remains at $5, but the price of *X* rises to $10.
j. Draw an indifference curve showing the new equilibrium.
k. What are the new equilibrium quantities?
4. Figure E.5–3 shows the budget line for a consumer with a $1,200 income who purchases only *X* and *Y*.
  a. What are the prices of goods *X* and *Y*?
  b. What is the equation for the budget line?
  c. The prices of *X* and *Y* remain constant and income increases to $1,400. Draw the new budget line. What is the equation for this new budget line?

Figure E.5–2

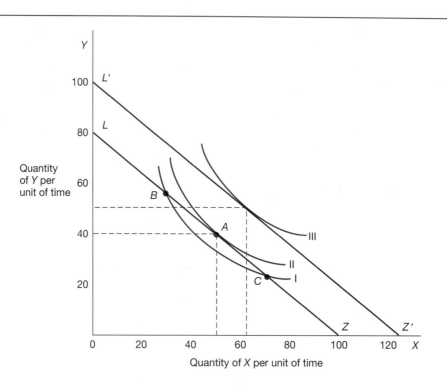

d. The prices of X and Y remain constant and income decreases to $960. Draw the new budget line. What is the equation for the new budget line?

e. The price of Y remains constant, income remains $1,200, and the price of X decreases to $20. Draw the new budget line. What is the equation for the new budget line?

f. The price of Y remains constant, income remains $1,200, and the price of X increases to $40. Draw the new budget line. What is the equation for the new budget line?

5. Suppose $MU_x = ay$ and $MU_y = ax$; $M = $ Income $= p_x x + p_y y$.

a. Fill in the following columns with answers that maximize consumer utility.

	(1) $M = 100$ $P_x = 10$ $P_y = 10$	(2) $M = 200$ $P_x = 20$ $P_y = 20$	(3) $M = 150$ $P_x = 10$ $P_y = 10$	(4) $M = 150$ $P_x = 10$ $P_y = 20$	(5) $M = 150$ $P_x = 10$ $P_y = 30$
x					
y					
x/y					

b. Using a preference map, graph each of the five utility-maximizing equilibria.

c. Explain your results when prices and income double between columns (1) and (2).

Figure E.5–3

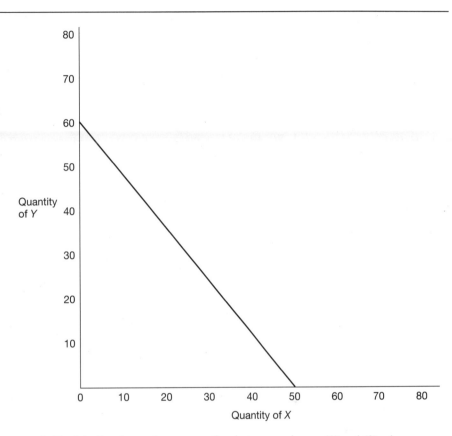

d. Explain the change in consumption between columns (1) and (3) when income is increased by 50.

e. In columns (3), (4), and (5), do your results seem reasonable after the price of Y is doubled and then tripled?

6. If a consumer's marginal rate of substitution is 4, at what rate is the consumer willing to trade Y for more X and remain indifferent. At what rate is the consumer willing to trade X for more Y and remain indifferent? What if the consumer's *MRS* = 1/4?

7. If the price of X is $6 and the price of Y is $2, at what rate does the market allow the consumer to trade Y for X? X for Y? What if the price of X is $9 and the price of Y is $3? What if the price of X is $4 and the price of Y is $2?

8. Use budget lines and indifference curves to analyze the effect of the following policies on the quantity demanded of some good, X.

   a. Government gives the individual $500.

   b. Government places a 5 percent tax on good X only.

   c. Government places a 5 percent tax on both goods.

9. A consumer is in equilibrium consuming zero X, a positive amount of Y, and spending the entire income. Assume typically shaped indifference curves.

   a. Why does the consumer buy no X? Explain in terms of the relation between the *MRS* and the price ratio.

b. Why does the consumer buy no *X*? Explain in terms of the marginal utilities of the two goods and the prices of the goods.

10. A consumer with an income of $100 is buying 15 units of *X* and 20 units of *Y*. The price *X* is $4 and the price of *Y* is $2. The marginal utility of the last unit of *X* is 40, and the marginal utility of the last unit of *Y* is 30.

   a. Is the consumer in equilibrium? Why or why not?

   b. At what rate does the market allow the consumer to trade *Y* for *X*? *X* for *Y*?

   c. At what rate is the consumer just willing to trade *Y* for *X* and remain indifferent? *X* for *Y*?

   d. What should the consumer do? Why? Answer in terms of what the market allows the consumer to do and what the consumer is just willing to do.

   e. Answer parts *a* through *d* of this question for a consumer with the same income, facing the same prices of the good, and purchasing the same amounts of the good, but for this consumer the last unit of *X* has a marginal utility of 60, and the last unit of *Y* has a marginal utility of 20.

11. *a.* A consumer is in equilibrium consuming two goods, *X* and *Y*. $P_x = \$4$, $P_y = \$10$, and $MU_x = 12$. What is the marginal utility of *Y*?

   b. A consumer is consuming 20 units of *X* and 40 units of *Y*. The marginal utility of the last units of *X* and *Y* is $MU_x = 20$ and $MU_y = 30$. The price of *X* is $4. The consumer should purchase more *X* and less *Y* if the price of *Y* is above_____ . Why? The consumer should purchase less of *X* and more *Y* if the price of *Y* is below_____ . Why?

   c. A consumer is purchasing 50 units of *X* and zero *Y*. The price of *X* is $20, the marginal utility of the last unit of *X* is 50, and the marginal utility of the first unit of *Y* would be 100. If the consumer is maximizing utility, the price of *Y* must be _____. Why?

   d. A consumer is purchasing two goods, *X* and *Y*, the prices of which are the same. The consumer would purchase equal amounts of both goods only if_____ .

   e. A consumer is purchasing no *X*. The marginal utility per dollar of all the other goods purchased is 8, and the marginal utility of the first unit of *X* purchased would be 24. Why doesn't the consumer buy any *X*? What would cause the consumer to purchase some *X*?

12. Figure E.5–4 shows the equilibrium for a consumer who spends the entire income of $400 on *Y* and buys no *X*.

   a. What is the price of *X*? The price of *Y*?

   b. Below what price (approximately) would the consumer buy some positive amount of *X*?

   c. At what price of *X* would the consumer buy 24 units of *X* and 35 units of *Y*?

13. A consumer has a choice of buying red marbles or blue marbles. The marbles are identical, except for color.

   a. Assume that the only use the consumer has for marbles is to put them in the bottom of a flower pot for drainage. Since dirt will cover the marbles, they will not be visible. Draw the consumer's indifference map.

   b. Assume that the only use for marbles is in producing light glitters, which require one red marble and two blue marbles to correctly filter the light. Draw the consumer's indifference map.

   c. Assume that this consumer is superstitious and believes that owning marbles that are not all the same color will bring bad luck. That is, he or she prefers

Figure E.5–4

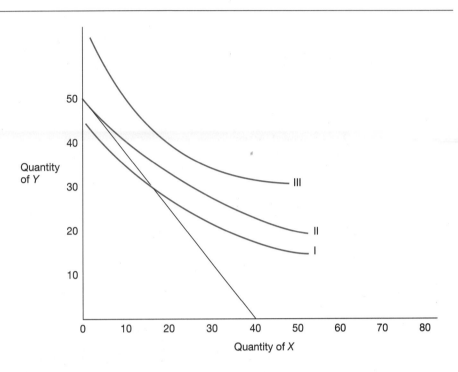

more marbles to less, but prefers any bundle of equal size containing only one color to one containing two colors. Draw this consumer's indifference map.

Analytical Problems

1. Researchers are intrigued by the fact that many of the people moving to small towns or into the country have willingly ignored economics to do so—passing up both better jobs and bigger paychecks. A lot of people are putting other concerns above jobs—a quiet scenic place that is safe for children, has less noise and congestion, and offers a slower pace of life. Are those people who move to small towns really ignoring economics? Use a preference map, plotting income on the vertical axis and small-town quality of life on the horizontal axis, to show how tastes are changing. Could you argue that the "price" of income is rising, relative to quality of life in a small town?

2. Increasingly, employees are being allowed to choose benefit packages from a menu of items. For instances, workers may be given a package of benefits that includes basic and optional items. Basics might include modest medical coverage, life insurance equal to a year's salary, vacation time based on length of service, and some retirement pay. But then employees can use credits to choose among such additional benefits as full medical coverage, dental and eye care, more vacation time, additional disability income, and higher company

payments to the retirement fund. How do you think flexible benefit packages will affect the employee's choice between higher wages and more benefits?

3. In many western states part-time ranchers raise cattle as a hobby. They work full time at blue- or white-collar jobs during the week and run the ranch during their spare time. Most of these part-time ranchers lose money on the venture. Illustrate the utility-maximizing equilibrium for these people with income (or profit) on the vertical axis and ranching on the horizontal axis. Are these people profit maximizers?

4. It was estimated that by 1994 there will be 70,000 more doctors than the number needed. Many doctors worry that unnecessary surgery will increase. Can medical surgery be either necessary or unnecessary? Isn't medical care like any other service; when the price falls the quantity sold increases? Using an indifference curve and budget line, show that when the price of medical care falls, more will be purchased.

5. When shopping for something such as groceries, consumers frequently only buy one brand of an item. For example, they generally don't buy some Tropicana, Kraft, and Minute Maid orange juice or some Folger's coffee and some Maryland Club coffee. For other items consumers often buy two or more brands. For example, they may buy some Pepsi and some 7UP or some Cheerios and some Kellogg's Corn Flakes or some Campbell's soup and some Progresso soup. How would consumer behavior theory explain each type of behavior?

6. The theory of consumer behavior would predict that, by and large, when people shop, they purchase the brand that they believe will give the highest marginal utility (or as a proxy the highest quality or quantity) per dollar spent on the brand. Could the following grocery shoppers conform to the theory (not do they, but could they)? Why or why not?

   a. When Jessica shops for most goods at the grocery store, she carefully compares the size or quantity and the price. For example, she always would buy the brand of paper towels that gives the most sheets per dollar. For some goods, however, price seems to make no difference. For example, she always buys Pepsi, even when Coke is priced lower.

   b. Donald generally chooses the brand with the highest price.

   c. On the other hand, Trisha generally chooses the brand with the lowest price.

   d. Barbara always takes $40 to the grocery store, then walks up and down the isles choosing groceries until the $40 is all spent.

   e. Steve carefully makes up a grocery list, which he takes to the store. However, he frequently does not buy some items on the list and spontaneously buys some items that are not listed.

   f. Chuck generally buys the brand that is "marked down," even if it isn't the lowest-priced brand.

7. Can you think of any example in which a consumer would not give up a single unit of a particular good, no matter what is offered in exchange? What type of goods would these be?

8. The notion that all consumers allocate their expenditures to equate price ratios to marginal rates of substitution, or marginal utility ratios, is unreasonable. Since consumers differ in terms of income, tastes, and preferences, they would follow different behavioral rules. Discuss.

9. Explain how the theory of consumer behavior developed in this chapter could be adopted to take account of the following cases:

   a. People give away money or goods-in-kind as charitable contributions.

   b. People typically don't like garbage or trash.

   c. People spend money on dentist visits, which they typically don't enjoy.

10. Have you ever made mistakes such as the following: studying too long for a test that turned out to be easy, not studying long enough for a test that turned out to be extremely hard, agreeing to go on a blind date that turned out to be miserable, buying a package of cookies that were so bad you threw most of them away, and not buying enough potato chips and soft drinks for a party? Does the possibility that people make mistakes necessarily contradict or negate the theory of consumer behavior? Discuss.

11. Suppose inflation causes the price level to double, but all prices do not change in the same proportion. If someone's income increases just enough so that he or she can buy precisely the same amount of each good that was previously purchased, will that consumer be worse off, better off, or equally well off? (Hint: use the two-good case with budget lines and an indifference curve.)

12. This question anticipates future material. Curly, Moe, and Larry go on a picnic. Curly and Moe each bring 9 pies and 12 sandwiches. Larry forgets to bring any food at all, and the others won't share. Larry, knowing that Curly's marginal rate of substitution of sandwiches (S) for pie (P) is 3 ($-\Delta S/\Delta P$) and Moe's *MRS* is 6, offers to trade Moe one pie for 5 sandwiches and to trade Curly 4 sandwiches for one pie, keeping for himself the leftover sandwich. Explain how all three stooges are made better off by the deal.

13. In this chapter we briefly mentioned preference change. Explain how the following could change a consumer's marginal rate of substitution (the slope of an indifference curve).

   a. Michael Jordan, Magic Johnson, and Larry Bird all announce that they have switched to Reeboks.

   b. Scientists discover that chicken, not beef, raises people's cholesterol level.

   c. A doctor tells a patient that drinking wine is the cause of the patient's stomach disorder.

14. Suppose it is possible for a group of people to have community indifference curves. If a city government spends money on crime prevention or pollution reduction, how is it possible for the city to have too little crime or not enough pollution reduction?

CHAPTER 6

Theory of Consumer Behavior: Changes in Income and Price

6.1 Introduction

Having developed the concept of utility maximization, we are prepared to analyze the effect of changes in two important determinants of a demand curve—the consumer's income and the price of the good. In Chapter 2 we emphasized that the theory of demand is concerned primarily with the effect of changes in price, other things held constant. One of the things held constant along a demand curve is income; but when prices change, there is a change in purchasing power. Even though the dollar amount of income does not change, the quantity of goods and services that can be purchased with a fixed income changes when prices change. For example, when the price of something you are currently purchasing rises, you are made worse off because you can no longer buy the same combination of goods and services with the same fixed income. Alternatively, when the price of something you are purchasing falls, you are better off because you can buy the same combination as before and still have some income left over to buy other things. In terms of the budget line, we pointed out in Chapter 5 that the maximum amount of good X a consumer could purchase with a given income was M/P_x. If the price falls to P_x', the consumer could purchase more—M/P_x', units—creating an increase in purchasing power. This increase in purchasing power is called a change in *real income*. With a constant money income, real income cannot be held constant when prices change. Thus, it is impossible to discuss the impact of a price change on consumer behavior without addressing how consumers are affected by changes in real income.

In this chapter, we will examine price and income effects in some depth, and we will discuss in detail the reasons economists assume that demand curves slope downward. When you finish this chapter, you should have a thorough understanding of the underpinnings of demand theory.

6.1.1 A Parallel Shift in the Budget Line

The first part of this chapter is devoted to analyzing in more detail the effect of changes in money income, which cause parallel shifts in the budget line, as discussed in Chapter 5. If the consumer was in equilibrium before an increase in income, after the increase there will be a new equilibrium on the higher budget line tangent to a higher indifference curve. The increase in income extends the set of the consumer's consumption possibilities, thereby making the consumer better off. The new equilibrium on the higher indifference curve is attained by following the same optimization rule—the marginal rate of substitution is set equal to the price ratio. The effect of a decrease in money income is analyzed similarly; the budget line shifts downward, and equilibrium is attained on a lower indifference curve since the set of consumption opportunities has decreased.

6.1.2 A Pivot in the Budget Line

The second part of this chapter is concerned with how consumers behave when the budget line pivots. A change in the price of a good, money income held constant, rotates the budget line—outward for a decrease in price, inward for an increase. This chapter will explain the consumer's reaction to a price change in more detail. Suppose a consumer begins in equilibrium then the price of the good decreases. Since the budget line rotates outward, the set of consumption opportunities available to the individual is increased, and the consumer is made better off. The good with the reduced price is now less expensive, relative to other goods. The consumer will tend to substitute consumption away from other goods to the now relatively cheaper good. Economists call this effect on consumption the *substitution effect*. The fall in price also increases the consumer's total consumption opportunities—more goods can be bought with the same money income. This includes all goods, but in particular the now less-expensive commodity. Economists call this part of the price effect the *income effect*.

The combination of these two effects leads to a new equilibrium situation, where the new budget line, which has rotated outward, is tangent to a higher indifference curve. The entire change is a combination of both the income and substitution effects. After the adjustment, the marginal rate of substitution equals the new price ratio.

The effect of an increase in price is symmetrical. The budget line rotates inward, leading to a new tangency on a lower indifference curve. The income effect follows, because the consumer now has a smaller set of consumption possibilities and is, therefore, worse off. Since the price of the good increases relative to that of other goods, the substitution effect involves a shift in consumption away from the now more-expensive good to other goods.

Figure 6–1   Income-Consumption Curve

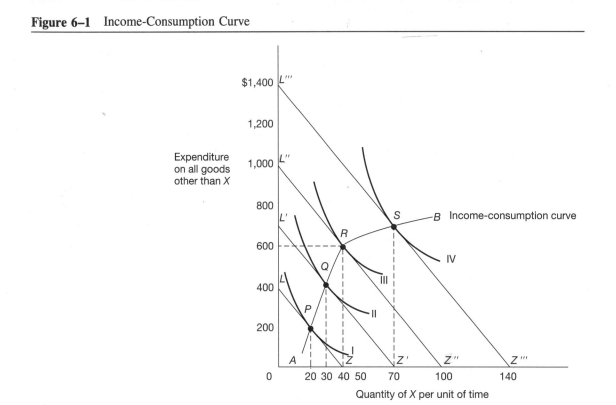

6.2   Changes in Money Income: Parallel Shifts in the Budget Line

In this section we analyze graphically the effect of changes in money income on
the quantity of a good purchased, holding the price of the good constant. As before,
we plot the quantity of some good, X, along the horizontal axis. However, rather
than plotting the quantity of some other good, Y, along the vertical axis, we plot
the expenditure on all goods other than X. The unit of measure along the vertical
axis is now dollars. Such a graph is shown in Figure 6–1.

When a consumer is choosing the quantity of good X and the amount to spend
on other goods, rather than the quantity of good Y, the budget constraint is

$$E = M - P_x Q_x,$$

where E is expenditure of all goods other than X and M is, as before, money income.
If the consumer buys no X and the entire income is spent on other goods, $E = M$
and the vertical intercept of the budget is M. As before, if the entire income is
spent on X, $E = 0$ and the consumer can purchase M/P_x units of X, which is the
horizontal intercept. The slope of the budget line is $-P_x$. Thus, for each unit of
X purchased, the consumer must give up P_x dollars spent on other goods.

6.2.1   The Income-Consumption Curve

In Figure 6–1, each indifference curve, I–IV, indicates the various combinations of X and expenditure on other goods that yield the same level of utility. Higher levels of utility are indicated by the higher-numbered indifference curves. Assume that the price of X is fixed at $10 per unit and that, initially, the consumer has an income of $1,000, indicated by budget line $L''Z''$. A consumer can spend all income on X and purchase 100 units, buy no X and spend $1,000 on other goods, or can purchase any combination along $L''Z''$. Each unit of X purchased forces the consumer to spend $10 less on other goods. The slope of $L''Z''$ is, therefore, $-$$10. From Chapter 5, utility is maximized at point R on indifference curve III, indicating that the highest available level of utility is attained at 40 units of X and $600 spent on other goods.

If income decreases to $700, the new budget line is $L'Z'$. Equilibrium is now at Q, with 30 units of X and $400 spent on other goods. A decrease in income to $400 shifts the budget line to LZ, causing the consumer to purchase 20 units of X and spend $200 on other goods. Finally, if income increases to $1,400 ($L'''Z'''$), the budget line is tangent to indifference curve IV at 70 units of X and $700. The figure illustrates that as income changes, the point of consumer equilibrium changes as well. The line connecting the successive equilibria is called the *income-consumption curve*, indicated by AB in Figure 6–1. This curve shows the equilibrium combinations of X and expenditure on goods other than X at various levels of money income, prices remaining constant throughout.

Definition

> The line connecting all the points showing consumer equilibria at various levels of money income with constant prices is called the *income-consumption curve*.

6.2.2   Engel Curves and Income Elasticity

Engel curves, named after the 19th-century German statistician Ernst Engel, show the relation between money income and the consumption of a particular good, other things, including the price of the good, held constant. These curves are closely related to income elasticity of a good, discussed briefly in Chapter 2, and are important for applied studies of economic welfare and for the analysis of family expenditure patterns. We can derive an Engel curve from the income-consumption curve.

The Engel curve pictured in Figure 6–2 is constructed from the income-consumption curve in Figure 6–1. Here, the quantity of good X is plotted along the horizontal axis, money income along the vertical axis. Point P' in Figure 6–2, showing that with an income of $400 the consumer purchases 20 units of X, is associated with point P in Figure 6–1. It follows that Q', 30 units of X at an income of $700, is associated with point Q. Likewise, R' and S' are equivalent to R and S, respectively. Not all income-consumption curves and Engel curves have the same general slope as this one. In some cases, the income-consumption curve may even bend backward, in which case the Engel curve will slope downward.

Figure 6–2   Engel Curve

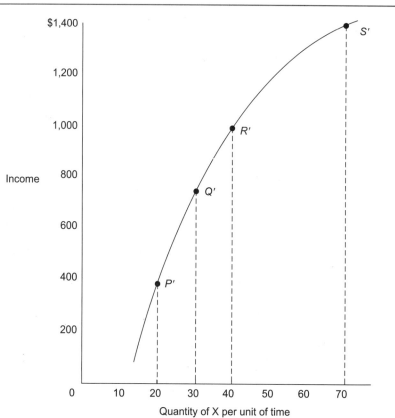

Definition

An Engel curve is the locus of points showing the equilibrium or utility-maximizing quantity of some good for each level of money income, the price of the good held constant. Such curves are readily derived from income-consumption curves.

The sensitivity of quantity demanded to changes in income, other things remaining the same, is measured by the coefficient of income elasticity (E_M). Specifically, the income elasticity of demand is the ratio of the percentage change in quantity demanded to the percentage change in money income. We write this as

$$E_M = \frac{\%\Delta Q_D}{\%\Delta M} = \frac{\Delta Q_D/Q_D}{\Delta M/M} = \frac{\Delta Q_D}{\Delta M} \cdot \frac{M}{Q_D} \gtrless 0.$$

Note that we do not know the sign of E_M, as was the case for demand elasticity. The sign depends on the sign of the term $\Delta Q_D/\Delta M$, which may be positive, negative, or zero. We can write this term somewhat differently as

$$\frac{\Delta Q_D}{\Delta M} = \frac{1}{\Delta M/\Delta Q_D},$$

where the denominator in the right-hand ratio is the slope of the Engel curve. Thus, E_M is positive or negative, according to whether the slope of the Engel curve is positive or negative.

Just as there was an arc elasticity formula for demand elasticity, there is also one for income elasticity, when there are discrete changes in the levels of income. Between two points on the Engel curve, or for any two income levels, the average elasticity is

$$\overline{E}_M = \frac{Q_1 - Q_0}{(Q_1 + Q_0)/2} \div \frac{M_1 - M_0}{(M_1 + M_0)/2} = \frac{Q_1 - Q_0}{Q_1 + Q_0} \div \frac{M_1 - M_0}{M_1 + M_0}$$

The subscripts 0 and 1 refer, respectively, to the initial and new quantity purchased and corresponding income levels.

Principle

The income elasticity of demand measures the sensitivity of the consumption of a good when income changes. Income elasticity may be negative, zero, or positive. The sign of the slope of the Engel curve and the sign of the elasticity of income coefficient, E_M, are always the same.

Economics in the News[1]

The Income-Consumption Line Gets Flat for Food Calories and Variety

In developing countries, whose populations are poor, the income elasticity of calorie consumption (Q_c) is substantially lower than the income elasticity of food expenditure (*FE*). In terms of the definition of income elasticities this means

$$\frac{\Delta Q_c}{\Delta M} \cdot \frac{Q_c}{M} < \frac{\Delta FE}{\Delta M} \cdot \frac{FE}{M},$$

where food expenditure is the amount of a household's income that is spent on food.

One explanation for these differences in income elasticities is that as incomes rise, consumers value food variety as well as nutrition, as measured by calorie intake. Thus, if we think of calories on the vertical axis and food variety on the horizontal axis, as shown in the diagram below, the income-consumption curve tends to get flat as income increases.

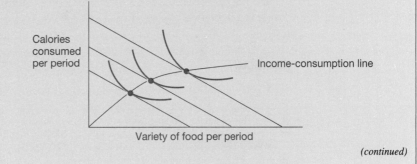

(continued)

[1]This report is based on Jere R. Behrman and Anil Deolalikar, "Is Variety the Spice of Life? Implications for Calorie Intake," *The Review of Economics and Statistics,* 71, no. 4 (November 1989), pp. 666–72.

Calorie intake becomes constant as income rises, but more income is spent on food in order to increase variety.

If this income consumption line applies to rich countries as well as poor countries, it suggests that food variety is an important part of any household's preferences. Also, governments and international agencies, such as the United Nations and World Bank, are faced with the prospect that efforts to increase calorie consumption in poor countries *with income increases,* or income policies in general, will be hampered by a household's desire to substitute variety for calories. Even in relatively poor countries, individuals do not behave as if adequate calorie intake is the only priority in their food consumption.

This behavior suggests that instead of changing income, calorie intakes can be increased more effectively by lowering the relative price of high-calorie foods. Reduced prices would cause consumers to substitute toward the higher-calorie food.

6.2.3   Normal and Inferior Goods

Looking at Figures 6–1 and 6–2, you can see that the relation between money income and the amount of the good consumed is such that, as income increases, the amount of the good consumed increases, the prices of all goods held constant. That is, in such cases, the income-consumption curves do not bend backward, and the Engel curve does not slope downward. Such a good is called a *normal good* over the relevant income levels. Because more of the good is purchased as money income increases, the income-consumption curve and the Engel curve are positively sloped for a normal good.

In the case of a normal good, the income elasticity of the good is also positive. From the formula for income elasticity shown above, $(\Delta Q_D / Q_D) \div (\Delta M / M) > 0$. Normal goods are given that name because economists in the past believed that an increase in income usually causes an increase in the consumption of a good—they believed this was the "normal" situation. However, an increase in income may well cause a decrease in the consumption of certain commodities at certain price ratios. These commodities are called *inferior goods.* For inferior goods, $(\Delta Q_D / Q_D) \div (\Delta M / M) < 0$. We contrast normal and inferior goods in the following definition.

Definition

A good is normal if its income elasticity is positive; it is inferior if its income elasticity is negative. The Engel curve for a normal good is positively sloped. The Engel curve for an inferior good is negatively sloped.

Figure 6–3 illustrates a good that is inferior over a certain range of incomes. Begin with an income shown by budget line *LZ.* Point *P* indicates x_1 is the equilibrium quantity of *X* for the consumer. Next, let income increase to the level shown by $L'Z'$, prices held constant. After the change, the position of consumer equilibrium

Figure 6–3 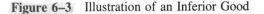 Illustration of an Inferior Good

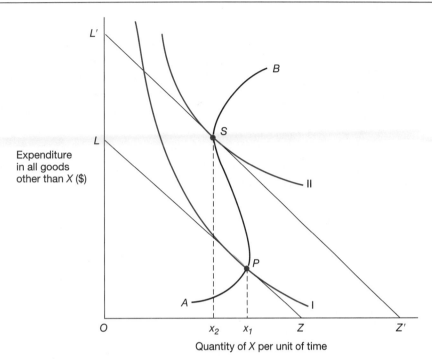

shifts from point P to point S. The consumer is better off, as indicated by the higher indifference curve. But the increase in income leads to a *decrease* in the consumption of X, to x_2. Thus, good X is inferior over the range of incomes denoted by LZ and $L'Z'$. Over this range, the income-consumption curve bends backward. Since this curve bends backward, the income elasticity of demand $(\Delta Q_D/\Delta M) \cdot (M/Q_D)$ is negative. Over this range of income the Engel curve also bends backward. Notice that over some ranges of income, the good may be normal for the consumer, such as movements from A to P and from S to B.

Inferiority and normality—and therefore, of course, income elasticity—vary over different ranges of income. Hamburger may be a normal good for one family over a particular range of incomes. It may be an inferior good over another range of incomes. Furthermore, the classification of goods as inferior or normal depends on the price ratio, which changes the slope of a budget line. At one price ratio, a good may have an income elasticity substantially different from the income elasticity at another price ratio. Economists frequently point out examples of inferior goods— margarine, hamburgers, and subcompact cars. As income increases, many people may reduce their consumption of these goods, but others may not. Therefore, remember that inferiority and normality are not inherent properties of the goods themselves. Income elasticities depend on preference patterns of consumers, prices, and the range of incomes.

Economics in the News

Recent Estimates Show that Beverages Consumed at Home Are Inferior Goods

It is widely recognized that as household income rises, households eat out more. In many high-income households both spouses are working professionals, which reduces the time a family has for cooking and eating at home. Therefore, no one should be surprised that the *at-home consumption* of many beverages shows a negative income elasticity, which of course means that they are inferior goods. This inferiority covers a broad range of drinks.

Dale Heien and Greg Pompelli recently published the income elasticities of eight beverage groups.[2] Their data come from 14,000 household surveys conducted in 1977 and 1978. The reported income elasticities are shown below:

Beverage Group	Income Elasticity
Coffee	− .19
Tea	− .04
Soft drinks	− .19
Beer	− .37
Distilled spirits	− .51
Wine	− .40
Juices	− .16
Milk	− .15

The drinks most sensitive to rising incomes are beer, distilled spirits, and wine. Tea, milk, and juices are least sensitive. These elasticities convey a great deal of information to producers. It tells them what happens across communities as per capita income changes.[3] Wealthier communities will consume less at home. Therefore, less advertising, for example, should be directed toward home buying (e.g., grocery specials). More effort should be given to placing the product in restaurants and with restaurant suppliers. Fast-food establishments tend to be dominated by one soft-drink company or another, for example, Pepsi at Pizza Hut and Coke at McDonalds. Wineries should more vigorously seek to have their wines placed on the lists of restaurants and, perhaps, to be labeled as the house wine.

6.2.4   Income-Consumption Curves and Demand Curves

Income changes, embodied in the income-consumption curve, shift the demand schedule for the good. Each equilibrium point on the income-consumption curve means there is a new demand curve. If the goods are normal, increases in income shift demand to the right. In the case of inferior goods, demand decreases or shifts to the left when income increases. Figure 6–4, Panels A and B show how demand shifts for a normal good as we move along the income-consumption curve.

[2]See D. Heien and G. Pompelli, "The Demand for Alcoholic Beverages: Economic and Demographic Effects," *Southern Economic Journal*, 55, no. 1 (January 1989) pp. 759–70.

[3]Heien and Pompelli also break down the income elasticities by region. The data set would even allow some income elasticity estimates to be made for counties and cities.

Figure 6–4   The Income-Consumption Line and Demand

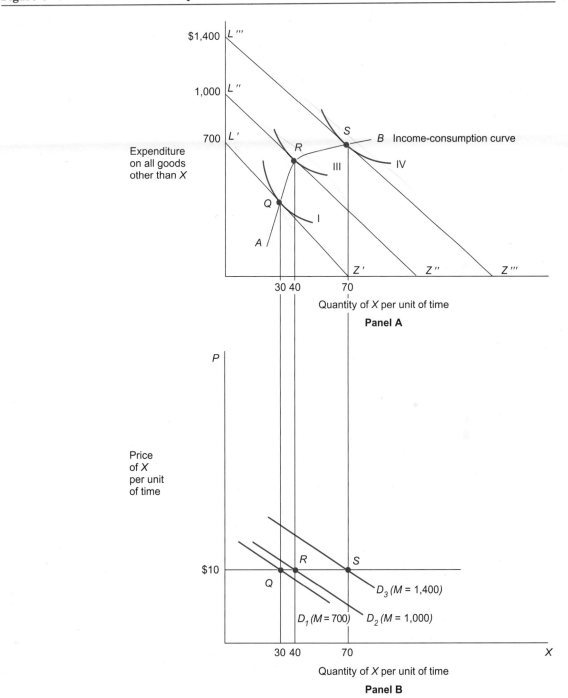

Figure 6–5   Price-Consumption Curve

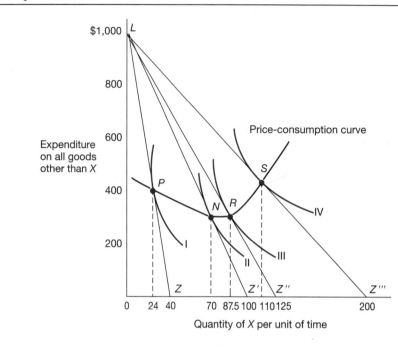

Panel A in Figure 6–4 is identical to Figure 6–1, except only points Q, R, and S are shown. As income rises from $700 to $1,000 to $1,400, the amount of X purchased also increases from 30 to 40 to 70 units. Demand is shown in Panel B, below the income-consumption picture, with the scale of the horizontal axis identical to that in Panel A. Since the price of X does not change, the quantities purchased are those quantities at the $10 price. For each Q, R, S, equilibrium point on the income-consumption curve there is a corresponding Q, R, S, equilibrium point on the three demand schedules D_1, D_2, and D_3. Because the same picture could be drawn at other prices, demand shifts to the right as income increases.

6.1   *Applying the Theory*

What does a preference map look like for a good that is neither normal nor inferior? This means that the elasticity of income is precisely zero and that as income changes, there is no change in the quantity purchased. Describe the income-consumption curve. Does the demand curve shift when income changes?

6.3   **Demand Curves: Pivots in the Budget Line**

The demand curve shows the effect of price on the consumption of goods. In this section, we hold money income constant and let price change in order to determine the effect of price changes on quantity purchased.

6.3.1   Price-Consumption Curves

Similar to Engel curves, demand curves are derived by moving the budget line and observing the various points of tangency to indifference curves. In this case, rather than a parallel shift in the budget line, there is a rotation of the line, as mentioned in the introduction to this chapter.

Figure 6–5 contains a portion of an indifference map for a consumer who can consume X (measured in units along the horizontal axis) and goods other than X. The total expenditure on these other goods is measured in dollars and is plotted along the vertical axis. The consumer has a money income of $1,000. When X is priced at $25 per unit, the consumer's budget line is LZ. This consumer can spend the $1,000 on other goods, can spend the entire $1,000 on 40 units of X at $25 per unit, or can spend at any point along LZ. You know by now that the consumption bundle represented at point P, where LZ is tangent to indifference curve I, is optimal. The consumer purchases 24 units of X, spending $600 on this commodity. The remaining $400 is spent on other goods.

Assume that the price of X falls to $10. Now, a consumer who wishes to spend all income on X can purchase 100 units. The budget line at the new price is LZ', with a slope of -10 rather than -25. The new equilibrium point of tangency is designated by N, where the individual consumes 70 units of X at a total expense of $700 and spends the remaining $300 on other goods. If price falls to $8 per unit, other things remaining the same, the new budget line is LZ'', with a slope of -8. At equilibrium point R, the consumer purchases 87.5 units of X. Note that $700 is still spent on X and $300 on all other goods. Finally, when the price of X falls to $5, the new budget line, LZ''', is tangent to indifference curve IV at point S. The maximum utility level is attained by spending $550 on 110 units of X and $450 on goods other than X. Therefore, each price decrease causes the consumer to purchase more units of X. The line joining points P, N, R, and S (and all other equilibria) is called the *price-consumption curve*. For a given money income, it shows the amount of X consumed as its price changes, other prices remaining the same.

Definition

> The price-consumption curve is the set of equilibrium points relating the quantity of X purchased to its price, money income and all other prices remaining constant. In the case shown above, the price-consumption curve also shows how expenditure on all goods other than X changes as the price of X changes.

6.3.2   Derivation of Demand Curves from Price-Consumption Curves

The individual's demand curve for a commodity can be derived from the price-consumption curve, just as an Engel curve can be derived from the income-consumption curve. The price-quantity relations for good X at points P, N, R, and S, and presumably for all other points on the price consumption curve in Figure 6–5, are plotted in Figure 6–6. The horizontal axis is the same (units of X), but the

Figure 6–6   Demand Curve

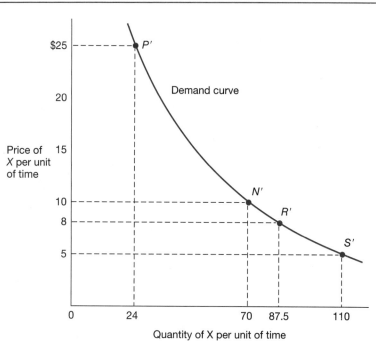

vertical axis now shows the price of X. When the price of X is $25, given by the slope of LZ, 24 units of X are purchased, indicated by point P' in Figure 6–6. If the price is $10, 70 units are purchased (point N'), and so forth. All other points on the curve are derived similarly. The line connecting these points is the demand curve for X.

Definition

The demand curve of an individual for a specific commodity relates the equilibrium quantities purchased to market price, money income and nominal prices of all other commodities held constant. The slope of the demand curve illustrates the law of demand: quantity demanded varies inversely with price—income and the prices of other commodities held constant.

6.3.3   Demand Elasticity and the Price-Consumption Curve

From the relation between the change in total expenditure on a good and a good's demand elasticity, we can determine by the shape of the price-consumption curve in Figure 6–5 that the demand curve in Figure 6–6 is elastic between $25 and $10, has unitary elasticity between $10 and $8, and is inelastic between $8 and $5. This can be done without actually calculating the elasticity. Recall from Chapter 3 that if the price of a good falls, total expenditure on the good increases (decreases) if the demand is elastic (inelastic). Total expenditure remains constant if the demand curve is of unitary elasticity. When price falls from $25 to $10, money income remaining constant at $1,000, equilibrium moves from point P to N in Figure 6–5. It is clear that the movement involves a decrease in expenditure on all goods other than X. Since money income remains constant, expenditure on X must rise and demand must be in the elastic range. The fall in price from $10 to $8 moves the equilibrium from N to R. Since expenditure on all other goods stays the same, with money income constant expenditure on X stays the same and elasticity is unitary over the range $10 to $8. The fall in price from $8 to $5 moves equilibrium from R to S; expenditure on all other goods now increases. Hence, expenditure on X decreases and demand is necessarily inelastic over this range. The demand curve in Figure 6–6 is elastic at high prices, becomes unitary, and becomes inelastic at lower prices.

6.4   Substitution and Income Effects

We will now set forth a more complete analysis of why demand curves slope downward. Recall from the introduction to this chapter that there are two effects of a price change. If price falls (rises), the good becomes cheaper (more expensive) relative to other goods, and consumers substitute toward (away from) that good. This is called the *substitution effect*. Also, as price falls (rises), a consumer's purchasing power increases (decreases). Since the set of consumption opportunities increases (decreases), consumers change the mix of their consumption bundles. This effect is called the *income effect*. We will analyze each effect in turn, then combine the two in order to see why demand is assumed to slope downward.

6.4.1   Substitution Effect

We begin our analysis of the substitution effect with a definition:

Definition

> The substitution effect of a price change is the change in the consumption of a good resulting from a price change if the consumer is forced to stay on the same indifference curve.

We want to emphasize that the substitution effect is the change in consumption caused by a price change *when the consumer is held to the original indifference curve*. Thus, the substitution effect comes from the movement of a budget line along one indifference curve. When the budget line pivots and the consumer changes from one equilibrium to another, the substitution effect is that part of the change in consumption due to the new slope of the budget line and not to its outward movement.

A numerical example may help distinguish the substitution effect from the total effect of a price change on a consumer. Suppose an individual with a $100 income regularly chooses between a sandwich (S) or the salad bar (B) at lunch. The sandwich lunch is $2, the salad bar is $4. Over several months this person chooses a sandwich 30 times and the salad bar 10 times. Suppose the marginal utility (MU_S)

of the last sandwich is 40; for the last salad the marginal utility (MU_B) is 80. This person is optimizing his or her utility, because (a) all income is spent:

$$(\$2 \times 30) + (\$4 \times 10) = \$100,$$

and (b) marginal utilities per dollar are equal:

$$\frac{MU_S}{P_S} = \frac{40}{2} = \frac{MU_B}{P_B} = \frac{80}{4}.$$

Now suppose the price of the salad bar falls to $2, so both the sandwich lunch and the salad lunch have the same price. Now, with the same combination of salad and sandwiches, the consumer is no longer in equilibrium for two reasons. First, for the same number of lunches all of the $100 income is not spent. At $2, salad expenditure is only $80. Thus, the purchasing power of the $100 income has risen, and the consumer can buy the same number of meals for $20 less.

The second reason the consumer is out of equilibrium is that the marginal utilities per dollar are no longer equal. That is

$$\frac{40}{2} = 20 < \frac{80}{2} = 40.$$

The utility per dollar on the salad is larger than it is for sandwiches. The consumer, in order to optimize and find a new equilibrium, should shift some lunch expenditure away from sandwiches toward the now less-expensive salads. This shift is called the substitution effect, and it would take place regardless of the fact that the consumer has $20 more to spend. Indeed, the government could tax this person $20, leaving only $80 to spend, and the substitution toward salads would still occur.

However, the fact that the consumer can buy the same number of meals for $20 less will probably cause the consumer to spend a little more on lunches and on other goods and services. This $20 is likely to get spread across the whole set of purchases made by the consumer. The extra salads bought by the consumer with part of this $20 is called the income effect.

6.4.2   Graphical Analysis of the Substitution Effect

In Figure 6–7, Panel A, *LZ* is the original budget line, giving an equilibrium at point *A* on indifference curve I. The equilibrium quantity of *X* is x_1. Now let the price of *X* *decrease,* so that the new budget line is *LZ'*. You know from the theory that the consumer will now move to a new equilibrium tangency on the new budget line *LZ'*.

But suppose we place the following restriction on the consumer: After the decrease in the price of *X*, the consumer's money income is reduced just enough to force a tangency to the original indifference curve I. That is, at the new price ratio given by the slope of *LZ'*, reduce income so that a budget line with the same slope (same price ratio) as *LZ'* is tangent to I. This new budget line is shown as *RT,* parallel to *LZ'*, but tangent to I. With the new budget line, *RT,* showing the new price ratio, the consumer maximizes utility at point *B,* consuming x_2 units of *X*.

Figure 6–7   Substitution Effects

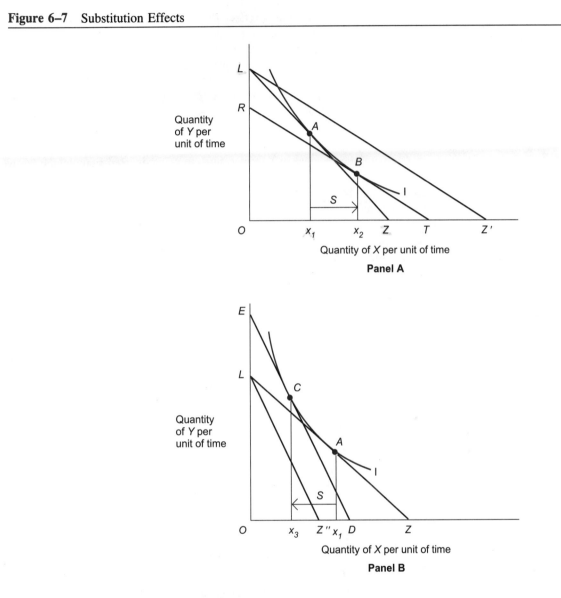

Panel A

Panel B

The consumer is neither better nor worse off, being on the same indifference curve as before. The movement from A to B, or the change in consumption from x_1 to x_2, is the substitution effect, designated by the arrow labeled S.

Considering the impact of a price change along an indifference curve, a decrease in price must lead to increased consumption of the good. That is, a fall in the price of X reduces the slope of the budget line. Because of the convex shape of indifference curves, the less steeply sloped budget line must become tangent to the original indifference curve at a greater quantity of X. Thus $\Delta X/\Delta P_x$, for the substitution effect only, must be negative.

Panel B shows the substitution effect for an *increase* in the price of X. As in Panel A, begin with budget line *LZ* tangent to indifference curve I at point *A;* x_1 units of good X are consumed in equilibrium. The price of X now rises, causing the budget line at the given money income to rotate to *LZ''*. Again we know that, money income held constant, the new equilibrium will be along *LZ''*.

Now, *increase the consumer's income* at the new price ratio, shown by the slope of *LZ''*, until a budget line with the new, steeper slope is just tangent to the original indifference curve I. This is shown by the budget line *ED,* tangent to I at point *C*. In this case, the consumption of X is x_3 units. The substitution effect is the movement from *A* to *C*, or the decrease in X from x_1 units to x_3, designated again by the arrow labeled *S*.

Considering the substitution effect only, the *increase* in the price of X causes a reduction in the consumption of X. This must always be the case. An increase in the price of X makes the budget line steeper, so the new point of tangency must come where the indifference curve is steeper. After a price increase, tangency must come at a lower consumption of X.

We have established the following principle:

Principle

The substitution effect is the change in the consumption of a good after a change in price, when the consumer is forced by a change in money income to consume at some point on the original indifference curve. Considering the substitution effect only, the amount of the good consumed must vary inversely with its price. That is, utility held constant, $\Delta Q_D/\Delta P < 0$.

6.4.3   Income Effect

While we have established the direction of the substitution effect, we cannot be as certain about how the income effect influences the quantity of X purchased. Before we examine the income effect, let us define it:

Definition

The income effect from a price change is the change in the consumption of a good resulting strictly from a change in purchasing power, that is, a change in real income.

The income effect is shown graphically in Figure 6–8. We begin with budget line *LZ*. The consumer is in equilibrium at point *P* on indifference curve I, consuming x_1 units of X. Let the price of X fall, causing the budget line to rotate outward to *LZ'*. We can isolate the substitution effect by reducing money income and forcing the new budget line at the new price ratio to move back until a new line with the same slope as *LZ'* is just tangent to I. Such a budget line is *AB*, tangent to I at *N*, where the consumer chooses x_2 units of X. In this case, the substitution effect of the price decrease shows an increase in the consumption of X from x_1 to x_2, shown as *S* in Figure 6–8.

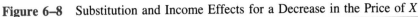

Figure 6–8   Substitution and Income Effects for a Decrease in the Price of X

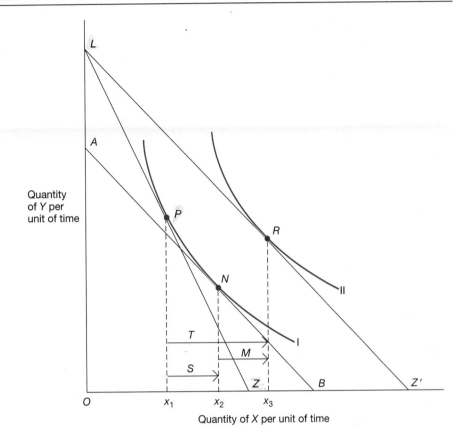

Now that we have isolated the substitution effect, let us return the money income to the original level by shifting the budget line from AB back to LZ'. Assuming that good X is normal, the increase in money income from the level shown by AB to that shown by LZ' causes the consumption of X to increase. This result is shown by the movement from N on indifference curve I to R on indifference curve II, or the increase in X from x_2 to x_3. This is the income effect. The income effect shows that the consumption of X increases from x_2 to x_3—the distance M in Figure 6–8. Whenever the income effect causes more X to be consumed after the income is returned and, therefore, reinforces the substitution effect, the good is normal.

6.4.4   The Total Effect of a Price Change

The total effect of the decrease in price that rotated the budget line from LZ to LZ' is the increase in consumption of X from x_1 to x_3. The total effect is broken up into the substitution effect (the distance x_1x_2) plus the income effect (the distance x_2x_3),

Figure 6–9   Income and Substitution Effects for a Price Decrease

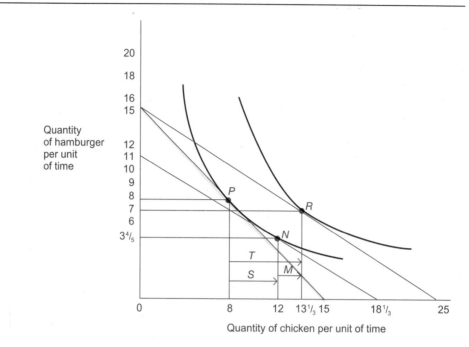

resulting from returning the money income we pretended to take away when isolating the substitution effect. In this case, the income effect reinforces the negative substitution effect because the good was assumed normal. Therefore, the total effect $\Delta X/\Delta P$, must be negative.

6.4.5   A Graphical Example of the Income and Substitution Effect

The total effect of the income and substitution effect can be illustrated with a graphical example. Suppose that good X is chicken and good Y is hamburger. The quantities of these two goods are plotted in Figure 6–9. Suppose that hamburger is selling at $2 per pound and remains at this price. Chicken is originally priced at $2 per pound. A household budgets $30 a month on these two kinds of meat. The initial budget line has a slope of $P_c/P_h = \$2/2 = 1$, and since at most $30 could be spent on each kind of meat, the intercepts are $30/2 = \$30/2 = 15$ pounds. In Figure 6–9 the household optimizes at point P, buying 8 pounds of chicken and 8 pounds of hamburger.

Now suppose the price of chicken falls to $1.20/pound. This pivots the budget line outward along the chicken axis. If the household spent $30 on just chicken, it could purchase $30/1.20 = 25$ pounds of chicken. Hence, the intercept on the chicken axis moves from 15 to 25. The consumer optimizes at R, purchasing 13 1/3 pounds of chicken and 7 pounds of hamburger. The movement from P to R is the total effect of the price of chicken changing from $2.00 to $1.20, shown as T in the figure. Chicken consumption increases from 8 to 13 1/3 pounds. Beef consumption falls from 8 pounds to 7 pounds. All of the household's income is consumed since $7 \times \$2.00 + 13 \ 1/3 \times \$1.20 = \$30$.

The total effect (T) can be divided into the substitution effect (S) and the income effect (M). The substitution effect is found by moving the new budget line, with endpoints 25 on the chicken axis and 15 on the hamburger axis, back toward the lower indifference curve until it is tangent to the lower curve. Tangency occurs at point N. The household purchases 3 4/5 pounds of hamburger and 12 pounds of chicken. The substitution effect (S) is an increase of 4 pounds in chicken consumption. Notice that this new lower budget line has an endpoint of 11 on the vertical axis. The intercept of the other two budget lines was 15. This is a decrease of 4 pounds of hamburger that can be purchased if all of the household's income is spent on hamburger. To obtain the tangency at N, income has effectively been reduced by $\$2 \times (15-11) = \$2 \times 4 = \$8$, or to \$22 instead of \$30, (i.e., $\$2 \times 11 = \$22$).

The income effect, captured by the movement between the two parallel budget lines in Figure 6–9, therefore represents a change in purchasing power of \$8. Because of the change in purchasing power, the consumer moves from point N to point R. Over and above the substitution effect, the household purchases 1 1/3 pounds more chicken (the change from 12 to 13 1/3 pounds). The overall effect on the quantity of chicken purchased, is $T = 5 \ 1/3$ pounds $= S + M = 4$ pounds $+ \ 1 \ 1/3$ pounds. The substitution effect is the movement from point P to point N on the same indifference curve. The income effect is the movement from point N to point R between the two parallel budget lines, or between the two indifference curves.

6.2 Applying the Theory

Relative to the substitution effect, do you think the income effect is very large? For what kinds of goods is the income effect likely to be small? For what kinds of goods is the income effect likely to be large?

6.4.6 The Income and Substitution Effect for an Inferior Good

For an inferior good more income means less consumption. Therefore when a price decreases and the real income goes up, the substitution effect increases consumption, but the income effect decreases it. The two effects work against each other. This situation is shown in Figure 6–10, where X is inferior over the relevant range. Again, begin with budget line LZ and equilibrium at P, with x_1 being consumed. The decrease in the price of X, as before, rotates the budget line to LZ', and as before, the substitution effect of the decrease in price is the increase from x_1 to x_2, or the movement from P to Q. Next, let the income be returned. As the budget line shifts from AB back to LZ' the consumption of X is reduced from x_2 to x_3 by the return of the money income. The income effect is the movement from Q back to R. The total effect is the change in X from x_1 to x_3. But the total effect is less than the substitution effect alone because the income effect, to some extent, offsets it.

Figure 6–10   Substitution and Income Effects for an Inferior Good

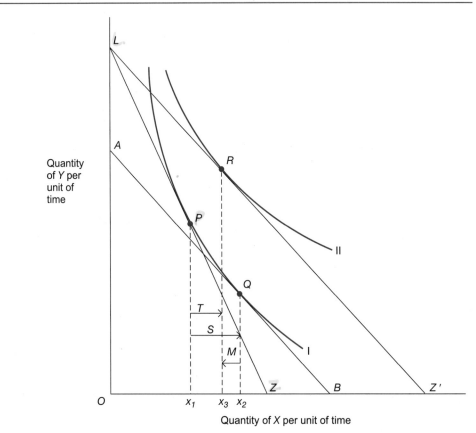

Quantity of X per unit of time

We can contrast a normal and inferior good in the context of this discussion by returning to the person choosing between a salad and a sandwich at lunch. When the price of the salad was cut in half, this person could buy the same number of lunches and have $20 of the original $100 to spend on other things. If part of this $20 went toward buying more salads at lunch, then salads would be a normal good. On the other hand, if the person decided to buy fewer salads as a result of the extra $20, salads would be an inferior good. The definition of a normal and an inferior good has not changed from that given earlier. A good is normal if more (less) is bought as income rises (falls). This reinforces the substitution effect. A good is inferior if less (more) is bought as income rises (falls). The income effect for an inferior good works in the opposite direction from the substitution effect.

6.3 *Applying the Theory*

When drawing the demand schedule, would the demand curve be steeper or flatter if the income effect were ignored? Does your answer depend on whether the good is normal or inferior?

Figure 6–11   Substitution and Income Effects for a Normal Good in Case of a Price Rise

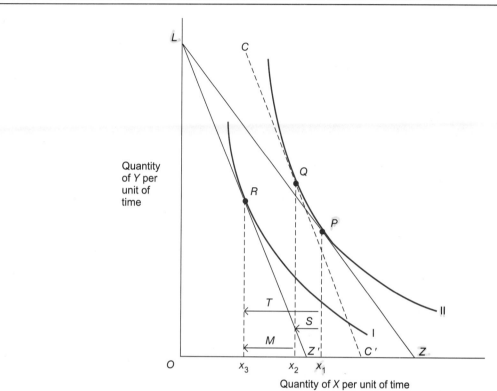

6.4.7   Substitution and Income Effects for a Price Increase

Let's review and extend the graphical analysis of the substitution and income effects by briefly considering the effects of a *price increase*. First, consider the case of a normal good, illustrated in Figure 6–11. The original price ratio is indicated by the slope of LZ. The consumer attains equilibrium at point P on indifference curve II, purchasing x_1 units of X. When the price of X rises, as indicated by pivoting the budget line from LZ to LZ', the consumer moves to a new equilibrium position at R on indifference curve I, purchasing x_3 units of X. The total effect of the price increase is indicated by the movement from P to R, or by the reduction in quantity demanded from x_1 to x_3, shown as T in the figure. In other words, the total effect is $x_1 - x_3 = x_1x_3$. This is a negative total effect, because quantity demanded is reduced by x_1x_3 units when price increases.

Coincident with the price rise, suppose the consumer is given an amount of additional money just sufficient to compensate for the loss in real income otherwise sustained. That is, the compensatory payment is just sufficient to make the consumer choose to consume on indifference curve II at the new price ratio. This new imaginary budget line is CC'; it is tangent to the original indifference curve II at point Q, but it reflects the new price ratio.

Figure 6–12   Substitution and Income Effects for an Inferior Good in Case of a Price Rise

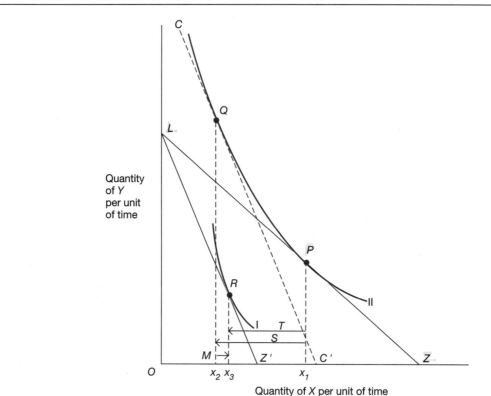

The substitution effect is shown by the movement from P to Q, or by the reduction in quantity demanded from x_1 to x_2. Now, let the consumer's real income *fall* from the level represented by the fictitious budget line CC'. The movement from Q to R (the decrease in consumption from x_2 to x_3) indicates the income effect. Since CC' and LZ' are parallel, the movement does not involve a change in relative prices. It is once more an income change, since the reduction in quantity demanded measures the change in purchases attributable exclusively to the decline in real income. The change in relative prices already has been accounted for by the substitution effect. In the figure you can see that X is a normal good; the decrease in real income causes a decrease in consumption. In this case, the income effect reinforces the substitution effect, as is always the case for a normal good.

Next consider a price increase for an inferior good. In Figure 6–12, an increase in price rotates the budget line from LZ to LZ'. Following the now familiar analysis, the consumer moves from point P to point R, decreasing the consumption of X from x_1 to x_3 (the total effect—T). The substitution effect, derived by giving the consumer just enough additional money income to compensate for the decrease in real income occasioned by the price rise, is from P to Q (from x_1 to x_2). The income effect is from Q to R (an *increase* in consumption from x_2 to x_3). This partial offset to the substitution effect is to be expected, since X is an inferior good and a decrease in income causes an increase in the consumption of X. We have established the following principle:

Principle

Considering the substitution effect alone, an increase (decrease) in the price of a good always causes less (more) of the good to be demanded. For a normal good, the income effect—from the consumer being made better or worse off by the price change—adds to or reinforces the substitution effect. The income effect for an inferior good offsets, or takes away from, the substitution effect to some extent.

In summary, for the Figures 6–8 through 6–12, when two goods are normal $T = S + M$, and the income and substitution effects move in the same direction. For an inferior good $T = S - M$, and the income and substitution effects operate in opposite directions.

6.5   Why Demand Slopes Downward

In graduate theory courses a popular test question asks the student to explain why demand curves slope downward. Many argue incorrectly that the principle of declining marginal utility, or a convex indifference curve, is all that is necessary. A better answer is that demand slopes downward because the good is normal or, if the good is inferior, the substitution effect is larger in magnitude than the income effect. Theoretically we cannot prove this explanation is always true, but no contradictory examples have ever been found for people.[4]

6.5.1   Demand for Normal Goods

In the case of a normal good, it is quite clear why price and quantity demanded are negatively related. From the substitution effect alone, a decrease in price is accompanied by an increase in quantity demanded, and an increase in price decreases quantity demanded. As we have shown, for a normal good, the income effect must add to the substitution effect. Both effects change quantity demanded in the same direction, and demand must be negatively sloped.

6.5.2   Demand for Inferior Goods

In the case of an inferior good, the income effect does not move in the same direction as, and therefore to some extent offsets, the substitution effect. As long as the substitution effect dominates or is larger than the income effect, demand is downward sloping. Could the income effect dominate the substitution effect, causing price and quantity demanded to be directly, rather than inversely, related? In other words, in Figure 6–10, could the indifference map be such that the income effect is so great that the equilibrium point on budget line LZ' falls to the left of x_1 rather than at R? In this case, could the income effect dominate the substitution effect,

---

[4]An example of the income effect having a larger magnitude than the substitution effect has recently been reported for rats. See R. C. Battalio, J. H. Kagel, and C. A. Kogut, "Experimental Confirmation of the Existence of a Giffen Good," *American Economic Review*, Vol. 18(4), September 1991.

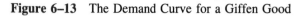

Figure 6–13 The Demand Curve for a Giffen Good

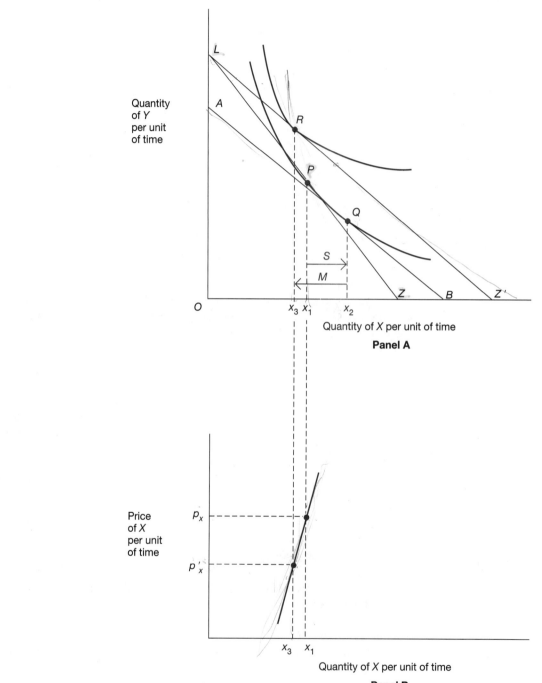

causing demand to slope upward? The possibility is illustrated in Figure 6–13. Notice that in Panel A the indifference curves are pressed together toward the top of the graph. When the price of X falls to p_x', and LZ pivots out to LZ', the utility-maximizing tangency on the budget constraint LZ' shows less total consumption of X. Purchases *decline* from x_1 to x_3. The substitution effect acts to increase consumption, but now the income effect is so large that less is bought. What we have illustrated is a superinferior good. In Panel B, where the demand is derived from the indifference map in Panel A, the demand curve slopes upward. As price falls, so does the quantity of X purchased.

Theoretically at least, such a circumstance is possible. Economists call such theoretical cases, where the domination of the income effect for an inferior good causes an upward-sloping demand, *Giffen's Paradox,* named for a 19th-century British civil servant who collected data on the effect of price changes.

But just because such cases are theoretically possible doesn't mean that they are likely or occur frequently—or that they occur at all in the real world. Some economists have noted that one way a young economist could advance rapidly in the profession is by discovering a Giffen good (no one has yet!). Cases involving positively sloped demands are probably theoretical curiosities—they certainly are not important in the real world.

It is easy to see that in most, if not all, conceivable cases, the substitution effect would tend to dominate the income effect. An increase in the price of a good makes this good more expensive, relative to all other goods. In the sense that all goods compete for a consumer's income, all other goods are substitutes. Even more directly, it would be extremely unusual if a good did not have reasonably close substitutes. People can and do change consumption patterns in response to changes in relative prices by substituting to and from other goods.

It would be unusual if an increase in the price of a good consumed substantially reduced a consumer's real income. The effect of the reduction in real income would be felt not only by the good with the increase in price, *but it would be spread over all other goods as well.* The impact of the change in real income from a price change for any *single good* would be rather small, if not minute. Therefore, it appears that the slight change in real income from price changes in inferior goods, combined with this slight change in real income being spread over all goods, would make it extremely unlikely that the income effect could overcome the substitution effect and cause demand to slope upward.

6.5.3   The Law of Demand

Economists feel so strongly about the domination of the substitution effect over the income effect that they speak of the *law of demand,* which says quantity demanded varies inversely with price, other things remaining the same.

Business people and those learning economics tend to harbor some skepticism about the law of demand. And there is evidence of alleged departures from this law. A new dog food is introduced at a low price. Prices are later raised and sales continue to climb. Buyers appear to be increasing purchases at higher prices. The maker of a nationally known pain reliever experiments with price by setting its price for a bottle of capsules first below the nearest competitors, then at the same price, and then above these prices. Sales do not change much, and, in fact, they increase slightly as prices are raised.

Do these and similar examples mean that the law of demand does not hold under these circumstances? These examples imply no such thing. The problem is one of ignorance.[5] Again, ask yourself the question: Is there anything you buy that you would buy more of at a higher price? Your answer is probably no—but, when uncertain (ignorant) about product quality, you may judge quality by price. This is not irrational behavior, and it is easy to explain why products that sell better at higher than at lower prices do not violate the law of downward sloping demand.

First of all, your time is valuable. Since time is scarce, no one uses it to become an expert on every item available. While you are shopping around gaining information about products, you could be working or enjoying some leisure time. The time spent shopping has value in the sense that you are allocating time (a scarce resource) away from other activities. Economists say that the time spent shopping has an opportunity cost, and the total cost of a good is the price of that good plus the value of the time spent shopping for it.

Second, people realize from past experience that price and quality are frequently, although not always, directly related. Price is often used in place of research on quality as an indicator of product quality. This would be expected when the monetary saving expected from buying the lower rather than the higher-priced item is small compared to the cost (in time) of gaining information. When absolute price variations among products are low relative to income, as would be expected in the case of relatively low-priced items, we expect people to do less systematic research and to judge quality more by prices. For more expensive goods, on the other hand, the absolute price variation is greater. This will make the cost of judging quality by price greater, relative to the cost of systematic quality research, for higher-priced goods. We expect consumers to depend more on research and less on price as an indicator of quality when purchasing high-cost (relative to income) items, such as housing, automobiles, and major household appliances. In other words, when the cost of taking price as an indicator of quality rises, fewer consumers judge quality by price.

As the returns to research on quality rise, people will rely more on research and less on price as an indicator of quality. This again would be the case for higher-priced goods where the cost of making a purchasing mistake is greater. The penalty for misjudging quality in an automobile is greater than that of misjudging a $5 bottle of aspirin. All of the examples of goods that sold better or as well after price increases that have been given are for low-priced goods—if the price of the goods had been increased much above the "going" price, sales would have fallen substantially. The aspirin at $10 a bottle would not have sold well when other brands were selling at around $5. In almost every example, the lower-priced good was well below the average price of similar goods, leading consumers to think it was not as good. The price was increased only to about the going price, never well above it, or the price increase was accompanied by a vigorous marketing campaign.

---

[5]Do not equate ignorance with stupidity. Ignorance means lacking knowledge about something. Even the smartest people are ignorant about many things, possibly through lack of interest. If we value the use of our time more in some other alternative than in learning about the diet of the ancient Incas, we will remain ignorant in that area. As in all things, overcoming ignorance has a cost.

Finally, when consumers believe that quality differences among different brand names are great, they will be more likely to buy higher-priced brands than when they expect little quality difference. That is, when consumers believe they will gain little quality at higher prices, they tend to pay lower prices. Marketing experiments on brands of razor blades, floor wax, cooking sherry, mothballs, salt, aspirin, and beer tend to verify this hypothesis.

We can easily explain these apparent exceptions to the law of demand. If consumers know two goods are exactly alike in every way (including prestige) and choose the higher-priced good, it would be an exception. For some goods, the imputed quality is judged by price when the cost of research on quality is high, relative to expected return. These are different goods at different prices in the minds of some consumers, and the cases cited are not violations of the law of demand.

Economics in the News

White Albino Rat Has Downsloping Demand Curve[6]

Economists have studied the choice behavior of animals. Pigeons, cats, guinea pigs, and rats have all been subjects of investigation. A number of experiments have been done with white rats. One has mapped the demand schedules for food pellets and water, goods labeled essential, and also for nonessential goods such as root beer and cherry cola. In these experiments the rats pressed a lever a set number of times to get a tiny cup of liquid or food. Prices could be changed by changing the number of lever presses or the size of the cup the animals were given. In the study a number of demand curves are traced for rats under different income and price conditions.

The subject rat labeled N3 is typical. In a 24-hour period the rat was allotted an income of 300 lever presses that could be spent on root beer or cherry cola. With one press a cup was passed through the cage wall. There was a lever and cup for root beer and a lever and cup for cherry cola. Lever presses were not changed, prices were increased or decreased by cup size. With the root beer, cup size was held constant at .05 cc. Cola cup sizes began at .05 cc, were increased to .10 cc, then reduced to .025 cc. The larger cup size is a price reduction, the smaller size represents a price increase.

The graphs in Figure 6–14 illustrate the actual reported behavior of this rat. The budget lines in Panel A show how the price of cherry cola (P_C) changes relative to the price of root beer (P_B). When cup sizes are .05 cc for both liquids, 300 press/.05 cc = 15 cc is the maximum possible consumption for each liquid. This is budget line Z. The rat consumes 1 cc of cola and 14 cc of root beer. When the price of cola falls and .10 cc is in each cup per press, the budget line pivots out to the schedule Z' and the rat goes to 25 cc of cola. Finally, when the price is raised to .025 cc per press, the budget line is Z''. The rat consumes virtually no cola as shown. These three points map into the downward-sloping demand curve in Panel B. As the price of cola falls, the rat consumes more. The graphs show that if the price of the two liquids is about equal, the rat prefers root beer. Nevertheless, instinctively this animal follows the law of demand. As price falls, the rat consumes more of the relatively less-expensive good. Such behavior is characteristic of other rats and other types of animals as well.

---

[6]This news is based on J. Kagel, R. Battalio, L. Green, and H. Rachlin. "Consumer Demand Theory Applies to Choice Behavior of Rats," in *Limits to Action: The Allocation of Individual Behavior*, J. E. R. Staddon, ed. (New York: Academic Press, 1980), Chapter 8.

Figure 6–14   Preferences and Demand for a Rat

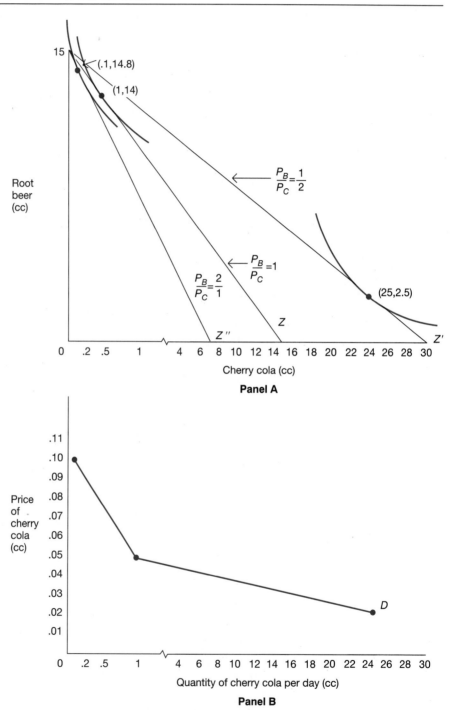

Panel A

Panel B

6.6   Summary

The basic principles of consumer behavior and demand have been developed in Chapters 5 and 6. To establish the shape of demand curves this chapter has explored the influence of a substitution and income effect when price changes. These two effects compose the two parts of how a consumer with a limited money income reacts to a price change. Almost always the substitution effect dominates the income effect. If the income and substitution effect are working to make the consumer move in the same direction, that is, to buy more or less of a good, then the good is normal. If they move the consumer in opposite directions, the goods are inferior. If the income effect is larger in magnitude than the substitution effect for an inferior good, then the good is referred to as a Giffen good. Such goods are rare, if nonexistent.

The substitution and income effect determine the shape, and more specifically, the elasticity of a demand curve. For a normal good, a large income and substitution effect will make demand more elastic. Small effects create a less elastic demand schedule. For inferior goods, the income effect causes demand to be less elastic than if the substitution effect were considered alone.

Income effects are studied independently of the substitution effect. The income-consumption curve is derived from connecting the different utility-maximizing points that come from changing income alone. These changes move the budget lines parallel to each other. If more of a good is consumed when income rises, the good is normal; if less is consumed, the good is inferior. Normal and inferior goods can be described by their income elasticity

$$E_M = \frac{\Delta Q_D}{\Delta M} \cdot \frac{M}{Q_D}.$$

If $E_M > 0$, the good is normal; $E_M < 0$ means the good is inferior.

An Engel curve shows all the equilibrium points for a consumer at different income levels. It is derived directly from the income-consumption curve. The Engel curve slopes upward if the good is normal, and it slopes downward if the good is inferior. The sign of the slope of the Engel curve and E_M are always the same. This is because $\Delta Q_D/\Delta M$ in the definition of E_M is the inverse of the slope of the Engel curve. Estimating the income elasticity of goods is important in many applied market studies. A reliable estimate of E_M helps economists and market researchers make predictions of market growth as per capita income changes in communities or regions. These predictions help producers make long-range production plans. Good predictions may prevent temporary short-run fluctuations in prices that disrupt markets.

Answers to *Applying the Theory*

6.1 For goods that were neither inferior nor normal, the quantity purchased would not change as income changed. For the quantity measured on the horizontal axis, the income consumption curve would be vertical. Also, the Engel curve would be vertical and the income elasticity of demand would be zero. Demand does not change as income changes. Indeed, this is a rare case when demand is independent of income.

6.2   Generally income effects are small because a consumer's total expenditure on any one good is a small part of his or her income. Therefore, the change in purchasing power for any price change is not likely to be large. This means that the parallel movement in the budget lines when the income effect and substitution effect are diagramed will not be large. The income effect will likely be larger, the greater a consumer's expenditure on the good whose price changes (e.g., gasoline, electricity, and housing). Also, the income effect is likely to be large for luxury items. Such goods are frequently, by definition, said to have small substitution effects and relatively large income effects. An example may be jewelry.

6.3   The demand curve would become steeper for a normal good because for any decrease in price, the increase in quantity purchased would not be as great in the absence of the income effect. For an inferior good, the demand curve would become flatter.

Technical Problems

1. Consider the following table showing income, the quantity of a good demanded, and the price of the good.

Quantity	Income	Price
100	$5,000	$16
120	6,000	16

Compute the income elasticity of the good using the arc formula. Next, suppose the price of the good changes so that the schedule is now as follows:

Quantity	Income	Price
150	$5,000	$10
130	6,000	10

Compute again the income elasticity of demand with the arc formula. Why has it changed, even though the change in income is the same?

2. If there is a single "all-important" commodity that absorbs all of the individual's income, what is its income elasticity? Explain your results using the definition of income elasticity.

3. Consider Figure E.6–1. Begin with the consumer in equilibrium with an income of $300 facing the prices $p_x = \$4$ and $p_y = \$10$.
   a. How much X is consumed in equilibrium?
      Let the price of X fall to $2.50; income and P_y remain constant.
   b. What is the new equilibrium consumption of X?
   c. How much income must be taken from the consumer to isolate the income and substitution effects?
   d. The total effect of the price decrease is _____. The substitution effect is _____. The income effect is _____.
   e. The income effect means good X is _____, but not _____.
   f. Construct the consumer's demand curve for X with money income constant.
   g. Construct the consumer's demand curve for X with the substitution effect only.
   h. Calculate the arc elasticity of demand for both the demand curves in parts f and g above. Which demand is less elastic?

4. Consider Figure E.6–2. Begin with the consumer in equilibrium with an income of $300 facing prices $p_x = \$4$ and $p_y = \$10$. Let the price of X fall to $2.50; income and p_y remain constant.

Figure E.6–1

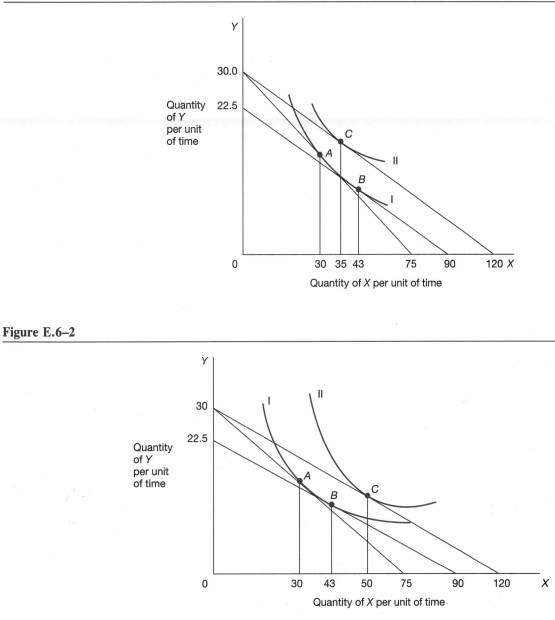

Quantity of X per unit of time

Figure E.6–2

a. What is the new equilibrium consumption of X?
b. The total effect of the price decrease is _____. The substitution effect is _____. The income effect is _____.
c. The income effect indicates that good X is _____.
d. Draw the consumer's demand curve with just the substitution effect (i.e., A to B).

Figure E.6–3

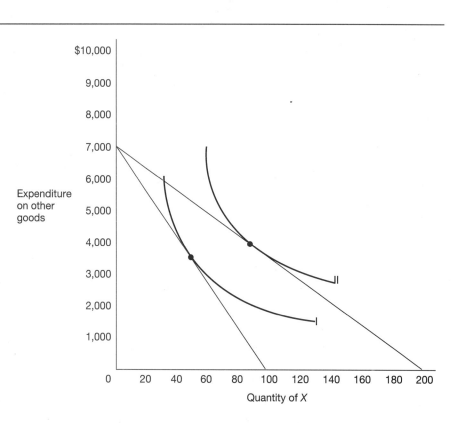

e. Draw the consumer's demand curve in the same diagram you did for part *d*, but consider both the substitution and income effects (i.e., *A* to *C*).

f. Calculate the arc elasticity of demand for both of the demand curves in parts *d* and *e*, above. Which demand curve is less elastic?

5. Consider Figure E.6–3. Begin with the consumer in equilibrium with an income of $7,000 facing a price of *X* of $35.

a. How much *X* is consumed?

Next let the price of *X* rise to $70.

b. How much *X* is consumed now? The total effect is _____. The substitution effect is _____. The income effect is _____.

c. The income effect indicated that good *X* is _____.

d. Draw the consumer's demand curve using only the substitution effect.

e. Draw the consumer's demand curve in the same diagram you did in part *d*, but hold money income constant and consider both the income and substitution effects.

f. Calculate the arc elasticity for both demand curves in parts *d* and *e*. Which demand is less elastic?

6. Consider Figure E.6–4. Begin with the consumer in equilibrium with an income of $1,200 facing a price of *X* of $15.

a. How much *X* is consumed? Now let the price of *X* rise to $24.

b. How much *X* is consumed now? The total effect is _____. The substitution effect is _____. The income effect is _____.

Figure E.6–4

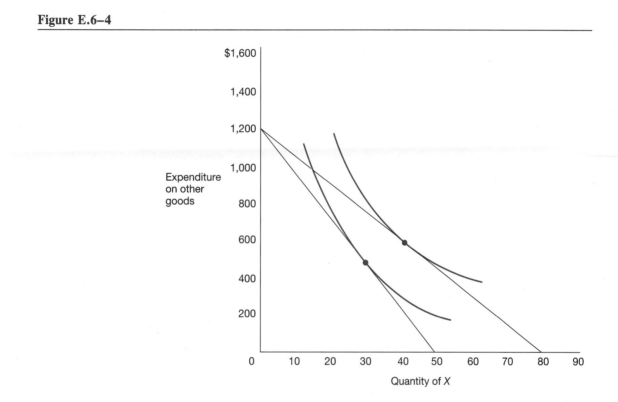

c. The income effect indicates that the good is _____.
d. Draw the consumer's demand curve using only the substitution effect.
e. Draw the consumer's demand curve in the same diagram you did in part *d*, but hold money income constant and consider both the income and substitution effects.
f. Calculate the arc elasticity for both demand curves in parts *d* and *e*. Which demand is more elastic?

7. Based upon your elasticity calculations in questions 3 through 6, compare elasticities of demand, money income constant and substitution effect only, for normal and inferior goods. Does the contrast seem reasonable? Why?

8. For the entire United States, assume that real per capita income rises over the next few years. Assume also that all relative prices remain the same. Draw what you think would be the appropriate Engel curve for the following commodities. Explain why you drew them with the shape you did.
   a. CD players.
   b. Beer.
   c. Hamburger meat and Hamburger Helper.
   d. Fish.
   e. All food.
   f. Personal computers.
   g. Hand calculators.
   h. VCRs.

9. Explain the statement: "It is possible for all goods and services to be normal, but never can they all be inferior."

10. Prove that in any consumer indifference map where the income-consumption curve is a straight line passing through the origin, the income elasticity of demand for each commodity is equal to unity.

11. Suppose at an income of $40,000 a year the average person consumes 25 gallons of soft drinks per year. The slope of the Engel curve at this income and quantity is .002.

   a. Explain why soft drinks are normal or inferior.

   b. Calculate the income elasticity of soft drinks.

12. Inflation causes the price level to rise 20 percent but prices do not rise in the same proportion. Will a consumer whose income rises enough to purchase exactly the same amount of each good that was purchased before the inflation be worse off, better off, or equally well off? Explain. (Hint: Use an indifference curve and budget lines for a consumer who purchases only two goods.)

Analytical Problems

1. Charitable contributions are deductible from income taxes. How would an increase in the tax rate affect charitable contributions? (Hint: Consider both income and substitution effects.)

2. As job opportunities and salaries for women have increased, what should be the effect on birth rates? (Hint: Consider both income and substitution effects.)

3. To reinforce the relevance of the substitution effect consider the following far-fetched situations.

   a. You eat lunch in the same restaurant every day and order exactly the same items: a ham sandwich for $2.00, an order of fries for $1.20, and a soda for $.80. One day when you begin to order lunch, you notice that the price of a ham sandwich has risen to $300, but you only brought the usual $4.00 to pay for lunch. A friend feels sorry for you and gives you $298 to make up the difference so you can now order what you usually do. What do you order? Why?

   b. You make up your grocery list and take just enough money to the store to buy everything on the list at the expected price. You play to buy 4 six packs of Pepsi at the expected price of $4.00 each. While you are shopping you notice that you have lost $14, but you also see that the price of Pepsi has fallen to $.50 per six pack each. How much Pepsi do you buy? Why?

   c. While you are at school you rent an apartment of a given quality for $800 a month. When you return to school for the new year, you find that the rent on all apartments is 50 percent lower, so an apartment of the same quality as you rented before now costs $400. Do you now choose to rent an apartment with twice the quality as before for $800 (previously $1,600)? Explain. What level of quality will you probably rent?

4. Cinderella has an income of $100 a week. Out of this income she always buys 6 pizzas at $8 each and 13 burgers at $4 each. Now her income falls to $70. Cinderella's Fairy Godmother takes pity on her and offers to perform a miracle: Raise Cinderella's income back to $100 or make the price of pizzas fall to $3 each. Which should Cinderella choose? Why?

5. In a more general sense, suppose a consumer is promised enough income to purchase a specified bundle of goods, say x_0 and y_0. At present, the consumer is unable to purchase these quantities because of the income constraint. The

consumer has the choice of seeing the price of X decrease until x_0 and y_0 can be purchased, or having income increase until the bundle can be purchased. Explain which option the consumer would prefer. What does it depend on?

6. Promotion contests, such as those that come in the mail from magazine publishers, sometimes say they will give prize winners a choice of the prize, for example, a new Mercedes or a vacation home, or the money equivalent of the prize, $50,000 or $250,000. If the money equivalent represents the actual market price of the prize, what should most people choose? Why?

7. After Iraq invaded Kuwait, gasoline prices rose dramatically—up to 50 percent. There were many effects of this increased price of gasoline. Explain the following effects in terms of the income effect, or the substitution effect, or both effects.

   a. People drove less and purchased less gas.

   b. People ate out less often.

   c. People had more tune-ups done on their cars.

   d. Bike sales went up.

   e. The sale of lottery tickets fell.

   f. People took vacations closer to home.

8. Critically evaluate the following statement with analysis: "A downward-sloping demand curve means the income effect is always smaller than the substitution effect, and the less elastic is demand, the less significant is the income effect."

9. After reading this chapter, two students get into a disagreement over the definition of inferior good. One argues that an inferior good exists when the substitution and income effects work in opposite directions when prices change in a preference map. The other argues that the definition of inferiority has nothing to do with prices. But on the Engel curve, an inferior good exists when the curve has a negative slope. Who is right?

10. Some economists argue that certain consumers buy goods simply because their price is high. Flaunting the product makes other people think the owner is wealthy. This is called the *snob effect*. Would the income effect be larger than the substitution effect when goods have snob appeal? What slope does the demand curve have? Are these goods examples of Giffen's Paradox?

CHAPTER 7

Applying Consumer Behavior Theory: Welfare and Substitution

7.1 Introduction

The preceding two chapters set forth the theory of consumer behavior, then used that theory to derive and analyze the determinants of demand. This chapter extends the use of the concepts of indifference curves and budget lines to analyze selected economic topics.

These topics were chosen because in these cases the application of consumer behavior theory not only led to a better understanding of the issues but actually extended the body of economic theory. The topics discussed in this chapter, while applying the tools of indifference curves and budget lines, will also help you learn about new tools used in economic analysis. Four topics are discussed. The first concerns the gains from trade between two parties, whether the parties are two individuals or two countries. The second topic discusses what is known in economics as consumer's surplus. Its basis comes from the theory of utility maximization. Consumer's surplus measures the benefits consumers receive from participating in a market. The next section demonstrates with an indifference map how people decide how much to work and how much leisure to enjoy. The analysis of this choice enables us to derive a labor supply schedule. Finally, the importance of substitution to a consumer's welfare is the last topic in this chapter. This section illustrates how consumers offset the effects of inflation by substituting away from the relatively expensive goods. This section also shows that income taxes give buyers more freedom to substitute than unit taxes. The increased ability to substitute puts individuals on higher indifference curves than would be the case with unit taxes.

7.2   The Gains from Exchange

Markets exist in an economy because individuals have different marginal rates of substitution between goods. The very reason there are buyers and sellers in a market is that parties place different values on the last unit of a good they possess. Different valuations lead to trade. A dentist, for example, may provide care for someone in return for bookkeeping services. At the margin, the dentist values bookkeeping more than the dental care he or she can give. A bookkeeper values dental care more than the value of keeping account ledgers. Of course most trades involve money in return for goods and services. Money exists because it is a commonly accepted good in exchange; it facilitates exchange. But the fundamental principle of exchange remains. Money is spent or traded because the marginal value of the dollars spent on a good is less than the marginal value of the good or service purchased. In this section, we analyze the gains from trade using utility theory.

7.2.1   Trade between Two Parties

Consider the following example. Two people consume only two goods, an endowment of which they receive every week. These goods are X and Y. Given preferences and the endowment to each person, the marginal rate of substitution for one person, say Allen (person A), is three X for eight Y or $MRS^A_{x \text{ for } y} = 8/3$. That is, Allen would be willing to exchange 3 units of X for 8 units of Y or 8 units of Y for 3 units of X and remain on the same indifference curve. Figure 7–1, Panel A, pictures the marginal rate of substitution for Allen. At point G on the indifference curve, Allen is willing to substitute at the rate of $8Y$ for $3X$.[1] This ratio, in essence, reflects an exchange rate between X and Y. As far as he is concerned $8Y = 3X$. The second person, Brenda (person B), has a different marginal rate of substitution. Suppose Brenda would exchange three X for six Y. She has an indifference curve slope such that the $MRS^B_{x \text{ for } y} = 6/3$. As shown in Panel B of Figure 7–1, this indifference curve at point E is not as steep as Allen's. At point E on the indifference curve, Brenda will substitute no more than 6 units of Y for 3 units of X. Brenda's exchange rate is, therefore, $6Y = 3X$.

Both people can benefit from trading. Allen views $8Y$ equivalent to $3X$, whereas Brenda thinks $6Y$ is the same as having $3X$. To start trading, Brenda could offer Allen 3 units of X and get 8 units of Y back. Allen would not be harmed and Brenda would be put on a higher indifference curve, because she would have accepted as few as 6 units of Y, but receives 8 units. In this trade, Brenda offers $3X$ and gets back $8Y$ from Allen, who is left indifferent. Brenda gets two more units of Y than would have been acceptable, and so she is put on a higher indifference curve in the exchange.

---

[1]Remember from Chapter 5 that the marginal rate of substitution is defined for one unit changes in X or Y, and as a consumer moves along an indifference curve, the slope (and therefore the MRS) is changing. Thus, stating that the MRS between two points is 8/3 in Figure 7–1 is an approximation of the MRS along this part of the indifference curve.

Figure 7–1   The Marginal Rate of Substitution for Two Consumers

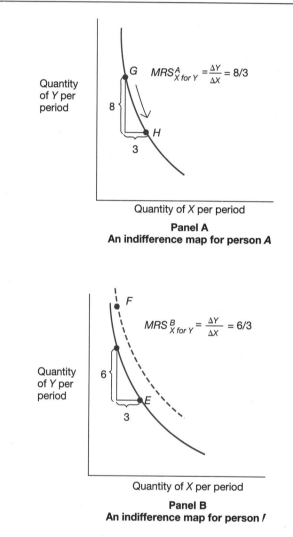

In Figure 7–1, we can trace through the effect of this trade on the indifference map for the two consumers. Allen receives three more X and gives up eight units of Y; Allen moves from point G to H and is left indifferent by the exchange. Brenda gives up $3X$ and receives $8Y$, and, therefore, she moves to a point like F in the map and is put on a higher indifference curve with 3 less X and 8 more Y. Notice that the trade put Allen on a flatter part of the indifference curve, whereas Brenda goes to a steeper segment of a new curve. The trade has lowered the MRS for Allen and raised it for Brenda. Continued trading would eventually make the MRS for each person equal.

Suppose Allen returned seven, instead of eight, units of Y to Brenda in the exchange. Now both people would benefit from the trade, and each would go to a higher indifference curve. Even if Allen went as low as six units of Y in the trade, Brenda would still make the exchange. At these rates ($3X = 6Y$), Brenda is left indifferent, while Allen is benefitted. As long as Allen returns between six and eight units of Y in exchange for three units of X, both individuals benefit from trade.

Any voluntary trade between Allen and Brenda, however, will always be in the same direction. Allen receives additional units of X while Brenda receives additional units of Y. The direction of trading will tend to equalize the marginal rates of substitution between the two traders. Because Allen is moving down an indifference curve, Allen's *MRS* decreases and the indifference curve becomes flatter. Because Brenda is moving up an indifference curve, Brenda's *MRS* increases and the indifference curve becomes steeper. The two consumers will continue to trade until their respective marginal rates of substitution are equal. It is only when the $MRS^A_{x \text{ for } y} = MRS^B_{x \text{ for } y}$ that a trade that helps one or both consumers without hurting one of them cannot be arranged. Trade stops when the marginal rates of substitution for Allen and Brenda are equal because any exchange that Allen suggests would be identical to one that Brenda suggests. Each would be willing to give up a unit of X for the same amount of Y, so no one would benefit from additional trade.

In this description of the benefits of trading, we have placed the notion of market exchange in a rather abstract context. However, either Brenda or Allen could be a firm, the other could be a customer, and one of the goods traded could be money. For example, McDonald's is willing to exchange hamburgers of a particular type for $1.50 each. If you are willing to trade more than $1.50 for a McDonald's hamburger, both you and McDonald's are made better off by the trade. The same analysis can be applied to any other type of exchange. Markets arise whenever the marginal rates of substitution are not equal. This is an important principle in economics.

Principle

If two individuals have differing marginal rates of substitution, both can be made better off in the sense of attaining a more preferred level of consumption by exchange. Only when the marginal rates of substitution are equal is there no further incentive to trade.

When two individuals have no further incentive to make trades, they are in an exchange equilibrium.

Definition

When two individuals have equal marginal rates of substitution, they have no further incentive to trade and are in exchange equilibrium.

7.1 Applying the Theory

Can you think of any good reason for blocking trade between two individuals? For example, governments have made it illegal to trade in pornography, drugs, automatic weapons, and so forth. Why are trades not allowed in these and other markets you may think of, if the marginal rates of substitution are different between individuals?

7.2.2 Pareto Optimality

Once two traders reach an exchange equilibrium, they will stop trading because trades that are mutually beneficial or trades that benefit one party while leaving the other indifferent are no longer possible. Traders that reach this state are described as having reached a *Pareto optimal* distribution of goods and services. All exchange equilibria are Pareto optimal; this occurs whenever the *MRS*'s for traders are equal. As two parties make trades that adjust their marginal rates of substitution closer together, they are described as making *Pareto* superior moves. This is a move that makes at least one person better off without making anyone else worse off.

Once two traders reach Pareto optimality, each can identify distributions of X and Y they would prefer. Even though mutually beneficial exchanges are no longer possible, they each prefer more to less. But getting more would mean exchange was no longer voluntary. One trader might say, give me all your Y in return for nothing. The other might consent, if severely threatened. Instead of trade, we usually call this *robbery*. There are lots of other terms we might give involuntary exchange; they all clearly convey the idea that someone is made better off by harming another. The essence of Pareto optimality is therefore that, once achieved, it is impossible to make further exchange without harming one party in the trade.

Principle

A Pareto-optimal distribution is one in which any change that makes some people better off makes others worse off. Thus, every exchange equilibrium is Pareto optimal.

To summarize, when there is voluntary exchange, Pareto optimality means that people will trade only if the trade makes the participants better off. If each person's *MRS* is the same, it is impossible to make both parties better off through trade.

The concept of Pareto optimality has wide applicability in economics. To economists, it represents a necessary condition for market efficiency. Whenever Pareto optimality does not exist, some redistribution of goods and services will help some individuals without hurting anyone else. It is important to realize that there are generally an infinite number of Pareto-optimal distributions between two traders. Any are possible, depending upon the original endowment. Hence, a Pareto-optimal distribution may have one trader relatively rich and another poor. More generally, the concept of Pareto optimality does not address the issue of fairness in endowments.

7.2 *Applying the Theory*

Is income redistribution—taxing the wealthy individuals and giving the money to the poor—Pareto superior? Can you think of any form of redistribution that does not satisfy the Pareto principle, but still you believe is worthwhile? Conversely, can you think of Pareto superior moves that are not worthwhile?

7.3 Consumer's Surplus

In this section, we develop the concept of consumer's surplus. Consumer's surplus actually measures the benefit a buyer receives from participating in a market or participating in an exchange. We can relate this measure to the area under the demand curve. After expressing it in this way, we can then show the relation between consumer's surplus and the value of a price rise or decline to a consumer using an indifference map. Consumer's surplus is a measure widely applied by economists, and it is one of the most important tools available in public policy studies.

7.3.1 The Paradox of Value

In his 1776 book, *The Wealth of Nations,* Adam Smith was troubled by the disparity between price and value. He asked: How is it that water, which is so very useful that life is impossible without it, has such a low price, while diamonds, a luxury, have such a high price? This question is known as the paradox of value. We can beg its answer by pointing out that the demand and supply for water intersect at a low price, while the market equilibrium for diamonds is established at a high price. Diamonds are scarce relative to demand, but water is not.

Smith would probably not have been satisfied with this answer. Even though demand and supply curves had not yet been used to describe markets, he knew that scarcity led to high prices, and abundance led to low prices. What bothered him was why something valuable to buyers did not fetch a high price in spite of its abundance. In 1776, economists had not yet comprehended that price in a market is determined by the *value of the last unit exchanged.* You know from the description of demand schedules and demand curves in Chapter 2 that the value individuals place on each unit of a commodity falls as they consume more.

Value is conceptually a much broader notion than price. Figure 7–2 can help you visualize the distinction between value and price. Think of each point on the demand curve as a measure of what an individual would pay for that unit of the good. So for unit Q_B, and no other unit, the consumer would pay as much as P_B, and for the Q_C unit, the value to the buyer is P_C. These points on the demand curve reveal the buyer's maximum willingness to pay. The demand curve shows how much a buyer is willing to pay for any number of units purchased of a particular

Figure 7–2   The Value of a Commodity

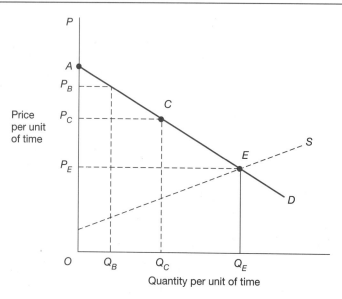

good.[2] The total value of Q_C units, for instance, is the sum of how much the consumer would be willing to pay up to and including the Q_C unit. Value in the figure would be the area under the demand schedule, $OACQ_C$. If, for example, you go to the grocery store and buy three apples, and if the first was worth $1.00 to you, the second worth $.80, and the third worth $.60, then the value of the three apples would be the sum $2.40. This amount of money would be roughly equal to the area under the demand curve for apples up to three apples.

You know, of course, that demand slopes downward, as shown in Figure 7–2. This means that the value of the last unit consumed is less than the value of those units previously consumed. If the market price of Q_E is P_E, the consumer will make purchases out to the Q_Eth unit in Figure 7–2. As long as value is greater than price, more will be bought. The value of the last unit—in this case the Q_Eth unit—is exactly equal to P_E, but units purchased up to the Q_Eth unit have the combined value equivalent to area $OAEQ_E$. This is the difference between price and value. Price measures the value of the last unit, not total value. The area under the demand schedule is an estimate of total value.

Principle

> Price is the value of the last unit purchased, because consumers continue to make purchases until value equals price. The area under the demand curve is an estimate of total value.

[2]This is not a precise claim because of the *income effect* when price changes. A better measure of willingness to pay would compensate the consumer for the income effect. A more thorough discussion of this aspect of demand is undertaken after consumer's surplus is defined.

Economics in the News

Smoking Bans on Airlines Reveal the Value of a Cigarette[3]

In February 1990 a new Federal law took effect. Smoking was totally banned on all commercial airline flights of less than six hours. The new law eliminates smoking on 95 percent of all flights in or originating from the United States. Previously, the ban applied to flights that took less than two hours.

Smoking is addictive. After acquiring the habit, many people value smoking much more than, say, the price of a pack of cigarettes. To escape the airline ban, some smokers creatively adjusted their airline travel in ways that cost more but allow them the opportunity to smoke. For example, instead of flying from Phoenix, Arizona directly to London, England, a flight that takes about six hours and does not allow smoking, smokers can fly first to Los Angeles, about a one-hour flight, smoke in the L.A. International Airport, then catch a flight to London. Smoking is allowed on that flight because flight time exceeds six hours. The added cost is $600. This added cost, plus the opportunity cost of the smoker's time, is what some Phoenix residents pay to avoid the six-hour ban. Clearly, the new law shows that for some people the value of smoking is much greater than the price of a pack of cigarettes.

There is an alternative to rescheduling. A smoker can simply pay the $1,000 fine for violating the law. United Airlines reported 14 violations to the Federal Aviation Administration in the first month the law was enforced. If rescheduling costs more than $1,000, violations are likely to be numerous. A high number of violators would be expected, for instance, on flights between Hawaii and California, a flight just short of the six-hour limit. Rescheduling more frequent stops is difficult, and other means of transportation (i.e., ship travel) are not good substitutes for airline travel.

7.3.2   Value and Expenditure

It is important to keep in mind the difference between value, which is the area under the demand schedule out to the last unit purchased, and how much is spent. What a buyer spends is the revenue, or income, to the seller. We discussed the revenue to a seller when we introduced elasticity of demand in Chapter 3. Recall that we measured total revenue (*TR*) as

$$TR = P \cdot Q,$$

where P is the market price and Q is the quantity sold. This is identical to the amount spent by a buyer. The expenditure is price times the number of units sold. What the buyer gives up as expenditure is income to the seller.

In Figure 7–2 if Q_E units are purchased by a consumer, we have defined the entire area under demand out to Q_E as value. The expenditure made by the consumer for Q_E units is $P_E \cdot Q_E$, or area OP_EEQ_E. The area of value must always be greater than the area of expenditure in order for the consumer to make a purchase. If value were just equal to the expenditure, the buyer would be indifferent about the purchase.

[3]The facts in this report are based on an account in *The Wall Street Journal,* April 23, 1990, p. B1.

Table 7–1   A Consumer's Willingness to Pay for Apples

Apple	Willingness to Pay for the Last Apple	Grocer's Price	Consumer's Surplus
1	$1.00	.40	$ .60
2	.80	.40	.40
3	.60	.40	.20
4	.40	.40	.00
5	.20		
Total consumer's surplus			$1.20

7.3.3   Consumer's Surplus and the Area under the Demand Curve

Economists who work on public policy problems frequently use consumer's surplus, measured as the difference between the maximum amount a consumer is willing to pay, or value, and the dollar amount actually paid for a commodity, or expenditure. To illustrate the concept of consumer's surplus, suppose you visit the grocery store to buy some apples. The grocer is capable of charging a sufficiently high price that you do not make any purchases, but at lower prices you will buy apples, and the lower the price the more you will buy. In other words, your demand curve for apples is downward sloping. Points on the demand curve have been tabulated in Table 7–1. We show a maximum willingness to pay for the first five apples. The value of the first apple is relatively high, $1.00, then the value falls to $.20, with the fifth apple. The demand curve from which this table is constructed is shown in Figure 7–3.

Suppose the grocer sells all apples at $.40. Regardless of whether the consumer is purchasing the first or fifth apple, the price is the same, as shown in Table 7–1. From the consumer's point of view, the supply curve is a horizontal schedule at the price of $.40. All the apples he or she could conceivably purchase are sold at this constant price. Consumer's surplus is the difference between what you are willing and able to pay, and the asking price. Since you are just willing and able to pay $.40 for the fourth apple, and the price of apples is $.40 each, you stop buying apples at this point on your demand schedule in Figure 7–3. For the first through third apples, however, Table 7–1 shows that you gain consumer's surplus from making the purchases. Total consumer's surplus is $1.20. There is no consumer's surplus from the fourth apple, since price equals value for this unit. For emphasis, we repeat the definition of consumer's surplus and relate it to demand curves.

Definition

Consumer's surplus is the difference between a buyer's willingness to pay and the market price.

Figure 7–3   Willingness to Pay and Consumer's Surplus

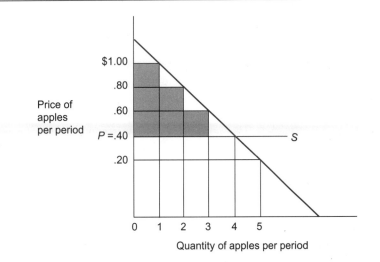

Consumer's surplus is graphed in Figure 7–3, when the consumer buys four apples. This is where the grocer's supply curve intersects demand. It is important to understand that you do not buy four apples because all four apples are valued at $.40 each. On the contrary, all but the fourth apple are valued more highly than $.40. You buy four because your willingness to pay for the fourth apple is just equal to the price of apples. More than four are not bought, because you are willing to pay only $.20 for the fifth, while the price is $.40.

You can see that in Table 7–1, we actually have subtracted price from the willingness to pay to get an exact measure of consumer's surplus. Adding up these amounts shows that the consumer's surplus from buying four apples is $1.20. This is also represented by the shaded region in Figure 7–3. If we had taken the area under the demand curve above $.40, we would have overestimated the surplus by the unshaded triangular areas between the price line and D. The estimate, however, becomes more exact as units of measure for the quantity become smaller. Say the grocer charged $.20 for each apple half. The consumer depicted in Figure 7–3 would then buy eight halves, and as the units are made smaller, the area between the price and the demand curve would become a much better estimate of consumer's surplus.

Principle

Consumer's surplus is estimated by the area between the demand curve and price.

7.3.4   Derivation of Consumer's Surplus from Indifference Curves

The theory of utility maximization will help you better understand consumer's surplus. Utility theory lends credibility to the concept of consumer's surplus and at the same time offers some criticism. For many years, economists were skeptical of using the area under a demand curve as a measure of the value a consumer places on a commodity. The cause of the skepticism was that a consistent story tying together consumer's surplus and utility maximization could not be told. It has been relatively recently that a rigorous derivation of consumer's surplus from indifference-curve theory has convinced many economists of the theoretical foundation of consumer's surplus.[4]

We now want to show the relation between consumer's surplus and the theory of utility maximization. With two graphs, we will show that the area under a demand curve is an estimate of how much money a consumer would pay to stay in the market. This amount of money is another way of viewing how much the buyer values the commodity. The best estimate of consumer's surplus is the area under a *compensated demand curve*. Compensated demand curves only show the substitution effect as price changes. Remember that the demand curves derived in Chapter 6 from the price-consumption curve included both the substitution and income effects.

Definition

A compensated demand curve shows the relation between price and quantity demanded when utility is held constant. The buyer remains on the same indifference curve as price changes. Hence there is no income effect.

To avoid confusion between compensated demand curves and the demand curves defined in Chapter 6, the demand curves that take into account both the income and substitution effects are called *ordinary demand curves*. In applied economics ordinary demand curves are most widely used to measure consumer's surplus because they are easier to estimate. Furthermore, if the income effect is not large, there is little difference between a compensated and ordinary demand schedule.

To see how the theory of utility maximization supports the concept of consumer's surplus, and to understand the relation between an ordinary and compensated demand curve, let us begin with an indifference map with two budget lines that reflect a price increase, as shown in Figure 7–4, Panel A. On the horizontal axis, we plot good X and assume X is a normal good. Along the vertical axis is expenditure on other goods. These other goods are simply labeled Y. What is not spent on Y is spent on good X. When the price of X is p_0 and the budget line is cz, suppose the consumer begins by maximizing utility at point u on indifference curve II. Expenditure on all other goods is Oy_0. The consumer purchases x_0 units of X. Expenditure on x_0 is distance cy_0 on the vertical axis. It is the amount left over from expenditure on Y. Now suppose the price increases to p_1. The consumer decides not to buy any X and optimizes at point c on indifference curve I. This is, of course, a corner solution. The two points c and u give rise to the *ordinary* demand curve D in Figure 7–4, Panel B. The corresponding points take into account both the substitution and income effects. At point c' in Panel B the price is p_1, and the consumer buys zero units of X. At point u' the price is p_0 and the consumer buys x_0 units of X.

[4]See R. Willig, "Consumer's Surplus without Apology," *American Economic Review*, 66, no. 4 (September 1976), pp. 56–69.

Figure 7–4

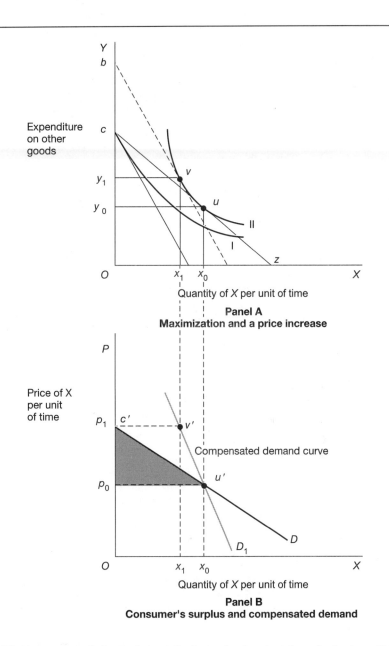

Panel A
Maximization and a price increase

Panel B
Consumer's surplus and compensated demand

The compensated demand curve is derived using just the substitution effect—a movement from u to v in Figure 7–4, Panel A. The two points on the compensated demand curve come from the original point u in Panel A and point v on the indifference curve II. In Panel B the compensated demand curve is labeled D_1.

In Panel B, as a result of the price increase from p_0 to p_1 and the consumer buying nothing, the consumer loses consumer's surplus equal to the area of the triangle $p_1 u' p_0$. This is the shaded region in Panel B of the figure. This area corresponds to a loss of utility from moving to the lower indifference curve I in Panel A. This loss can be measured in the preference map by asking: How much would a consumer be willing to pay in order to avoid the hike in price from p_0 to p_1? In Panel A, after the price increase, the consumer's utility declines to the level represented by indifference curve I. To return the person to indifference curve II, an increase in income equal to distance bc is necessary. So a consumer would be willing to pay income bc to avoid the higher price. Is $bc = p_1u'p_0$, the consumer's surplus lost in Panel B? The answer is no. It can be shown that bc is equal to the area under the compensated demand curve D_1 and between the prices p_0 and p_1. This is the area $p_0p_1v'u'$.[5]

The true loss in consumer's surplus is the area under the compensated demand schedule, not the ordinary demand curve. Thus, for a price increase, consumer's surplus represented by the area $p_1u'p_0$ underestimates the amount of income the consumer would exchange in return for the right to purchase commodity X at the lower price, p_0. If we repeated the analysis for a price decrease, we would deduce in a similar way that the consumer's surplus area under the ordinary demand curve and above price overestimates the amount a consumer would pay for the right to purchase the commodity at the lower price, rather than at p_0. In either case, however, the difference is not large if the income effect in Panel A is small.

Deriving consumer's surplus from indifference curves tells us that income effects distort the surplus estimate. The stronger the income effect, the less reliable ordinary demand curves are for estimating the true consumer's surplus. Conversely, the smaller the income effect the more reliable the estimate. For a price increase from p_0 to p_1, the income effect reduces purchasing power and thus leads to a greater change in the quantity demanded than if demand were the compensated curve. But because of the gain in purchasing power, if prices were returned to p_0, consumers are willing to pay more for the price decrease than is shown by the area under the ordinary demand curve.

[5]First, at point u in Panel A, the consumer can spend Oy_0 on other goods and therefore spend the remaining income, cy_0 on X. Hence, $cy_0 = Op_0u'x_0$ in Panel B. Remember that $Op_0u'x_0$ in Panel B is the expenditure made by the consumer for x_0 units. At point v in Panel A, the consumer spends by_1 on x_1; the budget line is higher because of the compensation provided to return to indifference curve II. Looking at Panel B, $by_1 = Op_1v'x_1$.

Finally, let the consumer be at point v again. A move from v to u is a movement along the same indifference curve, and the $MRS_{xfory} = \Delta Y/\Delta X = y_1y_0/x_0x_1$. To gain x_0x_1 more X, the consumer is willing to pay income y_1y_0. In terms of Panel B, this means that a movement from v' to u' on the compensated demand schedule is worth y_1y_0 to the consumer. Thus $y_1y_0 = x_1v'u'x_0$, the area under the compensated demand schedule between x_1 and x_0.

Putting all this together, we get an area in Panel B that corresponds to the distance bc in Panel A. This distance is the amount of income equivalent to the value a consumer placed on the low price, p_0, as opposed to p_1. Let's carefully focus our attention on the vertical axis in Panel A, the axis measuring the income held by the consumer after purchasing X. We want a measure for the distance bc on this axis. In a roundabout way we can get it. If we add and subtract some distances on this axis you can see that

$$bc = by_1 + y_1y_0 - cy_0$$

For each of the distances on the right hand side of this equation there are corresponding areas in Panel B. Substituting these areas:

$$bc = Op_1v'x_1 + x_1v'u'x_0 - Op_0u'x_0 = P_0P_1v'u'.$$

Economics in the News

Consumer's Surplus and an Increase in the Price of Chicken[6]

Grocery stores are increasingly automating checkouts at the counter. Instead of keying in prices, clerks are simply running the bar code on food packages across a light that reads the code. The code is then matched with a price in a data bank. These data bank prices are kept on a computer tape. By using these scanners, grocery stores have a history of quantities sold and prices.

Using these data, Oral Capps, an agricultural economist, has estimated the demand schedule for a variety of meats sold at one chain of grocery stores in Houston, Texas. The quantity demanded was assumed to depend mainly on the meat's own price, the price of other meats, and store advertising. For chicken, two points on the estimated demand curve are shown below:

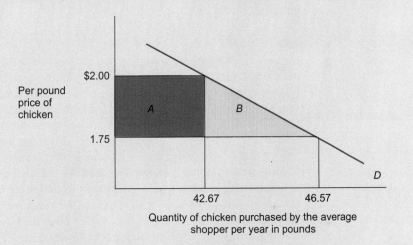

Quantity of chicken purchased by the average
shopper per year in pounds

Although the estimated demand curve is not linear, suppose we connect the two points with a straight line.

Consumer's surplus is the area between price and the demand schedule. So when price goes from $1.75/pound to $2.00 the loss in consumer's surplus is all of the shaded area in the above figure. This area represents what a consumer would pay to not have the price increase by the $.25 per pound. Alternatively, this area is a loss in benefit attributable to an increase in price. This area can be calculated as the sum of areas $A + B$. Area A is ($2.00 − $1.75) × 42.67 = $10.67, and area B is the area of a triangle. A triangle has area 1/2 × base × height. Substituting the numbers from the estimated demand gives 1/2 × (46.57 − 42.67) × ($2.00 − $1.75) = $1.95. The sum of the areas is $A + B$ = $10.67 + $1.95 = $12.62. Thus the average consumer loses $12.62 a year in consumer's surplus from the price increase.

---

[6]This account is based on Oral Capps, "Utilizing Scanner Data to Estimate Retail Demand Functions for Meat Products," *American Journal of Agricultural Economics,* 71 no. 3, August 1989, pp. 750–60.

7.4   The Labor-Leisure Choice

The tools developed in Chapters 5 and 6 can be easily adapted to analyze the theory of labor supply. This may seem strange, because indifference maps thus far have been used only to generate demand curves, not supply curves. However, we can drive a labor supply schedule if we consider a person's total supply of labor time to be the residual of the total time available less the person's demand for leisure. Hence the supply of labor is derived from getting the demand for leisure. The amount of time left over from leisure demand is working time. This is a good place to derive in detail a labor supply curve because indifference curves and budget lines are important tools in the analysis. Later in the text an entire chapter is devoted to studying labor markets. We shall take the labor supply curve as given in these later discussions, but you might want to refer back to this section as a review.

7.4.1   The Labor-Leisure Map

Figure 7–5, Panel A, contains a portion of an individual's indifference map between income and leisure. Instead of depending strictly on the quantity of goods, utility is now regarded as a function of how time is divided between working and leisure. Work, of course, increases an individual's income, measured on the vertical axis. Leisure is plotted along the horizontal axis. From the convex shape of the indifference curves I through IV in the figure, it is clear that we have assumed both income and leisure are considered desirable by the individual.

Before considering the problem of how the consumer maximizes utility, a word of explanation about the unit of measurement for leisure and the vertical line at the leisure amount L_m is in order. The unit of measurement along the horizontal axis can be hours per day, days per year, or any other period of time. Obviously, if the unit is hours per day, the maximum time for leisure is 24 hours. If the unit is days of leisure, the maximum is 7 per week or 365 per year. The line L_m indicates the maximum attainable units of leisure per time period, whatever the time period may be. If the individual chooses C' units of leisure per period, this person also chooses $C'L_m$ units for work; or if L_m units of leisure are chosen, this person does not work at all. The unit of measurement chosen for the horizontal axis clearly specifies the unit for the vertical. For example, when leisure is designated as hours per day, the vertical axis must measure income per day. Each indifference curve specifies the various combinations of income and leisure that yield the same level of satisfaction. For example, the consumer considers C' leisure (and, $C'L_m$ work) and income measured by the vertical distance $C'H$ equivalent to A' units of leisure (and $A'L_m$ work) and income $A'A$, since both points lie on the same indifference curve. The slopes of the curves indicate the rates at which an individual is willing to trade leisure for income. We assume, for analytical convenience, that both income and leisure are continuously divisible.

The budget lines are determined by the payment per unit of time. If the unit is hours per day, the budget line is determined by the individual's hourly wage rate; if days per year, by the earnings per day. Consider budget line Y_1L_m. If the individual

Figure 7–5   Indifference Curve Analysis of Labor Supply

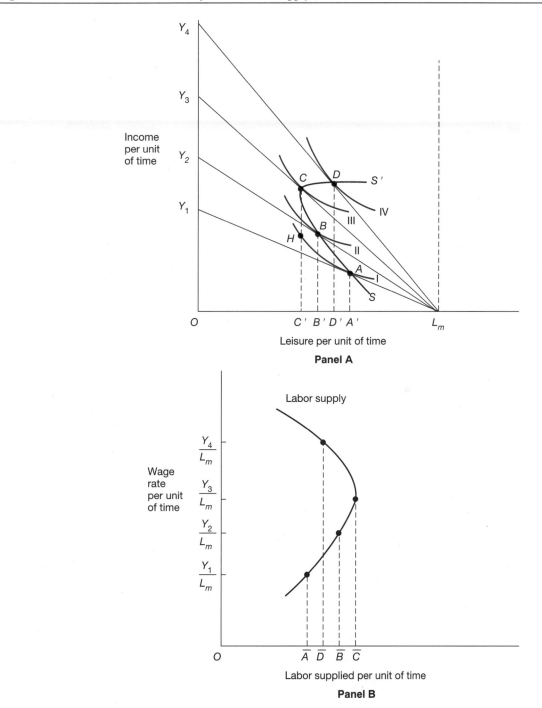

works the entire time period (say, 24 hours per day) and consequently takes no leisure, he or she could make Y_1 income per day; with no work, income would be zero, and leisure would be L_m on the budget line. The slope of the budget line in this case Y_1/L_m is the relevant wage rate of payment per unit of time. The "cost" of a unit of leisure is the sacrificed earnings for that period of time.[7] The lines Y_2L_m, Y_3L_m, and Y_4L_m are the relevant budget lines for higher wage rates, Y_2/L_m, Y_3/L_m, and Y_4/L_m, respectively. The leisure amount L_m is fixed, and the budget line pivots upward along the vertical axis as wage rates increase.

7.4.2 Labor-Leisure Choices

With a given wage rate, the highest attainable level of utility is at the point where the relevant budget line is tangent to the indifference curve. An individual with the wage rate indicated by the slope of Y_1L_m achieves the highest attainable level of utility at point A. He or she chooses the amount A' units of leisure, $A'L_m$ work, and receives an income of $A'A$. If the wage rises to the level designated by budget line Y_2L_m, the highest attainable level of utility is at B, where the individual works $B'L_m$ for an income of $B'B$ and enjoys B' leisure time. Points C and D indicate the equilibrium leisure, work, and income for the other two budget lines. The curve SS' connects these and all intermediate equilibria. Thus, SS' indicates the amount of time the individual is willing to work (or the amount of labor he or she is willing to supply) at each wage in a series of wages.

Beginning at a relatively low wage, the individual is willing to work more and consume less leisure as the wage rate rises. Since an increase in potential earnings causes leisure to cost more (in lost earnings), this person chooses less leisure and more work. After point C, however, further increases in the wage rate induce more leisure and less work. Leisure still costs more as the individual moves from C to D, so the substitution effect would make an individual work more and consume less leisure time, but because more leisure time is taken at D, it must be the case that the income effect causes the individual to consume more leisure with the increased earnings.

Just as we can derive demand curves from the price-consumption curve, we can derive supply curves from curves such as SS'. We may think of labor supply as the reverse of the demand for leisure. Figure 7–5, Panel B, shows the labor supply curve derived from the indifference map in Panel A. The distance $O\bar{A}$ in Panel B equals $A'L_m$ in Panel A and is the amount of work associated with wage rate Y_1/L_m, and so on. Since SS' changes direction at C in panel A, the labor supply curve bends backward at $\bar{C}$ in Panel B. Although in this case the individual chooses to work less as the wage rate increases at higher incomes, this need not be the case. A person's supply of labor depends on his or her indifference map.

---

[7]For simplicity, we assume a constant wage rate regardless of the amount of time worked. Certainly "overtime" work might be at overtime pay, or a second job could be taken at a lower wage than the primary job pays. We also assume that the individual is free to choose the amount of working time; sometimes this may not be the case.

7.3 Applying the Theory

Panel B of Figure 7–5 constructs the labor supply curve from points A through D in Panel A. The *demand* curve for leisure can also be constructed from Panel A. Sketch this curve. Over what ranges on the price consumption line SS is leisure a Giffen good?

7.5 Substitution and Inflation

One frequently encountered—and misunderstood—concept in economics is the consumer price index (CPI), computed by the Bureau of Labor Statistics (BLS). Wage contracts hinge on changes in the CPI, as do purchasing and construction contracts. Changes in the payment of social security and welfare benefits are based on the CPI, and stock and bond prices rise and fall based on favorable or unfavorable reports of the index. How well do changes in the CPI or other indexes reflect the impact of inflation on consumers? Do changes in a price index overestimate or underestimate the impact of inflation? Because price indexes are extremely important for economic policy, these questions are of paramount importance. We can use the tools developed thus far to see how well increases in the CPI actually measure the impact of higher prices on consumers.

7.5.1 The Consumer Price Index

First, let us define the CPI. In computing this index, the BLS uses a *Laspeyres indexing method,* which takes the ratio of the cost of purchasing a specified bundle of goods in one year relative to the cost of purchasing the same bundle during some specified *base* year. For example, suppose there are two goods X and Y, and the base year is 1980. The amount of each good consumed by a typical household in 1980, the bundle used for weighing, consists of x_0 and y_0. For 1990, a Laspeyres index (L) would be

$$L = \frac{p_x^{90}x_0 + p_y^{90}y_0}{p_x^{80}x_0 + p_y^{80}y_0} \gtreqless 1.$$

Note that the quantities in each year are the same, even though the consumption patterns of people actually might have changed. Superscripts on the prices represent the years. If there has been no change in prices, L would be equal to one, because $p_x^{90} = p_x^{80}$ and $p_y^{90} = p_y^{80}$. If prices, on average, have risen, L would be greater than one; if they have fallen, the index would be less than one.

The BLS, of course, uses more than two goods in computing the CPI. In fact, it uses a market basket based on what an average urban family of four consumes. More generally, when there are more than two goods, we may write L as

$$L = \frac{\sum p_i' x_i^0}{\sum p_i x_i^0},$$

Figure 7–6   Inflation and the Consumer Price Index

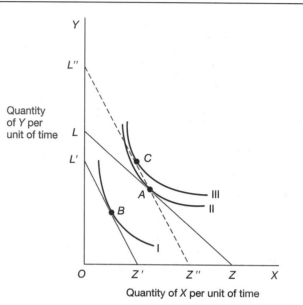

where p_i and p'_i are, respectively, the price of the ith good in the base year and its price in the year for which the index is calculated; x_i^0 is the consumption of the ith good in the base year.

Inflation, as measured by the change in the CPI, was approximately 14 percent in 1980, 10 percent in 1981, 6 percent in 1982, and 4 percent in 1983. Increases since 1983 have been about 4 percent. The CPI indicates that it takes about 4 percent more income to buy the same bundle of goods at the end of a year than it does at the beginning. Does this description give an accurate picture of the true effect of inflation? An indifference map and some budget lines will show that the answer depends on how much relative prices have changed over the year.

7.5.2   True Effect of Inflation

Let us return to the hypothetical two-good (X and Y) analysis. Figure 7–6 shows a particular individual's or household's equilibrium during the base period at point A on budget line LZ and indifference curve II. Let the prices of both goods increase, but let the price of X rise relative to the price of Y. If money income is held constant and the quantity of X is plotted along the horizontal axis, the budget line will shift backward and become steeper. The backward shift in the budget line reflects the fact that both prices rose; therefore, both the vertical and the horizontal intercepts of the budget line must decrease (move toward the origin). The increase in the steepness of the budget line reflects that p_x/p_y (the slope of the budget line) increases, because by assumption the price of X increased more than the price of *Y*. This new line is shown as $L'Z'$ in the figure. If the household had the same money income after prices changed, it would choose to consume at combination *B* on indifference curve I. Compared to point *A*, the household is clearly worse off.

The CPI shows how much additional income or expenditure the household needs to enable it to consume the *original bundle of goods* at the new prices, that is, to allow consumption at the old equilibrium, point *A*. As we noted, since the mid-1980s this would require about a 4 percent annual increase in income. In Figure 7–6, an increase in income that is just enough to shift the budget line to $L''Z''$ is needed. That is, $L''Z''$ has the same slope as the new line $L'Z'$, but there is enough additional income to allow the consumer to choose point *A*, the original consumption bundle. If this shift requires a 4 percent increase, this increase in income does not represent the true incidence of inflation. It actually overestimates the impact of a price increase.

You know from the previous analysis that, with budget line $L''Z''$, the combination shown at *A* would not be chosen. The household could increase utility by substituting *Y* for *X*, because the price of *Y* has decreased *relative* to that of *X*, even though both prices increased. The household would choose a point such as *C* on the higher indifference curve III and be better off. Because of the possibility of substitution, the increase in income needed to return to *A* would make the household better off than it was before. In this instance, the change in the CPI overestimated the effect of inflation.

To carry the analysis further, assume that both prices rise, but this time the price of *Y* increases by a greater percentage than the price of *X;* that is, p_x/p_y decreases. With money income constant, the budget line moves downward, but now it becomes less steep than *LZ*. Next, move the budget line with a lesser slope outward so that it passes through the original point *A*. The required increase in money income is the change in the CPI. The household once again can move to a higher indifference curve than II, this time by substituting *X* for *Y*. Once again, the change in the CPI overestimates the inflationary impact.

Finally, let both prices increase by precisely the same percentage. The budget line shifts downward, but the slope does not change; p_x/p_y remains constant. Now increase money income by the change in the CPI, so that the line passes through *A*. This budget line is the same as *LZ*. The household cannot reach a higher indifference curve by substituting. Utility is still maximized at the combination of goods given by *A*.

The only time the percentage increase in the CPI measures the amount that income must increase to make consumers exactly as well off as they were before a price change is when all prices change in exactly the same proportion. Only then does the increase in income given by the rise in the CPI exactly equal the increase necessary to make the consumer neither better nor worse off than without any inflation. Otherwise, the change in the CPI exaggerates the impact of inflation, due to consumers' ability to substitute. In such cases, if a consumer's income goes up by exactly as much as the rate of inflation, for example, as in a wage contract, inflation actually makes that consumer better off.

Figure 7–7   The Impact of Deflation

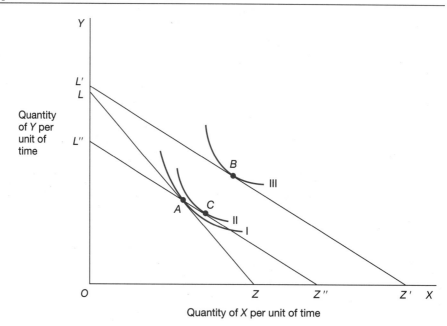

Quantity of *X* per unit of time

7.5.3   The True Effect of Deflation

Paradoxically, if all prices do not *decrease* proportionately, a fall in the CPI does not overestimate, but underestimates the impact of deflation. Deflation is represented by the decrease in income necessary to make a consumer neither better nor worse off than before the decrease in prices. To illustrate, begin with budget line *LZ* in Figure 7–7. The consumer maximizes utility by choosing the bundle of *X* and *Y* given by point *A* on indifference curve I. Now let the prices of both *X* and *Y* fall, but the price of *X* falls proportionately more than the price of *Y*. Suppose the price decline represents a fall of 10 percent in the CPI.

The budget line shifts outward to *L'Z'*. Since both prices decreased, both intercepts increase—move outward from the origin—and because the price of *Y* decreased relatively less than the price of *X*, p_x/p_y decreases, and the new budget line is less steep than *LZ*. The consumer chooses the bundle given at point *B* on indifference curve III and is clearly better off.

Suppose that after deflation the consumer's income is reduced 10 percent to reflect the 10 percent decline in the CPI. After the 10 percent reduction in income, the budget line shifts backward to *L"Z"*, which has the same slope as *L'Z'*, to reflect the change in relative prices, and passes through the original consumption bundle, *A*. The line must be shifted this far back so the original bundle can be purchased with the reduced income.

Clearly, *A* is not a utility-maximizing equilibrium. The consumer substitutes the relatively less-expensive *X* for *Y* and moves to a bundle such as *C* on indifference curve II. With a 10 percent decrease in the CPI and an offsetting 10 percent reduction in income, the consumer is better off. The decline in the CPI underestimates the true effect (in this case benefit) of deflation on consumers.

Given a 10 percent decrease in the CPI and in income, the consumer would substitute *Y* for *X,* if the price of *Y* falls relatively more than the price of *X.* Only if the prices of *X* and *Y* fall in exactly the same proportion does the decrease in the CPI exactly show the effect of deflation. The closer the price change is to a proportional change, the more closely the change in the CPI reflects the real impact of both inflation and deflation.

---

*Economics in
the News*

High Rates of Inflation Make Some Currencies Expensive[8]

There is a price for holding money in the form of cash or keeping money in a checking account. First, there is the opportunity cost of foregone interest. Currency could be invested in an interest-bearing account. Some checking accounts pay interest, but not as much as a certificate of deposit or a mutual fund account where the money has to stay put. Inflation is a second cost of holding money, and sometimes it is a very high cost. Inflation can be thought of as a declining market value of money. Money buys less; people notice inflation taking place by a general rise in prices. If the inflation rate is 5 percent for the year, then holding a dollar for a year means that a dollar can buy just $.95 worth of goods at the end of the year, or it would take $1.05 to buy the same goods. Besides the foregone interest given up by not investing the dollar, the price of holding the dollar with inflation is $.05. If the going interest rate is 7 percent, the price of keeping a dollar is the sum $.07 + $.05 = $.12.

In some countries, inflation makes it very expensive to hold the nation's currency. For example, in Argentina the 1990 inflation rate was about 6,000 percent. A 6,000 percent rate of inflation in the United States would mean that it takes $61.00 to buy what could have been purchased with a dollar a year earlier, or a dollar can buy between one and two cents worth of goods by year end. This is called *hyperinflation*, which makes it extremely costly to hold money. Under such conditions, people begin to buy and sell at prices marked in a foreign currency, such as the Japanese yen or U.S. dollar. Prices will be relatively stable in these currencies. People substitute away from the expensive home currency to a less-expensive foreign money. People may also forgo the use of money altogether and choose to barter with real goods. Shoes may be traded for fruit in a local market, a chicken may be exchanged for gasoline, and so on. The currency literally becomes too expensive to keep.

High rates of inflation and even hyperinflation are not unusual in developing countries. During the 1980s Brazil had steady inflation of about 200 percent per year, Mexico 90 percent, and Bolivia an astounding annual rate of 12,000 to 24,000 percent. Currencies help people trade. It is easier to buy gasoline with money than a chicken. But when the cost of holding money outweighs the benefits, buyers and sellers will resort to other means of trading.

---

[8]Information on the rates of inflation in developing countries is frequently reported in the weekly issues of *The Economist.*

7.6   Substitution and Taxation

The analysis in this section dates back to the work of Paul Samuelson 40 (or more) years ago.[9] Professor Samuelson compared the impact of taxing one item purchased by a consumer—say by a sales tax or a unit tax—as opposed to raising the same amount of revenue through an income tax. His conclusion was that taxation had the least impact on a consumer when income was taxed because an income tax did not restrict an individual's capability to substitute among goods and services. A sales tax, on the other hand, restricts substitution and, therefore, is more burdensome than an income tax.

7.6.1   Taxes in an Indifference Map

Figure 7–8 shows how a consumer allocates a monthly income between gallons of gasoline and expenditure on other goods. The value of the other goods on the vertical axis is simply measured in income not spent on gasoline. The consumer begins on budget line LZ. If no gasoline is purchased, this individual has $1,000 to spend on other things, which is the person's monthly income. The budget line LZ also shows that 800 gallons of gasoline can be purchased if zero income is spent on other goods. If 800 gallons can be purchased for $1,000 the price of gasoline must be 1,000/800 = $1.25. The consumer is in equilibrium at point A, spending $625 on other goods and consuming 300 gallons of gasoline a month.

Now suppose the state and federal governments tax gasoline so the price rises by $.75 a gallon to $2.00 a gallon.[10] The consumer still has $1,000 income if no gasoline is purchased, but since gasoline is more expensive, the budget line pivots inward. If the entire $1,000 were spent on gasoline, the maximum quantity that could be purchased would now be 500 gallons. The new budget line is labeled LZ' in Figure 7–8. The utility-maximizing equilibrium is now at point B on indifference curve I. The consumer spends $550 on other goods and purchases 225 gallons of gasoline. The government collects $.75 on each gallon sold, so the government's income is $.75 × 225 gallons = $168.75. The utility of the consumer declines because the tax moves the consumer to a lower indifference curve. In moving from point A to B, the consumer buys 75 gallons less gasoline and pays $168.75 in taxes.

Figure 7–8 can be used to illustrate that there is a way to collect the same amount of government revenue and leave the consumer on a higher indifference curve than curve I, though not so high as III. Let the tax be collected out of income, so that the government uses an income tax to get the $168.75. Since income declines but the price of gasoline remains the same, the budget line has the same slope as LZ and is shifted inward until the consumer has $831.25 to spend if no gasoline is purchased. The vertical intercept in Figure 7–8 is $831.25, as shown. The new budget line is L''Z''. If the entire income is spent on gasoline, 665 gallons can be purchased.

[9]Paul Samuelson, *Foundations of Economic Analysis* (Cambridge, Mass.: University Press, 1947). For further details, see Joseph Stiglitz, *Economics of the Public Sector,* 2nd ed. (New York: W.W. Norton, 1988), chapter 18.

[10]For the sake of argument in this discussion we shall assume that the government collects $.75 as its tax. Hence the burden of the tax is falling entirely on the consumer.

Figure 7–8   An Income Tax versus a Unit Tax

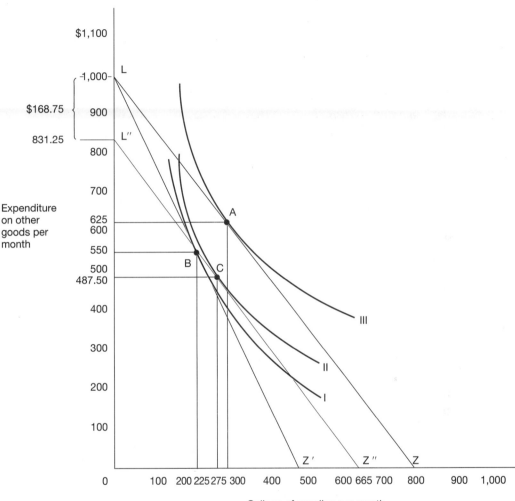

The equilibrium on budget line $L''Z''$ is point C. The consumer is on a higher indifference curve with the income tax than at equilibrium point B with the unit tax on gasoline, and is therefore better off. The consumer can never be worse off with an income tax than with the equivalent unit tax, because budget line $L''Z''$ goes through point B. This means the individual could consume at point B if this combination is desired. The reason $L''Z''$ goes through B is that the consumer pays an excise tax of $168.75, which we made, by construction of the figure, equivalent to the income tax.

Budget line $L''Z''$, therefore, allows the individual more latitude to substitute between other goods and gasoline. The increased capability to substitute lets the consumer reach a higher indifference curve, holding the amount of government revenue collected constant. Switching from an excise tax to an income tax is a

Pareto superior policy change. Consumers are helped, and the tax coffers are unaffected. If income taxes are a better way of collecting money, why do governments use excise taxes? There are at least a couple of reasonable answers.

First, it can be less expensive for governments to collect an excise tax than an income tax. There are far fewer gasoline stations than gasoline buyers. The government can hire a few tax collectors to go around every few months to collect the gasoline tax and enforce the law. Collection and auditing would become more expensive if this were done for an income tax on each wage earner. This expense must be weighed against the increased benefits to the consumer, and the choice ultimately requires subjective considerations.

A second reason comes from a desire on the part of government authorities to tax equitably. Often revenues are set aside for certain purposes. Taxes on gasoline, for instance, are usually collected for road building and maintenance. More recently, however, some of the tax money has been going into general expenditure funds to balance state and federal budgets. Those who use more gasoline pay more taxes, and these are the people who use the roads the most. They are most responsible for wear and tear and, in most cases, benefit the most when new roads are built. An income tax would not generally connect the road user with the tax. It could in principle, but the tax form would increase in complexity, thereby increasing the cost of collection even more.

Economics in the News

Taxing Cigarettes for a Healthier Society[11]

The Surgeon General during the Reagan administration, Dr. C. Everett Koop, stated that it was his objective to have a "smoke-free society" by the year 2000. In recent years, programs that educate Americans about the health hazards of smoking have been credited with reducing smoking by 1.5 percent a year. At this rate of reduction, 64 million people will still be smoking, on average, a pack a day by the year 2000.

But what about taxing cigarettes to reduce consumption? The purpose would not be to raise revenue for the government, but to reduce smoking. The economic theory just discussed shows that an excise tax would be better than an income tax for reducing consumption. The degree to which smoking would decrease depends, of course, on the elasticity of demand. Current price elasticity estimates are .6 to .7 for all smokers; they are higher for new smokers age 12–17, about 1.4.

In 1990 the excise tax on cigarettes was $.16 per pack, which generated about $4.7 billion in tax revenue. Currently the tax is $.32 per pack. Suppose the tax were raised to $.75/pack? Total cigarette consumption would decline by about 40 percent. If the tax were raised to $1.29/pack, consumption would fall by 50 percent. Tax revenue would rise to somewhere in the range of $13.3 billion to $18.6 billion. An excise tax may not be the most efficient way to raise revenue, but it would certainly be a more effective way to reduce smoking than "education." And instead of spending government revenues on education, revenues would be collected through the increased tax. These increased revenues could be used to support medical research.

---

[11]This news is based on two reports in *Fortune:* "Elasticity, It's Wonderful," February 13, 1989, p. 123–24 and "Smoking 101," February 27, 1989, p. 134.

7.7 Summary

This chapter has analyzed several economic topics using the theory of consumer behavior developed in Chapters 5 and 6. Many more topics can be and have been analyzed using these same tools. We consider those discussed in this chapter to be some of the most important topics toward which indifference maps further the study and application of economics.

The first application gave an insight into why people gain from participating in markets. Trading puts individuals on higher indifference curves, so they benefit from trade. Trades will continue to be made until respective marginal rates of substitution are equal. Whenever the *MRS*'s are equal, two consumers are defined to be in an *exchange equilibrium*. This equilibrium is *Pareto optimal*. Pareto optimality exists whenever any further exchange would harm at least one participant in the trade. If two traders were not in exchange equilibrium, a trade could be arranged that would help one or both individuals and hurt neither.

Consumer's surplus is an important tool in applied economics. It is a measure of how much a consumer benefits from participating in a market. Conceptually it is the area between the demand curve and the market price. Consumer's surplus is based on the notion that demand measures how much a consumer would be willing to pay for a good or service. Using an indifference map, we showed that an ordinary demand curve is an estimate of how much a buyer would be willing to pay. A better estimate is a *compensated demand* schedule. However, if the income effect is not large, compensated and ordinary demand curves are close to each other.

In section 7.4, we discussed how indifference maps can be used to analyze a choice between labor and leisure. The choices made can then be used to generate a *labor supply* curve. Economists believe that, in general, as wage rates rise, more labor and less leisure will result, but this does not follow from the theory of consumer utility maximization. As income rises, individuals may supply less labor to get a more desired mix of income and leisure. Thus the labor supply curve may bend backward. Have you ever been so busy working that you felt like you did not have time to spend the money you earned? This is the very reason labor supply curves may bend backward as income rises.

The last two sections of this chapter explain the importance of substitution when prices and income change. Price indexes do not accurately reflect how consumers are affected by inflation because the gains from substitution are not adequately measured by an index. The effects of inflation are generally overestimated, and the impact of deflation is underestimated by the consumer price index in the United States. In section 7.6, we showed that an income tax is a better way of collecting government revenue than an excise tax. An income tax allows more opportunity to substitute between goods and services, and in the process, a consumer can reach a higher indifference curve. There are some caveats here. First, an income tax may be relatively more expensive to collect, and second, an excise tax may be a fairer tax than an income tax, especially if the tax money is used for a special purpose.

Answers to   *Applying the Theory*

7.1   In many cases trade is blocked when there are "spillover effects" from the exchange. Even though the exchange benefits the individuals directly involved in the transaction, the trade harms, or has the potential to harm, those not directly involved. A drug trade leads to other crime because of addiction, for instance. The addicts steal to support a habit. Hence, increased crime is a "spillover" from the drug trade.

7.2   Income redistribution is not Pareto superior, but many governments do it. It is difficult to think of any kind of redistribution that is Pareto superior but undesirable. This is why the Pareto principle is universally appealing. Pareto superior exchanges put resources to better use. Anyone can think of redistributions toward themselves that are "worthwhile" but not Pareto superior. Would you like a check in the mail for $1 million from Uncle Sam? This redistribution of income does not satisfy the Pareto principle, but it would still be nice.

7.3   If leisure is not a Giffen good, then considering both the substitution and income effects, as leisure time becomes more expensive less should be consumed. On the price-consumption line SS' in Figure 7–5, Panel A, less leisure is taken along the curve between points A and C. Near point C at OC' units of leisure, the price-consumption line bends. Now as leisure becomes more expensive, more is consumed. This means the good is Giffen, and the demand curve is sloping upward.

Technical Problems

1. Joan and Jim are given a weekly endowment of burgers (B) and shakes (S) of $22B$ and $19S$ and $25B$ and $17S$, respectively. Joan's marginal rate of substitution ($-\Delta B/\Delta S$) is 4 and Jim's MRS is 6.
    a. What exchange would make Joan better off and Jim neither better nor worse off?
    b. What exchange would make Jim better off and Joan neither better nor worse off?
    c. Between what two rates of exchange would both be better off?
    d. What rates of exchange would make Joan better off and Jim worse off?
    e. What rates of exchange would make Jim better off and Joan worse off?
    f. In parts *a–e*, which moves are Pareto superior?
    g. If Joan and Jim continue to exchange burgers and shakes until they reach a Pareto optimal situation,
      (1) What would be a possibility for each person's MRS in this situation? Explain.
      (2) What would be a possibility for each person's consumption of burgers and shakes in this situation? Explain.
2. Calculate a Laspeyres price index for 1992 for an individual who consumed 4 dozen eggs, 60 pounds of meat, 2 pairs of shoes, 1 pair of jeans, and 30 movies per period in 1990 and use 1990 as the base year. Prices are given in the following table:

	1990	1992
Eggs/dozen	$ 1.20	$ 1.35
Meat/pound	1.25	1.65
Shoes/pair	45.00	55.00
Jeans/pair	38.00	45.00
Movies	4.00	4.50

What percentage increase in income would this consumer need to buy the same bundle of goods in 1992? Explain.

3. Explain precisely
   a. Why in every situation that is not Pareto optimal, a Pareto superior exchange is possible.
   b. Why in every situation that is Pareto optimal, a Pareto superior exchange is not possible.
   c. Why a Pareto optimal situation is not necessarily utility maximizing for the two individuals together.

4. Figure E.7–1 shows an individual's indifference map between leisure and income. Ignore indifference curve III for now and assume that curves I and II make up the map. The unit of time is one day of 24 hours. The wage rate is $3 per hour.
   a. How much does the individual choose to work? How much leisure does he or she consume?
   b. Let the wage rate rise to $5 an hour. Ignoring III, what is his or her work and leisure time? Suppose, at the wage rate of $5, the individual was taxed just enough to choose a point on the original indifference curve I.
   c. What is the substitution effect for the wage change from $3 to $5?
   d. Return the taxed income. What is the income effect?
   e. What is the total effect?
   f. In this example, leisure is a(n) (normal, inferior) good, and the income effect (offsets, reinforces) the substitution effect.
   g. Derive the associated supply curve for labor.
   h. Now let the relevant indifference map be I and III. Derive the new supply-of-labor curve for points A and D.
   i. Between curves I and III, for leisure the total effect of a wage increase from $3 to $5 is _____; the substitution effect is _____; and the income effect is _____.
   j. Leisure is now a(n) (normal, inferior) good.
   k. What can you say about the classification of leisure and a backward-bending supply of labor?
   l. Draw an indifference curve IV tangent to the budget line associated with $5 so that leisure is a normal good, but the supply of labor is not backward bending.

5. An individual can choose between income and leisure as depicted in Figure E.7–2. The maximum amount of time available in the period is OT, the first wage rate is indicated by the slope of MT; the new higher rate by the slope of RT. Regardless of the wage rate, the person works just long enough to earn income OI.
   a. Draw in the indifference curves at the two points of equilibrium.
   b. Is leisure a normal or an inferior good to the individual? Prove this graphically.

Figure E.7–1

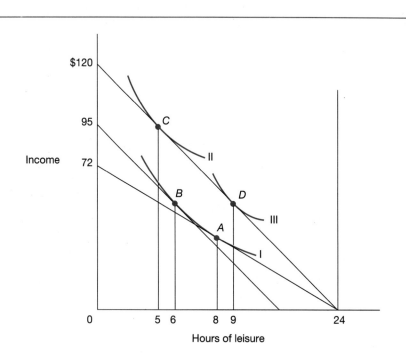

Figure E.7–2

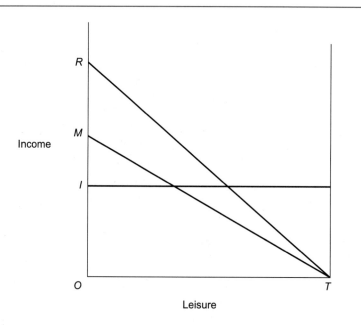

6. On an income of $100 per week, an individual can purchase good X (horizontal axis) at a price of $5 per unit and a good Y (vertical axis) also at a price of $5 per unit.

   a. On a graph draw the budget line, and assume the individual chooses to consume 10 units of each good, and call this point B.

   b. Price changes occur and P_x is now $4 and P_y is $10. The individual receives a cost-of-living increase enabling him or her to purchase the original bundle B at these new prices.

   (1) Draw the new budget line.

   (2) Is the individual better or worse off? Will more or less of good X be consumed? Explain.

   (3) What is the minimum cost-of-living increase that will enable him or her to be as well off at the new prices as at B? (Your answer will depend on the shape of your indifference curve.)

7. Suppose the rate of inflation for 1992 was 5 percent as measured by the consumer price index (CPI). Assume that you consume two goods X and Y and P_x and P_y both increased in 1992. Also assume that you were buying at the beginning of 1992 exactly the same market basket of X and Y represented in the CPI. If your income increased by 5 percent in 1992, were you made better off, worse off, or the same "under the following circumstances"? Prove using indifference curve analysis.

   a. P_X/P_Y increased.

   b. P_X/P_Y decreased.

   c. P_X/P_Y remained constant.

8. In each of the following cases, show graphically the equilibrium for the labor-leisure decision. Discuss that equilibrium.

   a. The individual is free to choose how many hours to work per day, the wage rate is constant, and this person has no source of income other than what is earned from work.

   b. The individual is not free to choose hours worked, but must work 10 hours per day or not at all, the wage is constant, and there is no source of income other than that earned from work.

   c. The individual is free to choose how many hours worked per day, the wage is constant up to eight hours, but double time is paid for all hours above eight, and there is no outside source of income.

   d. The individual is free to choose how many hours worked per day, the wage rate is constant, and the individual has an independent source of income that pays a constant amount per day.

   e. The individual must work 8 or more hours per day or not at all, the wage rate is constant up to 10 hours, but a double-time wage is paid for hours above 10, and the individual has an outside source of income.

9. Decide on the Pareto optimal or Pareto superior numbers in each of the following cases:

   a. Bill Davis loves bass fishing. It does not matter to him whether or not he catches anything; the important thing is getting out. The more trips, the happier is Bill. Mrs. Davis hates bass. The fewer fish brought home, the happier is Mrs. Davis. On his last outing, Bill caught eight fish. How many fish (in integer numbers) would be *Pareto superior* for the Davis household on the next trip? What is the *Pareto optimal* number of fish?

Figure E.7–3

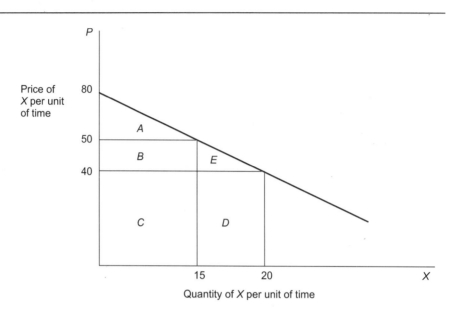

Price of X per unit of time

Quantity of X per unit of time

b. Suppose two people must work together in the same room. Jane likes the temperature exactly at 72°; her utility declines if it gets any hotter or colder. Ralph likes it hot, the hotter the better for his taste. Is 70° a Pareto optimal temperature? Is 75°? By applying the definition of Pareto optimality, list the range of temperatures that could be Pareto optimal.

c. Bob and Jane have three children. Bob would like to have more, but Jane's preferences are not to have any more. What number of children is Pareto optimal?

10. The demand curve in Figure E.7–3 has the equation $P = 80 - 2X$.

a. At a price of 40 what is consumer's surplus? Identify the areas and derive the dollar amount.

b. At a price of 50 what is consumer's surplus? Identify the areas and derive the dollar amount.

c. How much consumer's surplus is lost by the price increase? Identify the areas and get the dollar amount.

11. Use Figure E.7–4 to answer this question. Recall that consumer surplus is the area under demand and above price. Recall also that the area of a triangle is 1/2 × base × height. In the figure, demand curve D is the ordinary demand curve that includes both the substitution and income effect. For future reference, this good is a normal good.

a. If product price is $40, what is the consumer surplus, considering only the ordinary demand?

b. Let d_1 be the compensated demand, holding utility constant at the level associated with equilibrium at the $40 price. This demand is less elastic than D because the good is normal and d_1 does not show an income effect while D does. What is consumer surplus considering d_1 as the demand curve? Compare the two.

Figure E.7–4

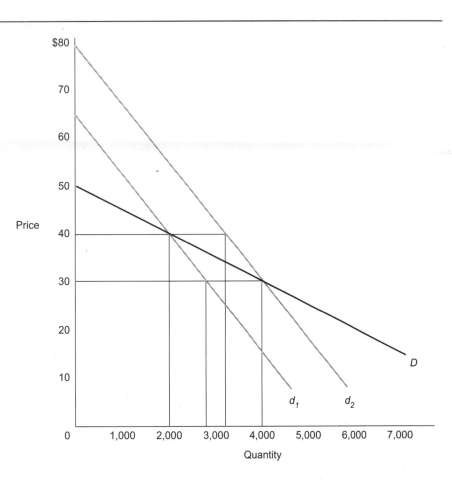

c. If price falls to $30, what is consumer surplus using *D?* What is the gain in surplus? Using *D* what would be the loss in surplus if price rises from $30 to $40?

d. Now, considering demand d_1, what is the consumer surplus if price falls from $40 to $30. What is the gain in surplus? Compare the two demands.

e. Now, d_2 is the compensated demand, substitution effect only, holding utility constant at the level associated with equilibrium when price is $30. Considering d_2, what is consumer surplus when price is $30? What is consumer surplus using d_2 when price rises to $40? What is the lost surplus? Compare this with the lost surplus when price rises along *D*, the ordinary demand?

   (Note: The gain in surplus when price falls from $40 to $30 is larger using *D* than using d_1. The loss when price rises from $30 to $40 is smaller using *D* than using d_2.)

f. Take the average of the surplus gain along d_1, the loss along d_2. Compare this with the equivalent gain or loss along *D*. (Note: This similarity gives additional evidence why economists consider changes in consumer surplus along an ordinary demand curve as a good indication of changes is welfare, even though consumer surplus along a compensated demand is theoretically a better measure of welfare when the income effect is not insignificant.)

Analytical Problems

1. Recall the paradox of value for which we used diamonds and water as an example. Using the paradox of value analysis, discuss why athletes such as Jose Canseco and Steffi Graf or entertainers such as Madonna and Bill Cosby make huge incomes, whereas people in occupations such as math teachers, nurses, and fire fighters, who are surely more valuable to society, make so much less.

2. Certain government entitlements such as Social Security payments are automatically given cost-of-living adjustments (COLAs) to offset the effect of inflation on the recipients. These COLAs are linked to the CPI. What are the implications of this linkage of COLAs to the CPI?

3. What type of country would be more likely to have a backward-bending supply of labor for the economy as a whole: an advanced industrial country or a much less developed country? Explain.

4. Over the last decade, there is evidence showing that, as more medical doctors practice in a community, the real price of medical care rises. Could this be the result of a backward-bending supply curve among physicians? Can you think of other causes for this trend?

5. Suppose prices increase by 10 percent over an entire 10-year period in a certain country. Then during 1 year, they increase another 10 percent. Would you expect changes in the consumer price index to overestimate the impact of inflation more or less from year to year or over a 10-year period? Explain.

6. In a recent interview, a marketer said that when a product is not selling you must either change the product, advertise, or reduce the price low enough to "create a demand for it." Can any of these selling strategies create demand? Discuss this question by using budget lines and indifference curves.

7. Social Security payments are presently tied to rises in the consumer price index. A given percent rise in the CPI is roughly matched by the same increase in payments to those receiving these benefits. Retired people spend most of their income on food and fuel, and these two items have been the major factors in CPI rises. Taking this into account, can retired people reach a higher indifference curve if Social Security payments are increased when the CPI rises? Argue analytically with an indifference map.

8. Jill and Jonathan are two children. Jonathan at first is happily playing with a teddy bear. Jill sees it and takes it for herself. This makes Jonathan unhappy; he cries and complains to his mother, who then makes Jill return the bear to Jonathan. But Jill complains that returning the bear to Jonathan is not fair. Is she right? Use the Pareto rule for optimality. What weakness is there in the Pareto rule for efficiency?

9. Suppose at the end of the semester your professor suddenly decides to change the final exam policy. The policy was that everyone would take the exam. Identify in the following list those changes that make the *class* unequivocally better off, those that would make the *class* worse off, and those for which the conclusion is indeterminate. Explain.

  a. There will be no final exam. Everyone receives as a final grade, his or her current grade.
  b. The final is optional. You may take your current grade as your final grade, or you may take the final.
  c. The final is mandatory, but it only counts if it improves your average.
  d. There will be a final, but points will be taken from the high-grade students and given to the low-grade students, until everyone has the same grade.
  e. The professor gives all students an A, regardless of their current grades.
  f. The final is mandatory, but there will be a makeup final if a student is not satisfied with his or her final grade.

PART IV

Production and Cost

CHAPTER 8

Theory of Production: One Variable Input

8.1   Introduction

Demand theory makes up only half the theory of price. The other half of the theory is supply: How much of a good or service are firms willing and able to sell at any given price. To make this decision firms must know how much it will cost to produce and sell given amounts of the good or service. The basic foundation of the theory of cost, and therefore of the theory of supply, is production theory, the subject of this chapter and Chapter 9.

Production, in a general sense, is the creation of any good or service. Production can take many forms: Ford Motor Company produces automobiles, a construction firm produces buildings, a doctor produces medical care, a city government produces police protection, your school produces education, and so on. Although we will develop the theory of production for a firm producing physical goods, the theories developed here are also applicable to the production of services and production by government agencies or nonprofit institutions, such as hospitals and universities. We will concentrate on the production of goods by firms because it is easier to specify the inputs used in the production process and to identify the quantity of output. For example, it is easier to specify the number of stoves produced by a factory or the amount of wheat produced on a farm than the amount of health care produced by a doctor, the amount of police protection produced by a local government, or the amount of education produced by a university. Keep in mind, however, that the basic principles always apply to production by institutions other than firms and to services as well as to goods.

This chapter begins with a discussion of some basic concepts of production. It then describes the simplest type of production process—when a firm is able to change the level of usage of only a single input—and shows how cost is related to single-input production. In Chapter 9, we will focus on the more complex process of transforming two or more inputs into the production of a single good.

8.2   Production Functions

With a given state of technology or knowledge, the quantity of output that a firm can produce depends on the quantities of the various inputs it uses. A *production function* shows the maximum amount of output that can be produced at given levels of input use.

Definition

A production function is a schedule (or table, or mathematical equation) showing the *maximum amount* of output that a firm can produce using any specified set of inputs, given the level of technology.

Production processes typically require a wide variety of inputs. They are not so simple as "labor," "capital," and "material". Labor can take many forms, from the least-skilled worker to top management. Capital can include buildings, trucks, different types of machinery, and so forth. Materials can be steel for automobiles, cloth for apparel, or chemicals for medicines. A firm employs many qualitatively different types of inputs. For simplicity, however, we will generally assume that only two broadly defined inputs are used—labor and capital. We will assume labor embodies all types of labor, capital consists of all physical equipment, and both inputs can be numerically measured.

We emphasize the importance of the words "maximum output" in the definition of a production function. A given combination of labor and capital can produce many levels of output, depending upon how intensively they are used. However, only the maximum possible output that the combination can produce is a combination on the production function. For example, suppose that a production function indicates that 10 workers using 2 machines can produce 100 units of output a day. Presumably the 10 workers could slack off a bit, and less than 100 units of output could be produced. This would not be a combination on the production function. Outputs that are less than the maximum output possible are not *technically efficient*.

Definition

A production process is technically efficient if the output that is produced is the maximum output possible from a given combination of inputs. All points on a production function are technically efficient.[1]

---

[1]Later in this chapter, we will contrast technological efficiency with economic efficiency, which means that a given output is produced at the lowest possible cost.

8.2.1 Short and Long Runs

When analyzing a firm's production decisions, it is convenient to introduce an important distinction. At a given point in time, inputs may be classified as fixed or variable. A fixed input exists when the quantity of a factor of production cannot readily be changed, even when market conditions indicate change is desirable. No input is ever absolutely fixed, no matter how short the period of time under consideration. Frequently, for the sake of analytical simplicity, economists hold some inputs fixed, reasoning that although these inputs could be adjusted, the cost of immediate variation is large enough to put them out of the range of consideration. Buildings, major pieces of machinery, and managerial personnel are examples of inputs that generally cannot be rapidly augmented or diminished. A variable input, on the other hand, is a factor of production, the quantity of which may be changed quite readily. Many types of labor services and the inputs of raw and processed materials fall into this category.

For the sake of analysis, economists use the presence of fixed inputs to decide when a firm is operating with a short-run or long-run production function. The *short run* refers to that period of time when the quantity of one or more productive inputs is fixed. Therefore, changes in output must be accomplished exclusively by changes in the use of variable inputs. If producers wish to expand output in the short run, they must do so, for example, by using more hours of labor service with the existing plant and equipment. Similarly, if they wish to reduce output in the short run, they may discharge certain types of workers, but they cannot immediately "discharge" a building or a diesel locomotive, even though its use may fall to zero.

The *long run* is defined as that period of time (or planning horizon) during which all inputs are variable. The long run, in other words, refers to that time in the future when output changes can be accomplished in the manner most advantageous to the producer. In the short run, a producer may be able to expand output only by operating an existing plant for more hours per day. In the long run, both labor and capital can be changed, additional productive facilities can be installed, and normal working hours restored, for example.

The short run and the long run do not refer to an actual difference in the time dimension or duration of the time period, in terms of weeks, months, or years. A factory might operate for many years with the same plant, even though the plant may be smaller than the owners desire. The firm is in the short run during this period. When it decides to build a new, larger plant and perhaps to expand the use of other inputs as well, it is in the long run. Once the new plant is built, it returns to the short run, a period that may last many more years. Think of the long run as a planning horizon. The firm plans in the long run, when all inputs can be varied. It produces in the short run, when some inputs are fixed.

We can summarize the short and long runs with the following:

Relation

The short run is the period of time during which some inputs are fixed (fixed inputs) and some inputs can be varied (variable inputs). The long run is the period of time during which all inputs are variable. Although the short run and long run refer to time, no actual time dimension in terms of weeks, months, or years should be inferred. The short run can be quite long, and the long run can be quite short. The period is specified only by the variability of inputs.

8.2.2   Fixed or Variable Proportions

Most production functions allow at least some inputs to be substituted for one another in reaching an output target. When substitution is possible, we say inputs may be used in variable proportions. There are two different ways of stating the principle of variable proportions. First, variable-proportions production implies that output can be changed in the short run by changing the amount of variable inputs used in cooperation with the fixed inputs. Naturally, when the amount of one input changes while others remain constant or do not change as much, the ratio of inputs will change. Second, when production is subject to variable proportions, the same output can be produced by various combinations of inputs— that is, by different input ratios. This may apply to the long run as well as the short run.

Most economists regard production under conditions of variable proportions as typical of both the short and the long run. When making an investment decision, for instance, a producer may choose among a wide variety of different production processes. As polar opposites, an automobile can be practically handmade, or it can be made by assembly-line techniques. In the short run, however, there may be some cases where output is subject to fixed proportions.

Fixed-proportions production means that there is one, and only one, ratio or mix of inputs that can be used to produce a good. If output is expanded or contracted, all inputs must be expanded or contracted at the same rate to maintain the fixed-input ratio. At first glance, this might seem the usual condition: one worker and one shovel produce a ditch; two parts hydrogen and one part oxygen produce water. Adding a second shovel or a second part of oxygen will not augment the rate of production. In such cases, the producer has little discretion about what combination of inputs to employ. The only decision is how much to produce.

In actuality, examples of fixed-proportions production are hard to come by. Certainly some "ingredient" inputs are often used in relatively fixed proportions to output. Otherwise the quality of the product would change. There is so much leather in a pair of shoes of a particular size and style. Use less leather, and you have a different type of shoe. In these cases, the producer has little choice over the quantity of input per unit of output. But fixed-ingredient inputs are really only an example of a fixed input in the short-run. Historically, when these "necessary" ingredients have become very expensive or practically impossible to obtain, businesses, generally under the lure of profits, have invented new processes, discovered new ingredients, or somehow overcome the problem of an increasingly scarce ingredient. As a consequence, we will direct our attention here to production where the producer has some control over the mix of inputs and will concentrate on production under variable proportions.

Table 8–1   A Long-Run Production Function

(1) Workers (L)	Capital (K)		
	10	20	30
	(2) Output	(3) Output	(4) Output
0	0	0	0
1	10	23	33
2	45	65	83
3	77	112	139
4	107	155	193
5	132	193	241
6	153	226	284
7	168	252	319
8	176	270	347
9	179	278	367
10	173	276	377

8.2.3   A Hypothetical Long-Run Production Function

A production function can be shown by a table, schedule, equation, or graph. We will begin our study of production functions with the hypothetical long-run function shown in Table 8–1. This production function, as you will see, illustrates several important principles of production. The firm uses only two types of inputs, labor (L) and capital (K) to produce its product.

The firm can choose among only three levels of capital (or machines): 10 units, 20 units, or 30 units. It can choose any number of workers, in increments from zero through 10. Column 2 in the Table shows the maximum amount of output that can be produced with each level of labor usage working with 10 units of capital. Columns 3 and 4 show the maximum amount of output that zero through 10 workers can produce with, respectively, 20 and 30 units of capital.

This production function reflects three assumptions commonly used in production theory: (1) No output can be produced with zero workers at any level of capital. (2) At a given level of capital, increases in the number of workers increase output up to a point. Beyond that point, hiring additional workers causes output to decline. For example, adding the 10th worker with either 10 or 20 units of capital causes output to fall, but not with 30 units of capital. The reason output declines with the 10th worker in the first two cases is possibly because so many workers using the smaller amounts of capital can cause the workplace to become congested, and workers get in each other's way. With 30 units of capital, there is enough capital for all the workers, so output does not begin to decline over the relevant range of labor, but it may begin to decline with further increases in labor. (3) The more capital used by any given number of workers, the larger the output that can be

Figure 8–1   Total Product of Labor at Three Levels of Capital

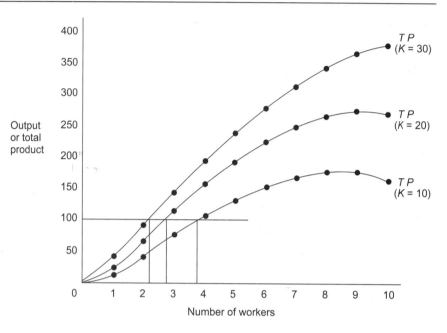

produced using that many workers. For example, four workers can produce 107 units of output with 10 units of capital, 155 with 20 units, and 193 with 30 units. As you can see, the output at every other amount of labor increases as capital is increased.

This production function allows labor and output to vary only discretely. Let us assume now that labor and output for zero through 10 workers can vary continuously at each of the three levels of capital. Thus, labor can take on any value between zero and 10, possibly by using part-time workers. Figure 8–1 shows each combination of labor and output in Table 8–1, but the points are connected in the graph to allow for continuous variation in labor and output. Output or *total product* (*TP*) at every level of labor using 10 units of capital is given by the curve *TP*(*K* = 10). The relation between labor and output is *TP*(*K* = 20) for 20 units of capital and *TP*(*K* = 30) for 30 units of capital. Output (*TP*) is plotted along the vertical axis, and the number of workers is plotted along the horizontal. These three total output or total product curves reflect the three assumptions noted above. No output can be produced with zero workers, no matter what the amount of capital. Output increases, up to a point, as the number of workers increases at each level of capital. As capital is increased, the maximum amount of output that a given number of workers can produce increases also. That is, *TP*(*K* = 30) is above *TP*(*K* = 20), which is above *TP*(*K* = 10).

The three curves in the figure also reflect two additional assumptions of production theory. First, output increases at an increasing rate for low levels of labor usage (the slope of *TP* increases). For example, with 20 units of capital, the first worker adds 23 units of output (from zero to 23), the second adds 42 units (from 23 to 65), and the third adds 47 (from 65 to 112). Then output increases at a decreasing rate as more labor is used (the slope of *TP* decreases). For example, output increases by 43 units (from 112 to 155) when the fourth worker is added, and it increases by 38 units when the fifth worker is added (from 155 to 193).

The second assumption illustrated by the graph is that given levels of output can be produced by more than one combination of capital and labor. For example, moving from an output of 100 on the vertical axis to each of the three *TP* curves, you can see that 100 units of output can be produced by approximately 2.25 workers and 30 units of capital, or 2.75 workers and 20 units of capital, or 3.75 workers and 10 units of capital. As you can see, other levels of output can be produced with more than one combination of labor and capital.

The production function shown in Figure 8–1 and Table 8–1 is clearly a variable-proportions production function. From one definition, different levels of a variable input (in this case labor) can be combined with a fixed amount of another input (capital) to produce different amounts of output. From the other definition, inputs can be used in different combinations to produce the same level of output. This will be the type of production function used in this and the following chapter. We turn next to further analysis of variable proportions production under the most simple conditions: a single variable input is used with a fixed input or inputs to produce different levels of output.

Economics in the News

Output and the Number of Workers on Wall Street

Is there a relation between a firm's output and the number of workers it hires? According to *Business Week*, "Wall Street Runs Scared," May 1, 1989, pp. 24–25, the answer is yes, at least on Wall Street. From mid-1988 through the first quarter of 1989, the average daily number of shares traded on the New York Stock Exchange had fallen approximately 20 percent. The number of announced mergers and acquisitions per quarter had fallen from 1,679 to 1,296, a decline of 23 percent. Wall Street analysts at the time were predicting that brokerage firms would substantially reduce the number of brokers, traders, investment bankers, and support staff they employed. Insiders believed that Drexel Burnham Lambert, one of the largest firms, would reduce its employees by as much as 40 percent. Other brokerage firms were already making such reductions.

This pattern followed the pattern set after the stock market crash of October 1987, when more than 17,000 Wall Streeters lost their jobs. Furthermore, during the previous financial expansion, most firms increased their work force significantly. When these brokerage firms do more business, they hire more employees. When they do less business, they hire fewer employees. What else could they do? It is hard to imagine them increasing or decreasing the size of their buildings as their sales expand or contract. And, what other important inputs do they hire?

A large number of other types of firms follow this pattern. When you hear that automobile sales are down, you typically hear also that many auto workers are unemployed. The same is true for steel, oil, retail trade, and other businesses. Every now and

(continued)

then you hear of a plant closing, but this is rare compared to the change in employees. The same is the case for expansion. Most firms expand by increasing the number of workers. It takes a relatively long time for a firm to decide to build a new plant or a new store. When it does, it must be the case that the firm believes that its sales increase will be rather permanent. Thus, the assumption that firms change their output by changing the number of workers appears to be a reasonably good approach to how actual firms behave in the short run.

8.3 Analysis of Production with a Single Variable Input

We now extend the theory of production in the short run. For simplicity, we will continue to assume variable-proportions production when a single variable input is combined with one or more fixed inputs.

8.3.1 Total, Average, and Marginal Product

Begin by assuming that the firm whose production function is shown in Table 8–1 and Figure 8–1 installs 20 units of capital (machines). The firm is now in the short run. Capital is the fixed input. The only way to change output is to change the amount of labor. The total product curve for labor is now $TP(K = 20)$ in Figure 8–1. The short-run production function, with labor the only variable input and capital fixed at 20, is reproduced from Table 8–1 in columns (1) and (2) of Table 8–2. Column (2) shows the maximum amount of output that can be produced using zero through 10 workers with 20 units of capital.

The *average product* of labor is the amount of output divided by that amount of labor employed. The average product of labor is obtained from the production function in columns (1) and (2) of Table 8–2 and is shown in column (3).

Definition

The average product of any input is total output divided by the amount of the input used. Thus, average product is the output-input ratio, or output per unit of input for each level of the input and the corresponding level of output.

It will be convenient later to use the notation AP_i for "the average product of the ith input." For labor, AP_L is the output per worker, or

$$AP_L = \frac{\text{Output}}{\text{Amount of Labor}} = \frac{Q}{L}.$$

As shown in Table 8–2, AP_L increases through the fourth worker when AP_L is 38.8 ($= 155/4$), then declines thereafter, but never becomes negative.

Marginal product is the additional output obtained from a one-unit increase in the variable input, with the use of all other inputs fixed. Marginal product is generally measured as the change in output from any small change in the variable input.

Table 8–2   Total, Average, and Marginal When Product Capital = 20 units

(1) Workers (L)	(2) Output (Q)	(3) Average Product (Q/L)		(4) Marginal Product (ΔQ/ΔL)
0	0	—		
			>	23
1	23	23.0		
			>	42
2	65	32.5		
			>	47
3	112	37.3		
			>	43
4	155	38.8		
			>	38
5	193	38.6		
			>	33
6	226	37.7		
			>	26
7	252	36.0		
			>	18
8	270	33.8		
			>	8
9	278	30.9		
			>	−2
10	276	27.6		

Definition

Marginal product is the change in output attributed to a one-unit change in input use. For small changes in the use of the variable input, it is estimated as the change in output per unit change in the input.

We will frequently use the notation MP_i for the marginal product of the ith input. For small changes in labor, we measure it as

$$MP_L = \frac{\text{Change in Output}}{\text{Change in Labor}} = \frac{\Delta Q}{\Delta L}.$$

Column 4 of Table 8–2 shows marginal product as labor changes by one unit.

As you can see in the table, marginal product in column 4 increases as labor increases at low levels of labor. Marginal product increases until $MP_L = 47$, when the third worker is added and output increases by 47. Then marginal product declines as additional workers are added up to the ninth worker, at which point output increases by 8 units. Since adding the 10th worker results in a decrease of two units of output, the marginal product is negative (-2). Marginal product would continue to be negative if more workers were added.

It is important to understand that we speak of the marginal product of labor, not the marginal product of a particular laborer. We assume all workers are the same in the sense that reducing the number of workers, for example, from eight to seven would cause the total product to fall from 270 to 252—regardless of which of the eight workers is released. The order of hiring or discharging makes no difference.

On closer inspection of the table you can see that for the first four workers when average product is rising, marginal product is greater than the average. After the fourth worker, when average product is falling, marginal product is less than average. This result is not a peculiarity of the table; it occurs for any function where the average peaks. To illustrate, if you have taken two tests and your grades are 70 and 80, your average grade is 75. If your grade on a third test is higher than 75—say 90—your average rises to 80. The 90 is the marginal addition to your total grade. If the third grade is less than 75, the marginal addition is below average and the average falls. This is the relation between all marginal and average schedules. In production theory, if each additional worker adds more than the average, average product rises; if each additional worker adds less than average, average product falls.

The short-run production function set forth in Table 8–2 specifies several common characteristics of marginal and average product in production theory. First, marginal and average products start out increasing, but then decrease, with marginal product becoming negative after a point. Marginal product reaches a maximum before the highest average product is attained. These relations result from the assumption that total product at first increases at an increasing rate, then increases at a decreasing rate, and finally decreases. The graphical exposition in the next subsection will further illustrate the relation between average and marginal product.

8.3.2   Average and Marginal Product: Graphical Approach

We now assume, as before, that labor and output vary continuously, and labor can take on any quantity from zero through 10. Both average and marginal product will vary continuously also. This assumption allows us to illustrate the properties of average and marginal product graphically.

In Figure 8–2, marginal and average product are plotted along the vertical axis and the amount of labor along the horizontal. The average product of each number of workers in Table 8–2 is plotted in the figure, then all points are connected to form the average product curve shown in the figure. The marginal product of each additional worker from Table 8–2 is plotted in the figure, then all points are connected to form the marginal product curve. Note that, following the form of the table, the marginal product of each additional worker is plotted between the two quantities of workers. For example, the marginal product of the eighth worker, 18, is plotted midway between the seventh and eighth, at 7.5 workers.

The figure shows that average product first rises, reaches a maximum between four and five workers, then declines. Marginal product rises, reaches a maximum at a smaller amount of labor, then declines, and finally becomes negative. When marginal product is above-average product, average product is rising, for the general

Figure 8–2   Average and Marginal Product ($K = 20$)

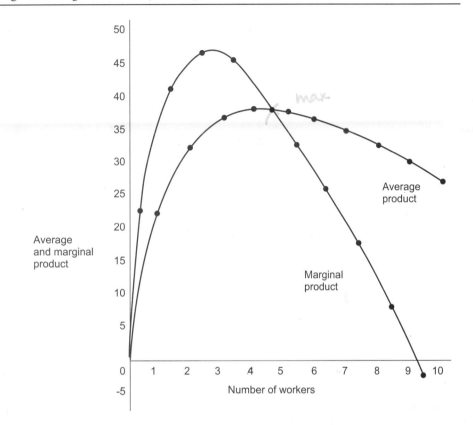

reason discussed above. When marginal product is below average product, average product is falling. Therefore, as is shown graphically, marginal product must equal average product when average product is at its maximum—when it stops rising and begins to fall.

8.3.3   Derivation of Average and Marginal Product Curves from the Total Product Curve

Thus far we have discussed the properties of total, average, and marginal product curves derived from a numerical production function. We now turn to the general properties of these curves, based on the typical assumptions used in production theory.

A total product curve for labor, the only variable input, is shown in Figure 8–3. This total product curve embodies the same assumptions about production used previously in this section: Output at first increases at an increasing rate as labor increases, output then increases at a decreasing rate, and finally output decreases as labor increases.

Figure 8–3 Derivation of Average Product from Total Product

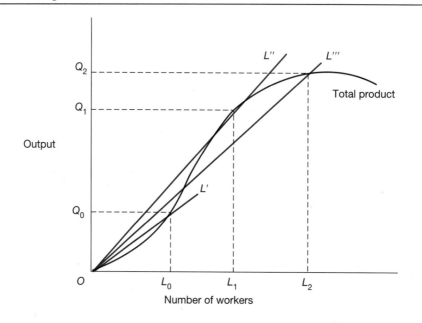

In the figure, Q_0 is the maximum amount of output obtainable when L_0 workers are combined with the fixed inputs. Likewise, L_1 workers can produce a maximum of Q_1, and so forth. Figure 8–3 shows that total output increases with increases in the variable input up to a point, in this case L_2 workers. After that, so many workers are combined with the fixed inputs that output diminishes when additional workers are employed.

The average product of L_0 workers is output per worker, or Q_0/L_0. In Figure 8–3 this is equivalent to the slope of the ray OL', passing through the origin and the point (L_0, Q_0). By inspection you can see that this slope is the ratio of the distance OQ_0/OL_0, which is simply the amount of output produced divided by the amount of labor used. In like manner, the average product of any number of workers can be determined by the slope of a ray from the origin to the relevant point on the total product curve; the steeper the slope, the greater the average product. The slopes of rays from the origin to the total product curve in Figure 8–3 increase with additional labor until OL'' becomes tangent to the total product curve at L_1 workers and Q_1 output; the slope decreases thereafter (for example, to OL''' at L_2 workers). Typical average product curves associated with this total produce curve, therefore, first increase, reach a maximum, then decrease.

As with average product, we can derive a marginal product curve from a total product curve. In Figure 8–4, L_0 workers can produce Q_0 units of output, and L_1 can produce Q_1. L_0L_1 additional workers, therefore, increase total product by Q_0Q_1. Because marginal product is measured only for small changes in the input, we can let L_1 become very close to L_0. The quantity Q_1 will then get very close to Q_0, and $\Delta Q/\Delta L$ will approach the slope of the tangent T to the total product curve. Thus,

Figure 8–4   Derivation of Marginal Product from Total Product

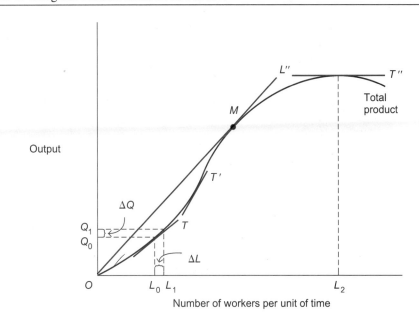

at any point on the total product curve, marginal product, which is the rate of change of total product as labor changes, can be estimated by the slope of the tangent at that point. By inspection, you see that marginal product first increases; for example, notice that T' is steeper than T. It then decreases, OL'' at point M being less steep than T'. Marginal product becomes zero when L_2 workers are employed (the slope of T'' is zero), and then becomes negative.

At point M, the slope of the tangent OL'' is also the slope of the ray from the origin to that point. As noted above, average product attains a maximum when a ray from the origin is tangent to the total product curve. Therefore, marginal product equals average product when average product is at a maximum. To repeat, as long as marginal product is less than average product, the latter must fall. When marginal product is greater than average product, the latter must rise. Average product must attain its maximum when it is equal to marginal product.

Figure 8–5 illustrates all of these relations. In this graph, you can see the relation between marginal and average products, and also the relation of these two curves to total product (TP). Consider first the total product curve. For very small amounts of the variable input, total product rises gradually. Then it begins to rise quite rapidly, reaching its maximum slope (or rate of increase) at point 1. Since the slope of the total product curve equals marginal product, the maximum slope (point 1) must correspond to the maximum point on the marginal produce curve (point 4).

After attaining its maximum slope at point 1, the total product curve continues to rise. Since output increases at a decreasing rate, the slope becomes less steep. Moving outward along the curve from point 1, the point is soon reached at which a ray from the origin is just tangent to the curve (point 2). Since tangency of the

Figure 8–5 Total, Average, and Marginal Products

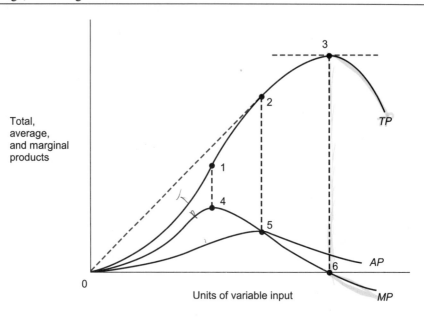

ray to the curve defines the condition for maximum average product, point 2 lies directly above point 5.

As the quantity of the variable input is expanded from its value at point 2, total product continues to increase. Its rate of increase is progressively slower until point 3 is finally reached. At this point, total product is at a maximum; thereafter, it declines. Over a tiny range around point 3, additional input does not change total output. The slope of the total product curve is zero; thus, marginal product must also be zero. This is shown by the fact that points 3 and 6 occur at precisely the same input value. And, since total product declines beyond point 3, marginal product becomes negative.

To emphasize these relations, consider the marginal and average product curves. Marginal product at first increases, reaches a maximum at point 4, and declines thereafter. It eventually becomes negative beyond point 6, where total product attains its maximum.

Average product also rises until it reaches its maximum at point 5, where marginal and average products are equal. It subsequently declines, conceivably becoming zero if total product itself becomes zero. Finally, marginal product exceeds average product when the average is increasing, and is less than average product when the average is decreasing.

8.3.4 Law of Diminishing Marginal Product

The slope of the marginal product curve in Figure 8–5 illustrates an important principle, the law of diminishing marginal product. As the number of units of the variable input increases, other inputs held constant, the marginal product of the input declines after a point. When the amount of the variable input is small relative to the fixed inputs (the fixed inputs are plentiful relative to the variable input), more intensive utilization of the fixed inputs by the variable inputs may increase the marginal product of the variable input. For instance, as you add more labor to a garden plot of fixed size, the marginal increase in vegetables grown may rise. Nonetheless, a point is reached where an increase in the use of the variable input yields progressively less additional product. Each additional unit has, on average, fewer units of the fixed inputs with which to work.

Principle

As the amount of variable input is increased, the amounts of other fixed inputs held constant, a point is reached where marginal product begins to decline. This decline is often referred to as the law of diminishing marginal product.

This is a simple statement concerning physical relations that have frequently been observed. Although it is not susceptible to mathematical proof or refutation, it is of some worth to note that a contrary observation has never been recorded. That is why it is called a law. Psychologists have found that the law holds true for study time.[2]

Economics in the News

How Firms Can Increase Productivity

Service industries—for example, hotels, restaurants, banks, hospitals, and so on—are quite labor intensive; that is, they use a great deal of labor relative to capital equipment, compared to manufacturing industries. During the 1970s and 1980s, labor productivity—essentially the average product of labor—rose at an extremely low rate in the service sector compared to productivity in manufacturing.

An article in *The Wall Street Journal*, "With Labor Scarce, Service Firms Strive to Raise Productivity," June 1, 1989, reported that rising wages in the service sector and expected higher wages in the 1990s were causing service firms to try to increase the productivity (average product) of their workers. Part of the explanation given for the lagging productivity in services was "the explosion of the service economy, which brought in disproportionate numbers of young inexperienced workers, . . . and service firms didn't invest as much in capital spending per worker as manufacturers did."

The Journal noted that service firms had responded to the labor shortages of the 1980s, particularly shortages of younger workers, in several ways. Many were raising wages, an obvious approach. Others were intensifying recruiting, offering various inducements to new workers. Some firms turned to immigrants, legal and illegal. Many employers were emphasizing nurturing current workers to cut turnover rates. For example, Pizza Hut changed its uniform to one more appealing to younger workers, improved kitchen air conditioning, and taught managers "to manage with a softer style." Other service

(continued)

---

[2]Do not make the common mistake, however, of saying that you stopped studying because diminishing returns (marginal product) set in. The term diminishing returns is frequently heard in noneconomic usage and is almost as frequently misused. Diminishing returns may set in with the first unit of study time, but you may continue studying. You cease studying when the marginal utility of the (expected) increase in grade (or the pleasure of studying) from an additional unit of study time is less than the expected marginal utility of using that time for something else.

companies increased the amount of training given new workers in order to increase their productivity. Some service companies, just as manufacturing firms were doing, were increasing worker productivity by installing new machines. For example, McDonald's was trying a new grill that cooks hamburgers on both sides, "a device that could eliminate the fabled hamburger flipper."

Many industries, however, were finding that new technologies increased their need for labor rather than diminished it. *The Journal* noted, "Lasting gains in productivity come only when service companies finally confront the issue directly, investing in technology or education or restructuring jobs so that each worker can do substantially more."

The Journal article used recent developments at a Sleep Inn Hotel, the first in a new franchise operation run by Manor Care Inc., as an example of the way firms were trying to raise labor productivity. The night clerk at the hotel, who previously watched TV, played solitaire, and worked crossword puzzles, began laundering sheets and towels in a washer and dryer installed behind the front desk. Previously, one full-time maid and a part-time worker did the sheets and towels in a separate laundry room, in which the laundry equipment did not have all of the labor-saving features of the new equipment.

To save on housekeeping staff, the Sleep Inn bolted night stands to the walls to eliminate vacuuming around the legs, took the doors off of closets, and installed round shower stalls, eliminating pesky corners that collect dirt. It was estimated that cleaning a Sleep Inn room, which was 70 percent the size of the industry standard, took 20 minutes compared to the typical 30 minutes in the industry. Computers were keeping track of each maid's time. Guests used their own credit cards to unlock their doors and a computer automatically turned on or off the air conditioning or heating when a guest checked in or out. The extensive use of asphalt and shrubbery saved labor by eliminating the task of mowing grass. In all, the 92-room hotel used only 11 workers, including the manager, as a result of these and several other labor-saving tricks. All of this was to increase profit and prepare for future labor shortages and the resulting higher wage rates.

Although *The Journal* article did not state it explicitly, the reason service firms such as Sleep Inn were trying to increase the productivity of labor was not simply to increase the average product of labor for its own sake. The purpose was to reduce these firms' costs of production. The higher the average product of labor, the lower the cost of producing a given amount of a good or service and, hence, the lower the average cost.

A numerical example can be used to illustrate the important relation between cost and average product. Suppose a hypothetical firm is using 10 workers and producing 1,000 units of output per day. The average product of labor is, therefore, 100. All other inputs are fixed in amount and must be paid a total of $500 a day. Suppose the wage of labor is $100 a day. The daily labor cost is $1,000, and the total daily cost is $1,500, the labor cost plus the cost of the fixed inputs. The average daily cost of operation, which is simply cost divided by output, is $1.50 (= $1,500/1,000). If the wage of workers had been $150 a day, the daily cost would have been $2,000, and the average daily cost $2.00.

Suppose the firm finds a way to increase labor productivity so that it takes only 5 workers to produce 1,000 units. The number and cost of the fixed inputs remains constant. Now the average product of labor increases to 200. Consequently, the daily labor cost of producing 1,000 units at the $100 wage falls to $500, the total cost falls to $1,000, and the average cost falls to $1.00. Clearly, with the lower total and average cost, the firm will make more profit, because of the higher average product. Thus, firms wish to increase the productivity of labor and their other inputs in order to reduce their costs. (We will develop the relation between average product and cost in much more detail in Chapter 10.)

8.4   Optimization with a Single Variable Input

An important part of production theory is explaining how the optimal combination of inputs is determined. This section develops that theory.

8.4.1   Unconstrained Optimization

You have already been exposed to the fundamental elements of optimization. The quantity of input demanded is determined by comparing the marginal cost of another unit to its marginal benefit, as discussed in Chapter 4. Suppose you own a business and a worker applies for a job. Would you hire this worker? The answer depends on how much extra revenue the worker would earn for your business. If the worker is expected to add more to revenue than you must pay in wages, the answer is yes. If the worker is expected to add less in revenue than the wages you must pay, the answer is no. The same reasoning applies to any factor of production. A firm would increase its use of a particular input of any type if the additional unit of input is expected to add more to revenue than it adds to cost. If the additional unit increases cost more than it increases revenue, no more of the input would be added.

It makes no difference whether the input is labor, capital, land, fuel, or something else. A firm increases its use of an input if the additional unit of input adds more to revenue than it adds to cost. The basic theory is simple because you already have learned a great deal about the importance of the margin in decision making.

Consider the following example: A firm sells its product at the going market price of \$1. It can hire one unit of the variable input, labor, at \$30 per day. If increasing its labor force by one more worker adds more than 30 units of output per day, the firm would hire the additional worker.

The amount an additional unit of input adds to total revenue is called marginal revenue product (MRP). That is,

$$MRP_i = \frac{\Delta \text{ revenue}}{\Delta \text{ input usage}} = \frac{\Delta Q \cdot P}{\Delta \text{ input usage}} = MP_i \cdot P$$

where P is the given price of the producer's output, Q, and MP_i is marginal product of input i. We can also define marginal revenue product as follows:

Definition

The marginal revenue product (MRP) of a factor of production for a producer is the addition to total revenue attributable to the addition of one more unit of the factor. Marginal revenue product is equivalent to marginal product multiplied by output price, when output prices are constant.

We will often add a subscript to MRP to denote the input to which we are referring. For instance, MRP_L is the marginal revenue product of labor.

Since each additional worker in the above example adds \$30 to cost, the marginal cost of the input is that wage rate. If the marginal cost of labor is the wage rate, w, the basic rule for hiring an extra unit is, if

$$MRP_L > w,$$

Table 8–3   The Marginal Revenue Product for Labor

Units of Variable Input	Total Product	Marginal Product	MRP
0	0	—	—
1	10	10	$ 50
2	30	20	100
3	50	20	100
4	65	15	75
5	75	10	50
6	80	5	25
7	83	3	15
8	84	1	5
9	81	−3	−15

the producer would add more of the input. If

$$MRP_L < w,$$

the firm would add no more of the input; it would, in fact, decrease its use. Optimization requires, when labor can be varied continuously,

$$MRP_L = w.$$

Let us consider another numerical example, this time in more detail. A firm sells a product at the going market price of $5 and employs labor at a wage rate of $20 per day. Table 8–3 lists the daily total product, marginal product, and marginal revenue product for zero through nine workers. Note that the marginal revenue product in the last column is simply $5 multiplied by marginal product. Suppose the wage rate is $20. Under these conditions, the firm hires six workers. It would not hire fewer than six, since hiring the sixth adds $25 to revenue but only costs $20. It would not hire seven workers, because revenue would only increase by $15, while cost would rise by $20. If, however, the wage rate dropped below $15 (say, to $14) the work force would increase to seven (an additional $15 revenue can be gained at a cost of $14). Or if wages rose above $25 but remained below $50, the firm would reduce the labor force to five.

The optimizing rule is illustrated in Figure 8–6. Suppose the marginal revenue product is given by the curve labeled MRP_L. The market wage rate is $\overline{w}$. The firm can hire as much labor as it desires at the wage rate of $\overline{w}$. Suppose the firm employed only L_1 units of labor. At that rate of employment, the marginal revenue product is the distance $L_1C = w_1$, which is greater than $\overline{w}$, the wage rate. At this point of operation, an additional unit of labor adds more to total revenue than to total cost. A profit-maximizing entrepreneur should add additional units of labor and, indeed, should continue to add units so long as the marginal revenue product exceeds the wage rate.

Now suppose L_2 units of labor were employed. At this point, the marginal revenue product, $L_2F = w_2$, is less than the wage rate. Each unit of labor adds more to total cost than to total revenue. A profit-maximizing entrepreneur should not employ L_2 units, or any number for which the wage rate exceeds the marginal revenue

Figure 8–6   Demand for a Variable Resource

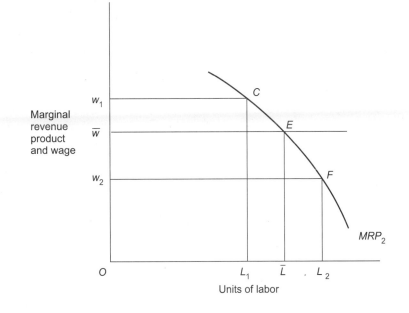

product. These arguments show that employing L units of labor leads to maximum net benefit to the producer.

In other words, given the market wage rate to the firm, a producer determines the quantity of labor to hire by equating the marginal revenue product to the wage rate. If the wage rate were w_1 in Figure 8–6, the firm would employ L_1 units of labor. Similarly, if the wage rate were w_2, the firm would employ L_2 units of labor.

Notice that Figure 8–6 only sketches that part of an MRP schedule that is derived from the downward-sloping portion of the MP curve. Figure 8–5 shows that the typical marginal product curve first rises, reaches a maximum, then declines thereafter, crossing the average product curve at its maximum. Since MRP is simply a constant commodity price multiplied by marginal product, it has a similar shape.

An optimizing firm would never choose a level of input usage where marginal product and, therefore, MRP are rising. To see why, suppose the wage, w, equals MRP where MRP is rising. The firm can add one more unit of labor and the MRP would be greater than the wage. Profits could continue to increase from additional units of labor, so long as MRP is rising. Hence, it must be the case that the optimal amount of labor is determined by the wage rate being set equal to MRP when the curve is declining.

8.4.2   The Constrained Optimization Problem

Constrained optimization leaves the decision maker with no real choice when only one input is variable. When there is only one variable input, the minimum cost of producing each level of output is the price of the variable input times the amount of the variable input needed to produce that level of output plus the cost of the fixed inputs, which is the same for every level of output.

For example, return to the production function shown in Table 8–2, when capital is fixed at 20 units. The cost of capital is the same at every level of output. Suppose the wage rate of labor is $100 per worker. If the firm wants to produce 155 units of output, it must hire four workers, as shown by the table. Thus the minimum cost, and the only cost, of producing 155 units of output is $400 plus the fixed cost of capital. Conversely, if the firm has a given variable-input budget of, say, $800 to spend, at $100 per worker the firm can hire only eight workers. From the table, eight workers can produce 270 units of output, which must be the maximum output that can be produced at an $800 cost of the variable inputs.

The cost-minimization or output maximization decision is more complicated when more than one input is variable. As shown in Table 8–1 and Figure 8–1, when the amount of capital is changed, the output that each given amount of labor can produce changes also. The total, average, and marginal product curves are derived holding the use of all other inputs constant and letting the use of only one input vary. When the use of any of these fixed inputs changes, the total product curve shifts, as shown in Figure 8–1, as do the average and marginal product curves.

If, as in Figure 8–1, the previously fixed input, in this case capital, can take on only a few different values, the cost-minimization problem is still relatively simple. The decision maker chooses the combination of inputs that can produce the desired output at the lowest cost. For example, as you saw in Figure 8–1, it was possible to produce 100 units of output with three combinations of labor and capital: 2.25 workers and 30 units of capital, 2.75 workers and 20 units of capital, or 3.75 workers and 10 units of capital. Suppose the price of labor is $10 per hour and the price of capital is $2 per unit per hour. The minimum cost of producing 100 units of output per hour is $57.50, using 10 units of capital at $2 each and 3.75 workers at $10 each. At other prices of labor and capital, the cost-minimizing combination might change.

The adding-up process becomes more complicated as the possible levels of capital usage increase, because there would be more total product curves for labor. Carried to the extreme, if capital is continuously divisible and can take on any value, as is the case for labor, there would be an infinite number of total, average, and marginal product curves for labor—one for each of the infinite possible levels of capital. Furthermore, there would be an infinite number of total, average, and marginal product curves for capital—one for each of the infinite possible levels of labor. Obviously calculating the input combination that leads to the lowest cost of producing a given level of output, as we did above in the simple example, would be virtually impossible under these circumstances. Furthermore, we wouldn't have a theory to explain how the cost-minimizing combination is determined.

Therefore, we need new tools of analysis to extend the theory of production in order to develop the rules for cost-minimization and output maximization when two or more of the inputs used can vary continuously. In the following chapter, we will discuss these new tools and set forth the rules. As you will see, the fundamental principles follow from the rules for constrained optimization, set forth in Chapter 4. You will also see that the principles and definitions developed in this chapter are important.

Economics in the News

How Productive Are U.S. Workers? Does It Matter Much?

In 1988 and 1989, many observers were seriously debating these very questions. Basically, the answer to the first question was, "Not as productive as we would like them to be." The answer to the second was a resounding, "Yes, it does matter. A lot."

Let's look first at what experts were saying about why worker productivity matters. Robert Samuelson, writing in *Newsweek,* June 26, 1989, argued that huge cuts in the U.S. defense budget, being proposed at the time, would not have nearly as large an effect on national wealth as improved productivity—the ability to produce more with the same number of workers. He noted that even very small increases in productivity—that is, output per worker—would overwhelm any reasonable reduction in defense spending. He estimated that a 1 percent annual productivity increase would lead to an increase in gross national product (GNP) of $50 billion a year; or, after compounding, over a decade, $525 billion more GNP per year. With a 1.5 percent increase in productivity, GNP per year would be $800 billion higher. This figure equaled the entire defense budget in 1989.

Princeton economist Alan Blinder, in *Business Week,* April 17, 1989, called the "miserably slow pace of productivity improvement" the chief economic malady in the United States at that time. He noted that the yearly 1 percent increase in output per worker since 1973 compared poorly with the 2.7 percent yearly increase over the preceding 15 years or the 2 percent yearly increase over the preceding century. Blinder estimated that with a 2 percent annual growth in productivity, real wages, net of inflation, double every 35 years; in a century, the standard of living increases sevenfold. With a 1 percent annual increase in productivity, real wages double only after 70 years, and the standard of living less than triples over a century. Obviously, an increase from 1 to 2 percent would make a difference.

Clearly, productivity matters in terms of wages and the standard of living. But, why was there such a slowdown? In his *Business Week* column, "Economic Trends" (May 22, 1989) Gene Koretz cites the increased importance of the service sector in the U.S. economy, relative to that of the manufacturing sector. He notes that in 1989, manufacturing productivity had been rising at about 3.5 percent a year for the past decade. During that period, productivity in services had risen only about half a percent per year. Services were responsible for practically all new jobs during the decade, and they accounted for over 70 percent of all private employment. The lower productivity increases in the important service sector dragged down increases in the economy as a whole.

Koretz noted that many observers believe low productivity is inherent in services. However, business economist Roger Fulton pointed out that, between 1979 and 1986, service output per worker in Japan, West Germany, France, Sweden, and Great Britain rose about 2 percent a year compared with 0.4 percent in the United States.

Why the difference? Citing MIT economist Lester Thurow, Koretz explained that during that period service industries in Japan and Europe invested much more heavily in new technology; capital per worker in Germany and Japan grew twice as fast as was the case in the United States. According to Thurow, the high capital investment resulted from higher service wages, compared to manufacturing wages, abroad relative to the ratio in the United States. The reasoning behind this conclusion is that higher wages for workers in German and Japanese service industries would have induced employers in these industries to substitute capital for the relatively more expensive labor. In the United States, where service wages were relatively lower, employers did not have the incentive to substitute as much capital for labor.

(continued)

In Japan and Germany, service workers in 1988 on average were paid, respectively, 93 and 85 percent as much as manufacturing workers. In the United States, they were paid 67 percent as much. It is possible then that service industries abroad substituted capital for the relatively more expensive labor. (We will cover this substitution effect that results from a change in input prices in more detail later in the following chapter.) Thus, a suggested cure for lagging U.S. productivity was higher service wages, which would lead to more capital investment in service industries.

Alan Blinder, in the previously cited *Business Week* (April 17, 1989) column, disagreed somewhat with the idea that more capital is the key to increasing worker productivity in the United States. He argued that since capital makes up only 25 to 30 percent of all inputs, even a large increase in capital investment would yield only small productivity gains. He therefore suggested that the solution is to take steps to cause labor, the much larger input, to work harder and better. That is, more output could result from essentially the same amounts of labor and capital. If this idea is correct, firms may not have been producing at points on their production functions. Blinder mentioned two ways that workers might be motivated to work harder and better: part of the worker compensation paid in the form of profit sharing rather than straight hourly wages and more worker participation in business decision making.

In an earlier *Newsweek* column (January 25, 1988), Robert Samuelson appears to agree that lagging productivity in services dragged down the productivity increases in the economy. He did not, however, point to lower investment in services or workers not working hard enough as the reason. Samuelson suggests several possible reasons for lagging productivity in services. First, although productivity in some parts of the service sector increased dramatically, communications, for example, other services cannot be improved. You can't automate a symphony orchestra or a baseball team. In other services in which quality is as important as quantity, or even more so (e.g., health care and education), productivity or output is difficult, perhaps impossible, to measure accurately.

Samuelson said that the computerization of much of the service sector may have slowed down productivity growth. He cited Lester Thurow's speculation that computers encourage number-crunching and memo-writing that increase costs but don't improve decision making. For some companies, improvements from computers may have been offset by higher training costs.

Finally, Samuelson argues that the huge expansion in service industries during the 1980s may have been the underlying reason for the decline in productivity in the service sector. During booms, firms tend to overexpand and overbuild; the overbuilding of stores and hotels was an example. Rapid expansion causes inefficiencies and mistakes. However, when the expansion began to slow down, these inefficiencies became more clear as sales declined, and firms began to do something about them, in order to increase productivity. The less-productive firms began to go out of business.

One possible reason for low productivity in services, not mentioned by any of the analysts discussed here, is simply the law of diminishing marginal product. As some of the authors noted, practically all of the new jobs in the economy during the 1980s were in service industries—according to Samuelson, 9 out of every 10 between 1982 and 1986. It is possible that hiring so many new workers in service industries caused marginal and average product to decline so much that productivity in the entire service sector also declined. This does not imply that the new workers were poorer workers; it only implies that as more workers were hired, marginal product fell.

(continued)

Thus, several reasons were proposed for the decline in productivity. These reasons do not, however, contradict each other. All are consistent with the theory of production discussed above. All could have had some responsibility for the decline, but how much responsibility should be assigned to each is a statistical question that may never be answered.

Lower investment in the United States, relative to capital investment in services in Japan and Western Europe, would have lowered average product in the United States. Firms may not have been producing at points on their production function because, for some reason or another, workers were not working hard or management was inefficient. The large increase in the number of workers could have caused the marginal and average product of labor to decline.

8.1   Applying the Theory

The Wall Street Journal, May 14, 1986, cited low productivity gains in U.S. manufacturing (3 percent) relative to much higher productivity gains in Japanese manufacturing (8 percent) as the primary reason for the higher cost of U.S. goods and, consequently, a reason for the trade gap between the United States and Japan. Another *Wall Street Journal* article, August 11, 1986, said that weak productivity gains in the U.S. service sector, relative to manufacturing, were the reason that the prices of services were rising much more rapidly at the time compared to the prices of manufactured goods. What would you expect to be the link between productivity and the price of goods and services? This question somewhat anticipates future material, but try to answer using the material in this chapter and your knowledge of supply and demand from Chapter 2.

8.5   Summary

This chapter has set forth the basic theory of production with a single variable input and all other inputs fixed in amount. Production with a single variable input provides the background for the theory of production when several inputs are variable. The theory of production forms the underpinning of the theory of cost.

Production is the transformation of inputs, such as capital, labor, and land, into goods and services, or the firm's output. The core of production theory is the production function. A production function gives the maximum output that can be produced by each combination of inputs in the production process. Each input-output combination on the production function is technically efficient, meaning that the output is the largest that can be produced at each level of input usage.

Inputs are classified as fixed or variable. The usage of a fixed input cannot be changed. It is the same at every level of output. A firm can change the amount of a variable input. To increase (decrease) output, it must increase (decrease) the amount of its variable inputs. In the short run, some inputs are variable and some are fixed. In the long run, all inputs are variable. No actual time dimension is implied by short run or long run.

Typically, as the use of a single variable input increases, output increases at an increasing rate, then increases at a decreasing rate, and finally may reach a point at which so much of the variable input is used relative to the fixed inputs that output declines with increased use of the variable input.

Two important concepts of production with a single variable input are average and marginal product: The average product of an input (AP) is the output per unit of the input, or total output divided by the amount of the input. Expressed as a ratio,

$$AP = \frac{Q}{I},$$

where Q is output and I is the amount of the variable input. The marginal product of an input (MP) is the additional output per unit increase in the input. For small increases in a variable input, marginal product can be expressed as the ratio,

$$MP = \frac{\Delta Q}{\Delta I}.$$

Graphically, the marginal product and average product curves typically rise, reach a maximum, then decline. Marginal product may become negative. The law of diminishing marginal product states that beyond some level of input use MP must decline. When MP is above (below) AP, AP is rising (falling); MP reaches its maximum at a lower level of input usage than the maximum of AP. When AP is at its maximum, marginal product equals average product. A change in one or more of the fixed inputs causes a shift in total, average, and marginal product curves; MP and AP change at each level of the variable input. Because only one amount of the single variable input can produce each level of output or because each level of output can only be produced with a single level of the variable input, constrained cost minimization or output maximization is trivial in this special case. The problem of profit maximization with a single variable input is not trivial: the firm chooses the level of the input at which its marginal revenue product equals the price of the input.

Cost minimization and output maximization are not trivial when two or more inputs are variable. In the next chapter, we will develop the analytical tools necessary for the theory of production with several variable inputs and set forth that theory. As you will see, the theory in this chapter provides a background for the analysis in Chapter 9.

Answers to *Applying the Theory*

8.1 Labor is an extremely important input in the production of most goods and an even more important input in the production of most services. Thus, the cost of labor makes up a very large part of the cost of production. If labor's productivity declines, firms must use more labor to produce a given output or can produce less output with a given amount of labor. In either case, the cost of production rises. This has an effect on supply similar to that of an increase in the wage rate of labor. In either case, supply falls. With a given demand, the fall in supply leads to an increase in price (see Chapter 2). This must be the line of reasoning suggested by the two *Wall Street Journal* articles.

Technical Problems

1. Fill in the blanks in the following table.

Usage of the Variable Input	Total Product	Average Product	Marginal Product
1	———	26	———
2	———	———	34
3	81	———	———
4	———	26	———
5	———	———	21
6	138	———	———
7	———	21	———
8	———	———	5
9	153	———	———
10	———	15	———

2. Fill in all three columns in the following table. Make your numbers conform to the conditions set forth below. Graph the average and marginal product curves.

Usage of the Variable Input	Total Product	Average Product	Marginal Product
1	100		
2			
3			
4			
5			
6			
7			
8			
9			
10			
11			
12			
13			
14			
15			
16			
17			
18			

Make your numbers meet the following restrictions:
   a. Marginal product first increases, reaches its maximum at 5 units of variable input, declines thereafter, and becomes negative after 17 units.
   b. Average product first rises, reaches its maximum at nine units, and declines thereafter.
   c. Marginal product equals average product at approximately the maximum point of the latter.
3. In the text, we calculated average and marginal product for labor when capital is 20 from the production function in Table 8–1 (shown in Table 8–2) and then plotted *AP* and *MP* (in Figure 8–2). Calculate *AP* and *MP* for labor when capital

is 10, and when capital is 30 from Table 8–1, then plot the *AP* and *MP* curves graphically. Compare these curves with the curves in Figure 8–2. What is the effect of increases in capital on the marginal and average product of labor, the only variable input?

4. The following production function shows the maximum output from one through eight workers, when combined with a given amount of the fixed input.

L	*Q*	*L*	*Q*
1	50	5	155
2	90	6	162
3	120	7	168
4	140	8	168

   a. Calculate the *AP* for each level of labor usage and the *MP* for each unit increase in labor.
   b. How does this production function differ from those discussed in the text? What is the relation between *MP* and *AP*?
   c. The total cost of the fixed inputs is $1,000. If the wage rate is $50, what is the minimum cost of producing each level of output?
   d. The total cost of the fixed inputs is $1,000 and the wage rate is $50. What is the maximum output that can be produced at a total cost of $1,250; $1,150; $1,300?

5. If the amount of labor increases from 20 to 30 workers and output increases from 1,000 to 1,500, what is the marginal product of labor over this range? What does this marginal product show?

6. If the total product curve is a straight line from the origin, what is the relation between marginal and average product?

7. Use the following figure (E.8–1) showing the average product of labor, the only variable input, to answer this question. Use the formulas in the text.
   a. What is the firm's output when average product is at a maximum? What is the marginal product at this output?
   b. What is the firm's output when 15 workers are used? What can you say about marginal product at this level of labor usage?
   c. Answer part *b* when 50 workers are used.

8. Assume that a curve is drawn showing, along the horizontal axis, the amounts of a factor *A* employed in combination with a fixed amount of a group of factors called *B*, and, along the vertical axis, the amount of physical product obtainable from these combinations of factors (see Figure E. 8–2).
   a. How can you find (geometrically) the amount of *A* for which the average product per unit of *A* is a maximum?
   b. How can you find (geometrically) the amount of *A* for which the marginal product of *A* is a maximum?
   c. Between the two points defined in parts *a* and *b*, will the marginal product of *A* increase or decrease as more of *A* is used?
   d. Between these two points, will the average product per unit of *A* increase or decrease as more of *A* is used?
   e. At the point defined in *a*, will the marginal product of *A* be higher than, lower than, or the same as the average product per unit of *A*? Give reasons.
   f. At the point defined in *b*, will the marginal product of *A* be lower or higher than the average product per unit of *A*? Give reasons.

Figure E.8–1

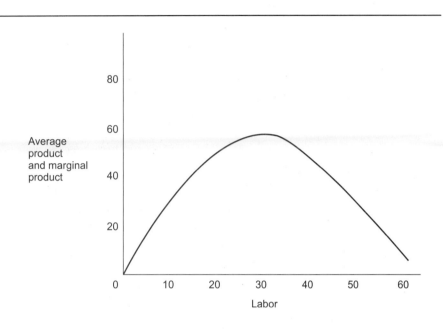

Figure E.8–2

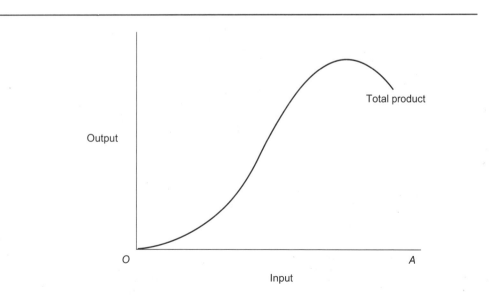

   g. How can you find (geometrically) the amount of *A* for which the marginal
        product of *A* is zero?
 9. Explain intuitively why the marginal product of a variable input may become
    negative. Give hypothetical examples.
10. Explain intuitively why a variable input is subject to the law of diminishing
    marginal returns. Give examples.
11. *a.* Suppose the average product of labor is 10. The firm hires 3 more workers,
        and output increases by 60 units. What happens to the average product of
        labor? Explain.
    b. A firm is hiring 10 workers and producing 100 units of output. The firm
        now expands to 20 workers and produces 180 units of output. What happens
        to the marginal product of labor? Explain.
12. A firm hires 50 workers: 25 are used to produce components of the product, and
    the other 25 are used to assemble the product. The marginal product of labor is
    higher in producing components than in assembling them. Explain how the firm
    can increase its output using the same total amount of labor.

Analytical Problems

 1. In discussions of worker productivity, the media generally speak in terms of
    average, rather than marginal, productivity. Why might this be so?
 2. Suppose a technological change occurs in an industry, and the result is that firms
    learn how to produce more output with given amounts of inputs. What would
    probably happen to the average product of labor? What would probably happen to
    the firms' costs? Explain.
 3. A manager refuses to hire more workers because diminishing returns would set in.
    What is wrong with this reasoning?
 4. When business is bad, firms generally reduce the amount of labor they hire and
    not the amount of most other inputs. When business is good, they increase the
    amount of labor, but not other inputs. Explain.
 5. Why is most of the material in this chapter on production with a single-variable
    input not relevant for a firm producing under fixed proportions (has a fixed-
    proportions production function)? Why is fixed-proportions production probably
    not relevant, even in the very short run?
 6. In the discussion of service firms increasing productivity in "Economics in the
    News," we set forth a numerical example showing how an increase in the average
    product of labor reduces the total and average cost of producing a given level of
    output. Explain intuitively the relation between average product and cost. (This
    question anticipates material in Chapter 10.) What are some other ways in which
    a service firm might increase the average product of labor? A hospital? A
    university? An auto-repair shop?
 7. What would happen to the average product of labor under the following
    conditions? Explain. What would happen to the firms' costs? Explain.
    a. Government imposes worker safety regulations on firms in the industry.
    b. The new union contract gives workers longer breaks and longer vacations.
    c. Improvements in the school system cause young workers to become better
        educated.
    d. Firms hire management consultants to teach managers how to better motivate
        workers.
    e. A profit sharing plan is made available to workers.

CHAPTER 9

Theory of Production: Two or More Variable Inputs

9.1   Introduction

In Chapter 8, we set forth the fundamentals of production theory when a firm can vary the usage of only one variable input. The usage of all other inputs was fixed in amount. As noted, the constrained cost minimization or output maximization problem was trivial, because only one level of input usage could produce any given level of output.

In this chapter, we will build upon the tools developed in Chapter 8 and analyze production when a firm uses two or more variable inputs. With a variable-proportions production function, a firm can produce a given level of output with many combinations of the variable inputs. In such cases, a firm will choose the combination of variable inputs that minimizes the cost of producing a given level of output or maximizes the output produced with a fixed level of cost. As you will see, the theory follows the basic format of constrained optimization set forth in Chapter 4.[1]

Throughout most of this chapter, we will analyze production under the assumption that only two inputs are variable. This assumption is made for graphical purposes. It is true, however, that the theory applies for any number of variable inputs. The theory will also apply equally well to both the long run and the short

---

[1]Those who have already gone through consumer theory will note many similarities between the concepts discussed there and the theory of production. Several users of this text have pointed out that they choose to cover production and cost theory before consumer theory. Therefore, we will not dwell on these similarities in this and the next chapter. For those students who have already studied consumer behavior theory, the relations should be rather obvious, because both are constrained optimization problems.

run. We can assume that the firm uses only two inputs, both of which are variable, and there are no fixed inputs. In this case, the firm is in the long run. Alternatively, we can assume that the firm uses two variable inputs in combination with other inputs, which are fixed in amount. In this case, the firm is in the short run. The results are the same under either assumption.

9.2   Characteristics of Production with Two Variable Inputs

This section and the next develop the concepts to be used to analyze a firm's cost-minimizing or output-maximizing decisions. We first set forth the characteristics of production with two variable inputs, labor (L) and capital (K). As noted, this situation may be considered the long run, when labor and capital are the only inputs, or when capital represents a combination of all inputs other than labor. It may also be the short run, when labor and capital are the only variable inputs, but some other inputs are fixed.

9.2.1   Production Isoquants

An important tool of analysis when two inputs are variable is the *production isoquant,* or simply the isoquant.

Definition

An isoquant is a curve or locus of points showing all combinations of inputs physically capable of producing a given level of output. Isoquants are derived from the production function. Therefore, each combination on the isoquant is technically efficient.

Recall from Figure 8–1 in Chapter 8 that more than one combination of labor and capital could be used to produce the same level of output. In that example, capital could be used in only three amounts, 10, 20, and 30 units. To derive the characteristics of isoquants, let us assume now that a firm can vary continuously the amounts of both labor and capital used to produce its product. Therefore, the firm's output varies continuously also. From the firm's production function, it is possible to produce 1,000 units of output with the following five combinations of labor and capital:

	Labor (L)	*Capital* (K)
A	2	12
B	4	8
C	6	5
D	8	3
E	10	2

Combinations A through E are only five of the infinite number of combinations that can be used to produce 1,000 units of output. These five combinations (points *A* through *E*) and other combinations are plotted as the isoquant [I (Q = 1,000)] in Figure 9–1. This isoquant shows for every amount of labor, plotted on the

Figure 9–1   A Production Isoquant

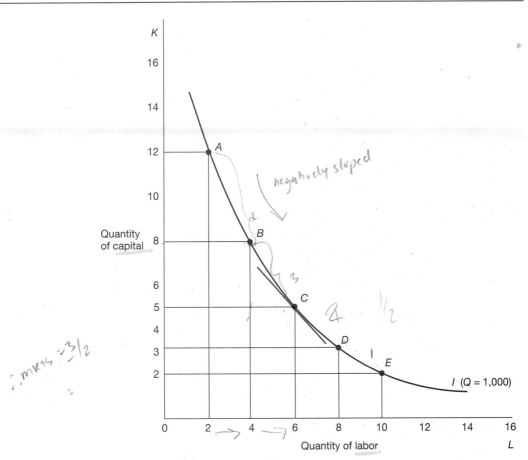

horizontal axis, the amount of capital, plotted on the vertical axis, that must be used if 1,000 units of output are produced. Conversely, it also shows how much labor must be used to produce 1,000 units of output for every amount of capital.

As illustrated in Figure 9–1, isoquants are negatively sloped, meaning that if labor is increased, capital can be decreased in order to keep output constant at 1,000 units. For example, if labor increases from 2 to 4 workers, capital can be decreased from 12 units to 8. Or, if capital is increased, labor can be decreased in order to remain on the same isoquant, keeping output constant. Increasing capital from 5 to 8 units requires, for example, a decrease in labor from 6 to 4, in order to keep output at 1,000.

Labor and capital vary inversely along an isoquant because the marginal products of both inputs are positive along an isoquant. An increase in labor, capital held constant, would therefore increase output. Capital can be reduced just enough to offset the increased output of the additional labor—since the marginal product of the reduced capital is positive, output falls when capital is reduced. The rate at which one input can be substituted for another along an isoquant is called the *marginal rate of technical substitution (MRTS)*.

Definition

The marginal rate of technical substitution of labor for capital is

$$MRTS_{L \text{ for } K} = -\frac{\text{Change in capital}}{\text{Change in labor}} = -\frac{\Delta K}{\Delta L},$$

holding output constant along an isoquant. In general terms, K is the amount of the input measured along the vertical axis and L is the amount measured along the horizontal. The minus sign is added in order to make *MRTS* a positive number, since $\Delta K/\Delta L$ is negative along the downward-sloping isoquant.

Over the relevant range of the isoquant, the marginal rate of technical substitution diminishes; that is, as more labor is used relative to capital, the absolute value of $\Delta K/\Delta L$ decreases along an isoquant. This can be seen in Figure 9–1. If labor increases from 2 to 4, capital must decrease from 12 to 8; so

$$MRTS_{L \text{ for } K} = -\frac{\Delta K}{\Delta L} = -\frac{-4}{2} = 2.$$

An *MRTS* of 2 means that capital must decrease by 2 units, per unit increase in labor. For a further increase in labor from 4 to 6, capital must fall by 3; $-\Delta K/\Delta L$ = 3/2. As you can easily calculate, moving from C to D and then from D to E, the *MRTS* is, respectively, 1 and 1/2.

The fact that the marginal rate of technical substitution diminishes means that isoquants are convex; that is, isoquants are bowed inward toward the origin or, in the neighborhood of a point of tangency, the isoquant lies above the tangent line, such as the tangent at point C in Figure 9–1. For extremely small changes in labor and capital, the *MRTS* is equal to the slope of the tangent. For example, as point D becomes closer and closer to point C, $\Delta K/\Delta L$ becomes closer and closer to the slope of the tangent at C. Thus, the slope of the tangent at C is the change in K per unit change in L, for small changes in L and K, when L equals 6 and K equals 5. It is easy to see that the slope of a tangent would become less and less steep as the input combination moves downward along the isoquant.

The characteristics of a typical isoquant are summarized in the general production isoquant shown in Figure 9–2. The isoquant I shows combinations of labor and capital that are capable of producing a specified level of output, for example, L_0 and K_0 or L_1 and K_1. The isoquant is downward sloping, indicating that as labor increases, less capital is required to keep output constant, or as capital increases, less labor is required. The marginal rate of technical substitution $(-\Delta K/\Delta L)$ is the rate at which labor can be substituted for capital, keeping output constant, and is given at each combination on the isoquant by the slope of a tangent at that point, such as the tangent at points A and B.

The reason the *MRTS* decreases along an isoquant is because, as labor increases, the additional labor has less capital to work with and labor becomes less productive. As capital decreases, the reduced capital is combined with more labor and becomes

Figure 9–2   A General Production Isoquant

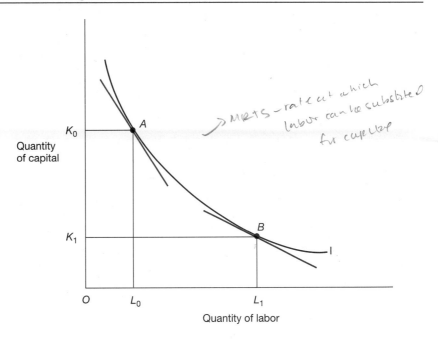

more productive. Therefore, for greater amounts of labor and reduced amounts of capital, more of the less-productive labor must be added to keep output constant. As labor increases relative to capital, greater amounts of labor are required to replace capital, and this means the *MRTS* must decrease. The concept will become more clear in the next subsection, in which we develop the relation between the *MRTS* and the marginal products of labor and capital.

9.2.2   Relation of *MRTS* to Marginal Products

We hinted at the relation of *MRTS* to the marginal products of labor and capital when we mentioned that the increased output from an increase in labor must be exactly offset by the reduction in output from a decrease in capital for movements along an isoquant. In fact, the exact relation can be established:

Principle

For small movements along an isoquant, the marginal rate of technical substitution equals the ratio of the marginal products of the two inputs:

$$MRTS_{L \text{ for } K} = -\frac{\Delta K}{\Delta L} = \frac{MP_L}{MP_K}.$$

To see the relation between the *MRTS* and the marginal products, consider a movement from point A to point B in Figure 9–1. Moving from A to B, $\Delta L = 2$

and $\Delta K = -4$. Since the marginal product of labor is the increase in output for a one-unit change in labor, the increase in output from a two-unit increase in labor is the increase in labor multiplied by the marginal product of each unit: $\Delta Q = \Delta L \cdot MP_L = 2 \cdot MP_L$. Likewise, the decrease in output for the four-unit decrease in capital is the decrease in capital times the marginal product of each unit: $\Delta Q = \Delta K \cdot MP_K = -4 \cdot MP_K$. The two changes in output must exactly offset each other to stay on the same isoquant, implying

$$\Delta L \cdot MP_L = \Delta K \cdot MP_K, = 2 \cdot MP_L = -4 \cdot MP_K.$$

Therefore, solving for $-\Delta K/\Delta L$,

$$MRTS = -\frac{\Delta K}{\Delta L} = \frac{4}{2} = \frac{MP_L}{MP_K}.$$

This relation holds for any small change in both labor and capital along an isoquant.[2] In general, since along an isoquant

$$\Delta L \cdot MP_L = \Delta K \cdot MP_K,$$

we can write

$$-\frac{\Delta K}{\Delta L} = \frac{MP_L}{MP_K} = MRTS_{L \text{ for } K}.$$

Since, as noted, along an isoquant K and L must vary inversely, $\Delta K/\Delta L$ is negative.[3]

This relation between the $MRTS$ and the ratio of the marginal products is important because it makes clear why the $MRTS$ diminishes, and it therefore explains the shape of an isoquant. As additional units of labor are added to a fixed amount of capital, the marginal product of labor diminishes. Furthermore, as shown earlier in Chapter 8, the marginal product of labor diminishes if the amount of the other input is diminished. Thus, two forces are working to diminish the marginal product of labor: (a) less of the other input causes a downward shift of the marginal product of labor curve and (b) more units of the variable input (labor) cause a downward movement along the marginal product curve. As labor is substituted for capital, the marginal product of labor must decline.

For analogous reasons, the marginal product of capital increases as less capital and more labor is used. With the quantity of labor fixed, the marginal product of capital rises as fewer units of capital are used. But, simultaneously, there is an

---

[2]We have violated our assumption about marginal product somewhat. The marginal product of an input is defined as the change in output per unit of change in the input, *the use of other inputs held constant*. In this case, we allow both inputs to change, and the marginal product is really an approximation. But we are speaking only of *slight* or very small changes in use. Thus, the violation of the assumption is small, and the approximation approaches the true variation for very small changes.

[3]It is possible that as more and more labor is used relative to capital, the marginal product of labor becomes negative and the isoquant bends upward. That is, because of negative marginal product, increases in labor reduce output and must be offset by increases in capital to keep output constant. Or, as more and more capital is used relative to labor, the marginal product of capital becomes negative, and the isoquant becomes positively sloped. Since both cases involve negative marginal product, and no firms would hire an input with negative marginal product, we will ignore these regions.

Figure 9–3   An Isoquant Map

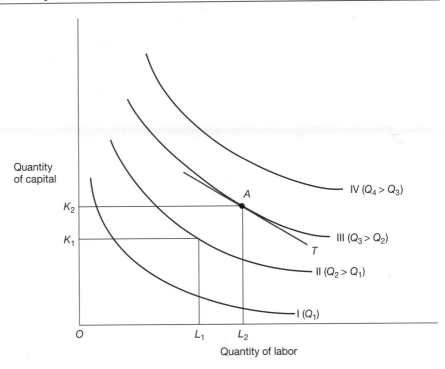

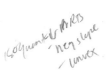

increase in the labor input, thereby shifting the marginal product of capital curve upward. The same two forces are present in this case: a movement along a marginal product curve and a shift in the location of the curve. In this situation, however, both forces work to increase the marginal product of capital. As labor is substituted for capital, the marginal product of capital increases. Thus, for increases in labor and decreases in capital, MP_L/MP_K and, hence, the $MRTS$ fall, because MP_L falls and MP_K rises.

9.2.3 Isoquant Maps

An *isoquant map* represents the family of isoquants derived from a production function. Figure 9–3 shows an isoquant map with four isoquants, each of which represents a different level of production or output. As before, labor is plotted along the horizontal axis and capital along the vertical. Each of the four isoquants has the properties discussed above: It is negatively sloped and convex, and it shows diminishing $MRTS$.

Any isoquant above and to the right of another isoquant is associated with a larger rate of output than that associated with the lower isoquant. For example, every combination on III, such as L_2 and K_2, can produce a higher rate of output (Q_3) than can be produced by any combination, such as L_1 and K_1, on isoquant II (Q_2).

Isoquants I through IV are only four of the infinite number of possible isoquants. Because labor and capital, and therefore output, can vary continuously, an infinite number of different outputs are possible. A different isoquant is associated with each level of output. The slope of each isoquant is the *MRTS* of labor for capital. This rate is shown by the slope of a tangent to the isoquant at the given combination of labor and capital; an example is the tangent line *T* to isoquant III at point *A*.

Figure 9–3 shows that isoquants do not have to be equal distance parallel to one another. Isoquants can get extremely close to each other, but they cannot intersect one another. It was stated that the production function gives only the highest level of output for any combination of inputs, so intersection would violate the definition of technical efficiency.

Isoquants show how a producer can substitute one input for another while keeping output constant. Isoquants and the *MRTS* are determined by the firm's production technology and the characteristics of the production function. We now turn to the way a producer can substitute one input for another, while keeping *cost constant.* This rate of substitution is determined by the prices of the inputs.

9.3   Isocost Curves and Input Prices

The rate at which a producer can substitute one input for another while holding cost constant is shown by an *isocost curve*.

Definition

An isocost curve shows all combinations of two inputs that can be purchased by a firm at a given level of cost, input prices held constant.

9.3.1   Specific Isocost Curves

Figure 9–4 shows three isocost curves that are associated with three different levels of cost. We will continue to assume that the two inputs are labor, plotted along the horizontal axis, and capital, plotted along the vertical, although the analysis applies equally well to any two productive inputs.

Assume that the price of labor, P_L, is $100 and the price of capital, P_K, is $200. The price of labor could be the wage rate per day. The price of capital could be the interest on money to buy equipment, or it could be a lease payment. The isocost curve associated with a cost of $200,000 and these input prices is the straight line labeled C' that goes from $K = 1,000$ to $L = 2,000$. To see why this is so, consider the case in which zero labor is hired. The firm can purchase 1,000 units of capital at a cost of $200,000, because $200 \times 1,000 = $200,000$. This is one point on the isocost curve, and it is the vertical intercept. Or, if the firm purchases zero capital, it can hire 2,000 units of labor, because $100 \times 2,000 = $200,000$; 2,000 is the horizontal intercept. Likewise, $K = 750$ and $L = 500$ is another point on the curve, because $200 \times 750 + $100 \times 500 = $200,000$. You can verify for yourself that ($K = 500$ and $L = 1,000$) and ($K = 250$ and $L = 1,500$) are two other points on the line.

Figure 9–4   Isocost Curves

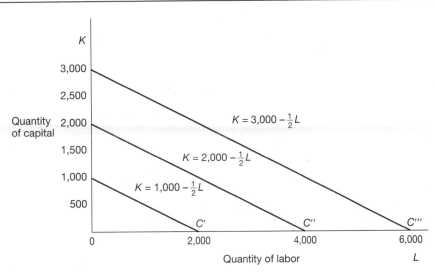

This isocost schedule can be expressed as the equation for a straight line. Since the expenditure on both inputs equals $200,000,

$$\$200 \cdot K + \$100 \cdot L = \$200,000.$$

Solving for K in terms of L,

$$K = \frac{\$200,000}{\$200} - \frac{\$100}{\$200} L = 1,000 - \frac{1}{2} L.$$

The vertical intercept is 1,000; the slope of the line, $-1/2$, is the ratio of the price of labor, P_L, to the price of capital, P_K, or the vertical intercept divided by the horizontal intercept, $-1,000/2,000$. The slope of the line shows how much capital must be reduced when labor is increased by one unit, holding cost constant. In this example, a one-unit increase in labor adds $100 to cost. To keep cost the same, $100 less must be spent on capital. Since the price of capital is $200, one half a unit of capital must be given up.

The isocost schedule with endpoints 2,000 units of capital and 4,000 units of labor, labeled C'', is the line associated with a cost of $400,000 assuming the same input prices. Since input prices are the same, the slope of this isocost schedule is the same as the slope of C'; that is, the ratio of the intercepts, 2,000/4,000, equals 1/2. At zero labor, $200 × K = $400,000, so the vertical intercept is now 2,000. The equation for this isocost curve is $K = 2,000 - (1/2)L$. You can verify that the curve labeled C''' is the curve associated with a cost of $600,000, and the equation for this line is $K = 3,000 - (1/2)L$.

A higher cost causes a parallel upward shift in the isocost curve under the same set of input prices. Therefore, any isocost curve lying above another is associated with a higher level of cost than the lower curve. The isocost curves in Figure 9–4 are only three of the infinite number of schedules when P_L = \$100 and P_K = \$200. The slope of these lines, P_L/P_K = $-1/2$, shows the rate at which the firm can substitute labor for capital or capital for labor under the given set of input prices at each level of cost. A one-unit increase in labor requires a decrease of 1/2 unit of capital to keep cost constant. A one-unit increase in capital, costing \$200, requires a two-unit decrease in labor to keep cost constant.

9.3.2 The Generalized Form

To generalize, if TC is a given level of total cost, P_L is the price of labor, and P_K is the price of capital, when the entire cost is spent on the two inputs,

$$P_L \cdot L + P_K \cdot K = TC.$$

Solving for K in terms of L,

$$K = \frac{TC}{P_K} - \frac{P_L}{P_K}L,$$

which is the equation for a straight line with a vertical intercept of TC/P_K and a constant slope of $-P_L/P_K$.

The characteristics of isocost curves can be summarized as follows:

Relations

An isocost schedule of the form

$$K = \frac{TC}{P_K} - \frac{P_L}{P_K}L$$

shows every combination of labor and capital a firm can purchase at a cost of TC when the price of labor is P_L and the price of capital is P_K. Alternatively, this equation shows the quantity of capital that the firm can purchase at each level of labor at a cost of TC. The vertical intercept of the isocost curve is TC/P_K. If TC increases (decreases), the isocost curve shifts upward (downward), but the slope, $-P_L/P_K$, remains unchanged.

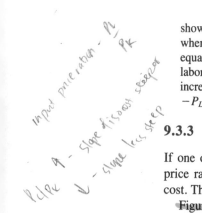

9.3.3 Changes in Input Prices

If one or both input prices change, causing an increase or decrease in the input-price ratio, P_L/P_K, the slope of an isocost curve changes for any given level of cost. The slope becomes steeper if P_L/P_K increases and less steep if P_L/P_K decreases.

Figure 9–5 shows the effect of a change in the ratio of input prices. In panel A, K_1L_1, K_2L_2 and K_3L_3, are three isocost curves associated with the input price ratio, P_L/P_K, and three different levels of cost. Panel B shows the effect of an *increase* in the input price ratio to P_L'/P_K'. Because P_L'/P_K', the slope of the isocost curves in panel B, is larger than P_L/P_K, the slopes of the isocost curves in panel B, K_1'/L_1', K_2'/L_2' and K_3'/L_3' are steeper than K_1/L_1, K_2/L_2 and K_3/L_3. The increase in P_L/P_K can result from an increase in P_L, a decrease in P_K, or a change in both prices that causes P_L to become relatively higher than P_K. Thus, the larger the ratio P_L/P_K, the steeper the set of isocost curves.

Figure 9–5   Changes in Input Price Ratio

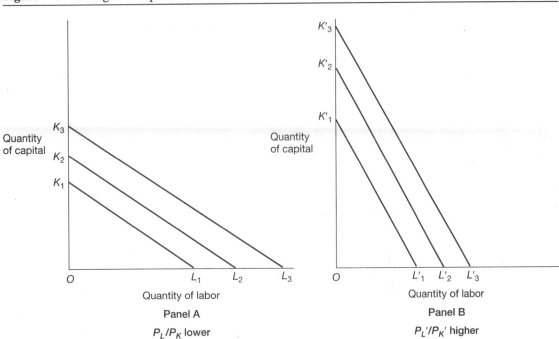

The effect of a change in the input price ratio can be summarized in the following:

Relations

If P_L/P_K increases, because of a relative increase in P_L or decrease in P_K, the isocost curve at each level of cost becomes steeper; a given increase in labor requires a larger decrease in capital to keep cost constant. If P_L/P_K decreases because of a relative decrease in P_L or increase in P_K, the isocost curve at each level of cost becomes less steep; a given increase in labor requires a larger decrease in capital to keep cost constant. The slope of the isocost, $-P_L/P_K$, shows the rate at which labor can be substituted for capital at a given level of cost; a one-unit increase in labor requires a decrease in capital of P_L/P_K units.

Now that we have discussed the properties of isoquants and isocost curves, we can combine these two concepts to show how the firm determines the combination of labor and capital that minimizes the cost of producing a given level of output or maximizes the output that can be produced at any given level of cost.

9.4   The Optimal Combination of Inputs

The core of production theory determines how a firm should combine inputs to produce a given level of output at the lowest possible cost, or how to produce the highest level of output possible at a given level of cost. We will first develop the

Figure 9–6   Optimal Input Combination to Produce Given Level of Output at Minimum Cost

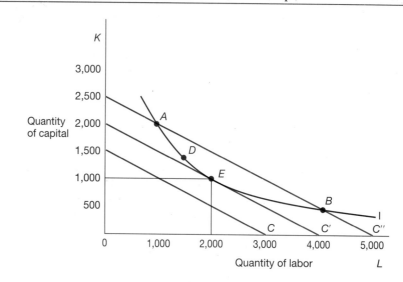

theory of the optimal combination of inputs using isoquants and isocost curves. Then we will show how this theory fits within the general framework of constrained optimization discussed in Chapter 4.

9.4.1   Production of a Given Output at Minimum Cost: The Graphical Approach

To analyze the problem of cost minimization graphically, suppose a firm wants to produce one million units of output per period of time. Combinations of capital and labor, the only two productive inputs capable of producing one million units of output, are shown by the isoquant labelled I in Figure 9–6.

The firm wants to find the input combination on the isoquant that costs the least. Assume, as before, that the price of capital, P_K, is $200 and the wage rate of labor, P_L, is $100. Thus, the slope of any isocost curve with these input prices is $-P_L/P_K$ $= -1/2$. Three of the infinite number of possible isocost curves with a slope of $-1/2$ are shown in the figure as C, C', and C''. From all possible curves, the firm wants to find the lowest (least-cost) isocost curve containing an input combination capable of producing one million units of output.

Clearly the isocost cost line C, with endpoints 1,500 units of capital and 3,000 units of labor, is not such a line, even though it is the curve associated with the lowest cost of the three lines in the figure. This line does not include any combination of labor and capital on isoquant I; therefore, C does not include any input combination capable of producing one million units of output. For the same reason, we can exclude input combinations on all isocost curves below C'.

Next, consider input combinations on the isocost line C'' with endpoints 2,500 and 5,000 on the vertical and horizontal axes, respectively. Two points on this line are on the isoquant: point A with 2,000 units of capital and 1,000 units of labor and point B with 500 units of capital and 4,000 units of labor. Combinations A and B, and any other combinations on the isocost curve, would cost \$500,000.

If the firm is using the combination at A, it could increase labor and decrease capital, moving along the isoquant to, say, point D. Output would remain constant, but clearly an isocost curve lower than C'' would pass through such a point. Thus, the cost of producing that output would fall. In fact, the firm could continue increasing labor and decreasing capital, moving downward along the isoquant and lowering cost, until point E is attained. At point E, the isocost line C' is just tangent to the isoquant at 1,000 units of capital and 2,000 units of labor.

Alternatively, if the firm begins at point B, it could move upward along the isoquant, adding capital and reducing labor. In this way it would lower cost while keeping output constant. And it would continue to lower its cost until the combination at E is reached, this time moving up the isoquant, increasing capital relative to labor.

Thus, any combination of inputs on an isocost curve above C' that can produce the desired level of output, costs more than the combination on C'. No combination on any isocost curve below C' is able to produce the desired level of output. We have, in other words, eliminated all input combinations other than 1,000 units of capital and 2,000 units of labor. This combination, at which the isocost curve is just tangent to the isoquant, is the lowest-cost method of producing the desired output. The cost of production would be $P_K K + P_L L = \$200 \times 1,000 + \$100 \times 2,000 = \$400,000$.

Tangency of the isocost curve to the isoquant means that the slopes of the two curves are equal. Recall that the absolute value of the slope of the isoquant is the marginal rate of technical substitution. The absolute value of the slope of the isocost curve is the input price ratio, P_L/P_K. Least-cost production, therefore, requires that the $MRTS$ of labor for capital be equal to the ratio of the price of labor to the price of capital. The market input-price ratio tells the producer the rate at which one input *can be substituted for another when inputs are purchased.* The marginal rate of technical substitution shows the rate at which the producer *can substitute in production* keeping output constant. If the two are not equal, at combinations such as A and B, a producer can lower cost by moving toward equality.

Principle

To minimize cost subject to a given level of production and given input prices, the producer must purchase inputs in quantities such that the marginal rate of technical substitution of labor for capital is equal to the input-price ratio (the price of labor to the price of capital):

$$-\frac{\Delta K}{\Delta L} = MRTS_{L \text{ for } K} = \frac{P_L}{P_K}.$$

Since the $MRTS_{L \text{ for } K}$ equals the ratio of the marginal products,

$$\frac{MP_L}{MP_K} = \frac{P_L}{P_K}.$$

9.4.2 Production of a Given Output at Minimum Cost: The Algebraic Approach

The above equilibrium condition, which was derived graphically, is closely related to the equilibrium condition for constrained optimization set forth in Chapter 4. Recall that constrained optimization requires that the marginal benefits per dollar spent on the last unit of each activity be equal for each activity. In the case of cost minimization, the activities are the amounts of labor and capital purchased and put into production, the constraint is the desired level of output, and the objective is to produce that output at the lowest possible cost.

Assume that the firm is at point A on the isoquant in Figure 9–6, using 2,000 units of capital and 1,000 units of labor. Clearly, at this input combination the absolute value of the slope of the isoquant, the $MRTS$, is greater than the absolute value of the slope of the isocost curve, $P_L/P_K = \$100/\$200$. Since the $MRTS$ equals the ratio of the marginal products, at point A

$$MRTS_{L \text{ for } K} = \frac{MP_L}{MP_K} > \frac{P_L}{P_K} = \frac{100}{200}.$$

Suppose, the marginal product of the last unit of labor is 1,000, and the marginal product of the last unit of capital is 1,500. A slight manipulation of the above inequality yields

$$\frac{MP_L}{P_L} = \frac{1,000}{100} = 10 > \frac{MP_K}{P_K} = \frac{1,500}{200} = 7.5.$$

The firm can reduce capital by two units, its output falls by approximately 3,000 (since $MP_K = 1,500$), and its cost of capital falls by \$400. To keep output the same (replace the sacrificed 3,000 units of output), the firm can increase labor by three units, increase output by approximately 3,000, and increase its labor cost \$300.[4] Thus, output would remain constant, but the net cost of production would fall \$100 (\$400 − \$300). As long as $MP_L/P_L > MP_K/P_K$, the marginal product per dollar spent on the last unit of labor is greater than the marginal product per dollar spent on the last unit of capital, and the firm could continue increasing labor, decreasing capital, and lower the cost of producing the one million units of output. As labor increases and capital decreases, MP_L falls and MP_K rises, until the cost-minimizing equilibrium is attained where

$$\frac{MP_L}{P_L} = \frac{MP_K}{P_K}.$$

This is equivalent to the equilibrium condition at point E in the graph, because this equality implies

$$\frac{MP_L}{MP_K} = MRTS_{L \text{ for } K} = \frac{P_L}{P_K}.$$

---

[4]Note that we used the term *approximately* for increases and decreases in output. We, therefore, ignored slight increases in marginal product for decreases in capital and slight decreases in marginal product for increases in labor.

In other words, the condition that MP_L/P_L equals MP_K/P_K means that the slopes of the isocost curve and the isoquant are equal.

Suppose the firm chooses the wrong input combination again. This time it chooses the combination at point B in the graph, at which the slope of the isocost curve is greater than the slope of the isoquant. Thus,

$$MRTS_{L \text{ for } K} = \frac{MP_L}{MP_K} < \frac{P_L}{P_K},$$

meaning, at this combination,

$$\frac{MP_L}{P_L} < \frac{MP_K}{P_K}.$$

The marginal product per dollar spent on the last unit of labor is less than the marginal product per dollar spent on the last unit of capital. The firm should reduce labor and increase capital in such a way as to keep output constant while reducing cost. The firm should continue substituting capital for labor, causing MP_L to rise and MP_K to fall, until cost is minimized at the combination shown at point E in the graph, where $MP_L/MP_K = P_L/P_K$.

Principle

The cost of producing a given level of output is minimized by using the combination of labor and capital at which

$$\frac{MP_L}{MP_K} = MRTS_{L \text{ for } K} = \frac{P_L}{P_K},$$

which implies that

$$\frac{MP_L}{P_L} = \frac{MP_K}{P_K}.$$

The marginal products per dollar spent on the last unit of each input are equal.

Economics in the News   **How Can the Pentagon Minimize Cost?**

During the spring and summer of 1989, there was considerable controversy about the funding of the new B-2 Stealth bomber. The U.S. Air Force planned to purchase 132 of these planes, which would be practically invisible to enemy radar, at a cost of $516 million each. In *Business Week* (April 17, 1989, p. 21), Dave Griffiths in his column "Why the Stealth Bomber Should Become Invisible" urged Congress not to appropriate funds for the Stealth. Griffiths's reasoning was based on the principle of cost minimization for a given level of national defense.

Griffiths argued that smaller advanced cruise missiles launched from available B-1 and B-52 bombers would have all of the deterrent capabilities of the Stealth. He said that the same Stealth technology could be used to make the missiles practically invisible, and

(continued)

they would be just as reliable. Although they would not allow quite as much time for recall as penetrating bombers, they would permit a president more flexibility than land- or submarine-based missiles. Finally, he stated that the Pentagon would save billions of dollars by choosing missiles launched from planes rather than B-2 bombers.

It must be pointed out, of course, that proponents of the Stealth were, at the same time, arguing that Stealth bombers were far superior to any available lower-priced deterrent systems. However, whether Griffiths was right or wrong is not the point here. The point is that economic theory—constrained cost minimization—is an extremely useful and effective approach to analyzing important policy issues. Griffiths, in effect, was asserting that the marginal benefits (usefulness as a deterrent) per dollar spent on Stealth bombers were less than the marginal benefits per dollar spent on missiles. The cost of a given deterrent level could be reduced by switching from bombers to missiles.

9.1   Applying the Theory

Newsweek, November 24, 1986, in a story about some changes being made by the Ford Motor Company, reported that in 1978 the company employed 506,000 people to make 6.5 million cars and trucks; in 1986, it was employing 370,000 workers to produce nearly the same number. Can you suggest three possible reasons for the drastic reduction in the number of workers employed to produce essentially the same number of vehicles?

9.4.3   Production of Maximum Output with a Given Level of Cost

Thus far we have assumed that the producer chooses a level of output then finds the input combination that permits production of that output at the least cost. As an alternative, we could assume the firm spends only a fixed amount on production and wishes to attain the highest level of output possible for that expenditure. Not too surprisingly, the results turn out to be the same as before.

This situation is shown in Figure 9–7. The isocost line *KL* shows every possible combination of the two inputs that can be purchased at the given level of cost and input prices. Four isoquants are shown. Clearly, at the given level of cost, output level IV is unattainable. Neither level I nor level II would be chosen since higher levels are possible with isocost curve *KL*. The highest level of output attainable with the given level of cost is produced by using L_0 labor and K_0 capital. At point *A,* the highest possible isoquant, III, is just tangent to the given isocost line. In the case of output maximization, the marginal rate of technical substitution of labor for capital equals the input-price ratio (the price of labor to the price of capital.)

Principle

In order to maximize output subject to a given cost, the producer must employ inputs in such amounts as to equate the marginal rate of technical substitution and the input-price ratio.

$$MRTS_{L \text{ for } K} = \frac{MP_L}{MP_K} = \frac{P_L}{P_K}.$$

Figure 9–7   Output Maximization for a Given Level of Cost

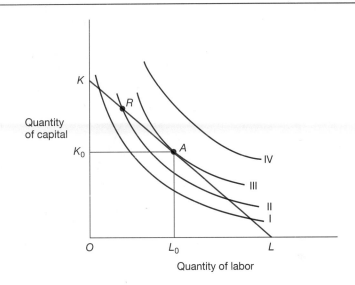

Suppose, in Figure 9–7, the producer chooses the combination of labor and capital at point R on isoquant II. Since the slope of the isoquant ($MRTS = MP_L/MP_K$) is greater than the slope of the isocost curve (P_L/P_K),

$$\frac{MP_L}{P_L} > \frac{MP_K}{P_K}.$$

The marginal product per dollar of the last unit of labor is greater than that of capital. The firm could spend \$1 less on capital and \$1 more on labor, for which the marginal product per dollar is higher. Cost would remain constant, while output increases. As long as the inequality holds, the firm could continue taking dollars away from capital and adding them to labor, thereby increasing output at the same cost. In other words, the firm is moving downward along its isocost curve and reaching higher and higher isoquants. As more labor and less capital are used, MP_L falls and MP_K rises until the combination L_0 and K_0 at point A is reached. At this combination, the firm produces the highest output possible at the given cost. Therefore, the equilibrium condition

$$MRTS_{L \text{ for } K} = \frac{MP_L}{MP_K} = \frac{P_L}{P_K},$$

implies

$$\frac{MP_L}{P_L} = \frac{MP_K}{P_K}.$$

As you have seen, the equilibrium conditions are the same for cost minimization and output maximization. Therefore, the equilibrium situation shown in Figure 9–8 applies to either problem. In the figure, the isocost curve KL is tangent to the isoquant I at $\overline{L}$ units of labor and $\overline{K}$ units of capital. This equilibrium gives

Figure 9–8   Generalization of Constrained Cost Minimization or Output Maximization

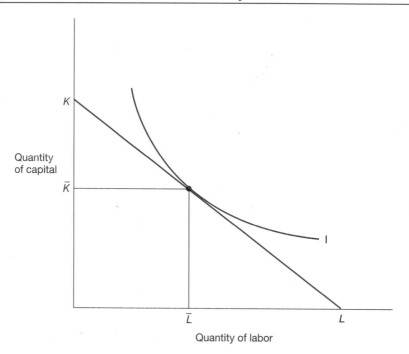

the cost-minimizing combination of inputs capable of producing the output associated with isoquant I. It also gives the output-maximizing combination of inputs
that can be purchased at the cost given by the isocost curve *KL*. In each case, the
equilibrium condition is

$$-\frac{\Delta K}{\Delta L} = MRTS_{L \text{ for } K} = \frac{MP_L}{MP_K} = \frac{P_L}{P_K}$$

or

$$\frac{MP_L}{P_L} = \frac{MP_K}{P_K}.$$

Economics in   **AIDS Research: A Movement along the Health Care Isocost Curve?**
the News

A huge amount of disease research is funded by federal grants, in large part from the
Centers for Disease Control (CDC), the National Institutes of Health (NIH), and the Drug
Abuse and Mental Health Administration (DAMH). These agencies have fixed budgets,
but receive grant proposals from researchers far greater than those budgets. The administrators try to allocate those budgets so as to maximize the research output (admittedly

(continued)

quite difficult to measure and even to conceptualize) attainable from a given level of expenditure or cost. Because the government cannot fund everything, these agencies must make trade-offs. In effect, they must choose a particular combination of research projects on their isocost line. This problem of fund allocation was destined to cause controversy, and it did.

As an article in *Newsweek,* "AIDS Research Gets the Grants," (March 6, 1989, p. 46) reported, many scientists were becoming jealous of AIDS researchers. Since 1984, when Congress began devoting funds to fight AIDS, total U.S. spending on AIDS research had grown from $61 million to $1.3 billion, an increase of 2,000 percent. By 1989, AIDS research was 8.5 percent of the NIH budget, 11.2 percent of DAMH spending, and 39 percent of CDC funding. Many scientists believed that these research dollars were dollars taken away from research spending on other diseases, such as Alzheimer's, Lyme, sickle-cell anemia, cancer, venereal disease, and tuberculosis. NIH added several hundred more staffers for AIDS-related work, while eliminating about 1,000 other positions. Federal spending on heart, blood, nutrition, and hepatitis research held steady or declined. Cancer specialists claimed that their research was hardest hit. Some argued that the cuts in federal spending could produce a crisis in other research fields within a decade.

Some experts, such as the director of the NIH and the chairman of the House sub-committee on Health and Environment, argued that there was not a dollar-for-dollar trade-off; all AIDS spending would not have been available for other diseases. However, the major argument centered around where the spending would have the greatest benefits. Some argued that many fewer Americans died from AIDS, 45,000 since the early 1980s, compared to, say, cancer, nearly 500,000 a year, and Alzheimer's, about 100,000 a year. These scientists believed that more research dollars should be spent on diseases with higher death rates.

Others strongly defended the spending on AIDS, saying it deserves even more. They asserted that AIDS research will bring about scientific advances in other fields, such as immunology, epidemiology, drug testing, development of animal models, and information about how tumors are formed.

All scientists wanted more total federal spending on health research in general, rather than being forced "to fight over pieces of the pie." Regardless of the rate of increase in total funding, scientists will probably continue to fight over pieces of the pie. The federal government and the relevant agencies must continue to allocate a given expenditure or cost among the different health-related activities, trying to maximize the benefits—in reduced death and suffering or side benefits—within the constraint of that expenditure. This problem, though much more serious than the typical production problem we discussed, nonetheless, is a constrained output maximization problem. Ideally, the marginal benefits per dollar spent on each research area should be the same for all areas. However, when comparing AIDS, cancer, heart, and other research, the benefits are extremely difficult to estimate, even though the people responsible continue to try.

9.4.4 Optimization with More Than Two Inputs

For analytical and graphical convenience, we have derived the optimization conditions for the case of only two variable inputs. This two-input case illustrates all of the important principles of production theory. The analysis can, however, be easily extended to cover situations with any number of variable inputs.

We have demonstrated that, for any two variable inputs, i and j, cost minimization and output maximization require the $MRTS_{i \text{ for } j}$ to equal the ratio of the input prices. Therefore, if the firm employs N variable inputs, for all possible pairs of inputs,

$$MRTS_{i \text{ for } j} = \frac{MP_i}{MP_j} = \frac{P_i}{P_j}$$

for inputs i and j, where P_i and P_j are the prices of the inputs. Or, expressed slightly differently,

$$\frac{MP_1}{P_1} = \frac{MP_2}{P_2} = \frac{MP_3}{P_3} = \ldots = \frac{MP_N}{P_N}.$$

That is, the firm simultaneously chooses the amount of each input, so that the marginal product per dollar spent on the last unit of each input is the same for all inputs.

When the combination of inputs is chosen so that the marginal rate of technical substitution equals the price ratio for all pairs of inputs, production is *economically efficient*.

Definition

Economic efficiency requires that a given level of production is produced at the lowest possible cost or the level of production is the highest level that can be produced at a given cost.

Note that economic efficiency and technical efficiency are not the same. Technical efficiency, you will recall, means that a given combination of inputs produces the maximum amount of output that combination is capable of producing. Every input combination and associated output given by the production function is technically efficient. Therefore, because isoquants are derived from a production function, every combination of inputs on an isoquant is technically efficient: the output associated with a given isoquant is the most that each combination of inputs on that isoquant can produce.

Only one combination of inputs on an isoquant is economically efficient. This is the combination that can produce the output at the lowest cost. Because a change in input prices would change the equilibrium combination of inputs, economic efficiency is determined by both the characteristics of the production function and the input prices.

9.5 The Expansion Path

A firm's cost depends on how much output it produces. If the firm is economically efficient in production, the cost of a given level of output is determined by the tangency between an isoquant and an isocost line. All of these points of tangency can be connected to form what is called an *expansion path*. An expansion path shows all of the efficient levels of output for different levels of cost, holding input prices constant.

Definition

The expansion path is the curve showing the economically efficient combination of inputs for each level of output, input prices held constant. Each combination is, therefore, the combination that minimizes the cost of producing a given level of output or maximizes the output from a given level of cost.

The expansion path is the curve showing how input usage changes as output changes, input prices held constant, when the cost of producing each level of output is minimized. Alternatively, the expansion path shows the output-maximizing combination of inputs at each level of expenditure, input prices held constant. Every point on the expansion path is economically efficient.

9.5.1   The Graph of an Expansion Path

A typical expansion path is shown in Figure 9–9. Isoquant curves I, II, and III represent three levels of output; KL, $K'L'$, and $K''L''$ are the isocost lines representing the minimum cost of producing each of the three levels of output. Input prices are not changing, so the input-price ratio is the same for each of the isocost curves. Since the input prices remain constant, the three isocost curves are parallel.

The cost-minimizing combinations of inputs are given by points A, B, and C, with, respectively, K_1 and L_1, K_2 and L_2, and K_3 and L_3 units of capital and labor. Each equilibrium point is defined by the equality between the marginal rate of technical substitution and the input-price ratio. The curve labeled EP, joining the three points of equilibrium, and by assumption all other points so generated, is the expansion path. Because the input-price ratio remains constant along the expansion path, the $MRTS$ remains constant also. Thus, the expansion path gives the optimal usage of labor and capital for each level of output, at constant input prices.[5]

An expansion path is derived under a fixed set of input prices. It therefore follows that a change in the input-price ratio will change the expansion path and, consequently, the optimal combination of inputs at each level of output. Figure 9–10 illustrates this change.

Isoquants I, II, and III are associated with three levels of output. Begin with an input-price ratio for labor and capital of $\overline{P}_L/\overline{P}_K$. At these input prices, the three isocost lines determining the cost-minimizing combination of labor and capital at each level of output are MN, $M'N'$, and $M''N''$. The slope of each is $-\overline{P}_L/\overline{P}_K$. The expansion path for this input-price ratio is EP_1.

Now assume that the input-price ratio falls from $\overline{P}_L/\overline{P}_K$ to $\hat{P}_L/\hat{P}_K$. Recall from the previous discussion that P_L/P_K, can decrease because of a decrease in P_L, an increase in P_K, or a change in both input prices that decreases P_L relative to P_K. This decrease in the input-price ratio causes the slope of the isocost lines in Figure 9–10 to decrease—that is, the isocost lines become less steep. The new, less steep

---

[5]The expansion path in Figure 9–9 indicates that the usage of both inputs increases as output increases. Because this is the normal case, such inputs are called normal inputs. It is possible, however, that the usage of one of the inputs might decrease as output increases over some range of output. An input, the usage of which decreases as output increases, is called an inferior input. Such inputs are relatively unimportant in production theory.

Figure 9–9 An Expansion Path

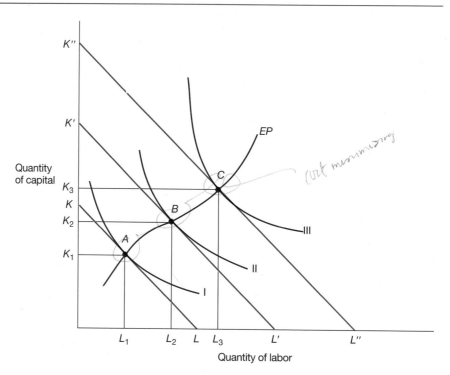

isocost lines that give the new, cost-minimizing combinations of inputs at each of the three output levels in the figure are *RZ*, *R'Z'*, and *R''Z''*. The new expansion path for the lower input-price ratio is EP_2, which lies below EP_1. Because the lower input-price ratio decreases the slope of the isocost curves, the point of tangency must be on a section of the isoquant that is less steep than before. Since each isoquant is less steep at the new points of tangency, more labor and less capital are used at each level of output. In other words, if P_L/P_K falls, the firm will substitute the relatively less expensive input, labor, for the relatively more expensive input, capital. This substitution effect causes the downward shift in the expansion path. On the other hand, if P_L/P_K increases, the isocost lines become steeper, tangency points occur on the steeper section of the isoquants, the firm uses less labor and more capital at each level of output, and the expansion path shifts upward.

9.5.2   Expansion Paths and Cost

The minimum cost of producing any given level of output can be derived from the expansion path, if the input prices are known. Suppose in Figure 9–9 capital and labor are the only variable inputs, $\overline{P}_L$ is the price of labor, and $\overline{P}_K$ is the price of capital. From the expansion path, the minimum cost of producing the output associated with isoquant I, is $\overline{P}_L L_1 + \overline{P}_K K_1$—the total cost of labor plus the total cost of capital. Likewise the minimum cost of producing the output associated with isoquant II is $\overline{P}_L L_2 + \overline{P}_K K_2$, and so on.

Figure 9–10   Changes in Input Prices and the Expansion Path

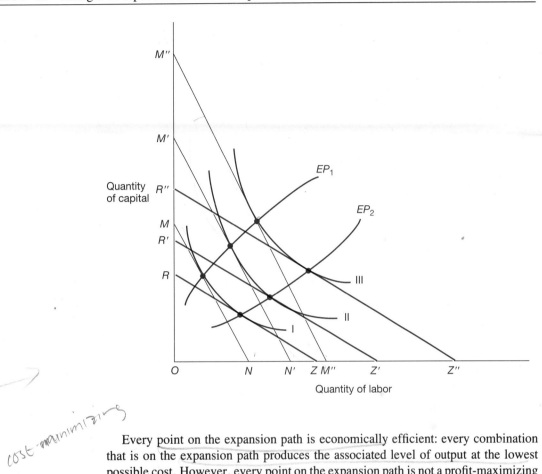

Quantity of labor

Every point on the expansion path is economically efficient: every combination that is on the expansion path produces the associated level of output at the lowest possible cost. However, every point on the expansion path is not a profit-maximizing combination of inputs. Only one level of output is the output that maximizes the firm's profit. The expansion path gives the firm's cost structure. To find the output that maximizes profit, the firm must consider both the cost structure and its revenue, which is determined by the demand for the firm's product. We will analyze the firm's profit-maximizing decision when we take up the theory of the firm, beginning in Chapter 12.

9.5.3   The Expansion Path and Fixed Proportions

Recall that we mentioned in Chapter 8 that a production function could possibly be characterized by production under fixed proportions. In this case, all inputs must be used in the same proportion regardless of output. An example would be, if 2 units of labor and 5 of capital are necessary to produce 100 units of output, 200 units of output require 4 labor and 10 capital, 300 units require 6 labor and 15 capital, and so on. If labor is limited to 2 units, no matter how much capital is added beyond 5 units, only 100 units of output can still be produced.

Figure 9–11   Production with Fixed Proportions

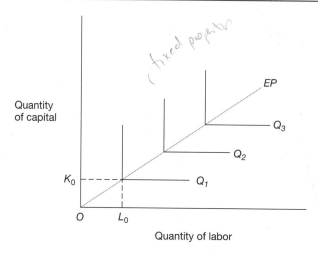

Figure 9–11 shows a set of isoquants and the expansion path for a fixed-proportion production function. The isoquants for outputs Q_1, Q_2, and Q_3 form right angles. Consider output level Q_1; this level is produced by K_0 capital and L_0 labor. If labor remains at that level while capital is increased, no more output can be produced. An increase in labor cannot increase output while capital remains fixed. Furthermore, Q_2, Q_3, and all other outputs require labor and capital to be used in the same ratio, K_0/L_0, no matter what the input-price ratio. The capital/labor ratio is the slope of the expansion path, *EP*, which is a straight line passing through the corner of each isoquant. The expansion path is therefore the same no matter what the input-price ratio is. As previously mentioned, fixed-proportions production is not particularly important in production theory, especially in the long run. Economists do use this concept from time to time in their analysis, but in this text we primarily treat production as characterized by variable proportions.

9.5.4 Returns to Scale

Economists are sometimes interested in the way output changes when all inputs are increased in the same proportion. For example, when all inputs are increased 10 percent, does output increase by more than, less than, or exactly 10 percent? The effect on output of a proportionate change in all inputs is called *returns to scale*.

Definition

Returns to scale measure the proportionate increase in output when all inputs are increased in the same proportion for a given production function.

More specifically, suppose output (Q) depends on only two inputs, L and K. Suppose the inputs increase by a constant proportion, say λ, and we observe the proportionate change (z) in output. Increasing labor and capital from L to λL and K to λK causes output to increase from Q to zQ.

CRT
Fixed-Proportion

RTS

1
variable proportion

We noted that, in the case of fixed-proportions production functions, if inputs are increased by a constant percent, output rises by the same proportion. More concisely, $z = \lambda$ in fixed-proportions production. This phenomenon is called constant returns to scale.

But returns to scale are often referred to when dealing with variable-proportions production functions. If all inputs are increased by a factor of λ and output goes up by a factor of z, then, in general, a producer experiences:

1. Increasing returns to scale if $z > \lambda$. Output goes up proportionately more than the increase in input usage.
2. Decreasing returns to scale if $z < \lambda$. Output goes up proportionately less than the increase in input usage.
3. Constant returns to scale if $z = \lambda$. Output goes up by the same proportion as the increase in input usage.

Economists often refer to returns to scale in two contexts. Returns may exist at the plant level or at the firm level, in which a firm may operate several plants. Frequently, there are increasing returns to scale over ranges of output at the firm level, but not for plants. For a proportionate increase in output at the firm level, it often takes proportionately less of an increase in administrative and selling personnel, while, at the plant level there may be constant or decreasing returns for the increase in output. Furthermore, returns to scale are not necessarily the same over the entire range of a variable-proportion production function. A production function may exhibit increasing returns over some part of the production function, decreasing returns over another part, and constant returns over still another part.

Do not conclude from this discussion of returns to scale that, with variable-proportion production functions, firms actually expand output by increasing input usage in exactly the same proportion. As you have seen, the very concept of variable proportions means that they do not necessarily expand in the same proportions; the expansion path may twist and turn in many directions.

Economics in the News

Mexican Maquiladora Industries Expanding

A practice started in U.S. manufacturing during the 1980s was the maquiladora program. This program involves U.S. manufacturing firms shipping parts (duty free) into Mexico, where the parts are assembled into the final goods in plants along the border. The goods are shipped back into the United States, and an import duty is paid only on the value added in Mexico; the goods are then sold in the United States.

Why would U.S. firms adopt this practice? (Let's ignore any tax implications and concentrate on production theory.) It may help to know that the maquiladora industries greatly accelerated during the 1980s when the peso plunged against the U.S. dollar, causing the dollar wages for Mexican workers to fall. *Newsweek,* "The Rise of Gringo Capitalism" (January 5, 1987, p. 40) stated that from 1982 to 1987 the average hourly wage in U.S. dollars for a maquiladora worker in Juarez fell from $2 to 75 cents. Clearly,

(continued)

during this period of falling Mexican wages, it became less costly for many U.S. firms to have their products assembled in Mexico.

But, why don't U.S. firms manufacture the components in Mexico also—that is, carry out all the production in Mexico? Again, ignoring any tax implications, we can reason along the lines suggested by the theory of production.[6] Suppose that a firm can divide its production process into two separate stages: processing, in which the components are manufactured, and assembly, in which the components are assembled into the final product. If the firm uses capital and labor in both stages, each stage has a separate isoquant map. The isoquants have different shapes, reflecting different marginal rates of substitution in the two stages. In the figures below, the two isocost curves in each panel, processing and assembly, are associated with the same total cost in each stage. The isocost curves for Mexico are much less steep than the curves for the United States, because the price of labor, relative to the price of capital, is much lower in Mexico. In panel A, a higher isoquant for processing can be attained in the United States than can be reached in Mexico at the same total cost. In panel B, a higher isoquant for assembly can be attained in Mexico than can be reached in the United States at the same total cost. Thus, at a given level of cost, more processing can be done in the United States and more assembly can be done in Mexico. Alternatively, the given level of processing can be done in Mexico only at a higher cost (the isocost must be shifted upward to reach tangency). Also, the given level of assembly could be attained in the United States only at a higher cost. It is therefore economically efficient to process in the United States and assemble in Mexico. The reason for the difference is that the price of labor, relative to the price of capital, is lower in Mexico and processing is relatively capital intensive, while assembly is relatively labor intensive.

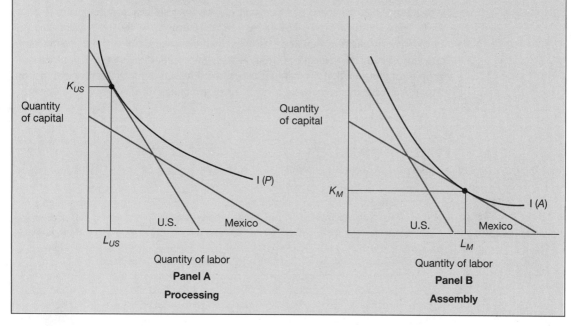

Panel A

Processing

Panel B

Assembly

[6]The following analysis is based upon "Manufacturing: Mexico's Maquiladora Industries," *The Margin*, November/December 1988.

9.6   Do Firms Behave This Way?

You may wonder how accurate a description of the behavior of actual firms the theory of production provides. Do firms really behave this way? If the question means, do firms know the precise level of each input that minimizes the cost of producing each output, the answer is clearly no. Firms typically don't worry about whether they should hire exactly 1,000 workers—not 999 and not 1,001—although a smaller firm might pay a considerable amount of attention to whether it should hire two or three workers. Firms don't try to minimize cost every day, or even every week. It takes time to respond to changing input prices; that is, much more time than it takes to read about such activities or than it takes your professor to graph the change on the blackboard. Certainly, firms don't use the graphs we have shown here, and most firms produce more than one product. Firms sometimes make mistakes.

The theory of production, however, is not designed to be a completely accurate description of how firms really behave. The theory is designed to explain how firms in general behave, not how any individual firm makes decisions. The theory shows how cost would be minimized or output maximized under ideal conditions in which the managers have complete information. The theory, therefore, is a model to analyze the behavior of actual firms that do not have complete information.

Nonetheless, firms do search for ways to reduce their cost—not continuously perhaps, but frequently. Observers have noted a strong tendency for firms to move toward the equilibrium conditions described by the theory. There is overwhelming historical evidence that as the price of an input rises, firms substitute other inputs for the higher-priced input. As labor costs rose in many industries or occupations, capital was substituted for labor. Substituting robots for labor in some manufacturing industries is a recent example. In countries where labor is relatively inexpensive and land is extremely expensive—for example, Japan and Western Europe—farmers use a lot of labor on relatively small farms or they import food products. In countries where labor is expensive and land relatively inexpensive—for example, the United States and Canada—farmers use a small amount of labor with a lot of capital on huge farms, where output per worker is very high. The theory of production set forth here predicts such behavior.

Furthermore, competition forces firms to try to produce at the lowest cost they can attain, given their information. If it is possible for a firm to reduce its cost but it doesn't, other firms will reduce cost and, consequently, will be able to underprice the firm that lags behind.

For all of these reasons, the theory of production is important for understanding firm behavior. We will, therefore, use this theory as a framework for developing the theory of cost in the next chapter and, hence, the theory of the firm in subsequent chapters.

9.7   Summary

In this chapter, we developed the tools necessary to analyze production with more than one variable input. In the discussion, we generally considered only two variable inputs, capital (K) plotted along the vertical axis for graphical purposes, and labor

(L), plotted along the horizontal. These may be the only inputs used by the firm in the long run or the only variable inputs used with fixed inputs in the short run.

An important graphical tool of analysis is a production isoquant, which shows combinations of two inputs (L and K) that are capable of producing a given level of output. Several isoquants make up an isoquant map. The higher the isoquant, the higher the associated level of output. Isoquants slope downward and are convex (become less steep with more of the input on the horizontal axis and less of the input on the vertical). An isoquant shows how one input can be substituted for another, while keeping output constant. The rate of substitution is given by the marginal rate of technical substitution ($MRTS$). The $MRTS_{L \text{ for } K}$ is the rate at which labor can be substituted for capital along an isoquant. Algebraically

$$MRTS_{L \text{ for } K} = -\frac{\Delta K}{\Delta L}.$$

For extremely small changes in input usage, the $MRTS$ is the slope of the isoquant at a point.

The marginal rate of technical substitution and the marginal products of the inputs are related as follows. The $MRTS_{L \text{ for } K}$ is equal to the ratio of the marginal products of the two inputs:

$$MRTS_{L \text{ for } K} = -\frac{\Delta K}{\Delta L} = \frac{MP_L}{MP_K}.$$

The $MRTS$ declines as more labor and less capital are used because MP_L declines and MP_K rises. This relation causes the isoquant to become less steep with more labor and less capital.

Another key tool of analysis is the isocost line, which shows how much capital can be purchased for each amount of labor hired at a given level of cost and at given input prices:

$$K = \frac{TC}{P_K} - \frac{P_L}{P_K} L,$$

where TC is the level of cost and P_L and P_K are the prices, respectively, of labor and capital. The slope of the isocost line is $-P_L/P_K$. The higher an isocost line, the higher the associated cost.

The combination of inputs that can produce a given level of output at the lowest cost, or the maximum output at a given cost, is that at which the desired isoquant is tangent to the lowest possible isocost line, or the desired isocost line is tangent to the highest possible isoquant. Since the two curves are tangent, their slopes are equal. Therefore, either optimizing rule requires

$$MRTS_{L \text{ for } K} = -\frac{\Delta K}{\Delta L} = \frac{MP_L}{MP_K} = \frac{P_L}{P_K}.$$

Or, expressed alternatively,

$$\frac{MP_L}{P_L} = \frac{MP_K}{P_K}.$$

For N variable inputs, the rule generalizes to

$$\frac{MP_i}{MP_j} = \frac{P_i}{P_j},$$

for every pair of inputs, i and j, or

$$\frac{MP_1}{P_1} = \frac{MP_2}{P_2} = \frac{MP_3}{P_3} = \ldots \frac{MP_N}{P_N},$$

where P_i is the price of the ith input. A combination of inputs at which cost is minimized or output is maximized under a constraint is economically efficient. Therefore, only the equilibrium point on a given isoquant is a point of economic efficiency.

The locus of all points of cost-minimizing or output-maximizing equilibrium points is an expansion path, which is a curve showing all combinations of inputs at which the cost of producing a given rate of output is minimized or the output attainable at a given level of cost is maximized, at a given set of input prices. Since input prices are constant, the $MRTS$ at each point on the expansion path is constant. All combinations of inputs given by the expansion path are economically efficient.

Since input prices remain constant along an expansion path, changes in the input-price ratio shift the expansion path. After a change in the input-price ratio, a firm uses more of the input that becomes relatively cheaper and less of the input that becomes relatively expensive at each level of output.

Finally, the cost of producing each level of output can be deduced from the expansion path. If L units of labor and K units of capital make up the optimal combination for producing a given output, and these are the only inputs, the cost of producing that level of output is $P_L L + P_L K$. We will greatly extend the analysis of production and cost in the next chapter, where we set forth the theory of cost.

Answer to *Applying the Theory*

9.1 One possible reason for the reduction in workers by Ford, and the one implied by the *Newsweek* story, is that Ford was not minimizing its costs previously. This may have occurred for two reasons. First, Ford may not have been technically efficient; it could have produced the same number of vehicles with fewer resources, including labor, or, for some reason or another, it could have produced more cars and trucks with the amount of resources it was using. Second, Ford may have been technically efficient but was not minimizing the cost of producing its chosen output. Perhaps, given the relative prices of resources, including labor, it was using too much labor and too little capital. Third, relative input prices may have changed between 1978 and 1986. If the wages of labor had risen relative to the price of capital, cost minimization would require more capital and less labor to produce a given quantity of cars and trucks. In the case of a company as complex as Ford, the answer is probably some combination of the three.

Technical Problems

1. Use the following figure, (E.9–1) showing a firm's isoquant for 500 units of output, to answer this question. Sketch isocost lines to make your estimates.
   a. If the combination of K and L changes from $45K$ and $5L$ to $30K$ and $15L$, what is the *MRTS*?

Figure E.9–1

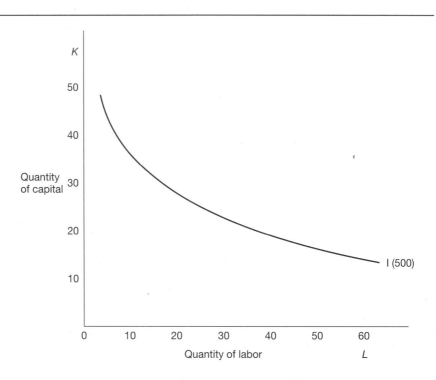

b. If the combination changes from 30K and 15L to 25K and 25L, what is the MRTS?

c. If the combination changes from 25K and 25L to 20K and 40L, what is the MRTS?

d. Why does the MRTS decrease as L increases relative to K?

2. If the price of capital equals the price of labor, the firm should use the same amount of each input in equilibrium. Answer true or false, and explain your answer.

3. A firm is using capital and labor to produce its product. The prices of labor and capital are, respectively, $P_L = \$5$ and $P_K = \$10$. The marginal products of labor and capital are, respectively, $MP_L = 50$ and $MP_K = 75$.

a. If the firm wants to continue to produce at the same level of cost, it could reduce its capital by one unit, increase labor by_____unit(s), and produce approximately_____unit(s) of additional output at the same level of cost.

b. On the other hand, if the firm wants to continue to produce the same level of output, it could reduce its capital by one unit, increase its labor by_____ unit(s), keep its output constant, and reduce its cost by $_____.

4. The following figure (E.9–2) shows the isocost line and isoquant for a firm that is minimizing the cost of producing the given level of output. The price of capital is $60 per unit.

a. What is the price of labor?

b. How much capital and labor does the firm use?

c. What is the total cost of production?

d. What is the MRTS in equilibrium?

Figure E.9–2

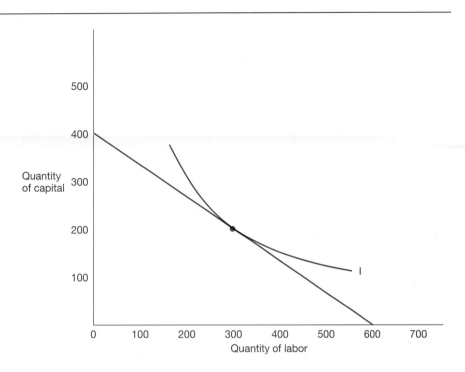

e. If the marginal product of labor is 80, what is the marginal product of capital?

f. Explain why the firm doesn't use 450 labor and 150 capital.

g. Explain why the firm doesn't use 225 labor and 300 capital.

5. A firm is producing a given level of output with capital and labor. The input prices are $P_L = \$4$ and $P_K = \$6$. The marginal products are $MP_L = 20$ and $MP_K = 30$.

a. If the firm wants to continue producing this level of output, what should it do?

b. If the price of capital rises to $8, and the firm wants to continue to produce this level of output, what should the firm do?

c. If, in the new equilibrium, the marginal product of capital is 32, what is the marginal product of labor?

6. The isoquant in the following figure (E.9–3) represents a firm's desired level of output. The prices of labor and capital are, respectively, $P_L = \$16$ and $P_K = \$12$. You may sketch isocost lines to make estimates.

a. If the firm wants to minimize the cost of producing this level of output, approximately how much labor and how much capital will it use? What will be the total cost of production? (Hint: Any isocost line with the slope indicated by the input prices has the same slope as all other isocost line.) What is the $MRTS$ in equilibrium?

b. Suppose the price of labor falls to $6, while the price of capital remains constant. How much labor and capital will the firm use to produce this level of output? What is the total cost of production?

Figure E.9–3

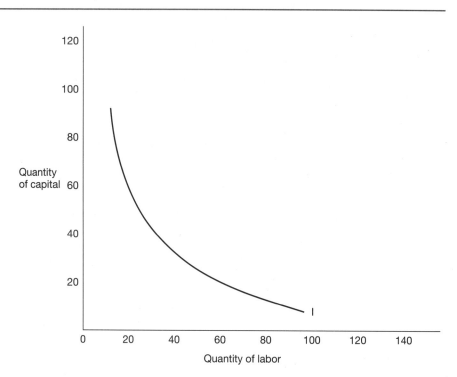

7. Explain the following statement: Every point on an isoquant is technically efficient, but only one point is economically efficient; every point on an expansion path is technically efficient and economically efficient, but only one point is profit maximizing.

8. The following figure (E.9–4) shows two types of isoquants that are not of the "typical" shape.

   a. What production characteristics would lead to an isoquant with the shape of I in Panel A? What is the *MRS* along this isoquant? If the firm wants to produce the output given by I at the minimum cost, there are three possible situations, depending on the input-price ratio. What are the three possible situations? (Hint: Experiment with different isocost curves for various input-price ratios.)

   b. What are the production characteristics that would lead to the isoquants in Panel B? What combination of labor and capital would the firm choose at each of the two levels of output? Explain. What would the expansion path look like? What is the marginal product of each input for movements along these isoquants?

9. In the following figure (E.9–5) *LZ* is the isocost curve and I is an isoquant. Explain precisely why combinations *A* and *B* are not efficient. Explain in terms of the relation of the ratio of the marginal products to the ratio of the input prices. Explain, in these terms, why the direction of substitution in each case, labor for capital or capital for labor, is optimal. Using the ratio of input prices

Figure E.9–4

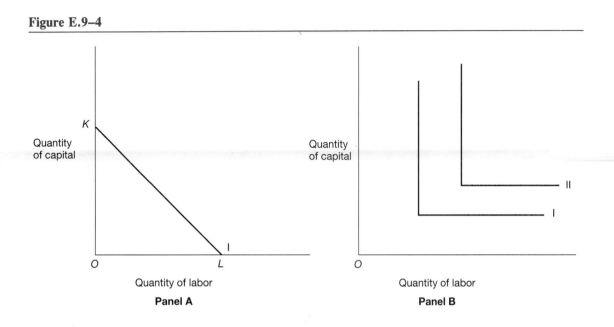

Panel A

Panel B

Figure E.9–5

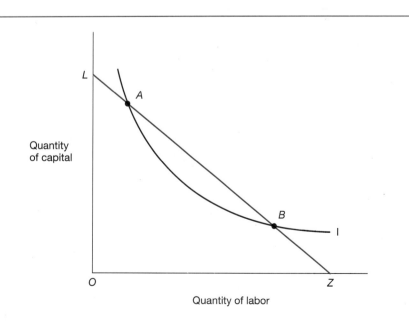

given by *LZ*, find and label the least-cost combination of labor and capital that can produce the output designated by I. In the above terms, explain why this combination is optimal.

10. Suppose that a steel plant's production function is $X = 5KL$, where X is the output rate, L is the amount of labor it uses per period of time, and K is the amount of capital it uses per period of time. Suppose that the price of labor is $1 a unit and the price of capital is $2 a unit. The firm hires you to figure out what combination of inputs the plant should use to produce 20 units. What is your answer? (Hint: $MP_L = 5K$ and $MP_K = 5L$.)

11. Explain the following statement: An expansion path can be derived under the assumption that the firm minimizes the cost of producing each level of output or that the firm maximizes the output attainable at each level of cost; the two expansion paths are the same.

12. A firm using only two inputs, labor and capital, is producing at a point on its expansion path. If the firm increases its capital and labor by 10 percent, its output will increase by 15 percent (increasing returns to scale). Explain why this method of increasing output could not allow the firm to produce the 15 percent increased output at a lower cost than would be attainable if it produces the higher level of output on its expansion path. Why would the combination chosen by increasing the inputs in the same proportion cost more?

13. This question anticipates material in the following chapter. The following figure (E.9–6) shows three isoquants in a firm's isoquant map, three points of equilibrium, and the firm's expansion path. Capital and labor are the only inputs.
   a. Begin with the firm producing the output associated with isoquant II, using L_0 labor and K_0 capital. Suppose the firm now chooses to produce the output associated with isoquant III but is restricted to the short run, in which capital is fixed at K_0 and labor is the only variable input. Explain why the cost of producing the larger output is higher in the short run, when capital is restricted to K_0, than would be the case if the firm was in the long run and could reach the new isoquant by moving along the expansion path. Compare the *additional* costs under the two conditions.
   b. Return to the original equilibrium on II with L_0 and K_0. The firm now chooses to produce the lower output associated with isoquant I, but is restricted to the short run with capital fixed at K_0. Compare the cost of producing the lower output with capital fixed at K_0 and only labor variable with the costs in the long run when both inputs are variable. Compare the *increase* in cost of moving from I back to II with capital fixed at K_0 with the *increase* in the cost of moving from I back to II when both inputs are variable and the movement takes place along the expansion path.
   c. Compare the cost of producing the output associated with II when the firm is in the long run and both inputs are variable with the cost of producing that output when the firm is in the short run and capital is fixed at K_0.
   d. Using the above results, can you make some general statements about costs in the long run and short run?

14. In a footnote we mentioned tangentially that under certain remote circumstances a firm could increase output efficiently and use less of some inputs at the higher output. The following figure (E.9–7) shows three isocost lines with constant input prices. The firm is originally in equilibrium on isoquant I, using L_0 labor and K_0 capital.

Figure E.9–6

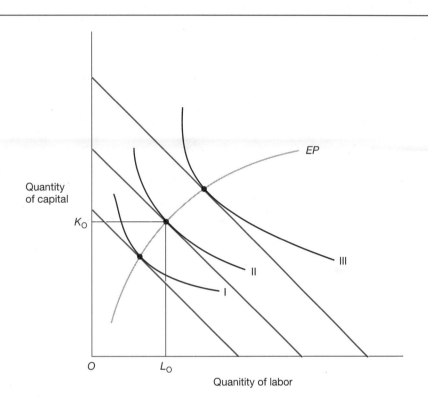

a. Draw in the figure (E.9–7) a new higher isoquant tangent to the highest isocost line where the firm uses less labor than L_0 but more capital than K_0.
b. Draw in the figure (E.9–7) a new lower isoquant tangent to the lowest isocost line, where the firm uses more labor than L_0 but less capital than K_0.
c. Draw the expansion path.
d. Is there anything about the isoquants you drew that violates any of the assumptions of production theory?
e. Could it be possible for the firm to produce more output by using less of both inputs? Explain.
f. Inputs that are used less, as output increases over a given range of input usage, are said to be inferior inputs. Could an input ever be inferior over the entire range of input usage? Explain.

Analytical Problems

1. An efficiency expert who examined a power company's plant said he believed the mill was being operated inefficiently. When the president of the company asked for examples, the efficiency expert said that, for one thing, the crane operators who were unloading coal from barges dropped about 10 percent of the coal into the river. If you were the president of the company, would you necessarily

Figure E.9–7

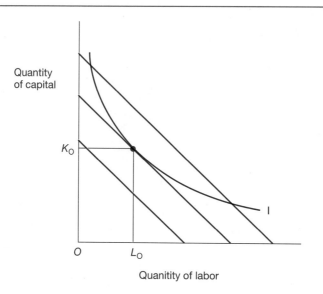

consider this circumstance evidence of inefficiency? Why or why not? What questions would you ask?

2. Several years ago, the United States was sending engineers and other technical experts to underdeveloped countries to advise these countries on the latest technological methods in manufacture and agriculture. They also assisted these underdeveloped countries in instituting modern technological methods. Can you explain why, in many of these countries, the advice and help were utter failures, causing great cost to the poorer countries. Why do you think, in many instances, the old-fashioned methods worked better?

3. A politician is running for office with a fixed campaign budget and a fixed amount of time to campaign. How would the principles developed here help the politician allocate the advertising budget among the different media and the time among the different segments of the voters.

4. A business executive says that in order to produce more output, the firm must use more of all inputs. When would this be true? When would it not be true?

5. Why would we say that a firm plans in the long run and produces in the short run?

6. Explain why nonprofit organizations would have an incentive to be economically efficient.

7. What factors might induce large manufacturing firms to increase their use of robots in the production process over the next decade? There are several such factors.

8. As energy prices rose during the 1970s, it appeared at first that firms were unable to decrease their use of energy. In other words, energy appeared to be used only

in fixed proportion. After a few years, however, firms were able to decrease their use of energy, as the theory says that they should. Explain why this lag in response might have occurred.

9. If you were in charge of awarding grants from a large foundation for medical research, how would you decide who gets the grants? There are many more applications for grants than the budget can fund.

CHAPTER 10

Theory of Cost

10.1 Introduction

Chapters 8 and 9 described the relation between a firm's production decisions and the cost of production. We discussed how a firm should use inputs to produce a given level of output at the minimum cost or the maximum possible output at a given level of cost. This theory applies in the short run, when one or more inputs are variable and the other inputs are fixed, and, in the long run, when all inputs are variable. This chapter will build on production theory in order to develop more completely the theory of cost.

Keep in mind that the primary purpose of cost theory is to aid in understanding how firms make their output and pricing decisions. In order to make such decisions, a firm must have information about the demand for the product it produces and the cost of producing that product. More specifically, it should know how much any given level of output will cost to produce.

We will first reintroduce a concept you encountered in Chapter 1—opportunity cost. Using this important concept we will show that in economic theory, cost involves a bit more than out-of-pocket expenses. Next, following the pattern of Chapters 8 and 9, we will set forth the theory of cost in the short run and show how cost is related to the production function. We then will turn to cost in the long run. Finally, we will describe how short-run cost and long-run cost are related.

10.2 The Opportunity Cost of Production

Most people have a general notion of what cost means. If someone asks you how much your new VCR cost, you might say $395, because that's what its price tag was. This amount may not, however, be the entire cost, because it does not include the value of the time you spent shopping for the VCR or possibly the transportation cost of going from store to store in order to compare prices. The full cost of the VCR would include all of these costs.

Similarly, if an owner of a firm asks the firm's accountant how much it cost to run the firm's plant last month, the accountant would add up all the owner's payments to the resources hired by the firm last month. The full cost, however, could be greater. Even if nothing was paid to the owner, the full cost would also include the value of the owner's time used to manage the firm and the value of any of the owner's other resources used by the firm last month but not directly paid for. In economics, how much something costs includes all opportunity costs.

You may recall from Chapter 1 that opportunity cost is the value of a resource in its next best alternative use. The full cost of production is the opportunity cost, which includes both *explicit cost* and *implicit cost*. Explicit cost is accounting cost. It is the amount paid to the resources a firm hires during a period of time. If the firm's owner owns resources that are used but not directly paid by the firm, these are implicit costs. Implicit cost is measured by the value of the owner's resources at their next best alternative use. An economist includes both explicit and implicit cost in the total cost of production.

To see the nature of implicit costs, consider two firms that produce a particular good and are in every way identical—with one exception. The first firm rents the building in which the good is produced, while the second firm owns its building and, therefore, pays no rent. An economist would say that both firms incur the same costs, even though the second firm has lower explicit or accounting costs. The costs are the same because using the building to produce the good costs the second firm income that could have been earned from leasing it at the prevailing rent, which is an opportunity cost. Since these two buildings are the same, presumably the market rentals would be the same. In other words, a part of the cost to the firm that owns the building is the amount that the owner sacrifices by not renting the building to another firm. To emphasize this point, consider what would happen if the building is destroyed by fire. To continue producing, the firm would have to replace the building or rent a similar building and pay the owner an explicit payment.

The above example involves the opportunity cost of capital—the building—owned by a firm, which is an implicit cost and should be included in the total cost of the firm. Another example of an implicit cost is the unpaid value of a business owner's time, which is used to manage the firm. Suppose the best alternative use of an owner/manager's time used to manage the firm is managing another firm for $80,000 a year. The sacrificed $80,000 is an opportunity cost and should be included in the yearly cost of the firm as an implicit cost.

Most implicit costs are measured by the best alternative return that could have been earned by the land or capital if it had not been used by the firm in the production process. The opportunity cost of someone's time is the value of time at its next best use. Measuring the implicit cost is typically, though not always, rather straightforward. The implicit cost of using land or capital owned by the firm is frequently what the firm would have to pay to rent equivalent land or capital. Alternatively, the implicit cost is the best return per period that could be earned from investing the money that could be received if the land or capital were sold. The implicit cost of the owner's time is more difficult to measure because the next best use of the time is not always clear. An owner may say the next best use is fishing. Or the owner could earn many times over what he or she earns now by doing something else, but the owner has no desire to change occupations. Generally, the best measure of an owner's time cost of management is the amount that the firm would have to pay to hire an equivalent manager.

Let us note in passing that the implicit cost of the services from a firm's land or capital is the sacrificed return, which is not always closely approximated by the amount paid for the land or capital. If the firm paid much more or much less for a piece of land than the land is now worth on the market, the implicit cost reflects the current value, not the past price of the land. For example, if a firm paid $1 million for the land, but the land now could be sold for $2 million, the implicit cost of using the land is the return that could be earned if the land is sold for $2 million and the return invested, not the return from investing $1 million. If the relevant rate of interest is 10 percent a year, the implicit cost is $200,000 not $100,000. The amount sacrificed, not the amount paid, is the determinant of implicit cost.

Similarly, although the implicit cost of an owner's time used to manage the firm is generally the amount the firm would have to pay to hire an equivalent manager, this is not always the case. The implicit cost could be higher. For example, suppose a rock singer acts as his or her own manager and, consequently, cannot give as many concerts or make as many recordings because of the time spent managing. If the singer would rather be singing than managing, the implicit cost of managing would be the sacrificed income, which presumably would be greater than the cost of hiring an equivalent manager.

To summarize, a firm often uses inputs in the production process that are not explicitly paid for. Economists value these inputs at their best alternative use and include this value in total cost as an implicit cost. This value is frequently, though not always, the amount that the firm would have to pay to hire these inputs if they were not owned or controlled by the firm's owner. Implicit costs are real and are important in decision making. Throughout this and the following chapters, we include both explicit and implicit costs when discussing a firm's cost of production, even though we generally do not specifically mention them separately.

Economics in the News

How Much Does It Cost an American Athlete to Be an Olympian?

In a column in *Sports Illustrated*, "Can You Spare a Job?" September 19, 1988, p. 78, E. M. Swift gave his answer: A lot more than most people think. Swift noted that the answer "depends on whether you're talking out-of-pocket expenses, which are easy to add up, or time lost in starting a career, which is hard to stick a price tag on." In other words, the cost is much higher if one considers both the explicit cost and the implicit cost, rather than explicit cost only. Swift pointed out that preparing to compete against

(continued)

the world's best athletes is a seven-days-a-week undertaking that leaves little time for pursuing a nonsports vocation.

Even though the time lost from a new career may be difficult to measure in dollar terms, the athletes quoted in the column were well aware that they were paying a very real implicit opportunity cost while they were training for the 1988 Seoul, South Korea Olympics. A rower chose to postpone his master's degree in computer science for several years. Another athlete almost dropped out when he realized that he would be competing for an entry-level job when his competitive career ended in his late 20s.

Swift mentioned that one possible solution to the high implicit cost borne by American athletes was the Olympic Job Opportunities Program (OJOP), created in 1977 to encourage businesses to hire athletes who were preparing for the Olympics and give the athletes sufficient time off to train. The participating firms would get quality employees for the future, satisfaction from helping the athletes, and prestige from participating in the program. The response, however, was not overwhelming for the 1988 Olympics. Of the hundreds of corporations contacted, only 95 chose to participate. Therefore, for the most part, the athletes themselves, except for a few in some "glamour" events, such as track, in which it was possible to earn money, had to pay the implicit cost themselves. For many, these costs were quite high, and who can say how many chose not to participate because of them?

10.1   Applying the Theory

A. Suppose you are a prospective Olympic athlete, finishing college, and deciding whether or not to continue training for the Olympics. How would you calculate the implicit cost? What factors would you consider in making your decision about whether or not to continue training? Can you put a dollar value on these factors?

B. *Sports Illustrated,* March 2, 1987, pointed out another example of implicit opportunity cost, this time for a basketball player. John Lucas had been an outstanding guard for the Houston Rockets, but, after twice testing positive for drugs, was banned from the National Basketball Association. During his mandatory stay at a drug rehabilitation center, he developed the John Lucas Fitness System, a training program for recovering addicts, alcoholics, the chronically depressed, and the elderly. After two years, Mr. Lucas was reinstated by the NBA and signed with the Milwaukee Bucks. Prior to the reinstatement, his fitness program had become extremely successful, after being franchised into several Houston hospitals. *Sports Illustrated* mentions that he sometimes jokes that his return to basketball may actually cost him money. How could this be the case, with the huge salaries that are being paid in the NBA?

10.3   Cost in the Short Run

As we did when developing the theory of production, we will begin our analysis of cost with the theory of cost in the short run, when one or more inputs are fixed and other inputs are variable. We will show how short-run costs are affected by the firm's output. We will illustrate the relation between cost and output with graphs of various types of cost curves and discuss why the curves are sloped the way they are. Two important purposes of the discussion of short-run cost are to develop further the relation between the production function and cost and to show how the shapes of cost curves are determined by the characteristics of production functions. As you will see later, the theory of cost provides a background for understanding how firms make short-run profit-maximizing decisions.

10.3.1   Short-Run Cost: One Variable Input

Let us begin, as before, with the simplest short-run situation—a firm combines one variable input with fixed inputs to produce various levels of output. In this way, we can illustrate most of the characteristics of short-run cost curves and their relation to the production function.

Assume that labor is the only variable input hired by the firm. The price of labor is $100 a day. The firm also uses a given amount of fixed inputs. It must pay these fixed inputs $3,000 a day no matter what its level of output. The $3,000 includes both an explicit payment to some of the fixed inputs and the implicit cost of the owner's capital and time spent managing the firm. Both are real costs to the firm and, therefore, are not differentiated in the analysis.

Variable, fixed, and total cost.   Columns 1 and 2 in Table 10–1 show a portion of the firm's short-run production function. These two columns give the amount of labor that must be combined with the fixed inputs in order to produce 100 to 900 units of output, in increments of 100.

The total variable cost of producing each level of output is shown in column 3.

Definition

> Total variable cost (*TVC*) is the amount paid for the variable inputs used to produce each level of output.

In this example, the total variable cost for each level of output is the price of labor (P_L), $100, times the amount of labor used to produce each level of output; for example, the *TVC* of 400 units is $100 times 26, where 26 is the number of labor days needed to produce 400 units of output. Each *TVC* in column 3 is obtained in this way.

Column 4 shows the fixed cost of producing each level of output, which is the same at each level of output. Fixed cost results from having some inputs unchanged in the short run.

Definition

> Fixed cost (*FC*) is the cost that is invariant with respect to output. This cost must be paid no matter what output the firm produces.

Since we assumed that the fixed inputs must be paid $3,000, the fixed cost at each output is $3,000. For each level of output, the variable cost is added to the fixed

Table 10–1   Total, Average, and Marginal Cost Schedule from a Production Function

(1) Labor (L)	(2) Output (Q)	(3) Variable Cost (TVC) $P_L \times L$	(4) Fixed Cost (FC)	(5) Short-run Total Cost (SRTC) TVC + FC	(6) Average Fixed Cost (AFC) FC/Q	(7) Average Variable Cost (AVC) TVC/Q	(8) Average Total Cost (ATC) SRTC/Q	(9) Marginal Cost (MC) $\Delta TVC/\Delta Q$ = $\Delta SRTC/\Delta Q$
0	0	0	$3,000	$ 3,000	—	—	—	
								> $10
10	100	$ 1,000	3,000	4,000	$30.00	$10.00	$40.00	
								> 5
15	200	1,500	3,000	4,500	15.00	7.50	22.50	
								> 3
18	300	1,800	3,000	4,800	10.00	6.00	16.00	
								> 8
26	400	2,600	3,000	5,600	7.50	6.50	14.00	
								> 12
38	500	3,800	3,000	6,800	6.00	7.60	13.60	
								> 16
54	600	5,400	3,000	8,400	5.00	9.00	14.00	
								> 22
76	700	7,600	3,000	10,600	4.29	10.80	15.15	
								> 30
106	800	10,600	3,000	13,600	3.75	13.25	17.00	
								> 40
146	900	14,600	3,000	17,600	3.33	16.23	19.55	

cost to obtain the short-run total cost (*SRTC*) of producing each level of output, shown in Column 5.

Definition

The short-run total cost (*SRTC*) of each level of output is the sum of the fixed cost and the variable cost at that output.

Columns 1 through 5 therefore show the relation between the short-run production function and short-run costs. To summarize, fixed cost remains constant and must be paid even if the firm produces no output. Variable cost and total cost increase as more output is produced, because more of the variable input must be used. It is always the case that

$$SRTC = TVC + FC.$$

Average cost.   The short-run total cost of production is important to a firm. However, one may obtain a greater understanding of a firm's costs by observing the behavior of short-run average costs. First consider average fixed cost (*AFC*), shown in column 6 of the table.

Definition

Average fixed cost is total fixed cost divided by output: $AFC = FC/Q$.

Because average fixed cost is a constant amount (here \$3,000) divided by output, AFC is relatively high at low levels of output and falls as output increases, as you can see from column 6. Thus, AFC declines over the entire range of output, as shown in column 6.

Average variable cost (AVC), in column 7, is the total variable cost of producing a given level of output divided by that output.

Definition

Average variable cost (AVC) is the variable cost of producing each level of output divided by that output: $AVC = TVC/Q$.

Column 7, which shows each variable cost in column 3 divided by the associated output in column 2, illustrates a typically assumed characteristic of average variable cost: AVC at first decreases as output increases (through 300 units of output), reaches a minimum (\$6 at 300 units of output), then increases thereafter. As you will see later in this chapter, this characteristic of AVC results from a general characteristic of the production function.

The final average cost calculation in Table 10–1 is average total cost (ATC), shown in column 8. The average total cost of producing each level of output is the total cost of that output divided by the output.

Definition

Average total cost is short-run total cost divided by output: $ATC = SRTC/Q$.

Average total cost in column 8 could have been calculated in two ways: dividing each $SRTC$ in column 5 by each output in column 2, or by adding each AVC in column 7 to each AFC in column 6. The reason $ATC = AVC + AFC$ is because $SRTC = TVC + FC$. Thus,

$$ATC = \frac{SRTC}{Q} = \frac{TVC + FC}{Q} = \frac{TVC}{Q} + \frac{FC}{Q} = AVC + AFC.$$

This latter method of calculating ATC helps explain the behavior of average total cost shown in column 8: ATC first declines as output increases (from 100 to 500 units of output), reaches a minimum (\$13.50 at 500 units of output), then increases thereafter. The minimum ATC is reached at a higher output than minimum AVC. Over the range of output at which AVC and AFC both decline, ATC (the sum of AVC and AFC) must obviously decline as well. But, even after AVC begins to rise, the decline in AFC swamps the rise in AVC and causes average total cost to continue to decline as output increases. Eventually, the increase in AVC more than offsets the decline in AFC. Thus, ATC continues to decline until it reaches its minimum and increases thereafter as the rise in AVC dominates the fall in AFC.

Marginal cost.   Marginal cost is the ratio of the change in variable cost or total cost to the change in output for a one-unit change or for a small change in output.[1]

Definition

> Marginal cost is the change in variable cost or, equivalently, the change in total cost divided by the change in output, when output is changed by one unit or by a small amount. Marginal cost is measured as the ratio
>
> $$MC = \frac{\Delta TVC}{\Delta Q} = \frac{\Delta SRTC}{\Delta Q}.$$
>
> Marginal cost is therefore the change in total or variable cost per unit change in output.

Let's assume in Table 10–1 that changes of 100 units of output are small changes. (Perhaps the firm produces many hundreds of units and this is just part of the entire range.) In the table, *MC* is plotted between the two relevant levels of output to emphasize that it is the marginal cost for a change in output, not for a given level of output. For example, since an increase in output from 100 to 200 units increases variable cost and, hence, total cost by $500, we measure marginal cost as

$$MC = \frac{\Delta TVC}{\Delta Q} = \frac{\$500}{100} = \$5.$$

This means that each additional unit of output from 100 to 200 increases cost by $5. Thus, the per-unit increase in cost is $5 over this range.

As you can see in the table, marginal cost first decreases, until it reaches a minimum of $3 between 200 and 300 units of output. Note that minimum marginal cost occurs before the minimum points on *ATC* and *AVC*. Marginal cost then increases for each increase in output after 300 units. You will see later that this characteristic of marginal cost follows from a general characteristic of the production function.

Finally, Table 10–1 shows the relation between *MC* and *AVC* and *ATC*. When *MC* is less than *AVC*, *AVC* falls; when *MC* is greater than *AVC*, *AVC* rises. When *MC* is less than *ATC*, *ATC* falls; when *MC* is greater than *ATC*, *ATC* rises. These relations hold for the reasons discussed at length in Chapter 8, where it was stressed that any time the marginal value is below (above) the average value, the average must decline (increase).

10.3.2   Graphs of Short-Run Cost Curves: One Variable Input

The properties of cost can be seen a bit more clearly using graphs. Therefore, assume that labor and output in the production function shown in Table 10–1 can vary continuously rather than in discrete increments of 100 units. Under this assumption, cost varies continuously also.

[1]Some economists reserve the term *marginal cost* for one-unit changes in output. For larger changes in output the change in cost is *incremental cost*. In this text we use marginal cost to refer to both one-unit changes in output and small changes in output. Marginal cost is determined by a change in either variable cost or total cost because the two changes are the same for a given change in output. Since fixed cost does not change when output changes, total cost must change by the same amount as the change in variable cost.

Figure 10–1

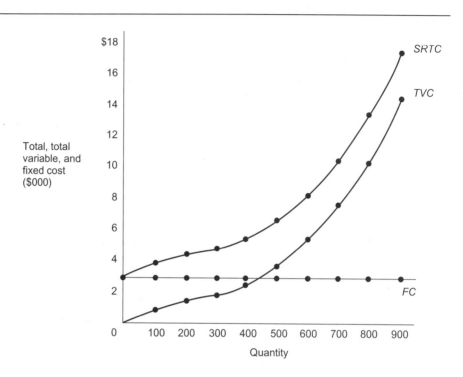

In Figure 10–1, the costs in columns 3, 4, and 5 are plotted for each output from zero through 900, in increments of 100, and then these points are joined by a curve to reflect continuity. Since fixed cost is constant at $3,000 for each level of output, the total fixed cost curve (*FC*) is a horizontal line at $3,000. Variable cost (*TVC*) is zero at zero output; it first increases at a decreasing rate, then increases at an increasing rate. Since short-run total cost (*SRTC*) is the sum of *TVC* and *FC*, *SRTC* is precisely $3,000 above *TVC* at each output level. Because *SRTC* is simply *TVC* shifted upward by a constant amount, *SRTC* has the same slope as *TVC* at each output. Therefore, *SRTC* also increases at a decreasing rate at first, and then it increases at an increasing rate.

Average fixed costs from Table 10–1 are plotted in Figure 10–2, and then the points are connected to reflect continuity. As you can see, *AFC* decreases over the entire range of output, because the ratio is a constant, here $3,000, divided by output. As output increases, *AFC* must decrease.

Average variable cost (*AVC*), average total cost (*ATC*), and marginal cost (*MC*) from Table 10–1 are graphed in Figure 10–3. Both average cost curves are U-shaped, first declining then rising with output. *AVC* reaches a minimum of $6 at 300 units of output, and *ATC* reaches a minimum of $13.60 at 500 units. Recall that *ATC* = *AVC* + *AFC*. Because *AFC* is large at low levels of output, *ATC* is much higher than *AVC* at these levels of output. As *AFC* becomes small at higher levels of output, *AVC* becomes closer and closer to *ATC*.

Figure 10–2   Average Fixed Cost Curve

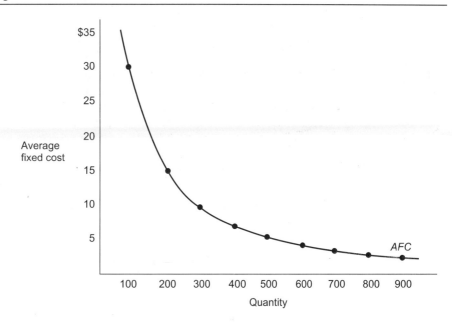

Figure 10–3   Average and Marginal Cost Curves

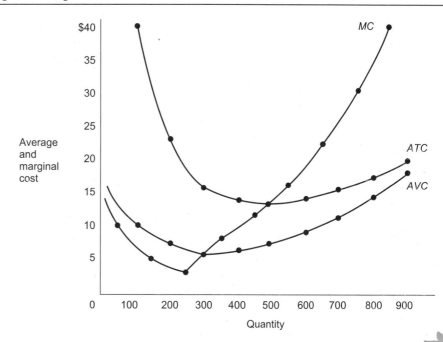

Marginal cost is plotted between each of two output levels to show that *MC* is the *additional* cost of *additional* units of output. Marginal cost first declines, reaching a minimum of $3 between 200 and 300 units of output, then rises thereafter. When *MC* is below *AVC* (*ATC*), *AVC* (*ATC*) is declining. Each addition to cost is less than the average and, therefore, pulls the average down. When *MC* is above *AVC* (*ATC*), *AVC* (*ATC*) is rising. Each addition to cost is greater than the average and, therefore, raises the average. Since *MC* is below (above) each average when the average is falling (rising), *MC* must necessarily cross *AVC* and *ATC* at their respective minimum points. This relation is shown in the figure.

The curves in Figure 10–3 illustrate all the properties of the types of short-run average and marginal cost typically assumed by economists. As mentioned previously, these properties follow directly from assumptions about the production function. We will now show you why.

10.4 Cost and the Production Function

If you know the production function and the price of labor, you can calculate average variable and marginal cost directly, without going through the total costs. This exercise will give some insight into why average and marginal cost are sloped the way they are shown in Figure 10–3.

10.4.1 Average Variable Cost and the Production Function

The production function from Table 10–1 is reproduced in columns 1 and 2 of Table 10–2. The average product (Q/L) and marginal product ($\Delta Q/\Delta L$) of labor are shown, respectively, in columns 3 and 5 of the table. Recall that the price of labor (P_L) used to obtain the cost schedules in Table 10–1 is $100. Dividing this price, $100, by the average product of labor at each level of output in Table 10–2, one obtains the dollar amounts shown in column 4 of the table. As you see, we have called the numbers in this column *average variable cost*. Comparison of column 4 in Table 10–2 to column 7 in Table 10–1, which gives *AVC* calculated directly from total variable cost, shows that the amounts are the same. *AVC* can be calculated in both ways, $AVC = TVC/Q$ or $AVC = P_L/AP_L$.

This result is not peculiar to this specific production function, but it holds in general when only one input is variable. Variable cost is the price of labor, P_L, times the amount of labor, L; or $TVC = P_L L$. Average variable cost is *TVC* divided by output, Q. Thus,

$$AVC = \frac{TVC}{Q} = \frac{P_L L}{Q} = P_L \left(\frac{L}{Q}\right).$$

The term L/Q is the amount of labor divided by output. Since average product (AP_L) is Q/L, L/Q is $1/AP_L$, which means

$$AVC = P_L \left(\frac{L}{Q}\right) = P_L \left(\frac{1}{Q/L}\right) = \frac{\text{Price of labor}}{\text{Average product of labor}}.$$

Table 10–2 Relations between Average and Marginal Product and Average Variable and Marginal Cost (P_L = $100)

(1) Labor (L)	(2) Output (Q)	(3) Average Product (AP_L) Q/L	(4) Average Variable Cost (P_L/AP_L)	(5) Marginal Product (MP) $\Delta Q/\Delta L$	(6) Marginal Cost (P_L/MP_L)
0	0	—	—		
				> 10.00	> $10
10	100	10.00	$10.00		
				> 20.00	> 5
15	200	13.33	7.50		
				> 33.33	> 3
18	300	16.67	6.00		
				> 12.50	> 8
26	400	15.39	6.50		
				> 8.33	> 12
38	500	13.16	7.60		
				> 6.25	> 16
54	600	11.11	9.00		
				> 4.55	> 22
76	700	9.21	10.86		
				> 3.33	> 30
106	800	7.55	13.25		
				> 2.50	> 40
146	900	6.16	16.23		

Recall from Chapter 8 that average product first increases, reaches a maximum, then decreases as the number of workers and the level of output increases. Since $AVC = P_L/AP_L$, AVC must decrease at low output levels when AP_L is increasing. AVC must increase at higher levels of output when AP_L is decreasing. It therefore follows that AVC reaches a minimum at the output level produced by the level of labor usage at which AP_L is at its maximum. As you can see in columns 3 and 4 of Table 10–2, this relation between AP_L and AVC holds for this specific example; AVC reaches its minimum at 300 units of output, where AP_L reaches its maximum.

10.4.2   Marginal Cost and the Production Function

Turning to marginal cost, the numbers in column 6 of Table 10–2 were calculated by dividing the price of labor, $100, by the marginal product for each change in the level of output. This column is titled *marginal cost,* and, as a comparison of column 6 in Table 10–2 and column 9 in Table 10–1 shows, the marginal costs in each column are the same.

This result holds in general. When we measure marginal cost as the change in variable cost divided by the change in output:

$$MC = \frac{\Delta TVC}{\Delta Q} = \frac{\Delta(P_L L)}{\Delta Q} = P_L \left(\frac{\Delta L}{\Delta Q}\right),$$

because P_L is constant. Marginal product is $\Delta Q/\Delta L$, so $\Delta L/\Delta Q = 1/MP_L$. Thus,

$$MC = P_L \left(\frac{\Delta L}{\Delta Q}\right) = P_L \left(\frac{1}{\Delta Q/\Delta L}\right) = \frac{\text{Price of labor}}{\text{Marginal product of labor}}.$$

Again recall that marginal product first rises, reaches a maximum, then falls, crossing average product at its maximum. From the above equation, over the range of output levels at which MP_L is rising, MC must fall; when MP_L falls, MC must rise over this range of outputs. Thus, the level of output associated with the highest MP_L must be the output at which MC is at its minimum. Again as you can see in columns 5 and 6 of Table 10–2 this relation between marginal product and marginal cost holds for the specific case illustrated; MC reaches its minimum between 200 and 300 units at output, where MP_L reaches its maximum.

Finally, when AP_L is at its maximum, it equals MP_L. Therefore, AVC ($= P_L/AP_L$) must equal MC ($= P_L/MP_L$) at the level of output at which average product is the highest. This means that MC must intersect AVC at its minimum point.

10.5 General Short-Run Cost Curves

The cost relations set forth for a single variable input are easily extended to the general short-run situation, in which two or more variable inputs are combined with fixed inputs. The fixed inputs are paid a fixed amount no matter what the level of output, so these payments are fixed costs. The use of the variable inputs varies with the level of output, so these payments are variable costs.

10.5.1 Short-Run Cost and Production

Regardless of the number of inputs that are variable and the number of inputs that are fixed, the short-run cost of production results from the constrained cost minimization process previously developed. Obviously, when only one input is variable and all others are fixed, there is only one level of the variable input that can be combined with the fixed inputs to produce any given level of output. As discussed previously, the amount of the variable input used to produce that level of output times the price of the variable input gives variable cost, which is added to fixed cost to obtain short-run total cost. Average and marginal costs are derived from the fixed, variable, and total costs.

When two or more variable inputs are combined with the fixed inputs, the cost-minimization process is similar to that set forth in Chapter 9. Suppose, for the sake of simplicity, that the firm uses two variable inputs, labor (L) and energy (E), which are combined with a fixed input, capital (K). Since capital cannot be varied, the payment to capital is a fixed cost. Let the price of labor be, as before, P_L, and let the price of energy be P_E. With the fixed amount of capital, the firm combines the variable inputs so that at each level of output the marginal rate of technical substitution of labor for energy ($MRTS_{L \text{ for } E}$) equals the input price ratio (P_L/P_E). Alternatively, the marginal products per dollar spent on the last units of each variable input are equal. That is

$$MRTS_{L \text{ for } E} = \frac{P_L}{P_E} \text{ or } \frac{MP_L}{P_L} = \frac{MP_E}{P_E}.$$

The resulting input combination, say L^* and E^*, gives the minimum variable cost of producing a given level of output, which is

$$TVC = P_L L^* + P_E E^*.$$

The short-run total cost for that level of output is this minimum variable cost plus the payment to capital, which is the fixed cost.

The process is the same for more than two variable inputs and/or more than one fixed input. The payments to the fixed inputs are the fixed cost. The minimum variable cost of producing any level of output is attained when the marginal products per dollar spent on the last unit of each variable input are equal. Variable cost is the sum of the prices of each input times its optimal level of usage for a given level of output. The total cost of producing that level of output is variable cost plus fixed cost, and it is the minimum total cost of that output.

10.5.2 Graphical Derivation of Average and Marginal Cost Curves from Total Cost Curves

Short-run total, average, and marginal cost curves when any number of inputs are variable and any number are fixed have the same generally assumed shapes as the curves discussed previously for the case when only one input is variable. (We will discuss the reasons for assuming these shapes, when more than one input is variable, in the next sections.) The average and marginal cost curves are easily derived geometrically from the total cost curves.

Fixed cost and average fixed cost.   Figure 10–4, Panel A shows a typical fixed cost curve, which is horizontal at FC. Average fixed cost (AFC) is fixed cost divided by the quantity of output (FC/Q). In Panel A, AFC for three levels of output, Q_1, Q_2, and Q_3, is given by the slope of a ray from the origin to the fixed cost curve at each output—points A, B, and C. Clearly, AFC decreases as output increases, because the slope of the ray decreases as output increases; that is, $FC/Q_1 > FC/Q_2 > FC/Q_3$. In Panel B, AFC is plotted as a continuously decreasing curve; points A', B', and C' correspond respectively to A, B, and C. When output is small, AFC is large. As output increases, AFC becomes smaller and smaller, until at very large levels of output the AFC curve approaches the horizontal axis.

Variable cost and average variable cost.   Figure 10–5 shows how AVC is derived geometrically from variable cost. Panel A shows a variable cost curve of the typically assumed shape. Variable cost (TVC) is zero at zero output and increases as output

Figure 10–4   Derivation of *AFC* from *FC*

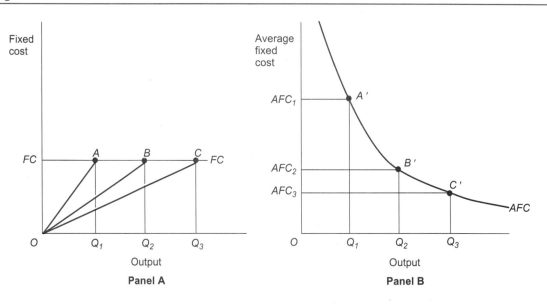

Panel A   Panel B

fig
10-5

increases; at first *TVC* increases at a decreasing rate then increases at an increasing rate. As is true of all "average" curves, the average variable cost of any level of output is given by the slope of a ray from the origin to the corresponding point on the *TVC* curve. (For example, *AVC* at output Q_1 is VC_1/Q_1, or the distance Q_1A divided by OQ_1, which is the slope of the ray OA.) As may easily be seen from Panel A, the slope of a ray from the origin to the curve steadily diminishes as one passes through points such as *A*, and it diminishes until the ray is tangent to the *TVC* curve at point *B*, associated with output Q_2. Thereafter, the slope increases as one moves from *B* toward points such as *C*. This is reflected in Panel B. Points *A*, *B*, and *C* correspond to the points A', B', and C' in Panel B. The curve *AVC* has a negative slope until output Q_2 is attained. After that point (B'), the slope becomes positive and remains positive.

The explanation for the U-shape of the *AVC* curve when there are several variable inputs is basically the same as that given for the situation of only one variable input. Suppose, for the sake of simplicity, that there are two variable inputs, as before, labor (L) and energy (E), and one fixed input, capital. The variable input prices are P_L and P_E. Thus, average variable cost is

$$AVC = \frac{TVC}{Q} = \frac{P_L L + P_E E}{Q} = \frac{P_L L}{Q} + \frac{P_E E}{Q} = P_L \left(\frac{L}{Q}\right) + P_E \left(\frac{E}{Q}\right).$$

Since the average products of labor (AP_L) and energy (AP_E) are, respectively, Q/L and Q/E,

$$AVC = P_L \left(\frac{1}{AP_L}\right) + P_E \left(\frac{1}{AP_E}\right).$$

Figure 10–5   Derivation of the Average Variable Cost Curve

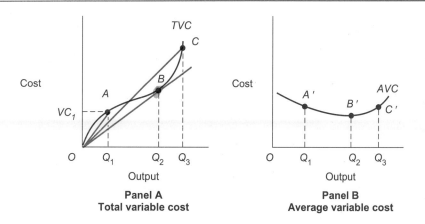

Panel A
Total variable cost

Panel B
Average variable cost

Similar to the one-input example, rising average products of the two inputs at first cause AVC to fall, but after some level of output, Q_2 in Figure 10–5, the general decrease in the average products of the two inputs causes AVC to rise. This example can be easily extended to any number of variable inputs. Rising average products, in general, cause AVC to decrease at first. Then when average products, on average, begin to decrease, AVC increases. For this reason, average variable cost is typically assumed to be U-shaped, first decreasing, next reaching a minimum, and increasing thereafter.

The average total cost curve (ATC) can be derived similarly from the short-run total cost curve ($SRTC$). $SRTC$ is simply the TVC curve displaced upward by fixed cost. in Figure 10–6, the slope of a ray from the origin to $SRTC$ is ATC at the relevant output. Thus, at output Q_4, ATC is the ratio of distances Q_4M/OQ_4. As you can see, the slope of the ray decreases, and, hence, ATC decreases, until output Q_5 is reached. Beyond Q_5, the slope of the ray increases, and, therefore, ATC increases. Thus, minimum ATC occurs at Q_5, at which ATC is Q_5N/OQ_5. Note that Q_5 is greater than Q_2 in Figure 10–5, at which AVC reaches its minimum. (To see this, notice that a ray from point F to $SRTC$ in Figure 10–6 has the same slope as a ray from the origin to TVC in Figure 10–5 at the same level of output. Clearly, the ray from F becomes tangent to $SRTC$ at an output lower than Q_5.)

Thus, ATC in Panel B is the average total cost curve associated with $SRTC$ in Panel A. The points M, N, and Z in panel A generate the points M', N', and Z'. ATC decreases at first because AFC and AVC both decrease; it then continues to decrease, because the decrease in AFC dominates the increase in AVC. When the increase in AVC begins to dominate the decrease in AFC, ATC begins to increase and increases thereafter.

Marginal cost.   The marginal cost curve can be geometrically derived from either the total variable cost or the short-run total cost curve. Since fixed cost does not change when output changes, marginal cost is either the change in total cost per unit change in output or the change in variable cost per unit change in output.

Figure 10–6   Derivation of the Average Total Cost Curve

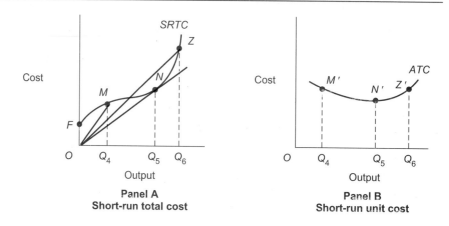

Panel A	Panel B
Short-run total cost	Short-run unit cost

Figure 10–7 illustrates how marginal cost is derived from a typical short-run total cost curve, which is the variable cost curve displaced upward by the constant fixed cost, F in the figure.

In Panel A, *SRTC*, as is generally the case, first increases at a decreasing rate, then increases at an increasing rate. Begin at output Q_1. As output increases from Q_1 to Q_2, total cost increases from C_1 to C_2, the movement from P to N along the curve. Marginal cost, $\Delta SRTC/\Delta Q$ is given by the ratio *NR/PR*. If the change in output becomes small, and the distance between P and N becomes smaller and smaller, the slope of the tangent at point N becomes a progressively better estimate of *MC* $(= NR/PR)$. At this point, and at any other point on the short-run total cost curve, the slope of a tangent to the curve at that point gives the marginal cost.

In Panel A, as output increases, the slope of *SRTC* decreases (marginal cost decreases) until point S at Q_3 units of output. Thereafter, the slope of *SRTC* increases, and, hence, marginal cost increases. The marginal cost curve in Panel B is constructed so that it reflects the slope of the short-run total cost curve. The tangents at points N, S, and T in Panel A give rise to the points N', S', and T' in Panel B. Marginal cost decreases until it reaches its minimum, at Q_3, then increases thereafter. At Q_4 units of output, point T in Panel A, the slope of *SRTC* is just equal to the slope of the ray from the origin at point T. Recall that *ATC* reaches its minimum when a ray from the origin is tangent to *SRTC*, and the slope of that ray is equal to *ATC* at that point. Thus, *MC* equals *ATC* at Q_4 units of output. In Panel B, *MC* would cross *ATC* at Q_4 units or point T', when *ATC* is at its minimum.

As was the case for *AVC*, the explanation for the slope of the *MC* curve is basically the same as that for the case of one variable input: The slope of *MC* is inversely related to the slope of the marginal product curve. Once again, assume two variable inputs, L and E, with prices P_L and P_E, and a fixed input, capital. Marginal cost, is, therefore,

$$MC = \frac{\Delta SRTC}{\Delta Q} = \frac{\Delta TVC}{\Delta Q} = \frac{\Delta[P_L L + P_E E]}{\Delta Q} = P_L \left(\frac{\Delta L}{\Delta Q}\right) + P_E \left(\frac{\Delta E}{\Delta Q}\right),$$

Figure 10–7   Derivation of Marginal Cost from *SRTC*

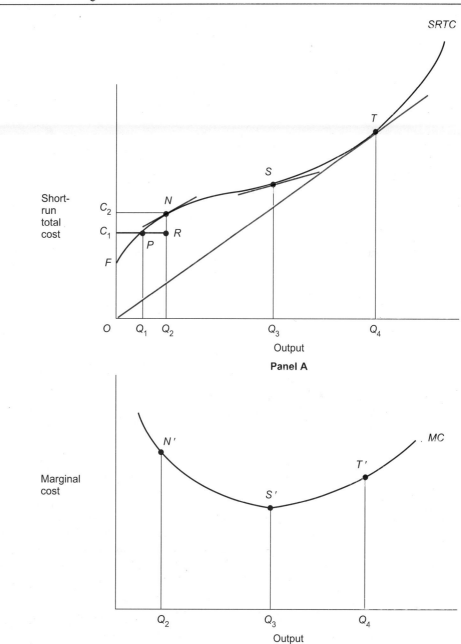

Figure 10–8   Relation of *MC* to Variable and Total Costs

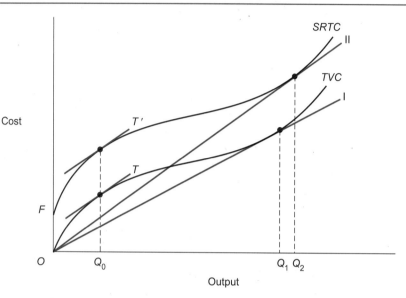

because input prices do not change. Since the marginal products of labor (MP_L) and energy (MP_E) are, respectively, $\Delta Q/\Delta L$ and $\Delta Q/\Delta E$,

$$MC = P_L \left(\frac{1}{MP_L}\right) + P_E \left(\frac{1}{MP_E}\right).$$

Similar to the one-input case, rising marginal products, in general, at first cause marginal cost to decline, but after some level of output, Q_3, in Figure 10–7, the general decrease in the marginal products causes marginal cost to rise. For this reason, *MC* is typically assumed to decrease, reach a minimum (at an output less than that of minimum *ATC*), then increase. This example can be easily extended to the case of more than two variable inputs.

Since *SRTC* is simply *TVC* shifted upward by the constant amount, fixed cost, we could have derived *MC* from the variable cost curve. In Figure 10–8, at output Q_0, the tangent (T) to *TVC* has the same slope as the tangent (T') to *SRTC*. Since the slopes of the two tangents at output Q_0 are equal, the *MC* at Q_0 is given by the slope of either curve. The same holds true for any other output level. The slope of ray I from the origin gives minimum *AVC*. At this point (output Q_1), ray I is just tangent to *TVC*; therefore, its slope also gives *MC* at output Q_1. Thus, *MC* = *AVC* when the latter attains its minimum value. Similarly, the slope of ray II gives minimum *ATC* (at output Q_2). At this point, the ray is tangent to *SRTC*; thus its slope also gives *MC* at output Q_2. Consequently, *MC* = *ATC* when the latter attains its minimum value. Finally, as is easily seen from Figure 10–8, *AVC* attains its minimum at a lower output than the output at which *ATC* attains its minimum.

The properties of the average and marginal cost curves, as derived in this section, are illustrated by the traditionally assumed set of short-run cost curves shown in Figure 10–9. The curves indicate the following.

Figure 10–9   Typical Set of Cost Curves

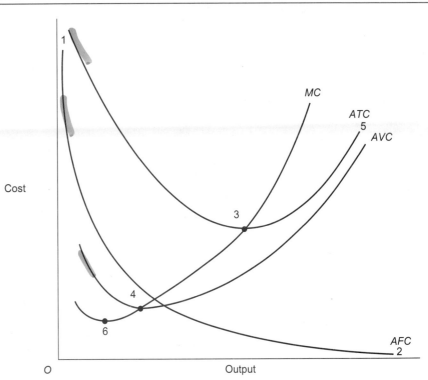

(a) *AFC* declines continuously, approaching both axes asymptotically, as shown by points 1 and 2 in the figure. (b) *AVC* first declines, reaches a minimum at point 4, and rises thereafter. When *AVC* attains its minimum at point 4, *MC* equals *AVC*. As *AFC* asymptotically approaches the horizontal axis, *AVC* approaches *ATC* asymptotically, as shown by point 5. (c) *ATC* first declines, reaches a minimum at point 3, and rises thereafter. When *ATC* attains its minimum at point 3, *MC* equals *ATC*, (d) *MC* first declines, reaches a minimum at point 6, and rises thereafter. *MC* equals both *AVC* and *ATC* when these curves attain their minimum values. Furthermore, *MC* lies below both *AVC* and *ATC* over the range in which the curves decline; it lies above them when they are rising.

This completes the analysis of cost in the short run. We have shown how short-run costs are related to the production function in the cases of one variable input, which illustrates all the typically assumed properties of short-run cost curves, and of several variable inputs. We now will turn to an analysis of cost in the long run when all inputs are variable and to the relation between short-run and long-run cost. We will return again and again to the short-run cost curves with the typical shapes set forth in Figure 10–9 when discussing a firm's short-run profit-maximizing decision in later chapters.

***Economics in
the News***   **Productivity and Input Prices Affect Costs**

The theory of cost implies that two factors affect cost—productivity, given by the production function, and input prices. A column in *Business Week,* "A Closer Look at U.S. Industry's Competitive Comeback" by Gene Koretz, July 25, 1988, p. 14, reinforces this conclusion with some evidence from the U.S. economy. This column reported that during the preceding year manufacturing productivity in the United States, measured by output per worker hour, increased 2.8 percent, placing it sixth among the 12 leading industrial nations. On the other hand, the increase in the hourly worker compensation was only 1.3 percent, the smallest increase of the 12 nations. These two effects enabled U.S. manufacturers to cut their unit labor costs 1.5 percent during the year, second only to Japan. Thus, the relatively small increase in productivity was, to a large extent, offset by the relatively even smaller increase in wages, enabling U.S. manufacturers to reduce average cost.

This result can be analyzed within the context of the previously derived relation between average variable cost and the ratio of the price of labor and the average product of labor. Recall that average variable cost is inversely related to average product and positively related to the price of labor; that is, $AVC = P_L/AP_L$. The relatively small increase in the average product of U.S. workers, relative to other countries, caused average cost to fall less than in many other countries. But the small increase in U.S. wages caused average cost to increase less than in other countries. Thus, the increase in average product, small as it was, was more than offset by the slight increase in wages and brought average cost down more than in any industrialized nation other than Japan.

10.2 *Applying the Theory*

Theoretically at least, the average product of labor and average cost are inversely related—other things being equal, the higher the average product, the lower the average cost and vice versa. Could you explain to your employer, without graphs or equations, why this relation would hold for actual plants or firms? What about the inverse relation between marginal product and marginal cost?

10.6 **Long-Run Cost and the Planning Horizon**

Now that we have completed the analysis of the fundamentals of short-run cost, when one or more inputs are fixed, we examine cost in the long-run, which, as you will see, is similar to cost in the short-run in some ways and different in others. Recall that the long run means that all inputs are variable, so no inputs are fixed. Therefore, in the long run all costs are variable, and there are no fixed costs.

10.6.1   **Long-Run Cost from an Expansion Path**

Because all inputs are variable in the long run, the firm must decide on the level of usage for each input. That is, the firm is planning for the future. For this reason, long-run cost is sometimes called the *planning horizon.*

Figure 10–10   Cost from an Expansion Path

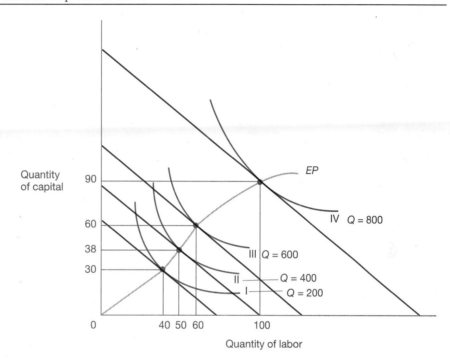

We begin analysis of long-run cost by assuming that an individual is just beginning a firm. One of the first things the owner must decide is the scale of operation
or the size of the firm. To make this decision, the owner must know the cost of
producing each level of output when all inputs are variable. Assume that the firm
will not be large enough to affect the prices of any inputs used in production. This
firm will use only two types of inputs, labor and capital. The price of labor (P_L)
is $80, and the price of capital (P_K) is $100.

To determine its long-run cost of producing each level of output, the firm,
theoretically, must know its expansion path, a portion of which is shown in Figure
10–10. This figure shows the cost-minimizing combinations of labor and capital
for four levels of output, 200, 400, 600, and 800. Recall that these cost-minimizing
input combinations are given by the tangency of the isocost curve, with a slope
$-P_L/P_K = -80/100$, to the isoquant associated with each level of output. For
example, 30 units of capital and 40 units of labor would be used to produce 200
units of output.

Columns 1, 2, and 3 in Table 10–3 show the cost-minimizing input combinations
from Figure 10–10. Because neither input is fixed, the firm would use none of
either input if it produces no output. Long-run total cost (*LRTC*) for each output
level is given in column 4. *LRTC* is simply the price of labor times the amount of
labor plus the price of capital times the amount of capital (*LRTC* = $P_L L + P_L K$)
for each input combination shown in Figure 10–10. Thus, the minimum cost of

Table 10–3 Cost from an Expansion Path (P_L = $80, P_K = $100)

(1) Output (Q)	(2) Labor (L)	(3) Capital (K)	(4) Cost (LRTC) $P_L L + P_K K$	(5) Average Cost (LRTC/Q)	(6) Marginal Cost ($\Delta LRTC/\Delta Q$)
0	0	0	0	—	
					> $31
200	40	30	$ 6,200	$31.00	
					> 8
400	50	38	7,800	19.50	
					> 15
600	60	60	10,800	18.00	
					> 31
800	100	90	17,000	21.25	

producing 200 units of output is $80 × 40 + $100 × 30 = $6,200. The other three costs are calculated in the same way.

The long-run average cost of producing each output (*LRAC*), shown in column 5, is total cost divided by output (*LRTC/Q*). Thus, *LRAC* at Q = 200 is $6,200/200 = $31. As you can see, average cost first decreases with output, through 600 units, then increases. Finally, long-run marginal cost (*LRMC*), in column 6, is measured by the change in cost divided by the change in output ($\Delta LRTC/\Delta Q$). An increase in output from 200 to 400 increases *LRTC* from $6,200 to $7,800; thus, *LRMC* is ($7,800 − $6,200)/(400 − 200) = $1,600/200 = $8. As always, we have shown marginal cost in the table between two output levels to emphasize that marginal cost is for the change in output and not for a given level of output. *LRMC* first falls as output increases, then rises. Comparing columns 6 and 5, *LRMC* is less than *LRAC* when long-run average cost is falling, and it is above *LRAC* when *LRAC* is rising. This is always the case for any average and marginal relation.

Thus far there is no conceptual difference between the arithmetic derivation of cost in the long run and cost in the short run, except that in the long run there are no fixed costs. This is also the case for the graphical depiction of long-run total, average, and marginal cost curves, as shown in Figure 10–11. Panel A of the figure shows the long-run total cost curve from Table 10–3 that is associated with the expansion path in Figure 10–10. The total costs of producing 0, 200, 400, 600, and 800 units are plotted, from the numbers in the table, along the vertical axis. Since output and, therefore, cost are now assumed to vary continuously, as does the expansion path, these points are connected to obtain the *LRTC* curve in the figure. Unlike the case for the short run, total cost is zero at zero output because there are no fixed costs. Cost first increases at a decreasing rate, then increases at an increasing rate. This shape is similar to that of short-run total and variable cost, but, as we will discuss below, for a different reason.

The average and marginal costs for the four levels of output in Table 10–3 are plotted in Panel B, then, to reflect the assumption that output and cost vary continuously; these points are connected with curves to obtain the long-run average

Figure 10–11   Long-Run Total, Average, and Marginal Cost Curve

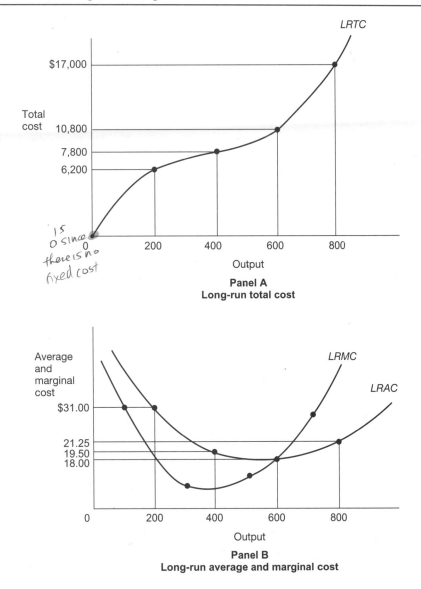

Panel A
Long-run total cost

Panel B
Long-run average and marginal cost

and marginal cost curves, *LRAC* and *LRMC*. As before, we plotted the marginal cost between each of the two levels of output. *LRAC* decreases, reaches its minimum at slightly less than 600 units of output, then increases. *LRMC* decreases, reaches its minimum at slightly more than 300 units of output, then increases. The shapes are similar to those of average variable, and marginal cost in the short run, but for different reasons. As is the case for all marginal and average relations, when

LRMC is less than *LRAC*, average cost is falling; when *LRMC* is greater than *LRAC*, average cost is rising. Thus, *LRMC* must equal *LRAC* at the minimum point on the latter.

10.6.2   Geometric Derivations of Long-Run Total, Average, and Marginal Costs

Figure 10–12 shows graphically the relation between a long-run total cost curve of the typically assumed shape (Panel A) and average cost (Panel B). Since average cost is total cost divided by the corresponding output, the long-run average cost of a particular quantity is given by the slope of a ray from the origin to the relevant point on the *LRTC* curve. For example, in Panel A, the cost of producing Q_1 is C_1. *LRAC*, C_1/Q_1, is therefore given by the slope of the ray designated I at point *P*. Average cost at Q_1 is plotted in Panel B at point P'. (Note that the vertical scales of the two graphs differ, but the horizontal scales are the same.)

From inspection of the *LRTC* curve, it is clear that the slope of a ray to a point on the curve decreases as output increases from zero to Q_2. Average cost must fall as output increases from zero to Q_2, as shown in Panel B. As output increases thereafter from Q_2, the slope of a ray to any point on the total cost curve increases. For example, at Q_3, the *LRAC* is given by ray III at point *S* in Panel A. Average cost of Q_3, C_3/Q_3, is plotted at point S' in Panel B. Thus, minimum average cost is reached at Q_2, where ray II is tangent to the cost curve at *M* in Panel A. This average cost is plotted at M'. Notice that the *LRAC* curve rises thereafter.

Relation

For the generally assumed long-run total cost curve, long-run average cost (*LRAC*) first declines, reaches a minimum, where a ray from the origin is tangent to the long-run total cost curve, and rises thereafter. (These relations are all shown in Figure 10–12.)

The derivation of long-run marginal cost is illustrated in Figure 10–13. Panel A contains a total cost curve shaped similarly to the one in Figure 10–12. As output increases from Q' to Q'', one moves from point *P* to point *Z* and total cost increases from C' to C''. Marginal cost, the additional cost of producing a small increase in output, is

$$LRMC = \frac{C'' - C'}{Q'' - Q'} = \frac{ZR}{PR}.$$

As *P* moves along *LRTC* toward point *Z*, the distance between *P* and *Z* becomes smaller and smaller, and the slope of the tangent *T* at point *Z* becomes a progressively better estimate of *ZR/PR*. For movements in a tiny neighborhood around point *Z*, the slope of the tangent is the marginal cost of output Q''.

As one moves along *LRTC* through points such as *P* and *Z*, the slope of *LRTC* diminishes until point *S* is reached at output *Q*. Therefore, the long-run marginal cost curve is constructed in Panel B so that it decreases (as the slope of *LRTC*

Figure 10–12   Derivation of the Average Cost Curve from the Total Cost Curve

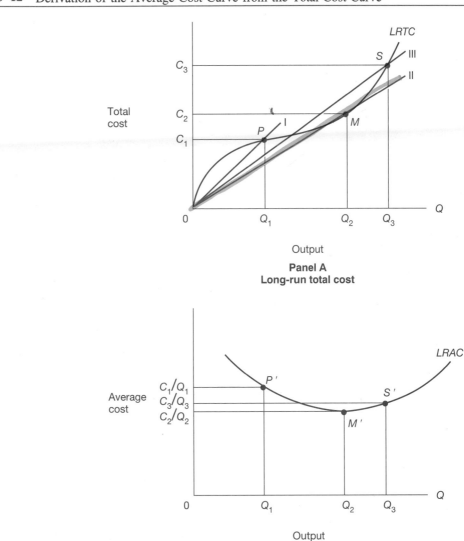

Panel A
Long-run total cost

Panel B
Long-run average cost

decreases) until output Q is attained and increases thereafter (as the slope of *LRTC* increases).

Notice in Figure 10–13, Panel A, we have brought ray II over from Figure 10–12, Panel A. As indicated in Figure 10–12, the slope of ray II gives minimum *LRAC*. At this point, the ray is tangent to *LRTC;* hence, its slope also gives *LRMC* at point M. Thus, *LRMC = LRAC* when *LRAC* attains its minimum value. Consider the relative position of *LRMC* and *LRAC* to the left and right of point M. Figure

Figure 10–13   Derivation of the Long-Run Marginal Cost Curve from the Total Cost Curve

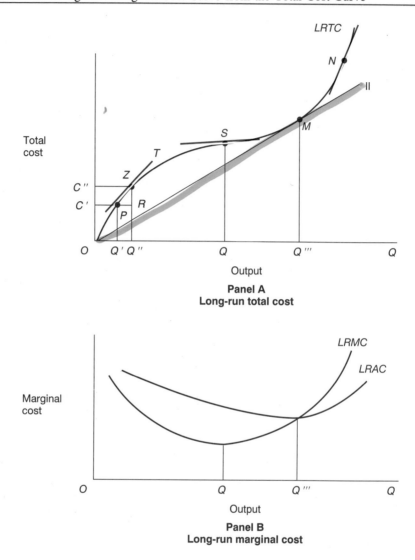

10–13, Panel B, illustrates the relation between the curves. Since the slope of *LRTC* is less than the slope of a ray from the origin to any point on the curve to the left of *M* in Panel A, *LRMC* is less than *LRAC* from the origin to Q''', as shown in Panel B. But because the slope of *LRTC* is greater than the slope of a ray from the origin to any point on the curve to the right of *M* (say at point *N*), *LRMC* is greater than *LRAC* at outputs larger than Q'''.

The characteristics of long-run cost curves are summarized in the following relations:

Relation

> (1) *LRTC* rises continuously, first at a decreasing rate, then at an increasing rate.
> (2) *LRAC* first declines, reaches a minimum, then rises. When *LRAC* reaches its
> minimum, *LRMC* equals *LRAC*. (3) *LRMC* first declines, reaches a minimum,
> and then increases. *LRMC* lies below *LRAC* over the range in which *LRAC*
> declines; it lies above *LRAC* when *LRAC* is rising.

10.6.3   Economies and Diseconomies of Scale

Recall that we mentioned above that the shapes of long-run and short-run cost
curves are similar but for different reasons. We now want to discuss in some detail
why the long-run average cost is typically assumed to be U-shaped, although, as
we will note, there is an exception.

Over the range of output in which long-run average cost is decreasing, the firm
is experiencing *economies of scale.* Over the range of output in which long-run
average cost is increasing, the firm is experiencing *diseconomies of scale.*

Definition

> A firm is said to have economies of scale if long-run average cost declines as
> output increases and diseconomies of scale if long-run average cost increases as
> output increases.

First consider why average cost falls as output increases. Adam Smith provided
one major reason in 1776—specialization. Proficiency is gained by the concentration
of effort. If a plant is extremely small and employs only a small number of workers,
each worker will usually have to perform several different jobs in the production
process. In doing so, workers are likely to move about the plant, change tools, and
so on. Not only are workers not highly specialized, but part of their work time is
also consumed by moving from one job to another. Important savings may be
realized by expanding the scale of operation. A larger plant with a larger work
force may permit each worker to specialize in one job, gaining proficiency and
decreasing or eliminating time-consuming interchanges of location and equipment.
There naturally will be corresponding reductions in the unit cost of production.

The physical characteristics of related pieces of capital constitute another force
giving rise to economies of scale. If several different machines, each with a different
rate of output, are required in a production process, the operation may have to be
quite sizable to permit proper "meshing" of equipment. Suppose only two types of
machines are required, one that produces the product and another that packages it.
If the first machine can produce 30,000 units per day and the second can package
45,000 units, output will have to be 90,000 per day in order to fully utilize the
capacity of all machines. The firm would operate three machines in production and
two machines in packaging.

This example, in essence, shows that investment frequently must be made in
"lumps." At the extreme, in some industries nearly all of the capital investment
must be made before any production can be undertaken. Such lumpiness can lead

to pervasive economies of scale. For example, suppose a railroad builds a line between two cities. Before the first run is made, tracks must be put down, stations built, and locomotives and cars purchased. To make 1 or 100 trips per period, the same capital investment is needed. Investment in this case is virtually independent of the output. Clearly, the more trips made per period, the less capital cost per trip. Lumpiness in investment leads to economies of scale.

Another physical element of capital that induces economies is that the cost of purchasing and installing larger machines is usually proportionately less than the cost of smaller machines. For example, a printing press that can run 200,000 papers per day does not cost 10 times more than one that runs 20,000 per day—nor does it require 10 times as much building space, 10 times as many people to work it, and so forth. For this reason also, expanding the size of the operation tends to reduce the unit cost of production. Another example of how larger capital investment acts to reduce average cost can be found when pipelines are built to transport crude oil, refined petroleum products, and natural gas. Capacity or volume of a pipeline varies with the square of the radius, while the circumference is a linear function of the radius. Thus, pipelines experience substantial economies of scale because the capacity to ship liquids rises much faster than the amount of steel necessary for construction of a larger cylindrical tube.

A final technological element is perhaps the most important determinant of economies of scale. As the scale of operation expands, there are qualitative changes in inputs. Consider the capital requirements for ditch digging. The smallest scale of operation is one laborer and one shovel. As the scale expands beyond a certain point, you do not continue to add workers and shovels. They are replaced by a modern ditch-digging machine or a backhoe. The capital-labor ratio thus rises with output. In this case, expansion permits the introduction of different inputs that tend to reduce the unit cost of production.

In summary, two broad forces—specialization and technological factors—enable producers to reduce long-run average cost by expanding the scale of operation.[2] These forces give rise to the negatively sloped portion of the long-run average cost curve. Why should it ever rise? After all possible economies of scale have been realized—why doesn't the curve simply stay horizontal?

The rising portion of *LRAC*, or diseconomies of scale, generally implies limitations to efficient management. Managing any business entails controlling and coordinating a wide variety of activities—production, transportation, finance, sales, and so on. To perform these managerial functions efficiently, the manager must have accurate information; otherwise, the essential decision making is done in ignorance. Hence uninformed decision making can lead to higher costs.

---

[2]This discussion of economies of scale has concentrated on physical and technological forces. There are monetary reasons for economies of scale as well. Large-scale purchasing of raw and processed materials may enable the buyer to obtain more favorable prices (quantity discounts). The same is frequently true of advertising. As another example, financing of large-scale business is normally easier and less expensive; a nationally known business has access to organized security markets, so it may place its bonds and stocks on a more favorable basis. Bank loans also come easier and at lower interest rates to large, well-known corporations. These are only examples of many potential economies of scale attributable to financial factors.

Figure 10–14   Various shapes of *LRAC*

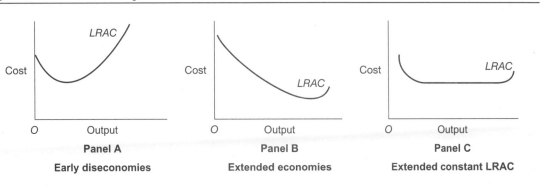

| Panel A | Panel B | Panel C |
| Early diseconomies | Extended economies | Extended constant LRAC |

Also, as the scale of operation expands beyond a certain point, top management necessarily has to delegate responsibility and authority to lower-echelon employees. Contact with the daily routine of operation tends to be lost, and efficiency of operation declines. Red tape and paperwork expand, and management is generally not as efficient. This increases the cost of the managerial function and, of course, the unit cost of production.

It is very difficult to pinpoint the reasons for diseconomies of scale and when they become strong enough to outweigh the causes of economies of scale. In an industry in which economies of scale are negligible, factors causing diseconomies may soon become of paramount importance, causing *LRAC* to turn up at a relatively small volume of output. Panel A, Figure 10–14, shows a long-run average cost curve for a firm of this type. In other cases, economies of scale are extremely important. Even after the efficiency of management begins to decline, long-run average cost may continue to fall for technical reasons over a wide range of output. The *LRAC* curve may not turn up until a very large volume of output is attained. This case is illustrated in Panel B, Figure 10–14.

In many situations, however, neither of these extremes describes the behavior of *LRAC*. Some economists and business people believe that the U-shaped *LRAC*, first decreasing, reaching a minimum, then increasing thereafter, does not accurately describe most production processes. They feel that, in many cases, a relatively small scale of operation enables a firm to capture all possible economies of scale. The long-run average cost is then constant over a wide range of output; eventually diseconomies are incurred at a large volume of output. In such cases, *LRAC* would decline over a small range of output, be horizontal over a large range, then rise, as shown in Panel C of Figure 10–14.

For analytical purposes, we will generally assume a "representative" U-shaped *LRAC*, such as the one shown in Panel B of Figure 10–13. This type of curve is typically used in economic theory. However, the shape of the long-run average cost curve of firms in a particular industry goes a long way toward explaining the number and size of firms in that industry. For example, if diseconomies are reached at a relatively low level of output, as in Panel A of Figure 10–14, one would expect the industry to consist of a large number of rather small firms. If firms are large, their average cost will be so high that they cannot compete with smaller firms. On the other hand, if, as in Panel B, average cost declines over a long range of output before diseconomies set in, large firms will have a great cost advantage over small firms, which would not be able to compete. In such cases, the industry would be made up of only a few extremely large firms, or possibly only one large firm. If firms experience constant returns to scale over a long range of output, as in Panel C, the industry would consist of firms of many sizes, from small to relatively large. No size over the range of constant average cost would give a firm a cost advantage over the other firms producing in this range.

Economics in the News

Huge Firms Try to Overcome the Problem of Diseconomies of Scale

The Wall Street Journal, January 29, 1988, reported that the giant computer manufacturer, IBM, was undertaking a massive restructuring program: "International Business Machines Corp., frustrated by three years of disappointing results, unveiled a sweeping effort to decentralize decision making at the world's largest computer company." The plan involved shifting a large part of the decision-making responsibility from the office of IBM's chairman to six main product and marketing groups. IBM had long been criticized for being too unwieldy. The chairman was spending too much time "resolving daily turf battles and log jams." Although IBM was still the overwhelming market leader in mainframe computers, its share in midrange products and personal computers had eroded badly. IBM's stock prices reflected the decline: Its stock lagged behind the Standard and Poor's 400 by 40 percent in 1986 and 10 percent in 1987. Its revenues had fallen in 1987, while many other computer firms experienced a large rise in sales.

It appears, then, that IBM was so large that it was experiencing managerial diseconomies of scale that caused its costs to rise. It's not as though the chairman and his staff were bad managers; the evidence indicates that the company had become so large that they were unable to solve every problem that came up. So diseconomies of scale because of management problems are real and not just a theoretical concept to justify drawing an upward sloping segment of the long-run average cost curve.

As noted, IBM's solution to the problem was to decentralize into six decision-making groups. No group would be "too-large." As the chairman said, "In many ways we now have several IBM companies."

Less than one month after the IBM article, *The Wall Street Journal*, February 19, 1988, reported that management consultants were predicting that other large companies experiencing similar problems would follow IBM's decentralization plan. *The Journal* pointed out that based upon history, it could be an expensive imitation. "In recent years an increasing number of companies have learned that pushing decision making down the ranks is a management luxury they can't always afford, especially in a competitive environment. The benefits can be undermined by staff duplication, marketing confusion, and out-of-control local units."

At the time, many companies were moving in the other direction. *The Journal* noted that for 50 years decentralization had come and gone several times, so its pitfalls were well known. The first pitfall is costly duplication. An example is Hewlett-Packard, which for many years had allowed its units to operate as minicompanies, and was trying to

(continued)

reverse the trend. The company had decided that the product duplication had become too costly in the face of strong competition. Johnson & Johnson, another large decentralized company, was having to make adjustments in order to reduce duplication.

Some companies found that small, decentralized sales forces can be inefficient when dealing with large customers. Minnesota Mining & Manufacturing (3M) is an example. This company previously sold its medical products through two divisions, which worked well when the buyers were individual doctors. When large hospital groups began making these decisions, 3M's sales strategy became inefficient. These buyers, interested in bulk purchases, preferred to deal with one sales representative.

The Journal reported that decentralization can also confuse customers when the individual units compete too much with one another. Furthermore, some decentralized companies found that managers tend to make decisions in the best interest of their units, which may not be in the best interest of the corporation as a whole. For example, a unit might seek short-term goals at the expense of the long-run goal of the company.

Thus, managerial diseconomies can become a serious problem for large companies. However, breaking the firm up into several smaller units can lead to problems also. It may be the case that firms can simply become too large, but there is little they can do about it, except shrink in order to reduce costs. An article in *Business Week*, March 27, 1989, "Is Your Company Too Big?" implies this and used steel manufacturing as an example.

When two large steel firms, LTV and Republic, merged in 1984, people thought that the huge increase in market share would "create dramatic cost efficiencies." It didn't. By 1986, LTV was in Chapter 11 bankruptcy, in large part due to the huge debt LTV incurred in the merger.

In contrast, Birmingham Steel in 1985 began buying small inefficient steel plants and converting them into "minimills." Birmingham was extremely successful and was making substantial profits by 1989. *Business Week* noted, "Behind Birmingham's success are typical small-company attributes: a genuine entrepreneur boss, flexible work rules, cost-efficient facilities, and narrow product lines. Such advantages allow Birmingham to make a ton of steel with only a third of the labor man-hours of large producers." Many experts were predicting that Birmingham and other small steel manufacturers would continue to increase their market share at the expense of the giant steel firms.

10.3   *Applying the Theory*

A. An article in *Newsweek,* May 1, 1989, reported that automobile companies were beginning to develop and build a car together, then sell the cars separately in the same segment of the market. "Mazda, for instance, builds the Ford Probe and the Mazda MX-6 in the same plant in Flat Rock, Michigan. The cars are essentially the same underneath but with different exteriors, and compete for the same buyers. The deal benefits both." Why would two separate firms that compete manufacture their products together?

B. *Newsweek,* June 8, 1988, "The Springfield 'Miracle'" discussed how the state of Massachusetts was steering new business to small manufacturers and developing worker training centers so the shops will have a steady stream of skilled workers. *Newsweek* noted, "In general, the smaller plants require workers with more flexible skills than large manufacturing facilities." Why?

C. *Newsweek,* January 5, 1987. In 1987, many large companies were hiring high-tech, specialty-design firms to innovate and design new marketable products for them. Why? Why didn't the large firms design their own new products?

10.6.4   Shifts in Cost Curves

Recall that a firm's cost curves are derived from the expansion path. Consequently, these cost curves will shift when the expansion path changes. The variables held constant along the expansion path are (1) the prices of inputs in the production process, which determine the isocost curves, and (2) the state of technology, which determines the shape of the isoquant map. Changes in these variables change the firm's cost. A firm's average cost curve will shift downward, as shown in Figure 10–15, when the price of one or more inputs decreases or when the state of technology improves—called technological change.

Technological change occurs when firms learn how to produce a given level of output using fewer resources, or to produce a larger output using the same amount of resources that previously produced a smaller output. The shift from *LRAC* (old) to *LRAC* (new) means that the firm can produce each level of output over the relevant range at a lower total cost and, therefore, at a lower average cost. A decrease in the price of an input would also cause such a downward shift, because the firm could then purchase any combination of inputs at a lower total cost. Thus, any given output, except zero output, could be produced at a lower cost.[3]

An increase in the price of an input or inputs would increase the cost of producing each level of output. Therefore, *LRAC* would shift upward. With respect to technology, it is inconceivable that firms would voluntarily carry out a technological change that would increase their costs, or that managers would suddenly forget how to combine inputs in the way that was previously efficient. However, such a change could be imposed externally. For example, governmentally enforced environmental or worker safety regulations could force a firm to change its technology in order to comply with the regulations. Firms might have to add capital that reduces pollution or change the machinery to make it safer. These enforced changes would increase the average cost of producing each level of output, thereby shifting the *LRAC* curve upward.

In discussing the effect of input price changes and technological change on a firm's cost curves, we have focused on the effect on long-run costs. We should note, however, that the effects in the short run are similar. Increases (decreases) in the prices of variable inputs would increase (decrease) short-run costs also. A technological improvement might also decrease short-run costs, but the major effects are more likely to be felt in the long run when the firm can vary the size of its plant.

---

[3]We did not include marginal cost in the discussion or the graph, even though in the vast majority of cases, when average cost shifts downward, marginal cost shifts downward also. However, for some unusual cases, average cost shifts downward but marginal cost shifts upward. This would probably be rare, but it is a theoretical possibility.

Figure 10–15   A Downward Shift in Long-Run Average Cost

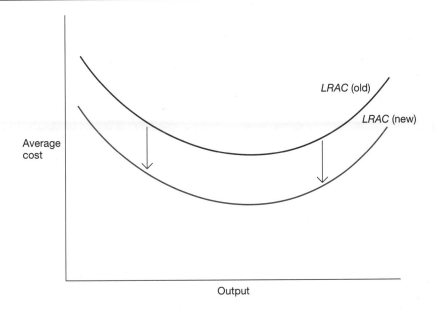

Economics in the News   **Forced Technological Change**

   In March 1989, California's south coast air quality management district adopted a new antipollution program for the Los Angeles area. (*Newsweek*, May 1, 1989) This program included more than 100 specific measures, but the major measure would do away with gasoline-burning vehicles. Municipal bus fleets would have to convert to clean fuel within two years. Within two more years other fleets such as taxies and rental cars would have to convert. By 2009, the order would extend to new cars sold to the public. Every filling station would have to have at least one pump with clean energy.

   The agency did not specifically designate any single clean fuel, but the plan's specifications were based on the assumption that it would be methanol—wood alcohol. Methanol is clean burning, but it was, at the time the program was adopted, used only by race car drivers and those who wanted a lot of power from its high octane. The problem was its high price. Methanol and gasoline sold for about the same price, but a gallon of gasoline produced 1.7 times the miles per gallon. *Newsweek* noted that buying methanol at 80 cents is equivalent to buying gasoline at $1.40.

   Thus, any regulation that forces firms such as bus companies to use methanol would shift the cost curves of those firms upward. This would have the effect of reverse technological change or technological deterioration. This is not to say that the potential pollution reduction would not be "worth it." It only means that the reduction comes at a price.

10.7   Relation between Short-Run and Long-Run Costs

Although we have discussed long-run costs and short-run costs separately, the two are closely related. In the long run, all inputs and, therefore, all costs are variable. The firm can choose the input combination that minimizes the cost of any level of output the firm chooses to produce. However, once the firm begins producing, it is in the short run. Some of the inputs are now fixed in amount—for example, the buildings and some capital—and, therefore, some of the costs are fixed. Now if the firm wishes to change its output from the level chosen in the long run, it cannot vary all of its inputs to attain the lowest cost of producing the new level of output. It can only change its variable inputs. Therefore, the cost of producing the new level of output is higher in the short run than would have been the case if the firm could have chosen the cost-minimizing combination of all inputs, rather than only the variable inputs. For this reason, cost in the short run exceeds cost in the long run for all output levels except one—the level of output chosen when the firm was in the long run and could choose the cost-minimizing input combination.

10.7.1   Long-Run and Short-Run Expansion Paths

The relation between long-run and short-run costs can be illustrated with two expansion paths. In Figure 10–16, $EP(LR)$ is the long-run expansion path when the prices of labor and capital are given by the slope of ZM and the other two isocost curves. The three isoquants $I(Q_1)$, $II(Q_0)$, and $III(Q_2)$ are associated with output levels Q_1, Q_0, and Q_2. Suppose the firm in the long run chooses to produce output Q_0. The tangency of $II(Q_0)$ and ZM gives the least-cost combination of labor and capital that can produce Q_0—L_0 and K_0. Once the capital is in place, the firm is in the short run, with capital being the fixed input and labor, the variable. As long as the firm continues to produce Q_0, short-run and long-run costs are the same.

Suppose, however, that the firm decides to increase its output to Q_2. Since capital is fixed at K_0, the only way it can increase its output is to increase its labor. As shown in the figure, with capital constant at K_0, the only feasible combination on $III(Q_2)$ is at point B, with the firm using $\overline{L}_2$ units of labor. This combination of inputs clearly costs more than the combination given by the long-run expansion path, K_2 and L_2. An isocost curve passing through point B and parallel to ZM and the other isocost curves lies above the isocost curve tangent to $III(Q_2)$. Thus, the cost of producing Q_2 in the short run, when capital is fixed at K_0, is greater than the cost in the long run, when both inputs are variable. Because the total cost of producing Q_2 is greater in the short run than in the long run, the average cost at Q_2 must also be greater in the short run.

Consider now the short-run and long-run marginal cost of increasing output from Q_0 to Q_2. At Q_0, short-run and long-run total cost is the same because the input combination is the same in each situation. From the above analysis, the short-run cost of producing Q_2, with capital fixed at K_0, is greater than the long-run cost of producing Q_2, when capital can be varied. Therefore, the cost of increasing output from Q_0 to Q_2 must be greater in the short run. Consequently, the short-run marginal

Figure 10–16   Long-Run and Short-Run Expansion Paths

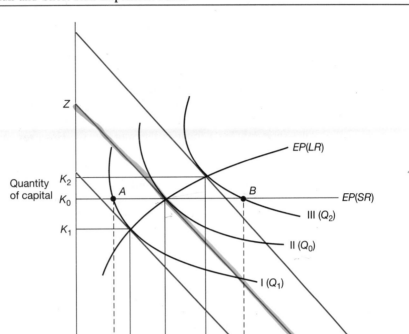

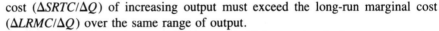

cost ($\Delta SRTC/\Delta Q$) of increasing output must exceed the long-run marginal cost ($\Delta LRMC/\Delta Q$) over the same range of output.

All of these derived cost relations must hold for any level of output above Q_0:

Relations

> When output is increased above the level at which the long-run cost-minimizing combination of inputs is chosen, total, average, and marginal cost are greater in the long run than in the short run.

Now return to the situation in which the firm is producing Q_0 with the cost-minimizing input combination L_0 and K_0. Suppose it then decides to reduce its output to Q_1 [given by isoquant I (Q_1)], but capital is still fixed at K_0. If the firm was in the long run and could vary both capital and labor, it would choose the combination at the point where I (Q_1) is tangent to the isocost curve, using K_1 units of capital and L_1 units of labor, the long-run cost-minimizing combination of inputs. Because capital is fixed at K_0 in the short run, the firm must choose the combination at point A, using K_0 units of capital and $\bar{L}_1$ labor. Because the isocost curve parallel to ZM passing through point A (but not drawn) is above the isocost curve tangent to $I(Q_0)$, the combination $K_0 L_1$ clearly costs more than the long-run cost-minimizing combination because it is on a higher isocost line. Therefore, the cost of producing Q_1 is greater in the short run, when capital is fixed at K_0, than it is in the long run when capital is variable. Because the long-run total cost of producing Q_1 is less than the short-run total cost, long-run average cost at Q_1 must be less than short-run average cost.

Finally, we can compare the short-run and long-run marginal costs of an increase in output from Q_1. Suppose the firm wishes to increase output from Q_1 back to original level Q_0. At Q_0, $LRTC_0$ and $SRTC_0$ are the same, because in both cases, the short-run fixed input is the same at K_0. However, long-run total cost at Q_1 ($LRTC_1$) is less than short-run total cost at Q_1 ($SRTC_1$). Increasing output from Q_1 to Q_0 increases the firm's cost more in the long run than would be the case in the short run, because the change in the long run begins from a lower cost than in the short run, and the movement ends at Q_0 where the cost is the same in both situations. Therefore, the marginal cost of increasing output from Q_1 is higher in the long run than in the short run.

Algebraically, since

$$LRTC_0 = SRAC_0 \text{ and } LRTC_1 < SRTC_1,$$
$$(LRTC_0 - LRTC_1) > (SRTC_0 - SRTC_1).$$

Because ΔQ is the same in both the long run and short run, marginal cost in the long run ($LRMC$) must be greater than marginal cost in the short run ($SRMC$):

$$LRMC = \frac{(LRTC_0 - LRTC_1)}{\Delta Q} > SRMC = \frac{(SRTC_0 - SRTC_1)}{\Delta Q},$$

from the above inequality. By the same analysis, it can be shown that at any output level below the output at which the long-run, cost-minimizing combination of inputs is used, marginal cost is greater in the long run than in the short run.

All of these derived relations must hold for any level of output below Q_0:

Relations

When output is below the level at which the cost-minimizing combination of inputs is chosen, total and average cost are lower in the long run than in the short run. Marginal cost is lower in the short run than in the long run.

10.7.2   Relation of Long-Run and Short-Run Cost Curves

Figure 10–17 illustrates in another way the relations, derived from Figure 10–16, between the short-run and long-run cost curves. In Panel A, $LRTC$ is the cost curve when all inputs are variable. It therefore shows the lowest possible cost of producing each level of output. Suppose the levels of capital (K_0) and labor (L_0) are chosen to produce output Q_0 at minimum cost. Now let $SRTC$ be the total cost curve when capital is fixed at K_0 and only labor is variable. Short-run and long-run cost are equal at Q_0, where $SRTC$ is tangent to $LRTC$. For reasons set forth in the discussion of Figure 10–16, $SRTC$ lies above $LRTC$ at all output levels greater than Q_0. At

Figure 10–17   Long-Run and Short-Run Cost Curves

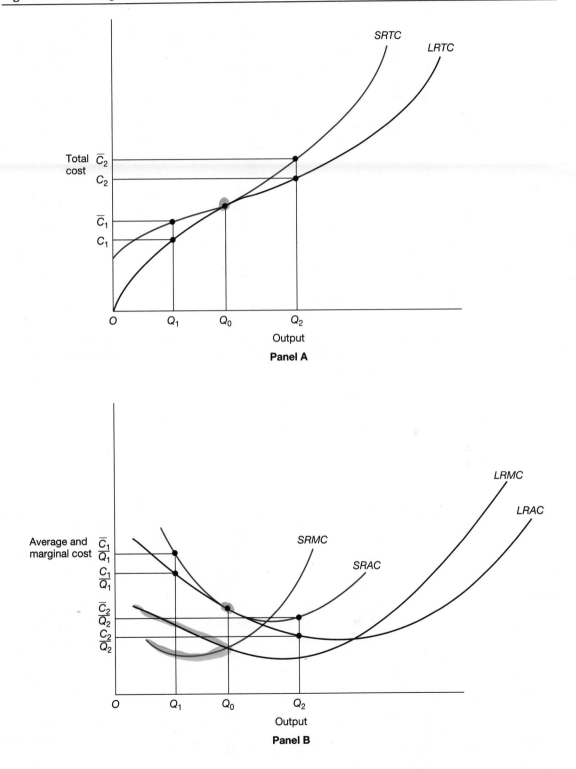

Panel A

Panel B

Q_2, for example, long-run cost is C_2 and short-run cost is $\overline{C}_2$ ($\overline{C}_2 > C_2$). Following the same reasoning, *SRTC* lies above *LRTC* at all levels of output below Q_0, such as Q_1. Here long-run cost is C_1 and short-run cost is $\overline{C}_1$ ($\overline{C}_1 > C_1$). At zero output, the firm must still pay its fixed cost in the short run, so *SRTC* is greater than zero when the firm produces no output. Long-run total cost is zero if the firm produces no output.

Panel B shows the relation between the short- and the long-run average and marginal cost curves associated with the total cost curves in Panel A. Since *SRTC* equals and is tangent to *LRTC* at Q_0, short-run average cost (*SRAC*) equals and is tangent to long-run average cost (*LRAC*) at Q_0 also. Because *SRTC* is greater than *LRTC* at every other level of output, *SRAC* is above *LRAC* at every other level. At Q_2, *LRAC* is C_2/Q_2 and *SRAC* is $\overline{C}_2/Q_2$; at Q_1, *LRAC* is C_1/Q_1 and *SRAC* is $\overline{C}_1/Q_1$.

Note from the figure that at Q_0, when *SRAC* and *LRAC* are equal and tangent, *SRAC* must be downward sloping. This follows from the geometry. Because at Q_0 *LRAC* is downsloping (economies of scales), *SRAC* must be downward sloping also in order to be tangent. Also, because the U-shaped *SRAC* must be downward sloping at Q_0, it must attain its minimum point at an output greater than Q_0.

Long-run marginal cost (*LRMC*) and short-run marginal cost (*SRMC*) in Panel B also illustrate the relations derived in Figure 10–16. From the previous analysis, at every level of output below Q_0, *SRMC* must lie below *LRMC*; at every level of output above Q_0, *SRMC* must lie above *LRMC*. Thus, *SRMC* must equal *LRMC* at Q_0 and cross *LRMC* from below. Alternatively, since *SRTC* is tangent to *LRTC* at Q_0 and the slope of a tangent to the total cost curve is equal to marginal cost at any output level, the two marginal costs must be equal at Q_0 because the slopes of the tangents to the two curves must be equal. Finally, from the previous discussion of the properties of short-run cost curves, *SRMC* must cross *SRAC* at the minimum point on *SRAC*.

10.7.3   Scales of Production

The discussion thus far has focused on only one set of short-run cost curves and their relation to the long-run cost curves. In the long-run, however, a firm can choose the scale of production that permits the lowest total cost and average cost for any level of output. Since the long-run cost curves are a planning horizon, firms are normally faced with a choice among quite a wide variety of scales of operation or short-run cost curves. In fact, if output can vary continuously, an infinite number of output levels and, hence, an infinite number of short-run cost curves are possible. Figure 10–18 shows a firm's long-run average and marginal cost curves (*LRAC* and *LRMC*). *LRAC* shows the lowest possible average cost of producing each level of output. Six sets of short-run average and marginal cost curves are also shown in the figure as $SRAC_1$, $SRMC_1$ through $SRAC_6$, $SRMC_6$. These curves are associated, respectively, with the least-cost combination of inputs for output levels Q_1 through Q_6. Along each of the short-run cost curves, some of the inputs are fixed, so the firm in each short-run situation can produce only one level of output at the lowest possible cost. The six sets of short-run cost curves in Figure 10–18 are not the only scales of operation a firm can choose. Many curves could be drawn between each

Figure 10–18   Average and Marginal Cost Curves

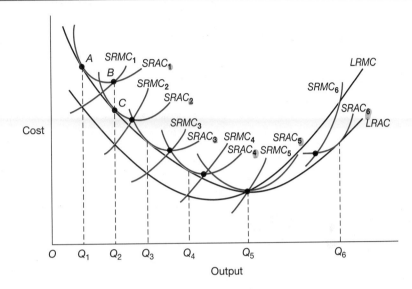

of those shown. These six curves are, however, representative of the large number that could be considered.

Figure 10–18 emphasizes that the *LRAC* curve is a planning device. Suppose the firm thinks the output associated with point $A(Q_1)$ in Figure 10–18 will be most profitable. The scale of operation represented by $SRAC_1$ will be chosen because it will allow production of this output at the least possible cost. For average cost given by $SRAC_1$, unit cost could be reduced by expanding output to the amount associated with point $B(Q_2)$, the minimum point on $SRAC_1$. If demand conditions changed so that this larger output was desirable, the firm could easily expand and would add to profitability by reducing unit cost. However, when setting future plans, the entrepreneur would choose the scale of operation represented by $SRAC_2$ because the firm could reduce unit cost even more. It would operate at point C, thereby lowering unit cost from the level at point B on $SRAC_1$.

The set of cost curves in Figure 10–18 illustrates the relations between short-run and long-run cost previously discussed for the case of a single short-run situation. Each of the six short-run average cost curves is tangent to *LRAC* at the output for which the long-run cost-minimizing combination of inputs was chosen. Each *SRAC* curve is above *LRAC* at every other output level. Each *SRMC* curve crosses *LRMC* from below at that output; *SRMC* is below *LRMC* at lower outputs and above *LRMC* at higher outputs. Each *SRAC* curve for outputs below that at which *LRAC* reaches its minimum point, at Q_5, equals and is tangent to *LRAC* where *SRAC* is negatively sloped and attains its minimum point at a higher level of output, at which *SRAC* equals *SRMC*. At any output above Q_5, *SRAC* equals and is tangent to *LRAC*, where *SRAC* is upward sloping and attains its minimum point at a lower output, at which *SRAC* equals *SRMC*.

Later in this text, we will return to the situation shown as $SRAC_5$ and $SRMC_5$. These are the short-run curves associated with the output at which $LRAC$ reaches its minimum point, Q_5. At this output, $SRAC_5$ is tangent to $LRAC$ at the minimum point on each curve. Also, at this minimum point, $SRMC_5$ equals $LRMC$. Thus, at the minimum point on $LRAC$, $SRAC = LRAC = SRMC = LRMC$.

The long-run average cost curve is a locus of points representing the lowest cost and, therefore, the lowest per-unit cost of producing each level of output. As you can see in Figure 10–18, the six short-run average cost curves, along with the many others that could have been drawn, trace out the long-run average cost curve. Thus, $LRAC$ is, in effect, an envelope of the $SRAC$ curves, which explains why $LRAC$ is sometimes called an *envelope curve*. The firm in the long-run determines the scale of operation with reference to this curve, selecting the short-run scale that leads to the lowest per-unit cost of producing the desired level of output.

Figure 10–18 illustrates the following.

Relations

(a) $LRMC$ intersects $LRAC$ when the latter is at its minimum point. One, and only one, short-run plant has minimum $SRAC$ that coincides with minimum $LRAC$ ($SRAC_5$). $SRMC$ equals $LRMC$ at this common minimum. (b) At each output where a particular $SRAC$ is tangent to $LRAC$, the relevant $SRMC$ equals $LRMC$. At outputs below (above) the tangency output, the relevant $SRMC$ is less (greater) than $LRMC$. (c) For all $SRAC$ curves, the point of tangency with $LRAC$ is at an output less (greater) than the output of minimum $SRAC$, if the tangency is at an output less (greater) than that associated with minimum $LRAC$.

10.8   Summary

Economists think of cost as being different from just out-of-pocket expense. Total cost must be viewed as the value of forsaken opportunities. Opportunity cost can be much larger than accounting entries. In many cases, accounting costs will not reveal the implicit costs of operation, which is another way of saying some opportunity costs are ignored.

The physical conditions of production and resource prices jointly establish the cost of production. If the set of technological possibilities changes, the cost curves change. Or, if the prices of some inputs change, the firm's cost curves change. Therefore, it should be emphasized that cost curves are generally, although not always, drawn under the assumption of constant input prices and a constant technology.

We have distinguished between cost in the short run and in the long run. In the long run all costs are variable. Some inputs are fixed in the short run, leading to fixed costs, as opposed to variable costs. The sum of variable and fixed costs is total cost in the short run. Average cost in either the long run or short run is found by dividing the relevant total cost by output. Marginal cost is the change in total cost per unit change in output. Marginal and average cost in the long run are not the same as marginal and average cost in the short run, because the usage of some inputs cannot be changed in the short run. Long-run cost is the lowest possible cost of producing each level of output. Short-run cost is the lowest possible cost at only one level of output and equals long-run cost only at that output. At every other output, short-run cost is higher than long-run cost.

Short-run average and marginal cost curves first decrease, then increase as output increases because, respectively, the average and marginal products of the variable inputs first increase then decrease. Economies and diseconomies of scale determine the shape of the long-run average cost curve. When there are economies of scale, the long-run average cost curve declines as output increases. Diseconomies of scale mean that average cost in the long run is rising as output increases. There are numerous technical causes of economies. Generally, capital costs do not rise as quickly as capacity. Also, because of specialization, labor becomes more productive as size increases. Diseconomies of scale seem to arise from difficulties in communication and coordination as an organization expands.

Now that we have set forth the theory of cost, we can turn to the analysis of how firms determine the output to produce and, in some cases, the price to charge. In deciding on its output and price, a firm must consider its revenue, that is, how much it will receive from selling the product, and its cost, or how much it must pay, explicitly or implicitly, to produce and sell the product. The difference is the firm's profit. The theory of consumer behavior explains the revenue or demand side of the calculation. The theories of production and cost explain the cost side. Together, these theories provide the framework for the theory of firm behavior, which, as you will see, is a straightforward application of the theory of optimizing behavior that was set forth in Chapter 4.

Answers to *Applying the Theory*

10.1.A This calculation could be quite complicated and would differ from person to person. In general, however, you would estimate what you would have to give up in order to train for and compete in the Olympics. What would a typical person with your major earn during the training period. How would your future income be affected by postponing entry into your chosen field? The implicit opportunity cost would be the dollar value of the best alternative use of your time. The explicit opportunity cost would be your estimate of any expenditures, over and above what you would have spent anyway, necessary for you to train. Clearly, any training reimbursement would be subtracted from the opportunity cost. All these costs can be estimated in terms of dollars.

The decision itself would be an unconstrained optimization problem, such as those discussed in Chapter 4. The marginal cost is the estimated opportunity cost. In estimating the marginal benefits, you would have to consider the probability of making the Olympic team, then estimate any additional revenue you would receive from having competed. The marginal utility from having competed is subjective, so it would be hard to put a dollar value on it. Nonetheless, the decision rule is, if the estimated additional benefits are greater than the estimated additional cost, continue training. If otherwise, don't continue training.

10.1.B Mr. Lucas clearly understood that by returning to the NBA the demands on his time would reduce, or perhaps even eliminate, the time he could spend managing or expanding his fitness centers. This potential loss of business income would be an implicit opportunity cost of playing basketball, and the reduction in income could partially, or perhaps totally, offset his salary in the NBA. Since he chose to play basketball, the marginal benefits must have been greater than the marginal cost.

10.2   When explaining this relation, the other thing to be held constant is the wage rate. The higher the average product of labor, the greater the total amount of output that can be produced by any given number of workers, when combined with the capital and other fixed inputs. From this it follows that the higher the average product of labor, the fewer workers that are required to produce a given level of output, and, therefore, with a given wage rate, the lower the labor cost of producing any given output. Thus, the total and, hence, average cost of producing that given level of output must fall.

The explanation for the inverse relation between marginal product and marginal cost, at a given wage rate, is similar. The greater the marginal product of labor, the more each additional worker adds to total output. Therefore, the higher the marginal product, the fewer workers that are required to increase output by any given amount, and the additional labor cost of any given increase in output is reduced. Thus, marginal cost is reduced because fewer workers must be added.

10.3.A   The most likely reason is to take advantage of economies of scale. A member of an auto consulting firm stated, "The main rationale is to spread and reduce cost." The market for each car was not large enough to produce a large enough number of each car to achieve these economies. The market for both cars was large enough. Other joint production combinations at the time were GM/Toyota, Chrysler/Mitsubishi, Ford/Yamaha, and Ford/Nissan.

10.3.B   Large firms can take advantage of specialization; they hire enough workers that each worker has to perform only one task. Smaller firms are not so specialized. The number of workers is so small that each must perform several tasks. Thus, the smaller firms want workers who can change tasks and perform more types of jobs.

10.3.C   Probably to take advantage of specialization and the fact that firms specializing in innovation and new product design have done enough of this task that they have learned to innovate more efficiently. This is similar to the reason that automobile manufacturers don't produce their own tires but buy them from tire manufacturers. This method can be more efficient.

Technical Problems

1. The first two columns in the table below give a firm's short-run production function when the only variable input is labor, and capital, the fixed input, is held constant at 5 units. The price of capital is $2,000 per unit and the price of labor is $500 per unit.

Units of Labor	Units of Output	Average Product	Marginal Product	Cost			Average Cost			Marginal Cost
				Fixed	Variable	Total	Fixed	Variable	Total	
0	0									
20	4,000									
40	10,000									
60	15,000									
80	19,400									
100	23,000									

a. Complete the table.

b. Graph the average variable cost, average total cost, and marginal cost curves.

c. What is the relation between average variable cost and marginal cost? Between average total cost and marginal cost?

d. What is the relation between average product and average variable cost? Between marginal product and marginal cost?

2. Fill in the blanks in the following table:

Units of Output	Total Cost	Fixed Cost	Variable Cost	Average Fixed Cost	Average Variable Cost	Average Total Cost	Marginal Cost
1	$	$ 100	$ 900	$	$	$	$
2					850		
3							700
4					800		
5						900	
6							1,500
7			7,900				
8						1,300	
9	14,000						

3. The following figure (Figure E.10–1) shows the average product (AP) and marginal product curves (MP) for labor, the only variable input hired by a firm. The price of labor is $1,200 per worker per period of time. Recall the following relations and definitions:

$$AP_L = Q/L, \quad MP_L = \Delta Q/\Delta L, \quad AVC = P_L/AP_L, \quad MC = P_L/MP_L.$$

a. When the firm hires 60 workers, what is the firm's output? What is average variable cost at this output?

b. Answer part *a* under the assumption that the firm hires 200 workers.

c. At what output is average variable cost at its minimum? What is average variable cost at this output? What is marginal cost at this output?

d. If fixed cost is $14,400, when AVC is at its minimum, what is average total cost?

4. The following figure (Figure E.10–2) shows the long-run expansion path for a firm using only capital and labor. The price of labor (P_L) is $10 and the price of capital (P_K) is $20. The figure shows three of the family of isoquants, I, II, and III, representing respectively, 100, 200, and 300 units of output and the cost-minimizing isocost curve for each of these output levels.

a. The firm in the long run chooses to produce 200 units of output. What is the cost-minimizing input combination? What is the total cost of production? The average cost?

b. Suppose the firm now in the short run with capital fixed at the amount given in part *a* when 200 units were produced, wishes to increase output to 300 units. What is the total cost of producing 300 in the short run? The average cost? The short-run marginal cost ($\Delta SRTC/\Delta Q$) over this range? Suppose the firm could be in the long run and vary both inputs optimally. What would be the long-run total, marginal, and average cost? Compare costs in the long and short run.

Figure E.10–1

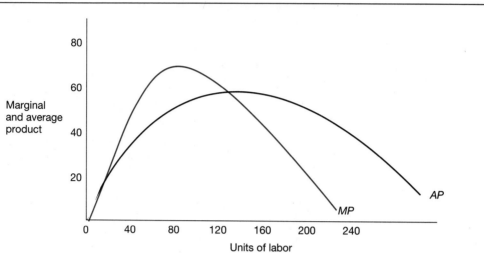

Figure E.10–2

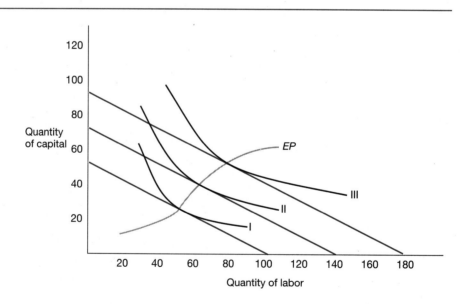

c. Return to the original long-run situation in part *a* when the firm was producing 200 units at least cost. Now let the firm reduce output to 100 in the short run when capital is fixed and only labor is variable. What are the short-run total and average costs of 100 units of output? What is the short-run marginal cost of increasing output from 100 to 200? What would the total, average, and marginal cost have been if the firm had been in the long run? Compare the long-run and short-run total, average, and marginal costs.

Figure E.10–3

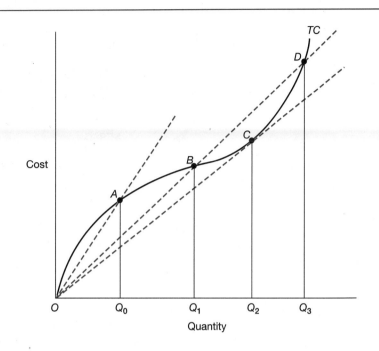

5. A firm is in the short run. Explain how each of the following events would affect the firm's average total, average variable, average fixed, and marginal cost curves. The firm's owner manages the firm and owns the building in which the firm produces its output.
   a. The wage rate of workers increases.
   b. The owner discovers a productivity-enhancing technological change.
   c. Government regulations force the firm to reduce its pollution emission.
   d. Government imposes a lump sum tax of $1,000 each period on the firm.
   e. The salary of managers of similar firms rises.
   f. The owner's spouse, who previously did not work, goes to work for the firm, but is not paid a salary.
   g. The rent of similar buildings rises.
6. Assuming the long-run total cost curve in Figure E.10–3 answer the following questions:
   a. When output is Q_0, average cost is the ratio _____ and is (greater than, less than, equal to) marginal cost.
   b. At output Q_2 average cost is the ratio _____ and marginal cost is the ratio _____ .
   c. Answer part a for output levels Q_1 and Q_3.
7. In the figure below (Figure E.10–4), *LRAC* and *LRMC* make up a firm's planning horizon. $SRAC_1$, $SRAC_2$, and $SRAC_3$ are the only three plant sizes available. These are called plant 1, plant 2, and plant 3.
   a. Draw accurately the short-run marginal cost curves associated with each plant. Recall the relation between short- and long-run marginal costs.

Figure E.10–4

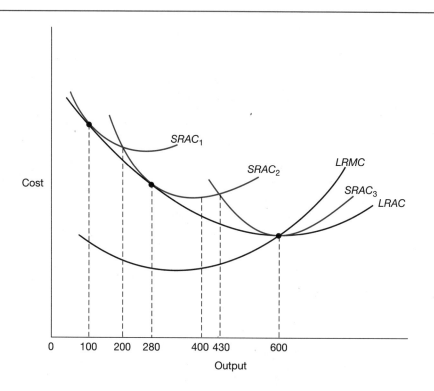

b. Plant 1 is designed to produce_____units optimally, plant 2 is designed to produce_____units optimally, and plant 3 is designed to produce_____ units optimally.

c. The firm would produce in plant 1 any output below_____. It would produce any output between _____and _____in plant 2.

d. $SRAC_2$ attains its minimum at 400 units. Suppose there was another plant (say 4) that could produce 400 optimally. Would the average cost curve associated with this plant attain its minimum above, below, or at 400 units?

e. The lowest possible per-unit cost is at_____units in plant_____. Why would the firm not use this plant to produce every other output since this is least per-unit cost?

8. At the output where short- and long-run average costs are equal, short- and long-run marginal costs are equal. Explain precisely why short-run marginal cost is higher than long-run marginal cost at greater output levels and lower at lower output levels.

9. A firm is hiring 20 workers, the only variable input, at a wage rate of $60. The average product of labor is 30, the marginal product of the 20th worker is 12, and total fixed cost is $3,600.

a. How much output is being produced?

b. What is marginal cost?

c. What is average variable cost?

d. What is average total cost?

e. At this output, is average variable cost increasing, decreasing, or constant? What about average total cost?

10. Why do we say that the firm plans in the long run and operates in the short run?

11. Why is short-run average cost never less than long-run average cost? Don't say because short-run total cost is never less. Explain why.

12. A firm's average variable cost is constant at $10. Fixed cost is $5,000. What do the firm's total, average, and marginal cost curves look like?

Analytical Problems

1. The board of directors of a large state university, after considering two sites for building a new basketball coliseum, chose to build on a plot of land the university already owned rather than on another tract of land that the university would have to buy. The reason given was that the chosen tract lowered the cost of the coliseum because it was free and the other would cost over $1 million. Analyze the reasoning.

2. *Modern Healthcare,* December 22, 1989, noted that hospital observers were extremely surprised that Cleveland Clinic named its top heart surgeon, Dr. Floyd Loop, as its new chief executive officer. One expert said, "[Dr. Loop is] one of the five or six best heart men on earth." He had done 10,000 open heart surgeries since joining the staff of Clinic. What is the cost of having Dr. Loop as the CEO? Explain.

3. *Newsweek,* March 20, 1989, described a new TV news show that a producer was making available as a teaching resource for high schools, particularly in poor areas. The schools received $50,000 worth of free equipment, including a satellite dish, a VCR, and color monitors. The 12-minute programs, designed for teenagers, were educational but contained four minutes of advertising aimed at high school students. School administrators liked the programs but did not like the advertising. One school principal stated, "If I had the option I'd go strictly for the instruction without the commercials. But this is America, and somebody's got to pay." Why wouldn't "somebody have to pay" if this wasn't America? What did the principal probably mean?

4. On a popular TV show of a few years ago, Kate and Allie, who ran a catering service, sued in small claims court to receive payment for a dinner they catered. The judge decided that they would receive only the cost of the food they prepared. Was this an economically correct decision? Explain.

5. About a dozen large banks control a huge part of the U.S. credit card business, to some extent from buying the credit card portfolios of smaller banks. A market analyst stated, "In this business only two things count, the cost of the money and economies of scale. The more cards you have out there, the lower the unit cost of processing each card. We are starting to see a coalescing of the industry." Analyze this statement. Why are there economies of scale? What was their effect? What is the cost of money? Why is it important?

6. A feature story on the CBS evening news, September 22, 1989, discussed a Clean Air Bill, on which the Senate was scheduled to begin debate the next day. The bill would force many firms to drastically reduce the amount of air pollution they were emitting. Some people argued that the bill, if passed, would substantially raise the cost of many firms, especially steel firms, and drive them out of business. Explain.

7. Suppose you could somehow measure the output of education from a college or university. Why might the long-run average cost curve at first show economies of scale? Why, after some size, might diseconomies set in? How can you account for the fact that some of our most distinguished universities are rather

small in terms of number of students, while other very distinguished universities are extremely large? How do you measure "distinguished"? The last part of this question may be very difficult to answer.

8. Suppose a person is trying to decide whether it is cheaper to drive a car to work or to travel by bus. How could the distinction between fixed and variable costs facilitate the comparison? What difference would it make whether

   a. The person owns a car?

   b. Depreciation of the car is purely a function of time rather than use?

9. Suppose there are a large number of producers in an industry, and all of them produce identical products that sell for the same price. Suppose the firms experience economics of scale. Would they have the incentive to expand? Why? Explain what would eventually happen to the number of producers.

10. In 1990, the U.S. government decided to take the battleships Iowa and Illinois out of service, which was expected to save $70 million a year. The Department of Defense believed that the move would not have an effect on U.S. naval power. Some critics opposed this on the grounds that the government had spent $400 million a few years before restoring these ships, and, since so much was spent, the government should keep them in service. Analyze this criticism.

11. We frequently see in the media arguments for a particular government project that follow along the line: If we can spend billions on new bombers, why can't we improve our educational system? If we can put people on the moon, why can't we build more homes? If we can . . . , why can't we . . . ? Analyze such arguments using the concept of opportunity cost.

12. Suppose you manage a business and have to make business trips of two to four days at least once a month. What factors determine the total cost of a trip? What factors would you consider when deciding whether your salespeople should travel by automobile or airplane? Are these necessarily the same factors that determine the cost of your own travel?

13. Many corporations pay employees, not just top management, bonuses based upon the company's profitability. (*Business Week,* November 7, 1988). Proponents of these plans claim these bonuses lower costs and increase the firms' net profits. How could this be so? Could it be the case that these firms were not minimizing cost prior to initiating the bonus plan?

14. An industry analyst stated, "And there's no doubt interest rates and tight money will affect real estate in 1990. But most U.S. companies finance their operation from internal cash flow, not borrowing." Explain why higher interest rates would affect a company's cost of operation, particularly the cost of investment, even though it finances from internal cash flow rather than borrowing.

15. A letter to Dear Abby (December 28, 1989) asked Abby's advice on the following question: "Dear Abby: My friend and I purchased four choice tickets for a major sporting event . . . at $100 each. . . . The value of the tickets has quadrupled. . . . We plan to attend the event and sell the other two tickets [for $400 each]. . . . Office cronies want to buy the tickets for their original price— $100 each. We insist on selling them for a price that we can easily get from others . . . [We] would appreciate your opinion."

    Abby's advice: Tell your office cronies . . . that they must be cuckoo to expect you to sell those tickets at your cost at this late date.

    Why is Abby's advice good economics? How much would they lose if they sold the tickets at the original $100 price?

PART V

Industrial Organization

CHAPTER 11

Market Structures

11.1   Introduction

As discussed in Chapter 1, economists frequently divide the economy into two broad sectors within which people make decisions: households and firms. Households purchase goods and services from firms and sell the use of their resources to firms. Firms purchase resources from households and use these resources to produce goods and services, which they sell to households.

You have already learned how households make purchasing decisions, and we discussed to some extent how they make decisions about selling the use of their primary resource—labor. You have also learned how firms efficiently use resources to produce goods and services. We now will analyze the profit-maximizing behavior of firms in the marketplace. This behavior determines what and how many goods and services to produce and, in many cases, the prices charged. We will also discuss the social implications of these decisions in different market environments. This study is called *the theory of the firm*.

The theory of the firm is a bit more complex, in one sense, than the theory of consumer behavior. Utility theory organizes practically all consumer behavior. No matter how wealthy or how poor, a consumer allocates a limited income to maximize utility. Although it is true that the larger the income, the more goods and services a person can consume, the theory of consumer behavior describes in general how choices are made. The difference between consumers and firms is more than a distinction between production and consumption. Firms compete in vastly different market environments. These environments are different for a small family farm, a huge corporate owned ranch, a plumber, a giant manufacturer such as General Motors or IBM, a local electric company, a small retailer, a large retail chain such as Sears or Krogers, and many, many other types of firms. Although these firms, as you will see, are similar in many ways, the conditions under which they sell their products can differ considerably.

In Chapter 1 we defined a market as a formal or informal arrangement in which buyers and sellers exchange goods, services, or productive resources. A market can be as well organized as a grain or cattle market in which buyers and sellers meet together—either in person or through computers—in a specified place to make exchanges. Or, a market can take the forms seen in the automobile, grocery, or recording industries in which buyers and sellers make exchanges in many widely separated places throughout the nation and the world. In some markets, buyers and sellers never meet in person—for example, when people order from catalogs or respond to TV ads by calling 800 numbers. As diverse as markets may be, they have one thing in common: people exchange goods or services in a market.

Because firms sell in such diverse market environments, there is no single, general theory to explain firm behavior. It would, however, be impossibly complicated to have a separate theory to explain the behavior of each separate firm or of firms in each separate market. Therefore, to analyze firm behavior and the functioning of markets, economists classify markets into four broad general categories called *market structures*.

Definition

> A market structure is a theoretical concept in which firms are classified for analytical purposes according to the important characteristics of the markets in which they sell their products.

Market structures differ primarily by the degree of available substitutes sold within the market and the amount of competition firms face. The degree of substitution and the amount of competition may not be totally related to a firm's size. A local electric utility may be relatively small but have little or no competition in the sale of electricity. On the other hand, a huge retailer such as Sears would have a great deal of competition and face many substitutes for its products in most cities. The type of market in which firms operate determines the theory that is applied to analyze both the behavior of firms and how well a market functions.

This chapter will introduce you to the four types of market structures you will be studying. It will discuss the characteristics that define each type of market structure and what types of firms fit into each structure. Keep in mind that it is not the purpose of economic theory to explain the behavior of a specific firm. Economic theory should explain and help us understand the behavior of firms, in general, within a given type of market structure and, therefore, the implications of that behavior. Before describing the characteristics of the four market structures, we will first discuss briefly why, in industrial economies, goods and services are typically produced by firms.

11.2   Why Do Firms Exist?

An economy could function without firms. Many such economies have existed in the past and some do even now. Years ago most households produced practically everything they consumed. Frontier households in the United States and Canada were virtually self-sufficient. Households today still produce many of the services they consume. Some examples are home repair, yard work, housecleaning, food preparation, childcare, and so forth. However, production of these services has changed from what it was 200 years ago. Home repair then, for example, did not involve going to the hardware store or lumber yard. The wood was cut, and even many tools were hand made. Today most of the goods used to produce these services—tools, mowers, vacuum cleaners, food, and so on—are produced and sold by firms. In fact, the vast majority of goods and most of the services that households consume are produced and sold by firms. Why?

To answer succinctly, most goods and services cost much less when they are produced by firms in relatively large quantities. The reason for the lower cost was discussed at some length in Chapter 10: economies of scale. As you saw in that chapter, firms can produce larger quantities at a lower average cost because of specialization of resources. A household that builds its own car or refrigerator or home could do so only at a cost considerably above the price at which it could purchase it in the market. Think of the implicit opportunity cost in terms of the time of the household members.

Think also of the variety of skills necessary to build a car, an appliance, or a house. If a household wished to be practically self-sufficient while enjoying a reasonably good standard of living, the household would have to possess a vast array of skills, mixed with large amounts of time; someone would have to learn medicine, dentistry, carpentry, plumbing, and on and on. There just isn't enough time available. Self-sufficiency comes only at the high cost of the forgone advantages of specialization.

We could, however, go a step further and let each household specialize in one part of the production process, then trade their products with other households for finished goods in the marketplace. This method would be more efficient than assembling all resources used to produce the household's goods under a single roof. But there would still be sizable transportation costs and other trading costs involved in such exchanges. People would eventually discover that these costs could be eliminated by bringing together all of the resources in one place and pooling their efforts in the production of goods and services. This system of production would give the advantages of specialization and division of labor, along with reducing transportation costs and the number of transactions made. If there were economies of scale, this cooperative form of organization would also produce at a lower cost and drive smaller scales of operation out of the market. Historically, this method of production did develop very quickly in the 19th century. It is often referred to as the *factory system.*

Actually, economies of scale can extend beyond those attainable in a single plant to economies over several stages of the production process in two or more plants. For example, some large manufacturing firms produce many of the components used to produce their products, then assemble the products in other plants, and possibly even own the retail outlets that sell the products. Some large oil firms pump the oil, refine it into finished products such as gasoline, and own many of the stations that sell the gasoline. Large retailers may take on the role of wholesalers in addition to their role as retailers. When firms own and control two or more stages of production and/or distribution, economists say these firms are *vertically integrated*. A primary reason for vertical integration is that economies of scale persist over two or more stages of the production process, and it may be less costly in general to coordinate production through one firm than to produce with each stage of production controlled by a different firm.

As you saw in Chapter 10, however, there are limits to economies of scale. As more production is carried out in a single firm, average cost can be reduced, but only up to a point. This is why we generally don't see all production centered in a single large firm. A single firm does not grow the wheat and other ingredients that are used in bread, then bake and wrap the bread, transport the bread to its stores, and sell the bread. The diseconomies of scale involved would raise costs and, consequently, prices. These diseconomies lead to different firms being involved in different stages of production.

In a formal business organization, people could cooperate and combine their skills with each person specializing in some aspect of the process. Cooperation of resources, however, is not the sole purpose of a firm. To understand a second important function of a firm, let us construct a simplified example. Suppose four of us chipped in and bought a boat in order to become commercial fishermen. We agree to split the profits equally. Fishing is hard work, and if one of us goofs off a little, we catch fewer fish than if all of us worked hard. Every fish the loafer does not catch costs the person doing the loafing only one fourth of the value of that fish, because its value is divided into four parts. Since the cost of goofing off is lower than would be the case if each of us received the full value of our product, we will goof off more, and production per worker will fall off. This incentive problem is common to any jointly owned and operated venture.

Someone would soon see the advantage of separating ownership from the operation of the business. The owners could contract with workers for a fixed amount of their labor per period in return for a fixed payment per period. Then if there was any shirking of duties, the worker could be fired. Separating the owners from the operation of the business offers a better means of control. Owners would claim any residual after the output was sold and the workers were paid, or they would suffer losses after all workers were paid. The owners, as residual claimants, could either assume the task of monitoring the workers to make sure they fulfilled their contract, or they could hire monitors, sometimes called managers, to do the job.

Therefore, firms are not simply forced upon a helpless society. They arise in an economy because they have been able to organize production more efficiently than other types of institutions. Generally, we think of the owners of capital as contracting with other resources and either hiring managers (monitors) or carrying out this task themselves. Although this may be the most prominent form of organization, it is not the only one. In many countries, the labor-managed firm is a frequently used form of organization; ownership and operation are purposely not separated. Sometimes, but less frequently, we find consumer-managed firms. The point here is that most production does take place in business firms. They exist because they offer an efficient way of organizing production. If some other, more efficient, way of organizing production were discovered, that organization would replace firms. Until then, economics texts will treat production and sales of goods and services as generally being organized in a business firm.

11.3   Market Power and Cross Elasticity of Demand

In the beginning of this chapter, we mentioned that the market environment in which firms sell their products can take many different forms. Because these environments can differ so much, it would be almost as complicated to have a theory designed to fit each individual market as it would be to have a theory to fit each firm. For this reason, economists analyze firm and market behavior within the framework of four broad rather general market structures. An extremely important concept determining which structure a given market and the firms selling in that market should be classified in is the amount of *market power* possessed by the firms in that market.

Definition

Market power is the capability of a seller to raise its price without losing all of its sales.

A useful measure of the market power possessed by firms in a given market is the *cross-price elasticity of demand,* a measure briefly discussed in Chapter 3. This section will discuss the concept of market power and the way cross-price elasticity helps define a market structure.

11.3.1   The Concept of Market Power

If firms have no control over the price they can charge for their products, economists say that these firms have *zero market power*. Such firms must take as given the going product price, determined in the market by demand and supply. Firms with no market power are frequently called *price takers* or perfect competitors.

Firms with no market power know that their output makes up such a small portion of total market sales that they can sell all they wish without having any effect whatsoever on the market price. If such firms attempted to charge a price even slightly higher than the market price, they would not be able to sell anything at all because buyers could continue to purchase all they wanted at the market price from other sellers. Such firms would never lower their price below the market price, because they know that they can sell all they want at the market's price. Selling at lower prices would mean unnecessary losses of profits. Examples of firms with zero market power—price takers—are most producers of agricultural products.

Firms that have some control over the price they can charge for their products are said to possess *market power*. Firms with market power can increase their price, maybe by only a small amount, without losing all of their sales. They can also lower the price they charge and increase the amount they can sell, even if only by a small amount. All firms that have some amount of market power face a downward-sloping demand for the specific product or products they sell.

Firms with market power are sometimes referred to as *price searchers*. Firms with market power or price searchers, in contrast with price takers who take the price as given and must decide only how much to produce, must determine what price to charge in addition to how much output to produce. A very broad range of firms of all different sizes possess market power of widely varying degrees. Retail stores have market power, as do municipal utility companies, automobile and computer manufacturers, soft-drink and beer bottlers, long-distance phone companies, and many more. All such firms have some degree of control over the price they charge for their products.

The amount of market power possessed by a firm—the degree of control it has over its price—is primarily determined by the availability of substitute products for the product the firm produces. If good substitutes are readily available to consumers, a firm would have little market power. If the firm raises its price by a small amount, it would lose a large amount of its sales to substitute products. If there are no good substitutes for a firm's product, it would have a great deal of market power. It could raise its price and not lose a large amount of sales to substitute products. Most retail stores, facing readily available good substitutes, probably have some market power but not a large amount. On the other hand, local electric or regional phone companies, without extremely good substitutes available, probably have much more market power.

When determining how much market power a firm possesses and how readily substitutes are available, "a great deal" and "not much" are not particularly precise measures. Fortunately, economists have developed a concept that is more precise.

11.3.2   Cross-Price Elasticity of Demand

Cross-price elasticity of demand is a measure of how substitutable other products are for one firm's output and, hence, how much market power the firm possesses. This measure also indicates directly whether two products are good substitutes and, therefore, whether or not the two firms producing these products are in the same market. More precisely, cross-price elasticity measures the sensitivity of the quantity purchased of one product to a change in the price of another product.

Assume two products, X and Y. The cross-price elasticity of demand between X and Y is determined by the ratio:

$$E_{xy} = \frac{\text{Percent change in quantity of } X \text{ demanded}}{\text{Percent change in the price of } Y} = \frac{\% \, \Delta Q_x}{\% \, \Delta P_y}$$

$$= \frac{\Delta Q_x / Q_x}{\Delta P_y / P_y} = \frac{\Delta Q_x}{\Delta P_y} \cdot \frac{P_y}{Q_y}.$$

(Note the similarity of the formula for cross-price elasticity and demand elasticity in Chapter 3.) The ratio, E_{xy}, can be positive, zero, or negative. If $E_{xy} > 0$, an increase in P_y causes an increase in the amount of X sold. Consumers switch from Y to X after P_y increases. Similarly, if $E_{xy} > 0$, a decrease in P_y causes a decrease in the amount of X sold. Consumers switch from X to Y after P_y decreases. If $E_{xy} > 0$, goods X and Y are *substitutes*. Consumers substitute from one good to the other after a change in the price of good Y.

Alternatively, it may be the case that when P_y rises, less X is purchased: $E_{xy} < 0$. In this case, consumers buy less of both Y and X when P_y rises. The two goods are then, by definition, *complements*. Goods that are complements—have negative cross-price elasticities—are generally goods that consumers consume together, such as automobiles and gasoline, cameras and film, and bread and butter. Finally, a change in the price of Y may have no perceptible effect on the amount of X sold. In this case, $E_{xy} = 0$, and the goods are said to be *demand independent*.

If E_{xy} is positive and the goods are substitutes, the larger is E_{xy}, the better substitutes are goods X and Y. A change in the price of Y has a large direct effect on the amount of X sold. If E_{xy} is positive but small, perhaps close to zero, the goods are not particularly good substitutes. A change in the price of Y has a direct but very small effect on the quantity of X sold.

We introduce the concepts of cross-price elasticity and substitution here, because cross-price elasticity helps determine whether or not two products are sold in the same market. And because a large positive elasticity indicates that two goods are easily substituted, the market power of each of the firms selling these goods is, therefore, likely to be weak; unless of course, the two firms collude in the market. In contrast, if a firm produces a product that does not have a high cross-price elasticity with other products, we can be reasonably sure that there are no good substitutes available; the firm is alone in its market, and the firm possesses a considerable amount of market power.

If E_{xy} is positive for a pair of products, the market power of each of the two firms producing the products falls as E_{xy} increases. For identical products, E_{xy} approaches an extremely large positive number, because any increase in the price of Y would drive all the sales to X. Alternatively, a firm's market power increases and becomes a maximum as the cross-price elasticity of its product with any other product goes to zero. In this case, no other products are viewed as substitutes for the product consumers presently purchase.

We have indicated no precise *numeral* relation between cross-price elasticity and the amount of market power possessed by a firm. We can only say that if this elasticity is, say, 6, the firm has less market power than if it is 2, and .4 indicates less market power than .2. Similarly, we have not pointed to any specific numerical value of cross-price elasticity that indicates whether or not two products are sold in the same market. We can only say that two products with a cross-price elasticity of 4 are more likely to be sold in the same market than if this measure is .3.

Antitrust legal cases do, however, make use of such numerical estimates as an indication of the amount of market power, and judges have specified numbers as indicating too much or not enough power to be in violation of antitrust law. Furthermore, statistical studies of particular markets have used cross-price elasticities to determine whether or not specific firms were selling their products in those markets.

Here we use only the theoretical relation between cross-price elasticity and the degree of market power and cross-price elasticity and the classification of firms in particular markets. More specifically, we will use the concept of market power as determined by the degree of substitutability between products as an important characteristic to distinguish among the different market structures within which we analyze firm behavior.

Economics in the (Old) News

United States v. E. I. du Pont de Nemours & Company[1]

On December 13, 1947, the Department of Justice brought suit against E. I. du Pont de Nemours & Company with the charge it had violated the Sherman Antitrust Act by monopolizing the sale of cellophane. Cellophane is a clear plastic wrap developed by Du Pont in the 1920s. The product was hailed as a major innovation in packaging. It was the only wrap "clear as plate glass, flexible, easily ripped open, [and] moisture proof."[2] By 1949, cigarette manufacturers would use nothing else, and 47 percent of all fresh produce, 35 percent of all meat and poultry, 34 percent of frozen foods, and 27 percent of crackers and biscuits were wrapped in the substance.[3]

There were, nevertheless, a number of other wrapping materials available in the post-World War II period—foil, glassine, paper, and films, such as Saran and polyethylene. Together, these alternative packaging substances were used more than 50 percent of the time by food processors.

The case was finally decided in 1953, six years after the suit was filed. Paul Leaky, Chief Judge of the U.S. District Court for the District of Delaware, wrote that the charge against Du Pont rested on two questions: "(1) does Du Pont possess monopoly powers; and (2) if so, has it achieved such powers by 'monopolizing' within the meaning of the Act."[4] Only if the answer to the first question was yes should the second be answered. The Department of Justice argued that cellophane had no good substitutes, and since Du Pont produced and sold 75 percent of all the cellophane in the United States, it possessed an illegal amount of monopoly power. Du Pont, on the other hand, claimed that all flexible wrapping materials should be included in the market because they were substitutes for cellophane. If the market was defined in this way, the company would have only 14 percent of the market. Judge Leaky based his decision on the cross-price elasticity of cellophane with other packaging materials. He concluded that the "facts demonstrate Du Pont cellophane is sold under such intense competitive conditions, acquisition of market control or monopoly power is a practical impossibility."[5]

The Department of Justice, not satisfied with this decision, appealed the case to the Supreme Court. A decision was reached in 1956 upholding the District Court. A majority of Justices defined the market broadly to include all flexible packaging material. The decisive evidence supporting the court's opinion was cross-price elasticity of demand. In their written opinion:

> If a slight decrease in the price of cellophane causes a considerable number of customers of other flexible wrappings to switch to cellophane, it would be an indication that a high cross-elasticity of demand exists between them; that the products compete in the same market. The court below held that the 'great sensitivity of customers in the flexible packaging markets to price or quality changes' prevented Du Pont from possessing monopoly control over price. . . . We conclude

(continued)

[1]351 U.S. 377 (1956).

[2]G. Stocking and W. Miller, "The Cellophane Case and the New Competition," *American Economic Review* 45, no. 1 (March 1955), p. 52.

[3]Ibid., p. 53.

[4]118 F. Supp. (D. Del. 1953), p. 54.

[5]Ibid., pp. 179–98.

> that cellophane's interchangeability with other materials mentioned suffices to make it a part of this flexible packaging material market.[6]
>
> High cross-price elasticity with several other products implies that there are good substitutes available and that the product in question is not alone in the market.

11.4 Characteristics of Market Structures

As mentioned previously, economists generally analyze firm and market behavior within the theoretical framework of four broad market structures. This section sets forth the important characteristics of the four theoretical market structures. As you will see, there is some overlapping of these market structures. Sometimes particular markets will exhibit characteristics of two structures. In such cases, the only thing we can do is classify a given market within the structure it more closely fits. In later chapters, we will set forth a theory or theories to explain, in general, the behavior of firms and markets within a given market structure, and the social implications of such behavior.

11.4.1 Perfect Competition

Perfect competition is probably the most frequently employed model of market structure. We begin by describing the most important characteristic of perfect competition: A perfectly competitive market is made up of a large number of relatively small firms selling identical products, so that each firm in the market has *zero market power*. That is, every firm takes the price determined in the market as given and is, therefore, a *price taker*.

Under perfect competition, no firm in the market, acting alone, has any effect on product price. The price of the product is determined by supply and demand in the market. Each firm recognizes that its output is indistinguishable from the output of every other firm in the market and that it is such a small producer that no matter how much it produces, the market price will not be affected. The firm therefore knows that it can sell as much as it wishes at the prevailing market price.

It is important to recognize that the assumption of every individual firm having no market power or being a price taker does not mean that all firms acting together do not have an effect on market price. You know from your study of supply and demand that this would not be the case. For example, any *one* firm knows that if it increases output 10 percent, market price would be unaffected; but if every firm increases output 10 percent, the price would certainly fall, because market demand is downsloping. Thus, a firm under perfect competition does not have to choose the price at which it sells; the price is determined in the market. Because each firm takes the price as given, it must only decide how much output to produce.

[6]351 U.S. 378 (1956).

A second characteristic of perfect competition is that it is relatively easy for firms to enter into and exit from the market. This characteristic means that there are no significant barriers to entry or exit. For example, there are no strict government licensing requirements that block new entry to keep firms in the market when they would rather exit.

Furthermore, no new entrant is required to make a huge capital investment, because all firms are relatively small. Nor do new firms have to set up an elaborate marketing system, the absence of which would keep them from selling their output. Also, firms that desire to exit from the industry and perhaps go into another business can do so without bearing a substantial cost. Many exit costs for firms in other types of markets are borne in the form of large sunk costs. Sunk costs are expenses that cannot be recovered once paid. Costs are not a barrier to entry or exit in perfect competition.

Markets that most closely fit the characteristics of perfect competition are agricultural markets. For example, a great many wheat farms sell their wheat in the wheat market, where the market price is determined by world supply and demand. Each firm produces only a tiny part of the total wheat supply. The wheat of a particular grade sold by one farm cannot be distinguished from the wheat of the same grade sold by any other farm. Nearly all food commodities are sold by a large number of growers in a national or international market. Thus the theory of perfect competition and the perfectly competitive market structure can explain rather well the behavior and performance of an important segment of the economy, the agricultural sector.

The theory of perfectly competitive firms and markets is important for two additional reasons. First, as you will see, perfect competition has several desirable features for consumers and for resource allocation in the economy. Economists therefore compare the performance of firms and markets in other market structures with those in perfect competition to see how these other structures measure up. They use perfect competition as a benchmark to judge the results of other firms and industries.

Second, the theory of perfect competition is the most simple theory of the firm and industry, yet it is also the most analytically rigorous. Therefore, economists sometimes use the theory of perfect competition to explain and predict the behavior of firms and industries that do not meet all of the requirements of perfect competition but come close.

As a passing note, we should mention that economists sometimes speak of *perfectly competitive industries,* which are related but not identical to perfectly competitive markets. A perfectly competitive industry consists of all the firms producing and selling in perfectly competitive markets, even though the firms may not be in the same competitive markets. Firms could be selling, for instance, in different geographical markets that are individually perfectly competitive. Thus we might speak of the U.S. beef industry, which is the collection of U.S. firms selling beef. The market these firms sell in may be national or more regional. Or we might speak of the world beef industry, which is the collection of all firms producing and selling beef in the world. In this text, we will sometimes define all firms selling in a perfectly competitive market as the industry. But keep in mind that industry is a description of what producers do, and does not necessarily refer to producers that are in the same market.

11.4.2 Monopoly

Perfectly competitive firms have the least market power (zero) of all firms in any market structure. Monopoly is the market structure in which firms have the most market power. Monopoly exists when only a single firm produces and sells a well-defined good or service for which there are no good substitutes.

Definition

> A monopoly market is a market in which one firm, called a monopoly or monopolist, is the only supplier of the good or service sold in that market. There are no good substitutes for the good or service.

The most important characteristic of monopolies is that they have considerable market power. The market demand for the product is the same demand facing the monopoly. Therefore, a monopolist is a price searcher. It has control over the price charged to buyers. The firm must choose both the output to produce and the price to charge for its product.

The reason that there is only one firm selling in a monopoly market is that entry by new firms into the market is difficult, if not impossible. Thus, a second characteristic of monopoly markets is the existence of substantial barriers to the entry of new firms into the market.

Barriers to the entry of new firms into the market can take several forms. Some have already been mentioned. One important type of barrier to entry for monopoly comes about when the long-run average cost of the monopoly continues to decline as more output is produced. In this case, a firm experiences economies of scale. Any new firm that attempts to enter into competition would have a higher average cost at lower levels of output. The monopoly could set a lower price—perhaps at its average cost—and drive the new firm out. If the new entrant comes in at the same size as the monopoly in order to produce at the same average cost, the market demand may not be large enough to support both firms, and one firm would be forced to leave. Such cases are often called *natural monopoly*.

The conditions for natural monopoly are shown in Figure 11–1. The demand curve is the market demand for a product. The long-run average cost curve for any firm that produces the product is *LRAC*, which indicates economies of scale over the entire range of demand. Suppose that a monopolist in the market chooses to produce and sell Q_M units of output and, from the demand curve, chooses a price of P. Because, from its *LRAC*, the average cost of producing Q_M is C_M, the price charged covers the monopoly's cost and the firm makes a profit. If a new firm chooses to enter the market at a smaller size, say producing output Q_E, its average cost would be C_E, which is much higher than P. Thus, the smaller firm could not cover its cost of production and would make a loss. The monopoly would drive out any small entrants. If a new firm chooses to enter at a large size, say producing Q_M, the market demand would not be sufficient to support both firms, and one firm

Figure 11–1   A Natural Monopoly

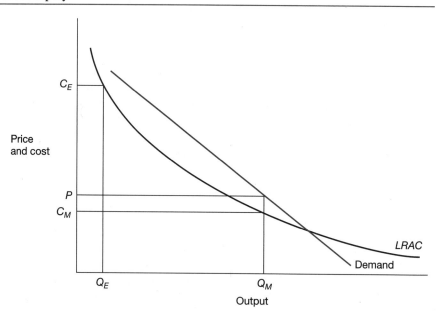

would have to exit. In such cases, the market can only support one firm. Hence monopoly must result because of demand and cost conditions.

Government licensing or franchising restrictions act as other barriers to the entry of new firms into a monopoly market. In such cases, a local or state government permits only one firm to supply a market. One reason given for government grants of monopoly is that these markets would be natural monopolies anyway. By licensing the monopoly and preventing entry, the government can retain some control over the monopoly, particularly over its pricing policies. In other cases, there is not such a clear reason for government licensing. We will examine such cases after we develop the theory of monopoly.

Another type of barrier to the entry of new firms into a monopoly market exists when a monopoly owns most or all of the raw material necessary to produce the product. No firm can enter into competition unless it is able to attain an alternative source of raw material or convince the monopoly to make some of the raw material available. Finally, entry into a monopoly market may be prevented during a period of time in which a monopolist holds a patent on the product or on the production process. This patent, issued by the federal government, gives the firm holding the patent the exclusive right to produce the product unless it chooses to sell this right to other firms. However, in many cases, patents are not a substantial barrier to entry because other firms can produce a product that is similar but not an exact duplicate.

Local or regional public utilities are the most important examples of monopoly today in the United States. In practically all such cases, the government either licenses and regulates the firm or owns the firm outright. Examples are electric companies, gas companies, some cable TV companies, and regional telephone companies. Until several years ago, AT&T had a licensed monopoly for long-distance telephone service. The U.S. Postal Service continues to have a monopoly in mail that is not labeled urgent.

Monopoly manufacturers are rare today. At one time, the Aluminum Company of America (Alcoa) had a monopoly in aluminum because it owned practically all of the known deposits of bauxite, a necessary ingredient in aluminum. The International Nickel Company (Inco), a Canadian firm, was a monopolist in the production of nickel for the same reason. In some Western industrial nations, air and rail transportation and TV broadcasting are government-owned or government-licensed monopolies.

Finally, just because a monopoly is the only firm in the market and faces no good substitutes for its product, we do not want to give you the impression that there are no substitutes at all for a monopolist's product. In general, there are. For example, natural gas is a substitute for electricity, mail is a substitute for the telephone, and vice versa. Satellite dishes are a substitute for cable TV. Even a monopoly bank or grocery store in a small town faces some competition from banks and stores in neighboring cities. National newspapers, such as *The Wall Street Journal* or *U.S.A. Today,* magazines, and television are substitutes for monopoly newspapers in large or small cities. The degree of substitutability and the amount of market power are, as noted previously, measured by cross-price elasticities.

The theory of monopoly is important for three reasons. First, it gives an insight into the way firms in an important segment of the economy, particularly public utilities, determine their price and output. Second, similar to perfect competition, monopoly, which is at the other end of the range of firms possessing market power, serves as another benchmark of comparison. Economists frequently compare theoretically the performance of perfect competition and monopoly because these market structures are the most clearly defined and distinguishable from each other.

Third, the theory of monopoly gives an insight into or first approximation of the way all firms with market power behave, or would like to behave. As you will soon see, firms in the other two market structures to be discussed do have some, though in some cases not much, control over their price and, therefore, have some market power. In these cases, the theory of monopoly provides a framework or initial approach to analyzing the way these firms make decisions about price and output. To understand these firm's decisions, it is necessary to understand the theory of monopoly.

11.1 Applying the Theory

The U.S. National Park Service grants an exclusive franchise to a seller of concessions and souvenirs within the boundaries of a national park. Companies bid for the rights to operate restaurants and shops in the park. The winning bidder pays a share of its profits to the Park Service each year. Is the franchise license a barrier to entry? Does the monopoly earn high profits?

11.4.3   Monopolistic Competition

A monopolistically competitive market structure, as the name implies, has characteristics of both perfect competition and monopoly. Like perfect competition, a monopolistically competitive market is made up of a large number of small firms, relative to the total market. Unlike perfect competition, each firm produces and sells a product that is similar to but somewhat different from the product sold by every other firm in the market. The difference may be in the actual product, the firm's location, the services provided by the firms, or the firm's advertising. Thus, consumers of the product of any firm in the market can distinguish that product from the product of any other firm. Because the products are differentiated and not homogeneous, each firm has some control over its price, although in many cases not much.

Since the product of every firm is similar to those of other firms in a monopolistically competitive market, the cross-price elasticity of demand between the product of a firm and the products of other firms is positive and relatively large. This is to say that the products of other firms are good substitutes for the product of any one firm. Thus each firm has some market power, but not a lot, and certainly not nearly as much as a monopoly possesses.

Another characteristic of monopolistic competition is that it is relatively easy for new firms to enter into and exit from a monopolistically competitive market. Typically, a new firm does not have to invest in a huge amount of capital to enter the market. Economies of scale over a large range of market demand do not exist. Also, because the capital needed to enter is not large, firms can easily leave a market and go into another business. This characteristic of easy entry and exit in monopolistic competition is extremely important in the development of the theory.

Important examples of monopolistic competition are retail and wholesale trade, particularly in relatively large cities, some banking, and small manufacturing. As an example of monopolistic competition consider the gasoline stations in a medium-sized or large city. Each station is fairly similar to every other station and sells similar goods and services. Nonetheless, there are differences in the stations. One station may sell Exxon, another Chevron, and another Texaco gasoline and products. Stations are located at different places. Gasoline from a station on the east side of a city is not a perfect, or even a particularly good, substitute for gasoline from a west-side station for a person who lives and works in the west side. But stations across the street from one another are good substitutes. Stations can also differ in the type of service they offer and the friendliness of employees.

Because of these differences, each station has some control over its price, as evidenced by small price differences for gasoline in most cities. A station could raise its price a penny or two a gallon and lose some but not all of its customers. Or a station could drop its price a few cents and gain some customers but not all the customers in the city. Thus, each station has a small amount of market power.

When the theory of monopolistic competition was developed in the 1930s, many economists predicted that this theory would prove extremely useful in analyzing firm behavior, because, they said, monopolistic competition is so much more realistic than perfect competition or even monopoly. This did not prove to be the case, however. Economists still use perfect competition and monopoly much more frequently as tools of analysis. As you will see when we set forth the theory of monopolistic competition, that theory does not differ much from monopoly, in the short run, or from perfect competition, in the long run. It therefore provides little additional insight into the way firms make decisions.

11.4.4   Oligopoly

An oligopoly market consists of two or more firms. Frequently, although not always, these firms are large, relative to the total market. The principal characteristic of oligopoly, and, as you will see, what makes oligopoly so interesting yet so difficult to analyze within a single theory, is the *interdependence among firms* selling in the market.

Interdependence among firms means that each firm knows that any change it makes in its price, output, advertising, marketing strategy, or other business activities will affect the profits of the other firms in the market. Each firm also knows that other firms will respond in some way or another to the change. However, the firm that is considering making the change does not know how its rivals will respond, but it does know their responses will in turn affect its own sales and profit so that it too may have to respond in a later period. Therefore, when making any change, a firm must consider the effect on its rivals and how these rivals will react.

Consider the interdependence between sellers in the automobile market, which is an oligopoly. If Ford decreases the price on most of its models by several hundred dollars, this will have a tremendous effect on the sales of GM, Toyota, and other car manufacturers. Ford does not know how these other firms will respond, but it must certainly take into account that they will respond. Ford must also consider how it will react to their responses.

As another example of the problem of interdependence, suppose Pepsi is deciding to expand its advertising campaign by adding a couple more rock stars, perhaps Madonna and Bon Jovi, to endorse Pepsi on TV. Pepsi does not know how Coke will respond. Will Coke continue advertising as before? Or will Coke call Pepsi's Madonna and Bon Jovi with Paula Abdul and George Michael and raise the ante with The New Kids on the Block? If so, Pepsi will have to respond, perhaps by seeing if it can find Elvis to counter The New Kids. These people cost a lot of money in an ad campaign, so the decision is not easy to make. Other oligopolists face the same type of interdependence problem, and they compete in many different ways.

If the above soft-drink example sounds like the description of a poker game, it is. The oligopoly problem is similar to games of chance such as poker, chess, or bridge, in which the players must consider their opponents' responses to a move or play and how these responses will affect their own patterns of play. Oligopoly has so many characteristics of such games that an important body of theory used to analyze oligopoly behavior is called *game theory*. The rival firms are characterized as players in a game in which each firm tries to predict what its rival will do, then acts on that prediction. As you will see, however, game theory is one of several tools used to describe oligopoly behavior. Interdependence has led economists to offer many different types of models of oligopoly behavior; no single theory of oligopoly exists.

Oligopoly markets can be characterized by either homogeneous products or differentiated products. In the above examples of automobile firms and soft-drink firms, the oligopolists sell a differentiated product. Automobiles are differentiated by their designs. Coke and Pepsi are similar, but consumers can distinguish between them, if not in a blind taste test at least by the differences in the bottle or can. Aluminum manufacturers are in an oligopoly market. The three large manufacturers sell in a homogeneous product market. Aluminum of a particular type from one manufacturer is the same as aluminum of the same type from another.

Oligopolists have market power. Each firm has some control over its price. In the case of oligopoly markets in which firms sell differentiated products, the cross-price elasticity is positive and relatively high. For firms in markets with a homogeneous product, the cross-price elasticity is extremely high. In such markets, however, firms are typically large relative to the total size of the market; thus, the sales of any single firm have an effect on the price and sales of the other firms. In oligopoly markets, each firm selects its own price and output, but, as you will see later in the text, this is not an easy task because of the interdependence among firms.

Entry into an oligopoly market is not easy because of barriers to the entry of new firms. These barriers are similar to, but not quite as restrictive as, the barriers discussed in the case of monopoly, when only one firm sells in the market. Because most oligopolies have economies of scale over a broad range of output, new entrants must be relatively large and must compete with large established firms. New firms must develop a marketing and service system, frequently nationwide, in order to compete. Because firms must be large in order to compete, the total market for the product generally can only support a relatively small number of firms. It is therefore difficult, but by no means impossible, for new firms to enter into competition with established firms in an oligopoly. Because of the large investment needed to enter an oligopoly market, exit from such markets can also be difficult and expensive.

We should note that the lines defining oligopoly are not as clear as the lines defining the other market structures. Some markets that have a large number of sellers at times exhibit interdependence among firms—the principal characteristic of oligopoly. For example, the sale of pizza in restaurants in most cities generally would be considered monopolistic competition. There are enough outlets for pizza that the decisions of one seller would have little effect on other firms. But, there can be exceptions. If Joe's Pizza begins to give away free Coke with its pizzas, Jane's Pizza, which is across the street, may respond by giving away free Pepsi. Or a price war may start in a neighborhood and spread through the city. Recognized dependency can exist even when there are numerous firms in the market. In some markets, dependency is fostered by trade organizations. These organizations keep sellers informed of industry events. Some organizations are local, for example, the real estate board for real estate agents. Some are national, like the American Petroleum Institute.

In some markets, firms that would otherwise be oligopolies get together, make decisions jointly, and act like a monopoly. This is collusion. Most collusive activities are illegal, but some joint ventures are allowed in the United States when capital investment is unusually large or American companies are attempting to enter international markets. As you will see later in the text, cooperative behavior is an important part of the analysis of oligopoly.

11.2 *Applying the Theory*

The Trans Alaskan Pipeline System (TAPS) was built through the cooperative efforts of eight oil companies. Investment dollars were pooled and construction designs were all agreed upon by the companies. All eight companies control the line, subject to state and federal regulation. Regulators approve shipping prices and, in general, access by nonowners cannot be denied. Is this oligopoly different from monopoly? In this example what are the advantages and disadvantages of such cooperation?

In general, what most people mean when they think of big business in the United States, Canada, Western Europe, and Japan is oligopoly. Most large manufacturers in the United States are oligopolistic. The automobile, breakfast cereal, steel, oil refining, cigarette, and chemical industries are examples of oligopoly. However, even though big business typically implies oligopoly, oligopolies can be relatively small. The few banks in a medium-size city are oligopolists, as would be the case for two independent newspapers in a city or the network TV stations. In all such cases there is a great deal of interdependence among firms, the most important characteristic of oligopoly.

---

*Economics in
the News*

Coke Takes Big Bite Out of Pepsi's Sales

The soft-drink market is a major example of interdependence among large oligopolistic firms. As you probably know, Coke and Pepsi dominate this market. These two firms are keenly aware of each other's marketing strategies, and the rivalry is frequently intense and personal.

In one Pepsi TV ad someone jokingly gives the great singer Ray Charles, who is widely known as being blind, a Diet Coke rather than a Diet Pepsi. Mr. Charles, after just one swallow, recognizes the switch and demands a Pepsi, which obviously, according to the ad, tastes much better. During the 1991 Super Bowl, Pepsi canceled some of its new elaborate commercials because of the war in the Persian Gulf. Coke responded by running extremely low-key ads, stating that it was not appropriate to run its usual light-hearted commercials two weeks after fighting had begun. Instead, Coke announced that it was donating $1 million to the USO. (Newspaper stories the next day actually reported this.)

On May 2, 1990, *The Wall Street Journal*, in "Burger King, in Big Blow to Pepsi, Is Switching to Coke," p. B1, reported that Burger King, the nation's second largest fast-food chain and Pepsi's biggest fountain customer, was changing to Coke in its restaurants. This switch represented a big loss to Pepsi, at least $270 million annually *The Journal* noted, and a big gain to Coca-Cola, which already had the business of McDonald's, the nation's largest fast-food chain.

(continued)

The Journal reported that Coke had used extremely direct attacks on Pepsi to obtain Burger King's business. Pepsi's next three largest fountain customers, Taco Bell, Pizza Hut, and Kentucky Fried Chicken, are chains owned by PepsiCo Inc., Pepsi's parent company. Coke's argument was that fast-food chains such as Burger King shouldn't use Pepsi because that use, in effect, supports a competitor. A Coke sales brochure for restaurant managers asked, "Is your soft-drink supplier satisfying your customers' hunger instead of their thirst?" Burger King said that Pepsi's ownership of rival chains was only one factor in its decision. This is probably true, because Burger King had approached both soft-drink companies looking for a better deal, and both firms submitted proposals.

No matter what the reason, Pepsi's share of the soft-drink fountain market fell from 26 percent to about 21 percent, while Coke's share rose from 60 percent to 65 percent. This competitive activity is a good example of the effects of interdependence among large oligopolies and how one firm's actions can have serious repercussions for its rivals.

11.4.5 Summary of Market Structures

The range of market power in the four market structures is shown in Figure 11–2. This figure summarizes most of the discussion in this section. Perfect competition, on the left, is characterized by the least market power possessed by its firms—zero. Monopoly, on the right, has the most market power. On the scale of market power, monopolistic competition is much closer to perfect competition than to monopoly. Because oligopolistic industries differ so much among themselves, this market structure covers a broad range of market power, from monopolistic competition practically to monopoly. In some oligopolies, firms are extremely competitive and, in others, firms act almost like monopolists. As we develop the theory of the firm, we will frequently discuss the implications of different degrees of market power for the firms themselves and for consumers.

11.5 The Assumption of Profit Maximization

A single thread that runs through the theories used to analyze firms in all of the market structures is the assumption that the goal of the firm is to maximize its profit. That is, other things remaining the same, firm owners prefer more profit to less, profit being the difference between total revenue and total cost. This does not mean that business people seek no other goals. However, an entrepreneur who ignores profits would be rather unusual. In any case, a firm generally cannot remain in business very long unless profits are earned. There have been several criticisms of the profit-maximizing assumption, but this assumption provides a general theory of firms, markets, and resource allocation that is successful in both explaining and predicting firm behavior. In short, the profit-maximization assumption is used first, because it works well and second, because it describes, to a large extent, the way firms actually behave.

The basic principles of profit maximization are straightforward and follow directly from the discussion of unconstrained maximization in Chapter 4. The firm will increase any activity so long as the additional revenue from the increase exceeds

Figure 11–2   Characteristics of Market Structures according to Amount of Market Power

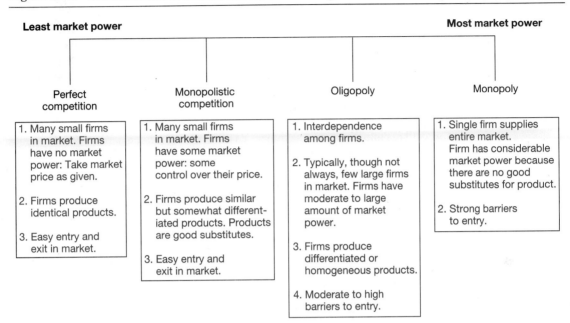

Least market power   **Most market power**

Perfect competition	Monopolistic competition	Oligopoly	Monopoly
1. Many small firms in market. Firms have no market power: Take market price as given. 2. Firms produce identical products. 3. Easy entry and exit in market.	1. Many small firms in market. Firms have some market power: some control over their price. 2. Firms produce similar but somewhat differentiated products. Products are good substitutes. 3. Easy entry and exit in market.	1. Interdependence among firms. 2. Typically, though not always, few large firms in market. Firms have moderate to large amount of market power. 3. Firms produce differentiated or homogeneous products. 4. Moderate to high barriers to entry.	1. Single firm supplies entire market. Firm has considerable market power because there are no good substitutes for product. 2. Strong barriers to entry.

the additional cost of the increase. The firm will contract the activity if the additional revenue is less than the additional cost. In other words, the firm sets marginal benefits equal to marginal cost.

A firm's profit is the difference between the total revenue it receives from selling its product and the total cost of producing and selling the product. In economics, profit means the return over *all* costs, which, as we pointed out in Chapter 10, include both explicit costs, the direct payments to the resources the firm hires, and implicit costs, the opportunity costs of using resources for which no direct payment is made. As we mentioned, implicit costs include a normal return or normal profit. Any return over and above the normal profit is called *economic profit,* or sometimes pure profit. This differs from accounting profit, which is the firm's revenue minus its accounting cost (explicit cost).

We should mention that the assumption that firms try to maximize profits does not mean economists believe that the owners of real firms do not have goals other than making the most possible profits. Some owners may not want to work hard enough to maximize profits. Others may want more security or to provide jobs for friends or relatives. Still others may want to serve their community or simply may enjoy owning their own business. Nevertheless, all owners want some profits, and it would be a peculiar owner who, other things being equal, does not prefer more profit to less. The theory of the firm is designed to explain firm behavior in general, not the behavior of specific firms. Profit maximization is the most general assumption that can be made about the motivation of firm owners in general. This assumption has provided the best basis for prediction and explanation of firm behavior that economists have yet devised. Until a more fruitful assumption can be thought of, economists will continue to assume that firms try to maximize their profits.

The assumption of profit maximization, however, does not mean that firms try to maximize their profit during every hour, or every day, or even every month. Sometimes short-term gains must be sacrificed for longer-term gains. At the extreme, a firm could sell shoddy merchandise or even cheat its customers for a short period of time and increase its profit during that time. However, when customers learn about this behavior, they stop buying its product and the firm goes broke. A firm typically has the incentive to maximize its profits over a long period. Therefore, we will assume that a firm maximizes its profit during a given period without putting a strict time dimension on the length of that period.

Economics in the News

Large Corporations Do the Right Thing

Newsweek, in the article "Doing the Right Thing," January 7, 1991, pp. 42–43, reported that many large business firms appear to have become much more socially conscious. The article gave several examples. The huge advertising agency J. Walter Thompson dropped its lavish employee Christmas parties at plush nightclubs such as New York's Palladin. In 1990, employees worked in soup kitchens, renovated low-income housing, and wrapped presents for hospital patients. The Sharper Image, a seller of $5,000 tanning beds and other Yuppie playthings, was selling *The Recycler's Handbook* and touting its use of biodegradable packing material. In its Ivory soap commercials, which previously emphasized cleaning properties, Procter & Gamble began to feature "heart-rending scenes of a young gymnast with Down's syndrome training for the Special Olympics." AT&T received a Corporate Conscience Award in 1990 for "its program to stop using ozone-depleting chlorofluorocarbons." U.S. West received the same award for "its employee support groups for gays, minorities, and veterans." *Newsweek* stressed that many other corporations were exhibiting "socially conscious" behavior.

Several questions arise from the discussion in this article and similar articles elsewhere. First, why did corporations suddenly decide that "greed is bad" and become good corporate citizens? Because a sudden miraculous conversion seems a bit out of the question, the answer would appear to lie elsewhere. Firm managers must have begun to think that "doing good" would be good for business. As *Newsweek* points out, studies have shown that the public is paying more attention to corporate behavior. A Roper poll found that 52 percent of a sample of U.S. consumers said they would pay 10 percent more for a so-called socially responsible product and 67 percent said they were concerned about a company's social performance when they shop. *Newsweek* cited the complaints from consumers that forced McDonald's to switch from polystyrene to paper containers. It appears that many corporations were using their social consciousness, or in some cases talking about their social consciousness, as a form of advertising to gain sales or to be able to charge more for their product. Doing good was seen, but not admitted, as a way to maximize profits.

If social responsibility or its appearance is a method of advertising, what types of firms would be most likely to use this approach? Perfectly competitive firms certainly

(continued)

would not, because the product of each firm is identical to that of every other firm in the market. Consumers would not know if they were buying from a socially responsible firm or not. A monopoly, facing no good substitutes, would probably not use this approach either, unless the monopoly was government regulated and thought that doing good would be pleasing to the regulators.

The firms most likely to use socially responsible behavior as a marketing device would be oligopolists who sell a differentiated product to consumers rather than to other firms that use the product in their own production. Other firms that purchase the product would probably be more influenced by the price and quality of the product rather than by other attributes of the product or the firm. Compare the previous references to companies that are "responsible" to Perdue Farms, USX, and Exxon, three companies that were given bad grades by a self-appointed "consumer watchdog group."

A third relevant question is why did firms believe that consumers would be swayed in their purchasing behavior by companies that did supposedly good things in the 1990s but not in the 1980s? Possibly, firms thought (possibly correctly) that consumers were being influenced by the media attention to the environment and other social issues. An additional, or possibly alternative, explanation may be the long, sustained period of economic growth in the U.S. economy. If socially responsible activities are a normal good, which seems likely, with a large income elasticity of demand, as people become better off they demand more of such activities and are willing to pay for them in the form of higher prices. Some companies recognize this and provide more of these activities.

At least one corporate observer, a professor of organizational behavior, did not feel that the social responsibility movement would necessarily pay off for corporate America, particularly for those companies whose "words speak louder than their actions." This professor also thought that "even the most socially conscious companies may not be able to offset the effects of recession. I don't know that being socially responsible gives you a leg up in hard times." This statement would be consistent with the hypothesis of a high income elasticity for corporate activities that are thought to be socially responsible. As income declines in a recession, people would demand less of these activities, and firms would eventually supply less.

We might note in closing that activities such as those mentioned here are not inconsistent with profit-maximizing behavior. These activities may well be undertaken by firms, particularly oligopolies, as a marketing tactic to gain sales from competitors in order to earn more profit, particularly in the long run.

11.6 Summary

This chapter is designed to give you a brief introduction to the theory of the firm and market structures. Goods and services are produced by firms rather than by individual households because this is generally the least costly, most-efficient method. Production by firms drives out other methods of production for most goods and services.

The analysis of firm behavior is carried out within the framework of four types of market structures: perfect competition, monopoly, monopolistic competition, and oligopoly. These market structures are defined by the number of firms in the market, how much market power firms have, whether the products are homogeneous or differentiated, how easy or difficult it is for firms to enter into or exit from the market, and the amount of interdependence among firms in the market. The one assumption that carries across all market structures is that firms try to maximize their profits.

It is frequently difficult to determine if two sellers are in the same market. Products are in a market if they are perceived by buyers to be good substitutes. The perceptions of consumers is the important determinant. Substitutability is often measured by cross-price elasticity. The term E_{xy} measures the percent change in sales of good X from a percentage change in the price of good Y. If E_{xy} is positive and large, the two products are close substitutes and, therefore, are defined to be in the same market.

Answers to *Applying the Theory*

11.1 The franchise license can be regarded as a significant barrier to entry *inside* the park. No other seller has a license; therefore, no other seller can operate inside the park. This does not necessarily mean that the seller inside the park has a great deal of market power. Other sellers can operate just outside park boundaries, and these sellers may be close substitutes. If there is active bidding for the franchise rights, large profits would not be expected. But because of other barriers, for example, satisfying strict capital and environmental restrictions, there may not be many firms bidding on franchise rights.

11.2 This type of legal cooperation between oligopolists is literally no different than monopoly. In this case, it was difficult for the firms to individually secure the funds for building the pipeline. Financing was much easier as a combined effort. Another advantage of cooperating to build one line is that there was an environmental impact from just one line rather than several. The major disadvantage is that there is little or no price competition among the operators. They charge the same rates subject to federal regulation.

Technical Problems

1. Would a cross-price elasticity of demand of 1.5 for the product of a firm and the products of its closest competitors indicate more or less market power for that firm than a cross-price elasticity of .6? Explain.
2. Which cross-price elasticity of demand in question 1 would indicate the higher probability that the firms are selling in the same market? Explain.
3. Explain precisely what a cross-price elasticity of demand of 1.5 means. A cross-price elasticity of demand of .6. A cross-price elasticity of demand of -2. A cross-price elasticity of demand of zero.
4. Answer true or false and explain your answer.
   a. A monopolist can raise its price without losing any sales.
   b. A perfectly competitive firm has no market power.
   c. Since each firm in a perfectly competitive market can sell all it wants at the prevailing market price, the demand for the product in the market is not negatively sloped.
   d. Oligopolists always have positive but very low cross-price elasticities of demand with other products selling in their market.

5. Within what market structure would the following firms probably be classified? Explain.
   a. NBC, CBS, and ABC.
   b. Shoe stores in a city.
   c. Miller and Anheuser-Busch.
   d. Large cattle ranches in Texas.
   e. The local cable TV company.
   f. Federal Express.
   g. The local electric company.
   h. Chase-Manhattan Bank.
6. Answer true or false and explain.
   a. If a firm takes in more than it pays out, it makes a profit.
   b. To make a profit, a firm must receive revenue greater than all of its opportunity costs.
   c. Firms always attempt to earn the maximum possible profit every day.
7. Answer true or false and explain your answer.
   a. People generally buy goods and services from firms because such goods and services are less expensive than if they were produced individually.
   b. Because goods and services are less expensive when produced by firms, it is foolish for people to produce some of the goods and services they consume.
8. Which of the following firms would be least or most likely to exhibit some "socially conscious" behavior? Explain.
   a. Farms, because farmers love the land.
   b. Aluminum producers, because they make an ecologically desirable product.
   c. Defense contractors, because they sell to the government.
   d. Large oil companies, because they worry about the public interest.
   e. Banks, because of the bad publicity over recent banking scandals.
   f. Automobile manufacturers, because they are naturally "socially conscious."

Analytical Problems

1. When discussing the reasons for the existence and importance of firms in the economy, we argued that production in firms can be carried out at a lower cost than production by individual households. However, we observe that some people do build their own houses, purchasing the materials and tools from firms but doing their own labor; others are mechanics for their own vehicles; and so forth. Many of these do-it-yourselfers say that they save money this way.
   a. In what sense might building your own home save money?
   b. In what sense might it be much more costly to build your own home (what is the opportunity cost)?
   c. In the context of utility theory, set forth above, why might it be rational for some people to build their own homes, even though it is truly more costly than hiring a professional contractor?
2. Explain why perfectly competitive firms would not be motivated to advertise, but many monopolistic competitors and oligopolists would be so motivated.
3. McDonald's, Burger King, and Wendy's are in every sense oligopolists in the national market. However, the individual outlets of McDonald's, Burger King, and Wendy's would be considered monopolistic competitors in most large city markets. Explain.

4. Suppose a firm selling in a perfectly competitive market chooses not to try to maximize profit, perhaps by producing at a higher cost than other firms selling in the market, because of a desire to voluntarily reduce pollution or to hire needy but less-productive workers. What would probably happen to this firm in the long run? Explain. (This question anticipates some of the theory to be set forth in Chapter 13.)

5. Suppose the firm in question 4 is a monopolist. How might the consequences for this firm differ from those above? Explain.

6. What might monopolistically competitive firms try to do to increase their market power—that is, reduce their cross-price elasticity of demand with other firms in the market? Why would such firms want to reduce their cross-price elasticity of demand? If some firms in this market are successful in increasing their market power by doing what you suggested, what would probably happen in the long run, after a relatively long period of time?

7. In what sense is the only department store in a small town a monopoly? In what sense is it not?

8. In what sense is the National Football League a monopoly? Are teams in the National Football League monopolies? In what sense is the National Football League not a monopoly?

9. The characteristics of specific markets can change over time. How has TV broadcasting changed over the past 15 years? What has happened to the market power of TV networks over that time?

10. Market power doesn't always reflect the number of firms in the market. There are thousands of professional singers and singing groups in the United States. Compare the market power of "Sally and the Sopranos" with that of Madonna and the New Kids on the Block.

CHAPTER 12

Theory of the Perfectly Competitive Firm

12.1 Introduction

In this and the following chapter, we will analyze the behavior of perfectly competitive firms and markets, the first of the four market structures discussed in Chapter 11. Recall from that chapter the fundamental characteristics of perfect competition:

1. Each firm selling in the market is small relative to the total market, and each firm produces a product identical to that produced by every other firm in the market. Therefore, every firm can sell all the output it wishes at the going market price, determined in the market by supply and demand. That is, each firm has zero market power and is called a price taker.

2. New firms can easily enter the market, and established firms can easily exit. That is, there are no significant barriers to entry or exit.

In our analysis of perfect competition, we will make the additional assumption that each firm has complete knowledge about the product it produces and the market in which it sells. Each firm knows the least-cost method of production, the market price of the product, the prices of the inputs used to produce the product, and the most advanced technology. Furthermore, while developing the theory of perfect competition, we will refer to the group of all firms selling in the market as a *perfectly competitive industry*. The use of the term *industry* is reasonable in this context because all firms produce identical or homogeneous products and because the term is pervasive in the literature.

As we noted in Chapter 11, the characteristics of perfect competition describe many important markets reasonably well—in particular, most agricultural markets. The theory of perfect competition is also important for two additional reasons: First, economists use this theory to compare the performance of markets in other market structures with that of perfectly competitive markets, which, as you will see, have several desirable features, especially for consumers. Second, economists at times use the theory of perfect competition to analyze the behavior of firms and markets that do not meet all the exacting standards of the theory. In fact, the theory of perfect competition is so simple, but so rigorous, and yields such good predictions that economists probably use this theory more often than any other in their analysis. Because the theory of perfect competition is used so much, we devote two chapters to its development: This chapter sets forth the theory of the perfectly competitive *firm*. Chapter 13 explores the theory of the perfectly competitive industry.

In Chapter 11, we stressed that firms attempt to maximize their profit, or revenue minus costs. In order to maximize its profit, a perfectly competitive firm, once it knows its revenue and cost conditions, has only two decisions to make: (1) whether or not to produce and (2) if it does produce, how much should it produce. Because it has no market power, the firm makes no pricing decision. Prices are determined by supply and demand at the market level. And because all products in the markets are homogeneous, firms do not advertise; such strategies would be useless. As you will see, the firm's profit-maximizing decision is a straightforward application of the theory of unconstrained maximization, set forth in Chapter 4.

As you learn about the theory of perfect competition, you may wonder from time to time how descriptive the theory is of the behavior of real firms and industries. Recall from Chapter 1 that generality can be achieved only by means of abstraction. No theory can be perfectly descriptive of real-world phenomena. The more accurately a theory describes one specific real-world case, the less accurately it describes all others. In any area of thought, a theoretician does not select assumptions on the basis of their presumed correspondence to reality. For example, physicists often assume away friction, even though a frictionless world is incomprehensible; and chemists analyze, as a matter of course, the chemical reactions between two compounds without considering the role of impurities—though impurities are always present. The conclusions of theory, not the assumptions, are tested against reality. This leads to a second point of great, if somewhat pragmatic, importance. The conclusions derived from the model of perfect competition have permitted accurate explanation and prediction of real-world phenomena. That is, perfect competition frequently works as a theoretical model of economic processes, even though it does not accurately describe any specific firm or industry.

Economics in the News

Financial Markets Are (Super) Competitive Markets

Every evening TV news broadcasts include a summary of the behavior of major financial markets during the day. The early morning news broadcasts typically feature a report on overseas financial markets prior to the opening of U.S. markets. Radio news throughout the day presents market reports from around the world. Newspapers generally devote several pages to the financial news.

(continued)

Judging by the amount of news devoted to their coverage, financial markets—stock markets, markets for foreign exchange, commodities markets, bond markets, and so on—are possibly the most important markets in the world. Of all the markets we are familiar with, none is more competitive than the financial markets. Consider the following characteristics of financial markets.

Homogeneous Products. Assets of like grade that are traded on financial markets are as homogeneous as products can be. A share of GM, IBM, or Exxon stock sold by one brokerage house is identical to that sold by any other. The same is true for bonds, foreign currency, commodities, and so forth.

Individual Traders Are Small Relative to the Market. Although one trader may hold a large percentage of the shares of a particular firm, the holdings of an individual trader relative to the total market are quite small. When one large stockholder held only two percent of GM stock, that was considered a relatively large holding. Traders in financial markets take the market price, as determined by supply and demand, as given and make their decisions based on these prices. Individual traders do not affect market prices.

Unrestricted Entry and Exit. In financial markets, entry generally occurs on the demand side of the market. The supply of a given stock is essentially fixed, and the demand for the stock determines its price. There are no barriers to entry. It is easy to enter the market and buy or sell financial assets. In fact, in financial markets, you can even sell securities you don't own—sell short—if you believe that the price is too high.

In addition to these characteristics, financial markets have the following special features that preserve the competitive market structure.

A Centralized Marketplace. Although traders need not travel any further than the computers on their desk tops, there is one central market rather than several small markets. Hence, every buyer has practically immediate access to every seller, and vice versa.

Widespread Information. There are many well-established, easily accessible institutions for collecting and distributing information about financial markets: *The Wall Street Journal*, the S&P Manuals, Moody's Bond Rating Service, Value Line, the Dow Jones Tape, CNBC/FNN, and so on. Indeed, financial markets come as close to perfect knowledge as markets are able to get.

No Constraints on the Price Levels. If participants in financial markets determine that the price is too high or too low, it will adjust immediately, and traders will be instantly aware of what has happened. There are no long-term contracts that tend to constrain price adjustments.

When you hear or read financial news reports, be aware that the markets being discussed are about as competitive as markets are capable of being.

12.2 Demand Facing a Perfectly Competitive Firm

From the theory of consumer behavior, a demand schedule or demand curve is a list of prices and quantities that a consumer, or group of consumers, would purchase at each price on the list per period of time. Demand curves for a product are downward sloping. A perfectly competitive firm sees the demand for its own output—though not for the output produced by the entire industry—in a much different way.

Figure 12–1   Derivation of Demand Facing a Perfectly Competitive Firm

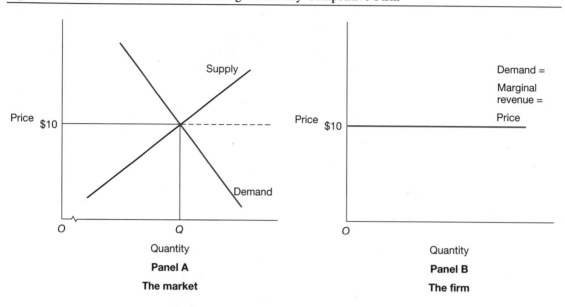

Panel A

The market

Panel B

The firm

Because each firm in the industry is so small relative to the total amount sold in the market, and products are homogeneous, it has no perceptible effect on the market price and is therefore a price taker. Each firm can sell all it wishes at the going market price.

Figure 12–1 illustrates how the demand facing each firm is derived. Panel A shows the equilibrium price and quantity as determined by supply and demand in the market for the product. Equilibrium price is $10 and the equilibrium quantity in the market is Q. As always, the demand curve for the market is downward sloping, and the supply curve is upward sloping.

Because no firm, acting alone, can affect market price, each firm takes as given the $10 market price determined by supply and demand and it can sell all it wants to produce at $10 per unit. If any firm raises its price above $10, it could sell nothing because every other firm is selling at $10. A lower price would result in a needless loss of revenue.

Thus, each firm sees the demand for its product as the horizontal line at $10, as shown in Panel B of the figure. Such horizontal demands are called *perfectly elastic demands*. They are perfectly elastic because, if the firm lowered its price by a very small amount, it could conceivably capture all the sales in the market if it could produce that much. Since the products are identical, every consumer would buy from the lower price seller. This means that the percentage change in quantity demanded from an extremely small percentage change in price would be virtually infinite. Therefore, the elasticity of demand would also be virtually infinite. Hence the name *perfectly elastic demand*.

The horizontal line at $10 in Panel B is also the firm's *marginal revenue curve*. Recall that marginal revenue (*MR*) is defined as the change in total revenue for a one-unit increase in output. For small increases in output, it is the ratio:

$$MR = \frac{\text{Change in total revenue}}{\text{Change in output}} = \frac{\Delta TR}{\Delta Q}.$$

In terms of Figure 12–1, the firm shown in Panel B, and every other firm, has a horizontal marginal revenue curve at $10. Each additional unit sold adds $10 to the firm's revenue, no matter how many units are sold. Hence, marginal revenue is equal to the price at which the competitive firm sells.

We should note that a horizontal demand facing a perfectly competitive firm does not contradict the law of demand—price and quantity demanded vary inversely. The demand for the product in the market is downward sloping, as shown in Panel A, and therefore the law of demand holds, as always, for the product.

The results of this section can be summarized as follows:

Relation

The demand curve facing a firm selling in a perfectly competitive market is a horizontal line at the level of market price. The output decision of an individual firm does not affect market price. In this case, the demand and marginal revenue curves are the same ($D = MR = $ Price); each additional unit of sales adds the market price to the firm's revenue. Demand is said to be perfectly elastic.

12.3   Short-Run Profit Maximization

We turn next to the output decision of a perfectly competitive firm in the short run. Clearly, since a perfectly competitive firm takes the market price as given, it has no pricing decision to make. It therefore chooses the level of output that yields the highest profit attainable at the given price and costs. In the short run, the firm has fixed costs, which are the same at each level of output including zero, and variable costs, which increase as the level of output increases. As noted above, the firm must decide whether to produce or shut down and produce nothing, then, if the firm decides to produce, it must choose the most profitable level of output.

First, we will simply assume that the firm has chosen to produce, then show, using a simple graph, how the most profitable level of output is chosen. Next, we will use a slightly more complex numerical example to illustrate how both decisions are made. Finally, we will generalize the decision-making process graphically.

12.3.1   Choosing the Optimal Level of Output

Suppose a perfectly competitive firm faces a market price of $10 for each unit of its product and has the marginal cost curve shown in Figure 12–2. The horizontal line at $10 is the firm's demand and marginal revenue curve. The marginal cost curve shows how much each additional unit of output adds to the firm's cost. The

Figure 12–2   Profit Maximization

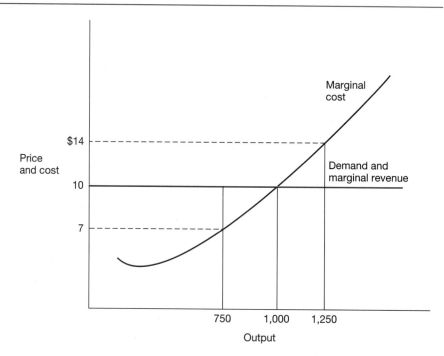

demand or marginal revenue curve shows how much each additional unit of output adds to the firm's revenue.

The firm's profit is its total revenue (how much it takes in) minus its total cost (how much it pays out, explicit and implicit):

$$\text{Profit} = \text{Total revenue} - \text{Total cost.}$$

Clearly, any increase in output that increases revenue more than it increases cost will increase the firm's profit. Or, any decrease in output that reduces cost more than it reduces revenue will also increase profit.

Suppose first that the firm decides to produce 750 units of output and the firm is making some positive level of profit at this output. However, the firm can increase its output by one more unit and make even more profit. Producing and selling the 751st unit would increase its revenue $10 (marginal revenue is $10) and increase cost slightly more than $7 (marginal cost at 750 is $7). Thus, profit will increase by about $3 (= $10 − $7) if the firm produces the 751st unit of output. Profit will also increase by producing each additional unit of output up to 1,000, because for each of these units marginal revenue is greater than marginal cost, so revenue increases more than cost. Because marginal cost is rising and marginal revenue is constant, each additional unit adds more to cost and, hence, less to profit than the preceding unit, but it does add a positive amount, so profit will increase. Therefore, the firm would not produce any level of output below 1,000 because marginal revenue exceeds marginal cost at each of these levels.

Now suppose the firm chooses to produce 1,250 units of output and earns some profit at this output. Since the 1,250th unit of output added $14 to cost (marginal cost at 1,250) and only $10 to revenue, it could decrease its output by one unit, and cost would decrease $14 while revenue decreases by only $10. Therefore, not producing and selling the 1,250th unit of output would increase the firm's profit by $4 (the $14 reduction in cost less the $10 reduction in revenue). And, for each one-unit reduction in output from 1,250 down to 1,000, the marginal cost of that unit is greater than the marginal revenue from selling that unit. Each reduction in output until 1,000 would raise the firm's profit.

By these arguments, for any output below 1,000, profit will increase if output is increased; for any output above 1,000, profit will increase if output is reduced. Thus, the most profitable level of output is 1,000 units, the output at which marginal revenue equals marginal cost.

Principle

The marginal revenue (*MR*) of a perfectly competitive firm is the horizontal, perfectly elastic demand at the market-determined price. The profit-maximizing firm should increase its output if *MR* is greater than marginal cost (*MC*) and decrease its output if *MR* is less than *MC*. Thus, the profit-maximizing output is the level at which

$$Price = MR = MC$$

The above analysis is not meant to imply that firms actually determine their profit-maximizing level of output by constantly varying their output and seeing what happens to profit. This approach, frequently used in economic analysis, is used only to demonstrate that the output at which $MR = MC$ is the profit-maximizing output by showing that every other output yields lower profits. Firms do, however, consider what will happen to their profit if output is increased or decreased, but the variation is seldom in increments of one unit.

12.3.2   Short-Run Profit Maximization: A Numerical Example

Suppose a perfectly competitive firm has the cost schedule for zero through nine units of output shown in the upper portion of Table 12–1. Assume that the market-determined price of this firm's product is $250 per unit. Because output varies discretely rather than continuously here, from the profit-maximizing rule developed in the preceding subsection, the firm should produce and sell seven units of output. The marginal cost of each unit of output through unit seven (column 7) is less than price, $250, which is marginal revenue. Because the marginal cost of the eighth unit of output ($296) is greater than $250, the firm should not produce this unit.

The fact that seven is the profit-maximizing level of output is easily verified in column 4 of the lower schedule in the table. The total cost of each level of output (from column 4 above) is reproduced in column 2 below. The total revenue, price times quantity, for each level of output is shown in column 3. Profit, which is total

Table 12–1   Short-Run Profit Maximization Cost Schedule

(1)	(2)	(3)	(4)	(5)	(6)	(7)
	Variable	Fixed	Total	Average Variable	Average Total	Marginal
Output	Cost	Cost	Cost	Cost	Cost	Cost
0	$ 0	$300	$ 300	$ —	$ —	$ —
1	100	300	400	100	400	100
2	150	300	450	75	225	50
3	180	300	480	60	160	30
4	260	300	560	65	140	80
5	380	300	680	76	136	120
6	540	300	840	90	140	160
7	764	300	1,064	109	152	224
8	1,060	300	1,360	133	170	296
9	1,464	300	1,764	163	196	396

Profit or Loss

		Price = $250		Price = $110		Price = $55	
(1)	(2)	(3)	(4)	(5)	(6)	(7)	(8)
	Total		Profit		Profit		Profit
Output	Cost	Revenue	(Loss)	Revenue	(Loss)	Revenue	(Loss)
0	$ 300	$ 0	− $300	$ 0	− $300	$ 0	− $300
1	400	250	− 150	110	− 290	55	− 345
2	450	500	− 50	220	− 230	110	− 340
3	480	750	270	330	− 150	165	− 315
4	560	1,000	440	440	− 120	220	− 340
5	680	1,250	570	550	− 130	275	− 405
6	840	1,500	660	660	− 180	330	− 510
7	1,064	1,750	686	770	− 294	385	− 679
8	1,360	2,000	640	880	− 480	440	− 920
9	1,764	2,250	486	990	− 774	495	−1,269

revenue minus total cost, for each output level is shown in column 4. You can see that the profit at seven units, $686, is higher than the profit at any other level.

Suppose now that the demand in the product market decreases, causing price to fall to $110. You can see from column 7 of the upper part of the table that the marginal cost of each additional unit of output through the fourth is less than $110, and the marginal cost of the fifth is greater than $110. Thus, if the firm produces any positive output, it will produce four units. However, from column 5 of the lower part of the table, total revenue at four units ($110 × 4) is $440, while total cost is $560 (from column 4 above). Therefore, as shown in column 5, the firm makes a loss (or negative profit) of ($440 − $560 =)− $120. As shown in column 6 of the lower table, the firm makes a loss if it produces any level of output at a price of $110, including zero units. But, the loss at four units of output is the smallest loss possible, at any level of output including zero.

Therefore, the firm should produce four units of output and not shut down and produce zero output. If it shuts down and produces nothing, it would receive no revenue, but it would still have to pay its fixed cost of $300. At zero output it would lose $300, as shown in column 6, which is a larger loss than would occur at four units of output.

Look at the decision in another way. At four units of output, the firm's variable cost is $260, shown in column 2 of the upper table. By producing four units of output, the firm could cover all of its variable cost ($260) out of its revenue of $440 (shown in column 5 of the lower part of the table) and have ($440 − $260 =) $180 left over to pay part of its $300 fixed cost. Thus, it would lose only ($300 − $180 =) $120 rather than the full $300 that it would lose if it shut down. As noted above, column 6 in the lower table indicates that $120 is the smallest loss possible when price is $110.

From the previous example, you can see that under certain circumstances a firm will produce a positive level of output rather than shut down, even though it would make a loss at every level of output. If it produces, the firm would increase its output as long as price (marginal revenue) exceeds marginal cost. At this optimal level of output, the firm can pay all of its variable costs from its revenue and still have some revenue left over to pay part of its fixed cost. It would lose less than would be the case if the firm produces nothing and loses all of its fixed cost.

Alternatively, a perfectly competitive firm would produce a positive output if, at the optimal level of output, the product price is greater than the average variable cost (AVC), even though it would make a loss at this, and any other, output. Since $AVC = TVC/Q$, $TVC = AVC \cdot Q$. Therefore,

$$\text{Revenue} - TVC = P \cdot Q - AVC \cdot Q = (P - AVC) \cdot Q,$$

which is positive if price is greater than average variable cost. In such cases, the firm could cover all of its variable cost from its revenue and have some revenue left over to apply to fixed cost. This would result in a smaller loss than would be the case if the firm would shut down and lose all of its fixed cost.

It follows from the above analysis that the firm would shut down, produce nothing, and lose its entire fixed cost, if revenue is less than variable cost (price is less than AVC) at every level of output. Such a case occurs in Table 12–1 when price is $55. If the firm produces when price is $55, it would produce three units of output, at which marginal cost is $30. As you can see from the lower table at this output, revenue is ($55 · 3 =) $165 and total cost is $480. Thus, the firm would lose ($165 − $480 =) −$315, as shown in column 8. If it shuts down, it loses only $300, its fixed cost. The firm would therefore choose to produce no output.

A comparison of column 2 in the upper table with column 7 in the lower shows that variable cost is larger than revenue at every positive level of output (and price is less than average variable cost, shown in column 5 of the upper table). If the firm produces any positive output, it would lose all of its fixed cost and the portion

Figure 12–3   Short-Run Profit Maximization

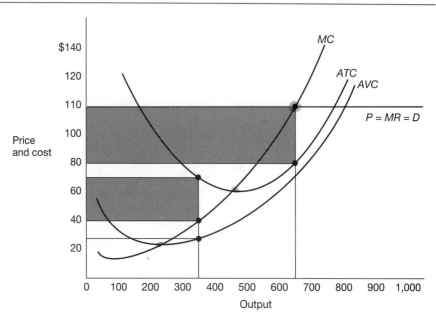

of variable cost not covered by revenue. The best the firm can do is shut down and lose all of its fixed cost.

The above analysis can be summarized in the following:

Principles

A firm should shut down, produce no output, and make a loss equal to its fixed cost, if at every level of output revenue is less than variable cost (price is less than *AVC*). If, over some range of output, revenue is greater than variable cost (price is greater than *AVC*), the firm should increase its output as long as price is greater than marginal cost ($P > MC$). If revenue is larger than total cost (price exceeds *ATC*) at this optimal output, the firm makes an economic profit. If revenue is less than total cost (price less than *ATC*) at this output, the firm makes a loss, but the loss is less than fixed cost, which it would lose if it produces zero output, because revenue is greater than variable cost (price is greater than *AVC*).

12.3.3   Short-Run Profit Maximization: Graphical Analysis

The profit-maximizing (or loss-minimizing) conditions for still another perfectly competitive firm in the short run are shown graphically in Figure 12–3. Here we assume that output and cost vary continuously, rather than discretely, as in the previous table. The curves *AVC*, *ATC*, and *MC* are, respectively, the firm's short-run average variable cost, average total cost, and marginal cost.

Suppose that the market-determined price (which is also marginal revenue and demand) is $110. From the preceding analysis, the firm can increase its profit by increasing its output if price (marginal revenue) is greater than marginal cost, or by decreasing its output if price (marginal revenue) is less than marginal cost. That is, it should increase output if output is smaller than that at which price equals MC and decrease output if it is larger than that at which price equals MC. It therefore follows from previous analysis that, if output can vary continuously, the firm maximizes its profits by producing the output at which

$$Price = MR = MC.$$

Thus, in Figure 12–3, the firm produces and sells 650 units of output per period in order to maximize its profit. Since price is higher than ATC at this output, the firm makes an economic profit. Total revenue is

$$TR = P \cdot Q = \$110 \cdot 650 = \$71,500.$$

At 650 units of output, ATC is $80, so total cost is

$$TC = ATC \cdot Q = \$80 \cdot 650 = \$52,000.$$

Thus, the firm's profit is

$$Profit = TR - TC = \$71,500 - \$52,000 = \$19,500.$$

We could, of course, also have calculated profit as

$$TR - TC = P \cdot Q - ATC \cdot Q = (P - ATC) \cdot Q$$
$$= (\$110 - 80) \cdot 650 = \$19,500.$$

Anytime price is higher than ATC at a given output, the firm makes an economic profit. Therefore, at any price above $69, the point of minimum ATC, the firm chooses the output at which price equals MC and earns the highest possible profit. If price falls below $69, the firm cannot make an economic profit at any level of output.

Suppose the price falls to $40. In this situation, the best the firm can do is to set price equal to MC and to produce 350 units of output. At this output, price is less than ATC ($70), so the firm makes a loss of

$$P \cdot Q - ATC \cdot Q = \$40 \cdot 350 - \$70 \cdot 350$$
$$= \$14,000 - \$24,500 = -\$10,500.$$

Producing 350 units of output and losing $10,500 is better for the firm than shutting down and producing nothing. If the firm produces zero output, its revenue is zero. Its variable cost is zero also, but it must still pay its fixed cost. Thus, if the firm shuts down, it loses all of its fixed cost. However, if the firm produces 350 units of output, its average variable cost is $25, so its variable cost is

$$TVC = AVC \cdot Q = \$25 \cdot 350 = \$8,750.$$

Since its revenue is $14,000, it can pay its variable cost and have

$$TR - TVC = \$14,000 - \$8,750 = \$5,250$$

Figure 12–4   Summary of Short-Run Profit Maximization

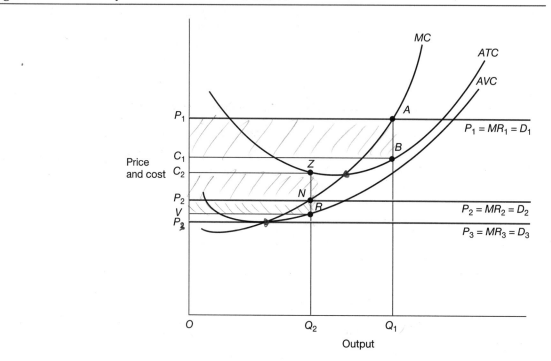

left over to pay part of its fixed cost. The firm loses its fixed cost minus $5,250, which is better than losing all of its fixed cost.

fig 12-3   If the price is below minimum *ATC*, $69, and above minimum *AVC*, $20, the firm produces the output at which price equals *MC* and makes a loss. At the chosen output, all variable costs are paid from revenue, and the remaining revenue is used to pay part, though not all, of its fixed cost. The firm loses less than its fixed cost, which it would lose if it produced nothing.

If price falls below minimum *AVC*, $20, the firm would shut down, produce nothing, and lose its fixed cost. This is better for the firm than producing a positive output. If price is below $20, revenue would be less than variable cost at any output. It would therefore lose all of its fixed cost plus that portion of variable cost that could not be paid from revenue, which is worse for the firm than shutting down and losing its fixed cost.

12.3.4   Graphical Summary of Short-Run Profit Maximization

All of the principles of short-run profit maximization for a perfectly competitive firm are summarized graphically in Figure 12–4. In the figure, *AVC*, *ATC*, and *MC* are, once again, a firm's short-run average variable, average total, and marginal cost curves. There are three possible scenarios.

If price is above the minimum point on *ATC*, the firm produces the output at which price equals *MC* and makes an economic profit. Suppose price is P_1. Output is Q_1, and total revenue is

$$TR = P_1 \cdot Q_1 = \text{Area } OP_1AQ_1.$$

Total cost at Q_1 is

$$TC = ATC \cdot Q_1 = C_1 \cdot Q_1 = \text{Area } OC_1BQ_1.$$

The firm's economic profit is

$$\text{Profit} = TR - TC = (P_1 - C_1) \cdot Q_1 = \text{Area } C_1P_1AB.$$

If price is between minimum *ATC* and minimum *AVC*, the firm produces the output at which price equals *MC* and makes a loss. Suppose price is P_2. Output is Q_2 and the firm's revenue is

$$TR = P_2 \cdot Q_2 = \text{Area } OP_2NQ_2.$$

Total cost is

$$TC = ATC \cdot Q_2 = C_2 \cdot Q_2 = \text{Area } OC_2ZQ_2.$$

The firm loses

$$TR - TC = (P_2 - C_2) \cdot Q_2 = -\text{Area } P_2C_2ZN.$$

If the firm shuts down it would lose its fixed cost (*FC*). If it produces Q_2, variable cost is

$$TVC = AVC \cdot Q_2 = V \cdot Q_2 = \text{Area } OVRQ_2.$$

It can pay all of its variable cost from its revenue and still have left over

$$TR - TVC = (P_2 - V) \cdot Q_2 = \text{Area } VP_2NR,$$

which it can use to pay part of fixed cost. Therefore, by producing Q_2, the firm loses less than *FC*.

If price is below P_3, at which price equals minimum *AVC*, the firm shuts down, produces nothing, and loses its fixed cost. The firm in the short run will, therefore, never lose more than its fixed cost.

12.3.5   Short-Run Profit Maximization in Practice

The following hypothetical example summarizes a perfectly competitive firm's short-run decision-making process in a somewhat different way from the preceding analysis. As you will see, the conclusions are identical.

Suppose the manager of an apparel firm is making production plans for the first quarter of 1993. The manager wants to determine how many moderately priced shirts to produce and realizes that in this particular segment of the market, this firm is only one of many firms producing a relatively homogeneous product, so it must take the market-determined price as essentially determined by supply and demand in the market. Based upon published forecasts of income and prices, purchased from a large econometric firm, the manager forecasts three prices under the best case, the worst case, and the intermediate case:

$$\text{Best} = \$20$$

$$\text{Intermediate} = \$15$$

$$\text{Worst} = \$10.$$

The firm's production manager determines that the short-run average variable and marginal cost functions have the following form:

$$AVC = 20 - 3Q + 0.25Q^2$$

$$MC = 20 - 6Q + 0.75Q^2,$$

where Q is sales expressed in 1,000 units. As you can probably determine, these equations are the typically assumed U-shaped curves used in the previous graphical analysis.

The first question to be answered is whether to produce or shut down, which requires knowledge of the firm's minimum average variable cost. Minimum AVC occurs at the output at which AVC equals MC:

$$AVC = 20 - 3Q + 0.25Q^2 = MC = 20 - 6Q + 0.75Q^2.$$

This is easily solved to obtain $Q = 6$; this minimum AVC occurs when output is 6,000. To determine the minimum AVC at this output, solve

$$AVC = 20 - 3Q + 0.25Q^2 = 20 - 3(6) + 0.25(6)^2 = \$11.$$

Since the best and intermediate price forecasts are above \$11, the firm would produce if these prices occur. If the worst forecast of \$10 occurs, the firm would produce no shirts because this price is below minimum AVC.

Next, the manager wants to know how much to produce at each of the higher prices. Looking first at the high price, \$20, optimal output is that at which the high price is equal to marginal cost:

$$P = 20 = MC = 20 - 6Q + 0.75Q^2.$$

Solving this equation (by factoring), the optimal—profit-maximizing or loss-minimizing—output is $Q = 8$, or, since output is expressed in 1,000 units, at 8,000 units of output. Thus, if the price is \$20, output is 8,000.

With the intermediate forecast, the optimal output occurs when

$$P = 15 = MC = 20 - 6Q + 0.75Q^2.$$

In this case, the solution is not as simple as was the preceding case, and the quadratic formula must be resorted to [the solution for y to the equation $ay^2 + by + c = 0$ is $y = (-b \pm \sqrt{b^2 - 4ac})/2a$]:

$$Q = \frac{-(-6) \pm \sqrt{-(6)^2 - 4(0.75)(5)}}{2(0.75)} = \frac{6 \pm \sqrt{6 + 4.6}}{1.5}.$$

The equation has two solutions: $Q = 0.93$ and $Q = 7.1$. At $Q = 0.93$ $AVC = 17.43, which is greater than the $15 price, and therefore cannot be optimal. At $Q = 7.1$, $AVC = 11.30, which is less than $15; thus, the optimal output at $P = 15 is $Q = 7.1$, or output is 7,100 units. Now, the optimal output at each price has been determined:

$$P = $20, \text{output} = 8,000$$

$$P = $15, \text{output} = 7,100$$

$$P = $10, \text{output} = 0.$$

Once the firm's output decision has been made, the calculation of total profit or loss is simple. Profit (loss) is total revenue minus total cost:

$$\text{Profit} = P \cdot Q - TC = (P \cdot Q) - (AVC \cdot Q + FC).$$

Based upon actual costs in 1992, the manager expects fixed costs for the shirt division to be $30,000 in the first quarter of 1993. The values for total revenue and variable cost depend on the forecast price and the corresponding optimal output.

If the high forecast of $P = 20 occurs, the optimal output is $Q = 8$, that is, 8,000 units. The average variable cost at this output is

$$AVC = 20 - 3(8) + 0.25(8)^2 = $12.$$

Therefore, profit will be

$$\text{Profit} = ($20)(8,000) - [$12(8,000) + $30,000] = $34,000.$$

If price is $20, the shirt division will earn a profit of $34,000 in the first quarter of 1993.

If the intermediate price of $15 occurs, output will be $Q = 7.1$, or 7,100 units. Average variable cost will be

$$AVC = 20 - 3(7.1) + 0.25(7.1)^2 = $11.30.$$

Total profit will be

$$\text{Profit} = ($15)(7,100) - [$11.30(7,100) + $30,000] = -$3,730.$$

If the intermediate price of $15 occurs, the shirt division will suffer a loss of $3,730 in the first quarter of 1993.

If the lowest estimate of $P = 10 occurs, the division will produce zero output, earn no revenue, incur no variable cost, and pay as a loss its entire fixed cost of $30,000.

In this section, we discussed the way a manager of a competitive firm, under rather stylized conditions, would make decisions when faced with three alternative price forecasts. The purpose is to reinforce the material presented thus far in this chapter. In the short run, a profit-maximizing perfectly competitive firm would make one of three choices.

1. Produce a positive level of output and earn an economic profit if $P > ATC$.
2. Produce a positive level of output and suffer a loss less than the amount of fixed cost if $AVC < P < ATC$.
3. Produce zero output and suffer a loss equal to fixed cost if $P < AVC$.

Figure 12–5   Derivation of the Short-Run Supply Curve of an Individual Firm in Perfect Competition

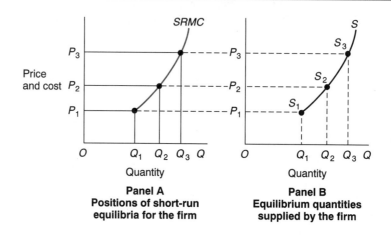

Thus, the illustration presented here mirrors the preceding discussion and graphical exposition.

12.4   Short-Run Supply and the Irrelevance of Fixed Cost

Using the concepts developed in the previous sections, it is easy to derive a perfectly competitive firm's short-run supply curve, which we do in this section. We will also emphasize an important point implied in the previous analysis: Fixed cost plays no role in the firm's decision-making process and, therefore, has no effect upon the firm's supply.

12.4.1   Short-Run Supply

Recall from Chapter 2 the definition of supply: A list of prices and the quantity producers are willing and able to sell at each price in the list per period of time, other things held constant. In Figure 12–5, Panel A shows, for a perfectly competitive firm, the marginal cost curve above minimum average variable cost. Any price below P_1 is below the minimum AVC, so the firm would supply zero output at such prices. Next, suppose the price is P_1; the corresponding equilibrium output is Q_1, where $P_1 = MC$. In Panel B, the point S_1 is associated with the coordinates P_1 and Q_1. This point represents the quantity supplied at P_1.

Next, suppose price is P_2. Equilibrium output in Panel A would be Q_2. We plot the point associated with the coordinates P_2 and Q_2 in Panel B and label it S_2. Similarly, other equilibrium quantities can be determined by assuming other prices (for example, price P_3 leads to output Q_3 and point S_3 in Panel B). Connecting all the points so generated, we obtain the short-run supply curve of the firm—the curve labeled S in Panel B. The supply curve is precisely the same as the short-run marginal cost curve above AVC. Because the firm would supply zero output at any price below P_1, the firm's supply is a vertical line—perfectly inelastic—at zero output over this lower range of prices. The following principle is therefore established:

Principle

> The short-run supply curve of a perfectly competitive firm is its short-run marginal cost for all prices above the minimum point on the average variable cost curve. For all prices below this point, quantity supplied is zero.

12.4.2   The Irrelevance of Fixed Cost

In the analysis of a perfectly competitive firm's profit-maximizing output decision, average variable cost, marginal cost, and average total cost all played a role, with marginal cost being the most important.

1. *AVC* tells the firm whether to produce or shut down. If price is below minimum *AVC*, the firm shuts down and produces nothing; if price is above minimum *AVC*, the firm produces a positive output.
2. *MC* tells the firm how much to produce if it produces a positive output. The firm equates price to *MC* to determine the optimal quantity.
3. *ATC* tells the firm how much profit or loss it makes, since profit is $(P - ATC) \cdot Q$.

Note that fixed cost plays no role whatsoever in the decision to produce. It is irrelevant in the decision-making process and, therefore, has no effect on the firm's supply. The reason fixed cost is irrelevant is because the same amount of fixed cost must be paid no matter what output is produced. It is impossible to change fixed cost. When a firm (or anyone for that matter) makes a decision, it weighs the marginal benefits and the marginal cost of the decision, then decides accordingly.

To see why fixed cost should be ignored, consider the following hypothetical example. A store, which is currently open eight hours a day from 10:00 A.M. to 6:00 P.M., is deciding whether or not to remain open until 10:00 P.M., an additional four hours. With the present store hours, it is receiving $50,000 a week in revenue. Its weekly variable cost is $30,000, and its fixed cost is $15,000. Thus, the store is earning a weekly profit of $5,000.

The manager estimates that the additional four hours will increase revenue $18,000, from $50,000 to $68,000, and variable cost $15,000, from $30,000 to $45,000. If the manager allocates 1/3 (4/12) of the $15,000 fixed cost ($5,000), to the additional four hours the store remains open, it would appear that increasing the hours would reduce profits by $2,000—the increase in revenue ($18,000) minus the increase in variable cost ($15,000) minus the relative share of fixed cost ($5,000) equals −$2,000.

This, however, is an incorrect approach. Clearly, because revenue would increase by $3,000 more than the increase in variable cost, profit would increase by $3,000. Profit with the longer hours is

$$TR = TVC - FC = \$68,000 - \$45,000 - \$15,000 = \$8,000,$$

which is $3,000 more than before. Fixed cost is the same as before and is subtracted from revenue to obtain profit. It does not matter how it is allocated. As long as the *additional* revenue is greater than the *additional* cost, the store should extend its hours. If the additional revenue is less than the additional variable cost, it should not.

Actual firms make similar types of decisions based on the same principle. Airlines schedule flights at times when demand is low, and frequently charge lower prices at these nonpeak hours. These flights would not be profitable if high fixed costs, such as the cost of the plane, are allocated. But the marginal cost is low—the additional crew and fuel cost. If the additional revenue is higher than the additional cost, the flight is profitable.

Theaters show movies in the afternoon, when demand is low, and charge lower prices, because the additional cost is lower than the additional revenue. Grocery stores stay open 24 hours a day for the same reason. Trucking firms make some hauls based on the same principle. In all such cases, once the fixed cost is committed, only the marginal revenue and marginal cost of any changes are relevant.

12.1   *Applying the Theory*

When individuals optimize, we know from Chapter 4 that when there are no constraints, the rule is to continue with an activity as long as $MB > MC$ and stop when $MB = MC$. When individuals make such decisions, do they pay attention to fixed costs? Do households have fixed costs? Are these costs relevant to the decision?

12.4.3   Summary

This completes the discussion of profit maximization by a perfectly competitive firm in the short run. The firm takes the market price, which is the firm's marginal revenue, as given. It chooses the output level at which price equals marginal cost, when price is greater than minimum average variable cost. If price is less than minimum average variable cost, it produces nothing and pays all its fixed cost. If price is above average total cost, the firm makes an economic profit equal to $(P - ATC)Q$. If price is between minimum average total and minimum average variable cost, the firm makes a loss, but not as large a loss as would be the case if the firm shut down.

Because the firm's marginal cost curve determines its output for any price above average variable cost, MC above AVC is the firm's short-run supply curve. At any price below minimum AVC the firm produces zero output. Since fixed cost is the same no matter what output the firm produces, fixed cost has no effect on the firm's output decision. Therefore, fixed cost has no effect on the firm's supply curve.

In the short run, firms are restricted because of past decisions about the levels of the fixed inputs and, hence, the amounts of their fixed cost. This is not the case in the long run when all inputs are variable. Therefore, a firm may be making losses in the short run, but in the long run, it may be able to make a profit. Or it may be making profit in the short run, but the firm may be able to make more profit if it moves into the long run. Therefore, to complete the theory of the perfectly competitive firm, we now turn to the firm in the long run.

Economics in the News

Fixed Costs Are Irrelevant

The *Houston Post,* "Low Fares Should Lift Air Profits," August 6, 1989, p. O1, announced that Continental Airlines had set off a summer fare war among the airlines by introducing cheap weekend fares: $75 nonstop flights on weekends. Seven other carriers matched the fares.

This story quoted several Wall Street airline analysts who discussed the reason for the fare cut. One industry analyst said, "Even though the $75 fares may not cover the actual airline seat cost, the plane is going to fly anyway and everything else is gravy." Another analyst agreed: "You're flying a lot of air around, and anything you put on that airline is a plus. I think it's a brilliant marketing plan." He also noted, "In the summer, weekends are the weakest. From Saturday morning through noon Sunday, most airports are deserted." Still another analyst pointed out, "If they're filling empty seats, it will add to their revenues."

Clearly, Continental and the other airlines that followed the fare cuts were not worried about the fixed cost of a flight. They had to pay that no matter how many passengers they carried. They set fares that would cover variable costs, which appeared to be quite low, and had some revenue left over. One analyst, as you will recall, called this "gravy." We call it revenue over and above variable cost, which is applied to fixed cost.

Another firm that made a decision to take an unusual action, based only on marginal cost and revenue, was a Los Angeles hospital that had fallen upon bad times. An article in *Modern Healthcare,* "One L.A. Hospital's Strategy: More Medicare, AIDS Cases," December 10, 1990, p. 40, reported that Queen of Angels–Hollywood Presbyterian Medical Center "is pursuing a decidedly different plan for a financial turnaround: It's taking in more Medicaid cases and AIDS patients . . . many administrators would regard such a plan as a blueprint for disaster." However, "Executives at [Queen of Angels] believe they can reduce operating expenditures and gain revenue by leasing out unused patient-care areas to other providers that are short on space . . . and by accepting referrals of patients that other hospitals don't want."

The article reported the Queen of Angels had been suffering a low, 64 percent, occupancy rate. "The new program, combined with internal cost reductions, are helping the hospital meet payments on its state-backed $75 million debt."

By filling beds that were previously empty, Queen of Angels was able to cover the variable cost of treating these new patients out of the increased revenues generated and pay off some part of its long-term debt—a large part of the hospital's fixed cost. This appears to have benefited both the hospital and also, of course, the new patients.

In the fall of 1989, many automobile dealers were complaining bitterly that rental car agencies, such as Hertz, Avis, and National, were seriously undercutting new car sales with sales of low-mileage rental cars. An article in the *Houston Post,* "Traffic Dispute," September 11, 1989, p. E1, offered a possible explanation for the recent trend. "A trend in the rental and auto manufacturing business . . . keeps an endless stream of new cars . . . cranking through rental fleets, only to emerge in a matter of months as low-mileage, used cars. As a hedge against the softening car market, the Big Three auto makers have made large investments in major rental companies. . . . In return they get supply agreements with the rental car firms that help keep auto plants operating and inventory under control." A Wall Street auto analyst suggested the reason: "The Auto companies feel compelled to take on these sales to *cover their fixed cost* [emphasis added],

(continued)

but these sales are not profitable. They can't get rid of their (expensive factory) robots. So they're flooding the car market with low-mileage residuals."

It appears that the analyst really meant that the auto manufacturers made these sales at a low price in order to cover the variable cost and have some revenue left over to apply to their fixed costs. The analyst did not mean that the auto makers covered all of their fixed costs. It was noted that the sales were not profitable (did not cover total costs, including all of the fixed costs), but the factories were stuck with expensive capital (robots) for which the firms were presumably paying a fixed cost. We would have to assume that even though the sales were not profitable, in the sense that revenues did not cover total costs, they were profitable, in the sense that variable costs and some fixed costs were covered, so that profits were higher or losses were lower than they otherwise would have been. If this was not the case, the firms would certainly not have sold cars to the rental agencies at the prices they did.

These stories indicate that firms do, in fact, ignore fixed costs in the short run, and make decisions based on marginal and variable cost.

12.5   Long-Run Profit Maximization for a Competitive Firm

In the short run, a firm is limited by its past decisions because some inputs are fixed in amount. In the long run, all inputs are variable, and firms are not constrained by the past. As you will recall, in the long run, a firm can produce any level of output at the lowest attainable cost. The long run represents a planning stage.

A firm operating in the short run may be at a scale at which it is not obtaining maximum possible profits, or it may be making short-run losses. It would then readjust its scale to the optimal size in the long run to earn the maximum possible profits. Or a firm may be at the planning stage prior to its entry into the market. It would be in the long run and would enter into the industry at the optimal size. Once plans have congealed and some fixed inputs are committed, the firm operates in the short run and continues to do so, until it makes another long-run change in its scale of operation.

This section sets forth the theory of the competitive firm in the long run. As you will see, long-run profit maximization is based upon exactly the same principle as short-run profit maximization. The only difference is that all inputs are variable in the long run.

12.5.1   Profit Maximization in the Long Run

In the long run, just as in the short run, the firm attempts to maximize profits by setting marginal cost equal to marginal revenue. In this case, however, there are no fixed costs; all costs are variable. As before, the firm takes a market-determined commodity price as given. This market price is also the firm's marginal revenue. As in the short run, the firm would increase output as long as the marginal revenue from each additional unit is greater than the marginal cost of that unit, and it would reduce output if marginal cost exceeds marginal revenue.

Figure 12–6   The Long-Run Adjustment Process

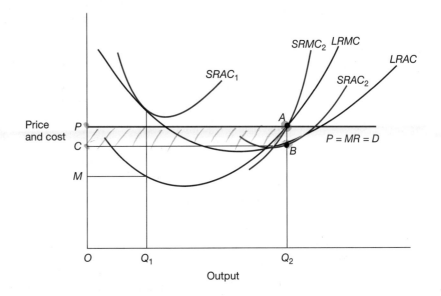

The long-run adjustment process of a competitive firm is illustrated in Figure 12–6. A firm's long-run average and marginal cost curves are, respectively, *LRAC* and *LRMC*. Suppose, however, this firm is now in the short run with the average total cost $SRAC_1$. Since the product price, *P*, is below $SRAC_1$ at every level of output, the firm is making losses in the short run.

If this firm goes into the long run, perhaps by building a new plant, it can make economic profits because price is above long-run average cost over a wide range of output. By the same argument as used for the short run, the firm can increase its profit in the long run by increasing its output as long as price (*MR*) is greater than long-run marginal cost. For example, at output Q_1, an increase in output in the long run would increase revenue by *P* but increase cost by only *M* (the long-run marginal cost at Q_1) and, thereby, increase profit. Similarly, the firm should increase output until Q_2, at which output price equals *LRMC*. Any further increases would reduce profit because *P* is less than *LRMC* at larger outputs.

Thus, the profit-maximizing equilibrium principle in the long run is the same as in the short run:

Principle

To maximize profit in the long run, a firm produces the output at which price (*MR*) equals long-run marginal cost.

Once output Q_2 is chosen, the firm would build its plant and commit any other fixed inputs so as to produce Q_2 at the lowest possible long-run average cost (and, therefore, the lowest total cost). After the plant is established, the firm is in the short run with the new average total cost curve $SRAC_2$, which is tangent to $LRAC$ at output Q_2. Similarly, short-run marginal cost ($SRMC_2$) equals $LRMC$ at Q_2, where marginal cost equals price. The firm is maximizing its economic profit, which is

$$P \cdot Q_2 - C \cdot Q_2 = (P - C)Q_2 = \text{area } CPAB.$$

The firm continues to produce and sell Q_2 as long as price remains at P and nothing causes the cost curves to shift. If, say, product price changes, the firm must adapt in the short run within the existing short-run conditions by choosing the output at which the new price equals $SRMC_2$.

This discussion illustrates the point previously discussed in Chapter 10: The firm plans in the long run and produces in the short run. The firm was producing with the cost given by $SRAC_1$. It decided to make a change and move to the cost structure given by $SRAC_2$, in which it could maximize its profit. Then the firm was producing once again in the short run.[1]

12.5.2   Other Long-Run Adjustments

In the preceding discussion, we assumed that a firm was making losses in the short run, but if it entered into the long run it could make a profit. It chose the output at which long-run marginal cost equaled price and entered a new short run, in which average total cost was tangent to long-run cost at the profit-maximizing output.

There are two other situations in which a firm would enter the long run in order to make a change. The first is when a firm is making an economic profit in the short run but could increase its profit by entering the long run. The second is when a new firm enters the industry. If price is above the minimum long-run average cost, the new firm can enter the industry at the scale that allows it to produce the output at which price equals $LRMC$, and make a profit. If price is below $LRAC$, all firms in the industry are making a loss, and no new firms would enter. In fact, as we will show in the next chapter, some existing firms will actually exit from the industry because they are not covering their opportunity costs.

Figure 12–7 shows three possible situations for a perfectly competitive firm in the long run. If price is P_1, the firm would produce Q_1, at which P_1 equals $LRMC$. The relevant short-run average total cost would be tangent to $LRAC$ at point A, and short-run marginal cost would equal $LRMC$ at point B. The firm would make an economic profit because price is greater than average cost, so total revenue is greater than total cost. In fact, at any price above minimum long-run average cost, the firm could make an economic profit in the long run.

---

[1]The discussion of Figure 12–6 ignored why the firm would choose the short-run cost conditions given by $SRAC_1$ in the first place. Since both short-run and long-run marginal cost are below average cost at Q_1, a price that equals marginal cost at this output would lead to losses. We used this situation to illustrate in the simplest way the transition from one short-run cost structure to another.

Figure 12–7 Three Long-Run Situations

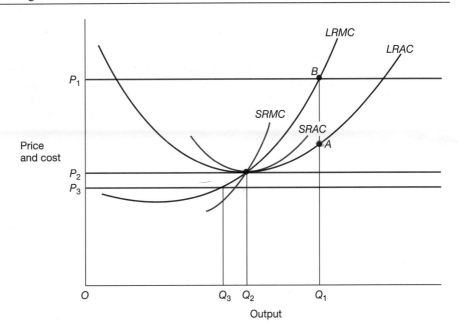

If price is P_2, price equals *LRMC* at the minimum point on *LRAC*. The firm produces Q_2 and makes zero economic profit. It does, however, earn a normal profit or normal rate of return because the value of the best alternative use of the firm's resources is included in cost. The relevant *SRAC* curve is tangent to *LRAC* at the minimum point on both average cost curves. Therefore, *SRMC* crosses *SRAC* at Q_2 also. When price equals *LRAC* at its minimum,

$$P = LRAC = LRMC = SRAC = SRMC,$$

and the firm receives no economic profit but does earn a normal rate of return. This situation will be extremely important for the discussion in the next chapter.

Finally, if price is below minimum *LRAC*, the firm would make a loss at any level of output. When price is P_3, the firm would produce Q_3, if it produces at all. No firm would enter this industry under such a condition, and, in fact, firms, unable to make even a normal profit, would leave the industry and put their resources in their next best alternative.[2] Since a perfectly competitive firm in the long run produces the output at which price equals long-run marginal cost, the long-run marginal cost curve is its long-run supply curve.

[2] This last situation, in which price equals *LRMC* below *LRAC*, is rather unrealistic and is included in the discussion primarily for illustrative purposes. No firm would enter the industry knowing it would make losses in this situation, and no established firm would make long-run changes that would lead to a loss. Established firms would, in the short run, produce at a price below minimum *LRAC*, if revenue is greater than variable cost. Then some firms might exit the industry in the long run, if such a situation persisted. Firms would not make long-run changes that they know would lead to losses.

12.6   Shifts in Cost Curves

We have, until now, emphasized how competitive firms change their output in response to market-determined changes in product price. Firms would also change their level of output if something caused a shift in their marginal cost curves. Recall from Chapter 10 that a firm's cost curves shift if the prices of some of the inputs it employs change or if the firm experiences technological change. Since a firm's marginal cost curve determines its output at any given price, the effect of changes in input prices and technology depends on how they affect marginal cost.

12.6.1   Changes in Input Prices and Technology

Here we will use short-run cost curves to illustrate how changes in input prices and technology affect a firm's output. However, the effect on the firm in the long run is practically identical. In Figure 12–8, MC_0 is originally a perfectly competitive firm's short-run marginal cost curve above its average variable cost (AVC_0); MC_0 is therefore the firm's short-run supply curve. From the preceding analysis, if price is P, the firm produces Q_0 units of output. If price is below minimum AVC_0, the firm shuts down and produces nothing.

Next, suppose the price of one of the variable inputs used by the firm decreases. (For now we assume that this firm is the only firm in the market affected by the input price change. As you will see in the next chapter, when all firms are affected, the situation is complicated somewhat.) After the fall in the input price, the marginal cost at each level of output decreases, as does average variable cost; it now costs less to increase output at any output level because one of the variable inputs is less costly.[3] This input-price reduction causes the marginal cost curve to shift downward to MC_1. Average variable cost, and hence minimum AVC, shift downward also to AVC_1. At the original price, P, the firm increases its output from Q_0 to Q_1 because of the decrease in marginal cost. Because minimum AVC decreases, the price at which the firm shuts down decreases also. Furthermore, at every relevant price, the firm wishes to produce more output than previously, as shown by the new marginal cost curve. Since the firm's supply curve is marginal cost above minimum AVC, the firm's supply increases from MC_0 to MC_1. Although we postulated that the decrease in marginal cost and the resulting increase in the firm's supply curve were caused by a reduction in the price of one of the inputs, the same effect would have resulted from a cost-reducing improvement in technology.

Next, let the prices of inputs return to their original level. The cost curves become, once again, MC_0 and AVC_0. With the price P, the firm again produces Q_0. Now assume that the price of one of the variable inputs increases. The increase in the price of the input raises the cost of producing any level of output and the cost of increasing output from any output level. Marginal and average variable cost therefore increase to MC_2 and AVC_2.

---

[3]There is a somewhat obscure theoretical possibility that for some inputs a fall in an input price increases marginal cost over some range of output, and vice versa. We ignore that possibility here and concentrate on the typical case.

Figure 12–8   Changes in Output in Response to Changes in Cost

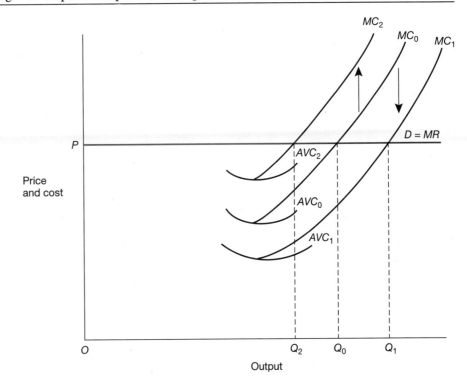

Now, at the product price P, the firm reduces its output from Q_0 to Q_2. Output would also decrease at any other product price, and the price below which the firm would shut down increases because AVC has risen. Thus, the increase in input price reduces the firm's supply curve to MC_2 above AVC_2.

We have developed the following relation:

Relation

When a change, such as a decrease in input price or an improvement in technology, reduces a firm's marginal and average variable costs, the firm's supply increases. It is willing and able to supply more at each product price. When a change, such as an increase in input price, increases a firm's marginal and average costs, the firm's supply decreases. It is willing and able to supply less at each product price.[4]

[4]You may have noticed in Figure 12–8 and in the previous discussion that we did not show or mention any effect on average total cost. Since ATC is the sum of AVC and AFC, ATC must shift upward (downward) when AVC shifts upward (downward) because AFC remains constant. The change in ATC, however, is irrelevant for the analysis of shifts in a firm's supply. Minimum AVC determines the price below which the firm shuts down, and MC determines how much the firm will produce if it does not shut down. Thus, these two curves alone determine the firm's supply. Average total cost is relevant only for determining how much profit or loss results at any price and output level.

Figure 12–9   Effect of an Excise Tax

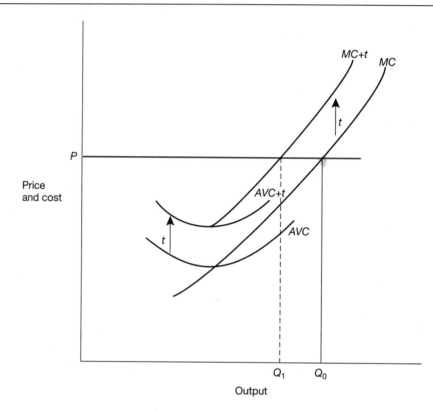

Output

12.6.2   Effects of Taxes, Subsidies, and Regulations

Thus far, we have discussed changes in a firm's output in terms of market-determined variables, such as product price or the price of inputs, or variables within the control of the firm, such as technological improvements. Government actions such as taxes, subsidies, or regulations can also affect a firm's cost and therefore its output.

Let us consider first the effect of a unit excise tax. Such a tax is simply a tax that requires firms to pay a specified amount to the government for each unit of output produced and sold, regardless of the price at which that unit of output is sold. The effect of such a tax is shown in Figure 12–9. A firm with cost curves MC and AVC, facing the market-determined price P, produces Q_0 units of output.

Now let the government impose an excise tax of t dollars per unit. For each unit of output sold, the firm must pay $\$t$ to the government. This has the effect of shifting the marginal and average variable cost curves upward by exactly $\$t$ at each level of output, to $MC + t$ and $AVC + t$ in the figure. To see why, suppose the marginal cost of producing another unit of output is $20 and an excise tax of $3 is imposed. The marginal cost of *producing and selling* that additional unit of output rises to $23; marginal cost, therefore, shifts upward by $3 at every level of output. By the same reasoning, average variable cost also shifts upward by $3.

In Figure 12–9, with the new marginal cost of $MC + t$, the firm reduces its output from Q_0 to Q_1. Because the minimum point on AVC rises by $\$t$, the price below which the firm shuts down in the short run rises by $\$t$ also. Thus, the firm decreases the quantity it produces when an excise tax is imposed. (Note that we could have obtained the same results from Figure 12–9 if we had assumed that the $\$t$ excise tax had reduced the price to the firm by $\$t$ per unit, the amount the firm must pay to the government. Analyzing the effect through cost is more consistent with the analysis when all firms in the market are subject to the tax.)

A subsidy has exactly the opposite effect. The government, wanting more of the product produced, pays the firm a specified amount for each unit of the good it produces and sells. This has the effect of shifting the marginal and average cost curves downward by exactly the amount of the subsidy. That is, the additional cost of producing and selling another unit of output is the marginal cost of production less the amount of the subsidy paid to the firm. Following the same line of reasoning used for a unit tax, the downward shift in the marginal and average variable cost curves induces the firm to produce more output and reduces the minimum price below which the firm will shut down.

A sales tax requires a certain percent of the price of a product to be paid to the government. In effect, the price received by the firm decreases, and the firm produces and sells less than before. As the effective price received by the firm decreases, the firm moves down its MC curve, causing the firm to produce a smaller output.

Lump sum taxes, such as a fixed license fee, and percent-of-profit taxes, such as a corporate income tax, have no effect on marginal or average variable cost and, therefore, have no effect on the firm's output. A lump sum tax requires the firm to pay the government a fixed amount no matter how much is produced. This is the same as an increase in fixed cost, and as is the case for all fixed costs, has no effect on output. Of course, in the long run, but not the short run, the tax could be high enough to cause the firm to go out of business.

A tax that requires firms to pay a percentage of their profits also has no effect on a firm's output because such a tax does not affect marginal cost. Suppose a profit tax of 25 percent is imposed. Now the firm can keep only 75 percent of its profit. One would assume that the firm would prefer 75 percent of its maximum possible profit to 75 percent of any lower level of profit. Since the firm was presumably maximizing profit prior to the tax by producing where price equals marginal cost, it would continue to do so.

Governmental regulations can take many forms—pollution controls, worker safety regulations, product safety regulations, regulations on the inputs used, and so forth. Only to the extent that such regulations shift the firm's marginal cost curve will they affect its output. A regulation that caused a once-and-for-all capital investment, such as the installation of pollution-reducing capital with no change in operating costs, would only raise a firm's fixed cost and would not change output. In contrast, a regulation that abolished the use of some type of pesticide on a farm, which would presumably make the firm less efficient or cause it to switch to a more expensive pesticide, would increase the marginal cost curve and induce the farm to reduce its output.

To summarize, if some type of change shifts a firm's marginal cost curve—input prices, technology, excise taxes, subsidies, and some governmental regulations—the firm changes its level of output. An increase in marginal cost decreases output, and a decrease increases output. Such changes also change the minimum point of average variable cost and, therefore, change the price below which the firm shuts down. Any change that does not affect marginal cost—lump sum taxes, percent-of-profits taxes and some governmental regulations—have no effect on the firm's output.

Economics in the News

Bad Times Are Good Times for Some Businesses

We hear a great deal about how a growing, healthy economy is good for business and slumps are bad. As is obvious from the preceding analysis, an increasing demand in a market is beneficial to firms selling in that market. A decreasing demand lowers price and either decreases profits or even leads to losses.

However, firms selling in some types of markets are actually made better off, at least temporarily, by economic slumps or declines. A story in *Newsweek,* "Pawnshops Make a Comeback," December 3, 1990, p. 44, reports how an economic downturn benefitted one type of firm, pawnshops. As you probably know, pawnshops lend money at extremely high interest rates to people who put up collateral such as jewelry, VCRs, computers, watches, and so forth. Borrowers pay up to a 36 percent yearly interest, because they are unable to obtain small loans from banks at lower interest rates.

Newsweek noted that the recession that began late in 1990 attracted many new customers to pawnshops—either as borrowers or as buyers of the goods put up as collateral for loans that were not repaid. "Bolstered by higher poverty rates, a sagging economy and a tightening economy, pawnshops are becoming lenders of last resort for a growing number of strapped consumers." One economist estimated that during the past year 1 in 10 Americans borrowed from pawnshops and that the number of pawnshops had increased by one third. Many pawnshops were relocating in the suburbs and, consequently, were attracting more middle-class and even upper-class patrons. People who wanted to tide themselves over until the next paycheck or were temporarily out of work were increasingly patronizing pawnshops when they were unable to obtain small loans from banks. Some small business owners even pawned their jewelry in order to meet a payroll.

Newsweek ended its article by posing a question: "Some industry observers denounce the double-digit interest rates as unconscionable. [Some were calling for regulations on interest rates.] Yet others say mandatory interest-rate regulation could drive companies out of business—and leave millions of borrowers with no borrowing alternative. To [some people], an expensive source of credit looks better than none at all." What do you think? How would such regulation be like a ceiling price? Who would benefit from interest-rate ceilings, and who would lose?

Obviously, pawnshops would not be the only beneficiaries of an economic downturn. You might take a look at Analytical Problem 5 at the end of this chapter for some other examples.

12.7   Summary

This chapter has set forth one of the most important tools of economic analysis—the theory of the perfectly competitive firm. The simple but crucial point of this theory is that the firm maximizes its profit by choosing the output at which its marginal cost equals the market-determined price, which is the marginal revenue of the firm. If price is greater than average total cost, the firm makes an economic profit, over and above its normal profit. In the short run, if price is less than average total cost but greater than average variable cost, the firm makes a loss but produces the output at which price equals marginal cost and loses less than it would by shutting down and producing nothing. If price is below minimum average variable cost in the short run, the best the firm can do is shut down, produce nothing, and lose all of its fixed cost. If price is below long-run average cost, the firm may exit from the market.

Anticipating future material in this text, the fact that the perfectly competitive firm produces the output at which price equals marginal cost has important social implications. The price of the product reflects how much consumers value the last units of the product—how much they are willing to give up rather than go without those units. Marginal cost measures how much it costs firms to produce the last units of output. Therefore, equilibrium in perfectly competitive markets means that the value people place on the marginal units of the good is equal to the amount it costs to produce the good. Perfect competition is the only market structure that results in this feature, as you will see later.

The theory of the perfectly competitive firm is relatively simple The theory of perfectly competitive markets or industries is somewhat more complex. When examining the functioning of markets, we must take into consideration the actions of all firms, not the action of only one firm. In the next chapter, we will develop the theory of perfectly competitive markets, which, as you would expect, is based on the theory set forth in this chapter.

Answers to   *Applying the Theory*

12.1   Certainly, individuals face fixed costs. Lease agreements on an apartment commit a person to a stream of payments, even if they do not live in the apartment over the entire lease agreement. Car payments, mortgage payments, minimum payments on credit cards, and minimum monthly charges on a telephone are other examples of fixed costs. Just as it is true for businesses, when individuals optimize, fixed costs should be ignored.

Technical Problems

1. If the market-determined price facing a perfectly competitive firm is $100, what is the firm's marginal revenue? Explain why.
2. Use the following figure (Figure E.12–1) to answer this question. This figure shows a perfectly competitive firm's short-run marginal cost (*MC*). Product price is $100.

Figure E.12–1

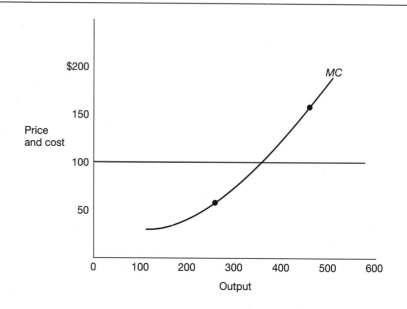

a. If the firm produces a positive output, how much should it produce? Explain.

b. Suppose, in the situation shown in the figure, the firm is producing 250 units of output. If the firm produces one more unit of output, what will happen to its total revenue? Its total cost? Its profit?

c. Alternatively, suppose the firm is producing 450 units of output. If the firm produces one less unit of output (moves from 450 to 449 units of output), what happens to total revenue? Total cost? Profit?

3. Use Table 12–1 from the text to answer this question. In the text, we explained why the firm produces seven units of output when price is $250, and makes an economic profit; and produces four units of output when price is $110, and suffers a loss.

a. If price is $200, how much will the firm produce? What are total cost and total revenue at this output? What is profit (loss)?

b. If price is $70, how much will the firm produce? What are total cost and total revenue at this output? What is variable cost at this output? What is profit (loss)? What would the firm lose if it shuts down?

4. Use Figure E.12–2, showing a firm's short-run average total, average variable, and marginal cost curves to answer this question.

a. If price is $175, how much does the firm produce? Explain why. What is total revenue? Total cost? Profit (loss)?

b. If price is $125, how much does the firm produce? Explain why. What is total revenue? Total cost? Profit (loss)?

c. If price is $100, how much does the firm produce? Explain why. What is total revenue? Total cost? Variable cost? Profit (loss)? How much does the firm have left over from its revenue, after paying its variable costs, to apply to fixed cost? How much would the firm lose if it shut down?

Figure E.12–2

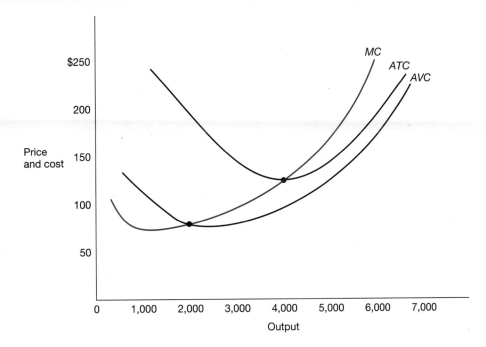

Figure E.12–3

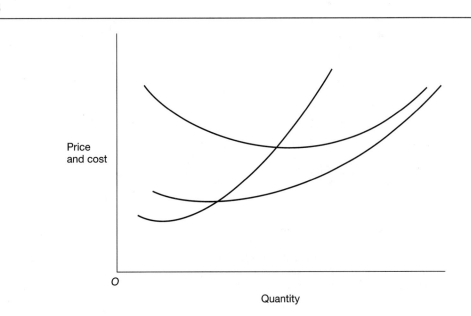

Figure E.12–4

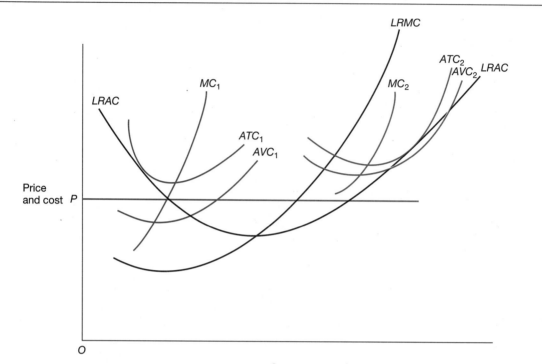

d. Below what price (approximately) would the firm shut down and produce nothing? Explain.

5. Figure E.12–3 on the preceding page shows a graph of a perfectly competitive firm's short-run cost structure.
   a. Label the three curves.
   b. Show a price at which the firm would make a pure profit. Show the quantity it would produce at this price and the amount of pure profit earned.
   c. Show a price at which the firm would continue to produce in the short run but would suffer losses. Show the output and losses at this price.
   d. Show the price below which the firm would not produce in the short run.

6. Suppose a perfectly competitive firm has a total revenue in a particular year of $4 million. Its total payments to inputs are $3 million. The firm owner also owns $4 million dollars worth of capital used by the firm. The going rate of return on capital is 10 percent. The owner does not manage the firm. What is the owner's rate of return on capital? What is normal profit? What is pure or economic profit?

7. Use the above figure (Figure E.12–4) to answer this question. In the figure, *LRAC* and *LRMC* are, respectively, a perfectly competitive firm's long-run average and marginal cost curves. Two short-run cost situations are shown by ATC_1, AVC_1, MC_1 and ATC_2, AVC_2, MC_2. The price of the product is P.

Figure E.12–5

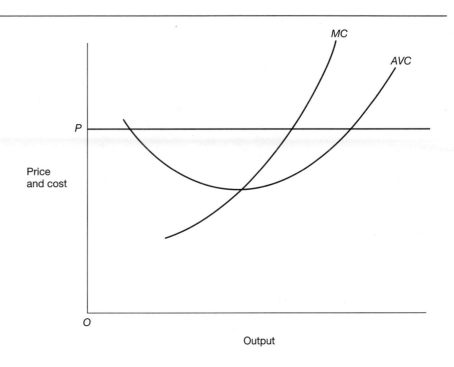

a. If the firm is in the short-run situation shown by ATC_1, AVC_1, MC_1, what is output? What is the firm's profit (loss)?

b. If the firm is in the short-run situation shown by ATC_2, AVC_2, MC_2, what is output? What is the firm's profit (loss)?

c. If the firm can move into the long run from either short-run situation, how much will the firm produce? What is profit (loss) at this output?

d. At the long-run profit-maximizing output, draw in the new short-run average total and marginal cost curves.

8. The figure above (Figure E.12–5) shows a perfectly competitive firm's average variable and marginal cost curves. Product price is P.

a. Show the firm's profit-maximizing output on the graph.

b. Show the new average variable and marginal cost curves if some of the input prices facing the firm decrease. Show the new output.

c. Show the new average variable and marginal cost curves if some of the input prices facing the firm increase (make sure the firm will continue to produce a positive output). Show the new output.

d. Explain what happens to the firm's supply in each situation (parts b and c).

9. Firm A and firm B both have total revenues of $100,000 and total fixed costs of $50,000; firm A has total variable costs of $80,000, and firm B has total variable costs of $110,000.

a. How much profit (loss) is each firm making? Should firm A produce or shut down? Why? What about firm B? Why?

    b. Firm C and firm D both have total revenues of $200,000 and total costs of $250,000; firm C has total fixed costs of $40,000, and firm D has total fixed costs of $70,000. How much profit (loss) is each earning. Should firm C operate or shut down? What about firm D? Why?

10. What is the short-run supply curve for a perfectly competitive firm? Explain.

11. A landscaping firm, whose owner had invested $1,250,000 in the firm, earned $150,000 in accounting profit last year. Which of the following statements are true? Which are false? Explain your answer for each.

    a. If the going rate of return on alternative investments is 15 percent, the firm should continue producing.

    b. If the going rate of return on alternative investments is 12 percent, the firm is earning zero economic profits.

    c. If explicit costs were more than $150,000, economic profit was negative.

12. Suppose the manager of a firm operating in a perfectly competitive market estimates the average variable and marginal cost functions to be

$$AVC = 10 - 3Q + 0.5Q^2 \qquad MC = 10 - 6Q + 1.5Q^2,$$

where *AVC* and *MC* are expressed in dollars, and *Q* is measured in 100 units. Fixed cost is $600.

    a. At what output is *AVC* at a minimum?

    b. What is the minimum *AVC*?

Suppose the market price is $10.

    c. How much output would the firm produce?

    d. What is profit (loss) at this output?

Now suppose the market price is $5.

    e. How much output will the firm produce?

    f. What is profit (loss) at this output?

13. Another firm selling in a perfectly competitive market estimates its short-run average variable and marginal cost functions as

$$AVC = 30 - 10Q + Q^2 \qquad MC = 30 - 20Q + 3Q^2,$$

where *AVC* and *MC* are in dollars and *Q* is units of output measured in 1,000 units. Fixed cost is $10,000. Based on marketing information, the manager believes the product price will be somewhere between $15 and $25, with $20 being the best estimate.

    a. How much output will the firm produce, and how much profit (loss) will it make at each price, $15, $20, and $25?

    b. Below what price will the firm shut down?

14. Sea-a-Rama loses money during the winter but does not shut down during these months. Explain why.

15. What would happen to a perfectly competitive firm's profit-maximizing output under each of the following situations. (Assume the firm is producing a positive output.) Explain your answers.

    a. The yearly license fee paid by the firm increases.

    b. A new consumer safety regulation forces the firm to hire a safety inspector for every 1,000 units of output it produces.

    c. The corporate profit tax increases.

d. The owner of the firm owns $1 million of capital used by the firm. The alternative rate of return increases from 8 percent to 12 percent.

e. The firm must pay a local tax of $1 for every unit of output sold.

Analytical Problems

1. We used financial markets as an example of markets that are perfectly competitive. In what sense are the following markets perfectly competitive? In what sense are they not?

    a. The market for video rentals in a large city.

    b. The market for orange juice.

    c. The market for bread in the United States.

    d. The gasoline market.

    e. The wheat market.

2. "It is silly to say that a firm would produce if it is making a loss. No firm would operate if it isn't making profits." Analyze this statement.

3. How can we say that a perfectly competitive firm faces a horizontal demand, when the law of demand states that demand curves for all products are downward sloping?

4. Would a perfectly competitive firm advertise? Explain. Why would a trade association representing a perfectly competitive industry (e.g., a wheat grower's association) want to advertise?

5. We used pawnshops as an example of firms that would expect to benefit from bad economic times in the country. Which of the following types of firms might be expected to benefit from bad times? Auto repair shops, automobile dealers, bus companies, video rental stores, canned food manufacturers, fruit growers. Explain.

6. How can economists say that firms should ignore fixed costs? These costs are real and must be the same as any other cost, such as the payments to workers. Explain.

7. A college student is thinking about dropping out of school and taking a job that has been offered. Which of the following should be a consideration in making the decision? Explain.

    a. I've already spent three years in college.

    b. I only have one more year until I get my degree.

    c. My parents have paid a lot of money to support me during the past three years.

    d. That new job will pay a lot of money.

    e. It will only cost $2,000 for my last year in school.

    f. I can make more money in the future if I stay in school.

    g. My grades have been rather low this year, but I haven't worked very hard.

    h. I really enjoy school.

8. In 1990, the President's Council of Economic Advisors issued a report on "the greenhouse effect," or global warning. This report relied heavily on marginal analysis—benefits versus costs—in its recommendation. How do you think marginal analysis was used in the report?

9. During the fall of 1990, after Iraq invaded Kuwait, oil prices rose dramatically, over 50 percent. Within six months oil prices returned to their preinvasion level. Theory says that an increased price leads to higher output, but very little new oil drilling took place in the United States during the period of high oil prices. Can you explain why not?

10. The following appeared in an article in *The Wall Street Journal,* April 19, 1983: "Amid dismal market conditions for heavy-duty and medium-duty trucks, International Harvester Company is selling many trucks below cost. Neil Springer, President of Harvester's truck group, denied in an interview that Harvester has led the price cutting, but acknowledged that it is selling some trucks below its (average) total cost. However, he noted that the sales (prices) cover such variable costs as labor and parts, even if they only pay part of fixed overhead costs. He said Harvester needs to sell below total cost to maintain its dealer organization, which he contends is stronger than it was in 1979. Mr. Springer also said the company is maintaining its market share, which is crucial to how Harvester would fare in a recovery."

   a. If you assume that officials at International Harvester know accurately all relevant cost schedules and their market demand schedule, explain precisely how they would determine optimum price and output in the short run. Use a diagram to show (a) output, (b) price, (c) total revenue, (d) total cost, and (e) total loss per period.

   b. During 1982, International Harvester incurred losses of $1.245 billion, a less than robust year economically. If Harvester is not "bailed out" with government subsidies, *explain carefully* what long-run adjustments you would predict for the company. Your explanation should include adjustments in terms of market demand, price, output, the relation between price and average total cost, and profit.

C H A P T E R 13

Theory of Perfect Competition:
The Industry

13.1 Introduction

Now that we have set forth the theory of the perfectly competitive firm, we will turn to an analysis of the functioning of perfectly competitive markets. The theory of perfectly competitive markets is slightly more complex than the theory of perfectly competitive firms, but, if you have a good grasp of the material in the preceding chapter, you should have little difficulty following the analysis in this chapter. To follow the generally accepted terminology, we will refer to all firms selling in a perfectly competitive market as a perfectly competitive industry. Thus, we can speak of all cotton producers selling in the cotton market as the cotton industry, and so forth.

We will begin the discussion of the theory of the perfectly competitive industry with the industry in the short run. In the short run, the industry consists of a fixed number of firms. Each firm uses some fixed and some variable inputs, and, therefore, has some fixed and some variable costs. Each firm produces the output at which the market-determined price equals marginal cost. Within this framework, we will develop the concept of short-run industry supply and analyze the effect of changes in each firm's cost on the quantity sold and price in the market. An important feature of this theory is the concept of producer's surplus, a concept closely related to that of consumer's surplus.

Next, we will finally make use of the important assumption that perfectly competitive markets are characterized by easy or unrestricted entry into or exit from the market. This assumption is crucial for the theory of the perfectly competitive industry in the long run. We will develop the theory of long-run competitive supply under the assumption that all firms are alike in their use of resources and technology.

We will then drop the assumption that all firms are alike and permit some firms in the industry to employ superior, or more productive, resources. As you will see, this assumption changes the theory very little. Finally, we will summarize the characteristics and some desirable features of perfect competition.

13.2   The Theory of the Perfectly Competitive Industry in the Short Run

Recall from Chapter 2 that we asserted that industry supply curves are upward sloping—quantity supplied varies directly with the price of the product. In that chapter, we briefly discussed why this direct relation between price and quantity supplied is typically assumed. Now we will set forth the proof. As you will see, the industry supply is derived from the firm's supply, discussed in Chapter 12. Then we will analyze the effects of changes in firms' costs on industry supply and, therefore, on price and quantity in the market.

13.2.1   Short-Run Industry Supply with and without Input Price Changes

Earlier chapters in this text showed that market demand is simply the horizontal summation of the demands of all consumers in the market. The derivation of market or industry supply in the short run is quite similar, but, as you will see, it is somewhat more complicated if the prices of some inputs change as the output in the market changes and firms use more or less of these inputs.

Assume first that the industry use of all inputs has no effect on the price of any input. Each firm takes the market price of each input as given and can purchase all it wants of that input at the going price. Furthermore, even if all firms in the industry increase or decrease their use of an input, the industry employment of the input is so small relative to the total use of the input by all firms in the economy that there is no effect on the input price. Assume that all firms in the competitive industry have identical cost structures. Finally, assume that the number of firms in the industry is fixed at 1,000.

Figure 13–1, Panel A shows the short-run marginal cost curve above average variable cost for a typical firm in the industry. If the product price is $15, this firm produces 100 units of output at which price equals marginal cost. Since there are 1,000 identical firms and each firm produces 100, the industry produces 100,000 units of output when price is $15. This combination is plotted as point A in Panel B. When price rises to $20, each firm increases its production to 125 units, as shown in Panel A. Thus, the industry produces 125,000 units of output when price is $20, as shown by point B in Panel B. Connecting all points so generated in Panel B, we have generated the industry supply curve. At each price, the firm produces the output at which price equals marginal cost. The industry produces an output equal to the output of each firm times 1,000. Thus, the industry supply in Panel B

Figure 13–1   Derivation of Industry Supply: Industry Has No Effect on Input Prices

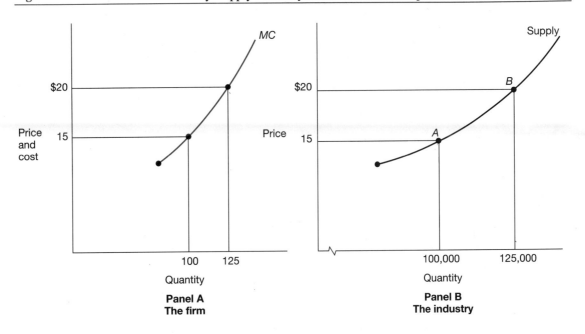

is simply the horizontal summation of all firms' marginal cost curves above average variable cost.

The derivation of industry supply is slightly more complicated when the prices of some inputs are affected by the industry usage of the inputs. Assume now that each firm is so small in the input markets that any one firm can change its input usage without having any effect on input prices, but when *all* firms in an industry *simultaneously* change their output and, hence, their input usage, there is a marked effect on input prices in some markets. For example, one small cotton textile manufacturer could expand production without affecting the world price of raw cotton. The relatively few additional bales purchased would not have a significant effect on the total demand for raw cotton. If all textile manufacturers in the United States simultaneously attempt to expand output by 10 percent, however, the demand for cotton would probably increase substantially, and the resulting increase in the price of cotton would be significant. When all manufacturers attempt to increase output, raw cotton prices would therefore be bid up; and the increase in the price of a variable input (raw cotton) would cause an upward shift in all firms' cost curves, including marginal cost.

As a consequence, the industry supply curve cannot be obtained by horizontally summing the marginal cost curves of all firms when industry usage has an effect on some input prices. As industry output and, hence, the industry usage of inputs expand, some input prices would increase, thereby shifting each firm's marginal cost curve upward and to the left. In such cases, the industry supply curve is more steeply sloped and, therefore, less elastic than the horizontal summation of all firms' marginal cost curves.

Figure 13–2   Derivation of Industry Supply: Industry Usage Affects Some Input Prices

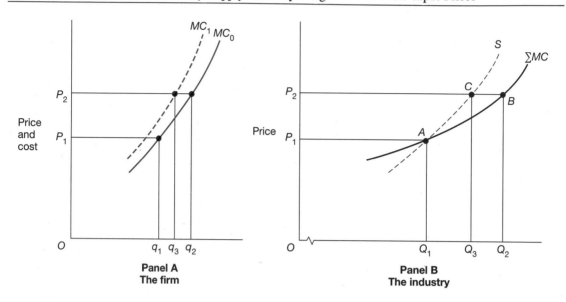

Panel A
The firm

Panel B
The industry

The derivation of industry supply in this case is shown in Figure 13–2. In Panel A, MC_0 is the short-run marginal cost curve of a typical firm in the industry. If product price is P_1, each firm produces q_1. If there are N firms in the industry, industry output at P_1 is Nq_1, which is equal to Q_1 in Panel B. Thus, point A is a point on the industry supply curve.

Now, let the product price increase to P_2. Each firm in the industry wants to increase output to q_2, where P_2 equals MC_0. Industry output would in this case expand along the curve labeled ΣMC (sum of the marginal cost curves) to point B at output Q_2, which is Nq_2. However, as all firms attempt to expand output together, they increase the use of inputs, and some input prices are bid up in response to this increase in demand. The increase in some input prices causes each firm's marginal cost curve to shift upward to MC_1 in Panel A. Therefore, rather than increasing output to q_2, where P_2 equals MC_0, they increase their output only to q_3, where P_2 equals MC_1. Thus, the industry increases its output only to Q_3, which is Nq_3, at point C in Panel B rather than to Q_2.

In Panel B, S is the industry supply curve. As you can see, S is steeper and therefore less elastic than the horizontal summation of all firms' marginal cost curves. Without more information on how much input prices increase, it is impossible to be more precise. Nonetheless, doubt is not cast on the basic fact that, in the short run, quantity supplied varies directly with price. The latter is all that is needed to draw a positively sloped market supply curve.

A decrease in product price has the opposite effect. As all firms contract their output and input use, some input prices fall in response, and firms' marginal cost curves shift downward. Each firm's output therefore decreases less than would have been the case if the marginal cost curve had not shifted. Consequently, the quantity supplied by the industry falls, but not by as much as it would have if some input prices had not fallen. (See supply curve S for prices below P_1.)

We have developed the following relation:

Relation

In the short run, with a fixed number of firms in the industry, industry supply is the horizontal summation of the marginal cost curves above average variable cost of all firms in the industry, when the industry has no effect on input prices. When the industry's usage of some inputs has an effect on the prices of these inputs, industry supply is steeper and less elastic than the horizontal sum of the firms' marginal cost curves.

Thus far in this section, we have shown that industry supply in the short run is upward sloping because each firm's marginal cost over the relevant range of output is upward sloping. Even if the marginal cost curves shift upward as industry output and, hence, input usage increases, the industry is still willing and able to supply more output as the price of the product increases. Thus, short-run supply is positively sloped.

13.2.2   Shifts in the Cost Curves

In Chapter 12, we described the effect of a change in input prices or a change in technology for an individual firm. Such changes increase or decrease the firm's marginal and average cost curves, which, respectively, decreases or increases the firm's supply. When there is perfect competition, the price of the product is not affected by the actions of any individual firm.

When a change in the price of an input or in technology affects not just one firm but all firms in the industry, the supply in the market shifts, and the price of the product changes. The change in product price causes each firm in the market to adjust its output so that the new marginal cost equals the new price.

Figure 13–3 illustrates the adjustment process. Assume that MC_0 in Panel A is the marginal cost curve above minimum average variable cost of each identical firm in the industry. Recall that if the industry as a whole has no effect on any input prices, supply is the horizontal sum of all firms' marginal costs. If, as the industry expands and uses more inputs, some input prices are driven up, industry supply is less elastic than the horizontal sum of MC, because, as all firms increase output in response to a product price increase, the increase in input prices shifts each firm's marginal cost curve upward and to the left.

In Figure 13–3, we assume for analytical simplicity that industry supply, S_0 in Panel B, is the horizontal sum of all firms' marginal costs. Supply and demand determine a price of P_0 in the market. In Panel A, the firm produces Q_0. If there are N firms in the industry and all firms are alike, quantity sold in the market is NQ_0.

Now, let the price of an input decrease. Each firm's marginal cost curve shifts downward to MC_1. Each firm would want to increase its output until P_0 equals

Figure 13–3   Effect of an Input-Price Decrease on the Firm and Industry

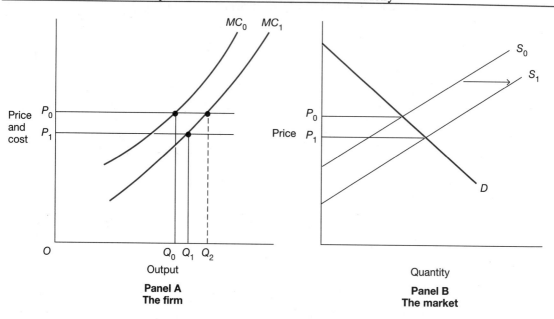

Panel A
The firm

Panel B
The market

MC_1 at output Q_2. However, the shift in marginal cost increases market supply from S_0 to S_1, the new horizontal sum of marginal costs. With the new supply, product price falls to P_1, and each firm produces Q_1, where P_1 equals MC_1. In this example, output increases as MC shifts downward, but not as much as would have been the case if supply had not increased, causing product price to fall, because all firms' marginal costs shifted downward.[1]

To summarize, a decrease in the price of an input or an improvement in technology that affects all firms in the industry shifts each firm's marginal cost curve downward. Industry supply increases, and product price falls. Each firm produces a larger output, and the quantity sold in the market increases also. A change that increases each firm's marginal cost, such as an increase in the price of an input used by all firms, has exactly the opposite effect. Industry supply decreases and causes product price to rise. Each firm produces less output, and quantity sold in the market decreases.

13.2.3   Effect of Taxes, Subsidies, and Regulations

In addition to changes in input prices and technology, government actions such as taxes, subsidies, or regulations can also affect cost, product price, and quantity sold. The effect of a unit excise tax, a per-unit tax on each unit of output sold, is

---

[1]The basic analysis would not have changed had we assumed that industry input usage has an effect on the prices of some inputs. Industry supply in Panel B would be less elastic, but the decrease in marginal cost would still cause supply to increase, causing a fall in the price of the product.

Figure 13–4   Effect of an Excise Tax

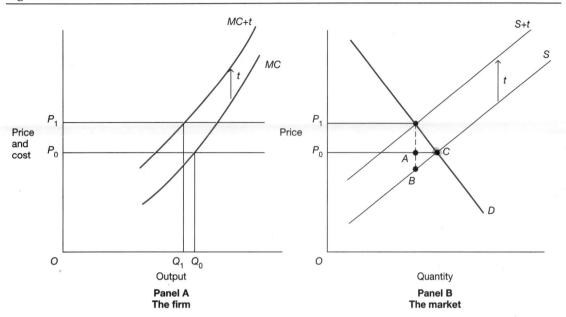

Price and cost

P_1

P_0

O Q_1 Q_0

Output

Panel A
The firm

Price

P_1

P_0

O

Quantity

Panel B
The market

shown in Figure 13–4. Assume as before that the industry has no effect on input prices. Before the tax is imposed, the curves labeled D and S in Panel B are, respectively, demand and supply in the market, with supply being the horizontal sum of all firms' marginal costs. The price of the product is P_0. In Panel A, a typical firm in the industry with the marginal cost curve MC produces Q_0 units of output.

Now, let the government impose an excise tax of t dollars per unit sold. For each unit of output sold, the firm must pay $\$t$ to the government. This tax has the effect of shifting the firm's marginal cost curve upward by exactly $\$t$ at each level of output; in Panel A marginal cost shifts upward to $MC + t$. As noted in Chapter 12, if the marginal cost of producing an additional unit of output is $12, the imposition of a $2 excise tax raises the marginal cost of producing and selling that additional unit to $14. The marginal cost of producing and selling every other additional unit of output rises by $2 also.

In Figure 13–4, because each firm's marginal cost shifts upward by t, industry supply in Panel B also shifts upward by exactly t, as shown by $S + t$. The tax has no effect on demand because sellers pay it and, presumably, consumers do not care how much of the price they pay goes to the firm and how much goes to the government. Thus, with the new supply, price rises to P_1. In Panel A, with the new price, P_1, and the new marginal cost, $MC + t$, the firm reduces its output from Q_0 to Q_1. Because all firms are identical and quantity sold in the market decreases, each firm reduces its output in the short run when the number of firms is fixed.

Clearly, as shown in Panel B, price in the market rises by less than t. At every level of output, $S + t$ lies precisely $\$t$ above S. Since price rises from P_0 to P_1, this much of the tax is passed along to consumers in the form of a price increase. That leaves the amount shown by the distance AB in Panel B to be paid by the firms.

13.1 *Applying the Theory*

In Figure 13–4, explain how the distance AB depends on the elasticity of supply and the elasticity of demand. Describe what happens as demand becomes more elastic. Describe what happens as supply becomes more elastic. You may want to review Chapter 3.

A subsidy has exactly the opposite effect of a unit tax. A government pays a subsidy to firms in an industry when it wants more of the product produced and sold at a lower price. A subsidy generally means that the government pays firms a specified amount for each unit of the good they sell. This has the effect of shifting each firm's marginal cost curve downward by exactly the amount of the subsidy. For example, if the marginal cost of producing another unit is $15 and the subsidy is $5 per unit, the marginal cost of producing and *selling* another unit is $10 because the firm receives $5 when that unit is sold. Because a subsidy shifts each firm's marginal cost curve downward by exactly the amount of the subsidy, industry supply (the sum of all marginal costs) shifts downward by exactly the amount of the subsidy. Price falls and quantity sold rises.

Taxes that have no effect on firms' marginal costs or the demand for the product have no effect in the short run on product price or quantity sold in the market. As discussed in Chapter 12, such taxes are lump sum taxes and percent-of-profit taxes. In the long run, however, these taxes could be high enough to cause losses and force some firms out of business. Furthermore, in the long run, firms could reduce their capital investment because projected profits from investments are reduced by lump sum taxes or profit taxes.

Recall from Chapter 12 that some types of governmental regulations affect firms' marginal costs, and some have an effect only on fixed cost. Only those regulations that affect marginal costs change product price and quantity sold in the short run. Such taxes shift the market supply curve. Regulations that increase firms' fixed costs do not change their output at any level of price, so they do not shift the market supply curve. Thus, they have no effect on product price and sales.

Economics in the News

Good News and Bad News for the Cereal Business

In this section, we have concentrated on the way changes in variables that affect firms' costs and governmentally enacted changes can affect prices, sales, and profits in industries. However, as an article in *Newsweek,* "Oat-Bran Heartburn," January 29, 1990, pp. 50–52, illustrates, we should not forget that changes in variables that affect demand

(continued)

can also have a huge impact. This article reported the effect of two scientific studies on the U.S. cereal industry.

In 1986, a Northwestern University study reported that oat bran was a highly successful method of reducing cholesterol. This study was followed by others that reached a similar conclusion; then the federal government warned people to keep their cholesterol down. According to *Newsweek,* "Customers stalked store shelves in search of oat bran and cereal companies scrambled to incorporate it in new products. Within a few months supermarket shelves bulged with [many new oat cereals]. By 1989 sales of oat-bran cereals rose to $247 million, up 240 percent from the previous year." Cheerios, a cereal that had always contained oat bran, became the top-selling cereal in the country. Obviously, the announcement of the health benefits from oat bran increased demand, which increased price, sales, and profit.

In January 1990, the *New England Journal of Medicine* published an article that concluded that oat bran may be no better than ordinary white flour at lowering cholesterol levels. This new study received the same publicity as the previous study and sent cereal producers scampering to handle damage control. Sales of oat-bran cereal fell off substantially as consumers searched for a new, miracle health food, such as rice or wheat. *Newsweek* concluded, "Whether 'the right thing to do' in the '90s is eating rice bran or amaranth—or even a whole-wheat bagel—one thing seems clear: marketers will be there to exploit it." Which is what we would predict.

13.3   Producer's Surplus

Producer's surplus is analogous to consumer's surplus, which we discussed in Chapter 7. Consumer's surplus, you will recall, is determined by market demand and, in fact, is measured by the area below the demand curve and above the market price. It is a measure of how well off consumers are when they buy at the market price rather than the highest price they are willing to pay. Producer's surplus is determined by market supply and, as you will see, is measured by the area above supply and below market price. It is a measure of how well off producers are when they sell at the market price rather than the lowest price at which they are willing to sell.

Definition

Producer's surplus is the difference between the market price producers receive from selling their products and the lowest price at which they would be willing to sell these units of output. Producer's surplus is measured by the area below the market price and above market supply.

13.3.1   Producer's Surplus and Market Supply

Figure 13–5 should give you some insight into the relation between producer's surplus and supply. In this figure, supply and demand in the market determine an equilibrium price and quantity of $30 and 1,000 units of output. Consider now the minimum price at which a firm would be willing to sell each unit of output from the first to the 1,000th.

Figure 13–5   Derivation of Surplus

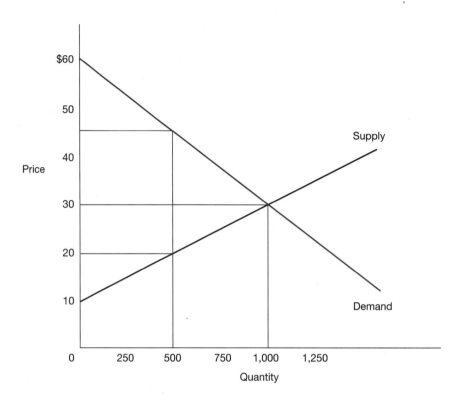

Look first at the lowest price a firm would be willing to sell the first unit. Remember that the market supply curve is derived from firms' marginal cost curves. Market supply therefore gives the marginal cost of producing each additional unit of output. As shown in the figure, the marginal cost of producing the first unit is $10. From the definition of supply, $10 is therefore the minimum price at which a firm would sell the first unit. Then, from the definition of producer's surplus, the producer's surplus from this first unit is the market price of $30, less the minimum price a firm would take, $10. Producer's surplus for the first unit is therefore $20.

Similarly, the minimum price at which a firm would sell the second unit is slightly more than $10, which is the marginal cost of the second unit. Thus, the producer's surplus from the second unit is slightly less than $20 because each unit can be sold at the market price of $30. Producer's surplus of each unit of output is derived similarly. For example, the marginal cost of (the minimum price a firm would take for) the 500th unit is $20. The producer's surplus from the 500th unit is $30 − $20 = $10. Each unit of output up to the 1,000th gives some positive producer's surplus, although producer's surplus declines with increases in output because of the upward-sloping supply curve. Since the marginal cost of the 1,000th unit equals the $30 market price, producer's surplus from this unit is zero.

We could add up the producer's surplus from each additional unit of output from the first to the 1,000th to obtain the total producer's surplus in the market. However, as is apparent from the graph, the area below the price of $30 and above supply from zero to 1,000 gives an extremely close approximation of producer's surplus. Since the supply curve is a straight line, this area is the area of the triangle with a base (b) of 1,000 and a height (h) of $30 − $10 = $20. Thus, producer's surplus is measured as the area of a triangle $(1/2) \cdot b \cdot h$, or

$$(1/2)(1,000)(\$20) = \$10,000,$$

which indicates that the benefit to producers from being able to sell each unit of output at the $30 market rather than at the marginal cost or minimum price at which they would be willing to sell is $10,000.

13.3.2   Total Surplus in the Market

The total surplus in a market is the sum of producer's surplus and consumer's surplus.

Definition

> Total surplus in a market is producer's surplus plus consumer's surplus. Producer's surplus is measured by the area below price and above supply. Consumer's surplus is measured by the area above price and below demand. Hence, total surplus is the area between demand and supply.

Producer's surplus indicates how much better off producers are by selling at the market price rather than the lowest price they would be willing to accept. Consumer's surplus indicates how much better off consumers are by buying at the market price rather than the highest price at which they would be willing to purchase. Total surplus, therefore, indicates how much better off both producers and consumers are by being able to sell and buy in the market.

The total surplus in the market shown by Figure 13–5 is easily determined. As you saw, producer's surplus in this market is $10,000. Consumer's surplus, the area below demand and above price, is the area of the triangle with a base of 1,000 and a height of $60 − $30 = $30. Consumer's surplus is

$$(1/2)(1,000)(\$30) = \$15,000.$$

Total surplus is $25,000 ($10,000 + $15,000), which measures how much better off all participants in the market are by being able to trade in the market.

13.3.3   Total Surplus is Maximized in Competitive Markets

Maximum total surplus is obtained when demand and supply freely determine price and quantity sold in competitive markets. Thus, the maximum total surplus obtainable in the market depicted in Figure 13–5 is $25,000. Any output below 1,000 decreases total surplus.

Suppose output is fixed at 500; or equivalently there is a price floor at $45. In either case, the equilibrium is at $45 and 500 units of output. The new consumer's surplus is measured by the area of the triangle

$$(1/2)(\$60 - \$45)(500) = \$3,750.$$

Thus, consumers lose surplus. The new producer's surplus, the area below $45 and above supply, is measured by the area of the rectangle with a height of $45 - $20 = $25 and a base of 500, which is $25 · 500 = $12,500, plus the area of the triangle with a height of $20 - $10 = $10 and base of 500, which is 1/2 · 500 · $10 = $2,500. Producer's surplus is $12,500 plus $2,500 = $15,000. The total surplus is now $3,750 plus $15,000 (= $18,750).

Note that consumers lose a surplus of $15,000 - $3,750 = $11,250. Producers gain a surplus of $15,000 - $10,000 = $5,000. However, the lost total surplus is $25,000 - $18,750 = $6,250. Some of the surplus is transferred from consumers to producers. However, there is still $6,250 of surplus missing. No one receives it, it is lost. The loss results from the restriction that does not allow output and price to be determined by demand and supply in the market. You can calculate this loss as the area of the triangle between 500 and 1,000 units and the price differential of 45 and 20. Alternatively, it is the area of the triangle below demand and above $30 from 500 to 1,000 plus the area of the triangle above supply and below $30 from 500 to 1,000. The amount represented by this area equals the loss of $6,250 and represents a net loss of total surplus.

As you will see when you work through the following "Applying the Theory," restrictions on the market such as ceiling and floor prices and excise taxes can cause a shift in surplus from consumers to producers or vice versa and always cause a net loss in total surplus. Furthermore, you will see in later chapters that the market under perfect competition leads to a larger total surplus than markets under any other market structure, other things remaining the same.

This completes the analysis of perfectly competitive industries in the short run. The most important aspect of this analysis has been the relation between the marginal cost curves of the firms in the industry and industry supply. This relation explains why short-run industry supply is upward sloping. We now turn to the analysis of the perfectly competitive industry in the long run.

13.2   *Applying the Theory*

Restrictions on the Market

This exercise is designed to show you how ceiling and floor prices and excise taxes can affect consumer's, producer's, and total surplus. Begin each part of the exercise with the original demand and supply curves shown in Figure 13–6 and no governmental intervention in the market.

a. In the original demand and supply situation, what are consumer's, producer's, and total surplus in the market?

Figure 13–6   Calculating Changes in Surplus

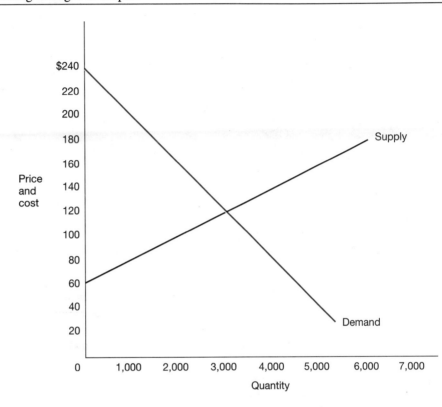

b. Let a floor price of $140 be imposed. No firm can sell below this price and producers can sell only what the market will buy. What are the new consumer's, producer's, and total surplus in the market? What are the changes in these surpluses from the original situation?

c. Eliminate the floor. Let a ceiling price of $100 be imposed. No firm can sell at a price above $100. What are the new consumer's, producer's, and total surplus? How are these changed from the original equilibrium?

d. Eliminate the ceiling price and let an excise tax of $60 be imposed. What are the new consumer's, producer's, and total surpluses? What are the changes in these from those in the original equilibrium? What is the government's tax revenue? What is the lost total surplus net of tax revenue?

13.4   Long-Run Competitive Equilibrium

In Chapter 12, we stressed that in the long run, when all inputs are variable, a perfectly competitive firm will produce the output at which the market-determined price equals the firm's long-run marginal cost. If a firm is in the short run, making economic profit, a loss, or a normal rate of return, it can often adjust in the long

Figure 13–7   Long-Run Adjustment Process

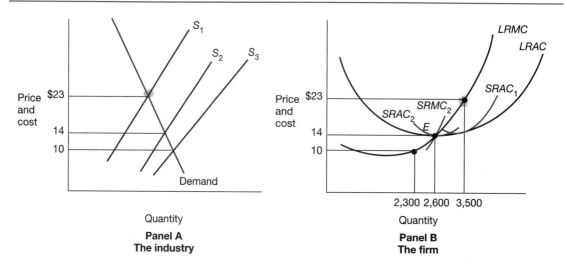

Panel A
The industry

Panel B
The firm

run to attain a more profitable situation. A firm making a below-normal rate of
return has two options: it can liquidate the business and transfer resources to a
more-profitable situation, or it can choose another more-profitable short-run situation, perhaps by changing plant size, and remain in the industry. Even a firm that
is making normal or above-normal profits may choose to change size in the long
run in order to increase profits.

We have not yet, however, discussed in detail the implications of the assumption
of easy entry into or exit from a perfectly competitive industry. This assumption
is crucial for the theory of the industry in the long run. If economic profits are
attainable, new firms will enter the industry. If losses are being made in the long
run, some firms will leave the industry. We will show in this section that all of
these adjustments in the size and number of firms in the industry in response to the
profit or loss incentive are key elements in establishing long-run equilibrium in a
perfectly competitive industry.

13.4.1   The Long-Run Adjustment Process

The process of attaining long-run equilibrium in a perfectly competitive industry
is illustrated in Figure 13–7. Suppose all firms in the industry are of identical size
(have the same cost structure), and potential entrants would be of identical size
also. Also assume for now that the industry as a whole has no effect on the price
of any inputs. (We will drop this assumption later.)

Begin with the demand in the market, as shown in Panel A, and the supply
curve S_1. The equilibrium price is $23. The long-run average and marginal costs
of each firm in the industry are, respectively, *LRAC* and *LRMC*. With a price of
$23, each firm chooses in the long run to produce 3,500 units of output. The

relevant short-run average total cost for each firm is $SRAC_1$, tangent to $LRAC$ at 3,500 units. Since price is well above average cost, each firm in the industry is making an economic profit. Total sales in the industry are given by the number of firms in the industry times each firm's output of 3,500.

Although each firm in the industry is in equilibrium, the industry itself is not. The existence of economic profit in this industry, a return in excess of that attainable elsewhere, attracts new firms into the industry. The entry of new firms increases industry supply in Panel A, and the increase in supply drives down product price. All firms adjust to the lower price. Firms will continue to enter as long as the price is high enough for them to earn economic profit. Thus, new entry will continue until supply has increased to S_2 and price has fallen to $14.

When the price is $14, it is equal to each firm's minimum long-run average cost at point E, as shown in Panel B. Each firm produces 2,600 units of output because price also equals long-run marginal cost at this output. No firm makes any economic profit, nor does any firm make a loss. Each firm makes a normal profit, which, as you know, is included in average cost. Because there is no more economic profit to be earned and firms make only a normal return, there is no longer any incentive for more firms to enter the industry.

The process of new entry might be very, very slow, or it might be very fast, depending on the mobility of resources in other industries. In any event, as time elapses, capacity will increase in the industry. As each firm adjusts to the reduced market price, the output of each will be smaller. Total output in the market is each firm's output, 2,600, times the number of old firms plus the number of new firms in the market. The larger number of firms, therefore, accounts for the larger output in the market as shown in Panel A. Since the new price, $14, equals both $LRMC$ and $SRMC_2$ at point E in Panel B, and this is a minimum point on $LRAC$ and $SRAC_2$, both the industry and its firms are in long-run competitive equilibrium, and neither economic profit nor loss is present for any firm.

If "too many" firms enter the industry and supply increases even further, say to S_3 in Panel A, price falls to $10, as shown in Panel B, and each firm makes a loss. Price is below minimum $LRAC$, and the best a firm can do is produce 2,300 units of output at which price equals $LRMC$. Firms cannot even earn a normal profit, and some will leave the industry and switch their resources to their best alternative use. Others will leave as their plant and equipment depreciate. As firms exit from the industry, supply will decrease, and it will continue to decrease as long as price is below $14. Thus, exit will continue until supply decreases to S_2 and price rises to $14, where firms earn a normal profit.

13.4.2   Which Firms Enter and Which Firms Leave?

As we emphasized above, when firms in an industry are making economic profits, new firms will enter the industry until price is driven down to minimum $LRAC$. When firms are making losses, firms will exit the industry until price is driven up to minimum $LRAC$. When price equals minimum $LRAC$, each firm earns a normal profit, and no entry or exit occurs.

A natural question arises from the theory. If all firms in the industry are identical, which firms leave when losses are being made? Identical firms mean identical losses. Similarly, if new firms are like existing firms, which firms enter when profits are earned? The answer to this question is not obvious, and only an answer that is suggestive can be provided.

A simple story gives some insight. Suppose your professor announces that $1,000 will be given away to the 20 students in the class after the lecture. The distribution pattern is this: the students can go to either room A or room B. Then $500 will be divided equally among those students in A, and $500 will be divided equally among those in B. How many students will be in each room? Obviously, 10 will be in each. If more than 10 are in one room and less than 10 in the other, some will leave the room that has more students and go to the other room until they are divided equally. Each student should receive $50.

Suppose the professor shows up after the students have arranged themselves and announces that a mistake has been made: there is $750 for those in A and only $250 for those in B. However, anyone who wishes can change rooms. What do you predict will happen? Obviously, five students leave room B and go to A. Once more, each should receive $50.

Which students would leave B and go to A? Which students would remain in B? Clearly, no one can predict this. The only prediction possible is that the final allocation will be 15 in A and 5 in B.

The predictions of this simple story are similar to the predictions of the theory of long-run competitive equilibrium. We can say that a perfectly competitive firm in long-run equilibrium will consist of as many firms as are necessary for price to equal each firm's long-run average cost at its minimum point. If price is above minimum *LRAC*, enough firms will enter to drive price down at this point. If price is below minimum *LRAC*, enough firms will exit to drive price up to this point. This is all the theory can predict; yet it is a rather strong conclusion. The theory cannot predict which firms will enter, which will exit, or which will remain in the industry. However, expectations about future profits and losses of firms in the industry may differ, and this may cause selected firms to stay and some to exit. Those who believe future prospects are down may exit. Those who are more optimistic may stay.

In terms of Figure 13–7, suppose that we know that on the demand curve in Panel A, at a price of $14, 520,000 units are demanded. Since long-run equilibrium requires that supply equals demand at $14, because this is minimum *LRAC*, 520,000 units of output will be sold in the market. Each firm produces an output of 2,600 in equilibrium. Therefore, in long-run equilibrium there must be 200 firms in the industry (200 × 2,600 = 520,000).

Clearly, if price is above $14, we know new firms will enter the industry, but we cannot predict which firms will enter. If price is below $14, we know some firms will leave the industry, but we cannot predict which firms will leave. All we can predict is that in long-run competitive equilibrium the price will be $14, each firm will sell 2,600 units of output, market sales will be 520,000, and the industry will consist of 200 firms.

*Economics in
the News*

Good News for Farmers? Probably Not for Long

Newsweek, "Tinkering with Nature," May 26, 1986, pp. 54–56, reported some seemingly revolutionary possibilities for genetic engineering in agriculture and possible implications of these experiments. For example, spraying bacteria on plants could possibly "lower the plant's freezing point—potentially saving farmers $1 billion a year now lost to frost damage."

Three years later, *Newsweek* predicted some trends for the 1990s: "Who said farming is a dying profession? Some experts predict that gene splicing could produce insect-resistant plants."

Suppose these genetic engineering experiments turn out to be highly successful. How will they likely affect farmers' income? Who would benefit the most?

Certainly technological breakthroughs that lower the costs of growing crops would benefit many existing farms in the short run by lowering their costs and, consequently, increasing their economic profits. However, these technological improvements would be readily available to all farmers. Because agriculture approaches the model of perfect competition, in the long run existing farms would expand their output of the crops for which the technological changes took place. More important, in the long run, new farms would enter these markets in response to the higher profits. As emphasized above, new entry would drive prices down until profits are competed back to a normal rate of return. Therefore, if farms, on average, were earning a normal profit before the technological improvement, they would earn only a normal profit after all the adjustments take place.

There could be two groups who would benefit. Consumers would end up paying lower prices in the long run because the technological improvement lowers the long-run average costs of the farms and price would fall to minimum *LRAC*. Second, the owners of land that is especially suited to growing crops that were affected by the technological improvements would, in the long run, see their land become more valuable. New farmers wishing to expand would bid up the price of this land.

13.4.3   Summary of Long-Run Equilibrium

Figure 13–8 summarizes the long-run equilibrium of a firm in a perfectly competitive industry. So long as the cost curves do not change, the only conceivable point of long-run equilibrium occurs at point *E*. Each firm in the industry receives neither economic profit nor loss. If the price in the market is above *P,* new firms will enter, and the price will fall. If price in the market is below *P,* some firms will exit, and price will rise. When price is *P* and each firm produces *Q,* there is no incentive for further entry or exit because the rate of return in this industry is normal, or equivalent to other investment opportunities. For the same reason, there is no incentive for a firm already in the industry to leave. The number of firms stabilizes, each firm operating in the short run with a plant size represented by *SRAC* and *SRMC*.

Firms will enter or leave the industry if there is either economic profit or loss. Since the position of long-run equilibrium must be consistent with zero profit (and zero loss), it is necessary that price equals average cost. For a firm to attain its

Figure 13–8   Long-Run Equilibrium of a Firm in a Perfectly Competitive Industry

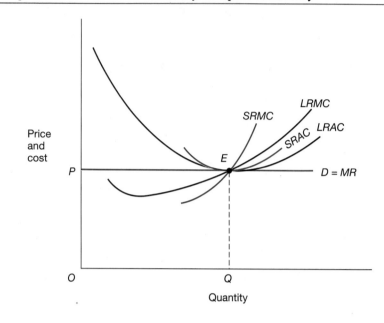

individual equilibrium, price must also be equal to marginal cost. Therefore, price must equal both marginal and average cost. This can occur only at the point where average and marginal cost are equal, or at the point of minimum average cost.

The short-run position could conceivably apply to any *SRAC* and *SRMC*. However, unless it applies only to the short-run plant that coincides with minimum long-run average cost, a change in plant size would lead to the appearance of pure profit, and entry would take place to reduce profits to their normal level.

13.5   Long-Run Industry Supply

The long-run analysis thus far has been concerned with the long-run equilibrium conditions of the firms and the adjustment process through which this equilibrium occurs. This analysis has been based on the assumption that expanded resource use by the industry does not bring about an increase in input prices. To carry the analysis further, this section will describe the supply adjustment process after there are changes in demand. We develop the long-run supply curve of a perfectly competitive industry when each point on supply is restricted to the condition of long-run competitive equilibrium. We will soon drop the assumption that the industry as a whole has no effect on the prices of any inputs by allowing such an effect to take place. However, we first maintain the assumption of no effect on input prices.

Figure 13–9   Long-Run Equilibrium and Supply Price in a Perfectly Competitive Industry Subject to Constant Cost

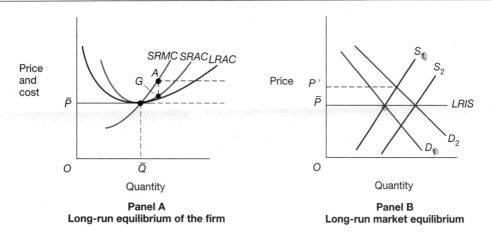

Panel A
Long-run equilibrium of the firm

Panel B
Long-run market equilibrium

13.5.1   Constant Cost Industries

A constant cost industry is a perfectly competitive industry that has no effect on the prices of any inputs used by the firms. Long-run equilibrium adjustment and long-run supply price under conditions of constant cost are explained by Figure 13–9. Panel A shows the long- and short-run conditions of each firm in the industry, while Panel B depicts the market as a whole. The original market demand and supply curves are D_1 and S_1. They establish a market equilibrium price of $\bar{P}$ dollars per unit. We assume that the industry has attained a position of long-run equilibrium, so the position of each firm in the industry is depicted by Panel A—the price line is tangent to the long- and short-run average cost curves at their minimum points.

Now suppose demand increases to D_2. With the number of firms fixed, the price will rise to P', and each firm will move to short-run equilibrium at point A. At point A, each firm earns an economic profit since price exceeds average cost by the amount AG per unit. New entrants are attracted into the industry, causing the industry supply curve to shift to the right. In this case, we assume that all resources used are so plentiful that increased use in this industry has no effect on the market price of resources. As a consequence, the expansion of old firms and entrance of new firms does not increase costs. The *LRAC* curve for all firms remains stationary. Complete long-run equilibrium adjustment to the shift in demand is accomplished when the number of firms expands to the point where the original equilibrium price, $\bar{P}$, is restored. This means in Panel B that supply increases to S_2. The firms in the market operate at the minimum point on *LRAC,* producing the quantity $\bar{Q}$.

In other words, since output is expanded by expanding the number of firms, each firm producing $\bar{Q}$ units per period of time at average cost $\bar{P}$, the industry has a constant long-run supply price equal to $\bar{P}$ dollars per unit. If price were above this level, firms would continue to enter the industry in order to reap the obtainable profit. If price were less than $\bar{P}$, some firms would ultimately leave the industry to avoid economic loss. In the special case where an expansion of resource use does not lead to an increase in resource price, the long-run industry supply price is constant. Thus, the long-run industry supply (*LRIS*) is a horizontal line at the long-run supply price, $\overline{P}$. In the long-run, price remains constant unless something occurs that shifts the firms' cost curves. A constant cost industry is characterized by a horizontal long-run supply curve.

13.5.2   Increasing-Cost Industries

We now drop the assumption that the industry as a whole has no effect on the price of any input in order to examine the adjustment process and the long-run industry supply when costs increase as the industry expands. An increasing-cost industry is a perfectly competitive industry that does have an effect on the price of some inputs, even though no firm in the industry, by itself, can affect any input prices. When an increasing-cost industry expands its output by using more inputs, its input usage in some input markets is large enough to increase the demand for the inputs in those markets and cause the price of those inputs to rise. Alternatively, a decrease in output and consequent decrease in input usage causes the prices of some inputs to fall.

The adjustment process and long-run industry supply of an increasing-cost industry are depicted in Figure 13–10. The original situation is the same as in Figure 13–9. The industry is in a position of long-run equilibrium, and D_1 and S_1 are the market demand and supply curves, respectively. Equilibrium price is P_1. Each firm operates at point E_1, where price equals minimum average cost for both the long- and short-run curves. Each firm is in a position of long-run equilibrium.

Let demand shift to D_2 so that price rises to a much higher level, P_2. The higher price is obviously accompanied by economic profit for the producing firms; new firms are consequently attracted into the industry, and the use of resources expands. Now suppose this expansion causes the prices of some resources to rise. The cost of inputs will increase for the established firms as well as for the new entrants.

Two forces act to bring the industry into a new long-run equilibrium. First, the entry of new firms increases supply in Panel B, causing the price of the product to decrease from P_2. Second, the increase in the prices of some inputs, caused by the expansion of output and input usage in the industry, causes the long-run average and marginal cost curves of each firm, new and old, to shift upward. Naturally, the process of equilibrium adjustment is not instantaneous. Nonetheless, as *LRAC* rises and price falls, each firm's profit is reduced from what it was when price was P_2 and $LRAC_1$ was each firm's average cost curve.

As long as there are economic profits, entry and adjustment continue until all firms have zero profit. The new product price, which is below P_2, will just equal the new minimum point of long-run average cost, which is above P_1. Such a point is given by E_2 on $LRAC_2$ in Panel A. Supply in Panel B has increased to S_2 and is equal to the new demand at the new equilibrium price, P_3.[2] As shown in Figure

---

[2]As Figure 13–10 is constructed, the minimum point on *LRAC* shifts slightly to the left as *LRAC* shifts upward. In fact, minimum *LRAC* can correspond to either a smaller or a larger output. The analysis underlying the exact nature of the shift involves an advanced concept not treated in this text.

Figure 13–10   Long-Run Equilibrium and Supply Price in a Perfectly Competitive Increasing Cost
Industry

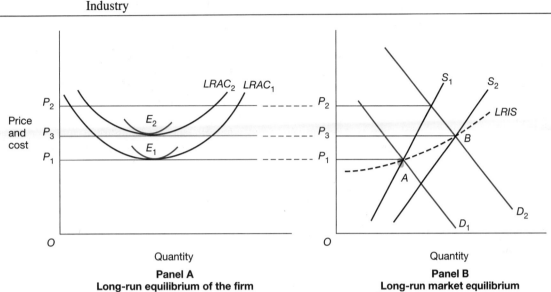

Panel A	Panel B
Long-run equilibrium of the firm	**Long-run market equilibrium**

13–10, the new equilibrium price, P_3, is about halfway between the old equilibrium price, P_1, and the price that prevailed immediately after the increase in demand, P_2. Actually, all we can say is that the new equilibrium price would lie somewhere between P_1 and P_2. Where the new price would end up depends upon the strength of the two forces bringing about the new equilibrium: the rising input prices that drive *LRAC* upward and the falling product price caused by the increase in supply from the entrance of new firms.

We should note that the two occurrences tend to work in opposite directions on the industry's supply curve. The rising marginal cost curve tends to shift the industry's supply curve to the left. But the entry of new firms tends to shift industry supply to the right. The forces causing a shift in the market supply schedule to the right (entry) must dominate those causing a shift to the left (rises in marginal costs); otherwise, total output could not expand, and there would not be a new market equilibrium price and quantity.

To see why supply must shift to the right after an increase in demand, let us assume that the opposite happens. In Figure 13–10, demand, as before, shifts to D_2. In the short run, price and quantity increase along with profits. The profits attract new firms, which, on entering, bid up resource prices. All cost curves rise. Suppose, however, that the leftward shift in all marginal cost curves dominates the tendency for an increase in supply caused by entry. Therefore, the new supply curve would lie somewhere to the left of S_1. If demand remains at D_2, price must be greater than P_3; firms must be making pure profits, and entry would continue. If the same process continues to occur, price will rise further, costs will rise, profits will continue, and entry will be further encouraged. Thus, a leftward shift in supply is not consistent with equilibrium. At some point, the entry of new firms must dominate the increase in costs, and supply must shift to the right, though not as much as it would in a constant-cost industry.

Therefore, for increasing-cost industries, new firms enter until minimum long-run average cost shifts upward to equal the new price. In the transition from one long-run equilibrium to the other, the long-run supply price increases from P_1 to P_3. This is precisely what is meant by an increasing-cost industry. The long-run industry supply curve is given by a line, *LRIS*, joining such points as A and B in Panel B. Thus, an increasing-cost industry is one with a positively sloped long-run supply curve. Alternatively stated, after all long-run equilibrium adjustments are made, an increasing-cost industry is one in which an increase in output requires an increase in long-run supply price.

13.5.3   The Possibility of Decreasing-Cost Industries and Technological Improvement

A decreasing-cost industry could theoretically exist, but the circumstances under which this could occur would have to be rather unusual. In such cases, an increase in industry output and input usage would decrease rather than increase the prices of some inputs. An increase in demand would raise the product price, lead to profits, and cause new firms to enter the industry, thereby increasing supply. Increased production would cause some input prices to fall, and, as a result, the long-run average cost curves of all firms would shift downward. The new minimum point on *LRAC* would be lower than before, so the new equilibrium price would be lower. As a result of the process, the long-run industry supply would be downward sloping. One must be very careful when identifying a decreasing-cost industry. Everyone can think of examples of products that have decreased dramatically in price while experiencing significant gains in sales. A recent example is the personal computer industry—prices have dropped as sales increased. The entire computer industry has experienced the same phenomenon. Earlier, color TV sets dropped in price as sales increased. This has also been the case for many other goods, such as VCRs and CD players.

These are not examples of decreasing-cost industries in the sense discussed above. In the cases of decreasing-cost industries, an increase in industry output reduces the price of some inputs. For such industries, costs fall because of reduced input prices. It is likely, however, that technological change caused the prices to fall in the above examples.

Recall that technological change lowers each firm's costs and, consequently, increases industry supply. Two possible situations are depicted in Figure 13–11. In Panel A, the demand for the product, D, remains constant over a reasonably long period of time. Begin with a long-run supply of S_1 and an equilibrium price of P_1. If technological change occurs, each firm's costs are reduced. At P_1, profits are earned and entry takes place to increase the supply curve to S_2, lowering price to P_2. Clearly, equilibrium output increases. Technological change continues, increasing supply to S_3, reducing price to P_3, and increasing output. Prices are falling in the market, but not because of declining input prices. In Panel B, the demand for the product increases from D_1 to D_2 to D_3. Because of technological change,

Figure 13-11   Effect of Technological Change

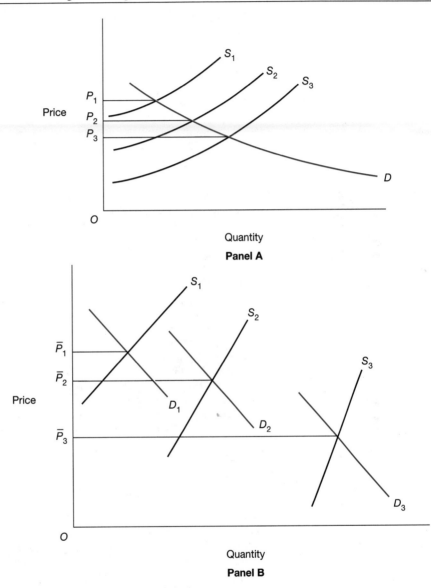

Panel A

Panel B

not because of a reduction in input prices from increased use, supply increases even more, from S_1 to S_2 to S_3. These shifts cause price to fall from $\overline{P}_1$ to $\overline{P}_2$ to $\overline{P}_3$.

Let us stress that these are not examples of decreasing long-run supply. The long-run supply curves were derived under the assumption that technology remains constant. In the situations depicted in Figure 13-11, and in the examples given here, it is the change in technology that is responsible for the shift in supply. To summarize this section, we have the following:

Relation

Constant, increasing, or decreasing cost in an industry depends on the way that input prices respond to expanded usage. If input prices remain constant, the industry is subject to constant cost; if input prices increase, the industry has increasing costs; and if input prices decrease, the industry has decreasing costs. The long-run supply curve for a constant-cost industry is a horizontal line at the level of the constant long-run supply price. The long-run industry supply curve under conditions of increasing cost is positively sloped.

Economics in the News

Entry and Exit in Financial Markets

Most of the 1980s were boom years for the U.S. economy. As the economy expanded, people borrowed more and more; lending institutions thrived and expanded. At the end of the decade, however, borrowing slackened considerably and many lenders were severely affected. The pattern followed the typical case of an industry that approached rather closely a constant-cost industry during a period of increasing and decreasing demand.

Business Week, "It's the Morning After for Mortgage Bankers," August 8, 1988, p. 66, reported the story of the mortgage banking industry. "Falling interest rates in 1986 and early 1987 touched off a frenzy of home buying and refinancing. That added billions in fat fees for mortgage bankers. And with intricate new ways to package mortgages into securities, dozens of newcomers were pouring into the business, from industrial giants such as General Motors Corp. and Owen-Illinois Inc. to pension funds and insurance companies. Attracted to the high fees and the chance to sell loans quickly and avoid credit risks, many thrifts, too, set up separate mortgage-banking units." In summary, demand increased, profits increased, and the number of firms increased.

In mid-1987, the demand for mortgage loans decreased—the building boom had slowed down—and, according to *Business Week,* too many firms were in the mortgage business. In one year, 10 percent of the nation's mortgage bankers lost their jobs or were reassigned. One large California company, Cal Fed, closed 14 of its 18 offices and announced that it would fold the rest into its saving offices. Other firms were going out of business, while still others were slashing capacity up to 50 percent by closing offices. The president of one large mortgage company said, "It will take another 12 to 18 months to wring out this excess capacity."

Wall Street brokerage firms rode a similar roller coaster during the 1980s. (See the *Houston Chronicle,* "Wall Street Brokerages Face Dry Spell," April 3, 1989, pp. 1B–2B.) The boom of the 80s brought huge profits to Wall Street brokers, but, according to the *Chronicle,* by 1989, "Their profits have been tightly squeezed by high interest rates, continued distrust of the stock market [from the crash of 1987] and a paucity of big merger deals." Many securities executives are discovering [that] . . . their core businesses are unprofitable because too many participants are chasing too little business. Competition has reduced profit to paper-thin levels in everything from mortgage backed securities to government and corporate bonds."

An increase in demand increased profits and induced entry. Then a decrease in demand reduced profits. There were too many firms. Most brokerages reduced their capacity, and some simply shut down, which is what the theory set forth here would predict.

13.6   Rent and Long-Run Competitive Equilibrium

Thus far in the analysis, all firms in an industry have been identical. Each firm, new and old, has the same cost structure. All economic profit is completed away in long-run equilibrium, where for each firm $LRAC = LRMC$ = Price.

But, what happens if some firms are different? Some firms hire better or more productive resources, or the resources owned by some firms are more productive than those of other firms in the industry. Some farmland is more productive than other land; surely the costs of the farms with more productive land would be lower than those of farms on other land, and surely they would make a profit even if other firms don't. What happens if the managers of some firms are better than those of others? If the location of some firms is better than that of others? These firms would have lower costs than others. Doesn't this make a difference? Don't these firms make a profit?

Actually, the existence of more productive land, management, location, or any other resource really does not make much of a difference in the theory, and these firms do not make a profit in the long run. Any differences in cost are due to differences in the productivity of one or more resources. Suppose that all firms but one in a competitive industry are alike; perhaps because of a more favorable location that lowers shipping costs, one firm has lower cost curves and would make a higher accounting profit than other firms.

The owner of the favorable location would surely raise the rent to the firm up to the point where the firm's economic profit disappears. If the original firm did not pay this higher rent, other firms would. In any case, the firm would be motivated to pay the higher rent since the owner would continue to make the equivalent of the next best alternative. Or, if the owner of the favorable location is also the owner of the firm, the firm's opportunity cost would rise because of the lucrative alternative of renting the location to some other firm.

In either case, the cost of the previously lower-cost firm would tend to rise. It would not rise above the cost of other firms because any higher rent would cause losses, and no firm would pay it in the long-run. The same type of argument applies to the superior manager; even if a manager-owner could lower the firm's costs, that manager could presumably lower the costs of other firms as well. The manager's salary would be bid up, or, if the manager is the owner of the firm, the opportunity cost of his or her time would rise. At equilibrium, all firm's long-run average cost curves would, therefore, reach their minimum points at the same cost, and no firm would make pure profit or loss, although some might have differing accounting payments.

Firms with even higher cost structures are generally "waiting in the wings" to enter the industry if demand increases and drives up prices sufficiently to cover their costs. These higher-cost firms could cover opportunity cost only at a higher price. If price increases enough to induce their entry, the owners of resources that allow the firms already in the industry to have lower costs than potential entrants will receive increased payments. Some firms that were making normal profits prior to the increase in price may begin to enjoy above-normal profits, which will, in the long run, be dispersed to the resources responsible for the profits.

The payments to the owners of the superior resources, over and above the amount necessary to induce these resources to be supplied in the market, are called economic rents, or simply rents. As an example, suppose a piece of fertile land has no use other than farming. Other than farming, the opportunity cost of the land is low. Therefore a low yearly payment would be sufficient to put the land into farming. But because the land is so fertile, farmers would bid the payments far above the low payment necessary to put the land into farming. The difference in payments is rent. People can earn rent for their labor services. Perhaps Michael Jordan would play professional basketball for anything above what he could earn, perhaps as a computer engineer. However, Mr. Jordan is such a good player and crowd attraction that he receives millions a year to play for the Chicago Bulls. The difference between the salary he would accept and what he actually gets is rent.

So firms can be different but still have the same minimum long-run average cost. Firms using superior resources must pay rents to these resources, which means the opportunity cost of the firm is higher. Firms with superior resources may well produce a greater output in equilibrium than firms using less productive resources. Nonetheless, the existence of rents means that all economic profit of all firms is competed away in the long run.

As we mentioned previously, because of scarce resources, it is possible that industry expansion could occur only through the entry of firms at a higher cost than firms already in the industry. If expansion takes place through the entry of higher-cost firms, the industry would have an upward-sloping long-run supply curve. As demand rises and causes product price to rise, firms that would have been unprofitable at lower prices enter. The economic profits of the old firms are captured as rents by the superior resources responsible for their lower costs. The final price is therefore higher, to accommodate the new firms, but each firm still operates at the minimum point on its long-run average cost curve.

Economics in the News   **Rents in Housing Markets**

USA Today, May 17, 1989, published a front-page story, "High Prices and High Rates Douse Markets," about the downturn in home prices. "An unwritten law has governed home prices through much of the '80s: Home prices go up, and they do so at least as fast as inflation. Not anymore." At the time, home prices nationwide were increasing less than the consumer price index, generally because of lagging demand brought about by rising interest rates. In many areas of the country, home prices were falling substantially.

The end of the news story made an interesting point: "No matter what the national trends are, real estate is first and last a local market." Softening in certain industries was causing lower housing prices in the Northeast. The resurgence of some manufacturing industries was buoying up many Midwest markets. Home prices in Houston and Dallas were rising, but they were falling in Tulsa and Denver.

What would cause such discrepancy in home prices among different regions or even among cities in essentially the same region? You don't see large regional price differences

(continued)

for furniture, appliances, food, and most other goods, except for small differences in transportation costs. If the price of soft drinks is much higher in Dallas than in Denver, firms would supply more soft drinks in Dallas, driving the price down there, and less in Denver, driving the price up there. The same is true for most other goods.

Housing is different. Bricks, lumber, electrical and plumbing supplies, and most other inputs into a house are relatively similar, except for shipping costs. If the real wages of construction workers differ by too much, some workers will leave low-wage areas and go to high-wage areas, thereby reducing the differences. But, houses are built on land, and the location cannot be shipped from one region or city to another. If Dallas is expanding and house prices there are rising, houses with a Denver location, where housing prices are falling, cannot be shipped to Dallas.

As an area of a city grows, the demand for housing increases, and housing prices rise. In response, contractors build new houses. As new houses are built, land becomes increasingly scarce, causing its price to rise. Because land cannot be shipped in from other regions, land owners receive more rent. The price of new houses rises, and because existing houses are a substitute for new houses, the demand for existing houses rises, and therefore their prices rise also. Thus, the owners of existing houses also benefit from the growth.

When the economy turns down in a region, the decreased demand for houses causes the price of homes to fall. Homeowners who move out of the city or region in response to the downturn cannot take their homes with them. They and most other home owners suffer a loss of wealth, as do land owners who find the price of their land falling because of the housing slump. In terms of the theory set forth here, it is sometimes difficult to exit from the market without suffering a loss, and in a growing market, it is difficult to enter into a market without paying a premium for land. The entire pattern of the housing market results from the immobility of one scarce resource: the location of land.

13.7   Summary

Perfectly competitive markets or industries are characterized by a large number of firms, each of which produces a product identical to that of every other firm. Product price is determined in the market by supply and demand; every firm takes the market price as given and can sell all it wishes at this price. In the long run, firms can easily enter into or exit from the industry.

In the short run, the firm produces the quantity where short-run marginal cost equals price, so long as price exceeds average variable cost. Therefore, marginal cost above average variable cost is the firm's short-run supply. If all input prices are given to the industry, industry short-run supply is the horizontal summation of all marginal cost curves. If the industry's (although not the individual firm's) use of the inputs affects the prices of some inputs, industry supply is less elastic than this horizontal summation. Any change that shifts firms' marginal cost curves shifts industry supply, thereby changing product price. Firms adapt by choosing the new output at which the new price equals the marginal cost.

In the long run, the entry and exit of firms force each firm to produce at minimum *LRAC*, where *LRAC* = *LRMC* = *SRAC* = *SRMC*. Profit is zero at this output, although each firm earns a normal profit. In a constant-cost industry, long-run industry supply is a horizontal line at the level of the firm's minimum long-run average cost. If the industry's use of inputs increases the prices of some inputs, the industry's long-run supply curve increases with output, and it is an increasing-cost industry.

The theory of perfect competition has two salient features. First, in equilibrium, the price of the product equals the marginal cost of each firm. This means that the value to society of the last unit of the good sold in a market, measured by the price, is just equal to the cost of producing that good, the marginal cost. For all units up to the last, the value of the good—its price—is greater than the marginal cost of producing that unit.

Second, in long-run equilibrium, market price equals minimum average cost. This means that each unit of output is produced at the lowest possible cost, either from the standpoint of money cost or resource use. The product sells for its average (long-run) cost of production; each firm, accordingly, earns the going rate of return in competitive industries—nothing more or less.

It should be emphasized that firms do not choose to produce the quantity with the lowest possible long-run average cost simply because they believe this level of production is optimal for society, and they wish to benefit society. The firms are merely trying to maximize their profits. Given that motivation, the market forces firms to produce at that point. If society benefits, it is not through any benevolence of firms but through the functioning of the market.

Finally, it is important to remember that the theory of perfect competition is not designed to describe specific real-world firms. It is a theoretical model that is frequently useful in explaining real-world behavior and in predicting the economic consequences of changes in the different variables contained in the model. The conclusions of the theory, not the assumptions, are the crucial points when analyzing economic problems.

Answers to *Applying the Theory*

13.1 Under the given supply conditions, the amount of the tax shifted to consumers in the form of higher prices and the amount that must be paid by the firms are determined by the elasticity of demand. If demand had been more elastic than D in the figure, market price would have risen less, quantity sold would have fallen more, and more of the tax would have been absorbed by the firms. (To see this, you can draw a less-steep, more-elastic, straight line demand that passes through the original supply at point C in Figure 13–4.) If demand had been less elastic than D, the price would have risen more than is the case along D, quantity would fall less, and less of the tax would be absorbed by the firms. (To see this, you can draw a steeper, less elastic, straight line demand through the original point at C in Figure 13–4.) Therefore, the better the substitutes for a good that is taxed, the more elastic is demand; the more elastic the demand, the less price rises, and the more quantity falls after an excise tax is imposed.

Now, hold demand fixed. If supply is more elastic than S in Figure 13–4 at point C, the distance AB would shrink. Consumers would pay relatively more of the tax. If supply is less elastic, the distance would be greater, and the firm would pay more of the tax.

13.2 *a.* Consumer's Surplus $(CS) = (1/2)(\$240 - \$120) \cdot (3,000) = \$180,000$.
Producer's Surplus $(PS) = (1/2)(\$120 - \$60) \cdot (3,000) = \$90,000$.
Total Surplus $(TS) = CS + PS = \$270,000$.

b. $CS = (1/2)(\$240 - \$140) (2,500) = \$125,000$.
$PS = (1/2)(\$110 - \$60) (2,500) + (\$140 - \$110) (2,500) = \$62,500 + \$75,000 = \$137,500$.
$TS = CS + PS = \$262,500$; Lost $CS = \$55,000$; Gain $PS = \$47,500$;
Lost $TS = \$8,500$.

c. $CS = (1/2)(\$240 - \$160)(2,000) + (\$160 - 100)(2,000) = \$80,000 + \$120,000 = \$200,000$.
$PS = (1/2)(\$100 - \$60)(2,000) = \$40,000; TS = CS + PS = \$240,000$;
Gain $CS = \$20,000$; Lost $PS = \$50,000$; Lost $TS = \$30,000$.

d. The entire supply curve must be shifted upward \$60. It now intersects the vertical axis at \$120. The new price is \$160, and the new quantity is 2,000.
$CS = (1/2)(\$240 - \$160)(2,000) = \$80,000$.
$PS = (1/2)(\$160 - \$120)(2,000) = \$40,000$.
$TS = CS + PS = \$120,000$.
Tax revenue $= \$60 \cdot 2000 = \$120,000$.
Lost $CS = \$100,000$; Lost $PS = \$50,000$; Lost $TS = \$150,000$; Lost TS net of tax revenue $= \$30,000$.
(Note that in every case of market intervention there is a net loss in total surplus that simply disappears.)

Technical Problems

1. The supply of labor to all firms in a perfectly competitive industry is reduced. Explain the effects on the wage rate, the quantity of labor employed, total industry supply of the commodity produced, and the price of the product.

2. If price falls below average total cost in the short run, the firm, in the long run, will do one of two things. What are these, and under what circumstances will each be done?

3. "Economists are silly to say that profits are competed away in the long run. No firm would operate unless it made profits." Explain.

4. Suppose every firm in an industry in long-run competitive equilibrium is assessed a lump sum tax.

   a. Since each firm is earning only a normal rate of return, will every firm go out of business? Describe the adjustment process in the long run.

   b. Under what circumstances will the price go up by the amount of the tax? Under what circumstances will it go up by less?

   c. If the price goes up by less than the tax, how does each firm, earning only a normal return, pay part of the tax? If it doesn't, who pays the part of the tax not shifted to consumers?

5. Explain the existence of rents in a perfectly competitively industry.

6. The short-run average variable and marginal cost curves of a perfectly competitive firm and supply and demand in the market are shown in the following figure (Figure E.13–1):

Figure E.13–1

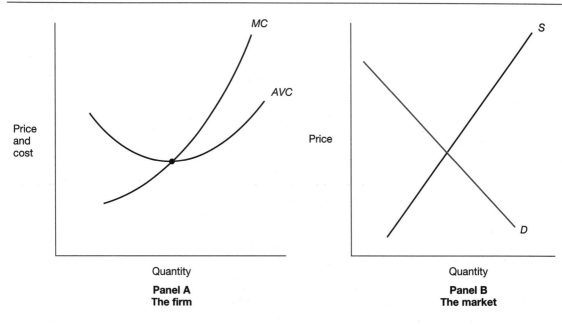

Panel A
The firm

Panel B
The market

a. Show on the graph the market price and output and the output of the firm.
b. The price of an input used by all firms in the industry rises. Show the new *MC* and *AVC*.
c. Show the new supply curve. Show the new price and firm output.
d. Describe how the adjustment process takes place for the firm and for the market.

7. The price in a constant-cost industry in long-run competitive equilibrium is $10. An increase in demand increases product price to $13.
   a. What is the price when the industry once more attains equilibrium?
   b. What is the new industry output? The new output of each firm?
   c. What happens to the number of firms in the market?
   d. Describe the adjustment process.

8. Answer problem 7 under the assumption that this is an increasing-cost industry.

9. Use the following figure (Figure E.13–2) to answer this question. The left side shows the *LRAC* and *LRMC* curves for a typical firm in an increasing-cost industry. The right side shows supply and demand in the market. Demand is originally D_0, and the industry is in equilibrium at a price P_0.
   a. Demand increases to D_1. Show the new price and the output of each firm.
   b. Describe what now happens and why.
   c. Show the new supply when the industry returns once more to long-run competitive equilibrium. Show the new *LRAC* and *LRMC* for the firm.
   d. Draw in the long-run competitive supply curve for the industry.

10. How can there exist a constant-cost industry when any firm that increases its output would experience an increase in cost? Explain.

11. Given your answer to problem 5, why would some resource owners in some firms earn larger rents than others? Could resources in some firms earn no rents?

Figure E.13–2

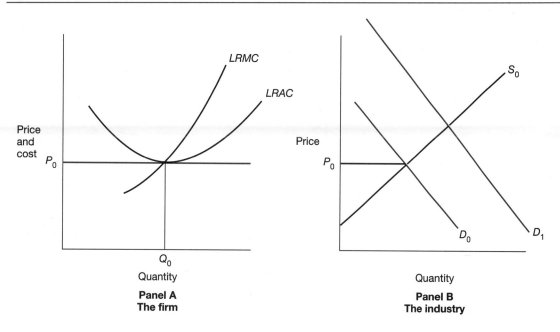

Panel A
The firm

Panel B
The industry

12. Explain how technological change would cause an industry to exhibit the characteristics of a decreasing-cost industry.

13. Explain why the short-run supply curve of a perfectly competitive industry is less elastic if industry usage affects the prices of some inputs than would be the case if all input prices are simply given to the industry as a whole. Why could it be the case that the input usage of any one competitive firm has no effect on input prices, while the usage of the industry does have an effect?

14. Use the following figure (Figure E.13–3) to answer this question. The graph shows the demand and long-run competitive supply curves for a perfectly competitive increasing-cost industry.

　　a. Show consumer's, producer's, and total surplus graphically.

　　b. What does the area below price and above supply mean?

　　c. If the price as shown is *P* but this industry had been a constant-cost industry rather than the one with the supply as shown, what would be the consumer's, producer's, and total surplus?

　　d. Let the industry be, once more, the increasing-cost industry as shown. Impose an excise tax on the industry, and show the new consumer's, producer's, and total surplus and the government tax revenue.

Analytical Problems

1. According to a story in the *Houston Post,* November 27, 1989, the residential maid industry is riding the crest of social and economic change. Sixty-four percent of all women over 35 work outside the home. This has resulted in annual growth of 20 percent for the maid industry since 1981. Explain why. The

Figure E.13–3

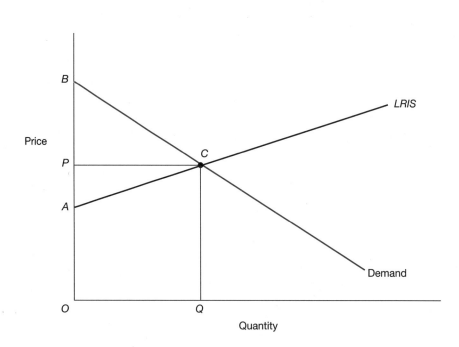

story didn't mention this, but what do you think happened to the wages of residential maids over this period? Explain. Would you think the residential maid industry is constant cost or increasing cost? Explain your answer. Does your answer conform with your answer to the wage question? Explain.

2. An article in *Newsweek* predicted that the American car market would be flooded with new cars in three to four years. Supply could hit 14 million while demand may be no higher than the current (at that time) 11 million. An auto analyst said that fiercely competitive prices may increase car sales well above conventional predictions. And looking ahead, there seems to be no way to avoid a market where there will be too many cars chasing too few passengers. So, what will come next—negative interest rates?

    a. Restate correctly the first statement quoted from the story.

    b. Would you have made the same prediction as the analyst?

    c. If price is "too high," is there any market in which too many goods are not chasing too few buyers?

    d. Other than the predicted fiercely competitive prices (probably meaning lower prices) what else could come next?

    e. Incidentally, car prices did not fall as predicted three to four years later. What do you think might have happened?

3. In 1985, *Time* stated, "The CD boom, like other electronic crazes before it, has been spurred by plummeting prices. Only two years ago, a machine [CD player] cost $1,000 and a disk about $20. But today retailers sell them for as little as $180, while disks cost $12 to $14. . . . sales have zoomed. An estimated

600,000 players will be sold this year, compared with 240,000 in 1984 and just 35,000 in 1983."

a. Is this a decreasing-cost industry? Explain.

b. What was probably occurring in this industry? Explain. There may be more than one answer.

4. During the early 1980s, video rental stores were generally rather small, charged high rental fees, and were generally quite profitable. By the late 1980s, most of the small stores had closed and the rental stores were typically large, were part of a nationwide system or were owned by major retailers, were charging much lower prices, and had huge selections. What probably happened in the video rental business during this time?

5. In the spring of 1985, farmers picketed the White House, demanding higher guaranteed prices and strict production controls. Participants argued that "We've got to have higher price supports so that we aren't forced to sell our products below the cost of production." Many stated that they couldn't make a profit under the present system. One farmer said, "Many of us are shoved out of business by forces beyond our control" (Associated Press, March 5, 1985). In this context, do you feel the model of perfect competition is working about as expected? Explain. If higher price supports had been imposed, would the farmers have made a profit? Distinguish between the short and long run.

6. During the 1970s, much crude oil in the United States was subject to a price regulation below the world price of oil. When the regulation was removed, most people predicted the price of gasoline would increase dramatically because the price of an ingredient input would rise. Gasoline prices in the United States did rise a little at first, but then either fell or remained constant. Explain why predictions of sharply rising gasoline prices were not correct.

7. Why don't very small wildcat oil producers advertise that they don't pollute the environment, whereas giants like Exxon and Shell do a great deal of this type of advertising?

8. Explain why, in the case of a decreasing-cost industry, one firm would have the incentive either to buy up the competitive firms or to expand, underprice the competitive firms, and drive them out of business.

9. The beef market is competitive. During periods of rising prices, ranchers keep more heifers from market to breed them and expand their herds rather than fattening them to slaughter weight for beef. Of course, it takes time for heifers to produce calves. Because of this, would you expect beef prices to fluctuate greatly or remain relatively stable? Explain your answer. A government economist said that improved government information on cattle numbers and both domestic and export demand will help stabilize the situation. Using your knowledge of the theory of competition, explain why this economist is probably wrong.

10. Agriculture is highly competitive. In the long run in competitive markets, profits are competed down to a normal rate of return. Nonetheless, we see a large number of extremely wealthy farmers and ranchers in this country and an even larger number who are doing quite well financially. Explain how this can be possible.

11. During the economic expansion of the 1980s, the amount of store space in regional suburban shopping malls increased by 95 percent while the population grew 13 percent and disposable income grew 40 percent, according to one study.

A Price Waterhouse study indicated that the United States had 40 percent more capacity than the population needs.

   a. How could someone measure how much capacity the population needs?

   b. What did the Price Waterhouse study probably indicate?

   c. What would you expect to occur?

12. The information in problem 11 is from an article in *Time,* April 11, 1988, p. 46. Some marketing analysts have argued that firms don't maximize profits; instead, they simply mark up their prices by a set percentage above cost. *Time* noted that 70 percent of all department store sales at the time were being generated by price markdowns. And retailers generally like to sell their merchandise for 40 percent more than its cost, but these days the margin has shrunk below 20 percent for many items.

   a. In light of this information, what would you conclude about the practice of setting fixed markup prices versus prices set essentially by markets?

   b. What might you conclude about the 40 percent markup retail firms like to get and the normal rate of return in the retail industry?

   c. Does your answer support or contradict your answer to problem 11? Explain.

13. If all of the assumptions of perfect competition hold, why would firms in such industries have little incentive to initiate technological change or to carry out research and development?

   a. What conditions would encourage research and development by competitive firms.

   b. Agriculture in the United States has made incredible technological progress in the 20th century, yet agriculture is extremely competitive. Is there a contradiction here? Why or why not?

CHAPTER 14

Theory of Monopoly

14.1 Introduction

The model of perfect competition is a useful analytical tool, even though the exacting conditions of the model seldom hold in the real world. The same statement applies to the model of monopoly. It is difficult, if not impossible, to pinpoint a true monopolist in real-world markets. Many markets closely approximate monopoly organization, and, consequently, the model often explains observed business behavior quite well.

Recall from Chapter 11 that a monopoly exists if there is only one firm that produces and sells a particular commodity or service, and there are no good substitutes available. Since monopoly is the only seller in the market, it has no direct competitors. Yet, as you will see, monopoly does not necessarily guarantee above-normal profits; it only guarantees that the monopolist can make the best of whatever demand and cost conditions exist without fear of new firms entering the market and competing away any profits.

Although monopolists have no direct competitors that sell the same product, they do have indirect competition. In the first place, all commodities compete for a place in the consumer's budget. Thus, to a certain extent, the monopolist's product competes with all other goods and services in the general struggle for the consumer's dollar. Second, though there are no close substitutes for the monopoly product at the price charged by the monopolist, some goods could become closer substitutes for the monopolist's product if price is increased. The presence of a monopoly therefore depends on relative prices between the monopoly product and other "poor" substitutes.

As we mentioned in Chapter 11, the theory of monopoly is important for three reasons. First, important markets are characterized by monopoly, if not exactly at least somewhat closely. The broadest example of monopoly would be public utilities. In municipalities, the electric company, the gas company, and sometimes the cable TV company are examples of monopolies. Regional telephone companies are essentially monopolies. Also, many cities have only one newspaper or, perhaps, two papers owned by a single firm. In small towns, there may be only one bank, or one hardware store, or even one grocery store. Certainly these virtual monopolies have some substitutes—natural gas can be a substitute for electricity, national newspapers for local papers, satellite dishes for cable TV, and so on. Nonetheless, these examples fit the definition of monopoly rather well, and the theory of monopoly provides a good explanation of how the firms behave.

Second, the theory of monopoly provides an excellent benchmark of comparison with perfect competition. Perfect competition is characterized by no market power or control over price. Monopoly is the market structure characterized by the most market power. After we set forth the theory of monopoly, we will compare the performance of monopoly to that of perfect competition. Using that comparison, we will discuss the features of monopoly that economists typically find undesirable and a few possibly desirable features.

Finally, the theory of monopoly is important because it provides a fairly good approximation or first approach to the behavior and performance of all firms with market power. By definition, any monopoly has market power because it is the only firm selling in a market. A monopoly must determine not only the quantity to supply but also the price to charge. Other firms with market power also determine the quantity to sell and the price to charge. The principal difference between monopoly and other firms with market power is that these other firms have less market power than monopoly because of the availability of better substitutes for the products they sell. Nonetheless, they use essentially the same principles as monopoly when attempting to choose the output and price that maximizes their profit.

14.1.1 Measuring Monopoly

Thus far in Chapter 11 and in this chapter, we have not given a precise measure of the amount of market power a firm must possess in order for it to be classified as a monopoly. We did emphasize in Chapter 11 that cross-price elasticity of demand determines how much market power a firm has by measuring the number and degree to which other products are substitutes. The lower the cross-price elasticity with other goods, the greater the market power of the firm. We would like to give you an exact cutoff that cross elasticities cannot exceed in order for a firm to be a monopoly. We would like to, but we can't. There simply isn't such a measure. Even the federal courts have been ambiguous on this point when ruling on antitrust cases. The courts have not been able to set forth a specific rule for determining whether a firm is or is not a monopoly.

For lack of a better, more-precise definition of monopoly we will have to stick by the one above: a monopoly is the single seller of a well-defined product without good substitutes.

Economics in the News

There Are Substitutes for Network Television

Even though cross-price elasticities are sometimes not helpful when it comes to identifying a monopoly, the underlying principle that monopolies do not have good substitutes is valuable. For many years, the three television networks, ABC, CBS, and NBC dominated American television. They are widely agreed to be close substitutes for each other by advertisers and viewing audiences, and for at least three decades, the 1950s, 60s, and 70s, they dominated television programming. For those wishing to watch television, the alternatives were essentially going out to a movie or reading a book. These choices were probably not good substitutes.

But beginning in the mid-1970s, cable television began to attract network audiences. Viewers, for example, could watch independent transmitters (e.g., WGN in Chicago) and public television. Pay channels could be brought into households, offering audiences additional substitutes. Sports, news, and documentary viewing have greatly expanded. In March and April of 1990, two months in a single year, the networks saw their audiences size drop by 7 to 8 percent (*The Wall Street Journal*, May 10, 1990). And all the networks are being forced to give back money to advertisers who prepay for a guaranteed audience size. Is the cause of the shrinking audiences the presence of cable television? Hard to say. More households have VCRs now. If the networks are showing reruns, a viewer can rent a movie. Movie theaters are in a renaissance. There are more theaters, generally with smaller seating limits, showing more movies. So, perhaps, the theater is becoming a better substitute for network TV as it becomes more localized.

In any case, network television is losing audiences. It can be reasonably inferred that good substitutes are therefore entering the TV market. Identifying them requires close observation of how TV audiences are behaving. For example, how is television time being spent by households? Do people spend more time watching cable TV? The behavior of advertisers is also important evidence. How are advertising dollars being allocated? Are more advertising dollars being spent on cable TV? Also, what about individuals in industries that are aligned with television? These would be the producers, directors, and distributors of films and TV series. To whom are they selling and targeting their work?

Generally, it is a collection of evidence that tells an economist what firms have large amounts of market power and are, ultimately, termed monopolies. Though a measured cross-price elasticity per se is difficult to put into practice, the principle is valuable.

14.1 *Applying the Theory*

Identify a seller that you think is a monopoly. Give it your best shot. Pick a company for which you think the strongest case can be made. Now identify all potential substitutes. Are they *good* substitutes? Give a reason for each answer.

14.1.2 Monopoly and Profit Maximization

The theory of monopoly follows directly from the theory of unconstrained maximization set forth in Chapter 4 and is, therefore, similar to the theory of profit maximization for a perfectly competitive firm. As in the case of the perfectly competitive firm, we assume that the monopolist wishes to maximize profit under the given cost and demand conditions. As you know, any firm can increase profit by expanding output, so long as marginal revenue from the expansion exceeds marginal cost. The firm would not expand if marginal revenue were less than marginal cost. The basic principle that profit is maximized by producing and selling the output where marginal cost equals marginal revenue is the same for any firm, monopolist or perfect competitor.

The difference between monopoly and competition is that, for the monopolist, marginal revenue is less than the price the unit sells for, and unlike the competitor, the monopoly cannot sell all it desires at the going market price. Because a monopolist is the only firm selling in the market, the market demand curve is the demand curve facing the firm. Though additional sales by a competitive firm do not lower the market price, a monopoly firm can sell more only if price falls. Therefore, the marginal revenue from an additional unit sold is the price of that unit less the reduction in revenue from lowering the price of those units that could have been sold at the previously higher price. The basic principle of profit maximization is, however, the same for the monopoly as for the competitive firm: profit is maximized at the output at which marginal revenue equals marginal cost.

14.2   Demand and Marginal Revenue under Monopoly

The fundamental difference between a monopolist and a perfect competitor is the demand and marginal revenue curves they face. We use a numerical example to show the relation between demand and marginal revenue for a monopoly. Suppose a firm has the demand schedule shown in columns 1 and 2 of Table 14–1. Price multiplied by quantity gives the total revenue obtained from each level of sales. Marginal revenue ($\Delta TR/\Delta Q$), in column 4, shows the change in total revenue, column 3, per unit change in output. The only time marginal revenue equals price is for the first unit sold. That is, at zero sales, total revenue is zero; for the first unit sold, total revenue is the demand price for one unit. In going from zero to one unit, the change in total revenue is therefore the same as price. Because the monopolist must reduce price to sell additional units, at every other level of output, marginal revenue is less than price. Note that in Table 14–1, marginal revenue falls as price declines and sales increase. Marginal revenue is positive through the fifth unit of output and then becomes negative as total revenue decreases with the sixth unit of sales.

The relation between marginal revenue and price can be more precisely stated with the help of Figure 14–1. A monopolist is thinking about lowering price by a small amount from P_0 to P; output will increase slightly by ΔQ units, or from Q to $Q + \Delta Q$ units. The change in total revenue (ΔTR) is the additional revenue the monopolist receives, area B, less area A in the figure. Area A is the revenue lost by selling the original Q units for less than P_0. Area B is the revenue gained by selling the additional units at P. This change in total revenue may be written as:

$$\Delta TR = \text{area } B - \text{area } A = P \cdot \Delta Q - \Delta P \cdot Q.$$

Table 14–1 Monopoly Demand and Marginal Revenue

(1) Units of Sales	(2) Price	(3) Total Revenue	(4) Marginal Revenue
1	$2.00	$2.00	$2.00
2	1.80	3.60	1.60
3	1.40	4.20	0.60
4	1.20	4.80	0.40
5	1.00	5.00	0.20
6	0.70	4.20	−0.80

Figure 14–1 Marginal Revenue When Demand Is Downward Sloping

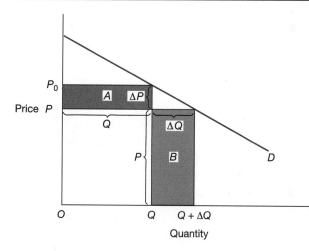

where ΔP is the absolute value of the change in price (in this case, the change in price is negative). Since marginal revenue is the change in total revenue per unit change in output, we divide the above equation by ΔQ to obtain

$$\frac{\Delta TR}{\Delta Q} = MR = P - \frac{\Delta P}{\Delta Q} \cdot Q,$$

where $\Delta P / \Delta Q$ is the absolute value of the change in price for a small change in quantity. This equation shows that marginal revenue is less than price.[1]

---

[1]We can use this equation to derive the equation for marginal revenue when demand is linear. Suppose the demand curve is of the form $P = a - bQ$. Then, the slope of demand is

$$\frac{\Delta P}{\Delta Q} = -b.$$

Also, we can substitute $(a - bQ)$ for P in this equation to write

$$MR = a - bQ - bQ = a - 2bQ.$$

Marginal revenue has the same price intercept, but twice the coefficient for slope.

Figure 14–2   Total Revenue, Marginal Revenue, Demand

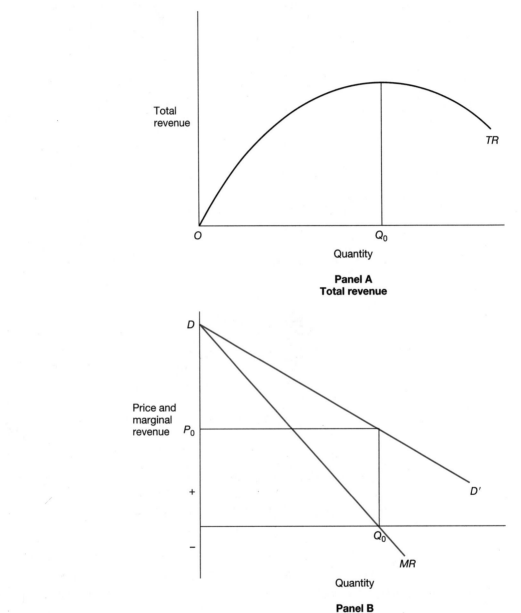

Panel A
Total revenue

Panel B
Demand and marginal revenue

Relation

Marginal revenue is the addition to total revenue attributable to an additional unit of output or sales. After the first unit sold, marginal revenue is less than price. In general, the relation between marginal revenue and price is

$$MR = \frac{\Delta TR}{\Delta Q} < P.$$

Figure 14–2 illustrates the relations between demand, marginal revenue, and total revenue for a monopolist with a linear demand curve. In Panels A and B, the scales of the vertical axes differ, but the horizontal axes are measured in the same units. Total revenue (Panel A) first increases when price is reduced and sales expand; it reaches a maximum at Q_0 and declines thereafter. Panel B indicates the relation between marginal revenue (MR) and demand. As mentioned above, MR is below price at every output level except for the first. (Since we have assumed continuous schedules, the two are equal infinitesimally close to the vertical axis.) The demand curve gives price at any output level; therefore, marginal revenue is always below the demand curve. Finally, when TR reaches its maximum, MR is zero (at output Q_0, price is P_0). At greater rates of output, MR is negative, since total revenue is falling.

We can use the above equation for MR to describe in more algebraic detail the relation between demand and marginal revenue. Because the above equation for MR is correct in general for any small change in quantity, we may rearrange some terms and write the equation using the formula for the elasticity of demand. Recall that $E_D = -\Delta Q/\Delta P \cdot P/Q$. Hence,

$$MR = P\left(1 - \frac{\Delta P}{\Delta Q} \cdot \frac{Q}{P}\right) = P\left(1 - \frac{1}{E_D}\right),$$

where E_D is the absolute value of demand elasticity at any quantity. From this equation, it is apparent that when marginal revenue is negative, demand is inelastic $(E_D < 1)$. When marginal revenue is positive, demand is elastic $(E_D > 1)$. Finally, when marginal revenue is zero, demand has unitary elasticity $(E_D = 1)$.

The movement from positive to negative marginal revenue as one moves down the demand curve follows from the definition of the elasticity of demand. As you will recall from Chapter 3, changes in total expenditure are related to demand elasticity. When demand is elastic, an increase in quantity (decrease in price) causes an increase in total expenditure. Over an inelastic segment of demand, an increase in quantity occasions a decrease in total expenditures, and in the unitary portion of demand, total expenditure remains unchanged. Since total consumer expenditure on a commodity is the same as the monopolist's total revenue, the relation of elasticity to marginal revenue follows directly. If marginal revenue is positive (negative), a small increase in sales leads to an increase (decrease) in total revenue. If marginal revenue is zero, a small change in sales does not change total revenue. A positive (negative) marginal revenue indicates that demand is elastic (inelastic) at that quantity. Zero marginal revenue indicates unitary elasticity. These relations are summarized in Table 14–2. They can also be seen in Figure 14–3, which shows a straight-line demand curve.

Table 14–2 Relations among Marginal Revenue, Elasticity, and Changes in Total Revenue

	(1)	(2)	(3)
Marginal revenue	Positive	Negative	Zero
Demand elasticity	Elastic	Inelastic	Unitary
Change in total revenue for an increase in quantity	Increase	Decrease	No change

Figure 14–3 Relations among Marginal Revenue, Elasticity, and Demand

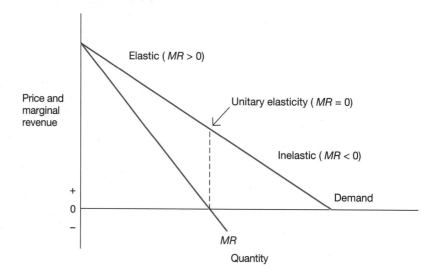

Relation

Since demand is negatively sloped, marginal revenue is negatively sloped and is less than price at all relevant quantities. The difference between marginal revenue and price will depend on the price elasticity of demand, as shown by the formula $MR = P(1 - 1/E_D)$. The maximum point on the total revenue curve is attained at precisely that rate of sales where marginal revenue is zero and elasticity is unitary.

14.3 Short-Run Monopoly Profit Maximization

The theory of monopoly profit maximization is similar to the theory of the perfectly competitive firm: The firm maximizes profit by choosing the output level at which marginal revenue equals marginal cost. In addition to choosing its output, a monopolist must also choose the price to charge. It chooses the price on its demand curve that conforms to the profit-maximizing output. Now that we have shown the marginal revenue conditions under monopoly, we can describe the short-run equilibrium conditions.

Table 14–3   Short-Run Profit Maximization

(1) Quantity	(2) Price	(3) Total Revenue	(4) Marginal Revenue	(5) Fixed Cost	(6) Variable Cost	(7) Total Cost	(8) Marginal Cost	(9) Profit
0	$—	$ 0	$—	$100	$ 0	$100	$—	− $100
1	80	80	80	100	20	120	20	− 40
2	75	150	70	100	32	132	12	18
3	70	210	60	100	40	140	8	70
4	65	260	50	100	52	152	12	108
5	60	300	40	100	70	170	18	130
6	55	330	30	100	95	195	25	135
7	50	350	20	100	125	225	30	125
8	45	360	10	100	163	263	38	97
9	40	360	0	100	208	308	45	57
10	35	350	− 10	100	260	360	52	− 10

14.3.1   Cost under Monopoly

Short-run cost conditions confronting a monopolist are similar to those faced by a perfectly competitive firm. The theory of cost follows directly from the theory developed in Chapter 10. Cost depends on the production function and input prices. The chief difference for a monopolist lies in the potential impact of output changes on input prices.

In the theory of perfect competition, we assume that each firm is very small relative to the total input market and can change its own rate of output without affecting input prices, just as any one consumer can change the amount of a good purchased without affecting its price.

However, if all firms in the industry change output and, therefore, the use of all inputs, the prices of some of those inputs may change, unless the industry is a constant-cost industry. The output of the monopolist, the sole firm in the industry, is the output of the industry. Certainly a monopolist, just as a competitive industry, may be so small relative to the demand for all inputs that its input use has no effect on price. Even a very large monopolist could purchase some inputs (such as unskilled labor) whose prices would not be affected by the monopolist's rate of use. On the other hand, there is a high probability that when a monopoly purchases some inputs, the firm's rate of purchase will have a definite influence on the prices of these factors of production. Despite the monopolist's possible effect on input prices, the cost curves are assumed to have the same general shape as those described in Chapter 10.

14.3.2   Profit Maximization: A Numerical Illustration

We begin the analysis of monopoly profit maximization with a simple numerical illustration. A monopolist's revenue and cost conditions are shown in Table 14–3. Columns 1 and 2 show the demand facing the monopoly. Quantity varies discretely in units of one from 0 through 10. The total revenue ($P \cdot Q$) at each price and output combination is in column 3. Marginal revenue ($\Delta TR/\Delta Q$) for each additional unit of output is in column 4. Marginal revenue is less than price for each unit of output after the first, at which price and MR are equal.

Fixed cost, as shown in column 5, is \$100. Variable cost (TVC) and total cost ($TVC + FC$) are in columns 6 and 7, respectively. (Average variable and average total cost are not given in the table, but you can verify that they have the typical U-shape.) Marginal cost ($\Delta TVC/\Delta Q = \Delta TC/\Delta Q$) for each additional unit of output is in column 8. As you can see, marginal cost first falls, reaches a minimum at 3 units of output, then rises. The profit ($TR - TC$) at each output level is in column 9. Clearly, an economic profit of \$135, when price is \$55 and output is 6, is more than that attainable at any other output and price combination.

It is easy to deduce this profit-maximizing combination of output, price, and profit without actually computing the profit attainable at every price-output combination. Begin at zero output, then increase output to one by charging a price of \$80. Profit rises from $-\$100$ to $-\$40$. Note that for the first unit of output marginal revenue, \$80, is greater than the marginal cost of that unit. Dropping the price from \$80 to \$75 results in an MR of \$70 and an MC of \$12. Profit rises from $-\$40$ to \$18. Again, for a price decrease to \$70, increasing quantity to three, MR, \$60, exceeds MC, \$8, and profit increases to \$70. For each decrease in price and increase in sales through the sixth unit at a price of \$55, MR is greater than MC, and, as you can see, profit increases. A further decrease in price to \$50 and increase in sales to seven units has a marginal revenue of \$20 and a marginal cost of \$30. Profit falls from \$135 to \$125. For further decreases in price and increases in sales MR is less than MC and profit decreases. Thus, price should be lowered and output increased as long as MR is greater than MC. No unit for which MR is less than MC should be produced and sold. This rule maximizes the firm's profit.

This example illustrates the following:

Principle

> To maximize profit when price and output vary discretely, the monopolist should reduce price and increase output as long as MR is greater than MC. No unit of output for which MR is less than MC should be produced.

14.3.3   Profit Maximization: A Graphical Illustration

Next, assume a monopoly for which price, output, and cost vary continuously. The revenue and cost conditions of this monopoly are shown graphically in Figure 14–4. Average total, average variable, and marginal cost have the typical shapes. Demand is a straight line, with marginal revenue lying halfway between demand and the vertical axis, reflecting that MR is twice as steep as demand.

Marginal revenue equals marginal cost at 8,000 units of output when both are equal to \$25. From the demand curve, the price at which the monopoly can sell 8,000 units of output is \$45. At every output below 8,000 and price above \$45, by the above rule, the monopoly can lower price, increase output, and increase profit, because MR is greater than MC. For example, when output is 6,000 and

Figure 14–4   Short-Run Profit Maximization

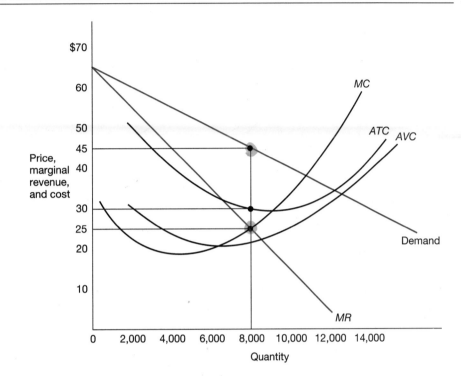

price is $50, marginal revenue is $35 and marginal cost is approximately $20. The firm can reduce its price to slightly below $50, increase its sales to 6,001, and increase its revenue by approximately $35, the marginal revenue from that additional unit of sales. This additional unit of sales increases the firm's cost by approximately $20, the marginal cost of the additional unit. Thus, the firm's profit increases $15 (= $35 − $20) because of the additional unit of sales. The firm can continue reducing price and increasing sales until it reaches 8,000 units of output, and profit will increase because *MR* exceeds *MC* over this range. The firm should not continue reducing price and increasing output beyond 8,000 because the marginal cost is greater than the marginal revenue beyond this output and profit would fall. Thus, the firm maximizes its profit by producing 8,000 units of output, at which *MR* equals *MC*, and setting a price at $45, which is the price given by the demand curve for 8,000 units of output.

Because price is greater than average total cost at this profit-maximizing level of output, the firm makes an economic profit. Total revenue is $P \cdot Q$ = $45 · 8,000 = $360,000. Total cost is $ATC \cdot Q$ = $30 · 8,000 = $240,000. Profit is $TR − TC$ = $360,000 − $240,000 = $120,000. Alternatively, profit can be calculated as $(P − ATC) \cdot Q$ = ($45 − 30) · 8,000 = $120,000.

In the above example, the firm makes an economic profit when it chooses the profit-maximizing output and price. This need not be the case, however. Just as is the case for a perfect competitor, a monopoly may produce a positive level of

Figure 14–5   Short-Run Loss Minimization

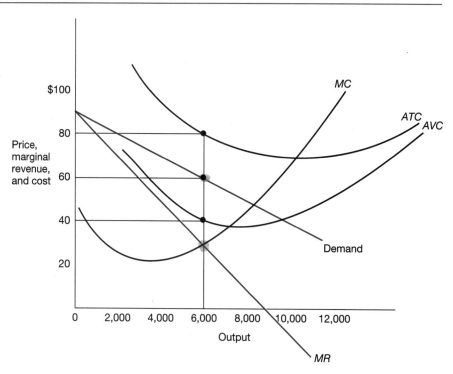

output in the short run, even though it is making a loss. Or, it may under certain conditions shut down in the short run and lose all of its fixed cost.

The situation of a monopoly making a loss in the short run is shown in Figure 14–5, which shows a monopoly's demand, *MR, ATC, AVC,* and *MC* curves. As you can see from the figure, demand lies below *ATC* at every level of output. Therefore, the firm cannot make an economic profit at any level of output because $P - ATC$ would be negative and would result in a loss. But, as we will show, the firm should produce a positive output because this results in a smaller loss than shutting down.

From the previous analysis, you know that the firm should produce 6,000 units of output because this is where *MR* equals *MC.* From the demand curve, the price is $60. Total revenue at this output is $P \cdot Q = \$60 \cdot 6,000 = \$360,000$. Total cost is $ATC \cdot Q = \$80 \cdot 6,000 = \$480,000$. The firm loses $TR - TC = \$360,000 - \$480,000 = -\$120,000$, which is equal to $(P - ATC) \cdot Q = (\$60 - \$80) \cdot 6,000 = -\$120,000$.

If the firm shuts down in the short run and produces nothing, it would earn no revenue, pay no variable cost, but would continue to pay all of its fixed cost. By producing 6,000 units of output and charging a price of $60, the firm's revenue, $360,000, exceeds its variable cost, which, as you can see from the graph, is *AVC* $\cdot Q = \$40 \cdot 6,000 = \$240,000$. Therefore, the firm can cover all of its variable

Figure 14–6   Short-Run Equilibrium under Monopoly

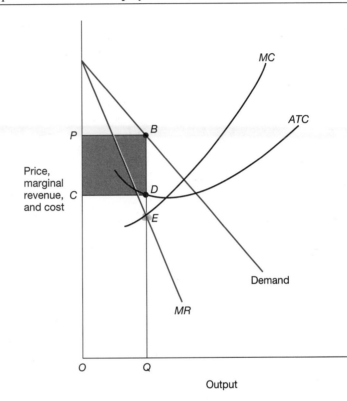

cost and have $360,000 − $240,000 = $120,000 left over to apply to its fixed cost. The firm would then make a loss of its fixed cost minus $120,000, which is better than a loss equal to all of its fixed cost.

If demand decreases even more and lies below AVC at every level of output, the firm should shut down and produce nothing. At every output, $P − AVC$ would be negative. Therefore, since the firm could not pay all of its variable cost from its revenue, it would have a loss equivalent to all of its fixed cost and the portion of variable cost not covered by revenue. It makes a smaller loss in the short run by producing no output and paying only its fixed cost.

14.3.4   General Graphical Exposition of Monopoly Profit Maximization or Loss Minimization

Figures 14–6 and 14–7 summarize graphically the monopoly profit-maximization and loss-minimization principles developed above. In Figure 14–6, demand lies above *ATC* over a range of output, so the monopoly can earn an economic profit. (In this case, because *AVC* is not necessary for exposition, it is omitted.) To maximize profit, the monopoly produces at point *E* where *MR* equals *MC*. It

Figure 14–7   Short-Run Losses under Monopoly

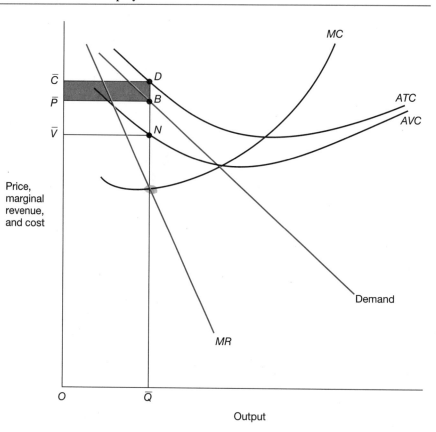

Output

produces an output of Q and, from the demand charges a price of P. At every output below Q, MR exceeds MC, and the firm could increase output, reduce price, and increase profit. At output levels greater than Q, MR is less than MC, so increasing output above Q and reducing price below P would reduce profit.

At the profit-maximizing output and price, total revenue, $P \cdot Q$, is the area of the rectangle $OPBQ$. Because the unit cost of producing Q is C, the total cost is $C \cdot Q$, or the area $OCDQ$. Economic profit is $TR - TC = (P - C) \cdot Q$ or the area $CPBD$.

In the example of Figure 14–6, the monopolist earns an economic profit. However, a monopolistic position does not always guarantee above-normal returns. If demand is sufficiently low, a monopolist may incur a loss in the short run. Figure 14–7 shows such a loss situation. Marginal cost equals marginal revenue at output $\overline{Q}$, which can be sold at price $\overline{P}$. Average cost is $\overline{C}$, so total cost, $O\overline{C}D\overline{Q}$, exceeds total revenue, $O\overline{P}B\overline{Q}$; hence, the firm makes a loss of $\overline{P}\,\overline{C}DB$. The monopolist would produce rather than shut down in the short run, since total revenue exceeds variable cost $O\overline{V}N\overline{Q}$; there is still some revenue ($\overline{V}\,\overline{P}BN$) left to apply to fixed cost. The firm would lose all of its fixed cost if it shut down. If demand decreases so that the monopolist cannot cover all of variable cost at any price, the firm would shut down and lose only fixed cost. This situation would occur if demand lies below *AVC* at every level of output.

14.3.5   Algebraic Summary of Monopoly Short-Run Profit Maximization

As we did for perfect competition, we now summarize a monopolist's profit maximizing decision algebraically. As before, the conclusions are identical to those of the graphical exposition.

We begin with a hypothetical example. Because of its exclusive patents, Leviathan Electronics possesses substantial market power in the product it manufactures—in fact, it is a virtual monopoly. The manager of Leviathan wishes to determine the output and the price for 1993.

The marketing department forecasts the demand for the product as

$$Q = 50 - (0.5)P$$

where Q is measured in 100,000 units. The corresponding inverse demand function is obtained by solving for P:

$$P = 100 - 2Q.$$

From this inverse demand function, the marginal revenue function is

$$MR = 100 - 4Q.$$

(Note that *MR* has the same vertical intercept as the inverse demand function ($100) and is twice as steep: This function corresponds to the above graphical relations.)

Once the marginal revenue function is obtained, the optimal level of output is determined by equating marginal revenue and marginal cost. The production department estimates the U-shaped average variable cost function as

$$AVC = 28 - 5Q + Q^2,$$

where again Q is measured as 100,000 units. The corresponding marginal cost function is

$$MC = 28 - 10Q + 3Q^2.$$

Equating *MR* and *MC*,

$$100 - 4Q = 28 - 10Q + 3Q^2,$$

two solutions are obtained: $Q = 6$ and $Q = -4$. Since $Q = -4$ is an irrelevant solution (the firm can't have a negative output), the optimal level of production is $Q = 6$. That is, the profit-maximizing or loss-minimizing output level, should the firm produce, is 600,000 units of output. Inserting this value of Q into the above inverse demand function,

$$P = 100 - 2(6) = 88.$$

Thus, the optimal price for 1993 is $88.

Using the estimated average variable cost function, *AVC* at 600,000 units of output is

$$AVC = 28 - 5(6) + 6^2 = \$34.$$

Clearly, since price, $88, is greater than *AVC*, $34, the firm's revenue must be greater than variable cost. Therefore, the firm will not shut down in 1993.

From past data, projected fixed costs for 1993 are $27 million. The total cost of producing 600,000 units of output is $TC = TVC + FC = AVC \cdot Q + FC = \$34 \cdot 600,000 + \$27,000,000 = \$20.4$ million $+ \$27$ million $= \$47.4$ million. Total revenue is

$$TR = \$88 \cdot 600,000 = \$52.8 \text{ million.}$$

The firm will make a profit in 1993 of

$$\text{Profit} = \$52.8 \text{ million} - \$47.4 \text{ million} = \$5.4 \text{ million.}$$

Suppose, however, projected fixed costs for 1993 had been $35 million. Leviathan would suffer a loss of $2.7 million. It should still produce because its revenue would exceed its variable cost of $20.4 million ($34 · 600,000). If the firm shuts down, it would lose its fixed cost of $35 million. This would be worse than producing 600,000 and suffering a loss of $2.7 million.

This hypothetical example illustrates the material presented thus far in this chapter. The short-run, profit-maximizing decision can be summarized in the following:

Principles

The demand facing a monopoly is the same as the market demand for the product, because the monopoly is the only firm selling in the market. Monopoly demand is therefore downward sloping. Marginal revenue is less than price for a monopoly at every level of output except the first. If marginal revenue is greater than marginal cost, the monopoly should reduce price and increase output. If marginal revenue is less than marginal cost, the monopoly should raise price and decrease output. If price, output, and cost vary continuously and the monopoly produces a positive output, it should, in order to maximize profit or minimize loss, choose the output at which $MR = MC$ and charge the price given by the demand at that output. Profit or loss is $(P - ATC) \cdot Q$, which is positive if P is greater than ATC or negative if P is less than ATC. If P is less than ATC but greater than AVC, the firm should produce. It can cover all of its variable cost from its revenue and have some revenue left to apply to fixed cost. If P is less than AVC, the firm should shut down in the short run and lose all of its fixed cost.

14.3.6 Monopoly Supply

Thus far, the primary difference between a monopoly and a perfect competitor has been the slope of the demand facing the firm: downward sloping for a monopoly, horizontal for a perfect competitor. Therefore, marginal revenue is less than price for a monopoly and equal to price for a competitor. Each type of firm chooses the output at which MR equals MC, but the monopoly also sets the price it charges. Either type of firm may earn an economic profit; either may suffer a loss.

Figure 14–8   Why a Monopoly Has No Supply Curve

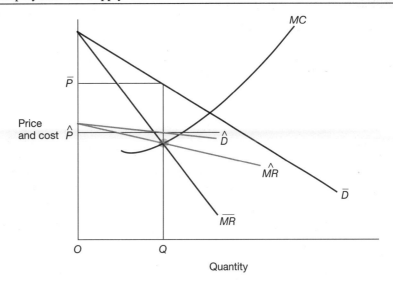

There is an additional difference between a monopoly and a perfect competitor. Recall that the supply curve for a perfect competitor is the marginal cost curve. It is tempting to say the same is true for a monopolist, but a monopolist does not have a supply schedule.

To understand why, recall the definition of supply from Chapter 2: a list of prices and the quantities that would be supplied at each price on the list per period of time. For a monopolist, any number of prices may be associated with a given level of output, depending on the position of demand at that output level.

To illustrate this point, assume first that demand and the associated marginal revenue are $\overline{D}$ and $\overline{MR}$ in Figure 14–8. (Remember marginal revenue depends on the elasticity of demand.) In this case, $\overline{MR}$ equals MC at output Q and price is $\overline{P}$. Next, let marginal revenue and demand be $\hat{MR}$ and $\hat{D}$. While marginal revenue again equals marginal cost at Q, in this situation, the commodity price is $\hat{P}$. By changing the slope of the demand and, therefore, MR curves, the same output, Q, can be sold at an infinite number of different prices. Thus, the monopolist has no supply curve.

Note that in Figure 14–8, the demand curve $\overline{D}$ is less elastic than $\hat{D}$, and the price associated with output Q is higher when $\overline{D}$ is the relevant demand. Another still less elastic demand with an associated MR curve crossing MC at Q would result in an even higher price. This does not imply that a monopoly would choose a price-quantity combination on the inelastic portion of its demand curve. A profit-maximizing monopoly must *always* choose a price and quantity on the elastic range of its demand schedule.

To see why a firm would produce on the elastic range of demand, recall the relation between marginal revenue and elasticity: When demand is elastic, MR is positive (a decrease in price causes an increase in revenue); when demand is

Figure 14–9   Long-Run Equilibrium under Monopoly

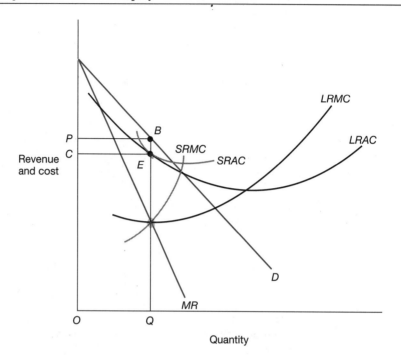

inelastic, *MR* is negative (a decrease in price causes a decrease in revenue). Marginal cost must be positive at every level of output: to produce more, the firm must pay more. At the equilibrium output, marginal revenue equals marginal cost. Because marginal cost is always positive, marginal revenue must also be positive when it is equal to marginal cost. Therefore, because *MR* must be positive at the equilibrium output, demand must be elastic at the equilibrium output.

To reinforce this conclusion, consider what a monopolist could do if, in fact, it was selling on the inelastic portion of demand. Since demand is inelastic, the monopoly could increase price and decrease output, causing total revenue to increase. The decrease in output causes total cost to decrease. The resulting rise in revenue and fall in cost would both act to increase profit. Thus, the monopoly could always raise price and increase its profit along the inelastic portion of demand. Consequently, it would never choose a price on this portion of the demand curve.

This concludes the analysis of a monopoly short-run, profit-maximizing decision. We now turn to monopoly profit maximization in the long run.

14.4   Long-Run Equilibrium under Monopoly

A monopoly exists if there is only one firm in the market. This statement implies that entry into the market is closed. If a monopolist should earn an economic profit in the short run, no other producer can enter the market in the hope of sharing

Figure 14–10   Change in Long-Run Equilibrium for a Monopolist

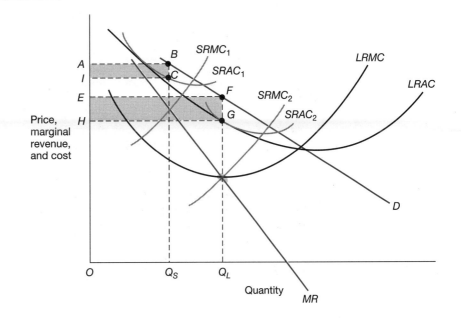

whatever profit potential exists. Therefore, profit is not eliminated in the long run through entry, as in the case of perfect competition. The monopoly does, however, make price and output changes in the long run.

A monopolist faced with the long-run cost and revenue conditions depicted in Figure 14–9 would build a plant to produce the quantity at which, by the above profit-maximization rule, long-run marginal cost equals marginal revenue. In each period, Q units are produced, costing C per unit and selling at a price of P per unit. Long-run profit is $CPBE$. This is the maximum profit possible under the given revenue and cost conditions. The monopoly operates in the short run with plant size indicated by $SRAC$ and $SRMC$.

Demand or cost conditions can change for reasons other than the entry of new firms, and such changes cause the monopolist to make adjustments. Assume that demand and therefore marginal revenue decrease. At first, the firm will adjust without changing plant size. It will produce the quantity at which the new MR equals $SRMC$, or it will close down in the short run if it cannot cover variable costs. In the long run, the monopolist can change capacity or plant size.

Long-run adjustment to equilibrium under monopoly must take one of two possible courses. First, if the monopolist incurs a loss, and if there is no plant size that will result in economic profit (or at least, no loss), the monopoly goes out of business. Second, if it suffers a loss or earns a profit with the original plant, the monopolist must determine whether a plant of different size (and, therefore, a different price and output) will lead to a larger profit.

The first situation requires no comment. The second is illustrated by Figure 14–10. *D* and *MR* show the market demand and marginal revenue confronting a monopolist. *LRAC* is the long-run average cost curve, and *LRMC* is the associated long-run marginal cost curve. Suppose, in the initial period, the monopolist builds the plant exemplified by $SRAC_1$ and $SRMC_1$. Equality of short-run marginal cost and marginal revenue leads to the sale of Q_S units per period at a price of *A*. At this rate of output, unit cost is *I*: short-run monopoly profit is represented by the area of the rectangle *ABCI*.

Since a pure economic profit can be reaped, the monopolist would not consider discontinuing production. Now the long-run marginal cost becomes the relevant consideration. The long-run profit maximum is attained when long-run marginal cost equals marginal revenue. The associated rate of output, Q_L units per period at the least unit cost, is the one represented by $SRAC_2$ and $SRMC_2$. Unit cost is accordingly *H*, and long-run maximum monopoly profit is given by the area of the shaded rectangle *EFGH*. This profit is obviously (visually) greater than the profit obtainable from the original plant size.

Generalizing, we have the following:

Principle.

A monopolist maximizes profit in the long run by producing and marketing the output for which long-run marginal cost equals marginal revenue. The optimal plant is the one for which the short-run average cost curve is tangent to the long-run average cost curve at the point corresponding to long-run equilibrium output. At this point, short-run marginal cost equals marginal revenue.

The profits reached by following the above principle are the highest the monopolist can attain; they can be attained because, in the long run, plant size is variable and the market is closed to entry.

Economics in the News

Monopolies of a Different Sort

In this chapter and in the part of Chapter 11 that discussed the characteristics of monopoly, we have characterized monopoly as a separate firm in and of itself. The firm produces a product and chooses an output and price that maximize its profit. Chapter 11 described some of the barriers to the entry of new firms that permit monopolies to continue to exist. The most prominent of these are economies of scale over a wide range of demand, which discourage entry. Examples are most public utilities. Some examples of monopoly from the past are AT&T, which had a monopoly of long-distance phone service through a government regulation, and some mineral producers, such as the Aluminum Company of America (Alcoa) and the International Nickel Company (Inco), which were monopolies because they owned virtually all of the raw material necessary for their products.

(continued)

At times, however, private firms, which are relatively competitive in one sense, choose to act as monopolies in a secondary stage of their business. Similarly, certain government agencies can act as monopolies in some of the services they sell. Although these "monopolies" are generally relatively small, taken as a whole they can make up a rather important segment of the economy.

Texas A&M University is one example of a branch of the government that has been accused of acting like a monopoly, and incidentally, many other major universities in the United States and Canada follow a similar behavior pattern. One would certainly not classify Texas A&M or other universities as monopolies in the sale of education. There are many competing universities, both public and private. Texas A&M is quite large as universities go, but it is not the largest university in the state.

Nonetheless, Texas A&M was accused recently of acting like a monopolist, not surprisingly by a group of students led by the student body president. The monopoly obviously was not for the sale of admission to students, who have many choices for their college education. The alleged monopoly was the campus bookstore, in the sale of common household items. (See *Bryan-College Station Eagle*, April 8, 1991.)

In the fall of 1990, the university franchised the bookstore to a private firm, but the contract stipulated a ceiling on the price of required textbooks. Nevertheless, revenues increased three-fold in less than a year. The student body president confirmed that students had been complaining about nonbook prices from the time the store had been franchised. A sample of prices for common household items given in the above newspaper story showed that the sample prices in the bookstore were between 21 and 70 percent higher than the prices of the same items in a grocery store adjacent to the campus.

The story noted, "Some at the university think [the private firm] raised prices on items like household goods, souvenirs, and office supplies to gain extra profits it won't get from book sales." What this translates to is that the private firm was prevented by contract from acting like a monopoly in the sale of textbooks, but it did exercise its considerable market power in the sale of other goods. The firm was by no means a pure monopoly in the sale of these goods; it certainly had, as noted, competition from sources off the campus. It did, however, have monopoly power on the campus because of its convenience for the large student population while they were on the campus and to those students who lived in campus dormitories. It exercised its market power by raising the prices it charged.

Have you ever wondered why soft drinks, candy, and popcorn are so high in movie theaters? Why souvenirs are so high at concerts? Why beer and hot dogs are so high at baseball games? Why meals and snacks are so high at airport restaurants? All of these concessions are monopolies. A movie theater or a ball park faces considerable competition from other types of entertainment, but once customers are inside, the concessions are monopolies. Consequently, they charge monopoly prices.[2] Thus monopoly in the economy is somewhat more pervasive than it would appear if one thinks only of monopolies as single sellers of all the products they sell.

---

[2]This statement is not quite correct. A movie theater must determine its ticket price, where it faces much competition, and its concession prices, where it has considerable monopoly power, simultaneously. The price of the ticket affects the demand for the concessions and vice versa. The theory that explains such prices, called a two-part tariff, is somewhat too complex for this text.

14.5   Multiplant Monopoly

We have thus far considered only firms—monopolies and perfect competitors—that produce a single type of product in a single plant. We will now consider a firm that produces in more than one plant. This section explores the theoretical issues associated with a monopoly operating several plants in the production of a particular product. While this analysis is straightforward, it has strong implications on how we should treat plants that have higher costs. Interestingly, less-efficient or higher-cost plants have the impact of shifting portions of a firm's entire marginal cost curve downward. This result holds for any multiplant firm in a competitive or monopoly market.

Suppose a monopolist produces output in more than one plant, with different cost structures. Consider first how a firm would allocate a given level of output among several plants. A firm will not sell output from a plant whose output *at the margin* has a higher cost than the other plant. The firm allocates a given output between two plants so that the marginal costs in both plants are equal.

Assume there are only two plants—A and B. In the short run, at the desired level of output, suppose the following situation holds

$$MC_A < MC_B.$$

Clearly, the firm should transfer output out of the higher-cost plant B into the lower-cost plant A. If, for example, the last unit produced in B costs $10, but one more unit produced in A adds only $7 to A's cost, that unit should be transferred from B to A. This transfer would lower the firm's total cost by $3 while keeping output constant. In fact, output should be transferred from B to A until

$$MC_A = MB_B.$$

We would expect eventual equalization because of increasing marginal cost. As output is transferred out of B into A, the marginal cost in A rises, and the marginal cost in B falls. It is easy to see that exactly the opposite occurs in the case of

$$MC_A > MC_B.$$

Output is taken out of A and produced in B until

$$MC_A = MC_B.$$

The complete situation is shown graphically in Figure 14–11. Demand for the product is *D*, and marginal revenue for the firm is *MR*. Total short-run marginal cost for the firm, $MC_A + MC_B$, equals marginal revenue at output Q_T. The product price is *P*, and marginal cost in each plant is *M*. Plant A produces Q_A units; plant B produces Q_B units. Because of the way that the curves were derived, $Q_A + Q_B = Q_T$. The firm is in equilibrium. Exactly the same principles apply for firms producing in more than two plants.

Suppose the monopolist did not have the higher-cost plant A. What would happen to prices in Figure 14–11? The intersection of *MR* and MC_B shows that this price would have to be above *P*. Ironically, the high-cost plant actually helps keep the monopolist's price down.

Figure 14–11   Multiplant Monopoly

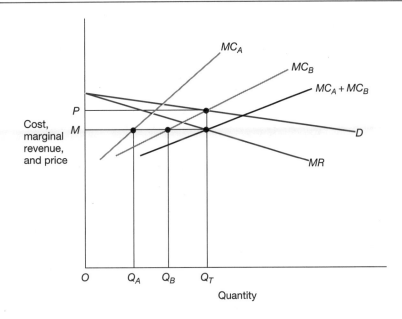

14.2 *Applying the Theory*

Frequently multiplant steel companies and multiplant auto companies decide to close plants. In Figure 14–11 how would the diagram be altered to illustrate a case of closing the high-cost plant?

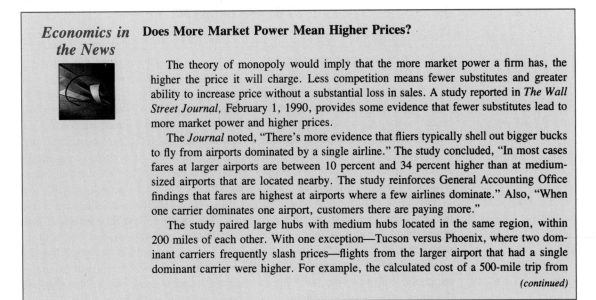

Economics in the News

Does More Market Power Mean Higher Prices?

The theory of monopoly would imply that the more market power a firm has, the higher the price it will charge. Less competition means fewer substitutes and greater ability to increase price without a substantial loss in sales. A study reported in *The Wall Street Journal*, February 1, 1990, provides some evidence that fewer substitutes lead to more market power and higher prices.

The *Journal* noted, "There's more evidence that fliers typically shell out bigger bucks to fly from airports dominated by a single airline." The study concluded, "In most cases fares at larger airports are between 10 percent and 34 percent higher than at medium-sized airports that are located nearby. The study reinforces General Accounting Office findings that fares are highest at airports where a few airlines dominate." Also, "When one carrier dominates one airport, customers there are paying more."

The study paired large hubs with medium hubs located in the same region, within 200 miles of each other. With one exception—Tucson versus Phoenix, where two dominant carriers frequently slash prices—flights from the larger airport that had a single dominant carrier were higher. For example, the calculated cost of a 500-mile trip from

(continued)

Atlanta was $111.25, but it was only $82.75 from nearby Birmingham. The same 500-mile flights from Cincinnati versus Columbus were $130.35 and $106.25, respectively, and from Dallas/Ft. Worth and Oklahoma City, $87.55 and $79.65, respectively. Other pairings from large and medium airports provided similar results, as did the actual fares charged from the two airports for flights to the same destination.

As noted, the larger-hub airports are typically characterized by a single dominant airline. This study provides evidence that these airlines use their market power to charge prices similar to those that a pure monopoly would charge. When airlines are faced with more competition at smaller airports, fares come down.

14.6 Summary

A monopoly exists if there is only one seller in a market, and there are no good substitutes for the seller's product. The degree of substitutability is frequently measured by the cross-price elasticity of demand between products. The larger the cross-price elasticity, the more substitutable the products are for one another. Because only one firm sells in the market, that market must be characteriazed by strong barriers to the entry of other firms into the market. These barriers to entry can take many forms, the most prominent of which is probably economies of scale—decreasing long-run average cost—over a wide range of output.

Marginal revenue is the addition to total revenue obtained from selling an additional unit of output. For a perfect competitor, marginal revenue is equal to price. Since a monopolist must lower price to sell more output, marginal revenue is less than price. In particular, the relation is given by $MR = P (1 - 1/E_D)$, where E_D is demand elasticity. If demand is elastic (inelastic), marginal revenue is positive (negative). A monopolist always maximizes profits on the elastic portion of demand. Since $MC > 0$, setting MC equal to MR requires $MR > 0$, which requires that E_D be greater than one.

The monopolist in both the short run and long run chooses the output at which $MC = MR$. In contrast to perfect competition, the market does not force the monopolist in the long run to produce the quantity at which long-run average cost is at its minimum and to charge a price equal to minimum long-run average cost and marginal cost. This does not mean that a monopolist will always earn profits. In the short run, a monopolist can suffer a loss or make a profit, depending on average cost and demand. If demand is nowhere above the average cost curve, the monopolist does not earn a profit and may even shut down if variable costs are not covered. In the long run, a monopoly will leave the market if demand is below long-run average cost at every level of output.

Finally, a multiplant monopolist will utilize less-efficient plants to reduce the marginal cost schedule and increase profit. Any multiplant profit maximizer will utilize plant capacity in such a way to equate the marginal cost of producing in each plant.

Not many true monopolies exist in the real world. The most prominent examples are public utilities, which are typically regional or local monopolies. Nonetheless, the study of monopoly behavior is extremely useful because it applies to all firms with market power. Market power is the capability to set price above marginal cost.

All firms with market power—and this includes all firms except perfect competitors—face a downward-sloping demand for their product. Such firms must choose both output and price in attempting to maximize profit.

All firms with market power would like to take the demand for their product as given, sell the output at which *MR* equals *MC,* and charge the price given by their demand for that output. In other words, all firms with market power would like to behave as a monopoly. However, as you will see when you study oligopoly behavior, some firms are prevented by the reactions of their rivals from behaving as a monopoly.

Notwithstanding some oligopoly behavior, the theory of monopoly is a good approximization to the behavior of all firms with market power. It is the first approach that we will make in the description of all firms with market power. We will also use the theory of monopoly to compare, from a social point of view, the performance of firms with market power to the performance of perfectly competitive firms and industries. As you will see in the next chapter, the ability to set price above marginal cost is the most important divergence for society as a whole between monopoly and competition.

Answers to *Applying the Theory*

14.1. A professional baseball team might be a good choice. Potential substitutes are nonprofessional teams playing locally. They can attract fans if professional ticket prices are increased. Other substitutes might be watching other teams on television or listening to radio broadcasts that cover other teams. It is possible that a fan may turn to following soccer or another sport if it becomes too expensive to follow baseball. Also, the quality of another sport may increase relative to baseball so that fans turn to it, even if there are no price increases at the baseball park. Deciding if good substitutes exist requires the collection of more evidence and making some judgment calls.

14.2 Say MC_A still represents the marginal cost of the high-cost plant. It can be so high that the sum $MC_A + MC_B$ would only require plant B in production.

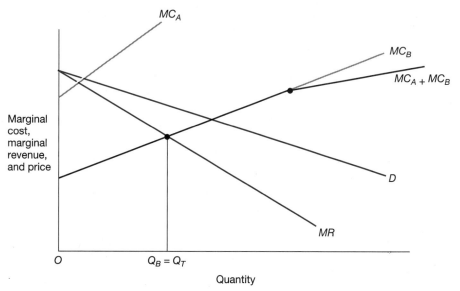

Technical Problems

1. The following table shows a portion of the demand facing a monopoly (columns 1 and 2) and the total cost of producing each level of output in column 2 (column 3).

(1) Price	(2) Quantity	(3) Total Cost
$20	7	36
19	8	40
18	9	46
17	10	53
16	11	61
15	12	71

   a. Calculate marginal revenue and marginal cost for each change in output.
   b. What are the firm's profit-maximizing levels of output and price?
   c. How much profit does the firm make?

2. Use the following figure (Figure E.14–1), showing a monopolist's demand, marginal revenue, and cost curves, to answer this question.
   a. How much does this firm produce, and what price does it charge?
   b. How much profit (loss) does the firm make?
   c. What are the two things this firm might do if it enters the long run? Explain.

3. Use the following figure (Figure E.14–2), showing a monopolist's demand, marginal revenue, and cost curves, to answer this question.
   a. What output does this firm produce and what price does it charge?
   b. What are total revenue, total cost, and total variable cost?
   c. What profit (loss) does the firm make?
   d. How much revenue does the firm have left to apply to fixed cost after paying its variable cost?
   e. What must be the firm's fixed cost?
   f. How much would the firm lose if it shuts down?
   g. What are the two options this firm might choose if it goes into the long run? Explain.

4. Use the following figure (Figure E.14–3), showing the average total cost, average variable cost, and marginal cost curves for a monopoly to answer this question.
   a. Draw in a straight-line demand curve and the associated marginal revenue curve with which the monopoly earns an economic profit. Show output, price, and the amount of profit earned.
   b. Draw a straight-line demand curve and the associated marginal revenue curve with which the monopoly suffers a loss but continues to operate in the short run. Show the output, price, and amount of loss. What will the firm do in the long run?
   c. Draw in a demand curve with which the monopoly shuts down in the short run. What will the firm do in the long run?

5. Explain why a profit-maximizing monopolist always (in theory) produces and sells on the elastic portion of the demand curve. If costs were zero, where would the monopolist produce?

6. Compare the perfectly competitive firm and the monopolist as to how each makes the following decisions:

Figure E.14–1

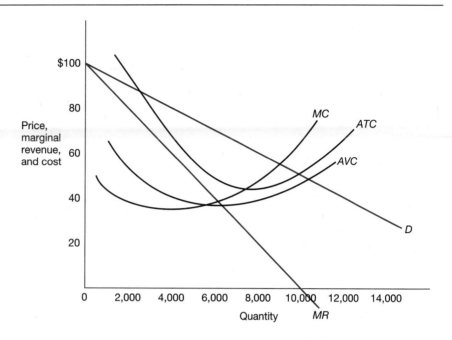

Figure E.14–2

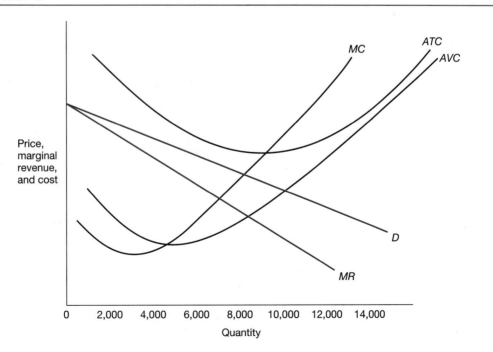

Figure E.14–3

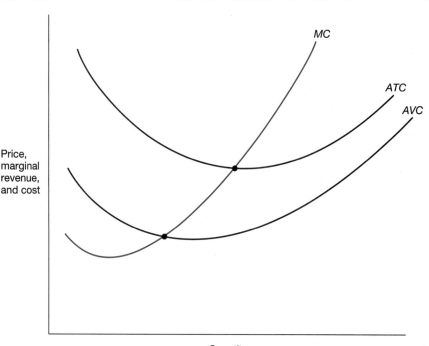

Quantity

    a. How much to produce.
    b. What to charge.
    c. Whether or not to shut down in the short run.
    d. What happens in the long run if losses persist.
  7. Suppose a monopolist has the demand curve $P = 40 - Q$ and marginal cost
    and average total cost are constant and equal to 10. There are no fixed costs.
    Find the profit-maximizing price and quantity. (Hint: $MR = 40 - 2Q$.)
  8. If a monopolist is not making enough profit, it can simply raise price until it
    does. Comment critically.
  9. There are two industries; one is composed of one firm, the other of 1,000 firms.
    At the point of equilibrium, the demand elasticity is 1.75 for one industry and
    .86 for the other. What industry has what elasticity? Why?
 10. If a firm is fortunate enough to be a monopoly, it will exploit this monopoly
    position by charging the highest price possible. Comment critically.
 11. Assume a monopoly with the demand and cost curves shown in the following
    figure (Figure E.14–4). The firm is in the short run with the plant designed to
    produce 400 units optimally.
    a. What are output and price?
    b. How much profit is made?
    c. If the firm can move into the long run, what will be output and price?
    d. How much profit will the firm earn?
    e. Draw in the new short-run average and marginal cost curves for the new
       level of output.

Figure E.14–4

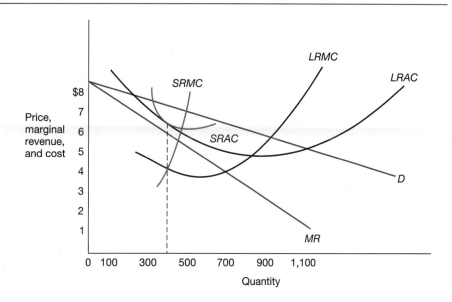

12. Suppose a firm has the following average variable cost, marginal cost, inverse demand, and marginal revenue functions:

$$AVC = 20 - 7Q + Q^2 \qquad MC = 20 - 14Q + 3Q^2$$

$$P = 56 - Q \qquad\qquad MR = 56 - 2Q$$

The firm's fixed cost is $22,500
 a. What are the profit-maximizing output and price?
 b. Should the firm shut down or produce? Explain.
 c. What is profit (loss)?

13. A monopoly is producing in two plants, A and B. The following figure (Figure E.14–5) shows the marginal cost curves for the two plants along with the monopoly's demand and marginal revenue curves.
 a. Draw precisely the total marginal cost curve.
 b. How much total output is produced?
 c. What price is charged?
 d. How much output is produced in each plant?

14. A monopoly is producing its desired output of 10,000 units in two plants, A and B. It produces 7,000 units in A and 3,000 in B. The marginal costs of the last unit in each are $MC_A = \$50$ and $MC_B = \$30$.
 a. What should the firm do? Explain.
 b. How will the firm attain its cost-minimizing equilibrium for 10,000 units of output.

15. Another firm owns two plants, C and D. It is producing its desired output of 1,000 units in plant C and nothing in plant D. The marginal cost of the last unit in C is $10. The marginal cost of the first unit in D would be $15. Is the firm minimizing cost? Explain.

Figure E.14–5

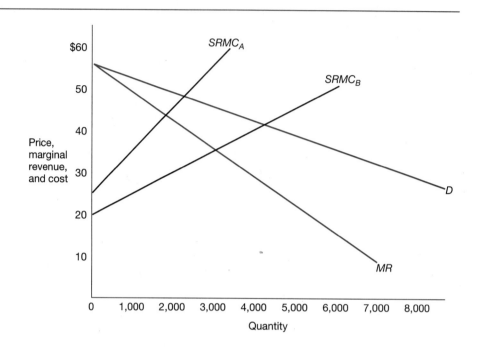

16. A monopoly has two plants, A and B, with the respective marginal cost functions

$$MC_A = 50 + 2Q_A \text{ and } MC_B = 10 + 6Q_B.$$

If the firm is producing 100 units of output in A and minimizing its cost of production, how much output should it be producing in B?

Analytical Problems

1. Explain why the cross-price elasticity of demand is a good indicator of monopoly power.
2. Compare the monopoly power of firms in each of the following groups of firms. Defend your answer.
   a. An Exxon station in a city, all Exxon stations in a city acting together, all gasoline stations in a city acting together.
   b. A shoe store in a city and a department store in the same city.
   c. An electric company and a cable TV company.
   d. The Chase Manhattan Bank and the First National Bank of Snook, Texas.
3. Comment on the following statement: When a monopoly is making a loss, it simply means that the stockholders are making less than a normal profit. Therefore, this really isn't a loss at all since the owners are not having to pay anything.
4. Suppose you are an adviser to a local government agency. The agency will grant a monopoly license to a firm to operate a profitable business. You are asked to

set a price at which the government will grant the license. How would you advise setting the price?

a. Assume you wish to maximize the government's revenue.

b. Assume the government will not set a price. How would you make the decision as to who gets the license?

5. The patent system conveys monopoly rights to some good or process. It is often claimed to be beneficial to economic growth because it encourages research. Are monopolies more likely to do research than perfectly competitive forms? Discuss.

6. In what sense is the only bank in a small town a monopoly? In what sense is it not? In what sense is GM or Exxon a monopoly? In what sense is it not? How about the U.S. Postal Service or your local electric company? If you were an adviser to a Supreme Court justice, how would you decide what does or does not constitute a monopoly? How would cross-price elasticity help you decide?

7. It has been suggested by a student that a monopoly would not advertise; one way of identifying firms in a strong monopoly position is by their advertising budgets. As monopoly power increased, advertising would decrease. Comment on this idea.

8. "Some entrepreneurs will start a successful business only to sell it." Is this reasonable behavior? Are such people forfeiting profits when the business is sold?

9. In 1945, Alcoa was found guilty of attempting to monopolize the aluminum market. Up to that time, the company maintained low markups and had a modest profit rate. Ironically, if Alcoa had set high markups and realized high profit rates before 1945, it probably would not have been found guilty. Can you explain why?

10. Large oil companies frequently advertise that they are very pollution conscious. Why do they do this? Why don't small wildcat drillers advertise that they are pollution conscious?

11. Firms and their unions frequently agree on public policy issues. Why would the three large U.S. auto manufacturers and the United Automobile Workers all lobby for tariffs and quotas on foreign automobiles?

12. This and the following question anticipate somewhat the material in the next chapter. The U.S. antitrust laws have been somewhat inconsistent, as has been their interpretation. However, there has been one point of consistency throughout: gaining a monopoly position in an industry is illegal per se, no matter how the monopoly position is attained. Why do you think that courts believe monopoly is bad?

13. Suppose a constant-cost, perfectly competitive industry is bought out by a monopoly that then operates each firm as a plant. The monopoly attempts to maximize long-run profit. Compare the two situations as to price, output, profit, and the overall effect on consumers of the product. (You may wish to use consumer's surplus to answer the last part of the question.)

CHAPTER 15

Behavior and Performance of Firms with Substantial Market Power

15.1 Introduction

Chapter 14 was primarily concerned with the profit-maximizing decisions of monopolies. A monopoly, in order to maximize its profit, chooses the output at which its marginal revenue equals its marginal cost and charges the price, given by its demand curve, associated with that level of output. We emphasized that this profit-maximizing decision process is a characteristic not just of pure monopolies but of all firms that have some degree of market power. This chapter will expand the analysis of the behavior of firms with market power.

The primary reason firms have market power is that other producers cannot enter the market and make at least normal returns. Or, other firms are able to enter the market but, for some reason or another, find entry extremely difficult. Entry is, in effect, blocked or impeded by barriers. Although there is some controversy over what constitutes a barrier to entry, for purposes of discussion, we will say that an entry barrier is any impediment that might prevent or hinder a firm from producing a particular product.

As you will see, barriers to entry can arise for several reasons. One of the most common barriers, economies of scale, comes from the production function. As a result of the production technology, the largest firm is the lowest-cost producer and can block smaller firms from entering the market. In some markets the brand loyalty of consumers, possibly brought about by advertising, can be a difficult, perhaps impossible, hurdle for new firms to overcome. Such barriers to entry can be *stra-*

tegically erected by a firm that is already producing in the market. This chapter will describe some of these strategic methods of fostering market power. We will specifically discuss the strategy of entry-limit pricing to illustrate how this behavior discourages competition from new firms.

Once a monopoly is secure in the market, a firm can undertake more sophisticated pricing strategies that increase returns above the profit-maximizing price determined by the intersection of marginal revenue and marginal cost. In Chapter 14, this was the price charged to everyone buying from a monopolist. As such, it is frequently called a *uniform price*. However, a monopolist can often increase profits by selling the same product for different prices to different groups of consumers. This is referred to as *price discrimination*.

Finally, we will discuss at some length the market performance of firms with considerable market power compared to the performance of firms selling in competitive markets. You will see that the crucial difference—both for the firms themselves and for society in general—is the ability of firms with market power to sell at a price above, sometimes far above, the firm's marginal cost. In fact, the amount by which price exceeds marginal cost is a result or consequence of the amount of market power possessed by a firm. The difference between price and marginal cost is sometimes used to measure the social cost of monopoly. We will not be able to say unequivocally whether monopoly is bad or good per se, but we will be able to introduce you to some of the issues involved in evaluating the behavior of firms that have market power.

15.2   Examples of Entry Barriers

It would be impossible to enumerate every reason why a potential producer finds it difficult or even impossible to enter a market. What forms a barrier to entry depends upon the market context in which it may arise. When discussing the characteristics of monopoly in Chapter 11, we briefly mentioned a few of the barriers to entry in monopoly markets. These barriers were economies of scale, government licensing and franchising, control of a necessary input in production, and patents. In this section, we will discuss at greater length some examples of how firms have actually used those and other barriers to achieve and maintain a monopoly position. We will also describe some entry barriers that can be erected through the strategic behavior of the firms themselves.

15.2.1   Economies of Scale

As emphasized in Chapter 10, economies of scale exist when a firm's long-run average cost curve is declining over a wide range of output levels. We explained briefly in Chapter 11 how economies of scale can protect a monopoly from the entry of new firms into the market, particularly if these potential new entrants would be relatively small. Now that you have a thorough understanding of monopoly pricing, we can discuss in more depth how economies of scale can inhibit or prevent entry.

Figure 15–1   Monopoly and Competitive Equilibria with Economies of Scale

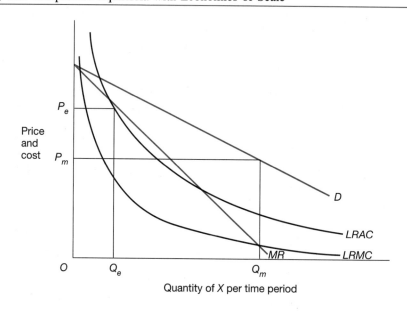

Figure 15–1 shows a case where there are pervasive economies of scale; the *LRAC* curve declines at every relevant level of output. If one firm operates in the market, profit maximization leads to output Q_m and price P_m.

Suppose a smaller firm enters the market, producing output Q_e with the *LRAC* and *LRMC* curves shown in the figure. The lowest price this firm can charge without making long-run losses is $P_e = LRAC$ at Q_e. Profits are normal, but this price is higher than the monopoly price already charged. For identical products, the new entrant will not make any sales. At the higher price, the entrant might attempt to convince buyers its product is better, but this usually means either increased costs for advertising or higher production costs. In both circumstances, costs will be higher, making successful entry all the more difficult.

Notice that the entrant's problem is intensified after it enters the market. Once its output, Q_e, is added to the monopoly output, Q_m, the total market output is greater. Price in the market must fall below P_m in order for the entire output to sell. The entrant, therefore, is always looking at a greater price difference than $P_m - P_e$ after entry has occurred.

Suppose the new firm enters the market and produces Q_m also. Price would certainly have to fall far below P_m, quite possibly below each firm's long-run average cost. Both firms would make losses, and, after a long and costly price war, it is highly probable that only one firm would survive. The survivor could then raise the price back to P_m and earn an economic profit. The potential entrant, knowing it would be in for a relatively long period of below-normal profit and that there is a good chance it would not survive the price war, would be strongly motivated not to enter the market.

When pervasive economies of scale like those shown in Figure 15–1 exist, it is difficult to maintain a competitive market, even if a large number of producers begin at a small scale. In fact, competition could exist only if producers were strictly prohibited from expanding. Imagine what would happen if they were not. Every firm would have the incentive to expand and move down the *LRAC* curve where unit costs would be lower, and, as a consequence, prices could be lowered. The larger firm could always undersell smaller firms and drive them out of business. Bigger firms would continue getting bigger, until only the largest firm remained. Such economies of scale are not conducive to the existence of perfect competition, because profit-maximizing incentives naturally lead each firm to try to dominate the industry. Eventually, the largest firm will drive the smaller ones out of the market. When a monopoly exists because of economies of scale, it is, as mentioned in Chapter 11, frequently called a *natural monopoly*.

Thus far, we have only considered the case in which economies of scale are so extensive that only a single large firm, a monopoly, can exist profitably in a market; this is the case of a natural monopoly. However, economies of scale can occur over a smaller, but still large, range of output, so that more than one firm, but still relatively few firms, can exist profitably. Because of economies, firms must be large enough to take advantage of the lower cost and prevent the entry of smaller, higher-cost firms. In contrast to the natural monopoly, however, the economies are not pervasive enough to cause a single firm to drive out all others. A few firms are large enough to take advantage of the lower cost attainable with large size, and these large firms can sell profitably in the same market. In such cases, economies of scale can lead to oligopoly in the market. These large firms may have considerable market power.

15.2.2   Input Barriers to Entry

Historically, an important reason for market power has been the control of raw-material supplies. If one firm (or perhaps a few firms) controls all of the known supply of a necessary ingredient for a particular product, the firm or firms can refuse to sell that ingredient to other firms at a price low enough for them to compete. Since no others can produce the product, monopoly results. For many years the Aluminum Company of America (Alcoa) owned almost every source of bauxite, a necessary ingredient in the production of aluminum, in North America. The control of resource supply, coupled with certain patent rights, provided Alcoa with an absolute monopoly in aluminum production. It was only after World War II that the federal courts effectively broke Alcoa's monopoly in the aluminum industry.

Another historical example of a firm that became a virtual monopoly because of its control of the only source of a necessary raw material is the International Nickel Company (Inco), a Canadian Company that owned the vast majority of known nickel deposits. Because of the discovery of large nickel deposits throughout the world, Inco now has many competitors worldwide. In fact, with the rise in the importance of international trade there are few, if any, firms that are presently monopolies because of their ownership of a raw material.

15.2.3   Capital Markets as Entry Barriers

A frequently cited barrier arises from capital markets. Established firms, perhaps because of a history of good earnings, are able to secure financing at a more favorable rate than new firms. Imagine how far a typical person would get by walking into a bank and requesting a loan for $20 million to start a large manufacturing company. Most bankers would take a dim view of this new company's survival. Knowing the new firm would be in the same market as other well-established companies, bankers would probably turn down the application. If the loan was made available, the interest rate for a new company would be above that paid by established firms. Capital markets pose a barrier for new firms when a large investment is necessary to enter a market. Nevertheless, many prospective entrepreneurs do find sources of capital, do start new companies, and do survive in the face of competition from established firms. Because of large capital requirements, input barriers are difficult, although not impossible, to overcome.

A related capital barrier sometimes exists because a substantial portion of the investment or capital costs facing a new firm are sunk costs. Sunk costs are costs that cannot be recovered if a firm exits from the market. The owners of a possible entrant into a market realize that they must bear a large capital cost if they are to be large enough to compete with the established firms. The owners also realize that there is some probability that they will not survive. If a large part of the investment expenditure cannot be recovered through the resale of the capital, these costs are sunk, and thus the owners would lose a large amount of their investment. For this reason, sunk costs can discourage entry and protect the position of the established firm or firms.

15.2.4   Barriers Created by Government

An obvious entry barrier is government. Allocations, licensing, and franchises are ways monopolies or firms with substantial market power are created by the government. Allocations, for instance, are granted to growers of many agricultural commodities to prevent the free entry of farmers into a crop market. The allocation tends to restrict output and raise the price of foodstuff, because entry cannot take place when short-run profits are earned. Licenses are granted to radio and television stations by the Federal Communications Commission (FCC), and only those stations possessing a license are allowed to operate. Locally, this confers immense market power on those stations that have FCC approval. Entrants can petition the FCC for a license to operate, but if those who are operating protest to the commission, the petition is frequently denied. Governments also grant exclusive franchises for city, county, and state services. For example, regional telephone and cable television utilities have market power in that they are the only regional producer of the product. By law, no other producer can exist.

Another legal barrier to competition lies in the patent laws of the United States. These laws make it possible for a person to apply for and obtain the exclusive right to produce a certain commodity, or to produce a commodity by means of a specified process that provides an absolute cost advantage. E. I. du Pont de Nemours & Company enjoyed patent monopolies over many commodities, cellophane being the most notable. The Eastman Kodak Company continues to hold numerous patents on its camera equipment.

Despite examples to the contrary, holding a patent on a product or production process may not be quite what it seems in many instances. In the first place, the holder of a product patent may chose not to exploit the monopoly position in the production of the product. If diseconomies of scale set in at a low level of production, the patent holder may find it more profitable to sell production rights to a few firms or to many. Second, a firm that owns a patented lower-cost production process may have a cost advantage over other firms in the market, but it may sell only a small part of the industry's total output at the equilibrium position. The new technique will lead to patent monopoly only if the firm has the capability to supply the entire market, or finds it profitable to do so. Third, a patent gives a firm the exclusive right to produce a particular, meticulously specified commodity, or to use a particular, meticulously specified process to produce a commodity. A patent does not preclude the development of closely related substitute goods or closely allied production processes. International Business Machines Corp. has the exclusive right to produce its patented computers, but many other computers are available, and there is competition in the computer market.

15.2.5   Brand Loyalties

On the demand side, older firms may have, over time, built up the allegiance of their customers. New firms might find this loyalty difficult to overcome. No one knows what the service or repair policy of a new firm may be. The preference of buyers can also be influenced by a long-successful advertising campaign; established brands, for instance, allow customers recourse if the product should be defective or short of its advertised promises. Although technical economies or diseconomies of scale may be insignificant, new firms might have considerable difficulty establishing a market organization and overcoming buyer preference for the products of older firms. A classic example of how loyalty preserves monopoly power can be found in the concentrated lemon juice market. ReaLemon lemon juice successfully developed such strong brand loyalties among consumers that rival brands evidently could not survive in the market. The situation was so serious that the courts at one time ordered ReaLemon to license its name to would-be competitors.

The purpose of this discussion is to expose you to several of the more common types of entry barriers and to illustrate the diversity of factors that prevent entry into a market and, consequently, foster market power. It is noteworthy that several of the barriers mentioned are somewhat influenced by the monopolist. The control of inputs and the development of consumer loyalties are effective barriers essentially erected by firms already producing in the market. In addition, market power can sometimes be gained by certain types of strategic behavior by incumbent firms. In the next section, we will discuss additional strategies that can keep potential entrants out of the market.

Figure 15–2   Entry Limit Pricing

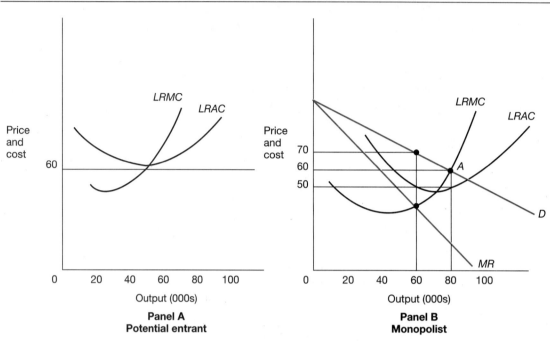

Panel A
Potential entrant

Panel B
Monopolist

15.3   Entry Limiting Strategies

The types of strategic behavior to be described here are price manipulation, carrying excess capacity, and producing multiple products. The theory to explain such activities has been developed recently both in economics and business. The topics discussed are designed to introduce you to the analysis rather than give you an in-depth understanding.

15.3.1   Entry Limit Pricing

Under some circumstances, a monopoly might charge a price below that at which profit is maximized and, therefore, produce and sell an output greater than that at which marginal revenue equals marginal cost. One such circumstance would be the case of a monopolist that, facing potential competition, lowers price in order to block the entry of potential competitors. Such pricing behavior is called entry limit pricing.

An example of a situation in which a monopoly might drop its price below the level that maximizes profit is shown in Figure 15–2. Panel B shows the demand, marginal revenue, long-run average cost, and long-run marginal cost curves for a monopoly. Panel A shows the long-run average and marginal cost curves that a potential entrant into the market would have. We have assumed that for technological reasons a potential competitor would suffer a cost disadvantage, relative to the monopoly. That is, long-run average cost of the potential entrant is higher than that of the monopoly at each relevant level of output.

If the monopoly attempts to maximize profit without regard for potential competition, it would set *LRMC* equal to *MR,* produce 60,000 units of output, and, from its demand curve, set a price of $70. Monopoly profit would be $(P - LRAC) \cdot Q = (\$70 - \$50) \times 60,000 = \$1,200,000$. However, even though the potential competitor has a cost disadvantage, it could enter the market by charging a price lower than $70 but above its long-run average cost and take away some of the monopolist's sales. If this occurs, the new entrant could make an economic profit and the monopoly would find that its profits are reduced.

The monopoly could, however, block attempts to enter the industry by setting a price of $60, which is slightly below the minimum point on the potential competitor's long-run average cost curve. In order for the competitor to make a profit, price must be above its *LRAC* over some range of outputs. Because the $60 price would be below its *LRAC* at every level of output, the competitor would make a loss if it came into the market. The competitor would have no incentive to entry; its entry is blocked.

The monopoly's profit, of course, would be lower in the long run as a result of decreasing its price to $60. The monopoly sells 80,000 units of output, as shown by its demand curve at point A. Its profit at that output is $(P - LRAC) \cdot Q = (\$60 - \$50) \cdot 80,000 = \$800,000$. The monopoly therefore sacrifices some immediate profit for a stream of lower but protected profit over a longer period of time. However, if the threat of entry is not great, the monopoly may not wish to sacrifice the stream of higher earnings now. In such a situation, the firm may decide to price and produce where $MR = MC$. If entry is easy, however, the monopoly may be well satisfied with lower profit at a lower price and higher output.[1]

15.1 *Applying the Theory*

If the monopolist could produce at any output as long as price was below $60, what would output be? What would profits be? Base your answer on Figure 15–2.

We should emphasize that entry limit pricing is possible and even feasible in the example just discussed, because the monopoly has a cost advantage over any potential entrant. It can therefore set a price low enough to block entry but still make an economic profit, although profits are lower than they would be without the threat of entry. If potential entrants would not be at a cost advantage, entry limit pricing would not be feasible, and the monopoly would have to search for some way other than price to impede entry—if that is possible.

---

[1] A complete analysis of this situation requires comparing the discounted future streams of profit with and without entry. We will not carry out this extension here because the concept of discounting has not yet been covered.

15.3.2   Capacity Barriers to Entry

A monopolist does not necessarily have to keep price low to block entry, and it may not want to if it can hold excess production capacity in reserve. This excess capacity signals to prospective competitors that the monopolist has the capability to quickly increase production and lower price if competition becomes a threat. It will take longer for an entrant to build a new factory in order to enter a market than it would for a monopolist to gear up idle capacity. By the time the new firm is ready for business, output in the market would be greater and the price would be lower from increased production by the monopolist.

Compared to a pricing strategy that blocks entry, it may be less expensive (more profitable) for a monopolist to hold its share of the market by keeping idle capacity. The choice depends on the difference between the costs over time of maintaining capacity and the stream of increased revenue from setting price above the relatively low entry limit price. If demand is not particularly elastic in the market, a small increase in production will cause price to fall greatly. Low elasticity would also mean a large sacrifice in revenue must be made to keep prices low. Consequently, a small amount of excess capacity may be a much less costly means to block entry.

15.3.3   Multiproduct Cost Barriers

When a firm produces more than one product and uses inputs in the production process that contribute simultaneously to the production of two or more goods, often the total cost of producing the goods together is less than producing each separately. Some obvious examples of cases in which an input produces more than one product simultaneously are cattle used to make beef and leather, a well that pumps crude oil and natural gas, and forests that produce wood for lumber and paper.

Less obvious examples arise from capital expenditures that contribute to the production of more than one product. Railroads, for instance, offer both freight and passenger transportation over the same tracks and between the same depots. These inputs are shared. The postal service shares its capital in sorting and delivering parcels and letters. In such instances, a single investment contributes to the production of more than one product. This is a common phenomenon among multiproduct firms.

Whenever it is less costly to produce products together rather than separately, costs are said to be *subadditive*. If we let $C(X)$ be the total cost of producing good X, and $C(Y)$ be the cost of producing good Y, cost is subadditive, if, for any amount of X and Y,

$$C(X) + C(Y) > C(X,Y),$$

where $C(X,Y)$ is the cost of producing the two goods together. For example, if the cost of producing 10 units of X separately is \$100 and the cost of producing 12 units of Y separately is \$180, the total cost of producing these amounts of the two goods separately is \$280. Cost would be subadditive if the total cost of producing $10X$ and $12Y$ together is less than \$280.

Subadditivity can create barriers to the entry of new firms into a market. Suppose there are three products, X, Y, and Z, with the following costs of production for a *specified* number of units of each of the three goods:

1. X, Y, or Z produced alone has a total cost of $10 for each of the specified number of units.
2. Any two products produced together have a total cost of $16 for the specified number of units.
3. All three products produced together in the specified amounts have a total cost of $23.

Therefore, since

$$C(X) = C(Y) = C(Z) = \$10,$$

$$C(X) + C(Y) + C(Z) = \$30.$$

Also, because

$$C(X,Y) = C(X,Z) = C(Y,Z) = \$16,$$

$$C(X,Y) + C(Z) = C(X,Z) + C(Y) = C(Y,Z) + C(X) = \$26;$$

and finally

$$C(X,Y,Z) = \$23.$$

Costs are subadditive because it is less costly to produce any two together rather than all three separately, and all three together rather than just two together and one separately.

If a firm produces any of the three goods separately, the price would have to be $10 or more for each of the specified amounts of the three goods. If a firm produces two of the goods together, it must receive a price of at least $8 for each amount of the two in order to cover costs. A firm producing X, Y and Z together can undersell any firm that is not, and it can still cover its costs. For instance, the seller with a total cost of $23 could set a price of $7.99 for the specified amounts of each of the three goods and not be undersold in the long run by anyone not producing the goods together. The total revenue would exceed the total cost. Those producers making two or fewer products together would be driven out of business. A firm must, therefore, produce all three products to successfully enter any one market, thus creating a barrier to entry. Generally, it is more costly to enter all three markets and produce all three products than it is to enter just one. The combined capital investment required to produce all three products would tend to discourage some firms from entering the three markets.

15.3.4 New Product Development As a Barrier to Entry

Sometimes a monopolist can block entry by introducing new substitutes for its own product in the market. As strange as this may sound, such a maneuver is greatly preferred to seeing new entrants introduce substitute products. Producing related products crowds the market with choices. As choices proliferate, the demand for each individual product decreases and becomes more elastic. This effect on demand makes it more difficult for a new firm to enter the market, since it would have a smaller demand for its product. Price and sales would be lower for the entrant than would be the case if the original firm had not introduced so many substitutes. It therefore becomes less likely under these conditions that total costs will be covered if a new firm comes into the market.

Historically, there are some interesting cases where firms with monopoly power sold multiple products expressly for the purpose of blocking entry. In the 1940s, American Tobacco, Liggett and Myers (L&M), and Reynolds, after being found guilty of conspiring to monopolize the cigarette industry, began independently introducing multiple cigarette brands to protect their respective market shares. Before the antitrust suit, the companies were purchasing low-grade tobacco at auctions in an effort to keep new entrants from introducing a low-grade, inexpensive cigarette. Apparently it was not used in cigarette production and nothing was done with the tobacco after it was purchased. When the suit was settled, the companies were ordered to cease and desist from this practice. Soon thereafter, the companies began developing their new brands.

A more recent example of brand proliferation to block entry can be found in the ready-to-eat cereal industry. In the mid-1970s the Federal Trade Commission (FTC) began investigating the big three cereal makers—Post, Kellogg, and General Mills— for possible anticompetitive behavior. The accusation made by the FTC was that these companies had generated multiple brands of cold cereal to deter entry. They had introduced a sufficient number of brands to cover the spectrum of tastes consumers had for cold cereals. No new firm could come into the market and carve itself a niche, because any type of cereal the firm could develop would face a close substitute from one of the other cereal makers. Nothing came of the FTC investigation, largely because it was very difficult to prove the intentions of the incumbent cereal makers, but the strategy, for whatever reason it was pursued, was a very effective deterrent to entry. These three large cereal producers still sell several different brands with slightly differentiated features.

An additional example occurs in the soft-drink market. Coke and Pepsi sell a wide variety of soft drinks, not all of which are colas. But just in the cola markets, for example, Coke sells regular Coke, Classic Coke, diet Coke, Caffeine Free Coke, Cherry Coke, and so on. Pepsi has its own competing broad range of beverages.

Economics in the News

Too Many Products Can Increase Costs

In the discussion of multiple products as an entry barrier, we noted that the simultaneous production of multiple products can reduce costs and therefore price. This practice can also discourage competitors from making competing products by crowding the market with substitutes. During the late 1980s, there was actually a trend toward fewer products sold by individual firms because product proliferation was actually increasing per-unit costs.

(continued)

In a column from *The Wall Street Journal,* "Want More Productivity? Kill That Conglomerate," January 2, 1990, Frank R. Lichtenberg, a professor at Columbia Business School, stated, "An important—and beneficial—way in which U.S. industrial structure changed in the 80s was a decline in the extent of corporate diversification, or the number of industries in which a firm operates." This represented a distinct change from the rapid increase in diversification that had occurred during the preceding 20 years. Lichtenberg's sample data showed that from January 1985, through November 1989, the mean number of industries in which firms operated declined by 14 percent, the proportion of firms that were highly diversified—operating in more than 20 industries—declined 37 percent, and the proportion of single-industry companies increased 54 percent. He attributed the change to two factors: Companies that were "born" during this period were much less diversified than companies that had "died," and already existing companies reduced the number of industries in which they conducted business.

Lichtenberg reported that his data for more than 17,000 manufacturing plants indicated that diversification has a negative effect on productivity—output produced per unit of inputs employed. "In other words, the greater the number of industries in which a plant's parent firm operates, the lower the productivity of the plant." You will recall from the theory of production and cost the inverse relation between changes in productivity and changes in cost. Lichtenberg stated, "Part of the sharp decline in U.S. productivity growth that occurred in the late 1960s and 1970s is therefore probably attributable to the conglomerate merger wave. Studies by other researchers have shown that corporate profitability also suffered as a result of diversification." He predicted that de-diversification should have a favorable impact on productivity.

Another article in *The Wall Street Journal,* "Firms Grow More Cautious About New Product Plans," by Alecia Swasy, March 9, 1989, noted that many large producers of consumer products, such as Campbell Soup, Nabisco, Kellogg, Quaker Oats, and Scott Paper, were decreasing or thinking about decreasing the rate at which they were introducing new products. Ostensibly these new products were designed to "fill the gap" for the purpose noted above. "Many packaged-goods companies are rethinking their strategies of flooding the markets with fresh entries. The high cost of getting a new product on store shelves—and pulling any failures back off—is slowing the rate of introductions this year." One of the reasons for the higher costs of introducing new products "stems partly from the fact that more retailers are charging hefty fees for putting new products on their shelves. Such 'slotting' fees can cost $1 million or more."

Certainly, if a firm with considerable market power expands its product line in order to provide a wide variety of different products, this strategy can discourage the entry of new competitors in the market. However, the firm must make a maximization decision involving marginal analysis: Will the marginal benefits of the new product exceed the marginal cost of introducing and marketing the new product? According to the article cited above, the answer is increasingly becoming no.

15.3.5 Summary of Strategies

Strategic behavior on the part of monopoly or firms with significant market power can arise in numerous forms. We have just scratched the surface of this area of economic analysis. You have seen that firms with monopoly power can take actions to block the entry of additional producers. These actions may take the form of setting relatively low prices, holding excess capacity against the threat of new production, producing multiple products to lower the cost per unit of output, and producing related products in order to reduce demand for a new entrant.

We have not discussed all forms of strategic behavior; many strategies are tailored to the particular market where the monopoly produces. The few mentioned should make it clear, however, that entry into a market is often not "naturally" impeded. It is blocked because those firms already in the market seek to keep new rivals out of the market.

15.4   Price Discrimination

Economists and business firms have long recognized that, if its buyers can be separated into separate groups with different elasticities of demand, a firm with monopoly power can charge different prices for the same product and increase its profits above what could be earned if it charged the same price to all buyers. In general, the more a seller knows about buyer preferences and the less easily buyers can trade among themselves, the greater the potential profit from setting different prices for the same good.

When consumers in a market do not pay the same price for the same product, the seller is price discriminating. There are two crucial points that should be noted in the definition of price discrimination. First, exactly the same product must have different prices. If the products are not identical, different prices do not indicate price discrimination. A vacation trip from Boston to Acapulco is not the same as a trip from Houston to Acapulco because transportation costs are different. Timing may also be important—a trip to Acapulco in winter is not the same as in summer. Demand is greater in the winter than it is in the summer, which raises the price of the vacation. Second, in order for price discrimination to exist, production and distribution costs must be equal. If costs are different, a profit maximizer who sets $MR = MC$ will usually charge different prices for a product. Costs may differ because of transportation charges, as mentioned. They may also differ because products are produced in different plants. In such cases the vintage of the facility or different labor contracts may make costs different.

It might seem that price discrimination would rarely exist. Not so. There are many examples of markets with price discrimination. A pharmacy giving discounts to senior citizens on prescriptions while other customers pay full price is practicing price discrimination. Theaters discriminate when they charge teenagers a lower ticket price than adults for the same showing. Hardware stores discriminate through their use of retail and commercial accounts. Commercial customers usually receive large discounts. Automobile dealers often charge different buyers different prices for identical cars. Medical doctors sometimes charge different patients different fees for the same treatment; the fees are frequently based upon the patient's income or insurance.

Definition

Price discrimination exists when buyers pay different prices for the same product and the different prices are not based upon differences in costs. Costs may differ if production costs, delivery expenses, or the time of sale are not identical.

This section describes the various types of price discrimination that can exist and sets forth the theory explaining each type. We begin with an analysis of third-degree discrimination, the most frequently encountered form. Under third-degree price discrimination, sellers charge different prices in separate markets based on the elasticities of demand in the markets. We then describe two more specialized forms of discrimination, commonly called first- and second-degree price discrimination.

15.4.1   Third-Degree Price Discrimination

Third-degree price discrimination exists when a firm can separate its customers into two or more separate markets, based upon the different characteristics of the customers. The firm then charges a different price in each market. The different markets are characterized by different demand elasticities. In order for a firm to practice price discrimination, the markets must be separable. If purchasers in the lower-price market are able to sell the product they buy at the lower price to buyers in the higher-price market, price discrimination will not exist for long. Arbitrage, or secondary trading among buyers, will soon restore a single, uniform price in the market. Goods that cannot be easily traded are more apt to have discriminatory prices than are those that can be easily transferred. For example, patients receiving medical care at a relatively low price cannot resell their care to other patients, but a lower-price buyer of some raw material or some good sold in a grocery store could, perhaps, resell it to someone in the higher-price market. Discrimination is more likely to occur in markets for services than in markets for material commodities.

As a first step in the analysis of third-degree price discrimination, we will show how a firm that practices price discrimination should allocate sales of a specified amount of its product among its different markets so as to maximize the total revenue it receives from these markets. To this end, we assume that a monopoly can divide the market for its product into two separate markets, called market A and market B. As a first approach, assume that the monopoly wishes to sell 10 units of its product and wants to allocate these 10 units between the two markets so as to maximize its total revenue.

Table 15–1 shows price, total revenue, and marginal revenue at each level of sales, from one through nine units of sales in each market. The problem is to determine how the firm should allocate the 10 units of sales between the two markets. Consider the first unit, quantity 1 in the first column; the firm can gain $45 ($MR_A$) by selling this unit in market A or $34 ($MR_B$) by selling it in B. Obviously, if it sells only one unit of output, it will sell it in A where the marginal revenue is higher. The second unit is also sold in A, because revenue increases by $35, whereas it would only add $34 in B. Since $34 can be gained in B and only $28 in A, unit three is sold in market B. Similar reasoning indicates that the fourth unit goes to B and the fifth to A. Unit six is sold in B, where the marginal revenue is $26, and unit 7 in A, where MR is $24. Eight is sold in A because the marginal revenue there is higher. Unit nine can go to either market since the marginal revenues ($18) are the same. We arbitrarily assign unit nine to market A, so unit 10 is sold in market B.

Table 15–1   Allocation of Sales between Two Markets

		Market A			Market B	
Quantity	Price	Revenue	Marginal Revenue	Price	Revenue	Marginal Revenue
1	$45	$ 45	$45(1)	$34	$ 34	$34(3)
2	40	80	35(2)	32	64	30(4)
3	36	108	28(5)	30	90	26(6)
4	33	132	24(7)	27	108	18(10)
5	30	150	22(8)	23	117	7
6	28	168	18(9)	20	120	4
7	25	175	7	17	119	1
8	22	184	1	14	112	−7
9	20	180	−4	11	99	−13

The 10 units of sales should be divided so that the marginal revenues are the same for the last unit sold in each market. The monopoly sells six units in A, charges a price of $28 in that market, and receives $168 revenue in the market. It sells four units in B, charges a price of $27 in that market, and receives $108 revenue. You can verify that the $276 total revenue from selling 10 units in the two markets by allocating six to A and four to B is higher than would be possible from any other allocation. You can also verify that if the monopoly wants to allocate 12 units of sales between the two markets, selling seven in A and five in B, where the marginal revenue from the last unit in each is $7, maximizes the total revenue from the 12 units of sales.

This example illustrates the following:

Principle

A firm practicing third-degree price discrimination allocates a given output among different markets in such a way that the marginal revenue from the last unit sold is the same in each market. The firm sells any additional unit in the market with the highest marginal revenue.

To illustrate this principle in a more general way, assume that a firm is selling a given level of output in two markets, I and II. The marginal revenue from the last unit sold in I is $30, and the marginal revenue from the last unit sold in II is $42, under the initial allocation:

$$MR_I = \$30 < \$42 = MR_{II}.$$

If the firm sells one fewer unit in I, its revenue there falls $30. However, if it sells that unit in II, its revenue in that market rises approximately $42, for a net gain in revenue of $12.[2] The firm should continue switching output from I to II as long as MR_I is less than MR_{II}. As more is sold in II and less is sold in I, MR_{II} decreases

---

[2]We said that revenue in II rises "approximately" $42 from the additional unit because we ignored the possibility of diminishing marginal revenue from that additional unit.

and MR_I increases, because of diminishing marginal revenue. Maximum revenue is attained when MR_I equals MR_{II}, and the firm should not continue reallocating. Thus, total revenue is maximized at a given level of output when

$$MR_I = MR_{II}.$$

It follows from the above analysis that if the firm allocates a given level of sales among more than two markets, the marginal revenue from the last unit in each market should be the same. For allocation among any number of markets, 1, 2, 3, . . . N,

$$MR_1 = MR_2 = MR_3 = \ldots = MR_N.$$

Intuitively, one would predict that, if there are two separate markets and the firm price discriminates, the higher price would be charged in the market with the less elastic demand, and the lower price would be in the more elastic market. Consumers in the more elastic market have access to better substitutes; therefore, price could be raised only at the expense of a large decrease in sales. In the less elastic market, there are poorer substitutes; higher prices bring less reduction in sales. The assertion that the higher price is charged in the less elastic market and the lower price in the more elastic market can be proved by using the following approach.

Let there be two separate markets for a monopolistically produced good; call these markets A and B. P_A and P_B are, respectively, the prices in markets A and B. MR_A and MR_B are the marginal revenues, and E_A and E_B are the absolute values of demand elasticity. Recall from the discussion of marginal revenue in Chapter 14 that

$$MR = P\left(1 - \frac{1}{E_D}\right).$$

We use this relation to prove that if $P_A > P_B$, then for the elasticities $E_A < E_B$. As stressed above, a discriminating monopolist divides output between the two markets so that the marginal revenues are equal in equilibrium. Thus,

$$MR_A = P_A\left(1 - \frac{1}{E_A}\right) = MR_B = P_B\left(1 - \frac{1}{E_B}\right).$$

If $P_A > P_B$, then by dividing

$$\frac{\left(1 - \dfrac{1}{E_B}\right)}{\left(1 - \dfrac{1}{E_A}\right)} = \frac{P_A}{P_B} > 1.$$

Since the monopolist would never choose a point at which MR is negative

$$\left(1 - \frac{1}{E_B}\right) > \left(1 - \frac{1}{E_A}\right).$$

Manipulation of this inequality yields

$$E_B > E_A.$$

Figure 15–3   Profit Maximization by a Discriminating Monopoly

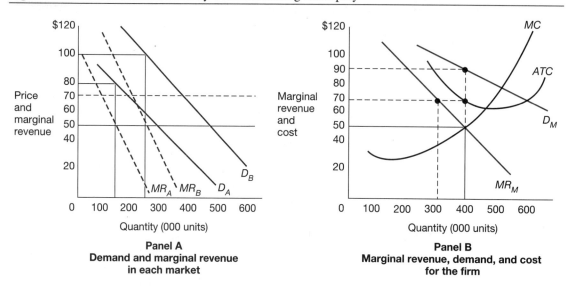

Panel A	Panel B
Demand and marginal revenue in each market	**Marginal revenue, demand, and cost for the firm**

Thus, whenever $P_A > P_B$, $E_B > E_A$ and vice versa. This proves that the more elastic market has the lower price.

So far, we have assumed that a discriminating monopoly allocates a given level of sales among markets so as to maximize revenue. We will now analyze graphically how a discriminating monopoly chooses the profit-maximizing level of output, allocates this output among markets, and chooses the profit-maximizing price in each market. Assume that the firm can separate its buyers into two distinct markets, A and B. The demand and marginal revenue curves in each market are shown as D_A and MR_A for market A, and D_B and MR_B for market B in Panel A of Figure 15–3. The firm's short-run marginal cost and average total cost curves are shown in Panel B.

The *horizontal* sum of the two marginal revenue curves in Panel A is shown as MR_M in Panel B. MR_M is constructed to reflect the condition that any given level of sales is divided between the two markets in such a way that the marginal revenue in each market is the same. For example, if the total output is 300, 100 units would be sold in market A, where $MR_A = \$70$, and 200 units would be sold in market B, where MR_B also equals $70. Thus, in Panel B, $MR_M = \$70$ at 300 units of output. An additional unit of output, the 301st, would have a marginal revenue of slightly less than $70 in either market. In Panel B, the market demand, D_M, is the horizontal sum of the two market demands in Panel A. This market demand is not necessary to determine the profit-maximizing sales and price in each market but is included for illustrative purposes later in the analysis.

The first step in the firm's profit-maximizing decision is to determine how much total output to produce. The profit-maximizing output is, as would be expected, that at which marginal cost equals total marginal revenue in Panel B. This occurs at 400 units of output, when $MC = MR_M = \$50$. Equating the marginal revenues in each market, the firm sells 150 units in A and 250 units in B, because at these outputs $MR_A = MR_B = \$50$. From the respective demands in Panel A, the firm charges a price of \$80 for the 150 units sold in market A, and a price of \$100 for the 250 units sold in market B.

If a firm can successfully price discriminate, as is the situation shown in Figure 15–3, it can always make more profit with price discrimination than it would made by charging one price in each market. From Panel B, the average or per-unit cost of the 400 units of output is \$70. Thus, the profit in each market is

$$\text{Profit in A} = (\$80 - \$70) \cdot 150 = \$1,500$$

$$\text{Profit in B} = (\$100 - \$70) \cdot 250 = \$7,500$$

Total profit is therefore \$9,000. If the firm acts like a typical monopoly and charges a single price for each of the 400 units, it would set a price of \$90, given by total demand, D_M, in Panel B. In this case, the monopoly profit would be

$$\text{Profit} = (\$90 - \$70) \cdot 400 = \$8,000.$$

Thus, the firm gains \$1,000 additional profit from discriminating.

Summarizing the results so far:

Principle

If a monopolist can divide the aggregate market for its product into submarkets with different price elasticities, the monopolist can profitably practice third-degree price discrimination. Total output is determined by equating marginal cost with aggregate monopoly marginal revenue. The output is allocated among the submarkets so as to equate marginal revenue in each submarket with aggregate marginal revenue at the $MC = MR$ point. Finally, price in each submarket is determined directly from the submarket demand curve, given the submarket allocation of sales.

15.4.2   First-Degree Price Discrimination—Perfect Price Discrimination

Under first-degree discrimination, the firm treats each individual's demand separately, and each consumer effectively represents a separate market. The firm then maximizes its profit given each individual's demand curve. In Figure 15–4, we have illustrated one consumer's demand function with its associated marginal revenue curve and the firm's marginal cost curve. In the normal case, the firm would maximize profit by selling the output where MR is equal to MC (i.e., an output of three units at a price of p_3). However, with first-degree price discrimination, the firm charges a different price for each unit sold to the consumer, depending on what the consumer is willing to pay. For the first unit of the product, the consumer is willing to pay p_1; so the firm makes a profit on this unit equal to the difference between p_1 and average cost at this output. For the second unit, the consumer will pay p_2 and so on.

Figure 15–4   First-Degree Price Discrimination

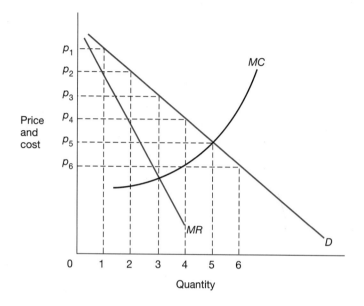

The firm will continue to sell to this consumer as long as the price the consumer will pay is greater than or equal to marginal cost. More specifically, under first-degree price discrimination, the firm will produce and sell to the level of output where the price of the last unit is equal to marginal cost. This is the output where the demand curve intersects the marginal cost curve. Since the monopolist does not have to lower price on every unit sold to sell one more at the margin, the demand curve is the marginal revenue schedule. In other words, since the firm charges a different price for each unit consumed, the addition to total revenue for a unit of the product will be the price charged for that unit. In Figure 15–4 it will not sell the sixth unit because the price the consumer is willing to pay (p_6) is less than the marginal cost associated with this level of production.

Figure 15–5 provides a comparison of profits with and without first-degree price discrimination. For simplicity, we assume that marginal cost is constant, so $MC = AC$. The consumer's demand and marginal revenue curves are, respectively, D and MR. Without discrimination, the firm will sell Q_S units at a price of P_S. Since average cost is constant, the firm's total profit is indicated by the rectangle P_SABC, the lightly shaded area shown in Figure 15–5.

Next, let the firm practice first-degree price discrimination. The firm will charge the consumer the maximum price he or she would be willing to pay for each unit purchased. Each unit sells for the highest price that can be obtained for that unit. The firm will sell up to the point where the price any consumer is willing to pay equals marginal cost; with price discrimination, the firm will sell Q_D units of output. For each unit, the firm charges the price on the demand curve, and profit is the

Figure 15–5   Profit with and without First-Degree Discrimination

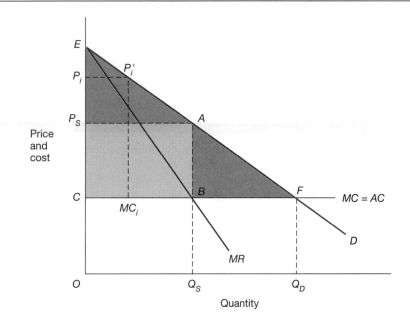

difference between that price and the corresponding point on the marginal cost curve (e.g., $P_i' - MC_i$). Total profit to the discriminating firm is the entire shaded area *EFC*. Obviously, price discrimination leads to a substantial increase in profit.

Though first-degree price discrimination would increase the firm's profits, it is usually not a realistic practice. Each individual consumer must be isolated and dealt with separately, which places tremendous informational requirements on the firm. Learning each consumer's demand curve can be an extremely costly endeavor. Also, once consumers realize that a seller is attempting to practice first-degree price discrimination they may intentionally understate their willingness to pay in order to get lower prices. Efforts by the monopolist to learn more about what each buyer will pay may be in vain.

15.4.3   Second-Degree Price Discrimination

First-degree price discrimination is expensive to implement, since, at least in theory, the firm must determine each individual's demand function. Second-degree price discrimination is somewhat simpler because every buyer is offered the same price discount as the quantity purchased increases. This form of discrimination can best be explained using Figure 15–6, where we again employ the simplifying assumption that marginal cost is constant. With second-degree price discrimination, the firm would charge every buyer P_1 for the first Q_1 units purchased. If consumers wanted to purchase more, they would then receive discrete discounts. In Figure 15–6, the

Figure 15–6   Second-Degree Price Discrimination

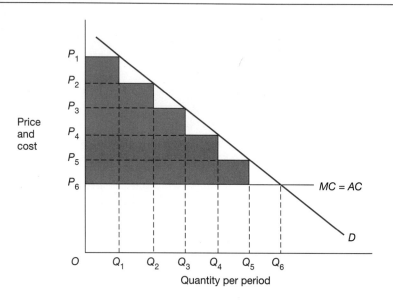

next Q_1Q_2 units would cost P_2, then price would fall to P_3 for the next Q_2Q_3 units, and so on. In effect, buyers are receiving quantity discounts. The discounts are offered as long as the price consumers are willing to pay exceeds marginal cost. The firm will sell a total of Q_6 units of its product with the last price tier at P_6 equal to marginal cost. Total profit is again the shaded area. Note the similarity between this case and the profits in first-degree price discrimination. In essence, second-degree price discrimination is an approximation of first-degree discrimination.

15.4.4   Summary

A firm with monopoly power practices price discrimination when it charges different prices to different buyers for the same product and the price differences do not result from differences in costs. Third-degree price discrimination occurs when a firm can separate its buyers into two or more groups and charges a different price to each group. The firm's total output is that at which marginal cost equals the market marginal revenue, which is the horizontal sum of the marginal revenues in each market. Output is allocated to the different markets so that marginal revenue is the same in each market. The price in each market is given by the demand in that market. For any two markets, the market with the lower elasticity has the higher price.

    First- and second-degree price discrimination are similar. Under first-degree price discrimination, consumers are charged the highest price they are willing to pay for each unit of the product. Under second-degree price discrimination, the firm establishes price tiers. Lower prices are charged on the last units as more is purchased. Second-degree discrimination is an offer of quantity discounts. Under first- and second- and third-degree price discrimination, the firm attempts to capture as much of each buyer's consumer surplus as possible. Actually, first-degree price discrimination allows the firm to capture all of the consumer surplus; in practice, however, this method of pricing is rare.

It is particularly crucial in any form of price discrimination that arbitrage—lower price buyers selling to buyers who would be charged a higher price—does not occur among buyers. An enterprising consumer could, if reselling is relatively easy, buy at a low price and sell at a higher price. The firm would at the limit find itself selling only at the low price.

Examples of price discrimination are not hard to find. Many drug stores discriminate by offering discounts on drugs to persons 65 and older. Retired persons probably have a higher elasticity of demand than other customers. Because they do not work, the value of their time may be lower, and they would tend to spend more time shopping for lower prices. Physicians sometimes charge higher prices to patients with higher incomes or more insurance; presumably these patients would have a lower demand elasticity.

Movies, plays, concerts, and similar forms of entertainment frequently practice price discrimination by offering lower ticket prices to younger buyers. Possibly younger people have a higher elasticity of demand for such forms of entertainment because they have available more substitute forms of entertainment. (It is not correct to say that different ticket prices for afternoon and evening performances are evidence of price discrimination. These are different products.) Airlines sometimes discriminate between vacation and business travelers, by charging a lower price if tickets are purchased well in advance. Business travelers often want to be more flexible and are not willing to commit over a long period of time. Other examples are electric companies that charge lower prices to industrial users than to households (although this price differential may reflect a difference in cost) and academic journals that charge a lower price to professors than to university libraries.

Sellers of durable goods, such as large appliances, sometimes attempt to practice first-degree price discrimination. Automobiles with the same characteristics have the same posted price—or sticker price—excluding shipping charges. As you probably know, dealers generally discount these prices. Except for the "hottest sellers," people seldom pay the full posted price, and different people pay a different price for the same vehicle. Consumers and the salespersons "bargain" with each other over price. Consumers try to get the lowest price they can. The dealer tries to practice first-degree price discrimination in order to charge each consumer the highest price that consumer is willing to pay. Certainly, it is impossible for the dealer to practice perfect first-degree discrimination because consumers try to conceal the highest price they would be willing to pay. Nonetheless, the dealer tries to find this price.

Sellers in markets in many foreign countries attempt first-degree price discrimination also. If you, as a tourist, have ever bargained in a foreign market or bazaar, you are familiar with the process.

*Economics in
the News*

Who Practices Price Discrimination, and Why?

In the text, we gave some general examples of the types of firms that practice price discrimination, particularly third-degree discrimination. Here we will be more specific.

In 1982, the Northern California Booksellers Association (NCBA) filed an unfair practices suit under antitrust law against Avon, the huge paperback book publisher (*Publisher's Weekly,* November 14, 1986, pp. 12–13.). The NCBA charged Avon with discriminatory pricing for giving a higher discount to major retailing chains, such as Dalton, Walden, and Crown, than it gave to independent bookstores. Avon's discount to Dalton, Walden, and Crown was 44 percent for mass-market books and 48 percent for trade paperbacks; its discount to independent bookstores was, respectively, 40 and 43 percent. Other large publishers were allegedly following a similar policy.

The NCBA argued that this discriminatory pricing policy put independent retailers at a severe competitive disadvantage. Avon's defense was that the price differential was not discriminatory because it was based upon differences in selling costs. The company argued that selling to major chains was less expensive, because of their centralized buying compared with the cost of maintaining a sales force that must call on many independent outlets. In October 1986, the judge in the case stated that booksellers, "find sales reps only marginally useful" and would choose to purchase from an Avon catalog if they were given the opportunity of doing so. He ruled that cost did not justify the higher discounts and that this price discrimination in favor of the major chains "has been a substantial factor in providing funds and other economic benefits which have contributed to the growth of these chains." The judge ruled against another Avon argument, that the paperback publishing industry was highly competitive, saying that the sale of paperback titles to independent booksellers is relatively noncompetitive.

It is interesting that the judge also noted that Avon's secrecy about the discounts created an inference that Avon did not have any objective criteria for granting discounts but did so in response to pressure from the chains. If this is correct, it would imply that Avon did not necessarily practice traditional third-degree price discrimination, but the major chains exercised monopoly power on the buyer's side of the market (called *monopsony power*) in pressuring Avon to give the larger discounts.

We noted in the text that airlines frequently price discriminate by charging business fliers, on average, higher fares than they charge nonbusiness fliers. Because fliers would not voluntarily reveal to an airline that they are flying on business, the markets are separated by requiring more advance notice and imposing more restrictions on tickets sold at the lower prices. The *Houston Post,* "Business Travelers Starting to Battle Expensive Air Fares," March 26, 1989, reported that businesses were taking measures to reduce their fares by subscribing to computer systems that constantly search for the lowest fares, hiring corporate travel managers, and joining business travel associations to lobby for lower fares and search for volume discounts. The *Post* noted that such measures were achieving moderate success, but as a travel supervisor for a large Houston bank noted, "With one major business carrier in Houston (Continental Airlines), we don't have a lot of bargaining power." This implies that the more monopoly power a firm has, the better it is able to price discriminate. Several corporate travel managers indicated that many of their firm's business travelers did fly on discounted fares but a very large proportion fly on short notice (one manager reported 75 to 85 percent).

(continued)

The following fare information in the article from the *Post* provides some evidence about the fare differentials. The fares are for a round-trip ticket on Continental Airlines from Houston to New York, leaving Monday, under four different purchasing situations (the fare differentials for American and Delta were similar):

Booking	Price	Restrictions	Penalty for Changes
14-day advance	$318	Stay Saturday night	100%
7-day advance	378	Stay Saturday night	25%
7-day advance	726	None	25%
1-day advance	924	None	None

The highest fare, not including first class, was almost three times as high as the lowest fare. The airlines rationalized the fare differences by noting that they restrict the number of seats available at the cheaper fares and because "The business traveler has to have a seat available at the last minute because they can't always plan ahead . . . for those last-minute reservations you have to price a number of seats accordingly." Such an argument would imply that seats available at the last minute are different products than seats available only in advance, and the price difference is justified by a difference in product quality. This is a difficult question to answer, but the evidence points rather strongly to traditional price discrimination, with some mitigating circumstances.

Newsweek, "The Initiative That Wasn't," December 1, 1986, p. 44, reported that American flower growers won a ruling from the International Trade Administration (ITA) that Costa Rica was illegally subsidizing exports and selling chrysanthemums to the United States for less than the price in Costa Rica. The ITA placed a 46 percent duty on Costa Rican flowers in order to protect American growers. While this pricing practice was ruled illegal, was it price discrimination? It appears so, because the flowers were surely the same in the two countries, unless they deteriorated during transportation; and the selling cost must have been less in Costa Rica than in the United States, because of transportation.

In his nationally syndicated column, "Insurance: Risks and Rights," September 15, 1987, William Raspberry, of the Washington Post Writers Group, discussed the increasingly important topic of whether differences in insurance premiums based on gender or age are evidence of price discrimination. He noted that premium differences may or may not involve civil rights violations. Raspberry begins, "Think of insurance as a product or service (which it is), and the idea of equal premiums for men and women makes sense. Think of it as a gambling venture (which it is also), and unisex premiums make no sense at all." He notes that if insurance is a product like cough syrup or car rental, insurers can be said to be discriminating—by charging higher rates—against women (in health insurance), against young males (in auto insurance), and against men (in life insurance). If insurance is like a gamble, the insurance company is protecting itself by demanding higher premiums if a teenager has a much greater chance of having a car accident or a woman figures to have either more or more-expensive health claims.

Raspberry supposes that what would seem like ordinary common sense at a gambling table comes off as a civil rights violation in the case of insurance, because insurance seems like a more necessary product than a gamble, and differential insurance premiums

(continued)

"sound unfair," usually to women, though not always. The legislatures of two states, Montana and Massachusetts, must have thought such rate differentials are unfair because they required unisex insurance rates. The Massachusetts insurance commissioner stated that rate differentials should be based only on "factors that are in people's control." As Raspberry interpreted this, "It's okay to charge a woman more for health insurance because she is a cigarette smoker, but not because she is a woman. It's fine to charge a youngster more because he is a reckless or inexperienced driver, but not because he is 19." Auto insurance rates in Montana "turned out to be a boon for young men, whose premiums came down, and a curse for young women, whose rates soared."

The city council of Washington, D.C., made it illegal for insurance companies to base health-care insurability on the results of tests for exposure to the AIDS virus. After a federal court upheld this ruling, a large number of insurance companies stopped writing new health insurance policies in the District.

Raspberry concludes that it might sound "like discrimination . . . [but] the differential policies start to make sense. . . . It strikes me as prudent and sensible for insurers-as-gamblers to weigh the likelihood of having to deliver a payoff. Mandatory coverage at ordinary rates may be a good deal for members of certain high-risk groups. But it is the rest of us, not the insurance companies, who will be stuck with the cost."

We agree with Mr. Raspberry. Different insurance rates to different groups based upon different risks is not necessarily price discrimination, in the sense discussed in the text; it is, in effect, different prices based upon different costs, even though the actual policies are the same.

15.5   Market Performance of Monopoly

Economists have done extensive research, both theoretical and empirical, comparing the social costs and benefits of monopoly and other firms with extensive market power, relative to perfect competition. As we have noted several times in this text, economists frequently use the theory of perfect competition as a benchmark of comparison for firms selling in other types of market structures. In this section, we will give a brief overview of this comparison. As you will see, it is theoretically possible to show, under somewhat stylized cost conditions, that the existence of monopoly rather than perfect competition in markets imposes a social cost upon society. We will present a bit of empirical evidence estimating the size of the social cost of monopoly in the United States.

However, once the assumption of the typically assumed U-shaped average cost curves are removed and the producer is allowed to experience pervasive economies of scale, it is not clear whether a market is better served by a firm or firms with considerable market power or by perfect competition. Lower costs of production may counterbalance the power of the monopolist to set price, resulting in a monopoly price lower than the price set under perfect competition. Moreover, under some cost conditions, a product may not even be produced unless the market is monopolized. Higher prices and increased revenues may be necessary to cover total costs. The choice is to go without the product or have it produced by a monopolist, which is to say perfect competition is not always a viable market structure.

15.5.1   Comparison with Perfect Competition

To facilitate the comparison of monopoly with perfect competition, let us briefly review the most important implications of the theory of perfect competition. Under perfect competition, the market price is the firm's marginal revenue. To maximize profit, each firm chooses the output at which marginal revenue and marginal cost are equal. Thus, price in the market equals marginal cost. In the long run, the market price equals minimum long-run average cost. Consequently, in the long run, the price is the lowest possible price at which the product could be produced. Also, in the long run, no firm makes an economic profit, but each firm covers its opportunity cost; that is, it makes only a normal profit.

For monopoly and all firms with market power, price is higher than marginal revenue. Since the firm chooses the output at which marginal revenue equals marginal cost, price must be higher than marginal cost. Furthermore, in the long run, a monopoly will charge a price that is higher than minimum long-run average cost, and there is no tendency for economic profit to fall to zero.

The most important difference between the two market structures for purposes of comparison is the relation between price and marginal cost. To see why this difference is important, consider the competitive market situation shown by the demand and supply curves in Figure 15–7. Begin first with the market in equilibrium; price is $50 and quantity sold is 1,000 units. The 1,000th unit sold costs exactly $50 to produce. That is, from the supply curve, the marginal cost of this unit is $50. Furthermore, because the price is $50, the last unit sold is worth exactly $50 to a consumer. Thus, the value to society of the last unit is $50, which is equal to the cost of producing this last unit.

In equilibrium, consumer's surplus, the area below demand and above price, is $28,000 (= (1/2) · (106 − 50) · 1,000). Producer's surplus, the area above supply and below price, is $15,000 (= (1/2) · (50 − 20) · 1,000). Total surplus in the market is therefore $43,000. We will now compare these results with those that would occur after a restriction on output is imposed in the market.

Suppose such a restriction permits producers to sell no more than 700 units of output. The new supply is the same as the original supply up to 700; supply is then vertical or perfectly inelastic at 700. With the new supply, price rises to $68.

From the demand curve, consumers would be willing to pay slightly less than $68 for another unit of output, the 701st. From the supply curve, the marginal cost of producing this 701st unit is slightly higher than $39. Thus, society is willing to pay about $29 more for an additional unit of the good than it would cost to produce that unit. In fact, for every additional unit up to the 1,000th, the value of that unit to society exceeds the cost of producing that unit.

Note also that the output restriction causes consumer's surplus to fall to $13,300 (= (1/2) · (106 − 68) · 700). This represents a loss to consumers of $14,700 in surplus. Producer's surplus is now $26,950 (= (1/2) · (39 − 20) · 700 + (68 − 39) · 700), representing a gain of $11,950. Thus, producers gain, but consumers lose from the output restriction. However, total surplus falls from $43,000 to $40,250 for a net loss in total surplus of $2,750. This lost surplus, which is shown geometrically in Figure 15–7 as the areas of the triangles labeled A (formerly

Figure 15–7   The Deadweight Welfare Loss from Output Restrictions

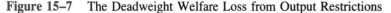

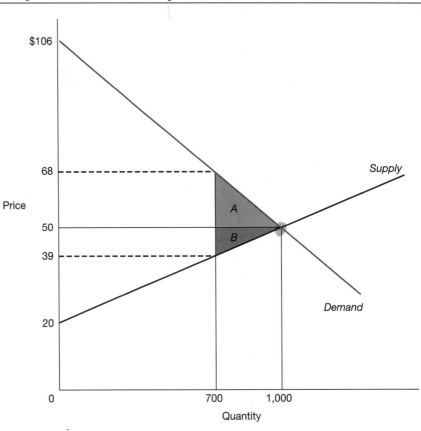

consumer's surplus) and B (formerly producer's surplus), simply disappears. It goes
to no one. Such losses after market restrictions are frequently called a *welfare loss*
or *deadweight loss* to society. A similar wedge between supply and demand was
discussed in Chapter 13.

Therefore, any restriction that causes output to fall will raise the price of the
product, causing the value to society of the last unit sold to exceed the marginal
cost of producing that unit. Such output restrictions also decrease consumer's surplus, may increase producer's surplus, and always reduce total surplus in the market,
causing a net loss in welfare.

The most common criticism of monopoly is that price is higher and output is
lower than in a perfectly competitive market. In effect, monopoly in a market has
the same consequences as the output restriction discussed above. This assertion is
based upon the situation depicted in Figure 15–8.

The monopoly shown in the figure produces Q_M and sets a price of P_M. Clearly,
price exceeds marginal cost, M, at this output. If we were to assume that this market
is organized competitively and that *MC* represents competitive industry supply,
supply equals demand at E. The competitive industry would, under these conditions,

Figure 15–8   Price and Output Comparisons

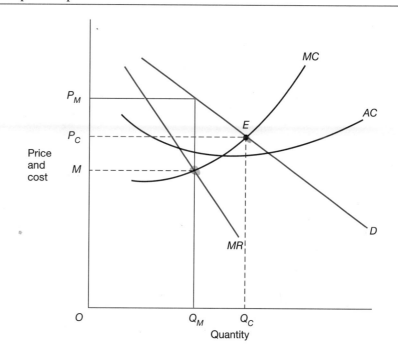

sell Q_C units of output at a price of P_C. The value to society of the last unit of output, P_C, is just equal to the cost of producing that last unit. In the case of monopoly, the value of the last unit, P_M, is greater than the cost of producing that unit, M.

Thus, under these specific conditions, monopoly restricts output and increases price above what it would be under competition. Under monopoly, society values additional units of output more than it would cost to produce those additional units. Under perfect competition, the value and cost of the last unit are the same. Imposing monopoly rather than competition in the market has the same effect as an output restriction in the market.

For reasons we have emphasized, the conclusion that price is higher than marginal cost is considered by economists to be the most important shortcoming of monopoly, from a social point of view. In fact, economists sometimes use the ratio of the difference between price and marginal cost to price—$(P - MC)/P$—to estimate the amount of monopoly power a firm possesses. The larger the percentage by which price exceeds marginal cost, that is, the larger the ratio $(P - MC)/P$, the more market power a firm is said to possess.

15.5.2   Surplus Loss from Monopoly

We have argued that in the case of monopoly, because the value of another unit of the good to consumers in the market exceeds the marginal cost of its production, society as whole would benefit by having more resources used in producing the

Figure 15–9   Surplus Loss from Monopoly

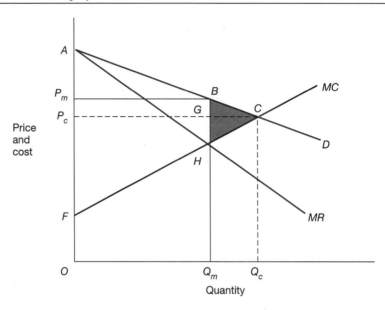

commodity in question. The profit-maximizing monopoly will not produce more because producing more would reduce profit. A perfect competitor produces the quantity at which the marginal cost of production just equals the marginal value of the good to consumers, not because of any innate social consciousness, but because the market forces this outcome on producers.

We can illustrate the loss monopoly causes society in the same way that we illustrated the loss from an output restriction in a competitive market: by using the tools of consumer's and producer's surplus. In Figure 15–9, suppose MC is the supply curve for a perfectly competitive industry. The industry would produce Q_c units of output, at which MC equals demand; price would be P_c. For the competitive market structure, total surplus—the sum of consumer's surplus plus producer's surplus—is the area $AP_cC + P_cCF = ACF$.

A monopolist would operate where marginal cost equals marginal revenue, selling Q_m units of output and setting a price of P_m. Under monopoly, total surplus is the area $ABP_m + P_mBHF = ABHF$. The producer gains some surplus while consumers lose some surplus, compared to the situation under competition. However, because the monopoly restricts output, the shaded area, BCH, represents a net loss in total surplus. Of this net loss, the loss to consumers is BCG, whereas the producer loses GCH. By restricting output and raising price, there is a transfer of surplus from the consumer to the producer equivalent to area P_mBGP_c. In total, the consumer loses the surplus represented by the sum of the areas $P_mBGP_c + BCG$. Since the monopolist gains the area P_mBGP_c, area BCG represents the net loss of consumer's surplus.

The monopolist is willing to forego the surplus represented by GCH to obtain surplus area P_mBGP_c. The transfer in consumer's surplus, P_mBGP_c, from higher prices, is greater than the loss of producer's surplus, GCH, from restricting output. By setting $MR = MC$ to maximize profits, a monopolist maximizes the difference between areas GCH and P_mBGP_c.

To summarize, within the theoretical structure imposed here, monopoly in a market has the same effect as an output restriction. A monopoly sells a smaller output and charges a higher price than would be the case under perfect competition. Under monopoly, but not competition, additional units of output have a higher value to consumers than the additional cost of producing these units, because price is higher than marginal cost for the last unit sold. Monopoly, compared to perfect competition, results in a transfer of some surplus away from consumers to producers, and there is a net loss of total surplus that goes to no one. This net loss of surplus is the welfare loss or deadweight loss of monopoly.

There is some reason to doubt, however, that MC can represent the supply curve of a perfectly competitive industry. The sum of a large number of firms' marginal cost curves is not necessarily the marginal cost curve of a single, much larger firm. In any event, a monopoly is more likely to earn a profit because it can effectively exercise some market control; output is restricted and prices are raised relative to perfectly competitive markets.

In long-run industry equilibrium under perfect competition, production occurs at the point of minimum long- and short-run average cost. The monopolist, on the other hand, utilizes the plant capable of producing its most profitable long-run output at the least unit cost. Only under rare circumstances in which marginal revenue intersects marginal cost at minimum long-run average cost would this plant size be the scale chosen by the monopolist.

15.5.3   Welfare Loss from Monopoly in the United States

In 1954, Arnold C. Harberger attempted to measure the welfare loss (lost surplus) from all monopoly in the United States.[3] Because of the relative tranquility of the period and the availability of good data, Harberger used the years 1924–1928 for his estimation. He assumed that those industries with higher than average returns on capital had too few resources invested (i.e., were monopolized), and those yielding lower than average returns had too many resources. In all industries, long-run average cost was assumed constant.

Harberger estimated how much better off society would have been if a transfer of resources had taken place to reduce monopoly price to average cost and increase output. This amount would equal the sum of all increases in consumer's surplus (area BGC in Figure 15–9) due to changing monopolies to competitive markets. There would not be any increase in producer's surplus at the margin since the $LRAC$

---

[3]See A. C. Harberger, "The Welfare Loss from Monopoly," *American Economic Review*, 34, no. 2 (May 1954), pp. 77–87. For some additional insights into this question, see F. M. Scherer, *Industrial Market Structure and Economic Performance* (Chicago: Rand McNally, 1971), chapter 17.

curve was assumed horizontal. The total welfare gain estimated from the resource transfer was $59 million; at the time less than 1/10 of 1 percent of the national income. In terms of 1954 income, this averaged less than $1.50 per person in the United States. When Harberger included certain intangibles in the data, the necessary transfer rose from 1.5 percent to 1.75 percent of national income, and the welfare loss rose to $81 million. (We might note that the welfare change does not consider the reallocation of income from the rest of society to the monopoly, area P_cP_mBG in Figure 15–9.)

In all the estimates, the total welfare loss came to less than 1/10 of 1 percent of national income, and in most instances, Harberger used assumptions that biased the estimates upward. This extremely low estimate was startling at the time. Aside from the transfer of resources from consumers to monopoly, it appeared that the total welfare cost was quite small.

A little more than a decade later, Gordon Tullock added new insights to the discussion by comparing the welfare loss from monopoly to the economics of theft.[4] It may be argued that if one person steals $100 from another, the theft simply involves a transfer of resources. However, the actions taken to carry out and prevent theft impose a large cost to society. Potential thieves would invest in resources— time, burglar tools, getaway cars, lookouts—until any additional resources would cost more than the marginal return in stolen assets from using these resources. (Even thieves can use a knowledge of economic theory.) Similarly, potential victims wish to protect their wealth. A potential victim would invest in preventive re- sources—watchdogs, locks, guns, and so forth—as long as the expected marginal saving from such resources is expected to exceed their marginal cost. Furthermore, the return to resources used in theft depends on the number of resources used in theft prevention, and vice versa.

Over time, society would attain an equilibrium amount of theft, which would probably be positive, since the prevention of all theft would cost too much. Even though the equilibrium amount of theft involves only transfers, the existence of theft will impose a considerable cost on society. The resources used to steal and to prevent stealing cost the individuals involved, and they cost society the use of those resources that could be used to produce other products. They are completely wasted from society's point of view—used only to cause or to prevent transfer of wealth, not to produce wealth.

Similar to theft, monopoly involves a transfer of resources from consumers to the producer. According to Tullock's analysis, the welfare losses estimated using Harberger's technique underestimate the true welfare loss from monopoly. Since the return from establishing a successful monopoly is frequently great, one would expect a potential monopolist to expend considerable resources attempting to mo- nopolize a market. In fact, entrepreneurs should be willing to invest resources in attempts to form monopolies until the marginal cost equals the expected return. After the monopoly is formed, others will invest resources trying to break the monopoly, which, in turn, means that the monopolist must use additional resources

[4]See G. Tullock, "The Welfare Costs of Monopolies and Theft," *Western Economic Journal* 5, no. 2 (June 1967), pp. 224–32.

trying to prevent the break. Just as successful theft encourages additional theft, successful monopoly encourages additional attempts to monopolize.

As Tullock noted, identifying and measuring the resources used to gain, break, and hold monopoly are quite difficult. It appears that a large amount of a very scarce resource—skilled management—is used toward this end. In any case, the Harberger estimates ignore this cost and therefore underestimate the social cost of monopoly.

15.5.4   A Closing Word about the Social Cost of Monopoly

Using the simple theoretical framework set forth here to compare monopoly and perfect competition, we have described why monopoly compares quite unfavorably. Relative to a perfectly competitive market, monopoly restricts output, charges a higher price, and does not operate at minimum long-run average cost. Furthermore, because monopoly restricts output, there is a net loss of total surplus relative to perfect competition.

The comparison between the two market structures is not so clear if production technology is characterized by continuous economies of scale in the long run. If economies of scale are present, the profit-maximizing incentive encourages firms to become larger and, as a consequence, fewer in number. A large number of firms could be maintained by making it illegal for a firm to become large, but this has serious disincentive effects for the profit maximizer. More important, it is not clear that a few firms (or even a single firm) producing the product is undesirable. Because of lower costs, these firms may charge a lower price than competitive producers.

As a matter of public policy, economists cannot say that perfect competition is more efficient and, therefore, more desirable than a monopolized market structure. This judgment cannot be generalized. Moreover, if we extended our comparison to the issues of research and development, employment, and inflationary impact, the relative advantages and disadvantages of the two market structures would become even less clear-cut.

Furthermore, economists today are not so concerned about the extent of monopoly in the economy as they were 15 to 20 years ago. International trade has, over the years, become increasingly important. Even if a few firms, or possibly only one, are responsible for the entire domestic production of some good, these firms frequently face intense competition from foreign producers. This foreign competition restricts the price that domestic firms can charge and increases the quantity available to consumers. Therefore, foreign competition limits the amount of market power possessed by domestic firms at home.

15.6   Monopoly Regulation and Taxation

Because some of the social effects of monopoly behavior are considered undesirable, governments sometimes attempt to regulate monopoly behavior by imposing price ceilings. This section analyzes the effect of price regulation on firms that have market power. This section also examines the effects of certain forms of taxation on the price, output, and profits of a monopoly.

Figure 15–10   Effects of Price Ceilings under Monopoly

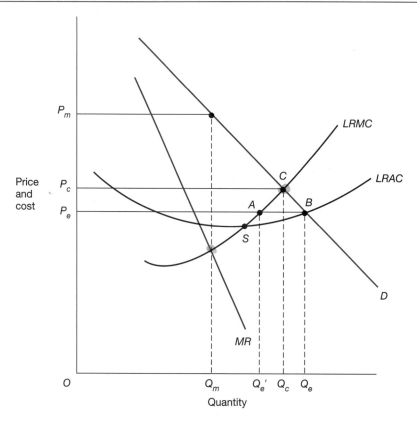

15.6.1   Price Regulation

If government believes a monopoly is charging too high a price, restricting output excessively, or making too much profit, it can set a price ceiling or price cap on the commodity. As you will recall from demand and supply analysis, a ceiling price set below equilibrium in competitive markets always causes a shortage of the good. However, a shortage might not result if there is price cap regulation for a monopoly.

Consider the situation shown in Figure 15–10. Under these demand and cost conditions, the nonregulated monopoly sells Q_m units of output at a price of P_m and obviously makes a profit. Assume that government, for some reason or another, believes that the price is too high and sets a ceiling price of P_c, below P_m. Now the horizontal line segment P_cC becomes the new demand up to the output Q_c. The marginal revenue curve up to Q_c is also the line segment P_cC. The firm can sell all it wishes at a price of P_c up to Q_c because, over this range, demand lies above P_c. It would certainly charge no lower price. At output levels greater than Q_c, the old demand and marginal revenue curves come into effect, because to sell more, the firm must lower its price. The entire new demand is given by the line P_cCD, and marginal revenue equals P_c up to Q_c.

Figure 15–11   Effects of Price Ceilings under Natural Monopoly

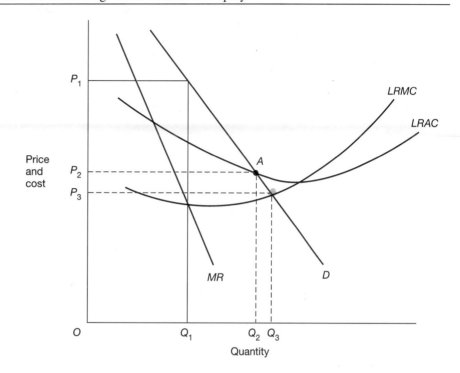

With this new demand, marginal revenue now equals marginal cost at point C. The firm sells Q_c units of output at a price of P_c. Because point C lies on the demand curve, the quantity demanded equals the amount the firm supplies, and the market is cleared. Profit certainly is lower than the profit before the ceiling price is imposed; since P_m and Q_m yielded maximum profit, any other price and output combination, including P_c and Q_c, must give less than maximum. Nonetheless, the quantity Q_c yields maximum profit under the constraint that price can be no higher than P_c.

With the ceiling price, the price is equal to marginal cost in equilibrium. If the price on the demand curve represents the market's marginal valuation of the commodity and marginal cost represents the cost of producing the last unit, marginal benefit and marginal cost are equal at the margin. In other words, the consumer's and producer's surplus in the market are maximized, and one of the results of perfect competition is obtained even though, in the long run, production need not take place at minimum average cost.

Other price caps would not give this result. For example, at any ceiling price set between P_m and P_c, price would equal *LRMC* at an output greater than the quantity the market would demand at that price. Therefore, the monopolist sells the quantity given by the demand curve at the ceiling price. Again, price falls from P_m and quantity increases from Q_m but, in contrast to P_c, price exceeds the marginal cost of the last unit sold.

If P_c causes price to fall, quantity to rise, and profit to diminish, why not lower price even further, possibly to P_e? At P_e the monopolist could sell Q_e and still cover costs, since $LRAC = P_e$ at Q_e. But the new demand and marginal revenue curve up to Q_e is P_eB; therefore, $MR = LRMC$ at A, and the firm would produce Q'_e, which is less than Q_e. Since quantity demanded at P_e is Q_e, a shortage of Q'_eQ_e results. In this case, the monopolist must allocate by means other than price. In fact, any price below P_c causes a decrease in quantity sold from Q_c, and a shortage occurs since quantity demanded exceeds quantity supplied at that price.

Under the condition assumed in Figure 15–10, the largest feasible output is attained when the ceiling price is set so that the firm produces the output at which marginal cost intersects demand. This result may not always be attainable with a ceiling price, in particular when the firm is a natural monopoly. Figure 15–11 illustrates such a case. Over the relevant range of demand, the firm is a natural monopoly: Economies of scale cause long-run average cost to decline beyond the point at which it crosses demand at point A.

The nonregulated, profit-maximizing monopoly sets a price of P_1 and sells Q_1. Suppose the government sets a price of P_3, the price at which $LRMC$ crosses demand. If the firm produces, it would produce Q_3, at which the new marginal revenue or price equals $LRMC$. However, because the ceiling price is below $LRAC$ at every level of output, in the long run, the firm would be forced out of business because it could not cover its total cost. In fact, the ceiling could be no lower than P_2 without forcing the firm to cease production. At a ceiling price of P_2, the firm would sell Q_2 units of output. Since price equals $LRAC$ at this output, the firm would make no economic profit. At this output, price is greater than marginal cost, with all of the negative implications discussed above. The firm would like to produce more—up to the point at which P_2 equals $LRMC$—but demand conditions would not permit it to sell this large an output.

15.6.2   Taxation

Governments place taxes on monopolies in order to regulate them and to raise revenue. We will examine here three common types of taxes: a per-unit excise tax, a lump-sum tax, and a percent-of-profit tax.

A per-unit excise tax means that for every unit sold, regardless of price, the monopolist must pay a specified amount of money to the government. Assume that the monopolist, whose cost curves $LRAC_0$ and $LRMC_0$ are shown in Figure 15–12, is charged a tax of k dollars for every unit sold. Total cost after the tax is the total cost of production (presumably the same as before) plus k times output; thus, average or unit cost must rise by exactly the amount of the tax, k dollars. The after-tax $LRAC$ in Figure 15–12 rises from $LRAC_0$ to $LRAC_1$, or by the vertical distance k. $LRMC$ also rises by k dollars. If it costs $LRMC_0$ to produce and sell an additional unit of output before the tax, after the tax it costs $LRMC_0 + k = LRMC_1$ to produce and sell that additional unit. This also is shown in Figure 15–12.

Before the tax is imposed, the monopolist produces Q_0 and charges a price of P_0. After the imposition of the tax, the cost curves shift vertically by the amount k to $LRAC_1$ and $LRMC_1$. Marginal cost now equals MR at output Q_1, so price rises

Figure 15–12   Effects of an Excise Tax under Monopoly

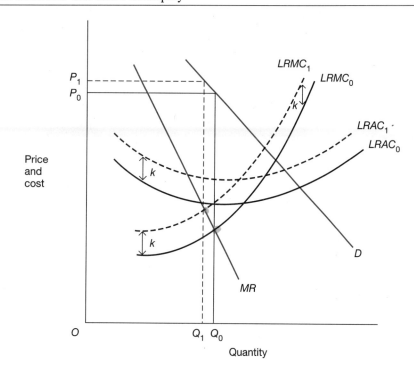

to P_1. Some of the tax, $P_1 - P_0$, is shifted to consumers in the form of a price increase, and the rest is borne by the monopolist. This effect differs completely from the effect of the ceiling price that causes price to fall and quantity to rise.

A lump-sum tax has a somewhat different impact on price and quantity. Assume that instead of imposing an excise tax on the monopolist, the government charges a license fee that remains the same regardless of quantity sold. The license fee is, therefore, a fixed cost to the monopolist. Average cost rises after the fee is imposed; at very small outputs, the curve rises more than it does at larger outputs because, the larger the output, the more units the fee is spread over. Once the fee is paid, however, no additional tax is charged for an additional unit of production per period—marginal cost remains unchanged. Since MC and MR do not change after the lump-sum tax, their point of intersection does not change, and price and quantity remain the same after the tax is imposed. The lump-sum tax does reduce profits and cannot be so large that it drives long-run average cost above demand. This would cause a loss and force the monopolist out of business.

A percentage-of-profits tax, just as the lump-sum tax, does not effect quantity or price. Assume that a monopolist must pay t percent of its profit (regardless of the profit) as a tax. Since t is presumably between 0 and 100, the monopolist keeps $(100 - t)$ percent of its profits after paying the tax. Revenue and cost curves remain the same. Before the tax is imposed, the monopoly chooses price and quantity so as to maximize profit. After the tax, it still chooses the same price and quantity so as to maximize before-tax profit, since $(100 - t)$ percent of the maximum profit is clearly preferable to $(100 - t)$ percent of some smaller amount of profit.

Tax regulation differs from price-cap regulation in several ways, even though profits are reduced in all cases. In particular, taxation, in contrast to some price caps, cannot force the monopolist to set price equal to marginal cost.

Before we end this discussion, there is a caveat that should be attached to lump-sum and percentage-of-profit tax theory. Even though the tax, within limits, will not affect short-run profit-maximizing behavior, these taxes can have long-run effects. In energy production, for instance, exploration and other forms of investment are undertaken in the hope of a future stream of profits. Firms would carry out exploration as long as the marginal cost of exploration is less than the expected marginal return. Any tax that reduces the expected return consequently reduces exploration, and anything that reduces exploration reduces future resource extraction (in the case of natural gas, the output of gas would fall in the future.) The situation is similar in the case of other forms of investment carried out in the expectation of a stream of returns in the future. A tax that is expected to lower the stream of returns in the future lowers investment. Reduced investment causes a reduction in future output. Therefore, while the tax on profit would possibly not affect current output, such a tax would affect future output, possibly quite significantly.

15.7   Summary

Monopoly can exist only when there are barriers to entry. Certain barriers naturally arise from the technology of production. Economies of scale lead to such types of barriers. Sometimes barriers arise from government. Franchises and patents are, in essence, government grants to monopolize a market. Finally, other barriers are controlled to some extent by the firms seeking to protect their share of the market. The control of critical inputs and brand loyalties are barriers that can be erected and influenced by an incumbent producer.

We discussed some strategic barriers in detail. Of importance was the practice of entry limit pricing. A firm can block entry by keeping price low and output relatively high. Profits are lower in the short run than if the strict profit-maximizing rule were followed, but in the long run, a monopolist may earn a higher, steady stream of profits. A monopolist can also block entry by producing multiple products. In some cases this will give a producer lower costs. If substitute products are made, it may also reduce demand to a potential entrant. In this way, product proliferation allows a monopolist to capture the market share that may have gone to a new entrant.

Price discrimination occurs when different prices are set for the same product. The practice leads to higher profits for the seller and generally more output. Third-degree discrimination occurs when buyers are separated into markets with different demand elasticities. The monopolist then maximizes profits in these markets. First-degree discrimination involves treating each consumer as if he or she is a market. All consumers are charged the highest price they are willing to pay for each unit of a product. This makes marginal revenue equivalent to demand, even though demand is downward sloping. Profits are maximized where $MR = D = MC$, a result very similar to the perfectly competitive outcome. Finally, second-degree discrimination approximates first-degree discrimination by setting price tiers or quantity discounts for a product.

The stylized monopolist chooses the output at which $MC = MR$. In contrast to perfect competition, the market does not force the monopolist in the long run to produce the quantity where long-run average cost is at its minimum and to charge a price equal to minimum long-run average cost. There is some loss of consumer's and producer's surplus. This does not necessarily indicate that price must be higher and quantity lower under monopoly than under perfect competition. We can only say that price under monopoly will not, in the absence of regulation, equal marginal cost.

This completes the discussion of the two extremes in the range of market structures: perfect competition, with the least market power, and monopoly, with the most. We have compared the performance of perfect competition with that of monopoly, although as we have stressed, a similar comparison holds for perfect competition and all firms with market power. We will now examine the behavior of the other two market structures: monopolistic competition and oligopoly. As you will see, firms in these structures are spread over a broad range of market power. Some firms have a rather small amount of market power and some have a great deal. As you will also see, in the case of oligopoly, there is no single, straightforward theory to explain firm behavior, as was the case for perfect competition and monopoly.

Answers to *Applying the Theory*

15.1 If the monopolist cannot charge a price higher than $60, then the demand curve is horizontal at $60 out to point A on the demand curve. Until 80,000 units are therefore produced, $MR = \$60$. The *LRMC* curve intersects MR when 80,000 units are produced. Therefore point A is profit maximizing and 80,000 units would be the profit-maximizing output. The monopoly could block entry with larger outputs but profits would be lower.

Technical Problems

1. List three barriers to the entry of new firms into a monopoly market that are essentially out of the control of the existing firms, and explain how each barrier can prevent the entry of new firms.

2. List three barriers to the entry of new firms into a monopoly market that are essentially under the control of the existing firm, and explain how each barrier can prevent the entry of new firms. What conditions must exist for these barriers to be effective?

3. Explain why a market structure with the characteristics of perfect competition could not exist in a market that would be characterized by natural monopoly without being imposed externally. What would happen to price and output if a natural monopoly is broken up?

Figure E.15–1

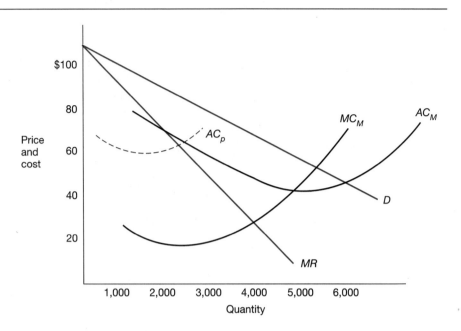

4. Figure E.15–1 shows the cost curves for a monopoly (AC_M and MC_M) and the monopoly's demand and marginal revenue curves. AC_p is the average cost curve for a potential entrant into the market.
   a. If the monopoly ignores the potential rival, what will be its price, output, and profit?
   b. What will happen to price, output, and profit if the potential entrant actually does enter the market at its minimum average cost?
   c. What will be the monopoly's price, output, and profit if it decides to keep price below the minimum average cost of the entrant?
5. This question deals with multiproduct economies and is based on the following information about products x, y, and z.

$$C(x) = C(y) \quad = C(z) \quad = \$10$$
$$C(x,y) = C(y,z) = C(x,z) = \$16$$

   The cost notation $C(\ )$ refers to a constant total cost for a specified amount of the product produced. What can the maximum $C(x,y,z)$ be in order for the technology to be subadditive across all three products?
6. Determine which of the following practices should be considered price discrimination. Which are not? Why are some of these pricing strategies not discriminating?
   a. Reserved seats are priced higher on airlines than standby seats.
   b. First-class accommodations on an airplane are more expensive than coach seats.
   c. Long-distance telephone service is more expensive from 8 A.M. to 5 P.M. than it is at other times.

Figure E.15–2

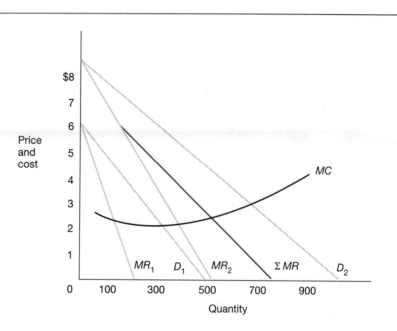

d. Children under 12 stay free at a hotel.

e. Young faculty members can purchase journals at a lower subscription rate than older members.

f. Consumers pay different interest rates at banks, depending on how much they earn.

g. Automobile loans at banks usually have a higher interest rate than home mortgages.

7. Assume that a monopolist can divide output into two submarkets, the demands and marginal revenues of which are shown in Figure E.15–2, along with marginal cost. ΣMR is the horizontal sum of the two marginal revenue curves.

   a. Find equilibrium output and price in each market.

   b. Which market has the more elastic demand?

   c. What would be price and output if the monopolist could not discriminate?

8. When will a discriminating monopolist with two separate markets do the following:

   a. Charge the same price in both markets?

   b. Sell the same level of output in both markets?

9. Figure E.15–3 shows long-run cost, demand, and MR for a monopoly.

   a. What are the firm's output, price, and profit?

   b. At what price cap would there be no excess supply or demand in this market? What would be the firm's output and profit with this price cap?

   c. What price cap could eliminate all economic profit but the firm could continue to earn a normal profit? What would be the problem with this price?

   d. Suppose a price cap is set at LRAC = demand. What would be the firm's output and profit at this price? What would be the problem with this price?

Figure E.15–3

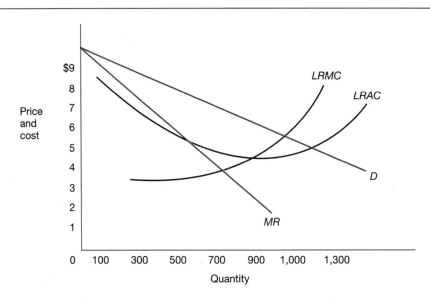

e. What would happen to price and output after an excise tax of $2 is imposed?

f. What would happen to price and output after a lump-sum tax of $1,000 is imposed?

g. What would happen to price and output after a lump-sum tax of $3,000 is
   imposed?

10. Figure E.15–4 shows demand, *MR*, and the long-run cost curves of a natural
    monopoly.

    a. Show on the graph the firm's profit-maximizing output and price.

    b. If a price cap is set so that demand = *LRAC*, show the firm's output if the
       government requires the firm to sell all that is demanded at this price. What
       is the problem, from a social point of view, with this price and output
       requirement?

    c. If the government sets a price cap so that demand = *LRMC*, what would be
       the problem with this price?

11. Suppose a theater can divide its customers into two markets, students and
    nonstudents. The elasticity of demand for students is 4, and the elasticity for
    nonstudents is 2. The theater's marginal cost per customer is constant at $6. If
    the theater practices third-degree price discrimination, what price will it charge
    to students? To nonstudents?

12. In Figure E.15–5 suppose *LRMC* is the long-run supply of a perfectly
    competitive industry.

    a. What will be the industry output and price?

    b. What will be consumer's, producer's, and total surplus in the market?

    c. Now suppose a single firm purchases all of the firms and operates as a
       monopoly. What will be price, output, consumer's, producer's, and total
       surplus? What will be the welfare loss.

13. Explain precisely what is meant by the welfare loss or deadweight loss from
    monopoly.

Figure E.15–4

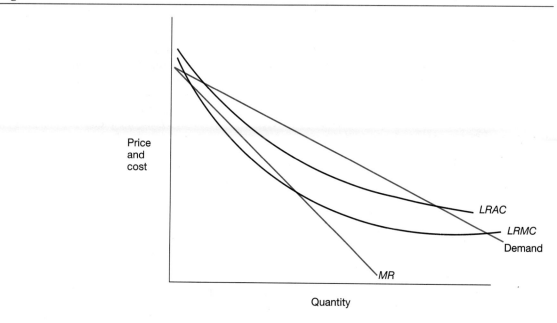

Figure E.15–5

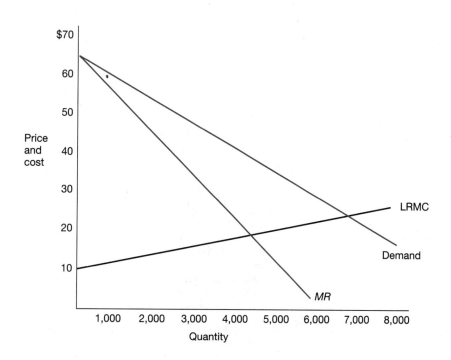

Analytical Problems

1. There is some overlap between some of the naturally imposed and some of the strategic barriers to entry that we discussed.
   a. Explain how for some of the naturally imposed barriers, it requires some type of strategic behavior on the part of the firm for these to be actual barriers.
   b. Explain how for some of the strategic entry barriers, it requires some externally imposed technological conditions for these to be actual barriers. For example, would a firm practice entry limit pricing if *LRAC* was constant?

2. What characteristics would be expected in the underlying production function for subadditivity to exist?

3. In a mailer announcing a national conference beginning on July 28 the following schedule of registration fees was included.

	By July 10	*After July 10*
1. Individual and corporate	$250	$300
2. College faculty, government, and nonprofit	100	150
3. Student	50	75

   As you see, there are six different fees. Which of the fee differences probably represent price discrimination and which possibly do not? Explain.

4. Some economists argue that a large number of firms is not necessary for competitive behavior in the market. All that is really needed is a viable threat of entry in a market where one or a few firms already produce. Evaluate this claim.

5. Why do faculty receive discounts from the university bookstore while students do not? (Don't just say price discrimination.) Why can price discrimination exist? Are all conditions necessary for price discrimination being met? Discuss.

6. In 1945, Alcoa was found guilty of attempting to monopolize the aluminum market. Up to that time, the company maintained low markups and had a modest profit rate. Ironically, if Alcoa had set high markups and realized a high profit rate before World War II, it probably would not have been found guilty. Can you explain why? This question was asked in Chapter 14. Has your answer changed after reading Chapter 15?

7. For many years, AT&T claimed that it could not provide overseas telephone service at reasonable rates unless it also provided domestic long-distance service. Justify this claim using the discussion of multiproduct monopoly.

8. In a letter to the editor, *The Wall Street Journal,* December 30, 1986, a corporate executive wrote:

   > [My professor in graduate school] explained that it was not primarily greed by which OPEC failed, . . . but because of OPEC's belief that it could maintain artificially high prices though collusion. . . . [He] then noted that only two monopolies, or cartel arrangements, have worked in modern industrial history. They were Nobel's dynamite dynasty, and AT&T until its recent dismemberment. The management . . . understood that a monopoly works, and can only work, by lowering prices each year, and not by raising them as OPEC was doing. . . . The prices and pricing strategies of Nobel and AT&T deterred effective competition for nearly 100 years.

   Explain the professor's analysis. Does it mean that Nobel and AT&T didn't try to maximize profit?

9. Frequent flyer coupons are given by airlines to customers based upon the number of miles these customers fly with that particular airline. These coupons can be redeemed for upgrades on flights and free tickets. The number of free flights is based upon the number of miles flown. Many fliers sold their coupons to other people. In 1987–1988 the airlines began to restrict frequent fliers from selling their coupons or tickets to others, sometimes even voiding the tickets of people other than those who were issued the coupons.

   a. Do frequent flier programs represent price discrimination? Why or why not?

   b. Why do you think airlines stopped letting others fly on tickets issued through the frequent flier program? Surely the airline did not care what the name of the customer sitting in a particular seat was.

10. Explain the difficulties involved if a government body sets the price for a public utility that is a natural monopoly.

11. Explain why economists historically have been opposed to monopoly.

12. The U.S. federal courts historically have said that monopoly per se is illegal and should be broken up. What do you see wrong with so-called "good" monopolies such as those mentioned in questions 6 and 8? Alternatively, why would the U.S. government regulate industries that approach, by most definitions, being competitive (e.g., insurance)?

13. In a market characterized by rapid changes in technology (e.g., calculators and computers), would there be less or more incentive to practice an entry limit pricing strategy? Explain your answer.

14. Suppose, because of economies of scale, a community wants one firm to be a monopoly in providing a particular service. The community lets different firms bid on how much they want to be paid for providing the service for a specified period of time. The lowest bidder then receives the contract. Will the monopoly earn profits over the contract period? Is this a good way of eliminating monopoly profits for certain public services?

CHAPTER 16

Imperfect Competition

16.1   Introduction

The two stylized market structures we have discussed so far, perfect competition and monopoly, are extremely useful economic tools, even though neither exactly depicts real-world producers. While not designed to describe actual markets, they are able to help us analyze many economic problems. Nonetheless, there are certain features of real-world markets not addressed by either model. Both models ignore the real-world situation of a large number of firms selling slightly different products. This type of market structure is known as *monopolistic competition*. It is somewhat monopolistic because product differentiation provides a firm with some market power; it is somewhat like perfect competition because there are many firms in the market and entry is easy. Many real-world markets are of the monopolistically competitive type. Most consumer services, prepared-food products, apparel, and household appliances are produced by monopolistically competitive firms.

The assumptions of monopoly and perfect competition also fail to deal with a market structure in which a few firms sell either identical or differentiated products. This market structure is referred to as *oligopoly*. Oligopolistic firms characteristically have large amounts of market power, but profit maximization is complicated by the fact that the actions of any one firm affect the profits and, therefore, the actions of the other sellers in the market, and this effect must be taken into account when a firm chooses its price and output. Many capital goods (i.e., machinery) and refined products are produced and sold by oligopolistic firms. Automobiles, aircraft, sugar, and aluminum also are oligopolistic industries.

We must stress that the distinction between monopolistic competition and oligopoly can become cloudy. The most obvious distinction between the two forms of market structure is that oligopolistic markets have a few firms, whereas monopolistically competitive markets have many. How do we decide that a market has "many" or "few" firms? In terms of the number of firms in a market, we really do not know when market structures become less like monopolistic competition and more like oligopoly. Whether a market is monopolistically competitive or oligopolistic depends less on the actual number of firms in a market and more on whether each firm recognizes that its actions will have a discernible impact upon its rivals. Put another way, the difference between monopolistic competition and oligopoly is determined by the degree to which sellers are interdependent. Even so, judging a market as oligopolistic or monopolistically competitive is subjective. But the recognition that profit depends on the actions of a producer's rivals is a critical boundary when moving from the theory of monopolistic competition to oligopoly.

This chapter first presents the theory of monopolistic competition and compares the results of the theory with the perfectly competitive model. Since both monopolistically competitive firms and oligopolistic firms frequently compete among themselves over who has the better product, we next discuss this type of competitive behavior. It is called nonprice competition and is the reason product characteristics are frequently altered. Oligopoly models are then presented, with emphasis on why there is no general theory of oligopoly. The chapter ends with a discussion of collusion or cooperative behavior.

16.2   Fundamentals of Monopolistic Competition

One of the notable achievements of economists who examined the middle ground between competition and monopoly was done simultaneously by an American economist, Edward Chamberlain, and a British economist, Joan Robinson.[1] They both contributed heavily to the modern development of economic theories of imperfect competition. At the time they published, neither economist knew of the other's work, but they both based their theories on a solid empirical fact: there are very few monopolies because very few commodities have no good substitutes; similarly, there are few commodities that have identical substitutes. In short, there exists a wide range of commodities that have close and not so close substitutes, and no perfect substitutes.

Chamberlain, who developed the theory of monopolistic competition, noted that because products are heterogeneous rather than homogeneous, perfect competition cannot exist. On the other hand, although heterogeneous, the products are only slightly differentiated. Each is a rather close substitute for others. Competition does exist, but it is not perfect, it is imperfect. Unlike perfect competition, monopolistic competition involves numerous sellers with buyers in the market who can distinguish among the goods sold.

It is important to note that the only difference between perfect competition and monopolistic competition is product differentiation. In the model of monopolistic competition, there remain large numbers of buyers and sellers, easy entry and exit into the market among sellers, and perfect information with respect to prices. You

---

[1]E. H. Chamberlin, *The Theory of Monopolistic Competition* (Cambridge, Mass.: Harvard University Press, 1933), and J. Robinson, *The Economics of Imperfect Competition* (London: Macmillan, 1934).

will see that this one change in the assumptions underlying perfect competition has profound effects on the behavior of sellers in the market.

As we discuss the theories of imperfect competition, keep in mind the definition of the market. A market is made up of sellers of goods that are easily substituted for one another by consumers. A market is frequently defined by the set of goods that share high and positive cross-price elasticities. In the case of monopolistic competition, a large number of firms sell easily substituted products.

16.2.1   Demand under Monopolistic Competition

We can best describe the market of a monopolistic competitor by describing what happens to a monopoly market as entry occurs. We will work in a very simple setting and focus on how the elasticity of demand changes as entry takes place.

Picture the demand facing a monopolist as D_m, the linear demand curve shown in Figure 16–1. The curve can be described by the equation for a straight line:

$$P = a - bQ.$$

The vertical intercept of D_m is at point a, as shown in Figure 16–1. The slope, $\Delta P/\Delta Q$, is $-b$.[2] If we call the elasticity of demand in the market E_D,

$$E_D = -\frac{\Delta Q}{\Delta P} \cdot \frac{P}{Q} = \frac{1}{b} \cdot \frac{P}{Q},$$

where we have substituted $-1/b = \dfrac{\Delta Q}{\Delta P}$ from the value of the slope $\dfrac{\Delta P}{\Delta Q}$ in the above equation. Since $\dfrac{\Delta P}{\Delta Q} = -b$, we have inverted the ratio for the substitution in E_D. The market elasticity, E_D, is the same as the elasticity for the monopolist.

Now, let a second firm enter the market and notice what happens to the elasticity of demand. Both firms produce an amount q_i, where $Q = q_1 + q_2$. For the moment, let us assume that the products are alike, so both firms charge the same price. The sum of the amounts each firm produces is total market output; so price in the market becomes

$$P = a - b(Q) = a - b(q_1 + q_2).$$

If either firm increases output by one unit, $\Delta P/\Delta Q = -b$, as before.[3] We have assumed that the two products are such close substitutes that the same price is charged for both. Each firm in the market has elasticity E_i:

---

[2]The slope $\dfrac{\Delta P}{\Delta Q}$ represents the change in P when Q changes by one unit. Hence, $\dfrac{\Delta P}{\Delta Q} = [a - b$ $(Q + 1) - (a - bQ] = a - bQ - b - a + bQ = -b$. Thus, $\dfrac{\Delta P}{\Delta Q} = -b$ and $\dfrac{\Delta Q}{\Delta P} = -\dfrac{1}{b}$ by inverting.

[3]Suppose, for example, the second firm expands by one unit. Then $\dfrac{\Delta P}{\Delta q_2} = a - b[q_1 + (q_2 + 1)]$ $- [a - b(q_1 + q_2)] = a - bq_1 - bq_2 - b - a + bq_1 + bq_2 = -b.$

Figure 16–1   Demand Shift after Entry

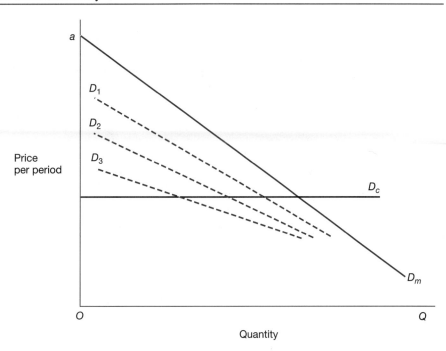

$$E_i = -\frac{\Delta q_i}{\Delta P} \cdot \frac{P}{q_i} = \frac{1}{b}\left(\frac{P}{q_i}\right).$$

The quantity produced by the firm, q_i, is in the denominator rather than Q.

To see better how E_i is related to E_D, we introduce the ratio q_i/Q as the market share of the ith firm. It is the proportion of the total market supplied by a single firm. For convenience, we set $s_i = q_i/Q$. For a monopolist, $s_i = 1$, but as firms enter the market, s_i becomes less than one. Under perfect competition, when there are many firms producing identical products, s_i becomes very close to zero. Thus, for imperfect competition, s_i ranges between one and zero.

Using the ratio s_i, we may rewrite the elasticity of demand for the firm (E_i) in terms of the elasticity of demand at the market level (E_D). With some substitution,

$$E_i = \frac{1}{b}\left(\frac{P}{q_i}\right) = \frac{1}{b}\left(\frac{P}{q_i}\right)\frac{Q}{Q} = \frac{1}{b}\left(\frac{P}{Q}\right)\frac{Q}{q_i} = E_D\left(\frac{1}{s_i}\right).$$

We can verify this equality by supposing that only one seller operates in the market. Then $s_i = 1$, and $E_i = E_D$. The elasticity of demand for a monopolist is the market's elasticity. Suppose there is perfect competition and s_i gets very close to zero. Then $1/s_i$ becomes very large, making E_i approach infinity. This verifies that under perfect competition the firm's demand curve is horizontal, and the elasticity of demand is infinite. Such a demand curve is labeled D_c in Figure 16–1.

This relation between a firm's elasticity of demand and the market elasticity indicates what demand looks like as a market becomes more competitive. At the extremes, there are D_m and D_c in Figure 16–1. If entry into the market occurs, each firm supplies a smaller share of the market; that is, s_i becomes smaller. The firm's demand curve must therefore shift to the left, and, as this shift takes place, the elasticity of demand increases. As entry takes place, each firm's demand curve both decreases and becomes more elastic than D_m. For illustration, entry shifts demand in the way shown by the dotted schedules in Figure 16–1. Demand moves from D_m to D_1, to D_2, and so on, and the more entry, the closer the demands get to the perfectly competitive demand, D_c.

However, product differentiation in monopolistic competition will prevent the firm's demand curve from becoming perfectly elastic. Perceived differences between goods make them less than perfect substitutes. For instance, toothpastes have different flavors and colors, and perhaps clean your teeth differently. Because consumers can identify these product characteristics for each producer, toothpastes will never become perfect substitutes. This means that the demand curve for a monopolistic competitor never becomes horizontal; some market power, perhaps only a small amount, is possessed by sellers. Because of product differences, firms capture different shares of the market. That is, s_i is different for each firm. From the formula, $E_i = E_D/s_i$, this means firms face different elasticities of demand. Partly because of this, and partly because costs are different, there are different prices in monopolistically competitive markets.

16.2.2   Short-Run Equilibrium

The theory of monopolistic competition is essentially a long-run theory. In the short run, there is virtually no difference between the model of monopoly and that of monopolistic competition. Each producer is a profit maximizer. With a given demand curve and a corresponding marginal revenue curve, the firm optimizes by equating marginal cost with marginal revenue.

When a longer view is taken, there is one essential difference between monopoly and monopolistic competition. In particular, a monopoly cannot be maintained if there is free entry. If economic profit is present in the short run for a monopolistic competitor, other firms will enter and produce a similar product, and they will continue to enter until all economic profits are eliminated.

16.2.3   Long-Run Equilibrium

Because entry takes place until profits are normal, we can proceed immediately to the analysis of long-run equilibrium in a monopolistically competitive market. A zero-profit equilibrium is reached when price equals *LRAC* and the firm cannot increase profits by raising or lowering price. This occurs when demand is tangent to *LRAC*. The tangency of demand and *LRAC* is an important feature of the model of monopolistic competition. You can see from Figure 16–2 that if demand inter-

Figure 16–2   Long-Run Equilibrium in Monopolistically Competitive Markets

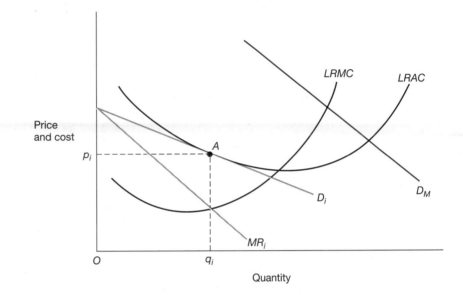

sected *LRAC,* prices would exist that could be above average cost, allowing firms to make above-normal profits. For instance, if the firm had demand curve D_M, profits would be maximized at a price well above *LRAC.* In a monopolistically competitive market, entry would occur, shifting demand to the left and making it more elastic, until the firm had a demand curve similar to D_i, just tangent to *LRAC.* Long-run equilibrium must exist at a point like *A* in Figure 16–2.

Equilibrium is depicted in Figure 16–2 with a *LRAC* curve that has some economies of scale at first, but diseconomies over larger ranges of output. Demand for a monopolistic competitor is not perfectly elastic, which means that the demand curve is never horizontal. Therefore, equilibrium cannot occur at the lowest point on *LRAC* but must occur on the downward-sloping portion of *LRAC*, before economies of scale are exhausted.

Point *A* must also be described by the intersection of *LRMC* and MR_i, where subscript *i* is used to represent a typical firm in monopolistic competition. The profit-maximizing rule must lead a monopolistic competitor to the highest possible profit, given the demand curve. If the firm produced an amount different from q_i, price would be below average cost, and profits would be below normal. Thus, q_i must be the profit-maximizing output.

Principle

> Long-run equilibrium in a monopolistically competitive market is attained when the demand curve for each producer is tangent to its long-run average cost curve on the downward-sloping portion of that curve.

16.2.4 Long-Run Equilibrium in Comparison with Perfect Competition

In long-run perfectly competitive equilibrium, total output is produced by a large number of small firms, each operating at the minimum point on long-run average cost. The product is sold at a price equal to minimum average cost, and it should be remembered that long-run marginal cost equals both price and average cost at this point. If demand should either increase or decrease, in the long run producers enter or exit, leaving each firm producing at the minimum point on its *LRAC* curve. It is impossible for any firm to lower average cost by either increasing or decreasing output. Therefore, costs are minimized for any level of industry output.

A monopolistically competitive firm is like a monopolist in that it faces a downward-sloping demand curve. At the same time, it is like a perfectly competitive firm; it faces market competition that competes away economic profit in the long run. The differences between the model of perfect competition and monopolistic competition result solely from product differentiation. Putting the desirability of product differentiation aside for the moment, we can show that monopolistic competition compares unfavorably with perfect competition on two accounts.

First, since demand is less than perfectly elastic, marginal revenue is less than average revenue. Profit is maximized where $MR = MC$ in the long or the short run, and price is not equal to marginal cost. From your study of monopoly, you know this causes a loss of total surplus (consumer's plus producer's surplus). Figure 16–3 shows this loss as the shaded region between demand and marginal cost. Given the demand for the firm's product, the willingness to pay for the product is greater than the marginal cost of production for $q_e - q_m$ units. Since potential buyers value the product at more than the marginal cost of production, this reduction in output represents a loss to society. A monopolistically competitive firm would never produce q_e in the long run. At q_e, LRAC is greater than p_e, and the firm would need a subsidy to break even and continue production.

The second criticism of monopolistic competition is that the long-run average cost of production is higher than it would be under perfect competition. In equilibrium, a monopolistically competitive firm produces at point A on *LRAC* in Figure 16–3. A perfect competitor would produce at B where *LRMC* = *LRAC* and *LRAC* is minimized. A monopolistic competitor does not exhaust economies of scale in production as a perfect competitor does.

Frequently, monopolistic competitors are accused of having excess capacity, but this is not the real issue. The firm chooses the most efficient plant size, as described by the *SRAC* curve in Figure 16–3. The average cost of producing quantity q_m cannot be lower whether the market structure is perfect competition or monopoly. The problem with monopolistic competition is that because of the downward-sloping demand curve, output is restricted and, as a consequence, economies of scale are not completely exhausted in the long run.

These two criticisms of monopolistic competition—relatively high long-run costs and a loss of total surplus—ignore product differentiation. Differences in product characteristics enable consumers to benefit from product variety. A choice among styles, colors, flavors, and qualities is a desirable feature of market structures. The

Figure 16–3   Monopolistic Competition versus Perfect Competition

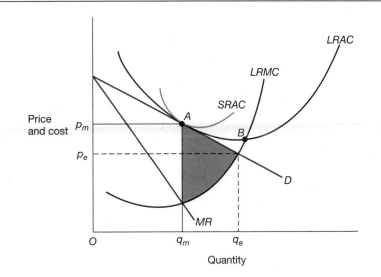

loss of surplus and the difference in the average cost of production is the price society pays for product variety. If consumers did not wish to pay this price, buyers would choose and producers would sell only one product type. Since product differentiation is so common, buyers in markets must be willing to pay the price for product variety. Some would argue that the social cost of monopolistic competition is less than or equal to the social benefit.

16.3   Nonprice Competition

Imperfect competition—both monopolistic competition and oligopoly—is frequently characterized by competitive behavior not involving price changes. Examples of nonprice competition exist whenever one firm compares its product to another. Such comparisons are usually made through advertising. A perfectly competitive firm would have no reason to resort to nonprice competition because it can sell all it wants at the going market price. Firms selling in markets with differentiated products frequently have the incentive to use methods other than price changes to increase profits. As you have seen, under monopolistic competition, free entry drives profits to zero in the long run. Nonetheless, a firm can sometimes delay or reverse this process by further differentiating its product from those of other firms— possibly by advertising or some other marketing strategy designed to increase the demand for the product. If the strategy is successful, the firm will enjoy above-normal profits, at least temporarily.

As you will see in the next section, in oligopolistic markets there is often a great deal of rivalry among firms. Because of strong interdependence among the firms, oligopolists hesitate to change prices frequently. Price changes can lead to unprofitable price wars. Oligopolies may therefore resort to less-threatening nonprice rivalry to raise their profits, but even this is not a completely safe strategy. Firms are sometimes forced by the actions of their competitors to make nonprice changes (such as expensive changes in styling designs) that they would not have undertaken if their rivals had not initiated the change. In the long run, profits may be normal because of such nonprice strategies.

Product differentiation opens an entirely new dimension of competition, unavailable, by assumption, to perfect competitors. If successful, such competition increases the demand for the product and, at any given price, causes the elasticity of demand to decline, allowing firms to charge higher prices for their products. This section discusses how product differentiation is a competitive decision variable. Firms can distinguish their products by the characteristics or qualities they attach to the goods they sell. Advertising plays a big role in a firm's effort to differentiate its product. It can either accentuate actual differences between products or create differences through the image that advertising lends to products.

16.3.1   Product Quality

Products can be thought of as a collection of attributes or features. An automobile can be described by its engine size, brakes, transmission, suspension, fuel efficiency, tires, head and trunk room, number of doors, color, and so on. These are all product features. They differ among automobiles and can be altered by the manufacturers to differentiate their products. Algebraically, product characteristics are variables (a_i), that are bundled in certain ways to make a particular product, Q. That is,

$$Q = g(a_1, a_2, a_3, \ldots, a_n) \tag{16-1}$$

where n is the number of possible attributes a product may have. How a producer selects these attributes determines the quality and nature of the product and the product's substitutability with other products in the market. The decision of a manufacturer to give an automobile all the product attributes that characterize a Cadillac Sedan De Ville will make the car an unlikely substitute for a Ford Mustang. In general, product differentiation determines the substitutability of products.

16.3.2   Product Differentiation

The idea that product attributes are a nonprice competitive tool is captured by letting all of the possible preferences consumers may have for a particular attribute be measured along a scale with endpoints arbitrarily labeled 0 and 1, as shown in Figure 16–4. Suppose this product attribute is sugar on breakfast cereal; then 0 is cereal with no sugar and 1 is cereal of virtually pure sugar cubes. The values 1/4, 1/2, and 3/4 mark equal distance points along this scale. Suppose that those who buy breakfast cereal are evenly distributed along this scale so that the number of individuals who want no sugar on their cereal is equal to the number who want their cereal half-sugared is equal to the number who want all sugar.

In the case of the first firm to produce cereal, it does not matter how much sugar is put on its product. It is the only cereal consumers can buy. Thus, we arbitrarily locate firm A on the scale as A_1. Since sugar is expensive, we place A_1 on the lower

Figure 16–4   Product Quality Measure

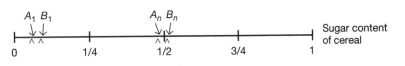

end of the scale. We use a subscript at this location because the firm may later want to change the sugar content of its cereal when other firms enter the market.

Rivalry begins when firm B decides to enter the market. The new seller knows the preferences of consumers, that is, the scale in Figure 16–4, and how much sugar firm A has on its product. The question is, how much sugar should B use to capture the largest possible share of the market? Market share is very important to profit maximization. Recall from Section 16.2 that the larger a firm's market share, the less elastic is demand and, consequently, the higher is price. Also, if there are economies of scale, increased sales allow a producer to move down the $LRAC$ curve and realize a lower average cost of production. Of course, at the margin, higher prices and lower product costs must be balanced against the marginal cost of increasing market share, which may, for example, involve advertising, or, in this case, using more sugar.

In Figure 16–4, you can see that at constant prices, B could capture most of the market by using a little more sugar than A. The best thing for B to do is enter with a product that is just to the right of A_1. We label this point B_1. Firm B captures all of the market to the right of A_1.

Firm A will, of course, not tolerate this for long. Its market share has been reduced to a very small part of the total market. Only those buyers with preferences between 0 and A_1 remain loyal to firm A's cereal. The firm could lower price or think about countering B's product by putting more sugar on its cereal. It can regain most of its lost market by moving just to the right of B_1. But then B will move to the right of A again, and A will then move to the right of B a second time. The leapfrogging will continue until one firm drops out of the market, or both firms end up with equal market shares at the midpoint of the preference scale. After a large number of moves, both firms will end up putting approximately the same amount of sugar on their cereal and supplying the amounts desired by the average buyer (i.e., at A_n and B_n).

The situation gets more complicated when a third firm enters the market. With a little experimenting, you will discover that firms will not find an equilibrium; they continually change the amount of sugar on their cereals. In Figure 16–4 add a firm C. It will locate to the right or left of the firm that has the largest market share. This leaves the firm in the middle with virtually no market. This firm will then relocate to increase market share and the leapfrogging never stops. This is not so unusual in the real world, considering how many "new" and "improved" labels producers put on their products. Often these improvements are nothing more than a slight adjustment in a product attribute, a change marketers hope will place them near their rival, but on the side of the preference scale that gives them the largest market share.

We have oversimplified things a great deal by considering product differentiation for only one product variable. Equation 16–1 shows that there are numerous product attributes for any one commodity. Realistically, there are all sorts of ways attributes can be mixed. Discovering the attributes that capture the largest share of the market requires sophisticated marketing techniques and, at times, just plain luck. The point of this simple model, though, is that product differentiation is a competitive tool that firms use to maximize profits. Differentiation can be as much a part of competition as price.

One further conclusion that can be drawn from the discussion surrounding Figure 16–4 is that nonprice competition can lead to the bunching of product attributes. In the case of the two firms in this figure, equilibrium occurred at the midpoint of the preference spectrum. Tastes could be better served with more product variety; say A moves closer to 0 and B closer to 1. Algebraically, it can be shown that, if consumers are evenly distributed along the scale, one firm should locate one quarter and the other three quarters of the distance between 0 and 1 to best serve consumer tastes in the market.[4] But there is no incentive for firms to behave in this way. The incentive to produce product attributes close to those of a rival can be easily seen in the physical location of businesses, television programming, automobile styling, and fashion apparel. Nonprice competition can frequently lead to what economists call *excessive sameness* in the market. Occasionally, a lack of product differentiation is unavoidable. In some markets, there is little than can be done to change the product. There is, for instance, little or no product differentiation in the facial tissue or aspirin markets, yet these markets fit the monopolistic competition model well. Advertising is a device used to highlight slight differences and, in some cases, even create them in the consumer's mind.

16.3.3 Advertising

Advertising has the capability of impressing a product's image on consumers, and consumers may choose to buy or not buy a product because of its advertised image. For example, people buy Rolex watches partly because of the image that successful, rich people wear these watches. If consumers are less interested in such a status symbol, they have the option of purchasing another brand. The Rolex status is a product attribute of the watch. The image is literally a feature of the product, just as style, color, and durability are.

Creating a product attribute through advertising can be an expensive proposition. For example, General Motors recently signed a $500 million contract to advertise on NBC over the next three years. The agreement allows GM to advertise on NBC's most popular shows. These programs generally have young audiences. John Hancock spent $1.6 million in 1990 to be the official sponsor of a college football bowl game. The exposure to the right audience is thought to be well worth the price. The sneaker company, L.A. Gear, currently has a $10 million contract with Michael Jackson to promote their shoes. To give a product a youthful image, to be connected

---

[4]There are some special assumptions about the preference map. See H. Hotelling, "Stability in Competition," *Economic Journal* 39 (March 1929), pp. 41–57; F. M. Scherer, "The Welfare Economics of Product Variety: An Application to the Ready-to-Eat Cereal Industry," *Journal of Industrial Economics* 28, no. 1 (December 1979), pp. 113–34.

Figure 16–5   Prisoner's Dilemma

		Suspect 1	
		Innocent	*Guilty*
		A	**B**
	Innocent	1: 0 years 2: 0 years	1: 2 years 2: 10 years
Suspect 2			
		C	**D**
	Guilty	1: 10 years 2: 2 years	1: 2 years 2: 2 years

with football, or another sport, or to have the product connected with a well-known rock star is fostering an image for the product that becomes an attribute of the product itself.

It is interesting that from a seller's viewpoint, rivalry can lead to excessive amounts of advertising. Specifically, if sellers could agree to restrict the amount of advertising they undertake—much of it done in response to a rival's ads in the first place—profits for sellers would rise. Advertising may be excessive because it is often a defensive tactic to maintain a seller's market share against the advertising of rivals. In many cases, it is a necessary cost of entry into a market, a cost that would be lower or even nonexistent if firms already selling in the market were not making heavy advertising expenditures.

How rivalry leads to unprofitable amounts of advertising can be illustrated by a model known as the prisoner's dilemma. The model is best described by the story that gives it its name. Suppose a crime is committed and two suspects are apprehended and questioned by the police. Unknown to the suspects, the police do not have enough evidence to convict the suspects without one of them confessing. So the police separate them and make each an offer known to the other. The offer is, if one suspect confesses to the crime and testifies against the other, the one who confesses receives only a two-year sentence, while the other who does not confess and upon conviction gets 10 years. If both confess, each receives a two-year sentence. Of course, if neither confesses, the probability is very high both will go free. Each could receive 2 years, 10 years, or go free (0 years), depending on what the other does.

Figure 16–5 shows the four possibilities of the dilemma. The upper-left and lower-right cells show the results if both plead innocent or guilty, respectively. The upper-right and lower-left cells show the consequences if one pleads guilty and the other innocent.

The problem is that the suspects cannot collude and decide to plead innocent. They must make their decisions based on their conjecture of what the other prisoner will do. If a suspect pleads innocent, he or she stands a chance of 10 years in prison if the other confesses. However, the worst that could happen if a prisoner confesses to the crime is two years imprisonment regardless of what the other does.

How prisoners actually plead depends on a number of factors; for example, whether or not the crime was committed by the accused, how well the prisoners

Figure 16–6   Advertiser's Dilemma

		Firm 1	
		Low	*High*
	Low	**A** π_1: 100 π_2: 100	**B** π_1: 150 π_2: 60
Firm 2			
	High	**C** π_1: 60 π_2: 150	**D** π_1: 80 π_2: 80

know each other, and the willingness of each to take risks, are just a few of the considerations affecting a prisoner's choice. Under many circumstances, however, the safest plea would be guilty, because the expected stay in jail would be minimized. Suppose the odds of the other prisoner pleading guilty are even; then over numerous such dilemmas the expected stay in jail if the prisoner did not confess would be five years $(0 \cdot 1/2 + 10 \cdot 1/2)$. On the other hand, by pleading guilty, the prisoner knows with certainty that the term would be only two years. From this calculation, you can see that there are incentives for both prisoners to plead guilty, and cell D becomes the equilibrium.

Imperfect competitors are caught in a similar dilemma when it comes to nonprice competition. Suppose the choice is to advertise a little or a lot. The relative advertising outlays determine profits. Low advertising by rivals keeps profits relatively high, but any single firm can increase profit at the expense of other firms if it advertises more while the others do not. It is thought by economists that in many imperfectly competitive markets, the total amount of advertising by all firms has little effect on total sales in the market.[5] That is, total market demand is relatively inelastic with respect to advertising. But, if any firm does little or no advertising while the other firms advertise heavily, that firm loses a substantial share of the market, and suffers reduced profit or even a loss.

To illustrate the situation, assume there are two rival firms that can choose high or low advertising levels. As with the prisoner's dilemma, there are four combinations of choices for the rival firms. In cells A through D in Figure 16–6, the profitability (π) of each combination is shown for the firms. If neither firm undertakes large amounts of advertising, profits are, say, $100 for each firm. They have equal costs and market shares. But you can see that there is a big temptation to increase advertising relative to that of the rival. Profits jump to $150, largely because the high advertising attracts business away from the low advertiser, whose profits fall to $60. To a small extent, profits also rise because the total market expands as a result of more total advertising. Cells B and C are not an equilibrium. The low advertiser can at least raise profits to $80 by following with a high advertising budget. In the long run, both firms end up with relatively higher advertising ex-

[5]See F. M. Scherer and D. Ross, *Industrial Market Structure and Economic Performance,* 3rd ed. (Boston: Houghton Mifflin, 1990), Chapter 16 for references.

penditures and lower profits. From each seller's perspective, there is too much advertising because they could both return to the low budget ad levels and receive $100 in profits.

If firms recognize the long-run effects of high advertising budgets, they might tacitly agree not to increase expenditures. Such an agreement is much more likely to occur when firms recognize their interdependence than when there are many firms with small market shares. An oligopolistic market structure is more apt to prevent advertising excessiveness, as measured by profits, than is monopolistic competition. However, once a rival decides to increase advertising, it is very difficult, regardless of the market structure, to avoid cell D in Figure 16–6. And it is very unlikely that, without an explicit agreement, firms will return to cell A.

Economics in the News

Athletic Shoemakers Caught in a Prisoner's Dilemma

Three athletic shoe companies rely heavily on celebrity endorsements in their advertising campaigns: L.A. Gear, Nike, and Reebok. The endorsements are expensive, typically costing a company $5–$10 million. Contracts guarantee stars a multimillion dollar fee plus a percentage of sales revenue (see *The Wall Street Journal,* May 23, 1990, p. B1).

The endorsement war was started by Nike when they contracted with Michael Jordan to do "Air Jordan" ads. This campaign was extremely successful and made Nike the biggest seller of athletic shoes with 26 percent of the market in 1990. The results prompted L.A. Gear and Reebok to react.

L.A. Gear announced in 1990 that they had signed Paula Abdul, who formerly endorsed Reebok shoes, to do video ads. L.A. Gear also has an endorsement contract with Michael Jackson. His contract is valued at more than $10 million. Reebok is countering with Madonna as an ad woman, and is in the process of preparing video ads with her. In response to the moves of these two companies, Nike has prepared numerous commercials with at least 12 professional athletes, notably Bo Jackson. L.A. Gear's market share is expanding; in 1990 it stood at about 15 percent. Reebok has 24 percent of the market.

A recognized problem with all of these endorsements is that buyers become confused over who endorses what brand. Ad agencies admit that consumers do not remember which celebrities endorse which shoes. New Balance, another athletic shoe brand, does not use celebrities because of what they call endorsement clutter. New Balance jokes about the other three companies relying heavily on celebrity ads. Their latest media campaign is "endorsed by no one," but "maybe that's why 38 NBA players are now wearing them. It certainly isn't because we're paying them a ton of money to appear in our ads." Even in this ad, New Balance makes the claim that many athletes are using their shoes.

Celebrity endorsements can be illustrated as a prisoner's dilemma. Referring to Figure 16–6, shoe companies begin in cell A with few or no endorsements. Nike moves out of the cell, either to B or C, with the Air Jordan campaign endorsements. Two other companies follow; and all move to cell D. It is not clear that the profitability of the ads is strong, particularly in light of buyer confusion over which stars endorse which shoes. It may be that profitability was higher before the endorsement campaigns began. Shoe executives are troubled. They realize that these ads are causing them to rely on the advertised image to differentiate their shoes. They believe there are important differences between shoe brands. These differences are becoming obscured by the celebrities. In the long run, it is these differences that guarantee a stable market share.

16.1   *Applying the Theory*

Hardy's is introducing a lean hamburger in response to McDonald's McLean Deluxe hamburger. Trace through a prisoner's dilemma scenario that begins with neither franchise having a "healthier" hamburger.

16.4   Interdependence in Oligopoly Behavior

Oligopoly is said to exist when more than one seller is in the market, but when the number is not so large as to render negligible the contribution of each. A market will have few enough sellers to be considered oligopolistic if the sellers recognize their mutual interdependence. In monopolistic competition and perfect competition, firms make decisions and take actions without considering how these actions will affect other firms and how, in turn, other firms' reactions will affect them. Oligopolists must take these reactions into account when contemplating a price change, a product change, or a new advertising campaign. Ford Motor Company must anticipate, for example, how GM and Chrysler Corporation will react when it introduces a new model because without doubt, Ford's actions will affect the demand for Chevrolets and Chryslers.

This, in short, is the oligopoly problem and the central problem in oligopoly analysis. The oligopolistic firm is large enough relative to the total market to recognize (*a*) the mutual interdependence of each firm's demand in the market and (*b*) the fact that its decisions will affect the sales of other firms, which, in turn, will cause them to react in a way that requires a new round of adjustments. The great uncertainty is how one's rivals will react.

Since so many industries meet the general description of oligopoly, it would, at first glance, seem that a general theory of oligopoly should exist. The problem in developing an oligopoly theory, however, is the same as the oligopoly problem itself. Mutual interdependence and the resulting uncertainty about reaction patterns make it necessary for economists to postulate specific assumptions about behavioral patterns; that is, specific assumptions about how oligopolists believe their rivals will react must be made before market outcomes can be predicted.

Therefore, an oligopoly equilibrium depends critically on the assumptions the economist makes in regard to the behavioral reaction of rival entrepreneurs. Since many different assumptions can and have been made, many different equilibrium solutions can and have been reached for oligopoly. There is no single "theory of oligopoly" in the sense that there is a theory of perfect competition or of monopoly.

A second complication encountered when modeling oligopoly is that oligopolists can produce homogeneous or differentiated products. As noted in the discussion of monopolistic competition, product differentiation is a major determinant of demand elasticity. As a consequence, just as a single model cannot simultaneously describe perfect and monopolistic competition, one model cannot describe oligopolies producing identical or differentiated products.

16.4.1   Types of Oligopoly Behavior

Broadly speaking, economists usually posit two contrasting patterns of behavior for oligopolists: they are assumed to be either cooperative or noncooperative. Co-operative oligopolies tend to accommodate changes made by rival firms. For instance, if a rival should raise price, a cooperative oligopolist would go along with the move and raise price too. Noncooperative behavior, on the other hand, does not accommodate such changes. If another firm raised price, rivals would keep prices low in order to attract sales away from the higher-priced producer.

Because of the possibility of differentiated or identical products, there are four general oligopolistic market structures. Two structures consist of a few noncooperating firms producing either (1) homogeneous or (2) differentiated products. Alternatively, there may be a few cooperating firms producing either (3) homogeneous or (4) differentiated products. If oligopolists produce the same products and do not cooperate, the market resembles perfect competition. Each producer's demand elasticity will be high because there are very close substitutes available. If each firm's output exhausts all economies of scale, price will be close to minimum long-run average cost. Cooperating oligopolists producing identical products jointly behave much like a monopoly. For instance, firms tend to act as one in the case of a price increase; since buyers cannot distinguish among products, it appears that industry price has risen as if a monopoly actually controlled production.

Product differentiation makes cooperation more difficult. In a cooperative agreement, price differences exist to account for differences in product qualities. Instead of settling on one common price for the market, cooperation now essentially entails some kind of agreement on the price of each product sold. Added to this increased difficulty over establishing prices is the opportunity for nonprice competition because of product differences. While oligopolists may have an agreement not to use price as a competitive tool, they may increase product quality to attract business away from rivals. This kind of competition is very difficult to control. Noncooperation would give a differentiated oligopolistic market the character of monopolistic competition, while cooperation would tend to result in greater economic profits. The most visible sort of cooperation when products are differentiated is leadership by a dominant firm in price or product changes. The largest firm in cooperative markets is frequently first to announce price and style changes that other firms in the market follow.

Oligopoly behavior, cooperative or noncooperative, is strongly affected by the threat of entry. If entry is easy, the gains from cooperation are low. High prices would only encourage new firms to enter the market. Prices in such markets tend to be low and cooperation to increase profits is minimal. If entry is difficult, and oligopolists have relatively secure market shares, over time it is much easier to cooperate and the gains from restricting output or raising price, for example, are greater. There is greater incentive to reach a noncompetitive agreement.

16.4.2   Tactic Collusion

Cooperative oligopolies are often said to be tacitly colluding. Tacit collusion is agreement without communication. For instance, steel producers may restrict their sales to specified geographical regions without meeting and openly dividing regions into designated marketing areas. A firm's geographic market in this case is understood from the ongoing relations it has had with its rivals over the years. Tacit collusion is distinct from the formation of a cartel or a trust. These latter types of collusion are open attempts to monopolize a market. Communication has taken place in order for the agreement to exist. Tacit collusion is not per se, or categorically, illegal, while a cartel is. Evidence of communication is the separating feature between tacit and explicit collusion.

Examples of tacit collusion are evident among manufacturers of consumer durables. For instance, oligopolists will often act together by changing their models annually at almost the same time. Washing machines, refrigerators, cooking ranges, and lawn mowers have annual changes that are announced by manufacturers at about the same time of the year. The same holds true for fashions when spring and fall designs are announced. For another example, ask yourself why makers of soft drinks and beer all use the same size cans and bottles, or makers of breakfast cereal package their product in the same size boxes. It is not because consumers all have a preference for the 12-ounce size. As far as anyone knows, cereal makers and bottlers have no explicit agreement that only this container size—along with a few others—is allowable.

The strongest examples of tacit collusion come from the prices oligopolists charge. In the service sector of the economy, there is a surprising amount of price uniformity, even though there is a wide variance in the quality of services. For instance, lawyers and real estate agents by and large charge the same prices for their services, even though the quality of their services varies from lawyer to lawyer or broker to broker. Explicit collusion is illegal in these industries and presumably does not take place, but a substantial amount of price uniformity nevertheless exists.

There is also the appearance of price leadership in certain oligopolistic markets. One firm leads the way for other rivals when prices are changed. At times it has been observed in the tire, oil, steel, and cigarette industries that when one firm announces a price change (usually an increase), the other producers follow along with the same percentage change. Generally in these markets it has been the firm with the largest market share that takes the lead in announcing a change. For instance, GM and U.S. Steel were recognized price leaders in the automobile and steel industries during the 1960s. However, as entry into these industries has taken place over the last 20 years, the leadership of these firms has declined. Price leadership works best as a form of tacit collusion when there are few firms and very little turnover among firms in the industry.

How does tacit collusion arise? What makes oligopolists cooperate without an explicit arrangement? The answer lies in the consequences of noncooperation. When it comes to selecting competitive strategies, the main difference between a monopolistic competitor and an oligopolist is the realization that what an oligopolist does will cause rivals to react. Oligopolists know that they are related to rivals in a prisoner's dilemma. Another new style or a lower price on old models may increase profits in the short run but reduce them in the long run.

Whether or not an oligopolist makes a change depends on the expected profits earned from making a move. Profits may increase substantially at first, but decrease in the long run after rivals react. How quickly rivals react in large measure determines how profitable a change will be. For cases where the stream of profits after making some change is expected to be less than it would be without the change, patterns of behavior are established among rivals. Oligopolists cooperate because, given the expected reaction of rivals, long-run profits are maximized by stable behavior. This is particularly true for behavior that, in the long run, will raise the costs of producers, because revenues are not likely to go up after rivals have adjusted.

16.4.3   Competition in Oligopoly

Oligopolists are profit maximizers; even when there appears to be a great deal of cooperation among rivals in a market, there is an incentive to make competitive moves that are not easily observed by rivals. Price changes are probably the most obvious moves. Since price is easily observed by rivals, tacit understandings not to lower price often occur. Nonprice competition, on the other hand, is not as easily noticed, and may be very difficult to emulate. Therefore, oligopolists are usually more competitive with respect to nonprice variables. For instance, an oligopolist's advertising budget is not widely known; a firm can incrementally increase the budget without inducing a reaction from rivals. Not surprisingly, oligopolists selling differentiated products tend to do a considerable amount of advertising.

Changes in product quality are often less perceptible than changes in price. A wine that is aged longer to give it a better taste, a few added inches between seats on an airplane, or fewer defective parts in a large shipment of equipment are quality changes not easily observed by rivals. Product-quality competition is particularly intense in service oligopolies, where product quality is difficult to judge unambiguously. Doctors and dentists, for instance, do not usually compete over the prices they charge patients, but the quality of their services and the waiting time in their offices vary a great deal. These are the dimensions where professionals usually compete. Certainly prices do fluctuate under oligopoly, particularly when it is noncooperative, but there is controversy over how much price flexibility exists among oligopolists in general. One thing is clear, however, there is more price flexibility under oligopoly than would exist if the market were monopolized.[6]

16.5   Theories of Oligopoly Behavior

There are numerous theories of equilibrium in oligopoly markets, each depending on a key assumption about how rivals will react to changes in either output or price by one firm in the market. By changing the assumed reaction rivals take, the equilibrium in the market changes. These popular models of oligopoly rivalry are not models of communicated collusion; they arise in a noncooperative environment. However, reactions may be quite accommodating. Outlined in this section are some of the market outcomes that may result when oligopolists compete and attempt to maximize profits. All of them will be described in a market setting called duopoly— two firms producing a homogeneous product.

---

[6]For discussion see G. J. Stigler, "The Kinky Oligopoly Demand Curve and Rigid Prices," *Journal of Political Economy* 55 (October 1947), pp. 432–49. Reprinted in G. J. Stigler, *The Organization of Industry* (Homewood, Ill.: Richard D. Irwin, 1968). Also see J. L. Simon, "A Further Test of the Kinky Oligopoly Demand Curve," *The American Economic Review,* 59 no. 9 (December 1969), pp. 971–75.

Table 16.1   Payoff Table

		Output Selected by the Other Producer									
		8	9	10	11	12	13	14	15	16	17	
Y o u r O u t p u t	8	292	258	225	192	158	125	92	58	25	−8	Collusive
	9	337	300	262	225	187	150	112	75	37	0	
	10	375	333	292	250	208	167	125	83	42	0	
	11	404	358	312	267	221	175	129	83	37	−8	
	12	425	375	325	275	225	175	125	75	25	−25	Cournot
	13	437	383	329	275	221	167	112	58	41	−50	
	14	442	383	325	267	208	150	92	33	−25	−83	
	15	437	375	312	250	187	125	62	00	−63	−125	Competitive (zero profit)
	16	425	358	292	225	158	92	25	−42	−108	−175	
	17	404	333	262	192	121	50	−21	−92	−163	−233	

16.5.1   A Payoff Table

Table 16–1 shows what is typically called a payoff table. It is similar to the prisoner's dilemma discussed earlier. The main difference is the number of entries across the top and left side. There are now 10 instead of 2. The numbers along the border in this table represent the output sold by each duopolist. Inside the table are profits earned by one of the duopolists. We have generated these amounts for each combination of outputs with a market demand of $P = 18.00 - (.42)Q$, where Q is the sum of the outputs of the two firms.[7] Also, marginal cost is assumed to be a constant $3.00 per unit, and fixed costs are approximately $37.50. To interpret the table, suppose you, as a duopolist, select an output of 11 and your rival picks an output of 10; your profit will then be at the intersection of row 11 and column 10 for a profit of 312.

This profit can be calculated from the demand equation and the assumptions that marginal costs are $3.00 and fixed costs are $37.50. Since total output is 21, the market price is approximately $P = 18.00 - (.42)21 \approx \$9.25$. By producing 11 units, your profit is the total revenue $9.25(11) ≈ $101.75 less the total variable cost of $3.00(11) = $33.00 and the fixed cost of $37.50, or 31.25, which is written as 312 in the table. Profit for your rival is $9.25(10) − $3.00(10) − $37.50 = $25.00. Since your rival's payoff table is the same as yours, the relevant profit is in row 10 and column 11. The entry is 250.

However, it is not very likely you will stay at an output of 11 if your rival continues to produce 10. Moving down the column, you see that you can do better by producing 12, 13, or 14. Your rival always sees you as the "other participant," choosing

[7]There is some rounding on this demand function. To construct the payoff table the demand equation is actually $P = 18.00 - (2160/5184)Q$.

values across the top of the table. If you choose a value of 13, for example, your rival may choose a row value to maximize profit and will produce 11 or 12 units of output. By looking at your table, suppose you see a choice of 12 made by the other participant. Looking down the left side of your table, since the other participant has chosen 12, you choose a value of 12 and earn profits of 225. Quite possibly at (12,12) neither of you has any incentive to make further changes. No output in the column under 12 yields a profit higher than 225. But the process of adjustment will continue until both duopolists have no further incentive to change their values.

16.5.2   Oligopoly Equilibrium

With respect to Table 16-1, several outputs can be identified as potential equilibria in the market, depending on how much cooperation there is. What actually happens in the market adjustment process is determined by how oligopolists think their rival or rivals will react to market changes in output or price. Expected behavior in economic theory is called a *conjectural variation*. Two firms in the market may think and actually behave like perfect competitors. This will lead to increases in output until a "perfectly competitive" equilibrium is reached in which each firm earns zero profit. In Table 16–1, this occurs at an output of 15 for each participant.

Firms may have a Cournot conjecture. In this case, each seller maximizes profit under the assumption the other will hold its output constant. Earlier, when we were describing the payoff table, we had implicitly made this assumption. Our thinking was that we chose the best output, given the output already chosen by the other participant. The last choice we discussed was what value to pick if the other person is at 12, and you chose 12. Both participants ended up at values of 12, which is called the Cournot equilibrium in the market.

Notice that profits are not zero as they were under the competitive assumption. Each seller now earns a profit of 225. Also, output is restricted. Under competition, the total amount sold by both would be 30. A Cournot equilibrium has a total output of 24. When we move from a market that is relatively competitive to one where there are a few firms, profits tend to be higher and output lower. No collusion is taking place, although the outcome may make us suspicious of collusion. When profit maximizers have a recognizable impact on market price and output and know their behavior affects the behavior of other sellers, they realize quite independently of each other that some reduction in output benefits all the sellers. As sellers realize this to one degree or another, the market moves toward the Cournot outcome.

A third potential equilibrium in the duopoly market described by Table 16–1 is called the collusive or monopoly equilibrium. It is achieved by the two firms behaving as if they were a single monopolist. A monopolist maximizes profit by setting marginal revenue equal to marginal cost (which is $3 in the table) for the market. This behavior gives each seller an output of 9, and profit per seller is 300. It is hard to imagine how this equilibrium could exist without some form of co-operation between producers, but cooperation may subtly evolve over time in any number of ways. The history of the market (e.g., how the firms first came to produce and compete with another) and accepted business practices often allow the firms to reach more collusive equilibria without any formal agreement or even communication over prices and output.

The relative outputs of the three oligopoly equilibria described so far can be related to each other by observing the diagonal connecting the collusive and competitive profit levels in Table 16–1. The greatest output comes in a competitive environment. Each firm produces 15 units for a total of 30. Total output is cut to 18 units if the two firms behave like a monopolist, and a Cournot equilibrium lies between these two points. Depending on the expected behavior, or conjectures of rivals in a market, a symmetric oligopoly equilibrium may exist anywhere along the diagonal line drawn between the collusive and competitive points. In many markets, however, the Cournot equilibrium appears to be attained relatively frequently.

We have explored oligopoly behavior in terms of rivals choosing output, but in many markets the value chosen is price. Once price is set, businesses usually try to sell all they can so long as price is greater than marginal cost. Some of the values in the table will change as a result; since the products are identical, the seller with the lowest price will get all the business. The competitive and collusive outcomes, however, are found in exactly the same way described above. Profits are either zero or maximized as if the firms were a monopoly. A Cournot equilibrium cannot be defined under these circumstances because firms do not choose output. However, it is possible to identify in more specific cases a Bertrand equilibrium when firms choose price rather than output. Very similar to Cournot, a Bertrand outcome results from each firm setting price and assuming rivals will keep their prices fixed. This assumption does not make it as easy as it was in the Cournot model to identify an equilibrium. For homogeneous products, the firm selling at the lowest price captures all of the market and becomes a monopolist. Therefore, to attract customers away from this firm, rivals will have to sell at a lower price. Eventually such a "price war" will lead to competitive prices. A Bertrand-type equilibrium will be different from the competitive equilibrium only when there are limits on the production capacity of the rivals or if the products are differentiated. If rivals cannot meet market demand at the prices they set, the Bertrand outcome will be similar to the Cournot equilibrium in the sense that total output is below a competitive equilibrium.

16.6   A Digression on Game Theory

The payoff table described in Table 16–1 is a tool commonly used in game theory. Game theory is the study of decision making when outcomes depend upon the behavior of two or more agents, for example, sellers in a market. Each decision maker has only partial control of the outcomes. Oligopoly market structures fall under the definition of game theory. So do actual games such as poker and bridge. Game theory is the theory of interdependent decision making. It has broad applications, not only in economics, but in virtually any political or social environment in which the outcome of an event depends on the choices made by several individuals. This section discusses some of the elementary features of two-person games.

Figure 16–7   A Decision Tree for Suspect 1

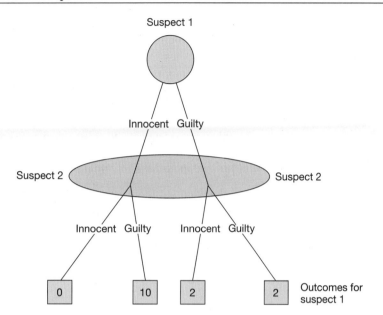

16.6.1   The Form of the Game

Table 16–1 is referred to as the strategic form of the game. For a single market period, the rows show all of one duopoly's choices or strategies, and the columns show all the strategies that can be used by the other firm. The intersection of the chosen strategies in one period gives the outcome of the game. When there are numerous choice periods, strategies are more complicated and therefore more difficult to describe. The collection of the sequences of choices a firm can make is called the strategy space $\{S\}$. A strategy is now represented by one sequence. For n periods of choices and a choice written as s_i for period i, $\{s_1, s_2, \ldots s_n\}$ would be one strategy.

A game can also be described by a decision tree. Figure 16–7 illustrates a decision tree for the prisoner's dilemma first described in the strategic form in Figure 16–5. At the top of the tree, suspect 1 has to choose how to plead: innocent or guilty. If the plea is guilty, this suspect testifies against the other suspect. Suspect 2 must also decide how to plea. The same choices given to 1 are given to 2. The bottom of the tree shows the outcomes realized by suspect 1 once all the decisions are in. Virtually any game can be represented in either its strategic form or its tree form. Decision trees are frequently called the extended form of the game.

16.6.2   Dominant Outcomes

Let us return to the prisoner's dilemma in the form shown in Figure 16–5. Suppose you are suspect 2 and you are choosing a row value. You can choose to plead innocent or guilty. Your objective may be to minimize the maximum possible time

in prison. By pleading innocent, the maximum is 10 years. The worst sentence
with a guilty plea is 2 years. Therefore, by minimizing the maximum loss, called
a *minimax* strategy, you choose guilty. The same game strategy for suspect 1 will
cause that person to plead guilty, and as a result sector D in Figure 16–5 becomes
the equilibrium point of the game.

A player's strategy is said to dominate another if it yields an outcome at least
as good against any strategy that an opponent may choose, with a better outcome
for at least one or more of the opponent's choices. In Table 16–1 we can check to
see that some of the strategies are dominated by others. Again, imagine that this
table describes two identical duopolists, and you are the duopoly choosing row
values.

Would you ever produce 8, your first row? The answer is no, because by
producing 9 units, you earn more profit no matter what output the other duopolist
produces. Hence the choice of 8 is dominated by 9. Since you never choose row
8, your rival would never choose column 8. Envision row 8 and column 8 being
crossed out. Now compare row 9 to row 10. Row 9 is dominated, so it becomes
an *inadmissable* choice. Row 9 and column 9 get crossed off the list of possible
strategies. Now look at row 17. It is dominated by row 16. (Remember that rows
and columns 8 and 9 have been crossed out.) And 16 is dominated by 15, 15 by
14, and 14 by 13.

Only rows 10 through 13 and columns 10 through 13 are left in the payoff table.
It has become a 4 × 4 table. Row 10 with four entries is dominated by row 11.
So this row and column get eliminated. Row 13 is dominated by 12, and finally
12 also dominates row 11. This leaves the entry at row 12 and column 12 as the
only undominated choice for a duopoly. The choice of (12,12) was also described
earlier as the Cournot equilibrium. Hence the Cournot point is the dominant solution
to the game.

16.6.3   Pure and Mixed Strategies

A pure strategy is a complete plan of action. How a player will react to an opponent
is set out in advance. Choices are conditioned by what a rival does, but once a
rival's move is known a player knows in advance what to do. Cournot behavior
represents a pure strategy. The strategy is: for whatever output a firm chooses, the
other firm chooses its output to maximize profits for that period. Output choices
are completely predictable when one firm knows the other follows this strategy.

Sometimes a firm may want to conceal its intentions. For instance, a potential
entrant into a market does not want an incumbent monopolist to know it is considering entry. The monopolist, if it anticipates entry, will act to make it more
expensive to enter or even cause the failure of the new firm.

As an example, consider the 2 × 2 payoff table in Figure 16–8. The entrant
can choose to enter either market A or market B. The current monopoly can take
action to block the entrant at the time of entry. If the monopoly guesses correctly
about which market the new firm tries to enter, it can guarantee the entrant's failure.
Thus at (A,A) and (B,B) the entrant gets zero profits as shown. If the entrant
chooses B but the monopoly anticipates A, the entrant earns 100 in profits. If the

Figure 16–8   Entry with a Mixed Strategy

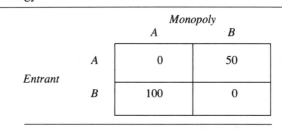

entrant chooses A but the monopoly anticipates B, the entrant earns 50. It is important to the entrant that the incumbent not correctly guess the entrant's move. The surest way to conceal intentions is to undertake a *mixed strategy*. In a mixed strategy, choices are left to chance.

The entrant chooses the market to enter by tossing a coin or rolling a die or using some other random method. Notice that the *minimax* result is zero, regardless of what market the entrant chooses. But suppose the entrant rolls a die and chooses market A if 1, 2, 3, or 4 comes up and market B if 5 or 6 shows. Now if the monopoly anticipates market A, the entrant earns on average $(4/6)(0) + (2/6)(100) = 33\ 1/3$. If the monopoly anticipates B, the entrant has expected earnings of $(4/6)(50) + (2/6)(0) = 33\ 1/3$. Thus, the minimax is 33 1/3, which is greater than 0. By randomizing choices, as shown, the entrant can guarantee average earnings are positive.[8]

16.7   Oligopoly and Cartels

The firms in an oligopoly may decide to overtly fix price and/or market shares. Explicit collusive behavior, necessary in the formation of a cartel, is illegal in the United States under the Sherman Act and other legislation. But antitrust litigation flourishes, indicating that such behavior is still thought to continue.

16.7.1   Cartels and Profit Maximization

A cartel is a combination of firms with the common goal of limiting the competitive forces within a market. It may take the form of open collusion whereby the member firms enter into contracts restricting price and other market variables. The cartel may be based on a secret agreement among members, or it can operate like a trade association or a professional organization. At this time, the most famous cartel is OPEC, a cartel of major oil-producing nations. To be successful, every cartel must have a way of enforcing the agreement that members of the group make. European

---

[8]This example is based on Andrew Coleman, *Game Theory* and *Experimental Games*, (New York: Pergamon Press, 1982), Chapter 4. For more discussion on mixed strategies and how to find the best probabilities when randomizing, see Coleman; Van Neuman and Morgensterin, *Theory of Games and Economic Behavior*, (Princeton, N.J.: Princeton University Press, 1953); Luce and Raiffa, *Games and Decisions: Introduction and Critical Survey* (New York: John Wiley & Sons, 1957).

Figure 16–9   Cartel Profit Maximization

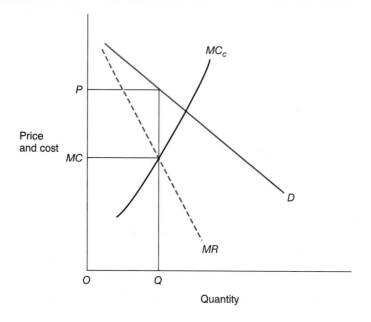

companies can form cartels and write a legally binding contract that courts will enforce. Other means of enforcement are more subtle. In OPEC, Saudi Arabia is such a large producer of high grade crude that it could increase output at virtually any time to ruin the business of stubborn members. Nonetheless, OPEC has frequently had problems enforcing its agreements. Many cartel agreements are, however, difficult to enforce because they are illegal. Any action taken to punish the violator may expose the whole operation to the authorities.

Let us consider the "ideal" cartel. Suppose a group of firms producing a homogeneous commodity combines their interests. A central management body is appointed to determine the uniform cartel price. The task, in theory, is relatively simple, as illustrated in Figure 16–9. Market demand for the homogeneous commodity is given by D, so marginal revenue is given by the dashed line MR. The cartel marginal cost curve in the figure is determined by the management body. If all firms in the cartel purchase their inputs in perfectly competitive markets, the cartel marginal cost curve (MC_c) is simply the horizontal sum of the marginal cost curves of the member firms. Conceptually, it is identical to the marginal cost of the multiplant monopoly discussed in Chapter 14. Otherwise, allowance must be made for the increase in input price accompanying an increase in input usage, and MC_c would stand further to the left than if all input markets were perfectly competitive.

In either case, suppose the management group determines that the cartel marginal cost is MC_c. The profit-maximization problem is identical to that for the monopolist. The cartel should operate where marginal revenue equals marginal cost. From Figure

16–9, marginal cost and marginal revenue intersect at point Q; thus, the market price, P, is the price established by the manager. The second, and probably the biggest, problem now confronting the cartel management is how to distribute the total sales of Q units among the member firms. The distribution of sales will determine each member's profit.

16.7.2   Cartels and Market Sharing

Fundamentally, there are two methods of sales allocation. One involves setting the cartel price, then letting firms maximize sales through nonprice competition. The other way of deciding sales is to set quotas. The former is usually associated with "loose" cartels. A uniform price is fixed, and each firm is allowed to sell all it can at that price. Firms cannot reduce price but can compete by other means. For instance, in many localities, doctors and lawyers have associations whose code of ethics is frequently the basis of a price agreement. Patients and clients then select a doctor or lawyer for reasons other than price. In this case, fostering and maintaining a good reputation is important to increased sales.

The second method of market sharing is the quota system, which has several variants. Indeed, there is no uniform principle to determine quotas. In practice, the bargaining ability of a firm's representative and the importance of the firm to the cartel are the more prominent elements in determining the quota. Bargained allocations are usually struck on two popular grounds. First, either the relative sales of the firms in some precartel base period or the productive capacities of the firms are used. As a practical matter, the choice of base period or the measure of capacity is also a matter of bargaining among members. The second basis is a geographical division of the market. Many of the more famous examples of cartels involve international market divisions.

Although a quota agreement is difficult in practice, in theory some simple guidelines can be laid down. Consider the cartel solution that was shown in Figure 16–9. MC_c is the horizontal summation of all firms' marginal cost curve. The cartel produces and sells the output level Q at a price P. The minimum cartel cost of producing Q, or any other level of output, is achieved when each firm produces an output at which every firm's marginal cost is the same and equals the common cartel marginal cost and marginal revenue. Each firm in the cartel shown in Figure 16–9 produces the output at which its marginal cost is MC. This solution is precisely that set forth in the case of the multiplant monopolist, discussed in Chapter 14.

To explain the allocation method in a little more detail, suppose that two firms in the cartel are producing at different marginal costs; that is,

$$MC_1 > MC_2$$

for firms one and two. In this case, the cartel manager could transfer output from the higher-cost firm 1 to the lower-cost firm 2. So long as the marginal cost of producing in firm 2 is lower, total cartel cost can be lowered by transferring production, and at any given price, profits will increase.

But this does not necessarily solve the problem of how profits are distributed. Once total output and its division have been decided on the basis of cost minimization, there may still exist the problem of allocating the profits across firms. If the cost structure for all firms is identical, the firms can, of course, simply share profits equally. But if cost differences exist, letting allocated production determine profit may not be satisfactory. There are sometimes tremendous incentives to increase production once prices are fixed in a cartel.

16.7.3   Short and Turbulent Life of Cartels

Unless backed by strong legal provisions, cartels in the United States are likely to collapse from internal pressure (before being found out by the Antitrust Division of the Justice Department). A few large, geographically concentrated firms producing a homogeneous commodity may form a successful cartel and maintain it, at least during periods of prosperity. But the greater the number of firms, the greater the scope of product differentiation, and the greater the geographical dispersion of firms, the easier it is to "cheat" on the cartel's policy. In times of marked prosperity, profit may be so great that there is little incentive to cheat. When profits are low or negative, there are increased incentives to secretly increase output and reduce price. These incentives make cartel agreements unstable.

The typical cartel is characterized by high (perhaps monopoly) price, relatively low output, and a distribution of sales among firms that enables most to operate at an output less than that associated with their minimum average cost. In this situation, any one firm can profit greatly from secret price concessions. Indeed, with a homogeneous product, a firm offering price concessions can capture as much of the market as desired, providing other members adhere to the cartel's price policy. Secret price concessions do not have to be rampant before the obedient members experience a marked decline in sales. Recognizing that one or more members are cheating, the formerly obedient members must themselves reduce price in order to remain in business. The cartel accordingly collapses. Without effective legal sanctions, the life of a cartel is likely to be brief, frequently ending whenever a business recession occurs.

The incentive of cartel members to increase output can be explained by using a kinked demand curve. The kink in the curve comes from the incentive structure of members within a cartel. Suppose the collusive organization has fixed a price that maximizes profit for the group. There is no longer an incentive for one oligopolist to cheat by raising price, because the other producers would probably not follow, even if they knew about the infraction. The cheater is imposing a self-inflicted punishment. If it should raise price, sales are rapidly lost to rivals. Thus, it is likely that demand is very elastic for a price increase, especially if the products are homogeneous.

There is, however, an incentive for members of an oligopoly to cheat by lowering price. If rivals do not follow the price cut, the cheater quickly gains additional sales from the other sellers. Figure 16–10 shows the potential gain for a member of a price-fixing cartel. Assume the price is fixed at P_0; the oligopolist, in this case, sells Q_0, but output may vary among members.

Figure 16–10   The Incentive to Cheat in a Cartel

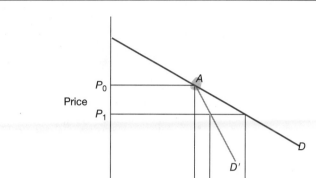

The demand facing the oligopolist, if other members do not follow either price increases or decreases, is the relatively elastic D schedule. If a price decrease is not followed, a lower price substantially increases sales. Similarly, if a price increase is not followed there would be a substantial decrease in sales.

   If members of the cartel, on the other hand, discover that a rival has lowered price, a reasonable reaction would be to match the lower price. This would protect their market share and punish the violator by reducing that firm's sales. In many cartels, this is the only means of enforcement. If rivals match a price cut, the demand curve below P_0 would be the much less elastic segment AD'. Customers would have no cause to change sellers if all firms sell at the same price. If the cheater is discovered and everyone matches the price, the gain in sales to one seller is relatively small. Output rises from Q_0 to Q_2 rather than to Q_1. This increase is due mainly to more *total market* sales because of the lower price charged by everyone in the cartel; each member gets a fraction of the total. Sales represented by Q_2Q_1 are those sales that could have been made if the price cut had gone undetected. These sales represent the incentive of a cartel member to cheat on an agreement. The more elastic is D, the larger the difference between Q_2 and Q_1, and the greater the incentive to cut price.

   Suppose that the amount Q_0Q_2 is extremely small. The total market demand is inelastic, and, as a consequence, total market sales increase only slightly after price is lowered to P_1. Also, suppose the sales increase from Q_2Q_1 is large, and it represents business attracted away from rivals. If this is a noticeable amount, rivals will suspect that someone has lowered price. A substantial increase in the output of one firm while others are losing sales at the fixed prices is another signal of cheating. A potentially large increase in sales from an undetected price cut is the incentive for cheating in a cartel, but, at the same time, it is the signal to other members that prices have been cut. The larger the increase in sales, the higher the probability of detection.

**Ivy League Universities Are Accused of Conspiracy to Fix Financial Aid
Amounts to Students**

In a press release issued by the Department of Justice, May 22, 1991, the Antitrust
Division filed suit charging eight Ivy League universities (Ivies) and the Massachusetts
Institute of Technology (MIT) with illegal conspiracy to fix the amount of financial aid
offered to prospective students. The Ivies immediately agreed to a settlement that they
would "no longer collude or conspire on financial aid." They also agreed not to discuss
with other universities future tuition or faculty salary increases. MIT was not a part of
the settlement.

All the Ivies, Brown, Columbia, Cornell, Dartmouth, Harvard, Princeton, Pennsylvania, and Yale, along with MIT were allegedly meeting on a regular basis to fix a
formula that determined how much a student's family could contribute to the cost of the
student's education. Then, in the spring of the year, the schools actually agreed on how
much a family could pay. The difference between that amount and each school's expenses,
tuition, room, board, and books was the aid offered to students. It was agreed by all the
schools to award aid based on need and not merit.

The Justice Department argued that the "collegiate cartel denied [students] the right
to compare prices and discounts among schools, just as they would in shopping for any
other service." The communication between the colleges allegedly led to the schools
reducing the aid packages to students who might otherwise have been offered more in a
more competitive market. In the settlement agreement, signed by all except MIT, the
Ivies cannot agree with any other colleges on the family's payment in a financial package,
nor can they communicate or exchange information with any college on the amount of
aid offered to potential students.

The cartel formed by the Ivies acted to reduce their cost of attracting the best students
to their programs, and, as a result, students paid more for an Ivy League education. From
the student's viewpoint, the schools were monopolizing the market for an Ivy education.
Less aid made the cost of such an education higher, and naturally "output" in terms of
applicants would shrink. According to the attorney general, "The most unfortunate aspect
of this conduct is that it had a disproportionate impact on those who needed the financial
aid the most." In selling education, the Ivies were taking away the price factor when
university educations were being considered by students. While they were apparently
successful in controlling this feature of the product it is unlikely that a fix on quality
factors were part of the conspiracy. Each school would still argue that it was better than
the others.

16.2 *Applying the Theory*

Over the past 10 years the U.S. Department of Justice has made it legal for oligopolists to undertake joint ventures in commercializing new products or entering
international markets. Name what you would consider advantages and disadvantages
of joint ventures.

16.8   Summary

Monopolistic competition and oligopoly are imperfectly competitive market structures that are characterized by a change in the assumptions underlying the theory of perfect competition. Monopolistic competition results from product differentiation. There are a large number of buyers and sellers, easy entry and exit by producers, and market participants have perfect information regarding prices.

Product differentiation confers a certain amount of market power on sellers. Because of this difference, the demand curve is less than perfectly elastic. However, since entry is easy, under the theory of monopolistic competition, economic profits are competed away. In equilibrium, the *LRAC* curve is tangent to the demand curve at a price higher than minimum average cost.

When products are differentiated, nonprice market strategies become an important competitive tool. Advertising and product-quality changes are two strategies that allow a firm to increase market shares and profits. The gains from such strategies are short run under monopolistic competition. In the long run, a successful move is generally matched, and profits in the market return to normal.

Because of interdependence, there is no complete theory of oligopoly. Oligopolies are characterized by few firms in a market. In contrast to perfect and monopolistic competition, barriers to entry must exist. Oligopoly sellers may offer homogeneous or differentiated products. Behavior in oligopoly markets is determined by how strongly rivals perceive their interdependence with other oligopolists. Broadly speaking, an oligopolist can be cooperative or noncooperative with rivals. The degree that oligopolists cooperate with each other determines, to a large extent, market prices and output. Oligopoly can closely resemble perfect competition, or monopolistic competition if products are differentiated. It can also approach monopoly if cooperation is close among sellers.

The most extreme form of cooperation is a cartel. Oligopolists explicitly agree on output, price, or both. In some cases, firms can be so well organized that behavior is closely akin to multiplant monopoly. But cartels are fragile because incentives to cheat are inherent within any agreement. A cheater can gain at the expense of other members if the firm is not caught.

Little has been said conclusively about the desirability of oligopoly for two reasons. It is difficult to be precise about the welfare effects of oligopoly when there is no single theory of oligopoly. Certainly there is no reason to believe that oligopolists will produce at minimum long-run average cost. Oligopoly requires more units of resources per unit of output than are absolutely necessary. Price is frequently higher than both average and marginal cost.

Furthermore, many resources can be devoted to nonprice competition under oligopoly, just as they can for monopolistic competition. If, as some say, many of these resources are "wasted," then too many resources are devoted to the effort. On the other hand, advertising and many quality and design differentials may be socially desirable. There is no clear evidence on either side. But the welfare criteria imposed are static. Dynamic considerations are also important.

Industrial research and development (R&D) has been essential in the development of our modern industrial economy and is essential to its continued viability and growth. Many argue, with considerable persuasiveness, that R&D usually thrives only in oligopolistic markets. Neither perfect competitors nor pure monopolists have the incentive; moreover, perfect competitors are usually not large enough to support research departments. Oligopolistic firms, on the other hand, always have the incentive. They want to improve the product or reduce its cost of production so as to increase profit relative to that of rivals. Such firms are typically large enough to absorb the short-run cost of R&D in order to reap its long-run payoff. All sorts of static welfare criteria may be violated, more or less with impunity, if the dynamic rate of growth is sufficiently rapid. Some economists, and all oligopolists, hold that oligopolistic market organization is essential for the dynamic growth of the economy.

Answers to   *Applying the Theory*

16.1   There are a number of ways the story can be told. Here is one. Suppose Hardy's and McDonald's are making profits, probably above normal because there are barriers to entry to starting a national chain of franchises. The franchises are in cell A, the upper-left corner. McDonald's decides that a market exists for "less fat" menu items, and it successfully sells a lean hamburger. McDonald's profits rise; business at Hardy's may decline. The two chains have moved to an off-diagonal cell. In response, Hardy's introduces a healthier hamburger. The chains move to the lower-right cell in the box. Both may earn higher profits, but the profits of McDonald's are not as high as before the introduction of Hardy's lean burger.

16.2   Joint ventures allow two or more firms to operate as a cartel in certain market endeavors. From society's point of view cartels operate much like a monopoly restricting output and keeping price high. And there is no nonprice competition that tends to improve product quality. You know, of course, this can cause duplicity or sameness in product qualities. However, there are advantages to joint ventures. Firms unable to undertake investment alone can raise the necessary capital together. The risk of a venture is also spread across a greater number of investors. Also, expertise can be shared, and the spreading of human capital across enterprises may increase the level of competition in the future.

Technical Problems

1. The smaller the seller's share in a cartel, the greater the temptation to cut prices in slack times. Why?
2. Describe the major features of monopolistic competition:
   a. How is it similar to monopoly?
   b. How is it similar to competition?
   c. What characterizes short-run equilibrium?
   d. What characterizes long-run equilibrium?
   e. What is excess capacity under monopolistic competition?
3. Assume that the bituminous coal industry is a competitive industry in long-run equilibrium. Now assume that the firms in the industry form a cartel.

   a. What will happen to the equilibrium output and price of coal? Why?

   b. How should the output be distributed among the individual firms?

   c. After the cartel is operating, are there incentives for the individual firm to cheat? Why or why not?

4. If you were attempting to establish a price-fixing cartel in an industry,

   a. Would you prefer many or few firms? Why?

   b. How could you prevent cheating (price cutting) by cartel members? Why would members have an incentive to cheat?

   c. Would you keep substantial or very few records? What are the advantages and disadvantages of each?

   d. How could you prevent entry into the industry?

   e. How could government help you prevent entry and even cheating?

   f. How would you try to talk government into helping? Under what conditions might this work?

5. Explain why we do not have a general theory of oligopoly. Given the absence of a general theory, what can we say about this type of market structure.

6. Advertising makes the demand curve faced by a seller less elastic. How might this fact be useful to a firm that desires to raise the price of a product without encouraging entry?

7. In many market structures, sellers behave alike without colluding. Use the prisoner's dilemma concept to explain apparent collusion.

8. The key difference between perfect competition and monopolistic competition is product differentiation. How does differentiation affect a market's structure?

9. According to some economists, there are too many gas stations and grocery stores. Is this in keeping with the theory of monopolistic competition? Why or why not?

10. Product variety is a desirable feature of markets, but it leads to market inefficiencies. Explain the costs of product variety.

11. Describe the difference between monopolistic competition and differentiated oligopoly. Do firms in each category behave differently?

12. During the Christmas holidays, the toy industry organized itself into a secret cartel. Use the kinked demand model to describe the incentive of each member of the cartel to cheat.

13. In Figure E.16–1 identify:

   a. The symmetric competitive (zero profit) choice for two players.

   b. The symmetric Cournot choice, assuming choices are outputs.

   c. The symmetric collusive/monopoly choice for two players.

   d. The dominant solution to the game.

Figure E.16–1

	6	*7*	*8*	*9*	*10*
6	50.0	40.6	31.3	21.9	12.5
7	57.8	46.9	35.9	25.0	14.1
8	62.5	50.0	37.5	25.0	12.5
9	64.1	50.0	35.9	21.9	7.8
10	62.5	46.9	31.3	15.6	00.0

Analytical Problems

1. Du Pont Company and Ethyl Corporation in the late 1970s and early 1980s would give a 30-day advance notice to customers when they raised prices. The companies also had a standing policy that they would match any price their rivals charged. Were the companies colluding to fix prices or behaving in a responsible, competitive fashion?

2. "One sure test that an industry is competitive is the absence of any pure profit." Comment critically.

3. Blue laws in some states restrict the sale of most consumer goods on Sunday. Consumers, by and large, oppose the law because many find Sunday afternoons the most convenient time to shop. Paradoxically retail merchant associations frequently support the law. The Houston Association of Retailers, for instance, has filed more than 40 lawsuits against violators, mostly large retailers. Discuss the reason for merchants supporting Blue Laws. Use the prisoner's dilemma.

4. In 1984, a grand jury investigated a possible collusive link between Dr Pepper Co. and Coca-Cola. A number of questions were aimed at determining whether the firms had a price-fixing conspiracy. At the hearings one business executive for Dr Pepper is quoted as saying, "[We have] a price strategy: Whenever Coke and Pepsi went up, we did." (*The Wall Street Journal,* August 13, 1984, p. 3). Does this practice tell you that the firms were illegally colluding? Might this have been price leadership? What about the Cournot model of behavior?

5. By applying the prisoner's dilemma model to advertising, some observers argue that to avoid the waste of resources on excessive advertising, some collusion should be permitted between firms. Comment.

6. A recent report shows that an aggressive advertising campaign by Pepsi has given the company an increased market share over Coca-Cola in food store sales. In essence, the "Pepsi Challenge" has lowered Coke's profits. Using the prisoner's dilemma model, show how Coke is likely to react to the challenge. What about advertising? What about taste?

7. Television critics frequently argue that TV series are too similar—there is too little variety. Assuming they are correct, explain this phenomenon in terms of the analysis in this chapter.

8. Restaurants in large cities seem to fit the basic model of monopolistic competition. But some restaurants are making substantial profits while others are going broke or barely breaking even. Is this consistent with long-run equilibrium? Why or why not?

9. In states where insurance rates are regulated, how do rate increases affect the income of insurance agents in the short run and in the long run? How does this result differ from the consequences of rate increases for a privately owned municipal electric or gas company? What about a telephone rate increase?

10. Many economists argue that more research, development, and innovation occur in oligopolistic market structures than in any other. Why might this be true? (Consider perfect and monopolistic competition and monopoly.)

11. It has been claimed by economist George Stigler that regulation in industries (e.g., the railroad industry) effectively acts to organize a cartel and foster cooperation among the regulated firms rather than restricting monopoly power. Do you consider this a realistic explanation of industry regulation? Present examples to support your point.

PART VI

Input Demand

17
Markets for Variable Inputs

18
Demand for Fixed Inputs:
Theory of Investment

CHAPTER 17

Markets for Variable Inputs

17.1 Introduction

We have developed a theory of markets that explains demand, supply, and market prices. A central part of this theory is the marginal cost curve and its reflection in the market supply schedule. Costs and supply depend, in turn, on the technological conditions of production and the prices of inputs. With minor qualifications, we have generally assumed that both are given. In this chapter, we will continue to assume that the physical conditions of production are technically given, but now we want to explore more carefully how the prices of inputs are determined.

Broadly speaking, input markets do not differ from any other market. Prices and the quantities sold are determined by the interaction of demand and supply. But there are important differences. First, on the demand side of the market, business firms rather than consumers purchase factors of production. The quantity of inputs used depends on the quantity of output sold by the firm. Sales, in turn, depend on the size of the market and whether producers are perfect competitors or have monopoly power. Input demand is therefore derived from and affected by the market conditions for the commodity. Second, supply, at least the supply of labor services, arises from individuals who are not only sellers of labor time, but are also consumers. Furthermore, in many input markets, the price of the input is the price of using the resource for a stipulated period of time, not the price of purchasing the resource.

You have already been exposed to the fundamental elements of input demand. The quantity of an input demanded is determined by comparing the marginal cost of another unit to its marginal benefit, as discussed in Chapter 4. Suppose you own a business and a worker applies for a job. Would you hire this worker? The answer depends on how much additional revenue the worker would earn for your business. If the worker is expected to add more to revenue than you must pay in wages, the answer is yes. If the worker is expected to add less in revenue than the wages you must pay, the answer is no. The same reasoning applies to any factor of production. A firm would increase its use of a particular input of any type if an additional unit of the input is expected to add more to revenue than it adds to cost. If the additional unit increases cost more than it increases revenue, no more of the input would be added. It makes no difference whether the input is labor, capital, land, fuel, or something else. The basic theory is simple because you have already learned a great deal about the importance of the margin in decision making.

17.2   One Variable Input and Perfect Competition in Input Markets

This section begins the theory of input markets with the simplest case. We assume that only one input, labor, can be adjusted by the firm, and this input is supplied by perfectly competitive agents. The competitive assumption ensures that there are no quality differences in the factor supplied and that individual suppliers do not control enough of the input to affect its price. On the other hand, we will allow the demand side of the market to be first perfectly competitive and then monopolistic. This change affects the marginal benefit of an input and, therefore, the demand for that input.

The theory developed here is applicable to virtually any productive service that is variable, although the most natural application is to the demand for labor. When we speak of the demand for labor, the demand for any variable factor of production is implied. The demand for capital is somewhat more complicated because investment decisions depend on the rate of interest. Investment will be given special consideration in the next chapter.

17.2.1   Demand of a Perfectly Competitive Firm

Any firm would increase the amount of labor used if the additional unit contributes more to the firm's income than to its cost. Consider the following example: a perfectly competitive firm sells its product at a market price of $1. It can hire each unit of the variable input, labor, at $30 per day. If increasing its labor force by one worker adds more than 30 units of output per day and hence more than $30 to revenue, the firm would hire the additional worker.

The amount an additional unit of an input adds to total revenue is called *marginal revenue product* (*MRP*). That is,

$$MRP = \frac{\Delta \text{ total revenue}}{\Delta \text{ input usage}} = \frac{\Delta Q \cdot P}{\Delta \text{ input usage}} = MP \cdot P,$$

where P is the given price of the producer's output Q, and MP is marginal product. We can also define marginal revenue product as follows:

Definition

The marginal revenue product (*MRP*) of a factor of production for a producer is the addition to total revenue attributable to the addition of one more unit of the factor. Marginal revenue product is equivalent to marginal product multiplied by output price, when output prices are constant.

Table 17–1   Marginal Revenue Product of Labor (MRP_L) and a Competive Firm's Demand for Labor

Units of Variable Input	Total Product	Marginal Product	MRP_L
0	0	—	—
1	10	10	$ 50
2	30	20	100
3	50	20	100
4	65	15	75
5	75	10	50
6	80	5	25
7	83	3	15
8	84	1	5
9	81	−3	−15

We will often add a subscript to *MRP* to denote the kind of input to which we are referring. For instance, MRP_L is the marginal revenue product of labor. In general, the *i*th input has MRP_i.

Since each additional worker in the above example adds $30 to cost, the marginal cost of the input is that wage rate. The marginal cost of another unit of input is generally referred to as the marginal factor cost (*MFC*) of the input.

If we let the marginal factor cost of labor be the wage rate, *w*, the basic rule for hiring an extra unit is, if

$$MRP_L > w,$$

the producer would add more of the input. If

$$MRP_L < w,$$

the firm would add no more of the input; it would, in fact, decrease its use. Profit maximization requires

$$MRP_L = w.$$

Let us consider another numerical example, this time in more detail. A perfectly competitive firm sells a product for $5 and employs labor at a wage rate of $20 per day. Table 17–1 shows the daily total product, marginal product, and marginal revenue product for zero through nine workers. The MRP_L in the last column is simply $5 multiplied by marginal product. Under these conditions, the firm hires six workers. It would not hire fewer than six, since hiring the sixth adds $25 to revenue but costs only $20. It would not hire seven workers because revenue would only increase by $15 while cost would rise by $20. If, however, the wage rate dropped below $15 (say to $14) the work force would increase to seven (an additional $15 revenue can be gained at a cost of $14). Or if wages rose above $25 but remained below $50, the firm would reduce the labor force to five.

Table 17–1 is recast as Figure 17–1. In the figure, MRP_L, the last column in Table 17–1, is graphed. The curve rises and then falls. It is not a smooth curve because we assume that a discrete number of workers must be hired, one,

Figure 17–1   Marginal Revenue Product and Demand for Labor in a Perfectly Competitive Market

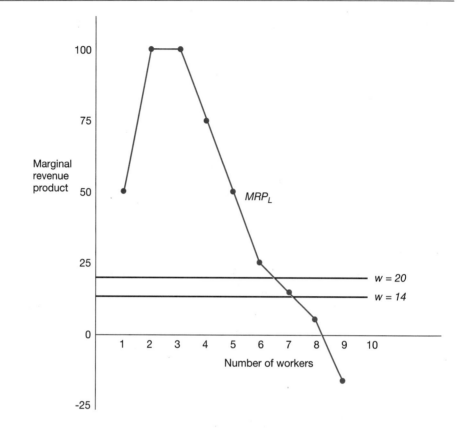

two, or three, and so on. Suppose the wage rate is $20 and the firm can hire all the workers it could possibly want at this wage rate. This wage then becomes the supply of labor to the firm. It is perfectly elastic at $20. Since the sixth worker contributes $25 to the firm's revenue and costs only $20, the sixth worker should be hired. Indeed, workers one through six contribute more than $20 to revenue, so a total of six workers should be hired. The seventh worker should not be hired since this worker contributes only $15 to revenue. If the wage rate fell to $14, the seventh worker should be hired as shown in the figure.

Assume now that the amount of labor hired can vary continuously rather than discretely. Perhaps the firm can hire part-time workers. Thus, any amount of labor is possible. Figure 17–1 shows that if part-time workers can be hired, the firm would like to hire 6.5 workers at the wage rate of $20/worker. The half-time worker would cost $10 for the half day. Now the employer has reached the precise point where $MRP_L = w$. If part-time labor were unavailable, stopping at six workers means $MRP_L > w$, but moving to seven causes $MRP_L < w$. So the employer stops at six.

17.1   *Applying the Theory*

Suppose the wage rate in Figure 17–1 rises to $75 per worker. How many workers does the firm hire? Assume that part-time workers can be hired.

Economics in the News

K-9 Cops Get Laid Off in Vermont[1]

In the spring of 1991, the Vermont legislature was facing a $50 million deficit. To save money it decided to lay off 7 of its 15-member dog cops. The dogs are actually owned by their state trooper masters, who are responsible for their care. But federal laws required the state to pay policemen 30 minutes of overtime a day for the time spent caring for the dogs. The annual bill for this overtime was $40,000 in 1990. Reducing the dog force by seven was estimated to save the state $20,000. From this estimate, the marginal cost, or wage rate, of a dog is constant at about $2,850 per year.

But state troopers argued that the dogs were responsible for the recovery of $80,000 in evidence (returned to owners) and $53,000 in drugs. Total recovery value is therefore the sum, or $153,000. If it can be assumed that *MRP* is constant, then the *MRP* of a dog is approximately $10,200 per year. Hence, $MRP = \$10{,}200 > w = \$2{,}850$. Rather than laying off dogs, it appears the state should have employed more.

The general profit-maximizing rule is illustrated in Figure 17–2. Suppose the marginal revenue product is given by the curve labeled MRP_L. It is a smooth curve, indicating that any fraction of the input can be employed. The firm can hire as much labor as it desires at the wage rate of $\overline{w}$, so the supply of labor to the firm is the horizontal line S_L. Suppose the firm employed only L_1 units of labor. At that rate of employment, the marginal revenue product is the distance $L_1C = w_1$, which is greater than $\overline{w}$, the wage rate. At point C, an additional unit of labor adds more to total revenue than to total cost. A profit-maximizing firm should add additional units of labor and, indeed, should continue to add units so long as the marginal revenue product exceeds the wage rate.

Now, suppose L_2 units of labor were employed. At this point, the marginal revenue product, $L_2F = w_2$, is less than the wage rate. The last unit of labor adds more to total cost than to total revenue. A profit-maximizing firm should not employ L_2 units, or any number for which the wage rate exceeds the marginal revenue product. These arguments show that employing $\overline{L}$ units of labor leads to profit maximization when the wage rate is $\overline{w}$.

Principle

A profit-maximizing competitive firm will employ units of a variable productive resource until the point is reached where the marginal revenue product of the input (output price times marginal product) is equal to the input price.

---

[1] This news is based on "Laid-Off Cops Gnash Their Teeth As State Cuts Budget to the Bone," *The Wall Street Journal,* Thursday, May 2, 1991, p. B1.

Figure 17–2   Demand for a Variable Resource in a Competitive Market

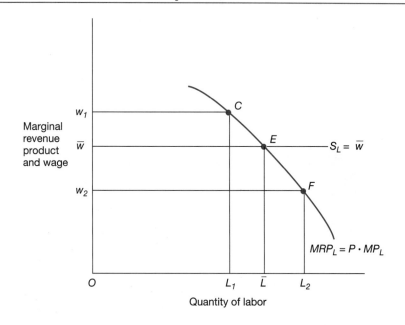

In other words, given the market wage rate or the supply-of-labor curve to the firm, a perfectly competitive producer determines the quantity of labor to hire by equating the marginal revenue product to the wage rate. If the wage rate were w_1 in Figure 17–2, the firm would employ L_1 units of labor to maximize profit. Similarly, if the wage rate were w_2, the firm would employ L_2 units of labor. By the definition of a demand curve, therefore, the marginal revenue product curve is established as the competitive firm's demand for labor when labor is the only variable input.

Before proceeding, we should discuss why the demand curve is downward sloping. Recall from the discussion in Chapter 8 that the typical marginal product curve first rises, reaches a maximum, then declines thereafter, crossing the average product curve at its maximum. Since *MRP* is simply a constant commodity price multiplied by marginal product, it has a similar shape.

A profit-maximizing firm would never choose a level of input usage where marginal product and, therefore, *MRP* are rising. To see why, suppose the wage, *w*, equals *MRP* where *MRP* is rising. The firm can add one more unit of labor and the *MRP* would be greater than the wage. Profits could continue to increase from additional units of labor so long as *MRP* is rising.

Principle

A competitive firm's demand curve for a single variable productive service is given by the downward sloping part of the marginal revenue product curve of the productive factor.

Table 17–2   Marginal Revenue Product for a Monopolist

(1)	(2)	(3)	(4)	(5) Additional Total Revenue per Unit of Additional Labor (MRP$_L$)	(6)	(7)	(8)
Units of Labor	Total Product	Commodity Price	Total Revenue		Marginal Product	Marginal Revenue	Marginal Revenue Product (MR × MP$_L$)
3	5	$50.00	$250	—	—	—	—
4	20	30.00	600	$350	15	$23.33	$350
5	30	25.00	750	150	10	15.00	150
6	38	22.00	836	86	8	10.75	86
7	44	20.00	880	44	6	7.33	44
8	48	19.00	912	32	4	8.00	32
9	50	18.50	925	13	2	6.50	13
10	51	18.00	918	−7	1	−7.00	−7

17.2.2   Market Power in the Commodity Market

The analytical principles underlying the demand for a single variable input are the same for perfectly competitive firms and firms with market power, but marginal revenue product is defined differently. Since commodity price and marginal revenue are different in markets in which firms have market power, the marginal revenue product will not be price times marginal product.

When a perfectly competitive seller employs an additional unit of labor, output is augmented by the marginal product of that unit. When a monopolist employs additional labor, output also increases by the marginal product of the additional workers. However, for a monopoly to sell the larger output, commodity price must be reduced; total revenue is not augmented by the price times the marginal product of the additional workers. Instead, $MRP_L = MR \cdot MP_L$, where MR falls as output increases.

Definition

Marginal revenue product for a firm with market power is the additional revenue attributable to the addition of one unit of the variable input. It is marginal revenue from the product times marginal product.

A numerical example might clarify this point. In Table 17–2, columns (1) and (2) show the output for various amounts of labor. Columns (2) and (3) together show the demand for the commodity that is produced by labor. As more is sold, price falls. Column (4) is the total revenue (product price times quantity) associated with each level of labor use. As shown in Column (5) MRP_L is calculated by finding the contribution to total revenue of one more worker from column (4). For example, the MRP_L of the fourth worker is $600 − $250 = $350. The next three columns, (6), (7), and (8), show another way of finding MRP_L. Column (6) is the marginal

Figure 17–3   A Monopolist's Demand for Labor

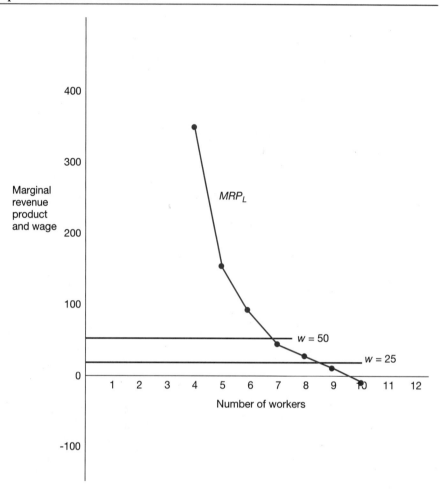

product of labor. It is the change in total production per additional unit of labor
from column (2). For example, the MP_L of the fourth worker is $20 - 5 = 15$.
Column (7) is derived from column (4). It is the change in revenue from producing
and selling one more unit of output. We have calculated marginal revenue in column
(7) by dividing the change in total revenue (column 4) by the increase in units
produced (column 2). MRP_L is also computed by multiplying marginal product
(column 6) times marginal revenue (column 7).

In this example, columns (6) and (7) show that marginal revenue product falls
because both marginal revenue and marginal product fall. Marginal revenue product
is the net addition to total revenue. In Table 17–2, the gross addition to revenue
from increasing labor from three to four units is 15 (the additional units of production) times $30 (the selling price of each unit of production), or $450. But to

Figure 17–4   Monopoly Demand for a Single Variable Service: Labor

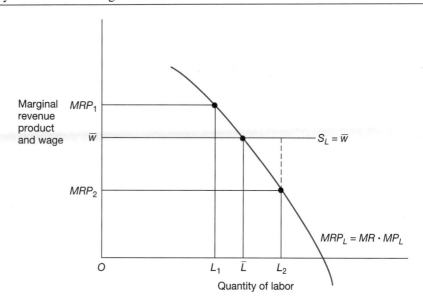

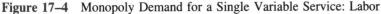

sell 15 additional units, price per unit must fall by $20. The "lost" revenue from the price reduction is 5 · $20 = $100, because five units could have been sold at a price of $50 each. This "loss" must be subtracted from the gross gain, or $450 − $100 = $350 = MRP_L.

Column (5) or (8) of Table 17–2 shows the monopolist's demand for labor, which is graphed in Figure 17–3. At each wage, MRP_L tells the monopolist how many units to hire. If the daily wage is $25, the monopolist would hire eight workers. Each worker up to the ninth adds more than $25 (the additional daily cost per worker) to revenue. The ninth adds $13, and would cost the firm $25 − $13 = $12 in lost profit. If wages rise to $50 a day, the firm would reduce labor to six units. Both the seventh and eighth worker add less than $50 to total revenue.

Figure 17–3 illustrates that at a wage of $25 the monopoly would like to hire about 8.5 workers, which is possible if labor varies continuously rather than discretely. In this case MRP_L is exactly equal to $25. But if no part-time hours can be arranged, the firm would only hire the eighth worker because the ninth causes MRP_L to fall below w.

To illustrate the demand for labor more generally, consider the marginal revenue product curve in Figure 17–4 when labor varies continuously. It must obviously slope downward because two forces act to cause marginal revenue product to diminish as the level of employment increases: (a) the marginal product declines (over the relevant range of production) as additional units of the variable service are added and (b) marginal revenue declines as output expands and commodity price falls. Thus, for the monopolist, marginal revenue product falls more rapidly than it does for a perfect competitor. Under perfect competition, output price remains constant, so only the declining marginal product causes MRP to decline.

By assumption, the monopoly purchases the variable input in a perfectly competitive input market. It views its supply-of-input curve as a horizontal line at the level of the prevailing market price, $\overline{w}$. Given the market price, $\overline{w}$, equilibrium employment is $\overline{L}$. Suppose the contrary, in particular that L_1 units of labor are used. At the L_1 level of utilization, the last unit adds MRP_1 to total revenue but only $\overline{w}$ to total cost. Since $MRP_1 > \overline{w}$, profit is augmented by employing that unit, and profit will continue to increase as additional units are employed, so long as marginal revenue product exceeds the market price of the input. A profit-maximizing monopolist would never employ fewer than $\overline{L}$ units of the variable input.

The opposite argument holds when more than $\overline{L}$ units are employed, say L_2; then an additional unit of labor adds more to total cost than to total revenue. In the figure $\overline{w}$ is greater than MRP_2 by the amount of the dashed line at L_2. A profit-maximizing monopolist would reduce employment until marginal revenue product equals input price. If only one variable input is used, the marginal revenue product curve will be the monopolist's demand curve for the variable input in question.

Principle

A producer with market power (all firms in imperfectly competitive markets) who purchases a variable productive resource in a perfectly competitive input market will employ that amount of the resource for which marginal revenue product equals the market price of the resource. Consequently, the marginal revenue product curve is the monopolist's demand curve for the variable resource when only one variable input is used. Marginal revenue product declines with output for two reasons: (1) marginal product declines as more units of the variable input are added and (2) to sell the additional output, the monopolist must lower the commodity price.

Economics in the News

The Marginal Revenue Product of Irrigation Water

A study by two agricultural economists, Ronald Lacewell and Duane Reneau, who estimated the marginal revenue product of irrigation water on farmland in four Texas High Plains counties, emphasizes that the marginal revenue product is essentially the demand curve for an input.[2] The *MRP* curve shows two features about the demand for a particular input:

1. The amount of revenue each additional unit of input adds to the producer's total revenue.
2. How much the producer is willing to pay for marginal units of the input.

Combined with the price of the input, the *MRP* curve shows how many units of the input a competitive producer will demand.

(continued)

[2]"The Value of Groundwater," *Water Currents,* Texas Water Resources Institute and the Texas Agricultural Experiment Station, Summer 1983.

Figure 17–5 Marginal Revenue Product Curves in Four Texas Counties

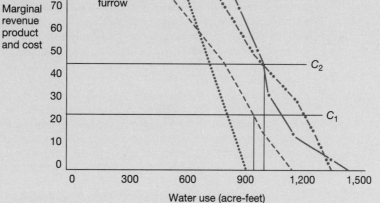
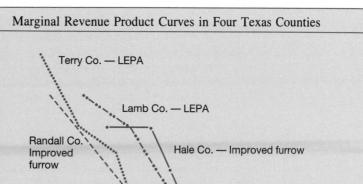

The study by Lacewell and Reneau is particularly interesting for those who might wish to apply the basic theoretical idea of input demand to real-world situations. In deriving the *MRP* curves displayed in Figure 17–5, the agricultural economists took into consideration the following factors that determine the relative benefit of water to a farmer who irrigates:

1. The type of irrigation system used.
2. The crop choice and market prices for the crop being produced.
3. The soil type.

In the counties studied by the economists, these factors were assumed to be held constant when deriving the demand for irrigation water. Obviously, the *MRP* of water will vary according to all three of these factors.

The basic approach used in the study was to estimate the marginal value of each additional acre-foot of water applied evenly over 1,000-acre farms in the four different counties. An acre-foot of water is the volume of water that would cover one acre of land to a depth of one foot. In order to get a representative *MRP* schedule for the typical High Plains farmer, Lacewell and Reneau used a composite of different crops combined with a composite average of market prices over a 20-year period. To take into consideration the effects of different soil types and irrigation technologies on *MRP*, four different counties were chosen, in which two different irrigation methods were used. One method, called improved furrow irrigation, is a variation of flood irrigation. The other, referred to as the LEPA (low energy precision application) method of irrigation, is a drip irrigation

(continued)

technique developed in Israel. The *MRP* curves estimated in Figure 17–5 can be considered fairly representative of those faced by farmers in West Texas using one of these irrigation technologies.

In this study, the price of water is the average cost of pumping groundwater to the surface. The lower the groundwater table, the greater the height it has to be pumped. The price of the input in each of the areas studied varies with different aquifer conditions. The lowest price was $22 per acre-foot in Randall County, and the highest price was $44 per acre-foot in Lamb County.

Figure 17–5 shows the low and high prices as C_1 and C_2, respectively. The intersection of the horizontal cost schedules and each *MRP* curve shows how much water farmers in each case will use. A Randall County farmer will use the amount of water where the $22 per acre-foot cost schedule intersects the Randall *MRP* curve. Therefore, the farmer will demand about 950 acre-feet of water per year. If more were used, the farmer would be adding more to total cost than to total revenue. If less were used, the use of additional acre-feet of water would add more to total revenue than to total cost.

The figure shows that a farmer in Lamb County, who uses the LEPA irrigation technique and faces a cost schedule of $44 will use a little less than 1,000 acre-feet of water per year. Despite the higher cost schedule, the MRP curve is further to the right than that of the Randall County farmer because of the more efficient irrigation technique. We observe that the *MRP* curves are literally demand curves for water from the perspective of the farmer. At any level of cost for groundwater, we can determine how much water each farmer demands.

The estimated *MRP* curves show how much water each of the four representative farms would buy if the unit cost of water rises to $150, which does not seem an unreasonable estimate for the cost of each acre-foot of water projected for the year 2000.[3] According to Figure 17–5, the use of the existing technologies would not allow the High Plains farmers to use any irrigation water at all under such conditions. Some of the options to consider are that farmers may

1. Go out of business.
2. Change to crops or cropping techniques that use much less water.
3. Change to more efficient irrigation techniques.
4. Find a less expensive input.

Alternatives (2) and (3) would both have the effect of shifting the *MRP* curve to the right. Under such conditions, it might be possible for one *MRP* curve to again intersect the unit cost curve of water.

Switching to surface water might be a less expensive substitute for underground water. This would lower the projected unit cost of irrigation water. Undoubtedly, farmers on the High Plains will have to choose some combination of the above options. In fact, they already are making such a transition, and many are changing to more efficient irrigation methods. Agriculturalists are researching new crop strains that use less water. In this research, they will be greatly assisted by new genetic-engineering techniques. Some farmers are shifting over to surface water by constructing small-scale reservoirs. The

(continued)

[3]Cost per acre-foot in Los Angeles is $250 per acre-foot. See *Business Week*, March 9, 1984, p. 104.

Texas Water Plan of 1968 even considered transporting surface water from the Mississippi River. It is questionable that such an expensive proposition could reduce the marginal cost of water, but the dream of such a plan "resurfaces" periodically in state and national legislative bodies.

17.3   Demand for a Productive Resource with More Than One Input Variable

When there are several inputs that can be varied in production, all but one are assumed to be held constant when deriving the firm's demand for a single variable input. When the usage of any other input—fixed or variable—changes, the *MRP* schedule will shift. After discussing all the parameters held constant when using *MRP* as a demand schedule, we will derive demand when the usage of other inputs changes.

17.3.1   Parameters for Marginal Revenue Product and Fringe Benefits

Several economic variables are held constant when the *MRP* schedule is defined as an input demand schedule. First, we hold the use of all other inputs constant. Recall from Chapter 8 that when the rate of use of another input changes, the marginal product curve of the other input shifts. If the use of another input changes, the *MRP* curve for a firm would therefore shift. We will discuss the derivation of input demand under these conditions more fully as an example of what happens to the demand schedule when the variables underlying the *MRP* curve change. A second variable held fixed is technology, because technological change will also shift the marginal product curve. Third, the demand schedule for the product is held fixed. In the case of the competitive firm, this means that product price does not change.

Until now, we have assumed that the wage bill is the total payment to the input; there are no additional or fringe payments, such as contributions to social security or to group insurance plans. This point requires some discussion. If you are an employer, the profit-maximizing rule of continuing to employ more of a variable input at the margin until *MRP* is equal to the input price makes sense, but in the case of labor, you might look at the wage rate or the price of an input in a slightly different way. In the real world, workers can cost an employer more than simply the money wage rate. There are certain additional payments to workers required by law, such as social security contributions, or perhaps paid by tradition, such as contributions to employee insurance policies or retirement plans. Other fringe benefits would be improvements in working conditions, noise controls, lounge facilities, and so on.

All of these additional payments are costs to the firm. Therefore, the total wage bill is the market-determined wage plus the cost of fringe benefits. In the United States, fringe benefits amount to about 25 percent of the wage bill. At any market-determined wage, if additional payments are made, fewer workers are hired than would be hired in the absence of such payments. However, as we will show, employers do not absorb all of the cost of the fringe benefits.

Figure 17–6 Individual Input Demand When Several Variable Inputs Are Used

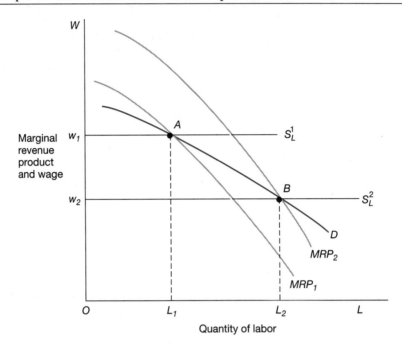

17.3.2   Adjusted Demand When More Than One Input Is Variable

In Figure 17–6, suppose that equilibrium for a perfectly competitive or monopoly firm is initially at point A. The market wage rate is w_1; the marginal revenue product curve for labor is MRP_1 when labor is the only input varied. When MRP_1 equals w_1, L_1 units of labor are employed. Now let the wage rate fall to w_2, so that the perfectly elastic supply curve of labor falls from S_L^1 to S_L^2.

When the wage rate falls from w_1 to w_2, the use of labor expands. However, the expansion does not take place along MRP_1. When the quantity of labor used and the level of output change, the use of other variable inputs changes as well. Under these conditions, labor's marginal product curve changes, and since marginal revenue product is equal to marginal product multiplied by the marginal revenue of the commodity, the marginal revenue product of labor curve must shift too.

Suppose it shifts to MRP_2. The new equilibrium is reached at point B, at which L_2 units of labor are hired. Other points similar to A and B can be generated in the same manner. The demand curve, D, is determined from successive changes in the market wage rate and the marginal revenue product curve. The input demand curve, although more difficult to derive, is just as determinate in the multiple-input case as in the single-input situation. The results can be summarized in the following principle:

Principle

> A firm's demand curve for a variable productive agent or resource when more than one variable input is used can be derived and must be negatively sloped. Even though demand is no longer the marginal revenue product curve, at every point on the demand curve, the wage rate still is equal to marginal revenue product.

17.4 Industry Demand for an Input

The industry demand for a variable productive service, in contrast to the market demand for a commodity, is not necessarily the horizontal summation of each producer's demand curve. In general, the process of summation for productive services is somewhat more complicated, because when all firms in an industry expand or contract simultaneously, the market price of the commodity changes.

The situation is analogous to the derivation of a perfectly competitive industry's supply curve from each firm's marginal cost curve. Recall that any firm can change its level of output without affecting input prices. When all firms attempt to vary output together, input prices may change and each firm's marginal cost shifts. Therefore, industry supply is the horizontal summation of these "shifted" supplies. In the case of input demand, any perfectly competitive firm can vary its inputs, and thus its output, without affecting commodity price. But when all firms attempt to change their use of an input and hence the output, the product price will change. Since each firm's demand for the input is derived holding commodity price constant, all input demands will shift.

17.4.1 Industry Demand under Perfect Competition

To illustrate the process of deriving industry demand, assume that a typical employing firm is depicted in Figure 17–7, Panel A. At the going market price of the commodity produced, d_1 is the firm's demand curve for the variable input similar to that derived in Figure 17–6. If the market price of the resource is p_1, the firm uses v_1 units. Aggregating over all employing firms in the industry, V_1 units of the input are used. Thus, point A in Panel B is one point on the industry demand curve for the variable input.

Next, suppose the price of the input declines to p_2 (it may be, for example, that the supply curve of the variable input shifts to the right). Other things equal, the firm would move along d_1 to point b' employing v_2' units of the input. But other things are not equal. When all firms expand their use of the input, total output expands. Or, stated differently, the market supply curve for the commodity shifts to the right because of the decline in the input's price. For a given commodity demand, commodity price must fall; and when it does, the *MRP* curve shifts to the left or the individual demand curve for the variable productive input decreases.

Figure 17–7   Derivation of the Industry Demand for a Variable Productive Input

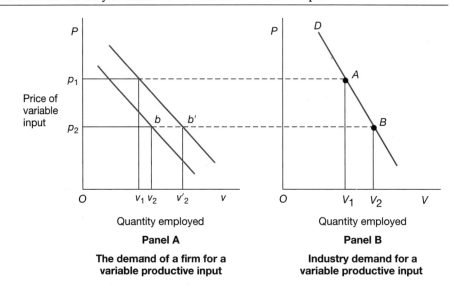

Panel A

The demand of a firm for a
variable productive input

Panel B

Industry demand for a
variable productive input

In Panel A, the decline in individual input demand attributable to the decline in the commodity price is represented by the shift left from d_1 to d_2. At the input price p_2, b is the equilibrium point, with v_2 units employed. Aggregating for all firms, V_2 units of the productive service are used and point B is obtained in Panel B. Any number of points such as A and B can be generated by varying the market price of the productive service. Connecting these points by a line, one obtains D, the industry demand for the variable productive service.

17.4.2   Industry Demand When There Is Monopoly Monopoly

If an industry is monopolized by a single firm, the monopoly demand for an input is the same as the industry demand. If several industries demand an input, the total market demand is the horizontal summation of every industry's demand, assuming that we ignore the effect of changes in commodity price in one industry on commodity price in other industries that demand the input.

17.4.3   Employment under Monopoly and Perfect Competition

We can use the concepts in the theory of input demand under monopoly and perfect competition to make a tentative comparison between industry employment under the two market structures. You know from Chapter 15 that under the same cost conditions, a monopolist restricts output and charges a higher price relative to a perfectly competitive industry. It should, therefore, come as no surprise that, under the same conditions, a monopolist hires less of an input relative to the competitive industry. Assuming the monopolist is unable to realize economies of scale, the degree of "inefficiency" attributable to a monopoly employer can be observed by comparing employment at any given wage to that in a perfectly competitive industry.

Figure 17–8   A Competitive Industry and a Monopoly Employer

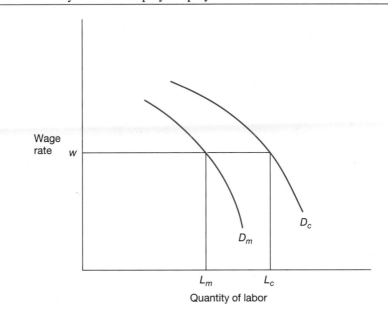

To make the comparison, we continue with the restrictive assumption that there is only one variable input—in this case, labor. We assume the same cost curves for both the competitive and the monopolistic structures. The same amount of labor is associated with a given level of input usage in either case. And, at any given amount of output and labor usage, the marginal product of additional labor is the same under either form of market organization. This might be the case if the monopoly simply organized the firms into individual plants and allocated output among the plants in the same way output would be divided among firms under competition.

Figure 17–8 compares labor demand under monopoly and competition, using the restrictive assumptions set forth above. Monopoly demand is D_m, which is the firm's *MRP* curve. D_c is the competitive industry's demand for labor. It takes account of the declining commodity price as all firms in the industry expand labor usage and therefore increase the quantity sold.

The D_c schedule will be greater than (lie to the right of) D_m, because at any given wage, output will be higher under competition than under monopoly. Or at any given level of labor, price times marginal product in a competitive market will exceed a monopolist's marginal revenue times marginal product. At a wage of w in Figure 17–8, the competitive industry will hire L_c workers while the monopoly will hire only L_m.

Keep in mind that this conclusion is derived under the assumption that costs are the same under monopoly and competition. If cost advantages were available to the monopoly but not to the competitive industry, more labor might be employed by the monopoly, at a given wage rate.

17.5   Supply of a Variable Productive Input

Variable inputs may be broadly classified into three groups: natural resources, intermediate goods, and labor. There are of course other inputs, commonly referred to as capital, but in the short run these inputs tend to be fixed. In this section, we describe the shape of the supply curve of these variable inputs.

17.5.1   Intermediate Goods and Natural Resources

Intermediate goods are those produced by one producer and sold to another, which, in turn, utilizes them in the firm's productive process. For example, cotton is produced by farmers and sold as an intermediate good to a manufacturer of fabric; the fabric, in turn, becomes an intermediate good in the manufacture of upholstered furniture. The short-run supply curves of intermediate goods are positively sloped because they are the marginal cost curves of manufacturers, even if they are variable inputs to others; and, as shown in Chapter 10, marginal cost curves generally have positive slopes. Natural resources may also be regarded as the commodity outputs of extractive operations. As such, they also have positively sloped short-run supply curves. In general, the supply of variable inputs is upward sloping. In most cases, inputs are produced just as any other good or service. The positive slope of supply indicates that at the margin it becomes more costly to provide another unit of the variable input.

17.5.2   Labor Supply

There are some special features about the supply of labor. In Chapter 7, we showed how an individual's supply of labor is derived from the indifference curves between leisure and income. In that chapter, we showed that, given a wage increase, an individual might choose to work more (sacrifice leisure) or to work less (take more leisure), depending on the shape of his or her indifference map. Therefore, an individual supply-of-labor curve may be positively sloped over some range of wages and negatively sloped over other ranges. The crucial question, however, is how the work force as a group behaves, that is, what is the shape of the market supply curve of any specified type of labor?

As an empirical matter, a firm, whether monopolist or competitor, can face two types of labor supply. In the cases discussed previously in this chapter, the supply of labor has been a horizontal line at the market-determined wage rate, indicating that the firm can hire all of the labor it wishes at the going market wage rate. In certain cases, firms do have some influence on the wage rate. In these instances, the firm faces an upward-sloping supply of labor, indicating that, in order to hire more of a certain kind of labor, the firm must pay higher wages. Under this set of circumstances, the firm is called a *monopsonist*, a situation which will be analyzed later in this chapter.

At the industry level, the labor supply curve also may be horizontal or have an upward slope. If the industry is small relative to the total supply of labor, the expansion of the industry may have no effect on the wage rate. The wage rate in this instance would be the industry's horizontal supply curve. There are, however, situations whereby the industry demand for labor is relatively large. Suppose an industry uses a specialized type of labor, specialized in the sense that the industry's use of the input affects that input's price. In the long run, the supply to the industry must be positively sloped; if there are a given number of people in a specific occupation and the firms in a particular industry desire more of that type, they must lure these people away by higher wages.[4]

The situation is similar when more than one industry uses a particular type of labor. If output is to be expanded in one or more of these industries, the wage of workers must increase in order to bid them away from other industries or occupations. When we consider the opportunities for workers in other industries or occupations, the supply of labor to an industry can be assumed to be upward sloping or at least horizontal (if the industry is quite small relative to the total demand), even if many workers in the work force have negatively sloped individual labor supply curves.

Economics in the News

Labor Shortages Spark Ways to Increase Productivity

The U.S. Department of Labor is predicting labor shortages in a number of occupations and labor force sectors by the year 2000. In any market, a shortage means there is excess demand. In the case of labor, there are unfilled job openings at the going wage. The obvious solution to a shortage is to raise wages. This is exactly what McDonald's is doing (*The Wall Street Journal,* June 1, 1989, p. A1), paying over $6 per hour as the starting wage in some cities. As another example, other companies are paying sign-up bonuses for experienced word processors to switch employers.

But some employers are using more subtle tactics. They are trying to make better use of the underemployed. The underemployed tend to be minority and female workers who are not employed to their full potential. Ortho Pharmaceutical, for example, surveyed their black employees and their female employees and found that most were in positions beneath their qualifications. In economic terms, their *MRP* was underestimated, according to Ortho, by about 20 percent (*Newsweek,* May 14, 1990, p. 37). The real *MRP* schedule lay to the right of that estimated. After discovering this problem, Ortho hired consultants to help overcome it. All Ortho executives and most employees attended workshops to help them understand on-the-job diversity.

Better use of minority workers is imperative for the future. According to the U.S. Department of Labor, native white men presently make up only 45 percent of the labor force. During the 1990s this number will decline to 39 percent. Only 15 percent of the

(continued)

---

[4]There are two possible exceptions, each leading to a horizontal industry supply-of-labor curve. First, if the industry is small, or if it uses only very small quantities of labor, its effect on the market may be negligible. That is, the industry may be to the market what a perfectly competitive firm is to the industry. Second, if there is unemployment in the particular type of labor under consideration, the supply of labor to all industries may be perfectly elastic up to the point of full employment. Thereafter, the supply curve would rise. The latter is a disequilibrium situation not encompassed in the analysis here.

people presently entering the work force are white men. As a matter of business survival, employers are being forced to overcome job discrimination.

A tight labor market is expected by firms in the service sector. Historically, this has been the sector of lowest productivity; productivity measured as output per worker or average product. Not only is labor about half as productive in nonmanufacturing as in manufacturing, but productivity growth is slower. In manufacturing, productivity is currently growing at about 3 percent a year. In nonmanufacturing, where four fifths of all workers are employed, growth is about 0.6 percent a year. Relative levels and growth of productivity are mainly due to the capital/labor ratio, which is lower in the service sector. Because the service sector is more labor intensive, labor shortages are likely to be greater in that area when shortages arise.

It is in the service industries that effective ways to overcome job bias must be found. Those companies that do it best will have a competitive advantage. Also, in these industries, new technologies will be used to increase capital and reduce labor. McDonald's, for example, is trying out a grill that cooks hamburgers on both sides at once, a device that reduces labor time per burger. Computer systems at banks are being installed to allow tellers to process checks in half the present time. Manor Care Inc., an operator of hotels, is cutting work forces by 13 percent with better-designed facilities. Rooms are designed to take 30 percent less time to clean.

Let us return to the determinants of the supply curves for labor. As population increases and its age composition changes, as people migrate from one area to another, and as education and reeducation enable people to shift occupations, rather dramatic changes can occur in the supply of various types of labor at various locations throughout the nation. These changes represent shifts in supply curves and are quite independent of their slopes. To describe the supply curve for a well-defined labor market, we must assume that certain parameters are held constant. In particular, some of the parameters underlying a labor supply curve are the population size, age, and education along with the preferences of members of the labor force, which will influence the proportion of the population working and the labor-leisure choice made by individuals.

Given any labor supply curve, the time period of adjustment after a wage change is one of the most important factors in influencing the elasticity of supply. If the salary in a particular occupation rises, people may choose to enter that occupation, but acquiring the needed skills takes time. Therefore, in the short run, supply may be quite inelastic. However, given the necessary period of adjustment, an increase in the relative wages in a particular occupation will attract additional people into that occupation, and supply will become more elastic.

In summary, we can say almost unequivocally that, except for the case of an individual worker, the supply of labor to a specific occupation is upward sloping. This positive slope reflects the fact that, at least in the long run, higher wages or benefits must be paid in order to attract more persons into the occupation. The longer the period of adjustment, the more people are induced to enter. The same thing applies to the supply of a particular type of labor in a specific area—city, state, region. When you hear people complaining that a city can't get enough teachers, or a county can't get enough doctors, or a college can't get enough professors, or a community can't get enough garbage collectors—and these are things you hear frequently—you should be able to suggest a solution. This is not to say the solution will be acceptable to those paying the bill. What people who make such statements generally mean is they cannot get enough of a particular type of worker at the going price.

17.6   Market Equilibrium

The demand and supply schedules of a variable productive service jointly determine its market equilibrium price. We have discussed the demand and supply curves of a variable input separately. By combining the curves, we can derive a market equilibrium for input markets.

17.6.1   Market Equilibrium for Variable Inputs

In Figure 17–9, D and S are the demand and supply curves for a variable input. Their intersection at point E determines the equilibrium price, w, and quantity demanded and supplied, v, in a particular input market.

If the price of the variable input (say, labor) exceeds w, more people wish to work in this occupation than employers are willing to hire at that wage. Since there is a surplus of workers, wages are bid down by the workers until the surplus is eliminated. If the wage rate is below w, producers want to employ more workers than are willing to work at that wage. Employers, faced with a "shortage" of labor, bid the wage rate up to w. The analysis is similar to that in Chapter 2. The only features unique to this analysis are the methods of determining the demand for and supply of variable productive services. Because input demand is based on the marginal revenue product of the input, the theoretical derivation of this equilibrium is labeled marginal productivity theory.

17.6.2   The Full-Wage Equilibrium

Earlier in this chapter, we spoke of the effect of fringe benefits—either externally imposed benefits such as social security payments paid by employers, or voluntary benefits such as improved working conditions or low-cost group insurance plans. Employers simply consider the added cost of the benefits as an addition to wages, and they adjust their use of labor accordingly. From that analysis, you may have the impression that employers absorb the entire cost of such benefits—that the only effect on employees is that fewer workers are hired, but those hired receive higher total wage rates (i.e., wages plus the value of the benefits). That is only part of the story. We neglected the supply side of the market in the analysis.

Remember that demand and supply determine the wage rates in markets. If working conditions in a particular market improve, or if there are additional fringe benefits paid to workers in this market, jobs in that market become more desirable relative to jobs in markets in which conditions do not change. The increased desirability of jobs in the market with improved working conditions will, at least in

Figure 17–9   Market Equilibrium Determination of the Price of a Variable Productive Service

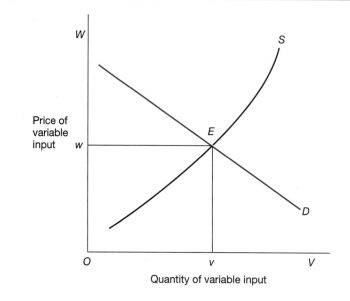

the long run, increase the supply of labor to that market. As you know, the increase in supply will drive down wages in that market relative to what they would have been in the absence of the increased desirability of the occupation. Thus, at least some of the cost of improved conditions is passed on to the workers involved. The proportion of the cost passed on depends on demand and supply elasticities and how the curves shift.

Let us consider the case of the northern Canadian mining and smelting industry. This industry mines and processes, among other things, zinc, nickel, gold, and lead. The mines and smelters are in rather desolate parts of the country, and working conditions have historically been harsh. Wages have had to be rather high to lure workers away from other more desirable occupations and geographical areas.

Recently, laws have been passed to make working conditions more amenable. Such laws are pollution, dust, and safety regulations in mines and smelters. Also, in order to attract labor, mining companies have voluntarily improved working conditions in other ways—improved housing, community improvements, and so on. These fringe benefits should be viewed as part of the total, or full, wage income for each worker. What is the effect of the additional benefits on the paid wage rate? Who really paid for fringe additions to the wages?

We can use Figure 17–10 to analyze the effect of fringe benefits on the market wage. Let D_1 be the total demand for labor in the northern Canadian mining industry. This demand reflects the relation between money wages only and the quantity of labor hired. That is, the wage rate on the vertical axis is the money wage rate and does not include the value of amenities. As noted above, employers simply add the cost of fringe benefits to the market-determined wage rate in choosing the amount of labor hired.

Figure 17–10 Effect of Fringe Benefits

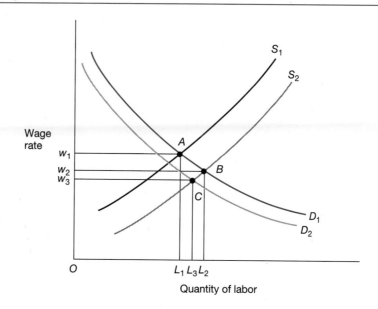

Let S_1 be the supply of labor to the industry prior to the imposition of additional benefits. Again, this supply is the relation between money wages and labor supplied; it is obviously upward sloping. The equilibrium wage and quantity of labor hired are, respectively, w_1 and L_1 at point A. Now, let fringe benefits be added. These benefits would be improved work conditions, such as added insurance benefits and improved housing. Suppose, just to take a somewhat extreme example, that the government absorbs all of the costs of such benefits. In this case, since the employer does not bear the added cost of hiring workers, we would not see a downward shift in input demand.

But, because of improved working conditions, the supply would increase say to S_2. That is, at each wage rate, more workers than before would be willing to work in the industry because of improved working conditions. Even though government pays for all of the fringe benefits, the wage rate falls to w_2. Workers themselves effectively absorb some of the cost of the benefits in the wage difference $w_1 - w_2$. Of course, the amount of labor hired increases to L_2. The equilibrium is at point B.

To be more realistic, if the companies themselves pay for most of the added benefits, they would be willing to hire fewer workers at each wage rate. That is, each worker costs more because of the added benefits. In this case, the demand for labor, D_1, would shift downward and to the left to D_2, resulting in even lower wages than w_2 and in fewer than L_2 workers being hired at point C (L_3 workers are hired at wage w_3).

Therefore, it is not necessarily the employer who absorbs all of the cost of fringe benefits. If the market works at all, the employees bear some part of the cost in the form of wages below the rate that would exist in the absence of benefits. The extent that wages are reduced because of fringe benefits depends on several factors: (1) the valuation by workers of the fringe benefits, reflected by the extent to which supply increases; (2) the elasticity of supply; (3) the extent to which demand decreases; and (4) the elasticity of demand.

To some extent, this analysis might explain why, in the absence of regulations and labor unions, wages differ from industry to industry. Other things being equal, if the wage rate for the same skill is higher in one industry than in another, workers would leave the low-wage industry and increase the supply of labor to the high-wage industry. In this way, wages would rise in the previously low-wage industry and fall in the previously high-wage industry, until wages were the same in both. Therefore, in the absence of external interference, the wages should be approximately equal in the two industries for equal skills. If, over the long run, one industry continues to pay higher wages than another, and there are no external interferences, then the working conditions for some reason or other—location, job risk, amenities, and so on—must differ between industries. The attractiveness of one industry relative to another affects relative wage rates for equal levels of skill.

17.7   Effects of Labor Unions and Minimum Wages

In many industries, workers belong to a labor union. A labor union is an organization that represents the interests of its member workers and supplies the labor of its members to potential employers. So far the theoretical discussion may seem far removed from the dramatic world of General Motors versus the United Automobile Workers. Indeed it is. A thorough understanding of labor markets requires one or more courses, not chapters in a textbook. With respect to unions, there is a substantial body of theory concerning the collective bargaining process, and an understanding of labor markets also requires an extensive knowledge of the institutional framework that labor unions and businesses operate within. This type of knowledge must be acquired in "applied" courses or contexts, just as other applied courses supplement other parts of microeconomic theory.

We can, however, give you some insight into the effect of unions on wages and employment by using the simple theory of labor supply and demand. The basic fundamentals of what unions can and cannot do are easily developed within this general framework. Furthermore, we can use this theory to analyze the effect of external interferences in the labor market, such as the imposition of a minimum wage.

17.7.1   Labor Unions

Consider any labor market with a positively sloped supply of labor. If the workers in this market are unionized, the union bargaining representative can raise wages in two ways. First, the representative could set a wage rate above equilibrium and guarantee the availability of workers at this price (up to a limit) while offering no workers at a lower price. Second, the union could limit the number of workers below the equilibrium number that would be hired in the absence of a union. This limitation, in effect, allows the market wage to rise.

Figure 17–11   Effects of a Labor Union in a Perfectly Competitive Labor Market

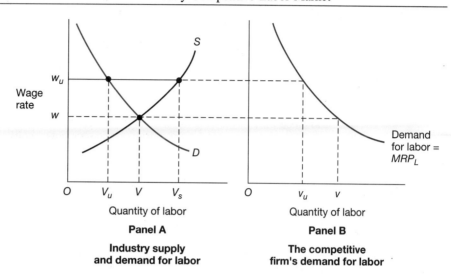

Panel A

**Industry supply
and demand for labor**

Panel B

**The competitive
firm's demand for labor**

Consider the first strategy. Suppose the labor market in question is perfectly competitive, so there are a large number of purchasers of this type of labor, and there is no union. The situation is depicted in Panel A, Figure 17–11, where D and S are the industry demand for and supply of labor, respectively. The market equilibrium wage is w, and V units of labor are employed. Each individual firm (Panel B), accordingly, employs v units. Next, suppose the labor market is unionized. If the union does not attempt to raise wages, the situation might remain as it is. However, gaining wage increases or other benefits is the reason for the existence of unions. Therefore, suppose the bargaining agency sets w_u as the wage rate in Panel A at the market level. Firms can now hire all of the labor they want at the rate w_u, as long as the industry does not hire beyond V_s on the labor supply curve. A total of V_u (where w_u equals demand) units of labor are employed, with each firm hiring v_u units. The result is an increase in wages and a decline in employment.

The fact that the imposed increase in wages causes a reduction in the amount of labor does not necessarily mean a union cannot benefit its members. If the demand for labor is inelastic, an increase in the wage rate will result in an increase in total wages paid to all workers, even though the number of workers employed declines somewhat. If the union can somehow equitably divide the proceeds of V_u employed workers among the V_s workers who want to work, perhaps by letting the workers work a shorter work week, all the workers will be made better off. The other side of the coin should be considered, however. Suppose the demand for labor is elastic; then total wage receipts will decline, and the union cannot compensate the workers who are unemployed from the increase in wage rates.

The second way for a union to raise wages is simply to limit the number of persons in an occupation. In terms of Figure 17–11, if the union could limit the number of workers to V_u and somehow prevent nonunion workers from working in the industry, pure market forces would cause the wage rate to be bid up to w_u.

Thus, limiting entry is an alternative way of raising wages. The problem here, of course, is that nonunion members can offer to work at lower wages and break the union. For this reason, the union must obtain, through threat of strike, boycott, or some other method, a contract with the firms preventing the hiring of nonunion labor. Or the union could get government to issue a limited number of licenses to work in the occupation, thereby restricting entry. The more difficult and time consuming it is to get a license, the more entry is restricted and the higher are wage rates. In either case, under reasonably competitive conditions, wage gains can be obtained only at the expense of reduced employment.

This analysis does not mean that unions deliberately set out to cause unemployment. They do considerable lobbying in Congress to restore full employment by expansionary monetary and fiscal policy and continually support full employment as an economic policy. The fact remains that wage gains in a specific industry are obtained at the expense of employment in that industry.

Economics in the News

Union Membership Is Declining

In 1973, 25 percent of the private-sector workers were members of unions in the United States. This percentage steadily dropped for 15 years, until in 1988 only 12 percent of the work force was unionized, and the trend continues toward a work force that is even less unionized. By the year 2000, the proportion of the private sector that will be unionized is predicted to fall below 5 percent (see *The Wall Street Journal,* April 17, 1990, p. A1).

What are the causes of this decline? Economists Stephen Bronars and Donald Deere say that the most important cause is reduced employment in unionized industries relative to increased employment in nonunionized fields. They argue that this shift in employment accounts for 95 percent of the downward trend. As this trend has been taking place, unionized workers have increased their earnings over their nonunionized counterparts. In 1973, a union worker earned 14.6 percent more than a nonunion worker at a similar job. In 1988, the difference widened to 20.4 percent. Thus, part of the reason for declining employment in unionized sectors of the economy may be due to the relative increase in wages.

17.7.2   Minimum Wages

A minimum wage is simply a floor price imposed above the intersection of supply and demand by government. The effect of a minimum wage rate is similar to the effect of a union. Those who retain their jobs in industries covered by the minimum wages are better off with the higher wage. Those who lose their jobs (i.e., the "surplus" labor) are worse off. These people must find work in other industries at less attractive wages. Therefore, a minimum wage makes some people better off and others worse off. The question is, who benefits and who loses?

Figure 17–12   The Effect of a Minimum Wage

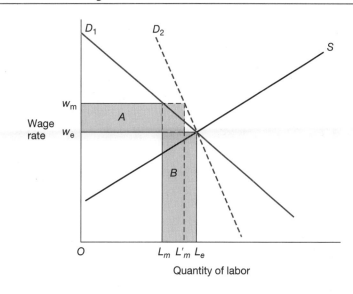

The amount of unemployment caused by a minimum wage depends on the elasticity of demand. To show this relation, let D_1 and S in Figure 17–12 be, respectively, the demand and supply of labor. In the absence of a minimum wage, equilibrium would occur at a wage of w_e with L_e units of labor employed. Once a minimum wage is imposed, you can see from the figure that the minimum wage of w_m reduces employment to L_m.

Although unemployment is created, labor as a sector can gain from the minimum wage. In other words, it is possible for labor to collectively receive total wages greater than before the minimum wage was imposed. Whether this happens depends on the elasticity of demand for workers. The minimum wage increases the total wage bill by area A in Figure 17–12, but decreases it by area B. The labor force as a whole gains if $A > B$ but loses if $B > A$. From Chapter 3 and the definition of elasticity, you know that when demand is inelastic, area A will be larger than area B, and it will be smaller if demand is elastic. It is easy to see that if demand is more inelastic, as shown by the demand curve D_2, employment would fall by only $L'_m L_e$, which is less than $L_m L_e$. Area B would become smaller, and area A would become larger by the area shaded in color. Labor as a sector therefore benefits more from a minimum wage as demand becomes less elastic.

Of course, even if the total wage bill does increase and labor as a sector is better off, those who are forced into unemployment are worse off unless those who work make transfer payments to those who are unemployed. If all workers were homogeneous, as in our theory, the impact would be randomly distributed. If, as in the real world, workers differ in productivity and in employers' feelings toward them, the least-productive workers and those most disadvantaged in their "reputation" with employers are the ones released.

Table 17–3   Input Supply and Marginal Factor Cost

(1) Price of Labor or Wage Rate	(2) Quantity of Labor Supplied	(3) Total Wage Bill	(4) Marginial Factor Cost	(5) Marginal Revenue Product
$10	5	50		
12	6	72	$22	$70
14	7	98	26	50
16	8	128	30	40
18	9	162	34	36
20	10	200	38	34
22	11	242	42	31

17.8   Monopsony: Monopoly in the Input Market

We have assumed thus far that firms, whether perfect competitors or monopolists, believe they can acquire as many units of an input as they want at the going market price. In other words, no single firm has a perceptible effect on the price of the input. This obviously is not the case in all situations. There are sometimes only a few purchasers (and in the limit one) of a productive service. When only a few firms purchase an input, each will affect input price by changing input use. We need to develop new tools to analyze the behavior of such firms.

For analytical simplicity, we consider only a single buyer of an input, called a *monopsonist*. However, the analytical principles are the same when there are a few buyers of an input, called oligopsonists.

17.8.1   Marginal Factor Cost under Monopsony

Since a monopsonist is the sole buyer of a productive service, the supply curve of the input is upward sloping. This means that in order to hire more of an input, the monopsonist must raise the price of that input. Since each unit of the input hired receives the same price, in order to increase the use of an input, the monopsonist must pay all units an increased price. Marginal cost is not simply the price of an additional unit of input purchased, but it is this price plus the increased payment to the units of input already employed. The total additional payment is called marginal factor cost.

Table 17–3 helps to clarify this point. Columns (1) and (2) indicate the labor supply to the monopsonist. Column (3) shows the total expense of hiring each amount of labor, and column (4) shows the additional expense of increasing labor by one unit. The firm can hire five workers at $10 an hour, six at $12, seven at $14, and so on. If five workers are presently employed, then to hire an additional worker, the wage rate must rise to $12 an hour, as shown in column (1). With five workers, the hourly wage bill is $50 an hour; with six, it is $72, as shown in column (3). Hiring the additional unit costs an additional $22 an hour, even though the wage rate rises by only $2. The additional worker costs $12, but increasing the

Figure 17–13   Supply and Marginal Factor Cost of Labor From the Numbers in Table 17–3

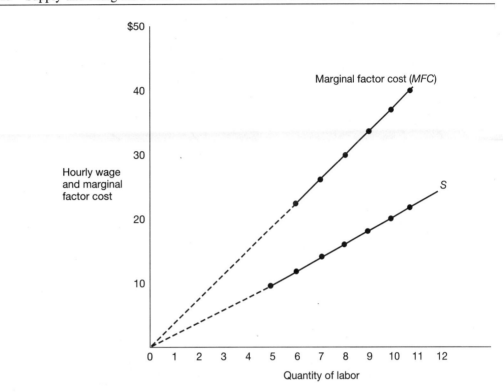

wage of the previous five workers from $10 to $12 increases expenses by 5 · $2 = $10. The sum is $12 + $10 = $22. We used the same analysis to derive each entry in column (4). You can see that column (4) shows the marginal increase in the total wage bill shown in column (3). Considering the addition of one unit of an input, the increased wage cost is the marginal factor cost (*MFC*). It includes the price paid to the additional unit plus the increase that must be paid to the units already employed. For every unit except the first, the marginal factor cost exceeds price.

Figure 17–13 provides a graph of the labor-cost numbers in Table 17–3. The supply curve *S* shows that to hire an additional worker the hourly wage must increase by $2 per hour. But every worker must receive this new wage, so the total cost of another worker must include the additional payment to the other employees. In the figure, the *MFC* schedule lies above the supply schedule. The two schedules spread farther apart as more workers are hired.

A more general version of the supply curve of a variable input and the marginal factor cost curve are shown graphically in Figure 17–14. The marginal factor cost always exceeds the supply price at all employment levels except the first unit. The marginal factor cost curve is positively sloped, lies to the left of the supply curve, and typically rises more rapidly than supply.

Figure 17–14 Marginal Factor Cost

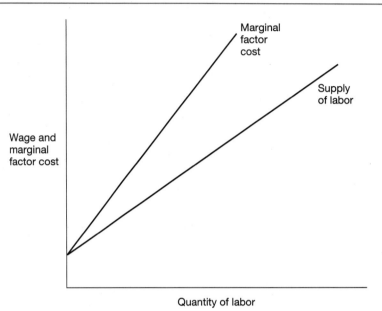

Definition

The marginal factor cost of an input to a monopsonist is the increase in total cost (and in total variable cost) attributable to the addition of one more unit of the variable productive agent.

17.8.2 Price and Employment under Monopsony

The relevant curves for price determination under monopsony are the *MFC* and the *MRP* curves, assuming there is one variable input. Suppose a firm is confronted with a positively sloped supply-of-input curve and the higher marginal factor cost curve. The situation is illustrated in Table 17–3 and in Figure 17–15. Using this table and graph, we will prove the following:

Principle

A profit-maximizing monopsonist will employ a variable productive service until the point is reached where the marginal factor cost equals its marginal revenue product. The price of the input is determined by the corresponding point on its supply curve.

The proof of this principle follows immediately from the definitions of marginal revenue product and marginal factor cost. Marginal revenue product is the addition to total revenue attributable to the addition of one unit of the variable input; the marginal factor cost is the addition to total cost resulting from the employment of

Figure 17–15   Price and Employment under Monopsony

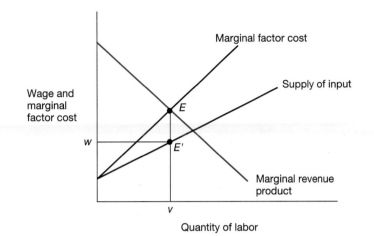

an additional unit. As long as marginal revenue product exceeds the marginal factor cost, profit can be augmented by expanding input use. On the other hand, if the marginal factor cost of an input exceeds its marginal revenue product, profit is less, or the loss greater, than it would be if fewer units of the input were employed. Consequently, profit is maximized by employing that quantity of the variable service for which the marginal factor cost equals marginal revenue product.

For example, assume only one variable input in Table 17–3. The marginal revenue product schedule for 6 through 11 workers is given in column (5). Each worker through the ninth adds more to hourly revenue (*MRP*) than is added to hourly cost (*MFC*). Thereafter, workers 10 and 11 add more to cost than to revenue. The firm hires nine workers.

17.2   *Applying the Theory*

In Figure 17–13 use Table 17–3 to graph the *MRP* in this specific case. Where does the *MRP* curve cross the *MFC* schedule? Does it confirm that nine workers are hired. If part-time labor could be hired, approximately how many workers are employed?

In the continuous case, the equality of *MRP* and *MFC* occurs at point *E* in Figure 17–15, and *v* units of the service are accordingly employed. At this point, the supply-of-input curve becomes particularly relevant; *v* units of the variable productive agent are associated with point *E'* on the supply-of-input curve. At this point, *v* units can be hired at a wage of *w* per unit. Therefore, *w* is the equilibrium input price corresponding to market equilibrium employment *v*. Whether the firm is a monopolist or perfectly competitive in the product market, it employs the variable input until the marginal value of the last unit equals the marginal factor cost of the input.

Figure 17–16   Competition, Monopoly, and Monopsony in the Labor Market

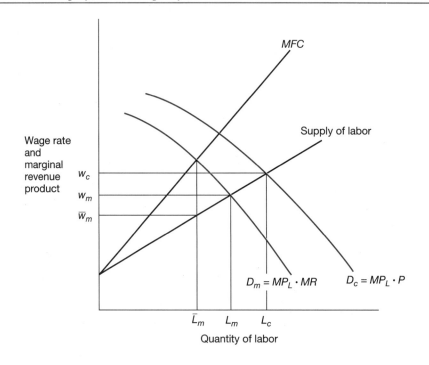

Recall from Section 17.3 that at a given wage rate, monopoly in the commodity market leads to fewer resources being employed in the input market relative to perfect competition. Each productive service is paid $MRP = MP \cdot MR$, which is less than $MRP = MP \cdot P$ for a perfect competitor, because marginal revenue is less than price. It can now be shown that when the input side of the market is also a monopsony, still fewer resources are employed than would be in the absence of monopsony. Remember, we are dealing with only one input, and the monopoly faces the same cost curves as the competitive industry.

Figure 17–16 illustrates how monopsony on the demand side reduces employment. As before, let D_c be a competitive industry's demand for labor, the single variable input. D_m is the monopolist's marginal revenue product curve for labor, under the assumption of an identical cost structure. The competitive industry equates the supply of labor with D_c; it hires L_c units of labor at a wage w_c. If the monopoly faced the same supply curve, it would hire L_m, which, of course, is less than L_c, and pay a wage of w_m. If the monopoly is also a monopsony, the firm reduces the amount of labor hired even more, to $\bar{L}_m$. The monopsony also pays a lower wage. The wage falls to $\bar{w}_m$. Let us note that, as in most comparisons of monopoly and competition, these conclusions are drawn under quite restrictive assumptions. It is likely that costs will differ between monopoly and competition, and this could reverse the relative positioning of the D_m and D_c schedules. In such cases, we could not make unambiguous comparisons between monopoly and competition.

Figure 17–17 Bilateral Monopoly

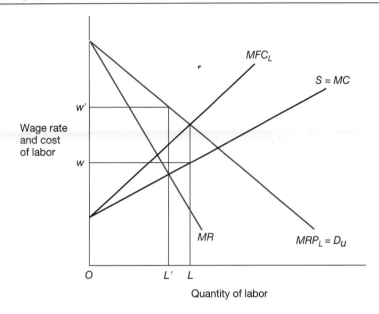

17.8.3   Bilateral Monopoly

An interesting aspect of monopsony behavior arises when the *seller* of the input is a monopoly. The input market is organized so that a single buyer of labor confronts a single seller of that resource, say a union. This situation, where a monopsonist hires a resource from a monopolist, is called bilateral monopoly. Examples of bilateral monopoly would be the United Auto Workers confronting General Motors, or, on a smaller scale, the only textile mill in a small town bargaining with a local union. This market structure yields no single equilibrium price or quantity. We can establish theoretical bounds between which the price and quantity will range, but the final results depend on the bargaining and political powers of the negotiating parties.

Figure 17–17 helps establish the bounds between which price and quantity will fall. To the union, the demand curve for its labor is the $MRP_L = D_u$ curve of the monopsonist. The union takes this as given. If this is the demand faced by the union, or labor monopolist, the marginal revenue curve can be easily derived. It is shown as MR in the figure. Suppose the union behaves as a profit maximizer and seeks to maximize returns to its organization, given its labor supply curve S, which represents the marginal cost of hiring another worker.[5] The union will set $MR = S$, offer L' units of labor to the single employer, and ask for wage w'.

---

[5]In Chapter 14, we showed that a monopolist does not have a supply curve. We assume, in this case, that the supply curve is provided by its union members, and the union takes it as given. In other words, the supply curve is outside its control.

We have already discussed the way the monopsonist behaves. It maximizes profits where $MFC_L = MRP_L$; thus, it wants to hire L units of labor and pay a wage of w. The equilibrium wage rate will lie somewhere between w and w', and the equilibrium amount of labor between L' and L.

We can illustrate how bargaining eventually determines the equilibrium wage and employment level. In Figure 17–17, the bargaining could begin with the union refusing to supply more than L' units of labor and the employer refusing to pay a wage higher than w. Then, if the employer wants more workers, a higher wage must be paid as part of the bargain. Employment moves closer to L units for the employer, and the wage rate moves closer to w' for the union. However, it might be the situation that $L < L'$. That is, the monopsonist wants to hire fewer workers than the union wants to sell and wants them at a lower wage.[6] In this situation, the bargaining position of the union is weakened. It wants both more workers hired and higher wages. No longer is a *quid pro quo* exchange viable.

17.9   Summary

We have covered a number of topics and developed several theories on markets for variable inputs in this chapter.

The most important concept about markets for variable inputs is that a profit-maximizing employer continues to use more of the input as long as marginal benefit is greater than marginal cost. Marginal benefit is the marginal revenue product (MRP) of the input, which gives the contribution to total revenue made by the last unit of input. For a perfectly competitive firm $MRP = MP \cdot P$, where MP is the marginal product of the input and P is the market price of the product sold by the firm. This price is taken as given. For a monopoly $MRP = MP \cdot MR$, where MR is the marginal revenue from selling another unit of output.

The marginal cost of a variable input is described by its supply curve. In many markets, an employer is a small purchaser of the input. For all practical purposes, it can buy as much of the input it wants at the going market price. In some markets the employer buys relatively large quantities of the input. Employers that buy so much of an input that they affect the price of the input are called monopsonies. When a monopsony hires an additional unit of input, marginal cost is the price of the last unit of input plus the incremental price hike in all the units currently employed. This sum gives rise to a marginal factor cost (MFC) schedule. A monopsony producer continues to purchase the input as long as $MRP > MFC$ and stops when $MRP = MFC$. The payment to the input is determined by the supply schedule of the input.

The sale of the labor input can be monopolized through a union. Any variable input however could be monopolized. Bauxite, for example, is an input in the production of aluminum, and for many years its sale was monopolized. The monopoly provision of an input is no different than the sale of any monopolized good. The seller operates where $MR = MC$ for the input. A monopoly seller of an input

---

[6]This would happen if the demand curve in Figure 17–17 was more inelastic, the supply curve more elastic, or both.

who sells to a monopoly buyer (monopsony) is in a bilateral monopoly market. Theory cannot predict the equilibrium amount of input employed, nor its equilibrium price.

We should end the summary with a warning. Do not simply draw the conclusion that input demand theory says that all workers get what they "deserve" or what they "ought to get." The theory says no such thing. It is a positive predictive or explanatory theory. It enables us to predict the effect of external forces, such as a change in the minimum wage or the unionization of an industry. It enables us to explain differences in wage rates among occupations. It does not allow us to say whether such differences are desirable from a social point of view. We cannot state that a distribution of income based on marginal productivity is somehow more "just" than any other distribution.

Many decades ago, economists got something of a bad name because of such moral judgments. People begin with a specific amount of resources that they own—capital, labor skill, social position, and so on. Who is to say that the original distribution of resources is somehow more just than any other?

On the other hand, we can't say that some other method of allocation or distribution may be more just, or may give people more closely what they deserve. We merely want to emphasize that variable input theory doesn't say anything about deservedness. It simply explains to a great extent why people receive what they receive. We can only say that society, or some part of it, believes that the resources owned by individuals are worth a certain amount. We hear and read that someone or some group deserves more income. For example, in a Wyoming newspaper (*Laramie Boomerang,* May 5, 1991) a reader wrote to the editor, "We pay professional athletes millions of dollars in salaries to 'entertain' us and some of our teachers get less than $20,000 a year to educate the future doctors, scientists, lawyers. . . . I don't think this is fair and I think it's time to change the system and put things right." In another Wyoming newspaper (*Casper Star Tribune,* June 15, 1991) a Jackson doctor is quoted as saying, "A pediatrician makes $50,000 to $60,000 a year. Many surgical specialists make 10 times that in net terms. That plainly is unfair. Those are inequities that plainly need to be corrected." Whether we agree with these opinions or not, our theory, and we, as economists, can say nothing about deservedness. Professional athletes and doctors and others receive their income because someone thinks the return from hiring them will be greater than, or at least as much as, the amount paid out. That is all we, as economists, can say.

Answers to *Applying the Theory*

17.1 The firm should hire four workers. At $75 per worker the supply schedule intersects the MRP_L curve at two points, 1.5 workers and four workers. But at 1.5 workers the MRP_L curve is everywhere below $75. The firm is taking a loss on these workers. To hire the second, third, and fourth worker, the first must be put to work. All workers are identical; it is not the case that the first is not as good as the others. The figure shows that to be productive above $75 per worker, it takes more than one worker. To produce well, it takes some team effort.

17.2 After graphing the MRP_L curve in Figure 17–13, nine workers are hired, because for the 10th the MRP_L curve goes below the MFC schedule. If part-time labor could be hired, it appears that 9.5 workers would be employed at a wage of about $19.

Technical Problems

1. Analyze some of the effects of a federal minimum wage. How do these effects differ from a state or local minimum wage?

2. Consider a firm using one variable factor of production. Table E.17–1 gives information concerning the production function [columns (2) and (3)], demand for output [columns (1) and (2)], and supply of labor [columns (3) and (4)] for the firm. Not all information will be used in each section of the problem. Add to the table any columns you wish.

   a. Suppose the firm is a perfect competitor in the output market and also a perfect competitor in the labor market. Draw a graph showing the demand for labor if the price of output is $3.50 per unit.

   b. How much labor would the firm use if the wage is $10.50?

   c. Suppose, instead, that the firm is a monopsonist in the factor market facing a supply curve for labor given in columns (3) and (4). This firm is a perfect competitor in the output market and the price of output is $3.50 per unit. How much labor would be used? What would be the wage? Explain your answers and graph your solution, showing on the graph how you got your answers.

   d. Now suppose the firm is a monopolist in the output market and a monopsonist in the input market where the demand for the output is given in columns (1) and (2) and the supply of labor is given in columns (3) and (4). What would be the profit-maximizing amount of labor used by this firm? What would be the market wage? Explain your answer and graph your solution.

3. Consider the monopolist-monopsonist shown graphically in Figure E.17–1. Labor is the only variable input.

   a. Show the equilibrium quantity of labor hired and the wage rate.

   b. We emphasized in the text that in the typically assumed case, a union that forces a wage increase will cause some unemployment. Suppose you represent such a union for this firm's employees. You can set any wage that you wish. In effect, you can simply set a wage and say to the firm, "You can

Table E.17–1

(1) Output Price ($ per unit)	(2) Sales (units)	(3) Workers Employed (units)	(4) Wage Rate ($ per unit)
10.50	5	5	4.00
5.36	10	6	4.25
5.00	14	7	4.50
4.00	17	8	4.75
3.00	19	9	5.00
2.60	20	10	5.25

Figure E.17–1

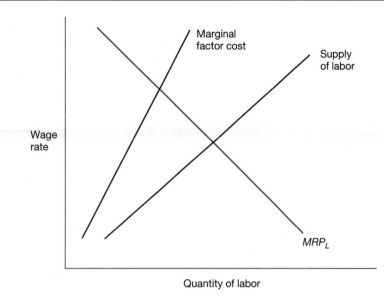

hire all the labor you wish at this wage rate, but below this wage you get none." The wage is given to the firm by you.

(1) Show on the graph the highest wage that you can set and cause no less labor to be hired than was hired in part *a* of the question.

(2) Show how much labor would want to work for the firm at this wage but would not be hired.

(3) Show the wage that maximizes the amount of labor hired. (At this wage, everyone who wants to work for this firm at the wage you set will be hired.)

Note: This problem shows a minor exception to the point made in the text. The same result could occur from a minimum-wage law. But the analysis in the text generally holds.

4. Explain why the demand of a competitive industry for an input is less elastic than the sum of the demands of all the firms in the industry.

5. Monopolization of an industry will reduce the demand for an input but will not change wages unless the monopoly has monopsony power. Comment.

6. What would be the equilibrium marginal product for an input that is free to a perfectly competitive firm; that is, the input costs the firm nothing?

7. After the first unit of an input hired, why is the marginal factor cost of that input to a monopsonist greater than the supply price of the input?

8. The demand for a factor of production depends to some extent on the demand for the products produced by the input. Explain the connection.

9. "Unskilled workers have low wages because their productivity is low." Is this precise? Give a more complete explanation.

10. The wage rate is solely determined by the marginal productivity of labor. In any case, the marginal productivity theory says that all workers get what they deserve. Comment critically.

Analytical Problems

1. You are attempting to get a labor union started. What conditions would make your job easier? What would make your job harder? Analyze the case of an individual firm, an industry, and an entire trade or profession.

2. Suppose that a particular firm in a competitive industry had a bigoted manager who refused to hire workers of a particular race, even though these workers are as productive as those of other races.
   a. Under what conditions could the firm so discriminate?
   b. Under what conditions could it not?
   c. Would a monopolist be more likely to discriminate? Why or why not?

3. There is a proposal that government should provide an incentive payment to firms that hire unskilled handicapped workers. The payment would be a fixed amount per unskilled handicapped worker per hour used. How would this effect the wage and number of unskilled handicapped people hired? If the payment is a lump sum regardless of the number of people hired, how would this affect your answer?

4. The fact that industries must pay a higher wage to get workers to work more means that none of these workers can have a negatively sloped supply of labor. Analyze.

5. Theft is an occupation. How would each of the following circumstances affect the number of thieves and their remuneration. Think in terms of *MRP* and labor supply.
   a. Higher minimum wages and broader coverage.
   b. Technological advances in the burglar-alarm industry.
   c. Longer sentences for theft.
   d. Economic prosperity.
   e. Recession.
   f. Laws restricting hours of work.

6. A member of Congress was quoted as saying that an increase in the minimum wage will not cause unemployment, since it will raise labor productivity. Comment critically.

7. There is a "shock theory" of minimum wage laws. They supposedly "shock" inefficient firms into becoming more efficient. The evidence is that after increases in minimum wages, firms purchase new capital equipment to use with labor. Comment. (Hint: Recall our theory of production.)

8. In many cities, the wages of school teachers are the same in all schools for teachers with similar experience. Why do schools in the wealthier areas of the city frequently get the best teachers?

9. A state government spent $3 million of state funds to send units of the National Guard to a riot-torn city. What is the relevant economic cost of sending these troops? What other items should be included?

10. Does it strike you as wrong that we do not compensate the brave men or women who climb a utility pole in a storm to restore electricity at least as much as we compensate the band leader on a television show? What about the nurses, paramedics, and enlisted military personnel who protect our lives and property? Are not these functions of more value to society? Comment.

11. Does Roger Clemons, a well-known baseball pitcher, make more than a high school teacher because he has more talent?

12. Compare a person's decision to increase his or her human capital by obtaining additional education or training with a firm's decision to invest in physical capital.

13. Professional basketball teams draft the top college players each year. If the drafted player wishes to play the sport—at least in the United States—he must sign with the team that drafts him. Most of the better players have agents. How does the theory of bilateral monopoly apply in this case? How are the beginning salaries determined? Would either party benefit if such a draft were declared illegal? Explain.

14. Some people say that, in general, firms do not spend enough time training their employees because management believes the employees will be bid away by other firms at higher salaries after they have been trained, so the training expenditure is allegedly wasted. Analyze this argument.

CHAPTER 18

Demand for Fixed Inputs: Theory of Investment

18.1 Introduction

In Chapter 17, when we discussed input markets in terms of labor and other variable inputs, we emphasized that the theoretical tools developed in that chapter apply to all inputs. Conceptually, the firm always maximizes profits by setting the marginal factor cost of an input equal to its marginal revenue product. When the firm is not a monopsony, marginal factor cost is the input price, and, when it is a perfect competitor in the final goods market, marginal revenue product is $MRP_i = P \cdot MP_i$ for the ith input. Generally, when a firm has market power, marginal revenue product is $MRP_i = MR \cdot MP_i$.

In this chapter, we focus on some additional considerations involved when inputs yield a stream of services over time. Typically, the purchase of such durable inputs is called investment. Examples of investment would be the purchase of machines and buildings. Expenditures on such items are often referred to as the purchase of capital. But there are other inputs that fit the definition of investment. Advertising and education are two additional examples of investment in production processes that, when purchased, will yield a stream of returns to the owner. The purchase of housing by individuals is investment. Whenever an input continues to yield services over multiple decision periods, interest rates become important in evaluating the benefits and costs of different investment alternatives. This chapter explores the theory of investment.

18.2 Multiperiod Analysis

We analyzed in Chapter 4 optimization within the context of a single period and have employed that context throughout the text. However, many optimization problems involve a stream of benefits or costs over time. Some examples are capital investment, durable goods that give benefits to consumers over time, and saving or lending. In such problems, a crucial variable in the decision-making process is the rate of interest. To show why the interest rate is so important, we introduce the concepts of future and present value.

18.2.1 The Existence of Interest

The decision to spend or save, or to buy now or later, depends critically on the rate of interest. Interest income is the cost of spending now. Income could be saved and spent in the future along with the interest payment. Therefore, future interest income is forgone when income is spent in the present.

Interest payments are closely connected with the process of capital accumulation. If people are willing to defer consumption now, called *saving,* and invest in a production process, they may be able to consume more at a later time than the amount originally forgone. If $C is invested in an activity and $(C + R)$ is received in the next period, R is the return on the investment of $C and represents the cost of consuming now. The rate of return on investment and interest are two sides of a coin. To illustrate this point, consider a simple example.

Suppose that in a very primitive society most of the people earn their living by fishing. The state of technology is so primitive that everyone fishes from the bank of a lake. One family deduces that if they had a boat, they could fish farther out in the lake and catch more fish. In order to build the boat, the family must sacrifice time that could be spent fishing and must, therefore, reduce consumption now in order to consume more later. This reduction in consumption represents an investment. Forgone consumption promises an uncertain but higher return later. The cost of continued fishing from the bank is the additional fish in the future that could be caught from a boat. The individuals who take the risk and decide to build a boat are called *entrepreneurs*.

The family might decide that they do not want to greatly decrease the amount of fish they consume while building the boat. They can still eat if other families will reduce their current consumption and give some of their fish to them. The problem is persuading other people to sacrifice some of their fish.

One method of persuasion is to agree to repay the fish after the boat is built and the catch becomes larger. But if people prefer consumption now to consumption in the future, the boat builders must agree to repay in the future more fish than they receive now while building the boat. The "lenders" of the fish require an additional amount to compensate them for the present consumption given up. The "borrowers" of the fish would, they hope, be able to repay more than they borrowed, because future catches should be larger. The additional amount of fish repaid represents the interest paid for the fish consumed now.

The fact that productive processes take time and people prefer to consume today rather than tomorrow results in a positive interest rate in most societies. Furthermore, the rate of interest will be determined by the increase in output made possible by deferring consumption and the risk of a particular venture. Interest rates are necessary to compensate lenders for giving up present income and for the risk they take if borrowers default on their promise to pay later. Remember that the family building the boat is not absolutely sure they could catch more fish by getting away from shore. Interest rates are affected by the possibility of forgoing consumption without any return at a later time. The more risky the venture, the higher the interest rate.

18.2.2 Future Value

To introduce the role played by interest rates in making multiperiod decisions, we begin by considering the rate of appreciation of a savings account over time. This rate of appreciation determines the future value of an asset.

Suppose you have $100 today, and the interest rate is 12 percent. If you invest the $100 at 12 percent interest, in one year you would have

$$\$100 + .12(\$100) = \$100(1 + .12) = \$100(1.12) = \$112.$$

The future value of $100 in one year is therefore $112. Obviously if the interest rate is higher (lower), the future value is higher (lower). If you hold the investment for two years, the future value would be

$$\$112 + .12(\$112) = \$112(1 + .12) = \$112(1.12) = \$125.44,$$

since you had $112 at the end of one year and invested this amount again at 12 percent. We can rewrite this expression for future value by substituting for the $112 you had at the end of the first year. Remember that at the end of the first year $112 = $100(1 + .12). Hence:

$$(1 + .12)\$112 = (1 + .12)(1 + .12)\$100 = (1 + .12)^2\$100 = \$125.44.$$

Similarly, the future value of the investment in three years is

$$(1 + .12)[(1 + .12)^2\$100] = (1 + .12)^3\$100 = \$140.49.$$

More generally, in n years the value of the investment would be

$$(1 + .12)^n\$100.$$

Generalizing further, the future value of investing $\$A$ at an interest rate r for n years is

$$FV = A(1 + r)^n.$$

Table 18–1 shows a comparison of future values of $100 over a 5-year to 25-year period for four different rates of interest. The future values increasingly diverge

Table 18–1 Future Values at Different Interest Rates

Interest Rate (percent)	Future Value of $100 at the End of				
	5 Years	10 Years	15 Years	20 Years	25 Years
3%	$116	$134	$ 156	$ 180	$ 209
8	147	216	317	466	685
12	176	311	547	965	1,700
20	249	619	1,541	3,834	9,540

for higher interest rates as the period of time becomes longer. This divergence shows the importance of the interest rate in making decisions involving time.

One such decision involves the cost of holding an asset. For simplicity, assume that you own an asset strictly for financial reasons. You keep the asset for its increasing market value and not because it provides you with a service. Such commodities are called sterile assets. Examples might be a bar of gold or a ton of coal. The question is: Should you keep the asset, which is appreciating, and sell it later, or sell it now? The answer depends on the future value of the asset. For simplicity, we assume that the asset costs nothing to store.

Suppose this asset could be sold now for $10,000, or it could be held for one year and sold for $11,000, an increase in value of 10 percent. It is obvious that if the interest rate is above 10 percent, you should sell the asset. For example, if the interest rate is 12 percent, you could sell the asset now, invest the $10,000 at 12 percent, and have $11,200 at the end of the year. You would be $200 better off than if you had held the asset. The cost (opportunity cost) of holding the asset is the potential $1,200 that could be earned as interest.

On the other hand, if the interest rate is below 10 percent, the asset should be held. If, for example, the interest rate is 8 percent, the $10,000 would bring only $10,000 (1.08) = $10,800, or $200 less than the potential gain from keeping the asset. You should therefore hold the asset if it is expected to appreciate at a rate greater than the relevant rate of interest; sell the asset if it is expected to appreciate at a rate less than the rate of interest.

18.2.3 Present Value

Now that we have discussed the concept of future value, we can discuss the related concept of present value. Consider how much you would be willing to take for the right to receive $1,000 one year from now. The promise of $1,000 one year in the future is worth less to you than $1,000 today. If you had $1,000 now, you could invest it at some rate of interest and have more than $1,000 in one year. How much less than $1,000 would you be willing to accept? At a 12 percent rate of interest, if you invest $892.86 now you would receive $1,000 in one year, because

$$\$892.86(1 + .12) = \$1,000.$$

Therefore, you would be willing to accept $892.86 for the promise to receive $1,000 one year in the future. You can invest $829.86 at 12 percent and have $1,000 in one year. The amounts $892.86 now and $1,000 in a year are equivalent.

At the same 12 percent rate of interest, you would be willing to accept $797.19 for $1,000 to be received in two years, because

$$\$797.19(1 + .12)^2 = \$1,000.$$

These amounts, $892.86 and $797.19, are the present values of $1,000 for one and two years, respectively. Generalizing, for the right to receive $1,000 n years in the future with an interest rate of 12 percent, a person would be willing to accept the present value (PV), where

$$PV(1 + .12)^n = \$1,000,$$

or

$$PV = \frac{\$1,000}{(1 + .12)^n}.$$

The $1,000 in the above ratio is a specific amount promised in the future, or what we have been calling future value. We can go a little further by writing the equation for present value as

$$PV = \frac{FV}{(1 + r)^n}.$$

This is the present value of some future return (FV) in n years with an interest rate of r.

Present value is the "discounted value" of a future income payment. As you can see, discounting means dividing the return by $(1 + r)^n$. The concepts of present and future values are linked by the rate of interest.

Let's now expand the analysis to consider the present value of a stream of future income payments rather than a single payment. Consider how much someone would pay for the following stream of income payments (each payment payable at year end).

Year	Income
1	$ 1,500
2	2,000
3	2,200
4	3,000
5	3,400
Sum	$12,100

No one would pay $12,100, the sum of the yearly incomes. The amount someone would be willing to pay depends on the present value of the income stream. Suppose the relevant rate of interest is 10 percent. Then, the present value of this income stream is

$$PV = \frac{\$1,500}{(1 + .10)} + \frac{\$2,000}{(1. + .10)^2} + \frac{\$2,200}{(1. + .10)^3} + \frac{\$3,000}{(1 + .10)^4} + \frac{\$3,400}{(1 + .10)^5}$$

$$= \$1,363.64 + \$1,652.89 + \$1,652.89 + \$2,049.04 + \$2,111.13$$

$$= \$8,829.59$$

Generalizing, let FV_t be the future value in the tth year and r be the rate of interest. The present value of the stream of future values is

$$PV = \frac{FV_1}{(1 + r)} + \frac{FV_2}{(1 + r)^2} + \frac{FV_3}{(1 + r)^3} + \cdots + \frac{FV_n}{(1 + r)^n}$$

$$= \sum_{t=1}^{n} \left(\frac{1}{1 + r}\right)^t FV_t.$$

We have now established the following principle:

Principle

The future value of investing $\$A$ for n years with an interest rate of r is

$$\$FV = \$A(1 + r)^n.$$

The present value of (the maximum amount that would be paid for) a future payment of $\$FV$ in n years is

$$\$PV = \frac{\$FV}{(1 + r)^n}.$$

The present value of a stream of income over n years is

$$PV = \sum_{t=1}^{n} \frac{FV_t}{(1 + r)^t},$$

where FV_t is the income to be received in year t.

The more heavily weighted toward the future are the income payments, the lower the present value of a stream of income. As an example illustrating this point, consider the following two streams of income, both of which sum to $10,000.

Year		Stream 1	Stream 2
1	....	$ 1,000	$ 4,000
2	....	2,000	3,000
3	....	3,000	2,000
4	....	4,000	1,000
Sum		$10,000	$10,000

At a 10 percent rate of interest, the present value of stream 1 is

$$PV = \frac{\$1,000}{(1 + .10)} + \frac{\$2,000}{(1 + .10)^2} + \frac{\$3,000}{(1 + .10)^3} + \frac{\$4,000}{(1 + .10)^4} = \$7,547.98,$$

while the present value of stream 2 is

$$PV = \frac{\$4,000}{(1 + .10)} + \frac{\$3,000}{(1 + .10)^2} + \frac{\$2,000}{(1 + .10)^3} + \frac{\$1,000}{(1 + .10)^4} = \$8,301.34.$$

The present value of stream 2 is almost $1,000 more than that of stream 1, even though the sums of the incomes are equal. The higher incomes are closer to the current year in stream 2. This means that they are discounted by a lower number than the higher incomes in stream 1. For example, in stream 1, the $4,000 income is divided by $(1.1)^4 = 1.464$, while the $4,000 amount in stream 2 is divided by only 1.1. Income closer to the present is worth more now than the same income further into the future.

As additional evidence of the increased impact of interest as the number of time periods increases, Table 18–2 shows the present value of $100 from the present to 25 years from now at four selected rates of interest. By comparing the rows of values, you can see that both time and increased interest have dramatic effects on present value.

18.1   *Applying the Theory*

Suppose someone promises to pay your family $1 a year forever. Is there a present value amount you would take now for this infinite stream of $1 payments?

18.2.4   The Price of Assets

We will now apply the theory of present value to the determination of the market value of an income-producing asset. When we speak of the asset's value, we generally mean the price that the asset can be sold for in the market. In the case of an income-generating asset, this value is determined by the present value of the stream of income the asset can be expected to yield over the relevant time horizon. Unless the asset has some other personal value to its owner in addition to the expected income, no one would pay more for the asset than the present value of its income stream. If the price of the asset is greater than its present value, a prospective purchaser could simply invest the money at the relevant interest rate and derive a net return greater than that expected from purchasing the asset. On the other hand, if the price is lower than the present value, the asset is expected to yield a net return greater than could be acquired from investing the money at the market rate of interest. The market price of the asset will be bid up or down until it is equal to its present value.

We can show the importance of present value in the following example. Suppose a real estate firm can buy a building for $1 million, then lease office space in the building to generate a net income of $50,000 a year for five years. (For analytical simplicity, assume that the rent is paid at the end of each year.) It is estimated that the wear and tear from use of the building (depreciation) will exactly offset appreciation in value due to inflation and that the building will sell for $1 million at the end of five years.

Table 18–2   Present Values at Different Interest Rates

Interest Rate (percent)	Present Values of $100 to Be Received at the End of				
	5 Years	10 Years	15 Years	20 Years	25 Years
3%	$86	$75	$64	$55	$48
8	68	46	32	21	15
12	57	32	18	10	6
20	40	16	6	3	1

If the market rate of interest is 10 percent, the present value of the building is

$$PV = \sum_{t=1}^{5} \left(\frac{1}{1.1}\right)^t 50,000 + \frac{1,000,000}{(1.1)^5} = \$810,461.$$

The asking price of this asset exceeds the value of the asset—the present value of the income stream. At a 10 percent interest rate, the firm would pay no more than $810,461 for the office building. Unless the present owner is willing to lower the price of the building, the real estate firm would be better off saving the $1 million at the 10 percent interest rate.

Economics in the News

Do You Take the Rebate or the Lower Interest Rate on a New Car Purchase?

In September 1990, General Motors offered a choice range of $500 to $1,000 in rebates or 3.9 to 7.9 percent on financing selected 1991 Buick, Pontiac, Chevrolet, and Oldsmobile cars and minivans. Suppose on a particular make and model the choice is between a $1,000 rebate and 7.9 percent financing on a four-year loan. If you went to your bank, the rate of interest would be 13 percent. You want to borrow $12,000 to pay the dealer now. Do you take the rebate or the lower interest rate?

The dealer tells you that at 7.9 percent, your monthly payments will be $292.39 for four years. Your bank tells you that for a four-year car loan at 13 percent the payments will be $321.93. Hence, each month you save $321.93 − $292.39 = $29.54 if you accept the dealer's financing. Over a year's time this amounts to $354.48. Suppose you could save the money and earn 10 percent; then discounted over a four-year period, the present value of the savings is approximated at[1]

$$PV = \frac{354.48}{(1 + .10)} + \frac{354.48}{(1 + .10)^2} + \frac{354.48}{(1 + .10)^3} + \frac{354.48}{(1 + .10)^4}$$

$$= \$1,123.65.$$

Rather than taking the $1,000 rebate, your savings would be greater by paying the lower interest rate.

---

[1]The present value is approximated because it is assumed you do not have the full $354.48 savings until the end of the year. However, if you earned 10 percent on the $29.54 as you saved the money each month, the *PV* would be $1,164.71. The discounted value is greater than that shown. For a somewhat broader discussion see E. Henry, "Manufacturer's Rebate or Cut-Rate Financing? Here's How to Tell Which Is a Better Deal," *Changing Times*, November 1990, p. 44.

18.3   Theory of Investment

The objective of any profit-maximizing firm that makes an investment is to obtain a stream of returns, the present value of which exceeds the cost of the investment. The firm first undertakes those available projects with the greatest differential between present value and cost. Since the stream of returns and payments must be discounted, the concept of present value enters into each investment decision. The rate of interest therefore becomes a key determinant of the amount of investment undertaken. It is an important variable in present value calculations, and it represents a minimum required return on any investment venture. A firm should invest in a productive asset only if the present value of the income stream generated by the asset is larger than that from investing the same expenditure at the going interest rate in an alternative financial asset.

18.3.1   Investment Decision Making

To show the importance of discounting in investment decisions, consider the following example. A research and consulting firm is thinking about installing a small computer in its office. The total payments on the computer will be $250,000 a year for three years. Beginning in the second year, the net revenue (after subtracting operating costs) generated by the computer is expected to be $90,000 a year for the next 10 years. At the end of that period of time, the firm estimates that the computer will have a salvage value of $50,000. For calculation purposes, the firm uses a discount rate of 5 percent. Should the firm install the computer?

First, calculate the present value of the stream of purchase payments as

$$\frac{\$250,000}{1.05} + \frac{\$250,000}{(1.05)^2} + \frac{\$250,000}{(1.05)^3} = \$680,811.$$

Next, the discounted stream of net returns for 10 years, beginning in the second year, is

$$\frac{\$90,000}{(1.05)^2} + \frac{\$90,000}{(1.05)^3} + \cdots + \frac{\$90,000}{(1.05)^{11}} = \$661,863.$$

Finally, the present value of the salvage or resale is

$$\frac{\$50,000}{(1.05)^{11}} = \$29,230.$$

The research firm should purchase the computer, since the net present value (*NPV*) is

$$NPV \text{ (return + salvage − cost)} = \$661,863 + \$29,230 - \$680,811$$

$$= \$10,282.$$

Of course, a different discount rate would change the present value of a particular investment. For example, keeping the same streams of cost and income as above, let the interest rate go up to 12 percent. With a 12 percent interest rate, the present value of the purchase payments of $250,000 over three years is $600,458. The new present value of $90,000 a year for years 2 through 11 is $454,036. Finally, at a 12 percent interest rate, the present value of the $50,000 salvage price at the end of the 11th year is $14,374. With the higher interest rate, the net present value of the investment is

$$NPV = \$454,036 + \$14,374 - \$600,458 = -\$132,048.$$

Since the net present value now has a negative value, the investment should not be made. The firm could do better by investing in an alternative project or placing the funds available for investment in an interest-bearing account.

This example illustrates an important point. For most investments, the payments are made in early periods, while the returns are spread over a much larger period of time. The higher the interest rate, the lower the present value of benefits, and therefore, high rates of interest tend to discourage investment.

Discounting and the concept of net present value are helpful for making decisions other than whether or not to invest. They help firms select among investment alternatives. To take another example, assume the same research firm is considering buying an office building for $1 million or renting office space in the same building at $60,000 a year for five years. For simplicity, assume rent is paid at the end of each year. The firm estimates that with inflation, the wear and tear on the building will offset the appreciation in value. The building will sell for $1 million at the end of five years. Should the firm lease or buy the building? Assume in this case the interest rate is 10 percent and, if the firm buys the building, the $1 million is payable immediately from assets owned by the firm.

The relevant stream of benefits and costs to compare is the discounted resale value of the building plus the present value of the stream of savings in rents (these savings add to profit—recall our discussion of opportunity costs) less the $1 million cost of the building:

$$NPV = \sum_{t=1}^{5} \left(\frac{1}{1.10}\right)^t \$60,000 + \frac{\$1,000,000}{(1.10)^5} - \$1,000,000 = -\$151,435.$$

Since the investment has a negative present value, the firm should not make the investment. It should invest the $1 million elsewhere, take the interest, and pay the rent. On the other hand, if the rate of interest is 5 percent, net present value of the investment is

$$NPV = \sum_{t=1}^{5} \left(\frac{1}{1.05}\right)^t \$60,000 + \frac{\$1,000,000}{(1.05)^5} - \$1,000,000 = \$43,295.$$

Since the net present value is positive, the firm should purchase the building.

To summarize our discussion, a firm undertakes investment to maximize a discounted stream of net income. Obviously, a profit-maximizing firm wants any new capital purchased to have a flow of returns the present value of which is greater than, or at least equal to, the present value of the flow of costs. Therefore, the discounted income and costs to a firm from an additional unit of capital are key variables in the investment decision-making process. The present value of the expected net revenue from capital depends on several variables such as the market rate of interest, the price of goods produced, the expected lifetime and rate of deterioration of the capital, the flow of services or capital productivity, the prices of other inputs employed, and so forth. A firm should invest in assets that have a lifetime net income stream with a positive (non-negative) present value; it should not invest in assets that have a net income stream with a negative present value.

18.3.2   The Firm's Demand for Investment

These principles allow us to develop a firm's demand for capital goods. Assume that a firm, during a particular time period, faces several investment opportunities. The firm may purchase capital goods either by selling debt instruments, for example, bonds, or by reducing its savings, held as, retained earnings. A firm's use of internal funds to finance investments does not change the cost of the investment. The opportunity cost of funds raised internally must be the relevant market rate of interest. We assume the firm may borrow or lend funds at the market rate of interest. While a firm is usually restricted in its borrowing by its overall net worth, we will assume this restriction is not a relevant barrier and ignore it in our analysis.

Even though a firm may know that several investment opportunities are profitable, it must have a way of ranking them in terms of how much profit they earn. The higher the percentage rate of return on each unit of capital, the more profitable the overall investment. Projects can be ranked by their rate of return from the highest to the lowest. As long as investment funds are not limited, the firm should continue to purchase capital until the rate of return on the last unit is just equal to the opportunity cost of investment funds.

There is one catch to ranking capital investment projects by their rate of return. What happens if the return on a project in one period is 10 percent, but 12 percent in the next? What is the project's overall rate of return? To derive the demand curve for investment, we introduce the concept of an *internal rate of return,* defined as

Definition

The internal rate of return from a particular investment is the interest rate that makes the net present value of that investment zero.

For example, suppose an investment costing $48,000 is expected to yield a net return (profit) of $20,000 a year for three years. To find the discount rate that makes the net present value zero, set

$$NPV = \sum_{t=1}^{3} \frac{\$20,000}{(1 + r)^t} - \$48,000 = 0.$$

Solving for r, the internal rate of return for this investment is approximately 0.12 (12 percent).

Now suppose the market interest rate is higher than 12 percent. From the above calculation, the net present value of the investment would be negative. For example, if the interest rate is 15 percent, the net present value is

$$NPV = \sum_{t=1}^{3} \frac{\$20,000}{(1 + .15)^t} - \$48,000 = -\$2,336.$$

Since net present value would be negative, the firm would not undertake the investment. At rates below 12 percent, the stream of returns is not discounted so heavily and the net present value would be positive; for example, if the interest rate is 8 percent, the net present value is

$$NPV = \sum_{t=1}^{3} \frac{\$20,000}{(1 + .08)^t} - \$48,000 = \$3,543,$$

and the firm should undertake the investment.

The firm's investment decision depends on the relation of the internal rate of return for a particular project and relevant market rate of interest. If the internal rate of return is higher than the market interest rate, the net present value at the market rate is positive, and the investment should be made. If the internal rate of return is lower, the net present value at the market rate would be negative, and the investment should not be made.

Consider another slightly more complicated investment opportunity. This one does not yield the same amounts of revenue per period and thus appears to have different rates of return on the amount of capital invested. Suppose, as before, the project cost is $48,000 paid at the beginning of the venture, but net profit returns are $20,000 for the first two years and $30,000 during the third year. The discount rate that makes net present value on the project zero is that rate for which

$$NPV = \sum_{t=1}^{2} \frac{\$20,000}{(1 + r)^t} + \frac{\$30,000}{(1 + r)^3} - \$48,000 = 0.$$

Because the return in period 3 has gone up, everything else remaining the same, the internal rate of return for the entire project life rises to nearly 20 percent. The internal rate of return calculations will give every investment project a rank according to the percentage rate of return earned on each dollar of capital, even when returns vary across periods.

The market rate of interest can be thought of as the return that could be earned if the investment is not made, because that is the return that could be earned if the same amount of funds were put into interest-bearing accounts or financial assets paying that rate of interest. Within this framework, the rate of interest is the opportunity cost of making a capital investment. Using the concept of the internal rate of return, we can derive a firm's demand for investment during a particular period.

Figure 18–1 shows the set of investment opportunities facing a hypothetical firm. In this case, the firm has four possible investment opportunities and can rank them according to the internal rate of return on each. The first and most profitable investment project involves a capital expenditure of K_1 dollars and has an internal rate of return of r_1. The second most profitable investment costs K_1K_2 dollars; it has an internal rate of return of r_2. Similarly, the other two investment projects cost K_2K_3 and K_3K_4 with internal rates of return of r_3 and r_4.

We should emphasize that the internal rates of return plotted along the vertical axis are the rates on each additional investment project, not the average rate of return on all investments up to that point. For example, r_2 is the internal rate of return for investment project two, that is, for increasing capital expenditure from

Figure 18–1   Alternative Investment Opportunities

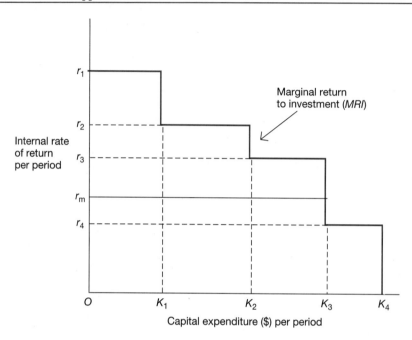

K_1 to K_2. It is not the average internal rate of return of the total expenditure of K_2 dollars. The schedule shown in Figure 18–1 is the marginal return to investment (*MRI*) schedule.

From the above discussion, if the firm has no limitation on its capital expenditure, it will undertake all projects that have an internal rate of return greater than the market rate of interest. It would undertake no projects for which the internal rate of return is less than this interest rate. If in Figure 18–1 the interest rate is r_m, the firm would undertake the first three projects. It would not undertake project four because it could purchase an interest-bearing financial asset with the K_3K_4 dollars and earn a higher return. Thus, the firm would invest K_3 dollars during the relevant period. Only if the interest rate falls below r_4, would the firm invest K_4 dollars. If the interest rate rises above r_3 but stays below r_2, investment three would not be made, and the firm would invest only K_2 dollars.

We have established the following principle:

Principle

A firm can rank potential investments according to their internal rates of return—the discount rate that would make the net present value of the investment zero. This ranking yields a marginal return to investment schedule (*MRI*). If investment funds are not limited, the firm should undertake those projects for which the internal rate of return is greater than the relevant rate of interest (i.e., when $r >$ *MRI*). Investment stops when $r =$ *MRI*. The *MRI* is the firm's demand schedule for investment.

Figure 18–2   Demand for Investment

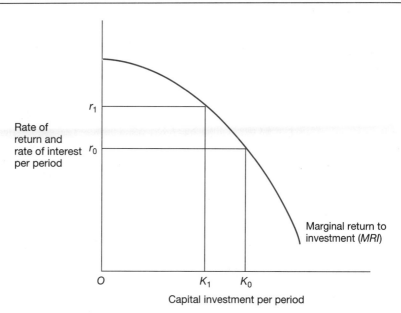

If the firm has only four investment projects available, the firm's demand function for investment looks something like Figure 18–1. However, most (if not all) firms have a wide variety of projects available. As you would expect, as more potential projects are available, the "stair-step" *MRI* function gets closer to a smooth and continuous demand function. If we assume that the investment projects are infinitely divisible, we can talk about the internal rate of return associated with an additional dollar expenditure on capital, and we can draw a continuous demand for investment as in Figure 18–2.

This figure shows the internal rate of return for additional (marginal) investment. Capital investment in the relevant time period is plotted along the horizontal axis; the internal rate of return on the marginal investment and the interest rate are plotted along the vertical axis.

Suppose the market rate of interest is r_0. Every additional unit of investment from zero to K_0 has an internal rate of return greater than r_0. From the previous discussion, if the internal rate of return exceeds the rate of interest, the investment is profitable and should be undertaken (if there is no limit on the amount of capital that can be raised by the firm). Any additional investment beyond K_0 dollars has an internal rate of return below the rate of interest and therefore should not be undertaken. Thus, with an interest rate of r_0, the firm would invest K_0.

By exactly the same type of reasoning, if the rate of interest is r_1, the firm should invest K_1 dollars. Likewise, at every other rate of interest the downward-sloping curve, showing the internal rate of return on each marginal investment, provides the optimal amount that the firm should invest at that interest rate. Thus, this marginal rate of return schedule is the firm's demand for investment.

Economics in the News

Investment in Housing, Interest Rates, and the S&L Crisis

For most households the biggest investment they make is in a house. About 65 percent of the families in the United States live in single-family dwellings. When such an investment is made, it is generally financed by a local savings and loan institution (S&L). Until 1982, S&Ls were restricted by law to lend only to households investing in single-family dwellings.

In 1980, the United States had 4,600 S&Ls.[2] This was the year that Congress removed interest rate ceilings that S&Ls could pay their depositors. Before 1980, rates were fixed at 5 percent, which was the highest rate a pass-book savings account could pay. At these low interest rates S&Ls were losing depositors. Brokerage houses and mutual fund organizations were attracting small investors into money market accounts. The interest paid on these accounts was not fixed and was higher than that paid on S&L or bank savings accounts. Small savers, therefore, moved their money to these new accounts. Consequently, S&Ls were running out of money to lend for housing. To keep their customers, the S&Ls lobbied for the capability to be more competitive on interest rates.

Banking institutions, including S&Ls, earn profit by loaning money to borrowers at higher interest rates than they pay savers. A loan on residential real estate is called a mortgage. In other words, S&Ls invest in mortgages. Typically, interest rates on mortgages are fixed for 30-year periods. Consequently, as S&Ls competed for savers by paying higher interest rates, profitability was reduced because the interest they received as income from mortgages was largely fixed. S&Ls were on the *MRI* schedule at a point below the going market rate paid in invested funds. In two years, beginning in 1980, the S&Ls suffered a massive profit drain. In 1980, their collective net worth was $32.2 billion; in 1982 it had fallen to $3.7 billion.

To help save the institutions, Congress passed the Garn-St. Germain Act (1982) allowing S&Ls to make nonresidential loans. They became much like banks, but without the commercial banking expertise. Many S&Ls are community owned and operated. To overcome losses, and in desperation, S&Ls tended to make high-yield, high-risk investments from junk bonds to solar energy technology. Many of these loans went into default. The profitability of S&Ls did not improve through the 1980s. As they failed, the Federal Savings and Loan Insurance Corporation, a government agency that guarantees against the losses of depositors up to $100,000, was left to pay depositors what the S&Ls had lost.

18.3.3   Industry Demand for Investment

The demand for investment by an entire competitive industry is similar to the demand of a firm. We assume that the investment opportunities facing all firms in an industry can be ranked by their internal rates of return, from highest to lowest. Thus, for the industry, the demand curve for investment also slopes downward.

However, the curve for the industry slopes downward for an additional reason. As you know, a competitive firm can invest and increase its output without lowering the price of the product; an entire industry cannot. If all firms undertake additional

[2]See J. S. Garden, "Understanding the S&L Mess," *American Heritage,* February/March 1991, pp. 49–68.

Figure 18–3   Effect of Taxation on Investment

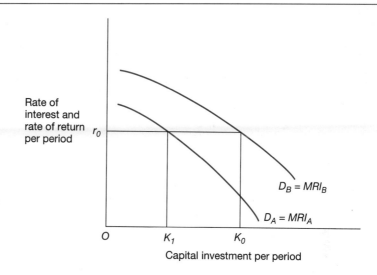

investment, the industry's output will increase and, because of downward-sloping product demand, the price of the product will fall. Since the price of the product falls with additional investment, the profitability, and therefore the internal rate of return from that investment, is less than it would have been had output price remained fixed. While we cannot obtain the industry's demand for investment by simply summing the demands of all firms, its general downward slope does not change. Firms invest until the marginal rate of return from investment equals the rate of interest. The lower the rate of interest, the more investment undertaken.

As is the case for any type of demand curve, if one of the factors held constant changes, the entire curve will shift. To generalize, anything that makes investments more profitable will increase the internal rates of return on investments and, consequently, increase the firm's demand for investment. Anything that makes investments less profitable will decrease the demand for investment.

For example, a large increase in wage rates would decrease present values (since it would decrease future net income) and therefore cause a decrease in internal rates of return on investment. Because the amount of investment forthcoming at any given interest rate would decrease, demand decreases. Technological improvement, on the other hand, would have the opposite effect.

The effect of a change in the rate of taxation on investment returns is shown graphically. In Figure 18–3, D_B, showing the before-tax internal rate of return on investment, is the demand curve for investment if the tax rate is zero. With no taxes and an interest rate of r_0, the industry would, with no credit restrictions, invest in K_0 units of capital. But taxation lowers the present value of expected income from any investment and, therefore, shifts the demand for investment downward. If taxation shifts this schedule to D_A in Figure 18–3, investment would fall to K_1 units for an interest rate of r_0. The difference between the two curves reflects the magnitude of the tax and the proportion of the tax that firms can shift to consumers. The larger the tax, other things being equal, the greater the effect on investment.

18.2 *Applying the Theory*

Investment is a flow of capital goods put into production. It is an addition to an economy's capital stock. For any positive level of investment does the capital stock necessarily grow?

18.3.4 Monopoly Demand in Capital Markets

The type of market in which the firm operates will also have an effect on the firm's demand for capital investment. If the investor is a monopolist, the firm's demand for investment will be the demand of the industry, since the firm is the industry. When considering an additional investment, the monopolist will know that the additional output from the investment will lower the selling price of the product. As the monopolist continues to invest in capital, the marginal return from the investment will be less than the value of the marginal product of the investment (price times marginal product) for any given amount of investment. Essentially, for the same reason that $MR < P$ and, therefore, $MP_L \cdot MR < MP_L \cdot P$ for labor, the marginal return on investment is less than would be the case for a perfectly competitive firm. Nonetheless, the investment decision made by a monopolist is no different than the one made by a perfect competitor. The monopolist will undertake investments so long as the internal rate of return is greater than the market rate of interest.

18.3.5 Monopsony Demand in Capital Markets

Monopsony in capital markets has no effect on the analysis of the demand for capital. Recall that monopsony in labor markets caused the marginal cost of labor to rise even faster than the slope of the supply curve for labor. The marginal factor cost of another unit of labor increased more quickly than did its price, because it was assumed that all labor received the same wage. For capital, a monopsonist faces an upward-sloping supply curve, but there is no MFC schedule above the supply curve, as there was for labor. A higher price for the marginal unit of capital does not necessitate paying a higher price for the units of capital already in use. The marginal factor cost of capital is the cost of the last unit purchased.

18.3.6 Demand for Capital in Summary

To summarize, the theory of investment differs in some ways from the theory of labor employment, even though the basics are the same. The profit-maximizing criterion, in essence, is no different; the firm carries out investment until the marginal return from investment equals its marginal cost. For capital, it is analytically more convenient to make the transition to rates of return because the input yields a stream of returns. So long as the internal rate of return exceeds the rate of interest, the present value of the stream of net returns is greater than the present value of the cost of investment. Thus, the optimal level of investment is that at which the internal rate of return equals the market interest rate.

18.4   Inflation and Investment

To this point, we have talked about interest rates without distinguishing between the real rate and the nominal rate. The nominal interest rate is the money rate actually paid in the market. The real rate is the rate of interest after an inflation (or deflation) factor is subtracted from (added to) the nominal rate. It is therefore net of inflation or deflation.

We now show that under certain assumptions, it is unimportant to specify whether a nominal or real rate is used. While the case is made for the rate of inflation, it applies equally well to deflation, a general decline in prices. For relatively low rates of inflation, as long as inflation has the same effect on interest rates as on the flow of returns, present value is unaffected.

18.4.1   Theoretical Effects of Inflation

To begin, we define r to be the real rate of interest and FV_t to be the real return from investment in period t. These are interest rates and income flows that are net of an inflation or deflation factor. Our analysis has dealt in terms of real variables. For instance, we have written present value as

$$PV = \sum_{t=1}^{T} \frac{FV_t}{(1 + r)^t},$$

where T is the time horizon limit. Now suppose inflation adjusts quoted prices and returns upward. The quoted, or nominal rate of return, includes an inflation factor, π. We write the nominal rate of interest as the sum of a real and inflationary component. Thus, the nominal rate of interest i is

$$i = r + \pi.$$

For example, suppose you have \$100 and you want a 5 percent increase in the purchasing power of that money at the end of the year. If the inflation rate is 10 percent during the year, at the end of the year you want

$$100 + 0.5(100) + .10(100) = (1 + .05 + .10)100 = (1 + r + \pi) 100.$$

To increase real purchasing power by 5 percent, the nominal rate of interest must be $i = r + \pi = 5\% + 10\% = 15\%$. We will assume that the return to investment or, more generally, the income flow FV_t is augmented by the same factor π and increases at this rate each period. If the real return in period one is FV_1, the money or nominal return in period two will be $FV_1 (1 + \pi)$, and, for any period t, it will be $FV_t (1 + \pi)^t$. Thus, the present value of a nominal income stream is written as

$$PV = \sum_{t=1}^{T} \frac{FV_t(1 + \pi)^t}{(1 + i)^t} = \sum_{t=1}^{T} \frac{FV_t(1 + \pi)^t}{(1 + r + \pi)^t}.$$

Now take a closer look at the denominator in the above equation. Notice that

$$1 + r + \pi = (1 + r)(1 + \pi) - r\pi.$$

The difference between the denominator, $1 + r + \pi$, and $(1 + r)(1 + \pi)$ is the product, $r\pi$. So, if $r = .05$ and $\pi = .05$, this term is .0025, a relatively trivial amount. In general, the lower the rate of inflation, the better $(1 + r)(1 + \pi)$ approximates $1 + r + \pi$. As the inflation rate becomes larger, the approximation is poorer. For a 50 percent rate of inflation and a 20 percent real rate of interest, $r\pi = .10$, which is much larger than .0025. In this case, $(1 + r)(1 + \pi)$ over-estimates the discount factor by a significant amount. As a consequence, the discounted present value of investment is underestimated by using $(1 + r)(1 + \pi)$ as the discount factor in the denominator.

Nevertheless, for low rates of inflation, we may write

$$PV = \sum_{t=1}^{T} \frac{FV_t(1 + \pi)^t}{(1 + r + \pi)^t} \approx \sum_{t=1}^{T} \frac{FV_t(1 + \pi)^t}{(1 + r)^t(1 + \pi)^t} = \sum_{t=1}^{T} \frac{FV_t}{(1 + r)^t}.$$

It follows that investors would, under the assumption that inflation rates are low, pay the same amount for a particular stream of returns as they would pay if inflation were zero. We would, therefore, say that under these conditions, inflation is neutral with respect to investment.

But, with high rates of inflation, the present value

$$PV = \sum_{t=1}^{T} \frac{FV(1 + \pi)^t}{(1 + r + \pi)^t} > \sum_{t=1}^{T} \frac{FV_t(1 + \pi)^t}{(1 + r)^t(1 + \pi)^t} = \sum_{t=1}^{T} \frac{FV_t}{(1 + r)^t}.$$

The nominal present value of a particular undiscounted stream of returns is greater than the real present value. You can see that if the rate of inflation is high, the numerator is increasing faster than the denominator. Since nominal present value increases with inflation, investors would be willing to pay more for a given real stream of income than would be the case with little or no inflation. Investment is, therefore, not neutral with respect to high inflation rates.

18.4.2 Actual Effects of Inflation

The above analysis does not mean that the amount of investment and the investment mix in an economy are in reality unaffected by inflation. This is far from the case. In the first place, inflation increases uncertainty about projected benefits and costs, and increased uncertainty will generally decrease the demand for investment. Investors may feel, for example, that the returns will not keep up with inflation. Or they may believe that the allowable depreciation rate of capital for tax purposes (which does not change with inflation) will not be sufficient to cover the replacement cost of the capital when the old capital wears out or is sold for salvage. While we have ignored to some extent capital replacement, this factor does play a significant role in investment decision making, and, because replacement must be made when the capital wears out, the increased cost will tend to have a negative influence on investment.

There is another way in which inflation combined with the tax structure may have a negative effect on investment. Under our existing tax structure, nominal, not real, income is subject to taxation. Therefore, if a firm purchases an asset and resells it later, all gains are subject to taxation, even though most or even all of the gains could be due to inflation. For example, suppose a firm purchases an asset for $100,000. The value of the asset increases during a year at the same rate as the rate of inflation, 5 percent. Thus, the firm sells the asset for $105,000, realizing a net gain of $5,000 which for the sake of illustration is taxed at a 34 percent corporate rate. The after-tax return is $3,300. The firm, in real terms, is $1,700 (.34 × 5,000) worse off however, since the $105,000 is worth only $100,000 in year-one dollars. In order to receive $105,000 after the inflation and taking account of taxes, the rate of return must be about 7.6 percent.

In a world of perfectly anticipated inflation, free of institutional constraints and regulations, the nominal rate of interest and income streams would adjust in an inflationary economy so that firms would realize present values on earning streams approximately equal to those without inflation. The nominal rate of interest would include the rate of inflation and the real rate of interest. But in the actual world with real firms, there frequently is uncertainty about how prices will change. Therefore, in this world, inflation can inhibit private investment. Sometimes, too, the interaction of inflation with the tax structure can compound the adverse impact of inflation.

18.5   Depletion of Natural Resources: Pricing over Time

An important investment decision is the decision to purchase a mineral deposit. During the past two decades, the topic of the depletion of natural resources has received a considerable amount of attention. We frequently hear that because there are finite supplies of certain natural resources, such as oil, gas, and coal, the world will soon run out of these minerals if current rates of depletion continue. Many economists assert that market forces can prevent such a disaster. Many policymakers argue that only governmentally imposed conservation will prevent or at least postpone such a doomsday. We can analyze the situation in much the same way we think about investment.

18.5.1   Rates of Extraction

Assume that a firm owns a mineral deposit such as an ore body or oil field and knows approximately the total amount of the resource that can be extracted. Suppose, also, that the firm expects the price of the natural resource to rise. Should the firm extract and sell some of the resource, or should it hold the resource for future sale? For analytical purposes, we will assume the relevant price for decision-making purposes is the sale price of the resource less the cost of extraction. We will also assume that the decision is simply whether or not to extract and not how much to extract. If the firm chooses to produce, we assume for now that the rate of extraction is predetermined.

From the discussion of the future value of assets, the decision concerning whether or not to produce depends crucially on the rate of interest. If the price is expected to rise at a rate lower than the rate of interest, the firm will produce. Under these conditions, the firm could extract the mineral, sell it, and then invest the returns at the market rate of interest, thereby gaining a larger return than could be realized by letting the deposit appreciate in value. If the firm expects the price of the resource to appreciate at a rate greater than the interest rate, the best course of action is to withhold extraction until the future.

We can condense the decision-making process into a single rule. If P_t is the future price in time period t, the future price under which the firm would be indifferent between producing and selling now or producing and selling in period t is

$$P_t = P_0 (1 + r)^t,$$

where r is the rate of interest, and P_0 is the present price of the resource. If price in period t is expected to exceed P_t, the firm should withhold production; if not, it should produce and sell.

Now let us examine what we would expect in the economy as a whole. Suppose the economy has a finite amount of a particular resource, and this resource is owned by many private firms. Suppose also that the industry has been producing at some particular rate. Now suppose some firms notice that the economy is rapidly depleting its supply of this resource. These firms would realize that the reduced supply in the future would probably cause future prices to increase more rapidly—let us say at a rate greater than the rate of interest. The firms would, therefore, withhold extraction in present periods in order to shift it to the future when price is expected to be above the break-even price. Expected prices thus change the rate of extraction.

But the decrease in present supply from the decrease in current production would, as you know, drive up current prices relative to future prices. How much would they be driven up? Suppose enough firms withhold production that the current price rises to the point that the future price is less than $P_0(1 + r)^t$; the future expected price does not exceed the value of the present market price invested for t periods. Some firms would then be induced to increase the current rate of extraction. We would expect the adjustment process to continue until the price expected in each future period equals the present price adjusted for interest.

When the price of the resource increases at the same rate as the rate of interest, the firms would have no incentive to increase or decrease production. If there is, in fact, a finite amount of the resource, equilibrium requires price to increase at approximately the same rate as the rate of interest. If price is rising less rapidly than the interest rate, firms will increase production now, driving down present prices relative to future prices. If the price is rising more rapidly than the rate of interest, firms will tend to decrease production now, driving up present prices relative to future prices. Market forces tend to force prices along an equilibrium path set by market rates of interest.

18.5.2 Resource Development

Certain factors tend to disrupt this equilibrium path. Discoveries of new deposits of the resource lead firms to believe that future prices will be lower than they would have been otherwise. These discoveries lead to increased current production and decreased prices. Also, increases in price tend to decrease the quantity demanded as consumers substitute away from the resource that is becoming more and more scarce and into resources with relatively lower prices.

In fact, the problem with the scenario of finite resource supply with prices increasing at the same rate as the rate of interest is that increasing prices lead to the development of products and technologies that can change the adjustment drastically. As we noted, increasing prices will decrease consumption of the resource. But the increased price will also lead to research to discover substitutes, and if such substitutes are discovered or invented, the demand for the resource will fall. Alternatively, if increased prices lead to new technologies, the supply of the resource can rise. Moreover, while all resources at any given time are, in fact, fixed in supply, the actual known reserves depend on the price of the resource. Take, for example, oil fields that were uneconomical to exploit when the price was $10 a barrel for crude. When prices rose to $30 a barrel, some of these fields became very economical and quite profitable.

A good illustration of these effects was a field in East Central Texas called the Austin Chalk. When most domestic crude was regulated and this oil was selling around $6 a barrel, no one could produce profitably from the field. The problem was that the Austin Chalk was of such low permeability that under the available technology it was unprofitable to drill in the area, even though geologists knew oil was there. After price was allowed to increase, drillers developed a new technology that permitted profitable drilling in a previously unprofitable area. What had not been considered reserves a few years before became reserves; the Austin Chalk became one of the more productive fields in the country—and a very profitable one at that—until oil prices fell once again.

Another function of higher resource prices is that they increase the incentive to explore and develop new resources. Exploration is similar to other inputs into the production process. Firms will carry out exploration to search for new resources as long as the expected marginal gain exceeds the marginal cost. Given a particular probability of success from exploration, the higher the price of the resource, the higher the expected marginal gain and hence, the more exploration that will be undertaken. The more exploration, the greater will be the reserves.

Principle

> If a mineral resource is known to be in finite supply, market forces will ensure that the price of the resource will increase at the same rate as the rate of interest. But the increasing price has two consequences. First, the higher price will induce firms to develop substitutes for the resource. Second, the higher price will induce more exploration, more production from previously unprofitable deposits, and the development of new technology to lower the cost of extraction.

The Art of Selling an Asset

Art has often been held as an investment by individuals and corporations. It is unlikely that it is a sterile asset since those who own paintings, sculptures, and so forth, usually enjoy their display. But as a sterile investment, the decision to hold on to a piece of art or to sell it is made by following the rule described above. If the owner thinks the price of the artwork will not rise as quickly as the rate of interest, then he or she should sell it.

In 1989, Paul Mellon, a major art collector in the United States, decided to sell 14 major works (*Forbes,* November 25, 1990). He auctioned his pieces through a New York art dealer, Cristie's. The dealer estimated the works would sell for $80 million. Only seven pieces sold for a total of $51 million, and just one of the pieces accounted for $25 million of this sum. The art world saw the sale as a signal that art prices were falling. To many investors, this was like putting a big block of company stock on the market. Paul Mellon had the reputation of being a shrewd investor. If he was selling, then people in the art world believed that art prices had peaked and it was time to sell. The result was that more art became available to the market, much of which was sold through Christie's or other such art dealers. In an auction, the seller can set a "reserve price," a minimum bid that must be made before the seller will part with the object. In many recent cases, the high bids have not reached the reserve price. The price of art has become "soft," and art dealers are encouraging potential sellers to wait.

This is a case of supply bringing forth more supply. If investors believe that prices will not rise in the future, they have an increased incentive to sell now. Selling now increases supply, which reduces prices and encourages even more art investors to sell. Art dealers are attempting to manage the market by discouraging owners not to sell. One way to do this is to simply not hold as many auctions. There are very few dealers who are representatives for people who hold extremely expensive works of art. There are also relatively few buyers, many of which are Western world museums. The interaction of these buyers and dealers may successfully change expectations. Expected future price increases may become greater, which will reduce the forthcoming supply of art and actually serve to bolster sagging art prices.

18.6   Summary

When there are costs and benefits over several periods of time, or more precisely when costs are incurred over numerous periods and benefits are realized over multiple periods, discounting is necessary for good decision making. Discounting is a tool that turns a future stream of payments and returns into a present value, and interest rates are the bridge between the present and the future. The fundamental formula connecting the future with the present is

$$PV = \frac{FV_t}{(1 + r)^t},$$

where t is the future time at which the value FV arises. The further t is away from the present, the smaller will be the present value. Given time, a smaller present value can be put into an interest-bearing account that with the earned interest will equal the future value at time t. Any stream of future values can be brought back to the present by using this discounting equation.

Discounting is an important tool for investment decision making. Investment is undertaken when an asset that delivers a stream of future returns is purchased. If the purchase price is greater than the PV of the future returns, the asset is too costly. If the price is less than the PV, a positive return is earned on the investment. Investment projects have an internal rate of return, which is the rate of return that equates the price of a project with its present value. The collection of internal rates of return yields the marginal return to investment (MRI) schedule illustrated in Figures 18–1 and 18–2. This schedule is the firm's demand curve for investment. Investment projects are undertaken up to the point at which the MRI curve is equal to the going rate of interest.

Discounting is not exclusively a means of deciding how much to invest: It also shows whether or not it is profitable to sell any asset. For example, you may be considering selling a certificate of stock. To decide whether or not to sell, you compare the returns on what you would receive from selling with the returns you would get from keeping the stock. To make the comparison, you bring the two streams of returns back to present. The same sort of comparison is made for a depletable resource. The decision to extract is determined by comparing the returns from the sale of the extracted commodity with holding the resource for future sale. Higher interest rates increase present extradition.

Rates of inflation that affect the future streams of costs and benefits the same way as the interest rate have no impact on the equation relating present value to future value. Interest rates with an inflation or deflation adjustment (π) are nominal interest rates (i). If the real interest rate is r, then $i = r + \pi$. The uncertainty of how inflation will affect interest rates and future values generally causes firms to undertake less investment. Another influence that causes lower levels of investment is higher taxes.

Answers to *Applying the Theory*

18.1. It might seem like there is no answer to this problem. But suppose the interest rate is 10 percent, then you want to find

$$PV = \sum_{t=1}^{\infty} \frac{1}{(1 + r)^t} = \sum_{t=1}^{\infty} \frac{1}{(1 + .10)^t} \,,$$

where the symbol ∞ means infinty. There are solutions to such problems. This series of payments approaches over an infinite time horizon the value $\frac{1}{r}$. Hence,

$$PV = \frac{1}{.10} = \$10.$$

You should be willing to accept $10 now for this stream of $1 payments.

18.2. No, the capital stock does not necessarily grow, because along with investment there is depreciation. Depreciation exhausts or reduces the capital stock. It is capital consumed in the production process. Only when investment is greater than depreciation does the capital stock grow.

Technical Problems

1. Assume an interest rate of 10 percent.
   a. What is the future value of $500 three years from now? Six years from now?
   b. What is the present value of $500 to be received three years from now? Six years from now?
   c. What is the present value of the income streams in the table that follows?
   d. Since both streams total $9,000, what accounts for the difference in present values?

Year	Stream 1	Stream 2
1	$5,000	$1,000
2	3,000	3,000
3	1,000	5,000

2. An ice cream distributor is thinking about buying another ice cream truck. The price of the truck is $20,000, and it is estimated that the truck will increase profits $4,000 per year for 10 years. Explain how the distributor should decide whether or not to buy the truck.

3. You are hired as an economic consultant to a firm that produces and sells wine. Over a relevant period, the wine gets better as it ages; therefore, the longer it ages, the higher the price the wine maker can get for the wine. Explain precisely the method you would use in order to advise the wine maker how long to age the wine before putting it on the market. Assume you have all the required technical information.

4. Assume the average price of oil is $25 a barrel, and the interest rate is 10 percent. The government wants to stockpile oil in reservoirs (assume they are free). What is the cost of stockpiling this oil over the next 10 years? What if the interest rate is only 4 percent?

5. Explain why the stockpiling cost mentioned in problem 4 is just as real a cost to the government—the taxpayers—as the actual cost of purchasing the oil or of storing the oil if such costs are not zero. Who would benefit and who would lose if this opportunity cost is ignored?

6. If the firm's investment decision is constrained by funding (or credit) limitations, how should it determine what projects to fund? Does your answer conform to the general rule for constrained optimization set forth in Chapter 4? Explain.

7. Suppose you own a deposit of a natural resource, the price of which is $2 a pound (price net of costs). The rate of interest is 12 percent. What would the price of the resource have to be in five years to make extraction holdbacks economical over this period? Answer the question under the assumption that the interest rate is 5 percent.

8. The current return from an investment is $10,000 per year. The real rate of interest is 5 percent, and the rate of inflation is 5 percent. Compare the present value of the return five years from now using the real and nominal rates of interest. (The return is expected to rise at the same rate as the rate of inflation). Make the comparison with a 50 percent rate of inflation.

Figure E.18–1

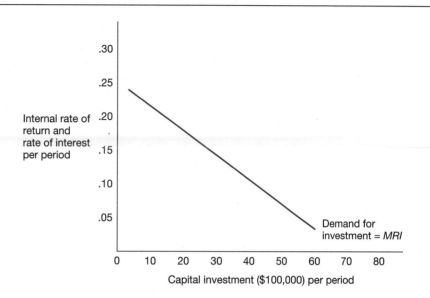

9. A firm can lease a piece of capital equipment for five years at $100,000 a year, or it can purchase the capital now, use it for five years, then sell it at the end of the period for one fourth of the purchase price. If the rate of interest is 10 percent, what is the maximum price of the capital at which it would be economical to purchase rather than lease?

10. Figure E.18–1 shows an industry's demand for investment before taxation. If the interest rate is 10 percent, how much investment will be undertaken? At the same rate of interest, how much will investment decline if a tax of 20 percent is placed on the return to capital? If the interest rate rises to 13 percent and the tax rate increases 50 percent, what happens to investment?

Analytical Problems

1. Nuclear power plants require large capital outlays to build and relatively small amounts of money to operate. During the many years of construction, they produce no electricity revenues whatsoever. In light of the time lag between money outlays and electricity revenues, explain why long-term interest rates are so important to public utilities in deciding if and when to build such plants. If prices are fixed by regulation, how would you expect inflation to affect the development of power plants?

2. The president of a large chemical firm recently stated that it was more profitable for his firm to pirate the inventions of other companies than it was to engage in original research. How does this behavior affect the value of R&D spending?

3. Use Figure E.18–2 to answer the following questions: investment per period in the U.S. gadget industry is plotted along the horizontal axis. The relevant rate of interest is r_0. Explain what happens to investment in the gadget industry if the following events occur:

Figure E.18–2

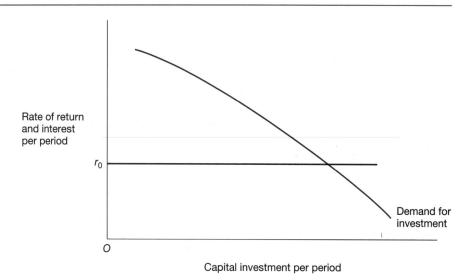

a. The government grants a subsidy to gadget producers.
b. A high tariff is placed on imported gadgets.
c. Strict pollution and safety controls are placed on the industry.
d. The Consumer Product Safety Commission finds that gadgets may be hazardous to your health.
e. Sweeping technological change occurs in the widget industry. (As you know, widgets are a good substitute for gadgets in most uses.)
f. The interest rate falls.
g. The rate of inflation increases.

4. What factors would go into a firm's decision to finance an investment via borrowing or using internal funds?
5. Why would we expect firms that produce capital equipment, for example, producers of metal-working machines, to lobby Congress for changes in the tax laws asking for more rapid depreciation?
6. At the time we were completing the revision of this text (August 1991), concern about the size of the federal deficit was being voiced by almost everyone. How might a very large federal deficit have an affect on private investment— investment by firms and individuals?
7. The tools we have developed for the investment decision can also be used in the firm's inventory decision. Why is this so? How would a firm go about deciding on the optimal inventory level?
8. The fact that you are attending a college or university indicates that you have made an investment decision. What kind of investment decision is this? What factors did you (at least implicitly) evaluate when making this decision? In what way would the decision to go to graduate school differ?

PART VII

Welfare and Market Imperfections

19
Welfare and Competition

20
Exchange Inefficiencies and Welfare

21
Behavior with Incomplete Information

CHAPTER 19

Welfare and Competition

19.1 Introduction

In the introduction to this text, we emphasized that economics is the study of choice. Because of scarcity, individuals must choose what goods to consume and decide the allocation of their time. Economics is concerned with the way people make these choices and the results of such behavior. From the theories about consumer behavior, we have been able to make predictions and to explain the observed behavior of individuals. To analyze market demand, we combined individual consumers and looked at their behavior as a group. In this way, much of the market analysis was based directly on the theory of consumer choice.

Supply theory is also based on the decision-making process of individuals, this time producers. Again, we combined producers into industries or markets, but behavior results primarily from the decisions made by individual firms, not the group as a whole. One exception we discussed briefly arose when firms combined into groups called cartels, and the group as a whole made decisions, or someone made the decision, such as how to distribute production and set price, for the group. For the most part, the decisions faced by this combination of firms are the same ones faced by individual producers, and to maximize profits the same decision rules apply.

The supply and demand of variable inputs are also decided by individual decision making. The supply of factors of production results from the choices of separate individuals, as does the demand for inputs by producers. In this context, we addressed the behavior of labor through unions, but, as in the case of cartels, we found the choices faced by a union were not much different from those confronted by a single worker. We have stressed and continued to observe that microeconomic theory is basically concerned with the choices of individuals and the economic consequences of these choices.

Economists are, however, concerned with whether or not these individual choices lead to socially desirable outcomes. Welfare economics studies how resources should be distributed in order to achieve the maximum well-being of individuals in society. Welfare economics is therefore concerned with what *ought to be* rather than with what *is*. To analyze the behavior of economic agents and make predictions is positive economics; it deals with what is. Normative or welfare economics focuses on policy changes that will increase the amount of benefit going to members of a society. The recommendations of welfare economists are severely limited unless they know the goals of a community or society. But taking goals as given, the welfare economist seeks the most efficient means of obtaining the desired outcomes. You will see in this chapter that the strongest principles in welfare economics are really conditions necessary for efficiency in production and distribution.

This chapter is only an introduction to the conceptual basis of welfare economics. A thorough study of welfare economics involves one or more courses, frequently at the graduate level, and requires far more rigorous treatment and rather complex mathematical analysis. This chapter is not intended to be analytical in nature, but rather, it should give you a feel for what welfare theory is. We begin with the concepts of social welfare and discuss their limitations. We then analyze the welfare effects of perfect competition. Competitive markets in which consumers maximize utility and producers maximize profits are considered welfare maximizing, independent of the distribution of goods and services.

19.2 Social Welfare

Groups of people—perhaps society as a whole—are faced with choices in much the same way as individuals are, and we frequently hear statements that would lead us to believe that a group of people can have a well-defined set of preferences. If preferences are well defined, this means they can be specified by an indifference map. We even hear statements implying that a nonhuman institution can have preferences.

We read and hear claims such as, "The 55 mile-per-hour speed limit is good," or "Selling grain, arms, or computers to other countries hurts the nation," or "The new tax package will be good for the country." Sports writers and coaches have been complaining for years that the National Collegiate Athletic Association rules are either too strict or not strict enough for college sports. None of these statements, and we are sure you have heard or seen a multitude of assertions similar to these, really makes any sense outside of a very narrow definition to be discussed in the following sections. The problem actually boils down to the fact that populations simply do not have utility maps or preference orderings. Individuals have preference orderings; groups generally do not.

Economics in the News

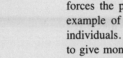

Aid to the Poor Is Up since 1960, but They Have Less Money to Spend

Poor people as a group, as any group of people, do not have a well-defined set of preferences. Individuals who are poor do have preference maps. Material aid to the poor takes many forms, but it can be classified as either a cash gift or goods-in-kind. A poor person can reach his or her highest indifference curve by receiving aid as income or cash. Goods-in-kind limit substitutability unless they can be readily sold. Limited substitutability forces the poor person to a lower indifference curve. Public welfare programs are an example of how preferences are imposed upon the poor as a group and the poor as individuals. Governments—local, state, and national—have become increasingly reluctant to give money to the poor. The rationale is that the "money will be used to buy beer or drugs." Children in the poor family will not get the proper food or proper medical care. In this case, the household may not represent the preferences of the members. Preferences diverge between the adults and young members, with the young possibly having no voice.

Public aid and programs are intentionally designed to make the poor consume food and medical care. Also, as drug addiction has become more widespread, less and less public aid is being made in the form of cash and more is being given in the form of food stamps and medicaid. Food stamps are vouchers that act as money in a grocery store. Alcoholic beverages and cigarettes cannot be purchased with these vouchers. Medicaid is a federal program by which doctors and hospitals bill the cost of medical care provided to the poor to the federal government. Hence, the poor now receive assistance from the government in three forms: money, food stamps, and medicaid.

Robert Moffitt in an article in the *National Tax Journal* entitled, "Has State Redistribution Policy Grown More Conservative?" June 1990, reported trends in how assistance is given to the poor. The following table is based on his data.

Monthly Aid to a Poor Family of Four

	1960	1968	1972	1974	1976	1978	1980	1982	1984
Cash	$483	$506	$512	$507	$500	$475	$436	$394	$388
Cash and food stamps	—	—	739	719	759	712	672	627	622
Cash, food stamps, and medicaid	—	—	—	—	935	893	852	827	806

All the figures are in 1982 deflated dollars. In real terms, aid to the poor increased from $483 in 1960 to $806 in 1984. But beginning in 1976, the total aid has been declining from the high of $935. Proportionately less of the package is in cash. While aid was given in cash only throughout the 1960s, the fraction has decreased to less than one half (48 percent) in 1984. The trend indicates that society is becoming less tolerant of the poor being given cash. Preferences are being imposed on the poor to receive more of their aid in the form of food vouchers and medical care and less of it in the form of cash.

19.2.1 The Concept of Social Welfare

A utility function for a group of people, or what is more commonly referred to as a social welfare function, is difficult to define or describe. This difficulty is mainly because preferences within a group encompass so many conflicting interests. In any group, from a nation, to a state, to a city, to a club, a policy or action that benefits one set of people may very well harm another set within the same group. One group in a society may wish to use resources to fight a war, while another wants more spent on highways and schools. Others may want more spent on housing and less on defense. The point is, we cannot say that a particular policy benefits an entire group if some in the group are made better off while others are made worse off. Therefore, we cannot make statements such as those mentioned above. Maybe we prefer a 55-mile-per-hour speed limit because it lowers the highway death toll, while you oppose it because you place a higher value on your time. One person may feel that all pornography must be banned, whereas for other people pornography is their only leisure activity. Many faculty members think the university would be better off with more books and journals in the library at the expense of student study space. Students may think more study space in the library would be better for the university. Who is the university? The faculty, the students, former students, the administration? In fact, could the entire student body ever speak as a unit?

Therefore, because actions taken by groups, or choices made by leaders of those groups, may harm some in the group and may help others, we cannot say whether the group is better off or worse off when a certain action is taken. This conclusion comes from the realization that we cannot compare changes in the utility of different people. If you gain 10 hamburgers and someone else loses a six-pack of his or her favorite soft drink, we can't compare your added utility with another person's loss in utility, because utility is neither measurable nor comparable. Even in the case of a social decision that takes $1,000 from one person and gives it to a poorer person, one cannot say that society's utility increases. No one has ever proven that the marginal utility of income diminishes with increased income. In economics, we do not recognize the concept of a social utility function or group preference ordering.

Any collective decision, whether the action of private producers or consumers acting together or governmental decision makers representing the electorate, which benefits some people at the expense of others, cannot be said to benefit or harm society as a whole, since we cannot compare changes in utility.[1] For the reasons given, it is therefore virtually impossible to define social welfare accurately, and in particular, it is impossible to define maximum social welfare.

---

[1] Although this statement is not quite accurate, it is very close to being so. Suppose a social action harms one person and benefits another. If the one who is benefitted is willing to bribe the one who is harmed sufficiently to compensate for the harm, both can be better off. This entire process is part of the subject matter in more advanced courses.

19.2.2   The Inconsistency of Group Preferences

To specify maximum welfare or increases in welfare, we would have to specify a utility function for society as a whole. Certainly, a society could vote on all possible organizations and distributions, but even this leads to complications. Consider the following simple hypothetical case. Suppose there are three individuals in a society who will vote on three possible events, A, B, and C. The preference orderings of individuals 1, 2, and 3 are as follows:

1. (ApB) (BpC) (ApC).
2. (BpC) (CpA) (BpA).
3. (CpA) (ApB) (CpB).

In the listing, (ApB) denotes that situation A is preferred to situation B. Note that each individual is rational in the sense that if A is preferred to B and B to C, then A is preferred to C. If this three-person society voted on events A and B, A would get a majority, as would B if they chose between B and C. But note that this society would vote for C over A, which would be inconsistent with the other two outcomes. If for society as a whole (ApB) and (BpC), then consistency would imply (ApC). But you see that this is not the case; thus, society seems to behave irrationally, while individual members maintain well-ordered preferences.

In any case, this simplified example shows that there can be inconsistency in determining social welfare by voting. Moreover, even with consistency in voting, we cannot say that majority rule must specify maximum social welfare. This method would involve interpersonal utility comparisons, and, as you know, economists cannot make such value judgments.

19.2.3   Pareto Optimality Revisited

Many, if not most, problems in public decisions involve economic choices; so surely economists must be able to say something about them. Actually, they can say very little. Economists cannot establish the goals of a society, nor can they say what is "good" for one person or for a collection of people. In general, economists can only address the issue of efficiency when individuals are aggregated and goals have been established. Efficiency within groups can be reduced to one prescriptive statement: If a change can be made such that one or more people are made better off and none worse off, the society's welfare will be increased if the change is made. We have already discussed this in Chapter 7 as the principle of Pareto optimality. "Better off" in this statement has a precise meaning.

Definition

A person is said to be better off in situation A than in situation B if he or she moves to a higher indifference curve.

Under the definition of Pareto optimality, whenever it is possible to increase the utility of one member of a group without hurting anyone else in the organization,

Pareto optimality does not exist. Such changes are considered Pareto superior. When the distribution of goods and services within the group can be rearranged only by harming someone, Pareto optimality is then finally achieved. To summarize:

Definition

A social organization is said to be Pareto optimal if there is no change that will benefit some people without making some others worse off. Changes that benefit one or more people in a group while leaving everyone else indifferent are Pareto superior moves.

This is a relatively weak concept in social welfare economics. To illustrate, suppose a new transcontinental highway is to be constructed. This will benefit millions of travelers. But it also forces the government to condemn (under the right of eminent domain) the homes of a few families. These families, of course, are paid a "fair market price" for their property. However, some of the families may be unwilling to sell for a fair market price; yet, they must sell by law, and as a consequence are made worse off. Millions may benefit and one may be harmed. Economists as economists therefore cannot say that the new highway increases or decreases social welfare. For this reason, economists are primarily interested in Pareto optimality because it expresses efficiency, and not because it serves as a social goal. The condition of Pareto optimality is the major component of what economists call welfare economics.

To summarize the implications of the concept of Pareto optimality:

Principle

(a) If a change will benefit one or more people without making anyone worse off, the change is socially desirable; (b) if a change helps some people and hurts others—the numbers are immaterial—no conclusion can be reached.

19.2.4   Consumer's Surplus in Welfare Analysis

When economists analyze the effects of policy changes—for example, in cost-benefit analysis—they frequently find the Pareto rule unhelpful. Unless consumers have identical preference patterns, in general, some people will benefit and some people will lose with any kind of social change. A much stronger tool in welfare analysis, and one that we also introduced in Chapter 7, is the concept of consumer's surplus. Recall that it is defined as the difference between what a consumer is willing to pay for each unit purchased and the actual market price. Graphically it is represented by the area between the demand curve and price. In the market, if this area representing consumer's surplus goes up for any sort of policy change, the change is considered beneficial to consumers as a group; if the area goes down, the change is harmful to them. You saw in Chapter 13 that producer's surplus can be used in the same way to judge the impact of a market change on producers as a group.

Figure 19–1   Welfare Consequences of a Price Ceiling and Floor

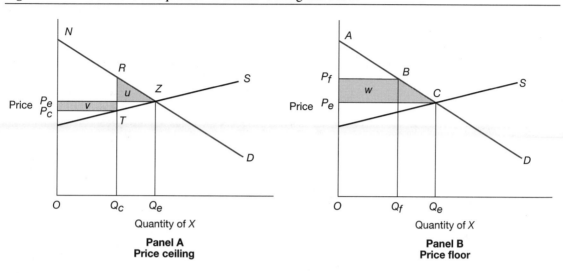

Panel A
Price ceiling

Panel B
Price floor

The use of consumer's and producer's surplus goes beyond the definition of Pareto optimality by looking at the net gain to consumers or producers from a change. Even though some consumers and producers might lose from a price increase (e.g., if on balance there is a gain in the total sum of consumer's and producer's surplus) the move is beneficial.

Let us be more specific and focus on consumer's surplus to see how surplus analysis violates the conditions of Pareto optimality. Suppose a certain commodity has an effective price ceiling; that is, price is set below the equilibrium market price. Panel A in Figure 19–1 illustrates the situation. With a price ceiling at P_c, consumer's surplus is P_cNRT. If prices were allowed to rise to the equilibrium price P_e, consumer's surplus would be P_eNZ. Consumer's surplus increases when the price rises if area u is greater than area v, and falls if area u is less than area v.

The reason we cannot use the concept of Pareto optimality to analyze the results of eliminating the ceiling is because the ceiling causes shortages. Some consumers get the product at P_c; others who want to purchase it at this price do not. If the ceiling is eliminated, those who purchased the product at P_c would be hurt, while those who could not buy it would be helped. On balance, it is impossible to use the Pareto criterion to say whether welfare rises if the ceiling is removed. Economists, however, frequently do compare areas such as u and v for the market demand curve, knowing full well that such a comparison is inconsistent with the definition of Pareto optimality.

The use of consumer's surplus is not always at odds with the definition of Pareto optimality, however. For instance, in Panel B of Figure 19–1, we show a price floor of P_f. Consumer's surplus is the area P_fAB when the price is kept at P_f. If the floor is eliminated, price would fall to P_e, and consumer's surplus would be P_eAC. Consumer's surplus rises by area w. In this case, since price is lowered for every consumer, everyone who buys the product can buy more at the lower price. Because no consumer is harmed, the price decrease is also beneficial to consumers by the Pareto criterion.

Of course, in each diagram we have ignored whether producers are made better or worse off by the policy change. In Panel A, when the ceiling is lifted, all producers are unambiguously helped. All can sell their output at higher prices and sell more on average. In Panel B, on the other hand, we cannot be certain of the effect of relaxing the price floor. Sellers produce more, but now prices are lower. Thus, the use of consumer's and producer's surplus requires great care at the market level. When surplus changes, some gain and some lose—we cannot determine whether welfare increases in the Pareto sense.

19.3   Pareto Optimality in Consumption

While the concept of Pareto optimality is a weak one, it does establish some useful guidelines necessary for the maximization of welfare in society. Pareto optimality is an efficiency condition, and a move toward Pareto optimality, a Pareto superior change, is simply a move to a more efficient allocation of goods and services. If an action is Pareto superior, we can unambiguously say that a group is made better off. We emphasize that an infinite number of resource allocations can be said to be Pareto optimal.

In Chapter 7, it was shown that equal marginal rates of substitution between two traders was Pareto optimal. Recall from that chapter that if the marginal rate of substitution for Allen (MRS^A) was 4 and the marginal rate of substitution for Brenda (MRS^B) was 2, then, as Brenda and Allen traded, their MRSs would become equal, but they could become equal anywhere between the rates of 2 and 4. Just as it is for two traders, no single allocation can be said to maximize social utility or be socially preferable to other Pareto optimal distributions. In this section, we want to discuss how economists apply the notion of Pareto optimality to market efficiency. We introduce the Edgeworth Box diagram, and then discuss the conditions necessary for Pareto optimality between two consumers and two producers in a market setting.

19.3.1   Pareto Optimality between Consumers

If for two goods X and Y, Allen has an $MRS^A_{x \text{ for } y} = \dfrac{\Delta Y}{\Delta X} = 4$, then Allen is willing to trade 4 units of Y for an additional unit of X. Allen is at a point on his indifference curve where the slope is 4. Alternatively, at the margin Allen views 4Y to be equivalent in utility to 1X; that is, $4Y = 1X$.

Allen can make Pareto superior trades with any consumer who has a different MRS. If Brenda has an $MRS^B_{x \text{ for } y} = 2$, then she is at a point on her indifference curve where she would be willing to give up 2 units of Y to get 1 unit of X and still remain on the same indifference curve. At the margin she views $2Y = 1X$. Figure 19–2 illustrates the marginal rates of substitution for Allen in Panel A and

Figure 19–2   Pareto Superior Movements for Two Consumers

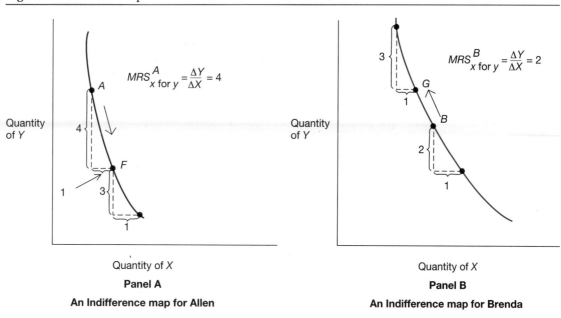

Quantity of Y

$MRS^A_{x \text{ for } y} = \dfrac{\Delta Y}{\Delta X} = 4$

$MRS^B_{x \text{ for } y} = \dfrac{\Delta Y}{\Delta X} = 2$

Quantity of Y

Quantity of X

Quantity of X

Panel A

Panel B

An Indifference map for Allen

An Indifference map for Brenda

Brenda in Panel B. Allen is at point *A* on his indifference curve. Brenda is at point *B* on her indifference curve.

Could Brenda and Allen make Pareto superior trades? Certainly, and there are an infinite number of such trades. All such trades move Brenda and Allen toward equal marginal rates of substitution, which means Allen moves closer to an *MRS* of 2 and Brenda moves closer to an *MRS* of 4. Thus, Allen will move down his indifference curve because at point *F* the *MRS* is 3. Beth will move up her indifference curve since at point *G* the *MRS* is 3.

Even without referring to the indifference curves pictured in Figure 19–2, it is easy to predict how trades should proceed. Allen could offer 3*Y* to Brenda for 1*X*. Brenda would have accepted 2 units, so she is made better off. Allen would have given up as many as 4 units of *Y* for one unit of *X*, so he is made better off by the trade. Thus, trade takes the direction of Allen obtaining more *X* and Brenda more *Y*. The direction of exchange is fixed. No Pareto superior trades in which Allen gets more *Y* and Brenda more *X* exist. In the trade just discussed, both consumers are made better off, so the trade is a Pareto improvement. Other Pareto superior trades could have been proposed. For example, Allen could have exchanged 4 units of *Y* for 1 unit of *X*. Brenda moves to a higher indifference curve while Allen remains indifferent. As long as no one is harmed in the trade, it is still a Pareto superior exchange. Brenda could have received 2*Y* for 1*X*. Now Allen is made better off while Brenda remains on the same indifference curve. The trade is Pareto superior and moves Allen to a higher indifference curve while Brenda moves upward along the same indifference curve. Any trade between 4*X* for 1*Y* and 2*X* for 1*Y* is Pareto superior.

Trading between Brenda and Allen will cease when their marginal rates of substitution are equal. No additional trades that benefit both people or one person without harming the other can be proposed. When the marginal rates of substitution are equal, consumers are defined as being in *exchange equilibrium*.

19.3.2 The Edgeworth Box

Economists frequently use a graphical method to illustrate all of the potential equilibria of exchange. We continue to assume only two people and only two goods. Each person has an initial endowment of each good, but each does not necessarily have the goods in the proportion that yields greatest satisfaction. To analyze the gains from exchange and exchange equilibrium, we use a graphical device known as the Edgeworth Box diagram, named for F. Y. Edgeworth, a famous British economist of the late 19th century.[2]

First, consider Figure 19–3. There are two consumption goods, X and Y; these goods are available in absolutely fixed amounts. In addition, there are only two individuals in the society, A and B (Allen and Brenda are now abbreviated); they initially possess an endowment of X and Y, but the endowment ratio is not the one either would choose if allowed to specify it. This problem is graphically illustrated by constructing an origin for A, labeled O_A, and plotting quantities of the two goods person A possesses along the vertical and horizontal axes as shown. Thus, from the origin O_A, the quantity of X held by A (X_A) is plotted on the horizontal axis and the quantity of $Y(Y_A)$ on the vertical axis. A similar graph for B, with origin O_B, is constructed beside the graph for A. These two basic graphs are illustrated in Panel A, Figure 19–3.

Next, rotate the graph for individual B 180 degrees to the left, so that it is actually "upside down" when viewed normally, as shown in Panel B. The Edgeworth Box diagram is then formed by bringing the two graphs together. The length of the X axis is the sum $X_A + X_B$, which is the sum of the initial endowments of good X for persons A and B, while the vertical length of the Y axis is the sum $Y_A + Y_B$, which is the sum of the initial endowments of good Y for persons A and B. The two graphs will form a "box" with the length and height equivalent to the sum of the endowments going to both individuals. Figure 19–4 illustrates the Edgeworth Box.

Point D in Figure 19–4 accounts for the total endowment of X and Y possessed by A and B. Person A begins with x_A units of X and y_A units of Y. Since the aggregates are fixed, individual B must originally hold $x_B = X - x_A$ units of X and $y_B = Y - y_A$ units of Y, where X and Y are total initial endowments of the two goods.

---

[2]It has been pointed out to us by a reader of the manuscript, Professor Rodney Mabry, that Edgeworth had nothing to do with the development of the Edgeworth Box diagram; the true originator was V. Pareto. Not being historians, we gratefully acknowledge this but yield to convention in naming the diagram.

Figure 19–3   Constructing the Edgeworth Box Diagram

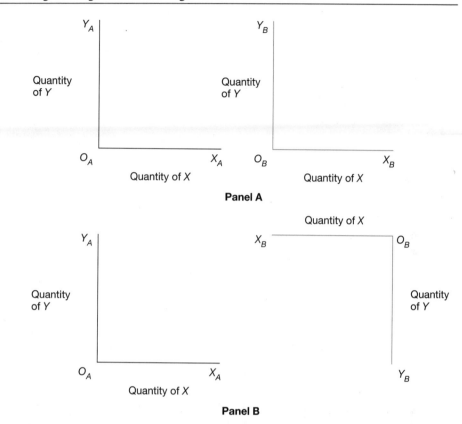

Every point in the Edgeworth Box completely describes the distribution of X and Y. Whatever part of the total person A does not have, person B holds. The closer point D is moved toward O_A, the more X and Y person B possesses. Moving D toward O_B indicates that person A has more of the total endowments.

19.3.3   Equilibrium of Exchange in the Edgeworth Box

As a first step toward defining equilibrium allocations that are Pareto optimal between individuals, consider an economy in which the exchange of the two goods takes place. If you like, you may think of the problem in the following context. There exists a small country with only two inhabitants, A and B, each of whom owns one half the land area. A and B produce nothing; they merely gather the foods X and Y that grow wild on the land. Each gathers only the food that falls on his or her land; but the two types do not fall uniformly. There is a relatively heavy concentration of Y on A's property and a relatively heavy concentration of X on B's land.

Figure 19–4   Edgeworth Box Diagram

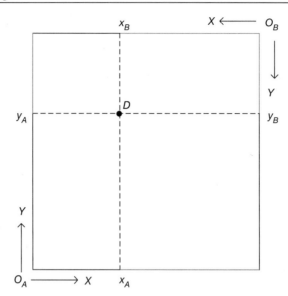

The problem of exchange is analyzed by means of the Edgeworth Box diagram in Figure 19–5. The dimensions of this basic box diagram now represent the scattering of foods, and we have added indifference curves for A and B. The curve I_A shows combinations of X and Y that yield A the same level of satisfaction. As usual, II_A represents a greater level of satisfaction than I_A; III_A is preferred to II_A; and so on. In general, A's well-being is enhanced by moving toward the B origin; B, in turn, enjoys greater satisfaction moving closer to the A origin.

Suppose the initial endowment is given by point D; A has x_A units of X and y_A units of Y. Similarly, B has x_B and y_B units of X and Y, respectively. The initial endowment places A on indifference curve II_A and B on curve I_B. At point D, A's marginal rate of substitution of X for Y, given by the slope TT', is relatively high; A would be willing to sacrifice, say, three units of Y in order to obtain one additional unit of X. At the same point, B has a relatively low marginal rate of substitution, as shown by the slope of SS'. Or, turning it around, B has a relatively high marginal rate of substitution of Y for X. Person B may, for example, be willing to forgo four units of X to obtain one unit of Y.

A situation such as this will always lead to exchange if the parties concerned are free to trade. From point D, A will trade some Y to B, receiving X in exchange. The exact bargain reached by the two traders cannot be determined. If B is the more skillful negotiator, B may induce A to move along II_A to point P_2. All the benefits of trade go to B, who moves from I_B to II_B. Or A might steer the bargain to point P_3, thereby increasing satisfaction from II_A to III_A, B's utility level remaining at I_B. Starting from point D, the ultimate exchange is very likely to lead to some point between P_2 and P_3, perhaps at a point such as P_4, at which two indifference curves, representing higher levels of utility for each, are tangent. Both therefore

Figure 19–5   General Equilibrium of Exchange

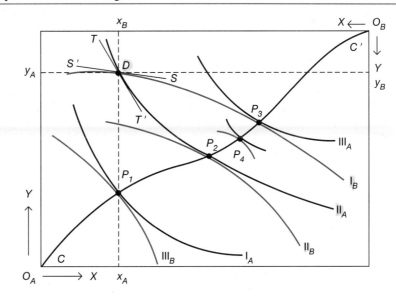

are made better off by trade. But the skill of the bargainers and their initial endowments determine the exact equilibrium point. Between points P_2 and P_3, one individual has been made better off without causing the other to become worse off, or both become better off in the sense of attaining a higher level of utility.

In the Edgeworth Box, exchange will continue to take place until the marginal rate of substitution of X for Y is the same for both traders. If the two marginal rates are different, one or both parties can benefit from exchange; neither party need lose. The exchange equilibrium can occur only at points such as P_1, P_2, P_3, or P_4 in Figure 19–5. The locus CC', called the contract curve in exchange, is a curve joining all points of tangency between one of A's indifference curves and one of B's. It is the locus along which the marginal rates of substitution are equal for both traders. We accordingly have the following principle.

Principle

> The general equilibrium of exchange occurs at a point where the marginal rate of substitution between every pair of goods is the same for all parties consuming both goods. The exchange equilibrium is not unique; it may occur at any point along the contract curve of the Edgeworth Box.

The contract curve represents all the possible Pareto optimal distributions between persons A and B in the sense that if the trading parties are located at some point not on the curve, one or both can benefit by exchanging goods so as to move to a point on the curve. To be sure, some points not on the curve are more preferable to one or the other party than are some points on the curve. But, for any point not on the curve, one or more attainable points on the curve are preferable to both parties. The chief characteristic of each point on the contract curve is that

Figure 19–6 Pareto Optimality in Production

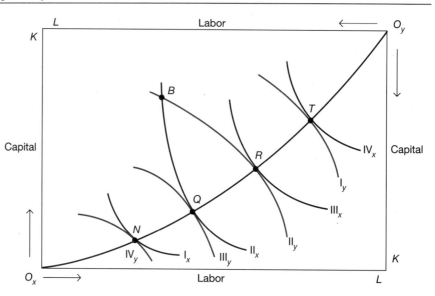

a movement along the curve away from that point must benefit one party and harm the other. Every distribution of *X* and *Y* that is represented by a point on the contract curve is said to be a Pareto-optimal distribution.

Principle

A Pareto-optimal distribution is one in which any change that makes some people better off makes others worse off. Thus, every point on the contract curve is Pareto optimal, and the contract curve is a locus of Pareto optimal points.

To summarize, the economics behind all of the graphical analysis simply says that people will trade only if the trade makes the participants better off. If each person's *MRS* is the same, it is impossible to make both parties better off through trade.

19.4 Equilibrium in Production

The analysis of equilibrium and Pareto optimality in production is quite similar to that of exchange. We can model production in the same way we did trade between two consumers. Suppose we have two firms producing two commodities with two inputs. We label the firms *X* and *Y*, and the two inputs, *K* and *L*, as shown in Figure 19–6.

19.4.1 Edgeworth Box in Production

We form an Edgeworth Box diagram similar to the diagram used to analyze consumer exchange. The *X* firm has the origin of its isoquant map at O_x; a portion of this firm's isoquant map is shown by isoquants I_x, II_x, III_x, and IV_x. The firm producing Y has the "turned around" isoquant map, with the origin at O_y. The isoquants for firm Y are shown by I_y, II_y, III_y, and IV_y. The total amounts of labor and capital available to the two firms are, respectively, $O_yL = O_xL$ and $O_yK = O_xK$; that is, labor is plotted along the horizontal axis and capital along the vertical.

Pareto optimality and equilibrium of production occurs at any combination of inputs where the marginal rates of technical substitution between labor and capital are equal for the two firms. This means the isoquants must be tangent so that $MRTS_x = MRTS_y$. To see why, suppose capital and labor are allocated between the two firms so that production takes place at point B. Firm X is producing the output given by II_x and firm Y, the output given by II_y. A reallocation of capital and labor between the two firms could move the production point to R—increased output for X with no decrease for Y—or to Q—increased output for Y with no decrease for X. Or both firms could increase output by moving to some combination between II_x and II_y, say to a point along the line QR. At any point at which the isoquants are not tangent, capital and labor can be reallocated so that one firm can increase its output without reducing the output of the other, or both can increase output.

The locus of points at which the isoquants are tangent is called the contract curve in production. If the firms are at a point on the contract curve, one firm can increase production only at the expense of a decrease in production for the other firm. To see this, assume that production takes place at point Q. Next, move in any direction to a point either on or off the contract curve, and note that the output of one firm must fall (move to a lower isoquant) while the output of the other must rise (move to a higher isoquant), or remain constant if the movement is along an isoquant.

It is obvious that the production equilibrium is not unique; it can occur at an infinite number of combinations on the contract curve. But each point on this curve represents a Pareto-optimal equilibrium. Production along the contract curve means that all resources are being used, and the production of one good can be increased only at the expense of a reduction in the production of the other good.

19.4.2   Production Possibilities Frontier

The contract curve in production is closely related to the theoretical concept of a *production-possibilities frontier*.

Definition

A production-possibilities frontier shows all combinations of goods and services that can be produced by a society when the society's resources are fully employed and all the goods and services are produced efficiently (i.e., using the cost-minimizing method of production). In a theoretical society in which only two goods are produced, the production-possibilities frontier is called the production-possibilities curve.

A production-possibilities frontier or curve indicates the opportunity cost of producing additional amounts of a particular good in terms of the amounts of other goods that must be given up if more of that good is produced. Considering a production-possibilities curve when only two goods, X and Y, are produced, every

Figure 19–7   Derivation of a Production-Possibilities Curve

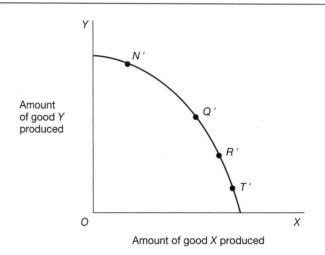

point on a production-possibilities curve corresponds to specific levels of output of goods X and Y. It shows the rate at which one of the goods must be given up in order for the society to produce more of the other good.

A production-possibilities curve is easily derived from a contract curve, such as the one shown in Figure 19–6. The derived curve illustrates the general features of any production-possibilities frontier or curve.

Consider point N on the contract curve in Figure 19–6. Firm X is producing the amount of X represented by isoquant I_X. Firm Y is producing the amount of Y represented by isoquant IV_Y. At point N, all resources are employed and the goods are produced efficiently because the isoquants are tangent. Relatively large amounts of capital and labor are used in the production of Y, and relatively small amounts are used in the production of X.

The respective amounts of goods X and Y produced at point N represent a point of the production-possibilities curve depicted in Figure 19–7. In the figure, the quantity of X is plotted along the horizontal axis, and the quantity of Y is plotted along the vertical. The combination of X and Y produced at N on the contract curve is represented as point N' on the production-possibilities curve in Figure 19–7.

We then move to point Q in Figure 19–6. At Q, the amount of X has increased, shown by the higher isoquant II_X, and the amount of Y has decreased, shown by the lower isoquant III_Y. Some labor and capital have been taken away from the production of Y and added to the production of X. The amounts of X and Y produced at point Q on the contract curve are plotted as point Q' on the production-possibilities curve. Point Q' represents more X and less Y. The quantities of X and Y produced when the isoquants in Figure 19–6 are tangent at points R and T are shown, respectively, as combinations R' and T' in Figure 19–7.

All other combinations on the production-possibilities curve are generated from the contract curve in the same way. As the society moves along the contract curve to higher isoquants in the production of X and lower isoquants in the production of Y, it moves downward along the production-possibilities curve, as less Y and more X are produced. The society can choose any combination on the production-possibilities curve, all of which represent efficient levels of production because the marginal rates of technical substitution are equal in the production of both goods.

The production-possibilities curve in Figure 19–7, derived from the contract curve in Figure 19–6, illustrates some important characteristics of production in any society. To obtain more of one good, some amounts of the other good or goods must be given up. This is because the society must move along its contract curve if more of a good is produced, and, as illustrated in Figure 19–6, resources must be shifted away from the production of one good into the production of the other.

Second, as shown by the decreasing absolute value of the slope of the production possibilities curve, for a given amount of increase in good X, increasing amounts of good Y must be given up as the production of X becomes larger and the production of Y becomes smaller; that is, the larger the amount of X and the smaller the amount of Y, the greater the opportunity cost of additional units of X in terms of sacrificed Y. We will return to this characteristic later in this chapter. Third, any combination of X and Y above the production-possibilities curve cannot be produced with the limited amounts of resources in the society. Finally, any combination of X and Y inside the production-possibilities curve does not represent a combination of resources along the contract curve because it is not produced efficiently; more of one good can be produced without giving up any of the other good, or more of both goods can be produced. Such a change in production could be a movement from a point off of the contract curve to a point on the contract curve, as discussed in the previous paragraphs.

19.1   *Applying the Theory*

List some factors that would cause the production-possibility frontier to shift outward. How can an economy produce more of everything?

19.5   General Equilibrium

We have described the equilibrium conditions between two consumers and two producers. When consumers maximize utility and are able to trade between themselves, they reach an equilibrium that is Pareto optimal. On the contract curve in exchange, the marginal rate of substitution for both consumers is equal. A very similar result was developed for producers. In this case, optimization led two producers in the Edgeworth Box to operate where their respective *MRTS*s are the same. If these slopes were different, it would be possible to increase the production of one or both outputs, holding the amounts of inputs fixed. We have observed, in short, that Pareto optimality is really not a condition of welfare as much as it is one of efficiency.

Having described the conditions of efficiency among consumers and the conditions for producers, we now examine efficiency across these two economic groups. Pareto optimality across producers and consumers is referred to as the general equilibrium condition.

Figure 19–8   General Equilibrium in Production and Exchange

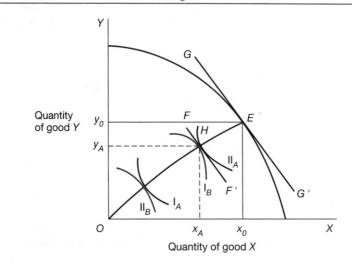

19.5.1   Pareto Optimality across Consumers and Producers

The problem of general equilibrium is as follows: Is there a set of prices at which the demands of consumers are voluntarily fulfilled by the suppliers who use all the productive resources that are voluntarily supplied at the going set of prices? If so, an efficient general equilibrium exists.

We could provide a fanciful example in which an auctioneer assembles all participants in the economy and "zeros in" on a set of prices in which all markets are in equilibrium. But this process is not even approximately descriptive of any real-world markets. However, competitive bids and counter bids in all markets do tend to push the economy toward an efficient general equilibrium. Needless to say, such an equilibrium is never, in fact, even approximately attained. There is, however, a tendency toward it; and, it is often useful to analyze the situation that would exist if markets were in general equilibrium.

General equilibrium occurs when equilibrium exists in both exchange and production. We can effectively combine the Edgeworth Boxes for production and exchange by placing the exchange box inside the production-possibilities frontier, which is derived from the production contract curve. Each point on the frontier is a point on the production contract curve. It determines what is available for exchange in the two-producer, two-consumer model. As Figure 19–8 shows, a tangent to the selected point on the frontier is the slope of the production-possibilities frontier, and the absolute value of the slope is called the *marginal rate of transformation*. Hence, the slope of the tangent at E represents the opportunity cost, in terms of sacrificed Y, of producing another unit of X. More precisely, the slope, $\Delta Y/\Delta X$, shows how much of good Y society must forgo to have another unit of X. Production at E, with x_0 units of X and y_0 units of Y, is Pareto optimal.

19.5.2   General Equilibrium in Production and Exchange

Optimality in exchange comes from letting consumers A and B distribute the x_0 and y_0 output. Pareto efficiency, as you already know, exists along the exchange contract line. Let the Edgeworth Box for exchange be Oy_0Ex_0, with x_0 and y_0 being, from the production-possibilities frontier, the total amounts of X and Y available. The origin for the consumer with indifference map I_A and II_A is at zero; the consumer with indifference map I_B, II_B has the origin at E. Clearly, there are an infinite number of possible allocations along the contract curve. But general equilibrium occurs when the marginal rate of transformation (MRT)—the slope of the production-possibilities frontier—is equal to the marginal rate of substitution for both consumers. Because we drop the negative sign on the slope of the MRS, we also do so for the MRT.

In Figure 19–8, general equilibrium exists at a point such as H. It is here that the slope of the tangent lines FF' and GG' are equal. Consumer A gets x_A and y_A units of output; consumer B gets $(x_0 - x_A)$ and $(y_0 - y_A)$ units. The amount of labor and capital used in production at E is determined by going back to the point on the production contract curve. Of course, there could be other, perhaps many other, points on the exchange contract curve where the slopes of the indifference curves are equal to the slope of GG'. The consumers will settle at such a point, and if there are several such points, the one chosen will depend on the original distribution of the two goods.

You might wonder why must $MRS_A = MRS_B = MRT$ in general equilibrium? First, if MRS_A is not equal to MRS_B, individuals A and B could trade and increase the utility of at least one person without decreasing the utility of the other. Therefore, whatever the output, MRS_A must equal MRS_B. Next, suppose MRS_A (or MRS_B) does not equal MRT. For example, let the MRS for each consumer be two and the MRT be three. Consumers are willing to take two more units of Y for one less unit of X, while producers can produce three more units of Y if they produce one less unit of X. It would, therefore, be possible for the producers to produce three more Y, give two to consumer A (or B) for the X lost to produce the additional three units of Y, reducing the production of X by one, and have one unit of Y left over. The extra unit of Y could be given to either person A or B to increase utility. Thus, welfare rises by the Pareto rule. Welfare can be improved as long as the absolute value of the slope of the production-possibilities curve is not equal to the common marginal rate of substitution in exchange.

19.6   Equilibrium in Perfect Competition

We now assume that there is perfect competition in every market and show that the set of input and output prices that exists will, in general, establish a Pareto-optimal organization for society. Thus, perfect competition is a sufficient condition for the general equilibrium we have just described.

19.6.1 Consumers in Competitive Markets

First, consider consumers. If there is perfect competition, all consumers face the same set of commodity prices. Since all consuming units set their *MRS* equal to the price ratio, the *MRS* of any one consumer is equal to the *MRS* of any other consuming unit. Since all consumers are just willing to exchange commodities in the same ratio, it is impossible to make one better off without making another worse off. Thus, a Pareto optimum is established among buyers.

19.6.2 Producers in Competitive Markets

Next, consider producers. In maximizing profit, entrepreneurs necessarily arrange the combination of inputs so as to minimize the total cost of production. Under perfect competition, the factor-price ratios are the same to all producers. Since each producer equates *MRTS* to the common factor-price ratio, the *MRTS* is the same for all. Consequently, there is no reallocation of inputs that would increase one producer's output without reducing another's. Again, a Pareto-optimal outcome is established.

19.6.3 General Equilibrium and Perfect Competition

For general equilibrium, the slope of the production-possibility frontier, or the marginal rate of transformation, represents the opportunity cost of producing another unit of either good. In other words, the opportunity cost of another unit of X is ΔY, and the opportunity cost of one more unit of Y is ΔX. Thus, the ratio

$$\frac{\Delta Y}{\Delta X} = \frac{\text{opportunity cost of } X}{\text{opportunity cost of } Y} \, .$$

When perfectly competitive firms maximize profits, they set the marginal cost of producing the good equal to its market price. Assuming that the marginal cost paid by the firm truly reflects the opportunity cost of the resources necessary to produce the last unit of output, we may write

$$\frac{\Delta Y}{\Delta X} = \frac{MC_x}{MC_y} = \frac{P_x}{P_y} \, ,$$

where the ratio on the far left is the slope of the production-possibility frontier. The first equality shows that the slope of the production-possibility frontier is equal to the ratio of the marginal costs. This equality explains why the production-possibilities frontier in bowed outward (i.e., the slope of the curve increases in absolute value). As the quantity of X increases, MC_x becomes larger. As the quantity of Y decreases, MC_y becomes smaller. Thus, increases in X and decreases in Y cause MC_x/MC_y to increase, and therefore the absolute value of the slope of the production possibilities frontier, $\Delta Y/\Delta X$, must increase.

The second equality between the marginal cost ratio and the price ratio comes from profit maximization under perfect competition. Each perfect competitor sets marginal cost equal to product price. When consumers maximize utility, they equate their

$$MRS_{x \text{ for } y} = \frac{P_x}{P_y}$$

so the marginal rate of transformation must therefore be equal to the marginal rate of substitution because both are equal to the ratio of market prices.

Finally, in this competitive general equilibrium, the number of hours of work voluntarily offered is exactly equal to the number of hours voluntarily demanded. An increase in wages would help some people, but some others would be unemployed. That is, an increase in wages would make some better off and some worse off. A decrease in wages would cause an excess demand. A change in wages from the general equilibrium level will upset both Pareto optimality and general equilibrium.

Let us reemphasize that Pareto optimality does not necessarily indicate maximum attainable welfare or the maximum attainable level of utility for society as a whole. As we stressed in this chapter, to specify maximum welfare, we would have to specify a welfare function for society as a whole. This we cannot do. Perfect competition does lead to a final Pareto-optimal equilibrium point, but this is an arbitrary point because any other point on the production-possibilities frontier also can be Pareto optimal in the sense of being efficient. The actual point attained depends on (among other things) the initial "starting point," or the initial distribution of income.

Government may (and generally does) become involved in deciding what the initial distribution of income will be. Although representatives may decide that the existing income distribution is preferable to any other distribution, or that some other distribution is more preferred, the role of an economist is not to decide what distribution is best, even under perfect competition. An economist's role does include pointing out the economic consequences of changing the distribution. All an economist can say is that if one or more people can be made better off by an action without anyone else being made worse off, the action makes the group better off.

Economics in the News

There Is a Difference between Efficiency and Fairness[3]

In 1990, Yale economist Robert Shiller and two Soviet social scientists, Maxim Boycko and Vladimir Korobov, asked New Yorkers and Muscovites what they thought about free markets. One of the questions was: "Is it fair for flower prices to rise on holidays, when demand is exceptionally high?" American and Russian responses were about the same: 66 percent of the Russians thought it unfair, as did 68 percent of the New Yorkers. Yet, in order for the market to operate efficiently, when demand increases, prices should rise if supply is upward sloping. There is the fundamental principle that markets are efficient if exchange is carried out to the point where marginal benefit is equal to marginal cost.

(continued)

---

[3]This report is based on the editorial by Alan S. Blinder, "Land of the Free: But Not of the Free Market," *Business Week,* September 10, 1990, p. 22.

A follow-up question was: "Should the government intervene to hold prices down even if it caused a shortage?" To this, 54 percent of the Russians thought so, but only 28 percent of the Americans. Americans practice capitalism, but often feel it is unfair.

This sentiment was made vivid by the rise in gasoline prices soon after the Iraqi invasion of Kuwait. The invasion caused a 6 percent reduction in the supply of oil. This reduction led to a $6 per barrel increase in the price of crude, which translated into about a $.14 rise in the price of gasoline. The national mood was that the increase was unfair. President Bush asked petroleum companies to hold down their prices, and Congress began investigations of price gouging. The market was working. This time the supply schedule was shifting to the left. The decrease in crude supply led to higher prices of refined products. This increase in prices is exactly what the model of perfect competition would predict. Adjustments were being made to bring about efficient allocations of crude oil. Nevertheless, the adjustments seemed unfair to many people. Fairness and efficiency are often two conflicting issues in markets.

19.7 Summary

The maximization of community utility or welfare, as we have called it in this chapter, presents difficult conceptual problems. There is no such thing as an aggregate utility function because indifference curves cannot be added across individuals. Indeed, any measure of group benefit runs into the problem of interpersonal utility comparison.

Economists have made their greatest contribution to the field of welfare economics through the condition of Pareto optimality. This rule really describes an efficient distribution of a scarce resource or product. Pareto optimality exists whenever it is impossible to help someone without hurting another person in the market. This definition led to the Pareto criteria by which economists judge a redistribution of goods: (a) If change will benefit one or more people without making anyone worse off, the change is socially desirable; (b) if a change helps some and hurts others—the numbers are immaterial—no conclusion can be reached by an economist.

In markets, Pareto optimality exists when consumers have the same marginal rates of substitution and producers have the same marginal rates of technical substitution. These properties were illustrated through the use of Edgeworth Box diagrams. Along the contract curve in an Edgeworth Box, it is impossible to improve the welfare of one economic agent without decreasing utility or production of the other. Therefore, all points along the contract curve are Pareto optimal. In markets where economic agents can freely trade, a point on the contract curve is reached; this point depends on the initial distribution of the items traded and to some extent on the bargaining acumen of traders.

General equilibrium exhibits the condition of Pareto optimality between producers and consumers. Markets are efficient first, if producers operate on the production-possibility frontier, and second, if the slope of this frontier, or marginal rate of transformation, is the same as the common *MRS* at which consumers trade.

General equilibrium is not a unique condition in an economy. There may indeed be many points on the production frontier that satisfy this rule.

Finally and most importantly, perfect competition by means of the price mechanism leads to a Pareto-optimal allocation of resources. Again, this allocation is optimal in the sense that it is efficient. Efficiency occurs when consumers maximize utility facing the same market prices and producers maximize profit when faced with common input prices and set marginal cost equal to the product price they observe in the market. A function of microeconomic theory is to determine the relative efficiency of various types of market organization. The major conclusion of this chapter is that competition can be efficient.

Answers to *Applying the Theory*

19.1   Producing more of everything means that the production-possibility frontier has shifted outward. Outward shifts can be caused by an improvement in technology. Technical advances, for instance, can make it less costly to produce a product. An increase in the stock of inputs can also push out the frontier. Greater quantities of inputs can expand an economy. The labor resource can be expanded by increasing the pool of people willing to work, but another way is through education, which in general increases the productivity of the individual.

Technical Problems

1. Explain why equality of marginal rates of substitution between any two goods for any pair of consumers implies that no consumer can be made better off without making some other consumer worse off. Why does perfect competition guarantee this result?

2. Assume two firms, each using capital and labor to produce two goods. The marginal rates of technical substitution between capital and labor are the same for each firm. Total capital and labor are fixed in amount. Explain why one firm cannot increase output without causing the other to decrease output.

3. Explain why there can generally be no social welfare function or social preference ordering.

4. There are two individuals, A and B, who consume two goods, X and Y. Consumer A's marginal rate of substitution between goods X and Y is two X for one Y. B's *MRS* is three X for two Y. In what direction will trade take place and between what two ratios?

5. In the Edgeworth diagram in Figure E.19–1, on the next page, point R represents the original allocation of goods X and Y between individuals A and B. Indicate:
   a. The feasible region of exchange and why this range is feasible.
   b. All points unacceptable to A and why.

6. Use the following consumption Edgeworth Box (Figure E.19–2) diagram to answer this question. For two individuals, A and B, A's initial endowment of Y is all of the Y and B's initial endowment of Y is zero. A's initial endowment of X is the distance $O_A\bar{x}$ and B's initial endowment of X is $\bar{x}$. A's $MRS = -\Delta y/\Delta x = 1/2$ and B's $MRS = -\Delta y/\Delta x = 2$ at the original endowment shown at $\bar{x}$.

Figure E.19–1

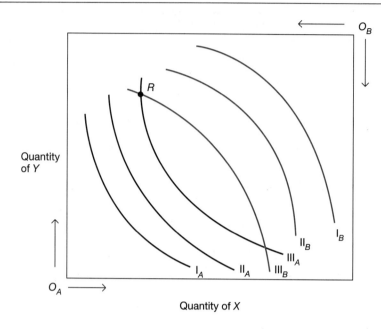

Figure E.19–2

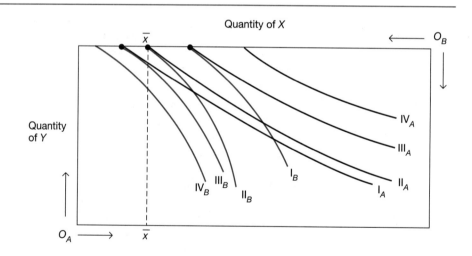

   a. If the two parties can trade, what will they do? Explain.
   b. Is this equilibrium Pareto optimal? Explain.
   c. What is the contract curve around this equilibrium? Explain
7. Explain how the production-possibility frontier is derived from the production
   Edgeworth Box.
8. Firm one produces good X and firm two produces Y. Both firms use labor (L)
   and capital (K) in the production process. For firm one, $MP_L = 10$ and MP_K

Figure E.19–3

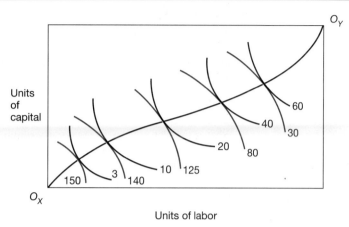

Figure E.19–4

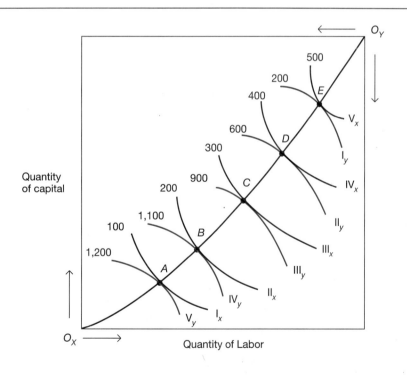

= 15. For firm two MP_L = 6 and MP_K = 12. What should the firms do from a
   social point of view?

9. Why is perfect competition desirable according to the Pareto optimality rule in
   welfare economics? Explain.

10. Given the contract curve for production in Figure E.19–3, construct a
    production-possibility frontier for X and Y. The numbers attached to each
    isoquant represent units of output.

11. Discuss the shape of the production-possibility frontier.
    a. Why is it concave (have an outward bulge)?
    b. Graphically sketch the marginal cost of producing X or Y from the production-possibility frontier. What is the relation between their shapes?
12. Use the production Edgeworth Box diagram (Figure E.19–4) on the preceding page to answer this question. This economy produces two goods, X and Y, using two inputs, L and K. The isoquants show the amount of X and Y produced at several points on the contract curve.
    a. Graph the relevant portion of the production-possibilities curve for X and Y (points A through E).
    b. What is the slope of the production-possibilities curve between each pair of points? Is this curve of the theoretically assumed shape? Explain what the "theoretically assumed shape" indicates (not geometrically but economically).
    c. What happens to the ratio of the marginal cost of X to the marginal cost of Y as X increases and Y decreases? Is this result consistent with the theory of cost? Explain.
    d. What happens to the capital/labor ratio in the production of each good as X increases and Y decreases?.

Analytical Problems

1. Frequently people talk about the goals of a city.
   a. Can a city have goals? Why or why not?
   b. Under what circumstances could you state unequivocally that a city was made better off by a particular activity?
   c. Suppose someone says the goal of a city should be to force the downtown merchants to beautify the downtown area. Can you see any possible trade-off or contradiction?
2. The federal government is very much involved in the redistribution of income. Some programs that transfer income are welfare, social security, and unemployment compensation. Pareto optimality takes the distribution of income as given. Discuss the rationale for income redistributions in light of the Pareto criterion.
3. Pareto efficiency and equity often work against each other in public policy analysis. For example, a particular distribution of goods may be efficient but not equitable if one consumer has most of the goods. Should efficiency be sacrificed to obtain a more equal distribution of goods and services?
4. Frequently a country's gross national product (GNP) is used as a measure of welfare. As GNP increases, the nation is considered to have an improved level of social welfare. Under what conditions, if any, can GNP be used as an indicator of welfare?
5. Some economists are very critical of the Pareto condition as a measure of welfare. The argument made is that utility is not independent of someone else's income. For example, if the Jones family next door gets a new color television, your utility may fall because of envy. The very fact that someone is happier may make another person more or less happy. Is there any validity to this argument? Can you think of examples where this seems to be true?
6. Welfare economics frequently makes use of the concept of Pareto optimality and Pareto-superior moves. Discuss the application of this criterion to some recent welfare problems and discuss the problem of evaluating alternative positions.

a. A tax on cigarettes that raises money for the government and presumably benefits smokers by encouraging them to smoke less.

b. An additional tax deduction for every family with children under the age of 12.

c. A tariff on foreign automobiles in order to protect the jobs of U.S. workers.

d. The opening of a free-trade zone with Mexico.

e. The comptroller of Texas announced in June 1991 that he had found $4.5 billion of waste in the state government budget. The governor of Texas then says that she will cut out this waste in order to reduce the state budget deficit without imposing an income tax.

7. In light of your answer to the above question can you think of a realistic law that the U.S. government could conceivably pass that would be a Pareto-superior law? By the way, at least one member of Congress voted against declaring war after the bombing of Pearl Harbor in 1941.

8. An economics student once commented, "It's practically impossible to think of a realistic Pareto-superior move that the government could make, so we must live in a Pareto-optimal world." Comment.

9. Competitive firms operate at the minimum point of long-run average cost and their marginal cost equals price; they are operating efficiently. A monopoly, in this sense, is not operating efficiently. If you find the monopoly unsatisfactory, suggest an alternative solution.

10. Analyze the following within the context of welfare economics (not as a rhetoritician).

a. Arguably, the greatest president of the United States spoke of a government "of the people, by the people, and for the people."

b. Another U.S. president, who was arguably in the top 5 or 10, spoke early in his term about one of the four freedoms of U.S. citizens as "freedom from want."

c. A later U.S. president told the American people to "Ask not what your country can do for you, but what you can do for your country." How would you go about finding out what you can do for your country?

d. In 1215 at Runnymede, when the English lords, high churchmen, and representatives of the city of London required King John to sign the Magna Carta, arguably one of the foundations of Western civilization, King John is reported to have asserted, "I can't sign this, it's not a Pareto-superior move!" The lords and others replied, "It is too." Who was right? By the way, many years before the English lords allegedly responded as King John did when Henry II laid the foundation of the English Common Law, which was not an insignificant achievement.

e. Can you think of a famous law, edict, or proclamation that was a Pareto-superior move?

CHAPTER 20

Exchange Inefficiencies
and Welfare

20.1 Introduction

In Chapter 19, we discussed how perfect competition leads to a Pareto-optimal distribution of goods and services. Although perfectly competitive markets are not characteristic of the real world, the competitive general equilibrium model serves as an excellent benchmark to compare the performance of real markets. We will examine here some of the reasons that markets do not achieve Pareto optimality. These reasons fall under the broad heading of market failure. In general, markets fail when exchange is impeded. We have discussed how markets become less efficient when prices are imposed by the government or firms have market power. These are two causes of market failure. In the next section, we analyze how government controls and monopoly cause market failure in the context of the general equilibrium model.

Market failure can also arise from the very nature of how certain goods and services are produced or consumed. In some cases, there exist peculiar features of consumption and production that make some goods difficult to trade in the marketplace. Because trade is difficult, exchange is impeded. One peculiar feature is that consumers of a good or service may not be able to exclude others from consuming the same good or service once it has been acquired. In other cases, producers, once they produce a product, cannot exclude people from enjoying the benefits of a product free of charge. You will see in this chapter that when there are such nonexclusion problems, a market, if it exists at all, does not lead to a Pareto-efficient outcome, even when there is perfect competition. When there is the inability to exclude someone from consuming a product, we have a *public good;* the existence of public goods leads to market failure.

Another source of market inefficiency results from external benefits and costs. Referred to broadly as *externalities,* this form of inefficiency arises when the ownership of valuable properties such as air, water, and sometimes land, is not well defined. In such cases, polluted water, air, or land is imposed on others without an agreed upon transaction. If individual ownership could be better defined, or a designated owner found to represent the interests of those individuals with a collective right to the resource, the transactions might be brought back into the marketplace and the source of the market failure corrected. This chapter discusses three reasons that cause markets to perform poorly. In the order they are presented, these causes of market failure are restrictions on competition, public goods, and externalities.

20.2   Restrictions on Competition

Markets may fail to provide a Pareto-efficient outcome because of a breakdown in competitive market structures. One source of breakdown is government control. Another is monopoly. As markets become more monopolized, there is a strong presumption that they also become less efficient. This point was already discussed in terms of consumer's and producer's surplus in Chapter 15. As firms gain more market power, they have an increased capability to set price above marginal cost. This earns them more profit, but causes a loss in total market surplus. In this section, we show that restrictions on competition arising from government price controls or monopoly violate the conditions for Pareto optimality. We then briefly discuss a caveat concerning making markets more competitive; this warning is widely known as the theory of the second best.

20.2.1   Monopoly Inefficiency

In Chapter 19, one of the Pareto rules for efficiency was that for consumers and producers,

$$MRS_{x \text{ for } y} = MRT;$$

that is, the slope of every consumer's indifference curve should be equal to the slope of the production-possibility frontier. The marginal rate of transformation, or the slope of the production-possibility frontier, is equivalent to the ratio of marginal costs, MC_x/MC_y. In perfect competition, this condition is satisfied through the set of equalities:

$$MRT = \frac{MC_x}{MC_y} = \frac{P_x}{P_y} = MRS_{x \text{ for } y}.$$

Profit maximizers set price equal to marginal cost in competitive markets. Likewise, utility-maximizing consumers equalize the slope of their indifference curves *(MRS)* with the same price ratio shown above. Competition thus leads to the equality of the *MRT* and the *MRS*s of consumers. If we focus on just the middle part of the above equalities,

$$\frac{MC_x}{MC_y} = \frac{P_x}{P_y},$$

and, rearranging terms, we can write this expression as

$$\frac{MC_x}{P_x} = \frac{MC_y}{P_y} = 1.$$

Both ratios are equal to one because perfect competitors set price equal to marginal cost.

This last relation helps explain why the existence of monopoly power is not Pareto optimal. In the case of monopoly, a firm sets price above marginal cost. Hence, for monopoly in both X and Y markets it is generally the case that

$$\frac{MC_x}{P_x} \neq \frac{MC_y}{P_y} < 1.$$

Not only are the ratios unequal, but they are both less than one. This means two things. First, the slope of the production-possibility frontier will not be the same as the slope of the consumers' indifference curves; and, second, since the ratios of marginal cost to price are less than one, the economy is operating inside the production frontier. Too few resources are being devoted to the production of goods in markets that are monopolized.

20.2.2 Government Controls

The same inference can be drawn when there are government price controls. Price floors cause prices to be above marginal cost, similar to the effects of monopoly. Price ceilings keep prices too low in the market. In both cases, too few resources are used in the production of the good. Also, taxes and subsidies distort the supply curve by shifting it, and therefore supply does not reflect the true cost of production in a market. Taxes appear to raise cost, and subsidies appear to lower cost. A tax will lead to fewer resources in production than is optimal; a subsidy to more resources. In both cases, inefficiencies are caused.

In summary, we have the following principle:

Principle

If there is not perfect competition, the market will not, in general, allocate the optimal amount of resources in the production of a good. An efficient equilibrium is not obtained.

Economics in the News

In Korea the Same American Products Have Different Prices[1]

American-made products find their way into South Korea through two channels. One is United States military bases that import the goods for troops stationed in the country. Soldiers and their families can purchase the goods at the base commissary at an average price that is about 25 percent below those at American supermarkets. The second way American goods enter South Korea is through nonmilitary importation. Manufacturers through authorized import-export licenses ship their products overseas. Generally, the goods are subject to import taxes when they enter the foreign country. Distributors shipping to South Korea pay a 15 percent import tax as well as local taxes and freight charges.

As a result of military and nonmilitary price differences, illegal markets have developed in South Korea. They are called *shijang*, or goblin markets (known as black markets in the United States). Prices on the goblin markets are set generally between the military price and the official price. The following gives some examples.

	U.S. Military Base Price	Korean Supermarket Price	Korean Goblin Market Price
Skippy peanut butter	$ 2.88	$ 6.90	$ 5.52
Johnson & Johnson baby oil	2.44*	6.76†	4.83*
Spam	1.81	3.15	2.76
V-8 juice (6-pack)	1.49	4.14	2.76
Aqua-Net hair spray	1.40	3.45	2.76
Chivas Regal	21.00	99.00	40.00

*14 oz.

†11.25 oz.

Source: *The Wall Street Journal*, "Korean Black Market Stymies U.S. Firms," July 19, 1991, p. B1.

Whenever consumers face different prices, in this case because of government controls, the market is not Pareto optimal and not in general equilibrium. The black-market prices are evidence of the market attempting to achieve equilibrium.

The goblin market is created by U.S. military personnel buying items on the base and then reselling them to intermediaries who sell illegally on the goblin market. Because three prices exist in the economy, consumers are behaving inefficiently. Some maximize utility by paying the military price, some maximize by paying the official supermarket price, and some maximize by paying the goblin-market price. The market is failing because of U.S. government subsidies and South Korean taxes. The goblin market is to date a relatively small piece of the total trade in South Korea. U.S. military bases in South Korea sell about $380 million in goods a year. About 20 to 33 percent goes into

(continued)

[1]This report is based upon "Korean Black Market Stymies U.S. Firms," *The Wall Street Journal*, July 19, 1991, p. B1.

20.2.3   Theory of Second Best

The previous principle seems to imply that society can be made better off anytime a monopolized or government-controlled market or markets can be made more competitive. From a policy point of view, the implication is that laws against monopoly or laws requiring the privatization of markets are beneficial. If there is any way policymakers can move, say, a monopolized market toward one that is more competitive, it would appear to be a Pareto-superior action because prices and marginal costs would move closer together. Some markets may never be competitive, but the more that are, it would seem the more efficient is production. Do we know for sure that Pareto efficiency will go up whenever a market is made more competitive?

The answer is, efficiency may not necessarily increase, and this is what the theory of second best is all about. This theory states that it is sometimes better to be at a point inside the production-possibility frontier than be at just any point on it. Such an idea was made widely known by R. G. Lipsey and Kelvin Lancaster.[2] Since then many technical arguments have followed, but the main idea can be explained quite easily with the help of Figure 20–1. Suppose we begin with a production-possibility frontier with endpoints $Q_y Q_x$ shown in the figure.

Even though community indifference curves do not exist in any consistent way, suppose for the sake of argument that society actually has a set of convex curves that look very much like those for a single consumer. In Figure 20–1 let W_1, W_2, and W_3 be three indifference curves for a society.[3] The curve with the highest level of benefit is W_3, and it is just tangent to the frontier at A. At point A we will assume that society's *MRT* equals the *MRS* for all individuals. Thus, point A represents an efficient, or Pareto-optimal, distribution of resources and outputs.

The presence of monopoly means production is not efficiently organized. There are too few resources in some industries and too many in others. Suppose that both the X and Y industries are monopolized, and society moves to a point inside the

[2]R. G. Lipsey and Kelvin Lancaster, "The General Theory of Second Best," *Review of Economic Studies* 24, no. 1 (1956–1957), pp. 11–32.

[3]We cannot, of course, theoretically derive these curves because of our inability to compare levels of utility across individuals. Remember utility is ordinal and not cardinal. We introduce these curves only to discuss relative levels of social welfare, which conceptually must exist, even though such schedules cannot be derived.

Figure 20–1 Theory of Second Best

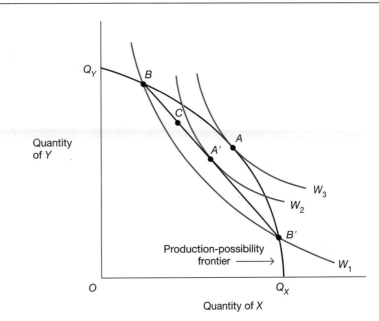

frontier along the straight line *BB'*. Where this point is on the line will depend in part on the degree of monopolization in each industry. Suppose society is at point *C*, inside the production frontier. Relative to point *A*, too much of good *Y* and too little of *X* are being produced. If, however, resources were allocated toward industry *Y*, the society could move back to the frontier, perhaps to a point such as *B*. This point represents a policy that makes the *Y* industry produce even more than it would produce at the efficient point, *A*.

However, if society has indifference curves like those shown in Figure 20–1, moving back to the frontier is worse than an interior solution. You can see that moving from point *B* to point *A'* would increase welfare for society from W_1 to W_2. If production is at point *C*, policymakers should attempt to increase output in industry *X* relative to industry *Y*. Given that neither industry is competitive, it is therefore not in the best interests of society to reach just any point on the production-possibility frontier.

There is no uniform agreement among economists concerning the role of government in making markets more competitive. Some argue that piecemeal policies will make matters worse. Others argue categorically for any policy that forces firms to price closer to marginal cost. Proponents of the latter policy maintain that when markets are relatively independent of one another, marginal cost pricing increases efficiency. The theory of second best applies most strongly when markets are closely related; that is, they either produce complementary goods such as bread and butter, or one market is an intermediate supplier of another as in the case of tiremakers supplying automobile producers.

20.3   Public Goods

The very nature of some goods and services makes it difficult, if not impossible, for markets to function efficiently. The problem centers around either consumers being unable to exclude others from consuming precisely the same good that they consume, or producers being unable to exclude consumers who do not pay for the product from enjoying the benefits of the product once it is produced. Such goods are called public goods. The existence of public goods can lead to market failure, because they hamper the incentive to trade.

Most goods do not suffer from the nonexclusion problem. When someone eats an apple or drinks a Coke, someone else can't eat the same apple or have the same drink. If you want these goods, you will have to buy units of them distinct from those consumed by someone else, and you therefore must pay a price for ownership and consumption that covers the cost of production. It is this exchange that creates and maintains markets. Certain goods, however, do not have the characteristics of apples and Cokes. For example, if your roommate hangs a clock in your apartment, you both gain and simultaneously consume the benefits of knowing what time it is. The clock is a public good. If someone consumes a public good, someone else can consume exactly the same good without reducing that person's consumption of it.

Definition

A public good exists when there is nonexclusion in consumption. That is, person A's consumption is not affected by persons B, C, or D also consuming the same product. The nonexclusion problem may arise once the product is produced, or when it is purchased.

Before we discuss public goods more thoroughly, we should mention that a solution to the problems arising from nonexclusion is generally not straightforward. We must also note that although this section discusses the provision of goods that do not permit exclusion, it is rarely the case that any good completely satisfies the definition of a public good. At some point, consumption by others does affect your enjoyment of the good. For instance, if everybody in your dormitory or apartment complex came into your room to look at your clock, your enjoyment of the clock would be affected. The congestion would greatly alter your lifestyle. Also, exclusion may be feasible at some point. To keep people from coming into your room to check the time, you could just close and even lock the door. Perhaps the only, and certainly the most widely cited, example of a true public good is the production of national defense. But some economists disagree even about this.

20.3.1   The Free Rider Problem

The easiest way to see how nonexclusion can lead to market failure is to look at nonexclusion at the time the good is produced. Nonexclusion in production arises when the producer of a good cannot prevent people who do not pay for the good from consuming it. Obviously, profit-maximizing firms will not produce a good unless they can withhold it if payment is not made. A park without limited access may be an example. A firm must pay the expense of producing the park, but it may have no control over park use after it is built. No control means no revenue, so profit-maximizing firms will stay away from such ventures.

Another frequently cited example is a lighthouse. While it might be technically possible to exclude nonpaying ships from the use of the lighthouse, it would probably be economically infeasible to do so. Or, consider the following example. Suppose that 1,000 families live along a river that floods every few years, causing these people considerable damage. An enterprising person could come along and offer to build a dam, charging these people an amount per year less than the expected value of the damage from flooding. Supposed you lived along the river; what would you say when asked to pay your share of the cost? Probably, "Forget it." There would be no incentive to pay. The dam could not be built to protect everyone else's property and not protect yours. So you could consume the benefits of flood control without paying the cost. You probably would not be the only one to figure this out. The entrepreneur would therefore have trouble collecting enough revenue to cover the cost of construction. Thus, a dam or a lighthouse that would benefit everyone more than it costs would not be constructed because of the inability of private firms to collect from those who do not pay. Or, getting back to the example of national defense, how could someone defend the entire nation from attack without defending St. Louis, Houston, Los Angeles, or any other individual city where the citizens do not choose to pay for defense?

Economists refer to these cases as examples of the free rider problem. Little or none of the good will be produced by private firms because these firms have no way of forcing the people who consume the goods to pay the price, so these people become free riders. When firms cannot collect a price for the goods they produce, there is no revenue to cover costs. Market failure results because the cost of these goods to society is less than the value society would place on these goods, but people, because of nonexclusion, have the option of consuming the good without making payment. Although value is greater than cost, revenue is not, and the good probably will not be produced by private enterprise.

To summarize, nonexclusion results when it is impossible, or economically infeasible, to produce and sell a good that has characteristics such that if some people pay for the good, others can consume the same good without paying for it. Once the good is produced, no one is willing to pay. Too little, or even none of the good will be produced, and the value of additional units of the good to society will be greater than the social cost of those units. Thus, a nonoptimal amount of the good will result.

The absence of exclusion is not the only reason why there is market failure when public goods are demanded. In some cases, public goods can be made private. A park, for instance, can have a fence built around it, so if visitors want in they must pay a toll at a gate. Those who do not pay, do not visit. The publicness of the good has been made more private, and free enterprise will participate in the production of the commodity. But when there is nonexclusion in production and consumption, it is not clear that exclusion should take place. When producers can exclude non-paying consumers, these people could still consume the good without decreasing its benefits to those who do pay. Within limits, for example, a park visitor who does not pay is not going to disturb others who may have paid. Congestion may be a problem as the park becomes crowded, but at the margin, one more visitor could be made better off at zero marginal cost to society. In this way, strict exclusion in the production of a public good ends up in too little production and prices that are too high.

Economics in the News

The Homeless Make It Plain That Public Transportation Is Not a Public Good[4]

Public transportation facilities have become a shelter of last resort for many of the homeless. They are setting up outdoor camps underneath highway and railroad bridges. In California, where the highway department prides itself on the vegetation planted along its freeways, the homeless are camping. In cities that have subway systems, the homeless are a common sight. They set up homes with old mattresses and cardboard walls in the dark but dry and warm parts of the rail line. Places close to bathrooms are the most popular, because on especially cold days the homeless can stay in these heated facilities.

Public transportation has some of the characteristics of public goods. Generally, the cost of one more person using the system is zero. Another way of putting it is that one additional rider does not interfere with the ride of others. But this is not true at all times of the day. During peak times when there is congestion, an additional rider does have an impact on other commuters. There is a capacity limit to a transportation system that is frequently reached during peak times. Transportation authorities are aware of the congestion problems caused by patrons and realize that there are limits to the "publicness" of public transportation. The homeless are, however, creating a new kind of congestion in the nation's transportation system.

In Oregon, highway viaduct camps are creating public safety hazards. Heat from fires has the effect of weakening bridge supports; smoke has caused traffic accidents. Some homeless are dismantling parts of the bridge and selling them as scrap. In California, the milling of homeless around the highways has caused pedestrian accidents. Campsites are littered with bottles, food containers, mattresses and human excrement. The camps are becoming places of disease, drugs, and violence. California is spending $200,000 annually to close out camps along the Los Angeles highways and to repair fences, sprinkler systems, and damaged shrubs. Many former subway riders in the East are now avoiding the system. The homeless beg for money, and by living in the system, they soil the facility. Depots smell bad and are becoming a source of disease. In Manhattan, cleaning crews in 1990 collected 85 pounds of hypodermic needles. The crews wear disposable coveralls and masks, and spray the homeless litter with bleach and water before touching it. Each "clean up sweep" costs the city of New York about $10,000. And riders are finding other ways to commute. New York estimates that the homeless camps are costing the subway system 37,000 riders a day.

Highway and transit authorities are responding to this new congestion problem by evicting people living there. This solution works temporarily; but the same or different homeless people (there are an estimated 750,000) are returning to the sites. In Oregon, California, and New York, authorities are constantly policing public facilities. Still the congestion remains and makes it plain that in this vein, highway and rail systems are not perfect public goods.

---

[4]This report is based on "Transit Systems Face Burden of Providing Last-Resort Shelter," *The Wall Street Journal,* July 18, 1990, p. A1.

20.3.2 Public Goods and Marginal Cost

An illuminating way of describing public goods is to stress that the marginal cost of letting an additional person consume the good is zero once it is produced. National defense, parks, and television signals are examples of goods that come close to fitting this description. Possibly outdoor concerts and fireworks are other examples.

If the marginal cost of letting another person consume the good is zero, the optimal price should be zero. It costs society nothing for these "additional" consumers to consume the good. If these consumers could have the good at zero price, they would be better off and no one would be worse off because none of society's resources would have to be used to take in an additional consumer. But the total costs of production are not zero, so how will these costs be paid at a zero price? Private producers must set a positive price to cover costs; hence, price will be greater than the zero marginal cost, and a less-than-optimal amount of the good is consumed. In other words, private production does not lead to a Pareto-optimal allocation of the good.

To put the issue another way, regardless of the total consumption of the public good, the same amount of society's resources must be used to produce it. It is reasonable to assume that for some consumers who elect not to purchase the public good, the marginal utility of the good is still positive. That is, for some consumers, in the case of a public good called A, a positive price leads them to a solution in their preference map, such that none of good A is consumed. Hence

$$\frac{MU_a}{P_a} < \frac{MU_b}{P_b} = \frac{MU_c}{P_c}, \text{ etc.,}$$

and $MU_a > 0$. That is, goods B, C, and so forth, are consumed, but no A is consumed, even though an additional unit of A would give positive marginal utility. Thus, if a zero price were charged to these consumers, some would consume good A. If A is a public good, they would be better off, and no one would be worse off because no more of society's resources are used when the good is consumed.

Principle

> If the production of some public goods is in the hands of private enterprise, social welfare is less than it otherwise would be because some consumers are excluded from the market when price is greater than zero. Since their consumption of the good is "free" to society in the sense that it entails no further resource sacrifice, society as a whole would be better off if these people would be allowed to consume the good at zero price, but under free enterprise, they are not allowed to.

20.1 *Applying the Theory*

Have you ever listened to a public radio station or watched public television? What is the cost of one more listener or viewer? Why do most such stations struggle to survive? A child listening to or watching broadcasts from a privately owned station may ask why there are so many commercials. What is your answer?

Figure 20–2 The Market for Private and Public Goods

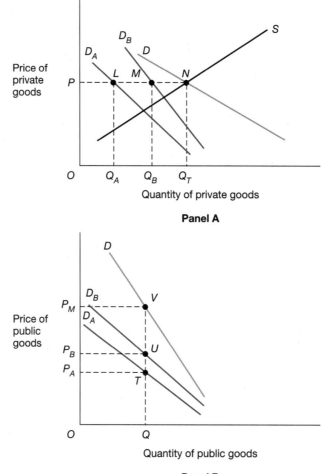

Panel A

Panel B

Because the marginal consumer can be brought into the market at zero marginal cost, the theory of public goods markets is different from the theory of the market for private goods. Recall that market demand for a private good is found by horizontally adding the demand curves for each individual, as shown in Figure 20–2, Panel A. We show two consumers, A and B. Market demand is D, the horizontal sum of the two demand curves D_A and D_B. For instance, at $P, Q_T = Q_A + Q_B$ or the sum of distances $PL + PM = PN$. A competitive market, after horizontally adding the demand curves of all individuals in the market, operates at the intersection of market supply and demand.

Public goods, however, are goods for which the same units of output can be consumed by different people at the same time. Individuals can pay for a good that other individuals are also willing to pay for. Take, for example, public parks. What is the demand for public parks? Ignoring possible congestion, park land is shared; the market demand must therefore be the sum of each person's demand curve for the *same* park land.

Consequently, in the case of public goods, demand curves must be summed vertically because each person consumes the same good. To see why, consider the situation shown in Panel B, Figure 20–2. Two consumers, A and B, demand some public good; their demands are, respectively, D_A and D_B. Consumer A is willing to pay P_A to use Q units of the public good. Consumer B will pay P_B for the same units. Thus, the two consumers together will pay $P_A + P_B = P_M$ for Q units. Summing the two demands over all amounts of good, we obtain the market demand for the public good, D. For example, $QT + QU = QV$ yields market demand. The optimal price and amount of the good are determined by the intersection of marginal cost and market demand. Price should be zero if the marginal cost of an additional unit is zero. But, as noted, this price would not cover total costs.

To summarize, public goods have features that may not permit markets to function efficiently. If producers cannot prevent free riders who do not pay for the good from consuming it, a less than optimal amount of the good will be produced. Or, if producers can exclude those who do not pay, but their consumption of the good would not reduce the consumption of those who pay, some people could be made better off without anyone being made worse off. Private production is not Pareto optimal. Many economists argue that in such cases government has a role to play in these markets.

20.3.3 The Role of Government

We should note that, sometimes, solutions can be found to the exclusion problem. Building a fence around a park and controlling access is one example of solving the problem. Radio signals, a second example, also suffer from nonexclusion. Anyone with a radio can consume them, so once the producer of radio waves sends a signal, it cannot be kept from anyone's consumption. We might think that radio stations would be terribly unprofitable businesses, but such is not the case. The problem of nonexclusion has been overcome by stations selling their air time to advertisers. They collect a fee for the commercials they broadcast for advertisers, and this fee covers the cost of producing the signals. In spite of these two examples, solutions to the exclusion problem are not always so straightforward. Governments, recognizing the fact that there may be some goods that are not optimally produced and consumed when the price is set by the competitive market mechanism, will sometimes produce these goods.

Government supplies many goods for which the marginal cost of adding another consumer is close to zero. Many public utilities, public transportation systems, and the provision of education have a cost structure in which the initial investment for production is large, but marginal cost is quite low. Efficient prices exist at the point where demand and marginal cost intersect, but these prices are not likely to generate enough revenue to cover total costs. So government pays the fixed cost or, in the long run, makes the necessary investment, then charges more efficient prices. The funds used to finance the "subsidized" enterprise are generated by taxes.

There are numerous examples of public goods for which consumers pay part of the cost of consumption, but not the whole cost. National parks are one example and the state provision of higher education is another. Even though tourists are charged an entrance fee, national parks are subsidized by tax revenue. At state universities, students pay tuition, even though the bulk of a university's expenses is covered by state taxes.

Governments will also supply goods that private firms would produce except for the difficulty or impossibility of collecting a price for them. This is the free rider problem. The previous example of the dam on the flooding river is such a case. No firm could charge consumers who "do not want" the flood protection, but government could collect enough revenue through taxation to build the dam. National defense, police and fire protection, and garbage collection are other examples of people allowing government to assume the role of providing such services, for which there can be free riders.

We should note in closing this section that there is considerable argument among economists about how large the role of government should be in providing public goods. In many cases, such as the examples of the park and the radio signal, the nonexclusion problem can be overcome. Prices will generally not be efficient when the good is privately produced, but the government financing of these same goods is not distortion free either. The taxes used to pay the cost of public goods will almost always cause market inefficiencies that we have for the most part left undiscussed in this text.

20.2 *Applying the Theory*

With respect to radio and television signals, how can these public goods be made private? In particular, how do pay TV companies like HBO and Showtime work to keep their signals private?

20.4 **Externalities**

We have covered very briefly some circumstances that do not necessarily provide a Pareto-optimal equilibrium for markets. In these cases, arguments have been made for some type of governmental intervention.

Quite possibly, a much more important problem of the market concerns the question of externalities, which occur when the private cost or benefit of some activity does not equal the total cost or benefit of that activity. A large part of the problem of externalities is closely related to the incomplete assignment of property rights.

In this text, we have generally assumed away the problem of externalities and the incomplete assignment of property rights. In this section, we will examine some aspects of these problems. Because these are complex problems, this discussion will merely touch on the major issues involved.

20.4.1   Definition of Externalities

Externalities occur whenever an exchange between two economic agents takes place outside the market place. The exchange of some good or service, in other words, is not agreed on by both parties to the transaction, yet the transaction is carried out anyway. Examples of externalities can be found in everyday life. Waking up to your neighbor's crowing rooster is an externality that may be desirable or terribly undesirable, depending on your sleeping habits. Roommates carry on a number of external exchanges that may be good or bad, depending on their points of view toward cooking, cleaning, bathing, and use of language. It is most likely that some of the externalities generated by your roommate are desirable and some are not so desirable.

We may think of externalities in terms of cost and benefits. A private cost or benefit is defined to be exclusive of any externalities generated by a particular activity. For example, a factory that dumps sewage into a river may not count the cost of water pollution when the costs of production are figured. Social costs would take into account the cost of pollution and should be thought of as the sum of private costs and the value of any externalities. Thus, the cost relation

$$\text{Social costs} = \text{Private costs} + \text{External costs}.$$

This same reasoning applies when we think about the benefits of an activity rather than the costs. Private benefit, like private cost, is determined exclusive of any externalities. Social benefit includes them; thus, the benefit relation

$$\text{Social benefits} = \text{Private benefits} + \text{External benefits}.$$

The social benefits of education, for example, are probably greater than the private benefits because of the externalities generated by an educated society. Education is directly related to more responsible behavior, which benefits one's friends, neighbors, and co-workers.

Depending on the problem under consideration, it is frequently more convenient to think of externalities in terms of either costs or benefits. But both of the above relations represent two sides of the same coin. Whenever there are externalities, social costs or benefits do not equal private costs or benefits.

Definition

An externality exists whenever the social cost or benefit of an activity is not equal to private cost or benefit.

Externalities, depending on their desirability or undesirability, carry more specific definitions. An external economy is said to exist when social benefit at the margin exceeds private benefit. When marginal cost equals private marginal benefits as shown in Figure 20–3, Panel A, marginal social benefit is above marginal cost at Q_0. More resources should be allocated to producing the commodity in question. The activity should be increased to Q_1, where marginal cost and marginal social benefit are equal. On the other hand, an external diseconomy exists when social

Figure 20–3   Divergence between Marginal Private Cost and Benefit and Marginal Social Cost and Benefit

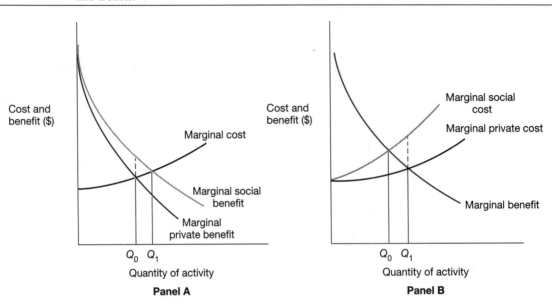

cost exceeds private cost at the margin. In Panel B of Figure 20–3, social cost is above private cost at the margin. When the private cost and marginal benefit curve intersect at Q_1, marginal benefit is less than marginal social cost. An undesirably large amount of resources is allocated to producing the commodity in question. In Panel B of the figure, the activity should be reduced by the amount Q_0Q_1.

Definition

An external economy exists when marginal social benefit is greater than marginal private benefit. An external diseconomy exists when marginal social cost is greater than marginal private cost.

At this time, it is quite reasonable to ask why private marginal cost and benefit diverge from marginal social cost and benefit. One major reason is that a problem of ownership or control of a certain resource exists. Briefly, this means that there is some scarce resource owned by a person, but for some reason the owner cannot charge a price for the use of this resource. And when prices cannot be charged, misallocation of resources results.

The now classic example of ownership externalities was originally brought up by the economist J. E. Meade in 1952.[5] A beekeeper raises bees for honey. The ideal location for beehives is in fields with lots of spring blossoms. While bees

---

[5]J. E. Meade, "External Economics and Diseconomies in a Competitive Situation," *Economic Journal* 62, no. 245 (March 1952), pp. 54–67.

make honey, they also pollinate blossoms, which, say for apple orchards, generates more fruit in the fall. Hence, both the beekeeper and the apple farmer benefit by being located close to one another. The beekeeper benefits because the apple blossoms are a source of nectar for the bees, and the apple farmer benefits from having the blossoms pollinated. But these benefits are not necessarily paid for in the market. Hence, for both the beekeeper and the farmer, social benefit is greater than private benefit. If ownership rights between the two parties were better defined, more efficient exchange might take place, but as it is, two few bees and too few trees exist.

An example of an external diseconomy, because of an improper assignment of ownership rights, might be pollution. Suppose a commercial fishing industry exists at the mouth of a river. Let a factory locate upstream. The factory dumps its waste into the river, killing some of the fish downstream and, consequently, lowering the amount of fish caught each day. Ownership of the stream's resources are often ambiguous, so the polluter is not made to pay for the dirty water. The private cost to the factory does not include the resulting reduced incomes of the downstream fishermen, and social cost is greater than private cost. Too much factory output is produced. There are many other examples of such external diseconomies—some as simple as this one while others are much more complex. In all cases, the remedy to the problem is usually difficult.

There is the danger of attributing too many problems to ownership externalities and simply saying that the marketplace does not ever allocate efficiently. One may or may not be happy with the results of the market, but market failures as a result of externalities must be treated carefully. We could, and many people do, carry the externality problem to a fallacy of the extreme. Certainly, if a large group of people drive big, fast cars, the price of gasoline rises. Some benefit; some lose. Selling wheat to other countries may increase the price of bread; again, some benefit, some lose. If you burn coal, the world has less coal. These activities are not externalities, however, because they are not external to the market. Selling more wheat to, say, the former Soviet Union, is a market transaction, frequently of such large proportions that the world price of wheat is affected. This, in turn, may cause the price of bread to increase. Events that increase demand or change supply are not externalities since the market is adjusting. Consumers and producers may not like these adjustments and may want government intervention to control them. But in these cases, the market is not failing, it is reacting.

20.4.2   Property Rights and Externalities

In most examples of externalities, the property rights of resource owners are not well defined. Problems arise because the production, investment, or even consumption decisions of some affect the income or utilities or others, through an implicit change in property use. No explicit transaction takes place that contracts for this exchange. We wish to stress that the problem of externalities becomes more serious as property rights become more ambiguous, or when no one has property rights in the case of some scarce resources.

The most complete concept of ownership rights, and that which we have assumed to exist throughout the text, is that owners can use their property in any way, subject to laws concerning injury to other parties. A less-complete right of ownership is the right to use the property of someone else to gain benefits from its use, but not to sell it or alter its form. Most rental properties and community-owned properties fall into this category, as do your classrooms, our offices, and some government properties, such as national parks.

There are many shades between the various forms of property rights, but these two are the principal categories. The right of ownership is never completely unrestricted. You may own a good but not be able to sell it above a governmentally fixed price. You may own land but not be permitted to build a swimming pool on it unless you build a fence.

As it turns out, most of the problems of externalities result from two situations. The first is incomplete or communal assignment of property rights, or even no assignment of property rights. The second problem results when certain uses of one's fully owned property have harmful effects on someone else's property.

20.4.3   Nonowned or Community-Owned Property

A scarce resource that is not owned is both overused and underproduced. Early settlers in the United States had no incentive to postpone chopping down trees or to plant forests. If one group did not chop the trees down, others would. What is the incentive to plant trees if no one owns them? Forests were destroyed. The American Bison, which were not owned, were almost made extinct, while cattle, which were owned, were not. Rivers, which were not owned, were polluted. No one owned the valuable whales, and they practically disappeared when whale oil was the major source of light and lubrication. Neither free enterprise nor human greed was the problem *per se*. The problem was that no one had the incentive to kill fewer whales so that the whales could reproduce at a rate sufficient to maintain the population. If any individuals took it upon themselves not to harvest another whale for oil, others would still continue. Similarly, there is no point in individuals planting trees if the ownership of the future forest is not specified.

As we have implied, publicly owned property gives rise to problems similar to those with nonowned property. A government- or community-owned property may not be used efficiently. Suppose that one community owned a large piece of property that is better suited for growing vegetables than for grazing cattle. If anyone can use the property, it will probably be used for grazing cattle, because if anyone can harvest the vegetables, growers would have to expend added resources to protect their crops. Cattle owners can drive their cows home from the community property at night.

Publicly owned property may not be put to its most efficient use, but this may not be bad for the society. The society may wish to have free beaches and parks rather than have private ownership of these scarce resources. People may prefer overcrowding to paying for the use of the facilities. Publicly owned resources will be put to different uses than those that would result from private ownership.

Economics in
the News

Property Rights and Fishing for Striped Bass[6]

In the case of fishing, property rights are often ill-defined, and over the years a number of controversies have arisen. In the Pacific Northwest, the right to fish for salmon has caused conflict between Oregon, Washington, British Columbia, and various Indian tribes. Presently, a complex set of interstate and international rules govern fishing seasons and catches in this area. Alaskan and Russian fishing boats have fought over fishing rights near the Aleutian Islands. The international agreement governing these rights appears to be constantly disputed.

The laws of property governing fish are complicated because fish migrate depending on seasons of the year and spawning habits. A community's claim to fish as a resource is made in spite of migration. Multiple claims arise, causing conflict in the harvesting and preservation of the resource. The example of striped bass illustrates property rights problems and the consequent externalities present in the fishing industry.

The striped bass, once a common entree on East Coast menus, is disappearing from the Atlantic waters. Over the last 15 years, the population of this fish has fallen 90 percent. The reason for the problem is two-fold. First, the spawning grounds of the striped bass are being destroyed, and second, since no state or individual has jurisdiction of the entire East Coast fishing ground, no one can regulate the conditions for catching the fish, and over-fishing has occurred. Both of these problems are discussed in turn.

When not spawning, striped bass roam the Atlantic seaboard from Maine to Florida, but in the spring they return to either the Hudson River or the Chesapeake Bay to lay their eggs. Most return to the Chesapeake, and this is the most serious source of the problem. Chesapeake water pollution has severely damaged their spawning ground, which has led almost to the total demise of the fish. Maryland is concerned with the problem, but has not been effective in controlling it because three fourths of the Bay pollution originates in neighboring states. Obviously, Maryland has no legal rights over people in these other states and, therefore, cannot impose restrictions on upstream polluters. The other states, of course, have little incentive to impose restrictions, since the pollution is not directly affecting them. An external diseconomy is thus destroying a valuable natural resource, and management is hampered by the absence of clear-cut property ownership and jurisdiction.

To make matters even worse, the small number of bass, roughly 7 percent, that spawn in the Hudson River stand to lose, at least temporarily, this breeding ground. Plans have been made to dredge the river for a $2 billion federally financed highway, housing, and parkland project. Controversy over the impact of dredging on the young bass population has so far slowed development. Seaboard states are pressuring New York to cancel the project, because striped bass in the Hudson are prospering. Environmentalists argue that the River's limestone watershed counteracts acidic pollution, thus protecting the breeding ground. Neighboring states fear the New York development would destroy Atlantic fishing for many years because at least 1 million young bass grow up in the Hudson waters before migrating along the New England coast. Upsetting the Hudson breeding grounds would, essentially, destroy New England fishing.

(continued)

[6]This news is based on David L. Yermack, "Striped Bass Issue Illustrates Problem of Unclear Jurisdiction," *The Wall Street Journal,* July 10, 1984, p. 29.

But no state has offered to help bear the cost of maintaining the Hudson breeding ground. Political pressure is being put on New York to drop the Hudson development project without offer of interstate compensation. Obviously, New York is balking. State residents feel that the entire cost of maintaining the quality of New England fishing is being put on New York. They are creating an external economy for the other states. While other states will benefit by New York's conservation policy, New York has no way of requiring compensation from these states. The problem, of course, is created by the absence of property rights over the fish. If New York residents knew who caught the Hudson Bay bass and, therefore, knew who benefitted from the state's protection of the fish's spawning grounds, a tax could, in principle, be levied to compensate the people of New York for maintaining the spawning grounds of the fish. But the fish cannot be easily tracked, and legally the state doesn't have the right to tax people in other states.

An additional problem arising from the lack of clear-cut property rights is the difficulty of obtaining uniform regulations on fishing along the Atlantic coast. Such regulations would go a long way to maintain or even increase the bass population. But because of the characteristics of migratory fish, such uniform regulations have not been set up.

To be sure, a number of states along the coast have begun to protect the bass. But differences in the restrictions states put on fishing dilute the effectiveness of any single state's effort. Once again, the absence of ownership reduces the incentive of any one state to take strong action, because no one state receives the full benefit of the restrictions it places on its fishing industry. Also, the most lenient state will benefit the most from the regulations of other states. All of the Atlantic States have adopted a minimum set of fishing restrictions written by the Atlantic States Marine Fisheries Commission. The guidelines, aimed at reducing each state's catch by 55 percent, ban fishing on certain dates, set minimum keep sizes, and regulate the size of nets and other equipment. Some states, notably Rhode Island, have gone far beyond these rules. In Rhode Island no one is allowed to catch a striped bass for three years. Maryland and Virginia, on the other hand, have kept the minimum standard. Other states regard this step as lenient, given the size and importance of the bass population around those states. "All of the states are playing the game of not wanting to give up more than anyone else," says Fred Schwab, New York's representative to the Interstate Striped Bass Management Project. Schwab is simply pointing out what we know will happen when there are no clear property rights in a valuable resource; there will be overuse of the resource.

20.4.4   The Assignment of Property Rights and Externalities

A fundamental economic and legal problem is the efficient assignment of property rights when the marginal social cost or benefit of some activity exceeds the marginal private cost or benefit. For example, when a factory pollutes, or group of factories pollute a publicly owned river, as noted above, the owners of property along the river downstream are damaged by this externality. The same problem could exist with air pollution. As mentioned previously, the polluting factories do not pay the full cost of pollution. The social cost is the total private cost plus the cost of the pollution to the property owners downstream. Or the full cost of production of a factory that is polluting the air is the total private cost of production plus the lowered values of the other people's property that is damaged by the smoke.

In some cases, the property rights problem is solved by adjustments in the marketplace. For example, mergers between firms across industries may internalize an externality. Recall the example of the beekeeper and apple farmer. Both provided each other with an external economy. The bees pollinated the apple blossoms, and the blossoms allowed the bees to make honey. Once it is understood by the farmer or the beekeeper that their work provides the other with a valuable benefit, there is an incentive to bring the externality into the market in order to produce more efficiently. The beekeeper, for instance, might begin a pollination service and offer to locate bees closer to apple orchards for a fee, or perhaps to pay the apple farmer for the right to keep the bees near the trees if the beekeeper benefits more from the arrangement than the farmer. Presently, pollination services do exist and flourish, for example, in the state of Washington.[7] If such transactions prove difficult to arrange, the beekeeper or apple grower might buy the other out. The two firms become one and the benefits of the externality are in this way internalized. Thus contractual arrangements in the market, or a merger, can eliminate externalities and a source of market failure.

Economics in the News

L.A. Residents Internalize an External Diseconomy[8]

Film crews are a common sight in the Los Angeles area. About 162 movies per year are made in Los Angeles. One of the prime locations is Hancock Park, a neighborhood of mansions. On one block in Hancock Park the homes have been used in films 82 times in the last eight years, on average a little more than 10 times a year.

Movie crews create external diseconomies for neighborhood residents. Trucks and cars are parked on both sides of the street for blocks. People are wandering through yards. Urinals are set up on street corners. Food service is provided to the crew right on the sidewalk and in the yards. Movie producers pay up to $6,500 a day to film in a mansion. The owners agree to vacate for the number of days a crew needs for the film. But, generally, the neighbors are unpaid. The external diseconomy created for the neighbors has caused them to take matters into the marketplace.

One TV crew asked, but then had to pay a homeowner $1,000 a day *not* to use a vacuum cleaner during film days. One homeowner demanded $1,000 a day to let a crew set up a light in her yard. It was bargained down to $400. A gardener was paid $50 not to run a leaf blower. In downtown areas, crews must have the parking spots vacated, and producers in some parts of the city must have permission from the shop owners to "use" the slots. The price has been as much as $1,000 a slot per day.

Since there are no property rights to the air waves, many residents are using them and then demanding payment to cease this use. They purposefully create an external diseconomy for the film crew in hopes of receiving payment in a market negotiation. Bar owners turn their music up louder. In Santa Monica, one owner received $400 per hour to keep it turned down. Another merchant runs a chain saw only when the film is running. He gets paid $100 early in the day to keep quiet, but later it is $50 per hour.

---

[7]S. N. S. Cheung, "The Fable of the Bees: An Economic Investigation," *Journal of Law and Economics* 16, no. 1, April 1973, pp. 11–34.

[8]For more vivid detail see "L.A. Residents Grow Ever More Negative Toward Film Crews," *The Wall Street Journal*, March 30, 1990, p. A1.

In other cases, the legal system can encourage a more specific definition of property rights. Class action suits, for example, in which groups of harmed individuals are represented in civil suits against a polluting factory, helped to redefine the ambiguous ownership of a resource. Through class action, the owner (owners) of property along a river might be compensated by a factory for polluting and, in this way, make up the loss in their property values. But this does not have to be the only legal solution to the property rights problem. Suppose the factory was simply given property rights to the river. Then, the downstream property owners could go to the factory and pay the owner to reduce pollution if the marginal cost was less than the marginal gain to them.

In either legal assignment of property rights, the pollution problem would be internalized by the market. When the rights are defined, compensation can be arranged to more efficiently take account of the externality. And regardless of how the property rights are assigned, the market will properly adjust to account for the externality. Whether the factory owner must pay downstream landowners, or the landowners pay the factory owner, pollution has an explicit opportunity cost attached to it. To pollute more, the owner must either pay the landowners or give up the payment received from them for not polluting. It really does not matter how the property rights are assigned so long as they are clearly defined. This conclusion is referred to as the Coase Theorem.[9]

The Coase Theorem critically depends on there not being transactions costs once property rights are assigned. What transpires after property rights have been assigned is affected by the number of parties involved. If 1,000 factories are damaging 10,000 fishermen downstream, it would be difficult and expensive to work out a transaction. Or, if 9,999 downstream property owners agree to bribe the factories not to pollute and one party does not agree, how could the nonpayer be excluded from the benefits? This is the familiar free rider problem. In the case of one damager versus one damagee, the solution would be simple if property rights are assigned. But the more parties involved, the greater the cost of making the transaction.

Another option is for government to force a "solution" by charging the damagers and, possibly, by compensating those damaged. An emission tax on all waste dumped into the air or water, for instance, would raise the private marginal cost of production to a level closer to the social cost. Taxes will tend to equate social cost with private cost, while subsidies will bring social and private benefit closer together. Surely a goal of zero air and water pollution is ridiculous. If there are diminishing marginal social benefits and increasing marginal social costs from reducing pollution, the solution is to have pollution at some optimal, but nonzero, rate. It is frequently the task of economists and engineers to determine that rate. Marginal costs are not easily measured, and, in the absence of a social utility function, marginal benefits are generally impossible to measure.

[9]In a very famous article by Ronald Coase, "The Problem of Social Cost," *Journal of Law and Economics* 3 (October 1960), pp. 1–44, it was shown that if one party is damaging another through its productive activity, the optimal amount of damage is the same regardless of the party to whom property rights are assigned, given zero transactions costs.

We have merely touched on the problem of external ownership effects. Many more examples and solutions could be discussed. The economics profession is certainly not in agreement about the problem or the solution. Neither is the legal profession. The sole purpose of this discussion is to make you aware of the problem and some possible solutions. We want you to think about the problem of externalities in economic terms.

Economics in the News

Subsidizing Organ Transplants: The Case of an External Benefit

One of the great medical miracles of recent years is the increasing use of an organ transplant—a heart, liver, or a kidney—to save human lives. These miracle operations receive a lot of attention in the press. Frequently, the local or even national media will call the public's attention to the impending death of a child unless an organ donor can be found.

Transplanting human organs is an incredibly expensive operation for recipients and most families must obtain financial support for the operation. To get some idea of how expensive transplant operations are: in the 1980s, a cornea transplant was priced between $3,000 and $5,000, a heart transplant cost from $50,000 to $250,000, a new liver $75,000 to $250,000, and the most simple kidney transplant started at $25,000.[10]

If a patient needs a new organ to survive, who should pay for the operation? This is an important question because the answer of who is willing to pay usually determines who receives the operation. At the present time, local and federal governments have played a limited role in financing transplants. The one area of exception is kidney dialysis and transplantation, which have been heavily funded through the Social Security Administration. By and large, however, transplant operations have been financed by the private sector, and families have relied on the donations of friends and relatives to pay for an operation. What role, if any, should the public sector have in providing organs to recipients who want them? Part of the answer lies in thinking about the external economies involved in organ transplants.

Certainly, there is tremendous private benefit from a transplanted organ. A patient without hope of living may go on to lead a healthy, productive life. Leading a productive life also benefits society; that is, some social benefit comes from an incapacitated member of the community returning to a normal lifestyle. The individual contributes as a citizen and as a productive input and consumer in numerous markets. Thus, society has an interest in the health of its members. This is why hospitals and medical research are frequently funded by local, state, and federal governments.

Suppose the government has decided to impose a more efficient equilibrium in the supply and demand for organ transplants. Society has decided to move the equilibrium closer to the point where marginal cost and the social marginal benefit of a transplant intersect. How should the government subsidize the operation?

We can illustrate graphically two kinds of public funding in paying for organ transplants. In Figure 20–4 on page 697, Panels A and B each show two demand schedules,

(continued)

---

[10]These figures are taken from "Organ Transplant Questions Remain," *Houston Chronicle*, September 2, 1984, Section 3, p. 1.

D_p and D_s. The lower schedule, labeled D_p, is the private demand for transplants; the higher schedule, D_s, is the social demand curve, which includes both the private and external benefits from a transplant. Disregarding for a moment any external economy from a transplant operation, equilibrium would occur at P_0 and Q_0 in both panels. (We ignore MC' in Panel A for now.) If all benefits, private and external, were counted, more operations would, of course, be undertaken. Using the D_s schedule as a measure of the social value of transplants, the equilibrium should be at P_1 and Q_1. The increase in operations is therefore $Q_1 - Q_0$.

One way to reach the higher equilibrium, and in most cases the least expensive method, is for the government to subsidize the patients by the amount $P_1 - P_0$; then Q_1 operations would be made, and the government would pay $Q_1 \cdot (P_1 - P_0)$ total dollars for transplants. This amount is shown as the shaded region in Panel A of Figure 20–4. The government directly pays each patient the difference between P_1 and P_0 when the operation is completed. This is usually the way most private insurance companies pay claims.

Panel B shows a second means to reach Q_1, but it will generally be more expensive than the payment method in Panel A. In this case, the government subsidizes the hospital cost of the operation. The original marginal cost schedule for operations MC. To move patients down the demand schedule, D_p, until Q_1 operations are reached, a new marginal cost schedule MC' is necessary. This requires that each operation at the hospital receive a subsidy of h as shown in Panel B. By comparing the panels, you can see that h is greater than $P_1 - P_0$, and since the number of operations is the same, the government spends more by paying hospitals part of the cost of the operation. Unless administrative costs are greater, it is less costly to pay patients rather than hospitals.

20.5   Summary

There are some goods for which exchange in the marketplace does not work well. Public goods have the characteristic that exclusion of consumption cannot be prevented once the good is produced or purchased. The principle of nonexclusion makes it difficult or impossible for a producer to collect revenue to cover the cost of production. Consumers, while enjoying the good, have no incentive to pay, since they can continue to consume without making payment. Public goods encourage consumers to become free riders. Ironically, the efficient price of some public goods should be zero. Because the marginal cost of letting another person consume the good, once it is produced, is zero, the price at the margin should be zero. Public goods are not a profitable venture for private enterprise. As a consequence, government produces many of the public goods in our society.

Externalities are another cause of market failure. They occur when exchange takes place outside of a market. Usually individuals consume something good or bad, depending on preferences, without paying or being compensated. Social benefit is greater than private benefit if there are external economies. Social cost is greater than private cost if there are external diseconomies. Most externalities result from an absence of property rights. Usually when property rights are well defined the market is able to adjust and internalize the externality. It can, however, be difficult to define property rights. As a consequence, the government taxes or subsidizes people to bring social cost and benefit closer to the private counterparts.

Figure 20–4   Organ Transplants As an Externality

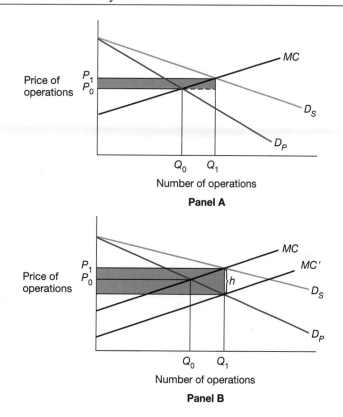

Panel A

Panel B

Restricted competition, through monopoly power or government controls, often stands in the way of Pareto-efficient production and distribution, but the theory of second best implies that making one market more competitive while others remain noncompetitive may reduce community welfare.

Answers to *Applying the Theory*

20.1   The marginal cost of one more person listening to the radio or tuning in a television signal is zero. Audio and video signals have characteristics of public goods. Public stations struggle because they rely upon donations. Listeners and viewers free ride. Young people and adults grow weary of the commercials (some are more exciting than the programs), but this is how a profit-making station earns its income. Stations sell audiences to advertisers who pay for the commercials.

20.2   With respect to pay television, most consumers pay for the signals through their cable TV company. The signal is privatized through its cable provision. Consumers must pay for the cable connection to their television. Many consumers circumvent the cable company by setting up satellite dishes that receive the signal directly from the HBO or Showtime transmission. The dishes are specially designed to receive signals other than the UHF or VHF signals that televisions are designed to pick up. Pay TV companies have responded by "jamming" the signals, so satellite dishes cannot receive a clear signal. There is an alternative measure for dish owners. They can now subscribe to the pay TV company for equipment that provides a clear signal. In any case, the technology exists to make radio and television signals private, but technology also exists to recreate them as public goods for the free riders.

Technical Problems

1. Why would a community-owned forest be depleted more rapidly than a private-owned forest?
2. Explain in what sense a national park is a public good and in what sense is it not.
3. Is your school library a public good? Could the time of year affect your answer?
4. Your roommate has a stereo. In what sense could this stereo have both positive and negative externalities to you?
5. Other than national defense, can you think of any pure public goods—goods with both producer and consumer nonexclusion?
6. What is the free rider problem connected with the existence of public goods? How can it lead to a market solution that is not Pareto optimal?
7. Why isn't every point on society's production-possibility frontier preferable to any interior point?
8. Explain why monopoly or oligopoly will not lead to a Pareto-optimal equilibrium. Explain why forcing a monopoly to produce more can reduce society's welfare.
9. What is the difference between external economies and diseconomies? Give an example of each. In which case are too few goods produced? Explain. In which case are too many goods produced? Explain.
10. In the Coase Theorem, it does not make any difference to society how property rights are assigned as long as they are assigned. Does it make any difference to the parties involved how property rights are assigned? Would a polluting factory rather pay landowners in order to pollute or would it rather be paid by the landowners not to pollute as much?

Analytical Problems

1. Suppose the social return to education is 8 percent, and the return to other investment is 10 percent. This shows too many resources are being used in education. Comment.
2. Suppose from time to time a certain theater has long lines for a particular movie and sometimes has to turn away customers. Is this evidence of market failure? Why or why not?
3. Suppose there are two classes made up of very similar students. In one class, each student receives the grade made on each test. In the other class, each student receives the class average on each test. These policies are known by all. In what class would you expect the higher average grade? Explain in terms of externalities, or the free rider problem.
4. In Texas, the state owns all the beaches. Analyze the following statements and determine whether they are true or false.
   a. If private individuals owned the beaches, poor and middle-income people would be denied access.

    b. Since the state can afford to clean the beaches, there is less litter than if they were privately owned.

    c. Since the state can regulate the beaches, it can keep off sleazy merchants, and the people using the beaches are better off.

    d. Since the state owns the beaches, more people use them, and the people are better off because a beach is a public good.

5. If bridges and highways are public goods, why do we see private enterprise building them and charging a toll? Do toll roads and bridges maximize consumer's and producer's surplus? Is a toll road or a toll-free publicly financed road better? (In your answer, consider the problem of congestion and the argument that "those who use the road should pay.")

6. In the bee–apple orchard example of externalities is there an incentive for one to buy out the other? Explain. What would be the externality problem if bees were bad for apples, but apple blossoms increased honey production by bees?

7. In our example of a factory polluting fisheries downstream, would the amount of property damage depend on when the fisheries were begun relative to the opening of the factory? Explain.

8. Other things being equal, would a monopolistic industry or a competitive industry that is producing an external diseconomy produce more of the diseconomy? Explain.

9. Airport noise is certainly a negative externality. Why would people choose to live near airports?

10. In Pennsylvania, a local restaurant owner took the prices off his menu and told customers to pay him what they thought the meal was worth. According to the owner, he isn't "losing a penny" by the new system (Associated Press, December 6, 1984). Has this owner created a public good with his restaurant? Do you expect him to stay in business by letting consumers decide value?

11. Many prison systems are becoming privately owned and privately operating institutions. Once a criminal is sentenced to serve time in jail, the state or federal government pays a corporation to hold the prisoner. (See *Newsweek*, May 7, 1984, p. 80 for a more detailed description.) Do you think private prisons can detain criminals as well as public institutions? Are prisons public goods? Do they have externalities that cannot be captured by the market? Why does the government own and operate prisons?

CHAPTER 21

Market Behavior with Incomplete Information

21.1 Introduction

Throughout this text we have assumed that all participants in a market have complete information about all relevant variables affecting that market. Firms know all prices, including input prices, the most efficient technology, and the productivity of all inputs they employ. Consumers have full information about all prices in the market and the quality of all goods and services they purchase. Most markets, however, are not characterized by complete information about price, product and input quality or performance, and other important market variables. The absence of complete information was not an important factor in the development of much of the theory developed in this text. The assumption of incomplete information would have complicated the theoretical analysis without adding much understanding of how markets function and allocate resources.

Clearly, the absence of full information does to some extent have an effect on the behavior of participants in markets, and consequently on market outcomes. This final chapter is designed to give you an overview of the way economists analyze market behavior when there is a lack of information. These theories of market behavior without full information are not meant to diminish the importance and usefulness of the theories of markets under complete information in explaining the functioning of markets. They are designed only to give you some understanding of the effects of incomplete information on the behavior of market participants.

In reality, most consumers do not know all prices of all goods and services. And they are frequently unsure about the quality of the products they buy. The same is true for producers who buy inputs. Often they are unaware of all the prices of inputs and are uncertain about the quality of inputs received from suppliers. In the case of prices, buyers can gather more information if they desire, but obtaining information is costly. As is the case for any other activity, an optimizing agent should gather information about price until the marginal benefit of more information equals the marginal cost of obtaining it. Thus, perfect information about all prices is not optimal.

With respect to quality, buyers can be unsure about the durability and performance of some products, particularly when they purchase big-ticket items such as automobiles, cameras, household appliances, expensive sports equipment, and so on. For many products quality is difficult to define and even more difficult to measure. In Chapter 16, we noted that quality can be defined as a collection of important product attributes such as durability. Purchasers of lawn mowers, for example, are interested in how easy a mower is to push, its safety features, its power, and the ease of starting. Listing these features is easy, but some aspects of a mower's quality may not be known until the product is operated. If the blade flies off and injures someone, the information that the mower is unsafe comes too late to be of much use. Just as in the case of price information, consumers can gather quality information, but only at a cost. Consumers can use rules of thumb or signals about a product to judge quality, but, as we will show, the use of these rules of thumb and signals can have a dramatic impact on market outcomes.

Firms also make decisions in the absence of complete information. They generally do not know with certainty what the demand for their product will be in the future. Nevertheless, they must make production decisions under this condition. When a firm hires workers, the manager does not have full information about the workers, for example, how hard and competently a given person will work. In terms of our current theory, the marginal product of a worker may not be known by an employer.

Economists have developed theories designed to explain how market agents make decisions in the absence of complete information and the effect of these types of decisions on market performance. We want to give you some feel for these theories here, without explaining them in great detail. We first introduce the tools economists use to deal with incomplete information, then discuss the way it affects utility maximization. Next we set forth some theories designed to explain how consumers deal with the absence of information. Finally, we discuss some problems that arise when those who pay others to do something do not have full information about the people they hire.

21.2   Expected Value and Attitudes toward Risk

Economists classify situations characterized by the absence of complete information as conditions of *uncertainty* and conditions of *risk*. Uncertainty exists when a person has absolutely no idea about how a present choice will affect future outcomes. The decision maker has an incomplete list of possible outcomes and cannot assign probabilities to any outcomes. Risk exists when a person has a complete list of all possible future outcomes of a choice or decision and is able to assign a probability to each outcome.

Probability is the likelihood of a future event taking place. If you roll a six-sided, unbiased die, you know there are six possible outcomes (1, 2, 3, 4, 5, 6), and there is an equal probability, one out of six or one sixth, that any of the six numbers will turn up. Because you know all possible outcomes and can assign a probability to each, the probabilities sum to 1. You have, of course, heard weather forecasters, say that there is a 40 percent chance of rain. Such a forecast means that out of a large number of days exactly like today it would rain on 40 percent of those days and not rain on the other 60 percent. Only two things can occur: It will either rain or not rain, and the sum of the probabilities, expressed as decimals, equals 1.

Practically all economic theories about behavior in the absence of complete information deal with behavior under risk. With risk there is still incomplete information because a decision maker cannot predict the future perfectly. There is, however, more information than there is under uncertainty. With risk, the decision maker has a list of future outcomes and the probability of each event occurring. In virtually all situations a person has some knowledge about the possible outcomes and some notion of the likelihood of each event occurring. Even when probabilities are estimated rather than known, the environment is risky rather than uncertain.

21.2.1 Expected Value

When economists analyze decision making under risk, they frequently use the concept of *expected value:*

Definition

Expected value is the weighted average of the values of all outcomes that can occur with the weights being the probability that each outcome will occur. If there are N possible outcomes that can occur from some activity, V_1, V_2, . . . V_N are the values of each outcome, and π_1, π_2, . . . π_N are the probabilities of each outcome occurring, the expected value from the activity, $E(V)$, is

$$E(V) = \pi_1 V_1 + \pi_2 V_2 + \ldots + \pi_N V_N.$$

As an example of expected value, suppose someone offers to let you roll a six-sided die, then pay you the dollar amount equal to the number rolled. If a six comes up, you receive $6, if a five, then $5, and so on. Each number has a probability of one sixth of coming up. If you rolled the die many times, you would, on average, be paid $1 one sixth of the time, $2 one sixth of the time, on up to $6. Therefore, on average your payment will be

$$(1/6) \cdot \$1 + (1/6) \cdot \$2 + (1/6) \cdot \$3 + (1/6) \cdot \$4 + (1/6) \cdot \$5$$
$$+ (1/6) \cdot \$6 = \$3.50.$$

With each roll of the die, you will receive only one of the possible amounts, but your average payment for many rolls would be $3.50. This average is the expected value of the event.

Decision makers frequently consider the expected value of an activity when risk is involved. For example, a firm might expect a given level of profit under one set of market conditions and another level of profit under a second set of conditions. If these two outcomes are faced over a number of periods, the expected value of profits is the profit under the first set of conditions times the probability of this event occurring plus the profit under the second outcome times the probability of it occurring. Although profits will vary from period to period, the firm can predict average earnings and make plans accordingly. When consumers are unsure of outcomes, expected benefits from different outcomes can be calculated. A consumer's *expected utility* (that is, the expected value of utility) measures on average the utility received from goods and services when a consumer makes choices in the presence of risk.

21.2.2   Attitudes toward Risk

People differ in many ways. One of the ways is their different attitudes toward bearing risk. These attitudes toward risk are identified and measured by the amounts that people are willing to pay for the opportunity to undertake a risky activity, relative to the expected value of the activity.

Consider the game, described above, in which you receive a dollar amount equal to the number that comes up after the die is rolled. The expected value of the game is $3.50. How much would you be willing to pay in order to play this game? There is no right or wrong answer, but your answer would reveal your attitude toward risk. If you are willing to pay exactly $3.50, you are said to be *risk neutral*. If you are willing to pay only some amount less than $3.50, you are *risk averse*. If you are actually willing to pay more than $3.50, you are *risk loving*. These three attitudes toward risk are defined more generally as follows:

Definition

> People who are willing to pay an amount exactly equal to the expected value of an event are risk neutral. People who are willing to pay only an amount less than the expected value are risk averse. People who are willing to pay more than the expected value are risk loving.

There are other forms of this game that can be used to determine a person's attitude toward risk. For example, suppose an alternative form of the game requires you to pay someone else the dollar amount that comes up on the roll of the die. Now your *expected loss* (the expected value of the amount you pay) is $3.50. If you are risk neutral, you would require a payment of $3.50 to play the game. A risk-averse person would require more, a risk-loving person less. Finally, a third way of presenting the game is as follows: The die is rolled, and as before, whatever number comes up is how much you pay. But now the question is, what amount would you pay *not* to play? Your expected losses are $3.50 as before. If you would pay this amount you are risk neutral. If you would pay more you are risk averse; to pay less makes you risk loving.

It is extremely unlikely that anyone is always risk neutral, risk averse, or risk loving in every situation. Depending on the situation, a person's attitude toward risk changes. For example, people play slot machines, which have an expected payoff less than the amount a person pays to play. Otherwise, the machine owner would not provide the machine. Therefore, people exhibit risk-loving behavior when playing slot machines. Yet most people who play slot machines probably have insurance on their car, home, or life. People who buy insurance are exhibiting risk-averse behavior. Insurance companies make money by charging premiums that are greater than expected losses. Anyone who buys insurance is therefore paying more over time than the expected losses. This is like the third presentation on rolling the die. You are risk averse if you pay more than the expected loss to not play. Insurance is like this game because you are paying a premium to not accept the risk of future loss. People bear risks practically all of the time, and their attitude toward bearing risk depends on the situation.

21.3 Expected Utility Maximization

We now discuss some fundamentals of the theory of utility maximization under risk. The essence of the theory is that people maximize *expected utility,* a concept closely related to expected value. If people maximize expected utility when risk is present, behavior depends on their attitude toward risk. Economists have generally assumed that when outcomes are risky, people make choices so as to maximize their expected-utility functions, subject to a budget or some other kind of constraint that may also have random components.

In this section, we set forth some basics of expected-utility theory and discuss how the theory explains behavior. We show how the theory is used to measure risk in a given situation and how a person can reduce risk. Recently, however, some scholars have become skeptical about how well expected utility theory explains actual behavior. We end this section with a discussion of a modified expected-utility function that psychologists believe describes behavior under risk better than the standard expected-utility function.

21.3.1 Expected-Utility Functions

An expected-utility function measures a person's expected level of satisfaction from choices that are subject to risk. Suppose risky choices yield an income, so income is a risky variable. Also, assume utility is cardinally measurable. For example, suppose utility is related to income by the function

$$U = U(M),$$

where M is income. If income can take on only two values, M_1 and M_2, with probabilities of π_1 and π_2, respectively, where $\pi_1 + \pi_2 = 1$, expected utility, $E(U)$, is

$$E(U) = \pi_1 U(M_1) + \pi_2 U(M_2).$$

Thus, expected utility is the sum of the utilities from each outcome weighted by the probability of the outcome occurring. Expected utility is the expected value of the different utilities. We will turn now to a hypothetical example to illustrate how expected-utility functions can be used to explain behavior.

Suppose someone owns and operates a movie theater and must rent films six months in advance. There are only two films available. One has already been released; based on past attendance and revenue figures, the owner can project with virtual certainty revenue of $23,000 per month from that film. The other has not been released yet, but has been advertised heavily. It could be a big hit and earn revenues of $30,000 a month. Or it could be a flop and earn revenues of only $16,000 a month. Based on experience, the owner places a 50 percent probability on the film's being a hit and a 50 percent probability on its being a flop.

From these estimates, the expected value *of income* per month from the risky film is

$$E(M) = (1/2) \cdot (\$16,000) + (1/2) \cdot (\$30,000) = \$23,000.$$

Based *purely* on the expected value of income, the owner would be indifferent between renting either film; each is expected to yield $23,000.

However, consider the owner's utility function from income, shown in Figure 21–1. The owner's utility, measured cardinally in unspecified units, is shown along the vertical axis. The level of income is measured along the horizontal axis. As you see, the utility function is concave; it has a positive slope but rises at a decreasing rate, indicating that the marginal utility of additional income declines as income rises. For example, when income increases from $12,000 to $16,000, the increase in utility is 3 units. For the next $4,000 increment of income to $20,000, the increase in utility is only 2 units.

The owner bases the choice of the film on expected utility. From the graph, the utility from the $23,000 that would be earned from the risk-free movie is 18 units. The utility from the $16,000 that would be earned if the risky movie turns out to be a flop is 15 units; if this movie is a success and earns $30,000, the utility would be 20 units. The expected utility from the risky movie with the 50–50 chance of being a flop or a hit is

$$E(U) = (1/2) \cdot U(\$16,000) + (1/2) \cdot U(\$30,000)$$
$$= (1/2) \cdot (15) + (1/2) \cdot (20) = 17.5.$$

Based on the expected utility of income, the owner would rent the risk-free movie with a utility level of 18 units rather than the risky movie with the lower expected utility of 17.5 units. The theater owner with the utility function shown in Figure 21–1, and anyone else with a utility function exhibiting diminishing marginal utility of income, is risk averse. The owner has the opportunity to obtain a film that guarantees $23,000 a month. Utility from the film is 18. More utility comes from a certain income of $23,000 than an expected value of income of $23,000. The owner clearly would not pay $23,000 for the risky movie, which by definition means the owner is risk averse. In general, a concave utility function, such as the one shown in Figure 21–1, illustrates risk aversion.

The convex utility function shown in Panel A, Figure 21–2, illustrates risk-loving behavior. The person with this type of utility function has increasing marginal utility of income. For example, a $4,000 increase in income from $16,000 to $20,000 increases utility from 22 units to 28, an increase of 6. But, an increase in

Figure 21–1 Expected Utility with Diminishing Marginal Utility of Income

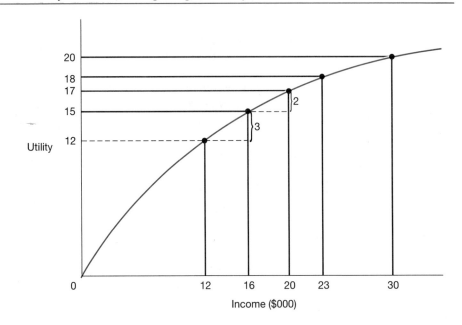

income from \$20,000 to \$23,000, an increment of only \$3,000, increases utility by 7 units, from 28 to 35.

Now consider the choice this person would make between a certain \$23,000 and an alternative that offers \$30,000 with a 50 percent probability and \$16,000 with a 50 percent probability. The \$23,000 income yields 35 units of utility. The expected utility from the risky income is

$$E(U) = (1/2) \cdot U(\$16,000) + (1/2) \cdot U(\$30,000)$$
$$= (1/2) \cdot (22) + (1/2) \cdot (56) = 11 + 28 = 39.$$

Utility is greater than the sure outcome of \$23,000 that yielded utility of 35. Individuals who are risk loving enjoy income and risk.

Panel B of Figure 21–2 illustrates a risk-neutral utility function. The person with this utility function has a constant marginal utility of income. An increase of \$4,000, from \$12,000 to \$16,000, increases utility from 16 to 22, an increase of 6 units. Likewise, a \$4,000 increase in income from \$16,000 to \$20,000 increases utility by 6 units, from 22 to 28. This risk-neutral individual would be indifferent between the choices of \$23,000 with certainty and \$30,000 with a 50 percent probability and \$16,000 with a 50 percent probability. The \$23,000 income would yield 32 units of utility. The expected utility from the risky incomes is also

$$E(U) = (1/2) \cdot U(\$16,000) + (1/2) \cdot U(\$30,000)$$
$$= (1/2) \cdot (22) + 1/2 \cdot (42) = 32.$$

Therefore, the expected utility from the risky income is identical to the utility from the certain income.

Figure 21–2   Risk-Loving and Risk-Neutral Utility Functions

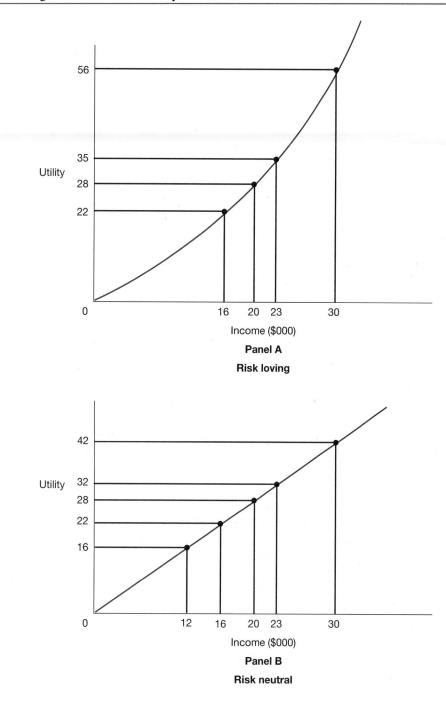

Panel A

Risk loving

Panel B

Risk neutral

We want to emphasize that the expected utility of income is *not* the expected value of income. In the above examples, the expected value of the risky income was always equal to the certain income. A risk-averse person will choose a certain income over a risky income with the same expected value, because the utility from the certain income exceeds the expected utility from the risky income. A risk-loving person will choose the risky income under the same circumstances, because its expected utility is greater than the utility from the certain income. A risk neutral person is indifferent between the two; the expected utility from the risky income equals the utility from the certain income.

21.3.2 Measuring Risk

A choice that has the possibility of different outcomes, each with a probability less than one of occurring, is said to be risky. A choice with a certain outcome is not risky. In the case of the theater owner, the film with a certain return of $23,000 is not risky. The film with possible returns of $16,000 and $30,000 with an expected value of $23,000 is risky. We have not, however, provided any measure of risk. There are several such measures, but they all are concerned with the spread of possible returns.

Risk is frequently measured by adding the weighted squares of an outcome's difference from the expected value; each term is weighted by the probability that it will occur. In the case of showing the risky film, the spread, or difference, of the worst case from the expected value is $-\$7,000$ ($= \$16,000 - \$23,000$). The spread of the best case from the expected value is $\$7,000$ ($= \$30,000 - \$23,000$). The square in each case is $49,000,000. The *variance* (σ^2) is found by multiplying each spread by the probability it will occur, in each case .5, and summing. Hence,

$$\sigma^2 = (.5) \cdot (\$49,000,000) + (.5) \cdot (\$49,000,000)$$
$$= \$49,000,000.$$

Sometimes risk is measured by the square root of the variance. This measure is called the *standard deviation*. In this case the standard deviation is $7,000.

The variance or standard deviation is sometimes used to compare the riskiness of different ventures. Suppose, for example, that the theater operator discussed above has the option of booking a film that has a worst-case scenario of $10,000 in monthly receipts with probability .25 and receipts of $40,000 with probability .75. The expected value is

$$E(M) = .25(\$10,000) + .75(\$40,000)$$
$$= 2,500 + 30,000 = \$32,500.$$

The spreads in monthly receipts are larger than the first option discussed above, so the variance must be larger. Calculating the variance,

$$\sigma^2 = .25[(10,000 - 32,500)^2] + .75[(40,000 - 32,500)^2]$$
$$= .25[(-22,500)^2] + .75[(7,500)]^2]$$
$$= .25(506,250,000) + .75(56,250,000)$$
$$= 126,562,500 + 42,187,500$$
$$= \$168,750,000.$$

The standard deviation is the square root, which is approximately $12,990.38. Thus, by the measure discussed here this pair of movies is more risky than the other. The variance and standard deviation are larger in this second scenario. The larger the variance, the greater is the measure of risk.

In general the variance of outcomes X_1 and X_2 with probabilities π_1 and π_2 and expected value $\overline{X}$ is

$$\sigma^2 = \pi_1(X_1 - \overline{X})^2 + \pi_2(X_2 - \overline{X})^2.$$

The standard deviation is the square root.

Frequently, decision makers are faced with the type of choice illustrated for the theater owner. A higher expected value is frequently associated with a higher variance, that is, a higher risk. In the movie example, the expected value was higher in the second choice, but the variance was also higher. Investors, as another example, are faced with the choice of one stock with a higher expected value than others but with a higher variance.

21.3.3 Diversifying

Risk can be reduced by booking multiple films. This involves maintaining two or more theaters. Indeed most theater complexes come in clusters of two or more. One reason for clustering is that there are economies of scale. Only one concession stand need be built for a group of theaters, and the same labor pool can service several theaters at the same time. These shared inputs reduce the average cost of operating each theater. Importantly, however, two or more theaters reduce or even eliminate the variance of monthly incomes. Suppose an owner operated two theaters; suppose also that receipts are affected by antigun legislation. But the owner has no way of knowing with certainty that such legislation and the surrounding publicity will be forthcoming in the next year. Films with violence attract relatively large audiences, but antiviolence campaigns reduce audience size. The owner guesses that the probability of forthcoming legislation is .5.

	Movie Type	
	Movie A	*Movie B*
Antigun legislation	$30,000	$10,000
No legislation	10,000	30,000

The above table illustrates how revenues depend on the presence of legislation and the publicity against violence. Movie B is full of violence and shooting. If there is publicity against such activity, the movie earns only $10,000 per month, otherwise it earns $30,000. Movie A is a human interest film. Without the legislation it earns $10,000. With the legislation, however, it yields $30,000 a month in revenues. Without legislation the violent film crowds out audiences for the human interest film. With the probability of legislation estimated at 50–50, the expected value of each movie is

$$(1/2) \cdot (\$10,000) + (1/2) \cdot (\$30,000) = \$20,000.$$

The variance of each movie is

$$\sigma^2 = (1/2) \cdot (\$10,000 - \$20,000)^2 + (1/2) \cdot (\$30,000 - \$20,000)^2 = \$100,000,000.$$

Suppose the two-theater complex shows both movies. Total earnings are no longer risky; one movie must earn \$30,000 and the other must earn \$10,000, regardless of whether or not the legislation is passed. Thus, income must be \$40,000. Because diversifying has led to no risk, the variance in this case is

$$\sigma^2 = (1/2) \cdot (\$30,000 + \$10,000 - \$40,000)^2 + (1/2)$$
$$\cdot (\$40,000 - \$10,000 - \$30,000)^2 = 0.$$

Thus, there is 0 variance.

This stylized example illustrates how risk can be reduced by diversification. Of course, it is rarely the case that the variance can be reduced to 0, as in this example. In general, however, when ventures have different distributions of outcomes, risk, measured by variance or standard deviation, can be reduced when an individual diversifies by choosing two or more of the ventures.

21.3.4   Reforming Expected-Utility Theory

Evidence from the observed behavior of individuals indicates that expected-utility theory does not adequately describe how people actually make decisions in the presence of risk. The French economist Maurice Allais in 1953 was the first to present a hypothetical problem that caused people to make choices that did not maximize expected utility.[1] More recently, two psychologists, Daniel Kahneman and Amos Tversky, have presented similar case studies to support the argument that individuals go through a more involved decision process than the simple maximization of expected utility when they face risk.[2] One of their case studies presented 72 people with the following two problems. The percentage of people opting for A or B in problem 1, and C or D in problem 2 is shown in brackets.

Problem 1

Choose between
A. \$2,500 with probability .33   B. \$2,400 with certainty
    2,400 with probability .66
    0 with probability .01
        [18]   [82]

Problem 2

Choose between
C. \$2,500 with probability .33   D. \$2,400 with probability .34
    0 with probability .67   0 with probability .66
        [83]   [17]

[1]Allais, M. "Le Comportement de l'Homme Rationnel devant le Risque, Critique des Postullats et Axiomes de l'Ecole Americaine," *Econometrica* 21 (1953), pp. 503–46.

[2]Kahneman, D. and Tversky, A., "Prospect Theory: An Analysis of Decision under Risk," *Econometrica* 47 (March 1979), pp. 263–91.

Thus 82 percent of the people chose option B in problem 1 and 83 percent preferred option C in problem 2. This pattern of behavior shows that people are not maximizing expected utility.

In problem 1, it was the case for most people in the study that

$$U(\$2,400) > .33 \cdot U(\$2,500) + .66 \cdot U(\$2,400) + .01 \cdot U(0),$$

where the inequality sign $>$ means "preferred to." It is widely assumed that the utility of nothing, $U(0)$, is zero. Hence we may rearrange terms by writing the above expression as:

$$U(\$2,400) > .33U(\$2,500) + .66U(\$2,400), \text{ or}$$
$$(1 - .66)U(\$2,400) > .33U(\$2,500), \text{ or}$$
$$.34U(\$2,400) > .33U(\$2,500).$$

This shows that when faced with problem 1, using expected-utility theory, people prefer a slightly greater probability of receiving $2,400 to the slightly lower probability of receiving $2,500. But problem 2 yields just the opposite conclusion. Again, assuming that $U(0) = 0$, choice behavior in problem 2 directly shows that

$$.33U(\$2,500) > .34U(\$2,400).$$

When faced with problem 1, the large majority of people preferred a 34 percent chance of receiving $2,400 to a 33 percent chance of receiving $2,500. When faced with problem 2, the large majority preferred a 33 percent chance of receiving $2,500 to a 34 percent chance of receiving $2,400. Therefore, preferences were reversed by changing from problem 1 to problem 2. Such preference reversals are inconsistent with the theory that people maximize expected utility when outcomes are not fully known. Preference reversals in the presence of risk have been documented in many different contexts by Kahneman and Tversky.

In light of this contradictory behavior, Kahneman and Tversky suggest that people follow a *prospect theory* when they make choices under risk. A full description of this theory is not provided here, but some of its main propositions are introduced. Under prospect theory people maximize a *value function*, which is different from a utility function. In a value function, subjective value is assigned to potential gains and losses. The behavior observed by the two psychologists suggests that losses are weighted more heavily than gains in an individual's value function.

Also, gains and losses are not simply weighted by the probability of an event occurring, but a value function has filters that adjust the probabilities. The filter adjusts some probabilities upward and some downward. For example, for two outcomes x and y that have probabilities of π and $1 - \pi$ of occurring, the value function V has values attached to x and y, written as $v(x)$ and $v(y)$ and filters w attached to the probabilities. Rather than maximizing expected utility, a decision maker chooses to maximize

$$V = w(\pi) \cdot v(x) + w(1 - \pi) \cdot v(y).$$

The values $v(x)$ and $v(y)$ attached to x and y are similar to the utility someone attaches to these outcomes. The main difference is that the probabilities are filtered by the w function. Also, for expected utility, the utility function has as its base 0, so that $U(0) = 0$. The value function is defined with reference to the person's

Figure 21–3   A Value Function

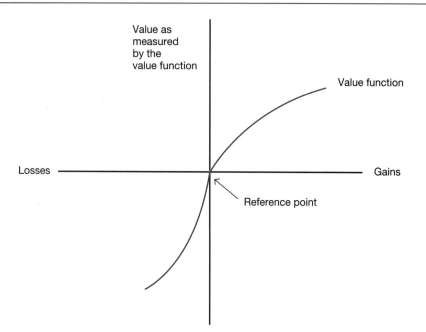

current income position. The value function can change altogether as a person's income position changes.

Figure 21–3 illustrates a value function. Value is plotted along the vertical axis. Gains and losses from the particular reference point are plotted along the horizontal axis; gains are to the right of the reference point, losses to the left. Kahneman and Tversky found that people are risk averse for gains, as shown by the concave shape of the value function to the right of the reference point. However, they found that people are risk loving in the case of losses. This is illustrated by moving left from the reference point, where the value function is convex. This portion of the curve is similar in shape to the risk-loving utility function shown in Figure 21–2, Panel A.

It may seem a little hard to believe that people are risk averse for potential gains while they are risk loving when faced with potential losses. Consider, however, the following evidence also presented by Kahneman and Tversky. There are two problems:

Problem 1

In addition to whatever you own, you have been given $1,000. You are now asked to choose between

A. $1,000 with probability .50	B. $500 with certainty.
0 with probability .50	
[16]	[84]

When faced with this problem, 84 percent of the people chose the certain $500, while 16 percent preferred the risky outcome with an expected value of $500. For most of the people

$$U(\$500) > .5U(\$1,000) + .5U(0),$$

which illustrates risk aversion for the gain. People preferred the certain outcome to the risky outcome with an equivalent expected value. Now consider:

Problem 2

In addition to whatever you own, you have been given $2,000. You are now asked to choose between

A. $1,000 loss with probability .50   B. a loss of $500 with certainty.
    0 loss with probability .50
         [69]   [31]

In this case, most individuals, 69 percent, preferred the risky choice with an expected outcome of $-\$500$ to the certain loss of $500. Thus, when facing losses, most people exhibited risk-loving behavior.

Research continues on the theory of choice in the presence of risk.[3] As this work continues, it is becoming more clear that explaining behavior in a risky environment is complicated. The simple theory of expected-utility maximization is adequate in some contexts, but it does not explain all observed behavior. Researchers continue to look for a cohesive theory that has testable propositions.

21.4   Information and Search

Markets may not perform well because consumers lack full information. Complete information includes knowledge on the part of all consumers about product prices and qualities, including the hazards associated with a product. For the average consumer, this level of knowledge is a practical impossibility. We describe here how incomplete information leads to price distortions in markets and possibly too few or too many resources devoted to the production of some goods.

21.4.1   The Benefits and Cost of Information

The theory of optimizing behavior concludes that the optimal amount of information for consumers occurs when the marginal benefit of its use is equal to the marginal cost of collection. As long as marginal benefit is greater than marginal cost, information will be gathered, but because marginal cost is positive, consumers will never collect information until the marginal benefit is zero. Figure 21–4 illustrates the marginal benefit (*MB*) and marginal cost (*MC*) of gathering information about a product. This information would include all knowledge about prices charged by

---

[3]See Mark J. Machina, "Choice under Uncertainty: Problems Solved and Unsolved," *The Journal of Economic Perspectives* 1 (Summer 1987), pp. 121–54.

Figure 21–4   Marginal Benefit and Marginal Cost of Information
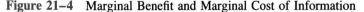

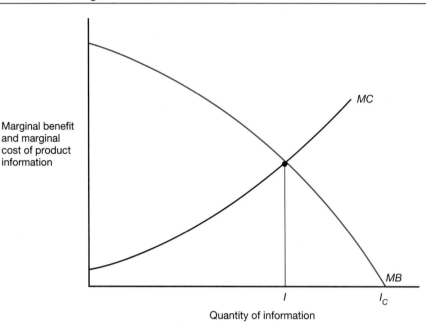

sellers and quality features about the product. At first the marginal benefit of such information is relatively large, but as a consumer continues to obtain more information and becomes more acquainted with the product's characteristics, additional pieces of information are less helpful. Hence the *MB* schedule declines.

The *MC* schedule rises, illustrating that the cost of collecting more information increases at the margin. The primary cost is, in many cases, the opportunity cost of time. As a consumer continues to gather more information, the value of next-best alternatives increases. At first leisure time may be used to search for lower prices and to collect more information about the product, but as more time is spent shopping, more valuable activities are forsaken, increasing the expense of finding information. Other costs of searching for or collecting information are direct costs such as telephone and transportation costs.

Because the *MC* schedule rises and the *MB* schedule declines, consumers optimize at the intersection of the two schedules. In Figure 21–4, a consumer gathers the quantity of information *I*. This is not perfect information. In Figure 21–4 perfect information would be where the marginal benefit of more information is zero, at I_C. Thus, a consumer who optimizes will, by the very process of optimizing, have less than complete knowledge about prices and product qualities.

This observation was first made by George Stigler in 1961.[4] Less than perfect information leads to price dispersion in markets. Identical products can have dif-

---

[4]G. Stigler, "The Economics of Information," *Journal of Political Economy* 69 (June 1961), pp. 213–25.

ferent prices across sellers because consumers are unaware that lower prices exist elsewhere. Similarly, products of relatively low quality can sell at relatively high prices because consumers are unaware that higher-quality products are available at lower prices.

Figure 21–4 allows us to make predictions about the quantity of information a consumer will obtain as the *MC* and *MB* schedules shift. As the income of a consumer rises, for instance, the opportunity cost of the person's time and therefore the cost of search will, in general, rise. This shifts the *MC* schedule to the left and the consumer will have less product information in equilibrium. Advertising that makes product information readily available to consumers will lower the *MC* schedule and increase *I* in the figure.

21.1   *Applying the Theory*

In Figure 21–4 what happens to the equilibrium level of information when the marginal benefit of information increases? What factors might be responsible for shifting the *MB* schedule in the direction you predict?

21.4.2   Search Goods and Experience Goods

Sometimes the information a consumer desires about a product or service does not become available until the individual begins consuming it. For example, when you are buying a car, you can make a thorough search of prices and features, carefully reading reports by the car magazines and consumer groups. Finally you settle on the automobile of your choice, but you cannot be sure that you have a reliable model until you drive it for a few months. Even though you purchase a car that by all reports is reliable, you could get a lemon. Goods that are infrequently purchased—for example, most consumer durable goods such as houses, cars, refrigerators, washers, dryers, and lawn mowers—are called *experience goods*.

There is a useful distinction between experience goods and *search goods*. Search goods have easily observable qualities, features that are known without consuming the product. Items that are frequently purchased fit into the search category. These would be most goods at a grocery store, apparel, and ordinary tools such as wrenches and hammers. For search goods, price is the relatively important factor in a consumer's decision to buy. The way search goods are advertised reflects the importance of price. When newspapers advertise grocery specials, it is the price that is highlighted for lettuce, carrots, and cuts of meat, not quality features. In contrast, for experience goods quality is more frequently advertised. Ads for experience goods often emphasize guarantees and warranties, and the brand name of the product. These features of an experience good are important because consumers often desire recourse in the event the product fails or does not meet expectations.

Certainly most goods have features that would make them search goods and features that make them experience goods. It is possible to gather some information about all products through search, but other information must come from experience. However, when experience is important, consumers will frequently use rules of thumb to estimate the experience forthcoming from the product. In other words, consumers evaluate the risk of consumption before a purchase is made using shortcut methods of judgment that may or may not be reasonable. These rules of thumb can have a large impact on the functioning of markets.

21.2   *Applying the Theory*

Some retailers guarantee that they offer the lowest prices in town. If a customer does find a lower advertised price, the retailer will pay the customer the difference between its price and the advertised price on the product sold. How do you think such a guarantee affects consumer search?

21.4.3   Rules of Thumb: The Akerlof Model[5]

Sometimes, when consumers have difficulty gathering information, they use rules of thumb to judge product quality and the price they are willing to pay for a product. These rules of thumb can have serious consequences for a market. As an illustration, suppose someone is in the market for a used car. A strong asymmetry of information in the market may exist between buyers and individual sellers. We assume for the sake of illustration that transactions are made between two individuals, and the seller can choose not to sell. Asymmetry of information means that buyers know little or possibly nothing about the automobile they see offered for sale, while the seller is fully aware of the car's history—true mileage, accidents, and routine maintenance, would be important pieces of this history.

Buyers, when they do not have much information about a product, are likely to adopt a rule of thumb to decide whether or not to make a purchase. Consumers use rules of thumb all the time. Brand names are associated with high- and low-quality products; a busy restaurant must have good food; stocks and bonds are bought and sold according to the phases of the moon. Some rules are good, some are not so good. In the example of a consumer buying a used car, suppose buyers know nothing about used cars and therefore assume that any car they see is an "average" quality used car. They then decide that the highest price they will pay is the price that delivers a car of average quality. The price asked by the seller is not used as a signal of quality.

Individual sellers, who actually know the quality of the cars offered for sale, will not sell high-quality cars at average-quality prices. They choose to keep the cars and drive them, hoping for prices to rise, or they let them depreciate to average quality. In any event, the high-quality cars in the used-car market are taken off the market. After a while, this changes the distribution of quality in the market, because average quality falls. Consumers eventually learn of this shift in overall market quality as they consistently overestimate average car quality. If they continue to

---

[5]This discussion is based on George Akerlof, "The Market for 'Lemons': Quality Uncertainty and the Market Mechanism," *Quarterly Journal of Economics* 84, no. 3 (August 1970), pp. 488–500.

hold onto their rule of thumb, they must adjust until prices are brought back in line with average quality. Thus prices fall, and once again, the relatively good cars are pulled off the market; average quality then falls again and later so does price. This cycle may continue until the market for used cars eventually disappears.

In this example, the important thing is not so much the lack of information as it is the unbalanced distribution of information between buyers and sellers. This asymmetry induces peculiar behavior on the part of consumers, which can be detrimental to a market's existence.

Of course, the problems associated with seemingly strange rules of thumb can be overcome if consumers are provided with more information. Sellers competing with one another to sell their automobiles have an incentive to supply potential customers with information about their products. Sellers can overcome these rules of thumb through guarantees, certification by an independent expert, reputation, and so on. We have presented a rather stylized story to illustrate a point. Rarely do consumers not know anything about the product they buy. However, the relative amounts of information that buyers and sellers have may literally determine the existence of some markets. More information is the key in some instances to generating greater exchange and stable equilibrium.

21.4.4   Evaluating Product Quality and Certification

The amount and distribution of information are not the only important features of information in a market setting. Consumers, even with information, may not be able to evaluate the information they have. Buyers, for instance, are often unaware of the side effects of chemicals in hair spray or floor wax; foods may contain harmful substances that are listed on the label, but whose names mean nothing to the shopper; and automobiles may have faulty designs that only an engineer can evaluate.

Just as a lack of information distorts the preferences of consumers, so will the inability to evaluate available information. When consumers are unaware of the full effects of dangerous products, they may be willing to purchase more of the commodity at the going price than they would under full knowledge. In other words, information without knowledge causes misperceptions, which distort the marginal benefit per dollar between two products. Better evaluation of information could bring consumers to a more efficient level of consumption.

In some cases, specific governmental bodies such as the Food and Drug Administration (FDA) and the Consumer Product Safety Commission (CPSC) are legislated to evaluate products. For instance, the CPSC annually inspects children's toys and alerts consumers to potentially dangerous features. Beyond this, the government agency often sets standards that eliminate the danger. Usually, the danger involved is reduced, but the cost to consumers is a more expensive product. For example, in the mid-1970s, the CPSC determined that baby cribs were unsafe because infants could slip through the crib bars. Consequently, it set a maximum distance between the bars of cribs. Manufacturers as a group were required to place bars closer together, which required more bars, so cribs became more expensive.

Such a change in product quality involves a trade-off to consumers. While required standards usually relieve buyers of evaluating the hazards of products, they also make manufacturers conform to designs that restrict product variety and/or make products more expensive. In the specific case of baby cribs, safety standards prevented consumers from buying less-expensive cribs that were undoubtedly not as safe as those that conformed with CPSC guidelines. But the choice was eliminated and less-expensive models may have suited some consumers' purposes and budgets.

Whether informational problems necessitate regulation is debatable. Many economists would argue that market failure from the absence of enough of the right kinds of information requires only additional information, not regulation. On the other hand, more is involved than simply acquiring a publication or reading a more informative description of a product. Once information is acquired, it must be studied, and if it is complicated or technically sophisticated, the costs associated with digesting the information can be high. Under these circumstances, many economists argue that safety and quality regulation are beneficial functions of government.

Economics in the News

Service Guarantees Are Not Always a Good Signal of Quality[6]

Guarantees can signal that a product is of better-than-average quality. But writing a guarantee that is a true signal of quality can be difficult, especially in service industries. Providers of services, for example, hotels and banks, find it difficult to define good service, let alone guarantee it. The simple promise, "satisfaction guaranteed or your money back," lets the buyer define satisfactory service. Many sellers, however, are unwilling to accept so much buyer control of a guarantee. Their fear is that buyers will use the service, then argue that it was not satisfactory in order to obtain a refund. Interestingly, studies show that consumer cheaters make up no more than 3 percent of the people who might cash in on a guarantee.

Some service providers have been able to define and measure good service. Consequently a guarantee can have meaning and can effectively signal quality. Pizza Hut, for example, guarantees that pizzas sold at lunchtime will be ready in five minutes or the next one is free. First Interstate Bank pays customers $5 if they find a mistake on their monthly statement or if the automatic teller machine breaks. General Motors guarantees customers an oil change and lube job in 29 minutes or the next one is free. Service guarantees that are unable to define good service are inadequate signals of quality. The German airline Lufthansa guarantees that passengers will not miss connecting flights excluding situations beyond the control of the airline. The two most common causes of flight delays are bad weather and air-traffic-control delays, which are beyond a carrier's control. What else is or is not uncontrollable is debatable. McDuff Electronics has a

(continued)

---

[6]This news is based on "More Firms Pledge Guaranteed Service," *The Wall Street Journal,* July 17, 1991, p. B1.

written guarantee that the firm will sell electronic equipment at the lowest prices, but the guarantee includes a paragraph of exceptions to the promise. To the consumer it appears the retailer has difficulty defining what the lowest price can be.

Some service providers do not provide a clear definition and promise because they fear customers will take advantage of loopholes. Copper Mountain ski resorts in Colorado, one of several within easy driving distance of Denver, would refund lift ticket money until 10 A.M. if conditions were not good. Many skiers, wanting to hit at least one more resort in a day, would ski Copper Mountain between 8 and 10 in the morning, claim the snow was not good, and get the refund. They would then buy an afternoon pass elsewhere. The guarantee was short-lived. While such examples do exist, most clienteles, as noted above, are honest, and watered-down guarantees rather than signaling quality communicate that the vendor is dishonest. Guarantees without immediate response can also backfire. Texaco once offered a $5 in-store certificate to dissatisfied customers. But customers were required to mail in an application that described the reason for dissatisfaction and the name and description of the employee responsible for the poor service. Texaco had very few written responses.

21.3   *Applying the Theory*

There is asymmetric information in the housing market. Sellers are more completely aware of defects than buyers. The buyer must "experience" the good before learning about these defects. Describe some ways this asymmetry can be overcome.

21.5   Principal–Agent Relationships

A lack of information or asymmetry of information can make it difficult to negotiate working relationships between two parties. Legal contracts between individuals often involve one person acting on behalf of another. Professional football players, for example, have a contract with a representative who acts on the player's behalf at wage negotiations. The player is the principal in the contract and the representative is the agent. Such representatives are often known as sports agents. Many other types of working agreements call for an agent working for a principal. The principal is the employer and the agent is effectively the employee. Other examples of principal–agent relationships are a homeowner hiring a real estate agent to sell the owner's house, a person with legal difficulties hiring an attorney, and stockholders of a corporation employing managers.

The absence of information in such relationships makes it difficult for principals to know if the agents are fulfilling their obligation. Is the sports agent really negotiating the best salary for the player? Is the real estate agent working hard to find a buyer? Is an attorney giving the best effort? The inability of the principal to monitor the agent hinders an accurate assessment of the agent's effort.

Economics in the News

There Can Be Heroes in Principal–Agent Relationships[7]

Principal–agent relationships are entered into every day and are usually taken for granted. For example, when people ride a bus, the riders collectively are principals who contract with the bus company, the agent, to act as a carrier. Contractual obligations must be satisfied. The company must employ responsible and certified drivers. Buses must be comfortable, safe, and carry a minimum number of passengers. The company must service designated routes and set a schedule that they meet in a timely manner. These conditions are all part of the principal–agent relationship between passengers and public transporters.

Under principal–agent relationships it is generally easy to satisfy minimum requirements; for example, bus drivers must be experienced and have a chauffer's license for driving. But some agents can exceed these requirements. On August 4, 1991, Armando Helliger, a Greyhound bus driver, disarmed and captured a would-be hijacker of his bus and passengers. After the suspect commandeered his bus and robbed the passengers, the driver wrestled the gun away from the thief, then shot and wounded him with the thief's own gun as he was running away. It was the first time the driver had held and fired a gun.

The passengers all hailed the driver as a hero. Helliger disagreed and took issue with the label. "I don't think of myself as a hero," Helliger told reporters. "I was scared." Hero or not, Helliger did exceed the contractual responsibilities of his principal–agent relationship.

Another principal–agent relationship often taken for granted is that between a student and a teacher. Students are the principals; teachers are the agents. Schoolteachers are contractually responsible to teach their students. But there is a problem in determining how the responsibility of the teacher is satisfied. Sometimes fulfillment of the contractual obligation is measured by the success of students on examinations. The better students perform, the more capable the agent; but this is less than a perfect measure of how successful the agent's work is. One problem involved in the student–teacher relationship arises because the student is capable of damaging the relationship by refusing to learn. Several years ago, NBC news interviewed a retiring teacher. The reporter asked her, what is a good teacher? Her response: "A satisfactory teacher tells students what they need to know. A good one explains it to them, but a great teacher, ah, a great teacher inspires students."

21.5.1 Moral Hazard

Agents, of course, are aware of the principal's position. The absence or asymmetry of information often creates a climate of mistrust between contracting parties. The source of the mistrust is widely referred to as *moral hazard*. Moral hazard is the incentive of agents to shirk their responsibility because the principal is unable to know if the agent is really working. The agent maximizes profit by maximizing

[7]This news is based on Associated Press Reports, Monday, August 5, 1991 and Tuesday, August 6, 1991.

the difference between the cost of the work effort on behalf of the principal and the payment. The optimal work effort may even be nothing for the agent, which harms the principal.

For example, suppose a professional football player offers his player rep or agent a fixed fee, say $10,000, to negotiate a contract with a team. The agent, with minimal effort, can negotiate a $100,000 contract and be paid $10,000. But with more effort, which costs the agent money, a bigger contract could be negotiated for the player. With $5,000 in expenses on plane fare, telephone, hotel, and so on, the agent could work hard at the bargaining table and negotiate a $200,000 contract for the player. The player is better off with twice the salary, but the agent has no incentive to negotiate such a contract, because the player rep's profit is only $10,000 − $5,000 = $5,000. The agent is better off with minimal work effort.

The agent in this example is exhibiting moral hazard. The contract between the player and agent has been essentially short-circuited. Moreover, the player has difficulty finding out that the agent shirked responsibility. The agent can simply say to the player that the team owners were tough and would not bargain. The player has no way of checking the agent's story or in general monitoring the agent.

Moral hazard arises in a large number of principal–agent agreements, on the part of both the agent and the principal. A moral hazard exists when either party to an agreement has an incentive not to abide by all provisions of the agreement. An agreement that is frequently used as an example of moral hazard for an agent is the sale of insurance. A principal buys insurance from an insurance company, the agent, in order to avoid or reduce a potential loss. In the case of property insurance, the insurance company is responsible for any damage or loss that may occur. Because a loss would be covered by insurance, the principal who owns the property does not have as great an incentive to protect the insured property from damage as would be the case if the principal had to bear the entire expense of a loss. The property owner may be lax in taking measures to prevent fire, theft, or vandalism. Such measures cost time and money, and the owner is not responsible for the loss. Or, in the case of health insurance, the principal may not take all the precautions that would be the case if the principal had to pay all medical expenses. The insured person may smoke, eat a non-nutritious diet, not wear a seat belt, or fail to exercise. In such contractual agreements the principal has the incentive to shirk responsibility.

21.5.2 Efficient Payment Schemes

One way of correcting the moral hazard problem inherent in principal–agent agreements is to find a different method of paying the agent, or compensating the principal in the case of insurance. Suppose that instead of paying the player rep a flat $10,000 fee to negotiate a contract, the player offers a commission on the negotiated salary. If the player offered the agent k percent, the agent has the incentive to negotiate a relatively high salary, because the higher the salary the higher the commission paid to the agent. The agent may not negotiate the highest salary, however; at some point the agent's cost of negotiation may rise faster than the marginal rise in commission. It would then perhaps be in the interest of the player to pay the agent's expenses. The offer would be to pay expenses plus a commission. The player would want to pay expenses with a commission until the marginal payment was equal to the expected marginal gain in salary from the negotiated contract. It is unlikely that a perfect payment scheme can be found, but tying the agent's payment to the principal's gain works in the direction of making incentives between the agent and the principal more compatible. Compatible incentives decrease the necessity of the principal monitoring the agent.

In the case of insurance, incentives are aligned by requiring the insured party to pay a deductible when the insured property is damaged. An automobile policy for example, has a $100 or more deductible in the event of collision damage. This means that the driver pays the first $100 or more of the damage cost and the insurance company pays the balance. A sufficiently large deductible will cause the insured principal to protect the property, in this case the automobile, from damage. Insurance policies generally cost less as the deductible increases. The price goes down partly because the balance paid by the insurance company in the event of damage has been reduced by the amount of the deductible. More importantly however, the price is reduced because there is less moral hazard as the deductible increases. The higher the deductible, the more careful the property owner is. The same effect occurs in the case of deductibles on home and medical insurance.

21.5.3 Integration

Besides linking performance to payment, another way of overcoming principal–agent conflicts is to bring the principal and agent together under one manager. A single manager can merge the interests of two parties. Whenever the interests of the parties are merged or combined, there is *integration*.

To see how integration dissolves principal–agent problems, consider the following example. Suppose a movie studio that produces a number of films during a year distributes the films to independent theaters. The studio has a contract with the theaters to show the films. The studio is the principal in this example; the theaters are the agents. The studio owner does not know if the theaters as a group are showing the films at prices and runs long or short enough to maximize profits for the studio. Without a great deal of information about demand at each theater, the studio cannot construct a payment scheme that makes the incentives of the theaters compatible with those of the studio. To achieve maximum profits, the studio can merge with the theaters. The principal and agents then come under one management. Managers will then set prices and runs to maximize the joint profits of production and exhibition.

Mergers actually solve several problems that arise through contracting. The moral hazard problem disappears because there are no longer principals or agents. Both are now one party. The necessity of lawsuits over nonperformance of the contract is also overcome. Before the merger, if a theater decided not to show a film it was under contract to exhibit, the studio would sue to recover damages. Lawsuits are expensive and time-consuming. After a merger, a theater manager who chooses not to show a film is simply a stubborn employee. Instead of a lawsuit, the manager gets fired. In general, the firm goes about its business much more expeditiously after integration.

Finally, because important information is no longer held by only one party in negotiations, integration results in the elimination of the entire strategic negotiation process. This process can be very expensive. The process is also a barrier to many mutually beneficial contracts. Rather than expend the cost of negotiation with a risky outcome, potential principals and agents may simply forgo the relationship.

21.6   Summary

This chapter has provided a description of individual behavior when there is incomplete information. However, the description is not complete. The theory of behavior with less-than-perfect information continues to develop. This chapter has presented several topics that highlight how an absence of information complicates the decision-making process. When outcomes are risky the current theory describing behavior is the maximization of expected utility. Expected utility is defined as the weighted utilities of the different outcomes, where the weights are the probabilities of the different outcomes occurring. With respect to income, if the utility function is rising at a decreasing rate (concave), the individual is risk averse; if the utility function has a constant slope, the person is risk neutral; and if the function is rising at an increasing rate (convex) a person is risk loving.

Individual behavior is not always consistent with expected-utility theory. Psychologists have shown that behavior sometimes depends on the potential gains and losses of a risky venture. Individuals are likely to be risk averse with respect to gains and risk loving with respect to losses. Behavior is difficult to predict because it depends on the reference point of the individuals.

Decision makers do not optimize by gathering perfect information about prices and product qualities. This lack of information leads to price dispersion in markets and fosters imperfect competition. Sometimes information cannot be obtained unless the good is consumed. These are experience goods, as opposed to search goods, which have quality characteristics that can be determined by inspection.

In the case of experience goods, there is often an uneven distribution of information in the market. This asymmetry of information may exist, for example, in the used car market. Sellers know quality, but buyers are ignorant. As a result buyers will be use rules of thumb to evaluate quality, and these rules can restrict exchange, as discussed in the Akelof model. Broader exchange can be restored if sellers who offer high-quality products offer guarantees. Certification by private or government organizations can also signal high quality. If relative qualities can be objectively assessed, the lemons problem is overcome by the increased information.

An absence or asymmetry of information causes conflict of interest between principals and agents in contract agreements. The inability of one party to monitor the other leads to moral hazard. One party may gain from shirking responsibility. More efficient payment schemes can resolve the conflict. Payment should be tied to performance. Integration of principals and agents can also overcome moral hazard and other problems associated with contracts.

Answers to   *Applying the Theory*

21.1 An increase in the marginal benefit of information shifts the *MB* schedule in Figure 21–4 to the right. If the *MC* schedule does not shift, more information will be collected. A factor that may shift the *MB* schedule to the right is rapid product development. The personal computer industry has undergone rapid technological change that has led to numerous product improvements. Learning about these changes benefits consumers, which is modeled as a rightward shift in the *MB* schedule.

21.2 Guarantees that offer the lowest price on retail goods are likely to limit search. If consumers believe the guarantee, they are likely to conclude that the retailer does have the lowest prices. This shifts the marginal benefit from searching schedule in Figure 21–4 to the left. Individuals will search less and gather less information about the product.

21.3 Builders of new homes offer guarantees of their workmanship. The guarantees provide repairs at no charge for as long as a year. Sellers of older residences can voluntarily supply a list of known defects. In California and Maine such a list is required by state law. Buyers of older homes can also buy insurance against unknown defects. Frequently the policy premium is paid by the buyer. Of course, a potential buyer can hire an inspector with building experience to look for defects.

Technical Problems

1. Suppose an individual has a utility function for income (M) that is $U = M^2$. This person has potential future incomes of 100, 150, and 200 with respective probabilities of .5, .25, and .25.
   a. Calculate expected utility.
   b. Calculate the variance of expected utility.
   c. Is this person risk averse, risk neutral, or risk loving? Explain.
2. Suppose an individual has a utility function for income (M) that is $U = M$. Is this person risk averse, risk neutral, or risk loving? Explain.
3. Suppose an individual is facing the following two potential income streams with probabilities shown:

M_1	Probabilities	M_2	Probabilities
30	1/3	0	1/4
60	1/3	60	1/2
75	1/3	120	1/4

   a. Calculate the expected value of each prospect.
   b. Calculate the variance of each prospect.
   c. Which prospect would you choose? Does utility depend on both expected value and risk (measured by variance)? Explain.
4. In Figure E.21–1 a consumer gathers I^* quantity of information. Describe how the *MB* and/or *MC* schedule shifts and the equilibrium I changes if the following events take place:
   a. The consumer retires and has more time to search.
   b. The consumer receives a job promotion that means more income and longer hours at work.

Figure E.21–1

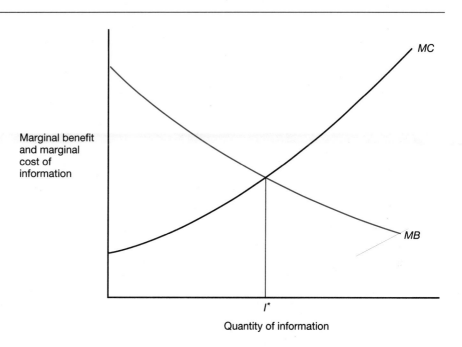

Quantity of information

c. The consumer relocates to the country and now commutes further to work in the city.
d. The government fixes all prices and sets strict quality standards.
e. The consumer lives in a country that has recently privatized industry; companies now set their own prices.
f. A new technology causes wide variances in the production costs of firms in an industry.

5. For each of the following principals or agents, only the agent or principal is specified. Provide the agent or principal that matches, and then for one of the pairs specify briefly the relationship contract.
   a. Fireman.
   b. Big-game hunter.
   c. Doctor.
   d. Football player.
   e. Landlord.
   f. Auto mechanic.

6. The utility function in the following figure (E.21–2) shows an individual's utility for given levels of income. Use this figure to answer the following questions:
   a. Calculate this person's marginal utility of income for an increase in income from $10,000 to $20,000; for an increase from $40,000 to $50,000; for an increase from $80,000 to $90,000.
   b. Is this person risk averse, neutral, or loving? Explain.
   c. If this person is confronted with a risky project with a .4 probability of receiving $25,000 and a .6 probability of receiving $85,000, what is the expected income from this project?

Figure E.21–2

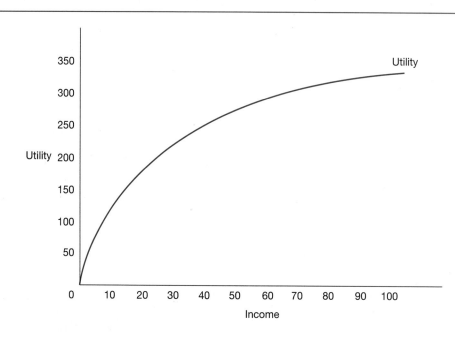

d. What is the expected utility from this project?

e. What is the utility from a certain income equivalent to the expected income from this project?

f. If confronted with a choice between this risky project and a guaranteed income equal to the expected income, which would this person choose? Explain.

g. Approximately how much income would this person have to be promised with certainty to make the person indifferent between the certain income and the risky choice?

7. Explain the difference between a search good and an experience good.

8. Many economists would say that there is a trade-off between governmental regulatory agencies designed to protect consumers from shoddy merchandise and unregulated business. Explain the trade-off.

9. Explain how mergers or integrations can reduce or even eliminate some principal–agent problems.

10. In which of the following cases might integration be used to eliminate a moral hazard in a principal–agent relationship. Explain the principal–agent relationship and the moral hazard in each case. For the instances in which integration is not feasible, what type of arrangement might be used to reduce moral hazard?

   a. A wholesaler supplies auto parts to an automotive parts store.

   b. A person's insurance agent handles retirement annuities accounts and medical insurance.

   c. One insurance company has the group medical insurance for all the employees of a large university.

   d. A used car dealer sells you an automobile.

     e. A large steel manufacturer buys iron ore and coal from other firms and sells steel to manufacturers of consumer durables.

     f. A congressman represents the residents of a congressional district.

11. Why would people hold relatively low-yielding bonds, blue chip stocks, and high-risk growth stocks in their investment portfolio? Why not simply pick the best investment?

Analytical Problems

1. You are accused of committing a crime and you hire a attorney to defend you. You want the attorney to minimize the criminal penalty. How do you, as a principal, pay the attorney, your agent, to act in your best interest? Suggest pay-for-performance plans.

2. You have been damaged because a supplier failed to supply you with necessary materials for your factory. Suggest methods of payment and delivery for materials that make the supplier more responsible.

3. Explain precisely the difference between uncertainty and risk. Why do you think economists generally ignore decisions made under uncertainty and concentrate their analysis on decisions made under risk?

4. Hotels, motels, and restaurants might be called the agents for the principals, who are their customers.

     a. In what sense are the principals faced with moral hazard?

     b. Some hotels, motels, and restaurants earn the majority of their income from repeat business. Others, for example those near major tourist attractions such as Yellowstone Park and Disneyland, essentially serve one-time customers. Which type of hotels, motels, and restaurants do you expect would give the best service? Explain.

     c. Why would you expect that large motel chains, such as Holiday Inn, might actually own and manage the motels near popular tourist attractions rather than franchise them to independent owners. Why might franchised motels be more prevalent where there is considerable repeat business (e.g., a downtown motel)? Explain.

     d. In light of your answers, explain how a reputation effect might reduce the moral hazard problem between principals and agents.

5. Using the discussion of search theory described here, explain why high-priced goods, such as major appliances, probably have a lower variance in price across the city than low-priced goods, such as can openers or toasters. Explain.

6. During the early 19th century, when most people lived in small towns or cities or rural areas, there was essentially no demand for governmental regulatory agencies designed to protect consumers from shoddy merchants. Many argue that there is such a need now. Explain.

7. In the case of risky projects, explain the difference between maximization of the expected value of utility from income and maximization of the expected value of income. When would the two be the same? When would they be different?

8. In the discussion of expected utility, the text made two points about observed human behavior. In your own words discuss why:

     a. People exhibit risk-averse behavior under some conditions and risk-loving behavior under others.

     b. Some people are risk loving in the case of losses and risk averse in the case of gains.

9. Explain why diminishing marginal utility of income leads to risk-averse behavior? Why would people experience risk-averse behavior? Why would people experience diminishing marginal utility of income? Would the utility from an increase in income differ according to the time period involved. If so, why? If not, why not?

10. If two types of goods sell at essentially the same price and one is a search good and the other is an experience good, which good would probably exhibit the greater price variance? Explain.

11. A university food service is losing money. It raises prices the next academic year to break even. Fewer students take a meal plan, cost per student rises, and the food service goes deeper into debt. Prices are raised again and the same things happens. Describe the food service's problem in terms of the Akerlof model. Make recommendations that would help correct this deterioration of the market.

INDEX